W9-BLH-415

THE PAPERS OF

Andrew Jackson

•

HAROLD D. MOSER,
EDITOR-IN-CHIEF

MAJOR GENERAL ANDREW JACKSON
FURST.F.

THE PAPERS OF

Andrew Jackson

VOLUME V, 1821–1824

HAROLD D. MOSER

DAVID R. HOTH

GEORGE H. HOEMANN

EDITORS

•

THE UNIVERSITY OF TENNESSEE PRESS

KNOXVILLE

•

*The paper in this book meets the minimum
requirements of the American National Standard
for Permanence of Paper for Printed Library Materials.*
♾
*Binding materials have been chosen
for strength and durability.*

•

Library of Congress Cataloging in Publication Data
(Revised for vol. 5)

Jackson, Andrew, 1767–1845.
The papers of Andrew Jackson.
Vol. 2 edited by Harold D. Moser and Sharon Macpherson.
Vol. 5 edited by Harold D. Moser, David R. Hoth,
George H. Hoemann.
Includes bibliographical references and indexes.
Contents: v.1. 1770–1803. —v. 2. 1804–1813—[etc.]
—v. 5. 1821–1824.
1. Jackson, Andrew, 1767–1845.
2. United States—Politics and government—1829-1837—Sources
3. Presidents—United States—Correspondence
I. Smith, Sam B., 1929–
II. Owsley, Harriet Fason Chappell.
III. Moser, Harold D.
IV. Title.
E302J35 973.5'6'092 79-15078
ISBN 0-87049-219-5 (v. 1: cl.: alk. paper)
ISBN 0-87049-441-4 (v. 2: cl.: alk. paper)
ISBN 0-87049-650-6 (v. 3: cl.: alk. paper)
ISBN 0-87049-778-2 (v. 4: cl.: alk. paper)
ISBN 0-87049-897-5 (v. 5: cl.: alk. paper)

Advisory Board

Publication of
The Papers of Andrew Jackson
was assisted by grants from
THE LADIES' HERMITAGE ASSOCIATION
THE UNIVERSITY OF TENNESSEE
THE NATIONAL HISTORICAL PUBLICATIONS
AND RECORDS COMMISSION
THE TENNESSEE HISTORICAL COMMISSION
and
THE PROGRAM FOR EDITIONS OF THE
NATIONAL ENDOWMENT FOR THE HUMANITIES,
AN INDEPENDENT FEDERAL AGENCY

In memory of
Betty Hoth
A Loving Mother

Contents

For the page number on which each document of The Papers begins, see the Calendar.

Illustrations

Frontispiece: Andrew Jackson, congressional medal presented March 16, 1824. Etching by Jules Jacquemart after engraving by Moritz Fürst. From J. F. Loubat, *The Medallic History of the United States, 1776–1876* (2 vols.; New York: n.p., 1878), 2:Plate 47. Courtesy of The Special Collections Library of the University of Tennessee, Knoxville.

Following page 232.

Andrew Jackson, oil on canvas by Robert Street. Courtesy of Sedalia Public Library, Sedalia, Missouri.

Henry Marie Brackenridge, photograph of miniature by unknown artist. From William F. Keller, *The Nation's Advocate: Henry Marie Brackenridge and Young America* (Pittsburgh: University of Pittsburgh Press, 1956), frontispiece. Courtesy of the University of Pittsburgh Press.

George Walton, oil on canvas by Matthew H. Jouett. Courtesy of The Historic Mobile Preservation Society Archives, Mobile, Alabama.

George Mercer Brooke, oil on canvas by Gilbert Stuart. Courtesy of George M. Brooke, Jr.

James Gadsden, oil on canvas by Ralph E. W. Earl. Courtesy of The Hermitage, Home of Andrew Jackson, Hermitage, Tennessee.

Nathan Towson, oil on canvas by Rembrandt Peale. Courtesy of Maryland Historical Society, Baltimore.

Henry Atkinson, miniature by unknown artist. Courtesy of Illinois State Historical Library, Springfield.

Richard Ivy Easter, oil on canvas by Ralph E. W. Earl. Courtesy of The Hermitage, Home of Andrew Jackson, Hermitage, Tennessee.

Samuel Houston, watercolor on ivory by Joseph Wood. Courtesy of San Jacinto Museum of History, Houston, Texas.

James Jackson, oil on canvas by unknown artist. Courtesy of Charles P. Jackson.

George Wilson, photograph of portrait by unknown artist. From *Tennesseans: Nineteen Hundred and One and Two* (n.p.: Speed Publishing Company, 1902), p. 16. Courtesy of The Special Collections Library of the University of Tennessee, Knoxville.

Patrick Henry Darby, oil on panel by Matthew H. Jouett. Courtesy of The J. B. Speed Art Museum, Bequest of Mrs. Marie Louise Darby, Louisville, Kentucky.

John Donelson (1755–1830), oil on canvas by Ralph E. W. Earl. Courtesy of The Hermitage, Home of Andrew Jackson, Hermitage, Tennessee.

Josiah Nichol, oil on canvas by [Ralph E. W. Earl?]. Courtesy of Robert Douglass Nichol.

Andrew Jackson, charcoal on paper by Thomas Sully. Courtesy of The Detroit Institute of Arts, Gift of Mrs. Walter O. Briggs, Detroit, Michigan.

Henry Clay, oil on canvas by Charles Bird King. Courtesy of The Corcoran Gallery of Art, Museum Purchase, Gallery Funds, Washington, D.C.

John Caldwell Calhoun, oil on canvas by Charles Bird King. Courtesy of The Corcoran Gallery of Art, Museum Purchase, Gallery Funds, Washington, D.C.

John Quincy Adams, oil on canvas by Thomas Sully. Courtesy of National Gallery of Art, Andrew W. Mellon Collection, Washington, D.C.

William Harris Crawford, oil on canvas by Charles Willson Peale. Courtesy of The High Museum of Art, Gift of Mr. and Mrs. Granger Hansell, Atlanta, Georgia.

The Letters of Wyoming, to the People of the United States, on the Presidential Election, and in Favour of Andrew Jackson (Philadelphia: S. Simpson & J. Conrad, 1824), title page. Courtesy of Dartmouth College Library.

James Monroe, oil on canvas by John Vanderlyn. Courtesy of The National Portrait Gallery, Smithsonian Institution, Washington, D.C.

George Hay, oil on canvas by Cephas Thompson. Courtesy of Ash Lawn–Highland/The College of William and Mary, Charlottesville, Virginia.

William Drayton, oil on canvas by Samuel F. B. Morse. Courtesy of White House Historical Association, Washington, D.C.

DeWitt Clinton, oil on canvas by Rembrandt Peale. Courtesy of Historical Society of Pennsylvania, Philadelphia.

Ezekiel Whitman, engraving by unknown artist. From *The Green Bag*, 7(October 1895):471.

The People's Ticket, endorsement of the candidacies of Andrew Jackson and John C. Calhoun. From *Cincinnati Advertiser*, June 23, 1824.

Daniel Pope Cook, engraving by unknown artist. Courtesy of Chicago Historical Society, Chicago, Illinois.

Ninian Edwards, oil on canvas by James Reeve Stuart. Courtesy of Chicago Historical Society, Chicago, Illinois.

A Foot-Race, etching by David Claypoole Johnston. Courtesy of The American Antiquarian Society, Worcester, Massachusetts.

Rachel Jackson, oil on canvas by Ralph E. W. Earl. Courtesy of The Hermitage, Home of Andrew Jackson, Hermitage, Tennessee.

Andrew Jackson, oil on canvas by Ralph E. W. Earl. Courtesy of The Hermitage, Home of Andrew Jackson, Hermitage, Tennessee.

Introduction

ANDREW JACKSON, 1821–1824

My comfortable farm . . . is the only contentment for me." That was a refrain for Andrew Jackson during the years 1821–1824, the period covered by this fifth volume of *The Papers of Andrew Jackson*. But Jackson's efforts to retire—to "live free from the bustle of public life & scenes of intrigue and corruption"—eluded him for all but a brief time during these years. His notion that a person owed public service when called upon kept him from retiring to the Hermitage.

Jackson was, as he wrote, "wearied with public life." Chronically dissatisfied with his overseers, he wished to give more attention to his farms in Tennessee and Alabama. The education of his adopted son, Andrew, Jr., now in his teens, and several other wards entrusted to his care, also demanded his attention. He and his spouse, Rachel, were both in their mid-fifties, and neither enjoyed good health. In fact, Jackson had already conceded that he probably could never regain his health; he could only "prolong" his life, if at all, through "private ease, or happiness," which he found "inconsistant" with life as a public man. Jackson had already given more than a decade to public service, much of it at "great private sacrifice," and his public career had been controversial, the subject of several congressional investigations. At this stage, Jackson wrote that he simply wanted to spend his days at home with his wife, son, and friends, "amonghst the farmers of the country," where virtue lay.

In 1821, circumstances allowed Jackson to retire from public life, at least officially. The congressional investigations of the Seminole War, which had once threatened to disgrace him, were complete, and though the Senate's report had been very critical, Jackson considered his memorial on the matter a sufficient response. The reduction of the army which the government was putting into effect would leave only one major general, and Jacob J. Brown had claim on that position by virtue of seniority. Meanwhile, the Spanish Cortes had finally ratified the Adams-Onís Treaty, which the United States Senate then promptly reratified. Back in 1819, in anticipation of the treaty's approval, President James Monroe had asked Jackson to oversee the transfer of Florida from Spain and to establish a government in the new territory, and now he repeated the offer. The governorship of Florida would serve as a fitting tribute to Jackson's long service in the Gulf region and, as such, would allow him to retire gracefully from the military. It would also provide him with income for a while longer and allow him to dispense patronage to friends forced out of the military by its reduction. Jackson accepted the appointment on the understanding that he would resign after organizing Florida's government.

The Florida post proved disappointing to Jackson. The expense of setting up a household at Pensacola consumed his income as governor. President Monroe generally ignored his recommendations for appointments, leaving the retired General in doubt about his standing with the administration. Moreover, Jackson's actions landed him in heated disputes with former Spanish officials over custody of court records and with one of Monroe's appointees over jurisdiction. As a consequence, Jackson left Florida without regret in early October.

Returning to Tennessee, Jackson seemed on the brink of the retirement he had so long sought. As he and his family settled in at the Hermitage, he forwarded his resignation of the Florida governorship to Monroe on November 13. Even now, however, he was to be denied the peace for which he longed. Disturbing news about a possible congressional investigation of his acts as governor reached him from Washington, arousing his sense of honor. To vindicate his reputation, Jackson sought in early 1822 to withdraw his resignation so that he could meet the charges against him. Congress, however, showed little real interest in the investigation, and only printed the documents on the matter, allowing the question to die. By mid-March 1822, Jackson again might have looked forward to a genuine retirement, but for his developing presidential candidacy.

Jackson's candidacy came to life in July 1822, when the Tennessee legislature officially nominated him for the presidency. Jackson's response was consistent. The presidency was too great an honor and too important a duty to be declined. Corruption had become rampant in Washington and needed to be rooted out. The scrambling for office in the second Monroe administration sickened him. It distressed him that cabinet officers used the spoils of office to further their own careers and ambitions rather than laboring exclusively for the country's good. Patronage had become an engine of corruption to boost one's candidacy. Jackson himself would set a better example: he would not seek office, but he would serve as an instrument of the people's will if they willed it.

During the early stages of the campaign, Jackson may have found this stance compatible with his longing for retirement. Though necessarily in the public eye, he resided far from the political vortex that was Washington, and for much of 1822 he remained a more or less passive observer of the political scene, absorbed with the private concerns of running his plantation and overseeing the estate of his ward Andrew J. Hutchings.

Soon, though, his sense of honor and his commitment to public service thrust him toward a more active role. However gently the editors supporting other presidential aspirants criticized his candidacy, their comments increased Jackson's desire to win vindication from the people. At the core of Jackson's concern was the prospect that Treasury Secretary William H. Crawford might succeed Monroe. The likelihood that Crawford would use a nomination by the congressional caucus to obtain the presidency, in defiance of the popular will, called to Jackson's sense of duty. Apart from the question of cabinet succession, Jackson personally admired two of the other candidates, John Quincy Adams and John C. Calhoun, though he thought little of a third, Henry Clay. But no one better embodied Jackson's fears for his country than Crawford, a man he had distrusted and detested since Crawford's tenure as secretary of war in 1815 and a politician supported by most of Jackson's enemies in Tennessee. As the head of the department with the most extensive patronage, Crawford had the greatest opportunity for corruption, and, Jackson concluded, Crawford was willing to use spoils and the congressional caucus to steal the election from the people. As Jackson's political intelligence reported the groundswell of popular support that would transform him from a favorite son of Tennessee into a top contender, the General found himself increasingly involved in the campaign, if only to defeat Crawford.

In 1823 and 1824 Jackson generally acted in ways that improved his presidential prospects, though he usually attributed his decisions to nonpolitical considerations. The crucial moment came in late September 1823. Earlier in the year Jackson had convinced himself that he could not serve his country effectively as minister to Mexico and rejected an appointment that some saw as a ploy to remove him from the political scene, but that decision had not conflicted with his desire to relax among family and friends at the Hermitage. In September, however, Jackson learned that Tennessee's incumbent Senator John Williams, a Crawford ally, could not be beaten for reelection by any who had offered against him. Friends sought out Jackson, and he rushed to Murfreesboro, where he won election to the Senate. Once again the call of public duty would separate Jackson from wife and family, even though he had serious concerns about Rachel's response to the separation. Borrowing money to finance his trip, Jackson traveled to the very center of political corruption, the national capital.

Thereafter, though he claimed to avoid "the intrigue of caucus, or president makers," Jackson filled his letters with political reports and calculations. Stifling his natural combativeness, he achieved a détente, if not always peace, with such enemies as Thomas Hart Benton, Henry Clay, Andrew Erwin, and Winfield Scott, demonstrating thereby that he was capable of self-control and not the savage "with a Tomahawk in one hand, & a scalping knife in the other" that some expected. After his nearly unanimous nomination by the March 1824 Pennsylvania convention at Harrisburg catapulted him to the front rank among the candidates, Jackson took a still more active role in the campaign. He cemented his Pennsylvania support with a public letter endorsing "judicious" protection for American industry, and, behind the scenes, he actively coordinated responses to assaults against his reputation by opposition editors and pamphleteers. It was, Jackson insisted, a great sacrifice, but one justified by the threat of "caucus mongers" thwarting the national will. And in the end his sacrifice was rewarded: Jackson won a plurality of the popular and the electoral votes. "Having been supported by the majority of the people" in November 1824, Jackson awaited the pending vote for president in the House of Representatives with the assurance that Henry Clay had been eliminated and William H. Crawford stood "no chance." With that done, Jackson assured his friends he would be "content" with the outcome.

The conflict between Jackson's desire for retirement and his sense of public duty forms a major theme of the documents in this volume. As he wrestled with this tension, Jackson used language that displayed many of the rhetorical trademarks later identified with Jacksonian democracy: an almost mystical confidence in the virtue of the common people and a fear of any entrenched elite. Jackson came to view himself as the instrument of a grassroots movement to purify American politics from the corruption of political intrigue and private ambition. As he saw it, his victory would restore the design of the founding fathers, a government reflective of the will of the voters and accountable at all times to the public.

ACKNOWLEDGMENTS

This volume of *The Papers of Andrew Jackson,* like the four preceeding, is the product of a major collaborative effort involving thousands of institutions and individuals. The list is too long to mention each separately, but to all of those who responded to our requests for documents and for help with annotation, we are grateful, and especially to those furnishing manuscripts for this volume.

Several institutions deserve special mention, mainly for the magnitude of their contributions. Chief among these are the Library of Congress, the National Archives, the Tennessee State Library and Archives, and the John C. Hodges Library, University of Tennessee. At the Library of Congress, John McDonough, Manuscript Historian, has assisted the project at every turn: he has made the Library's Jackson collection readily available, he has answered innumerable research questions, and he continues to share with us his extensive knowledge. At the National Archives, the research staff of the National Historical Publications and Records Commission, and particularly Timothy Connelly, have been indefatigable in unearthing documents and answering difficult questions. Our demands at Hodges Library, University of Tennessee, have been incessant, but Nancy Laemlein, formerly in Interlibrary Loans, the entire staff of Interlibrary Loans, and James B. Lloyd, Bill Eigelsbach, Nick Wyman, and Bobbie Painter in Special Collections have always gone out of their way to service our requests and to make their collections available. The staff of the Tennessee State Library and Archives—and especially Marylin Bell-Hughes, Fran Schell, and John Thweatt—has been equally cooperative and helpful.

We are also deeply obligated to several individuals who have assisted us far beyond any normal expectations: to Bill Cook in Lebanon, to Fletch Coke in Nashville, to Jerry W. Cook in Wartrace, all in Tennessee, and to Milly Wright in Florence, Alabama. To each of them we offer our sincere thanks.

Our sponsors have seen to it that the work continued, and our indebtedness to them is great and our appreciation sincere: to Jim Vaughan, Executive Director, and Sharon Macpherson, Deputy Director for Research, at The Hermitage, to Frances Jackson, Regent, and Ann Robinson, Vice-Regent, and to past regents, to the Board, and to the membership of the Ladies' Hermitage Association; to the National Historical Publication and Records Commission, Nancy Sahli, Acting Executive Director and Program Director, and Richard N. Sheldon, Assistant Director for Publications; to the National Endowment for the Humanities, Research Programs Division, and especially Douglas M. Arnold; to the Tennessee Historical Commission, Herbert L. Harper, Executive Director, Robert E. Corlew, Chairman, and Linda T. Wynn, Administrative Assistant; and finally, to our fiscal agent, the University of Tennessee-Knoxville. At the University, we are fortunate to receive the encouragement and support of Joseph E. Johnson, President, and William T. Snyder, Chancellor; but we are particularly appreciative of the Office of the Dean, College of Liberal Arts—Deans Lorman A. Ratner and Charles O. Jackson, Administrative Assistant Phyllis Cole, and Executive Assistant Ann Robinson-Craig—for their patience, understanding, and guidance in the day-to-day administration of the project.

The supporting staff of the Jackson papers has made our work easier and, indeed, more pleasant. As graduate research assistant, Joseph C. (Clint) Clifft has saved us an immeasurable amount of time in running down leads—he has proved indeed as indefatigable as the permanent staff. Wyatt Wells, assistant editor, has brought his wide reading and critical eye to bear upon these pages. In addition, Jesús F. de la Teja has continued to provide invaluable assistance with Spanish documents; and, above all, Dorothy Brooks has generously kept the office running while the editors were too engrossed in Jackson to notice anything else. Without the assistance of each, the volume would be considerably less than it is. To each, thanks.

Editorial Policies

PLAN OF WORK

The goal of the Papers of Andrew Jackson is to bring together the literary remains of Andrew Jackson and make them accessible to both the general reader and the serious scholar. An international search of almost 6,000 repositories, contacts with hundreds of private collectors, and an examination of newspapers, magazines, journals, and monographs have yielded a collection of some 100,000 documents. To make this material available, complementary letterpress and microfilm series are being published.

The microfilm publication, thirty-nine reels issued in 1987, is a supplement to the Library of Congress Andrew Jackson Papers and the National Archives microfilm series. It includes *all* Jackson documents found in the project's search to that date and *not* included on those two publications. The entire body of Jackson papers in the three publications—the Supplement, the Library of Congress Presidents' Papers Series, and the National Archives records—can be accessed through *The Papers of Andrew Jackson: A Guide and Index to the Microfilm Editions* (Scholarly Resources, Inc., 1987). Microfilm supplements will make available newly located documents when sufficient numbers accumulate.

The letterpress series will be a selective edition of sixteen volumes, accompanied by a cumulative index. With its annotations, it will stand alone as a unit, but it will also facilitate access to the much larger body of material available on the microfilms. Each volume will include a calendar in which all unselected documents, except the most routine, will be described by their writer or recipient, subject matter, provenance, and location on the film collections. The letterpress series will thus serve as an indispensable guide to the entire body of papers.

EDITORIAL METHOD

In the interest of stylistic continuity in the letterpress series, the present editors have adopted generally the editorial practices established in the previous four volumes.

The editors have broadly defined "papers" as outgoing and incoming correspondence, financial records, deeds, records of litigation, speeches and essays, memoranda, and military orders. In addition the editors have included in the Calendar all of Rachel Jackson's correspondence, whether or not with Jackson, and a small number of particularly significant third-party items essential to the understanding of otherwise obscure events in Jackson's life. All documents are listed in the Calendar following The Papers, with page numbers indicated for those selected, and writer or recipient, provenance, and subject matter described for the others. Certain routine documents have been omitted from the calendar, notably ration returns, orders for payment of military accounts, passes, military furloughs, and muster rolls. With few exceptions, the routine military correspondence, signed by aides-de-camp on Jackson's orders, has also been omitted unless the letter was part of a chain including letters directly to or from Jackson.

Documents in this volume are arranged in chronological sequence. The only exception is with enclosures, which generally appear immediately following the document they accompanied. All letters are reproduced in full, except when the only surviving text is incomplete. If several copies of a document are available, the editors have relied upon the recipient's copy (whether AL, ALS, or LS) for the text. Where that is missing, they have selected the most authoritative manuscript available. Generally, printed copies have been used only in the absence of manuscript versions, or when the manuscript has been mutilated or is a badly garbled copy. In several instances, variant manuscript copies of documents have been found containing additional text. If short, it has been incorporated into the document, with attention called to the source of that portion in footnotes. When lengthy or when some portion of the document may still be missing, the text source has been identified in an unnumbered provenance note immediately following that portion. Texts are taken from the first cited source.

The prime consideration in preparing the documents for publication has been fidelity to the original text. With the few exceptions noted below, the editors have made an effort to reproduce the papers exactly as written with all their peculiarities of spelling, capitalization, and punctuation. To aid readability, dashes after commas, semicolons, colons, or periods have been omitted. Abbreviations, including the commonly used ampersand and contractions, have been allowed to stand as written, with expansion in square brackets only when necessary for the understanding of the modern reader. Apostrophes below the line have been raised to their modern position above the line, and superscripts have been dropped to the line, retaining punctuation as in the original. Addressees' names, often written at the end of a document, have been omitted, as have words inadvertently repeated in the text. Dates written at the end of a document have been transferred to the beginning; interlineations and marginalia have been incorporated into the text as indicated by the writer.

Occasionally, bracketed matter has been introduced into the text to clarify otherwise questionable or unrecognizable words, to supply characters in mutilated documents, to indicate with ellipses a missing portion of a document (italicized in these last two instances), and to insert the full name(s) of persons. Dates and names furnished by the editors for undated, misdated, unsigned, and unaddressed documents are also enclosed in brackets, with a question mark if conjectural. Significant cancellations have been incorporated in angle brackets.

Immediately following each document is an unnumbered note giving the provenance of that item and, if appropriate, identifying the writer or recipient. Significant postmarks, address instructions, endorsements, and dockets have also been included here. The symbols used in this note appear in the List of Abbreviations. The document's location on microfilms is also noted in parentheses, with reel number alone referring to the Jackson Papers on the Library of Congress Presidents' Papers Series; with reel and frame number separated by a hyphen, to the Jackson Papers Series (Scholarly Resources, Inc., 1987); and with a M or T number followed by a hyphen and reel number, to the National Archives publications, which are conveniently listed in the Repository Symbols of this volume.

Introductory notes and footnotes are used to supply context and continuity and to identify persons, places, and events, usually at their first appearance in the text. Persons sketched in the *Dictionary of American Biography* and the *Biographical Directory of the United States Congress, 1774–1989* have been identified only briefly, and symbols at their names in the index have been used to direct the reader to additional biographical information in those publications.

DOCUMENT SYMBOLS

AD	Autograph Document
ADS	Autograph Document Signed
AL	Autograph Letter
ALS	Autograph Letter Signed
AN	Autograph Note
ANS	Autograph Note Signed
DS	Document Signed
LC	Letterbook copy
LS	Letter Signed

REPOSITORY SYMBOLS

A-Ar	Alabama Department of Archives and History, Montgomery
AFlT	University of North Alabama, Florence

CCamarSJ	Saint John's Seminary, Camarillo, Calif.
CSmH	Henry E. Huntington Library, San Marino, Calif.
CtY	Yale University, New Haven, Conn.
DLC	Library of Congress, Washington, D.C.
DNA	National Archives, Washington, D.C.
	RG 15, Records of the Veterans Administration
	RG 21, Records of the District Courts of the United States
	RG 21, M1214, Minute Books of the U.S. Circuit Court for West Tennessee, 1818–39, and of the U.S. Circuit Court for the Middle District of Tennessee, 1839–64
	RG 45, Naval Records Collection of the Office of Naval Records and Library
	RG 45, M124, Letters Received by the Secretary of the Navy: Miscellaneous Letters, 1801–84
	RG 46, Records of the United States Senate
	RG 59, General Records of the Department of State
	RG 59, M40, Domestic Letters of the Department of State, 1784–1906
	RG 59, M116, State Department Territorial Papers, Florida, 1777–1824
	RG 59, M179, Miscellaneous Letters of the Department of State, 1789–1906
	RG 59, M439, Letters of Application and Recommendation during the Administration of James Monroe, 1817–25
	RG 59, M639, Letters of Application and Recommendation during the Administration of Andrew Jackson, 1829–37
	RG 60, General Records of the Department of Justice
	RG 75, Records of the Bureau of Indian Affairs
	RG 75, M15, Letters Sent by the Secretary of War Relating to Indian Affairs, 1800–24
	RG 75, M208, Records of the Cherokee Indian Agency in Tennessee, 1801–35
	RG 75, M234, Letters Received by the Office of Indian Affairs, 1824–81
	RG 77, Records of the Office of the Chief of Engineers
	RG 84, Records of the Foreign Service Posts of the Department of State
	RG 94, Records of the Adjutant General's Office
	RG 94, M565, Letters Sent by the Office of the Adjutant General, Main Series, 1800–90

	RG 94, M566, Letters Received by the Office of the Adjutant General, 1805–21
	RG 94, M567, Letters Received by the Office of the Adjutant General, Main Series, 1822–60
	RG 94, M688, United States Military Academy Cadet Application Papers, 1805–66
	RG 98, Records of United States Army Commands, 1784–1821
	RG 107, Records of the Office of the Secretary of War
	RG 107, M6, Letters Sent by the Secretary of War Relating to Military Affairs, 1800–89
	RG 107, M22, Register of Letters Received by the Office of the Secretary of War, Main Series, 1800–70
	RG 107, M220, Reports to Congress from the Secretary of War, 1803–70
	RG 107, M221, Letters Received by the Secretary of War, Registered Series, 1801–70
	RG 107, M222, Letters Received by the Secretary of War, Unregistered Series, 1789–1861
	RG 156, Records of the Office of the Chief of Ordnance
	RG 217, Records of the United States General Accounting Office
	RG 233, Records of the United States House of Representatives
DSI	Smithsonian Institution, Washington, D.C.
FHi	Florida Historical Society, Tampa
FU	University of Florida, Gainesville
ICHi	Chicago Historical Society, Chicago, Ill.
IGK	Knox College, Galesburg, Ill.
IHi	Illinois State Historical Society, Springfield
IaDaM	Davenport Public Museum, Davenport, Iowa
InFwL	Lincoln National Life Foundation, Fort Wayne, Ind.
InU-Li	Indiana University, Lilly Library, Bloomington
KyLoF	Filson Club, Louisville, Ky.
LN	New Orleans Public Library, New Orleans, La.
LNHiC	The Historic New Orleans Collection, New Orleans, La.
LNT	Tulane University, New Orleans, La.
LU	Louisiana State University, Baton Rouge
MBU	Boston University, Boston, Mass.
MHi	Massachusetts Historical Society, Boston
MWiW-C	Williams College, Chapin Library, Williamstown, Mass.
MdHi	Maryland Historical Society, Baltimore
MeB	Bowdoin College, Brunswick, Me.
MeSaco	Dyer Library, Saco, Me.

MnHi	Minnesota Historical Society, St. Paul
MoIT	Harry S. Truman Library, Independence, Mo.
MoSHi	Missouri Historical Society, St. Louis
MoSW	Washington University, St. Louis, Mo.
Ms-Ar	Mississippi Department of Archives and History, Jackson
MsSM	Mississippi State University, State College
N	New York State Library, Albany
NHi	New-York Historical Society, New York City
NN	New York Public Library, New York City
NNC	Columbia University, New York, N.Y.
NNPM	Pierpont Morgan Library, New York, N.Y.
NWM	United States Military Academy, West Point, N.Y.
NbO	Omaha Public Library, Omaha, Neb.
NcD	Duke University, Durham, N.C.
NcU	University of North Carolina, Chapel Hill
NjHi	New Jersey Historical Society, Newark
NjMoHP	Morristown National Historical Park, Morristown, N.J.
NjP	Princeton University, Princeton, N.J.
OClWHi	Western Reserve Historical Society, Cleveland, Ohio
OrU	University of Oregon, Eugene
PBL	Lehigh University, Bethlehem, Pa.
PHC	Haverford College, Haverford, Pa.
PHi	Historical Society of Pennsylvania, Philadelphia
PPiU	University of Pittsburgh, Pittsburgh, Pa.
PPRF	Rosenbach Foundation, Philadelphia, Pa.
PU	University of Pennsylvania, Philadelphia
PWbH	Wyoming Historical and Geological Society, Wilkes-Barre, Pa.
SpSAG	Archivo General de Indias, Seville, Spain
T	Tennessee State Library and Archives, Nashville
TBHay	Haywood County Archives, Haywood County Court, Brownsville, Tenn.
TDWe	Weakley County Archives, Weakley County Court, Dresden, Tenn.
TFWi	Williamson County Archives, Williamson County Court, Franklin, Tenn.
THer	Ladies' Hermitage Association, Hermitage, Tenn.
THi	Tennessee Historical Society, Nashville
TJMad	Madison County Archives, Madison County Court, Jackson, Tenn.
TMPPM	Pink Palace Museum, Memphis, Tenn.
TMSh	Shelby County Archives, Shelby County Court, Memphis, Tenn.
TNDa	Davidson County Archives, Davidson County Court, Nashville, Tenn.

TNJ	Jean and Alexander Heard Library, Vanderbilt University, Nashville, Tenn.
TPHen	Henry County Archives, Henry County Court, Paris, Tenn.
TSBe	Bedford County Archives, Bedford County Court, Shelbyville, Tenn.
TU	University of Tennessee, Knoxville
TUOb	Obion County Archives, Obion County Court, Union City, Tenn.
TxU	University of Texas, Austin
UPB	Brigham Young University, Provo, Utah
Uk	British Library, London, England
ViU	University of Virginia, Charlottesville
ViW	College of William and Mary, Williamsburg, Va.
WHi	State Historical Society of Wisconsin, Madison

SHORT TITLES

Annals of Congress	*The Debates and Proceedings in the Congress of the United States* .... 42 vols. Washington, D.C., 1834–56.
ASP	*American State Papers: Documents Legislative and Executive, of the Congress of the United States* .... 38 vols. Washington, D.C., 1832–61.
Bassett	John Spencer Bassett, ed., *Correspondence of Andrew Jackson.* 7 vols. Washington, D.C., 1926–35.
Calhoun Papers	Clyde N. Wilson et al., eds., *The Papers of John C. Calhoun.* 22 vols. to date. Columbia, S.C., 1959–.
Clay Papers	Melba Porter Hay et al., eds., *The Papers of Henry Clay.* 10 vols. and Supplement. Lexington, Ky., 1959–92.
FHQ	*Florida Historical Quarterly.*
Heiskell	Samuel G. Heiskell, *Andrew Jackson and Early Tennessee History.* 2 vols. Nashville, Tenn., 1918 (1st Edition); 3 vols. Nashville, Tenn., 1921 (2nd Edition).
House Journal	U.S. Congress, House of Representatives, *Journal of the House of Representatives*
HRDoc	U.S. Congress, House of Representatives, *House Documents.*
HRRep	U.S. Congress, House of Representatives, *House Reports.*

Jackson	Harold D. Moser, David R. Hoth et al., eds., *The Papers of Andrew Jackson.* 5 vols. to date. Knoxville, Tenn., 1980–.
mAJs	Microfilm of *The Papers of Andrew Jackson*, Supplement (forthcoming).
NYPLB	*Bulletin of the New York Public Library.*
Parton	James Parton, *Life of Andrew Jackson.* 3 vols. New York, 1860.
Register of Debates in Congress	U.S. Congress, *Register of Debates in Congress.* 14 vols. Washington, D.C., 1825–37.
Richardson *Messages and Papers of the Presidents*	James D. Richardson, ed., *A Compilation of the Messages and Papers of the Presidents, 1789–1897.* 10 vols. Washington, D.C., 1896–99.
SDoc	U.S. Congress, Senate, *Senate Documents.*
Senate Executive Proceedings	U.S. Congress, Senate, *Journal of the Executive Proceedings of the Senate.*
Senate Journal	U.S. Congress, Senate, *Senate Journal.*
THQ	*Tennessee Historical Quarterly.*
TPUS	Clarence E. Carter and John Porter Bloom, eds., *The Territorial Papers of the United States.* 28 vols. Washington, D.C., 1934–75.
Writings of Sam Houston	Amelia W. Williams and Eugene C. Barker, eds., *The Writings of Sam Houston, 1813–1863.* 8 vols. Austin, Texas, 1938–43.

Chronology

1821

Jan 8	Creek delegates at Indian Springs signed treaty ceding a portion of tribal lands in Georgia to the United States
Jan 16	Presided at Nashville dinner honoring George Washington Campbell, recently returned as minister from Russia
Jan 17	Moses Austin received grant of land in Texas for settlement
Jan 18	Met with delegation of Cherokee Indians representing the Creek Path towns
Jan 23	Andrew Erwin filed amended answer in lawsuit *Jackson* v. *Erwin*
Jan	Benjamin Lundy commenced publication of *Genius of Universal Emancipation*
Feb 4	Stopped overnight at Samuel Savage's plantation, en route to Tennessee from Alabama
Feb 6	Attended court at Franklin, Tennessee
Feb 8	Returned to Hermitage
Feb 19	Senate reratified Adams-Onís Treaty
Feb 24	Mexico proclaimed independence from Spain
Feb 28	Congress passed land relief act allowing adjustments in the terms of purchase of public lands; became law March 2
March 5	James Monroe inaugurated as president for second term
March 10	Commissioned to receive Florida from Spain and as governor of the territory
April 14	Left Nashville with Rachel Jackson and party for New Orleans aboard the *Cumberland* en route to Florida
April 22	Arrived at New Orleans
May 1	Attended public dinner in his honor at Blakely, Alabama
May 3	Attended public dinner in his honor at Mobile, Alabama
May 9	Arrived at Cantonment Montpelier
June 9	James G. Forbes arrived from Cuba carrying orders authorizing José M. Callava to arrange the transfer of West Florida to the United States
June 16	Moved quarters to Manuel Gonzalez's house northwest of Pensacola

July 10	Robert Butler received the transfer of East Florida to the United States
July 12	Moved quarters to Galvez Springs, two miles west of Pensacola
July 17	Entered Pensacola; received West Florida from Spain for the United States
Aug 10	Missouri admitted as a state
Aug 22	Ordered arrest of José M. Callava for failure to produce documents in the Vidal case
Sept 20	James Jackson and John Coffee concluded agreement for sale of AJ's Evans Spring farm in Alabama to Richard C. Cross
Oct 4	Attended public dinner and ball in his honor at Austin's Tavern in Pensacola
Oct 8	Left Pensacola for Tennessee
Nov 4	Arrived at Hermitage
Nov 9	Honored at public dinner in Nashville
Nov 13	Resigned governorship of Florida
Nov 23	Attended public dinner in Nashville honoring Governor William Carroll
Dec 15	Agents of the American Colonization Society purchased the tract of land in West Africa that would become Liberia
Dec 18	South Carolina legislative caucus nominated William Lowndes for president

1822

Jan 3	Returned to Hermitage from Florence, where he had employed Stephen Sharrock as overseer of his Big Spring farm
Feb 5	Thomas G. Watkins visited the Hermitage and obtained a reconciliation with Jackson
Feb 28	Ordered dismissal of Stephen Sharrock as overseer at Big Spring farm
March 14	Employed Egbert Harris as overseer at Big Spring farm
April 6	First issue of Philadelphia *Columbian Observer,* edited by Stephen Simpson, published a laudatory sketch of Jackson, whom it would soon support for president
April 22	House of Representatives passed resolution calling for investigation of the war department contract for stone for the Rip Rap Shoals of Virginia
May 4	James Monroe vetoed bill for repair of the Cumberland Road
June 19	United States formally recognized independence of Gran Colombia, first Latin American state so recognized

June 22	Returned from visit to Alabama
July 2	Denmark Vesey, a free black, was executed at Charleston, South Carolina, for plotting a slave revolt
July 4	Accepted sword voted by the Tennessee legislature in 1819 to honor his War of 1812 service
July 23	Having bought out the Nashville *Clarion,* Patrick Henry Darby published the first issue of the Nashville *Constitutional Advocate,* which supported Jackson's presidential candidacy and pursued Darby's private feuds
July 27	Nominated for presidency by Tennessee house caucus
Aug 3	Nominated for presidency by Tennessee senate caucus
Aug 7	The *Washington Republican and Congressional Examiner*, supportive of John C. Calhoun and opposed to William H. Crawford, commenced publication
Sept 25	Returned from Alabama to Hermitage
Oct 7	Admitted as member, and elected Grand Master, of Masonic Grand Lodge of the State of Tennessee
Oct 20	Delegates of the European powers met in first working session of the Congress of Verona; formal sessions concluded December 14
Oct 27	William Lowndes died at sea while en route to England
cNov 17	Left Florence to return to Tennessee
Nov 18	Henry Clay nominated for president by caucus of Kentucky legislature
Nov 20	Arrived at Franklin, Tennessee, en route home from Alabama, and remained for burial of Rachel Donelson Eastin, a niece, who had died there a few hours previous
Nov 24	Returned to the Hermitage
Dec 12	United States recognized independence of Mexico.

1823

Jan 6	Nicholas Biddle elected president of Second Bank of the United States
Jan 8	Attended public dinner at Nashville commemorating the Battle of New Orleans
Jan 20	First of a series of letters disclosing the "A.B." plot appeared in the *Washington Republican*
Jan 27	Confirmed by U.S. Senate as Envoy Extraordinary and Minister Plenipotentiary of the United States to Mexico
cFeb 12	Visited Gallatin, Tennessee, to arbitrate a mercantile dispute involving Samuel K. Blythe, Hardy M. Cryer, and Samuel Gwin
March 15	Declined formally the appointment as minister to Mexico

cMarch 15	First letter of "Wyoming" published in Philadelphia *Columbian Observer*
March 19	Mexican emperor Agustín de Iturbide abdicated throne
April 7	French army invaded Spain to restore monarchy; resistance crushed by August 31
April 8–12	Presided over special meeting of Grand Lodge of the State of Tennessee Masons at Nashville
July 10	Honored at Murfreesboro public dinner
July 13	Thomas H. Fletcher's "Political Horse Racing" appeared in the *Richmond Enquirer*, reprinted from the *Nashville Gazette*
July 24	Attended sale of town lots at Florence, Alabama, by the Cypress Land Company
Aug 9	Returned home from Alabama
Aug 30	Elected a vice-president of newly established Nashville Bible society
Sept 18	Florida Indians signed Treaty of Moultrie Creek with United States commissioners
Sept 19	Signed agreement settling his lawsuit against Andrew Erwin regarding Duck River lands
Sept	William H. Crawford suffered stroke
Oct 1	Elected to the United States Senate
Oct 2	Tennessee house passed resolutions condemning presidential nominations by congressional caucuses; senate concurred November 15, and the governor was directed to submit resolutions to other legislatures
Oct 7	Reelected as Grand Master Mason and presided over regular meeting of the Grand Lodge of the State of Tennessee
Oct 23	Arrived at Hermitage after visit to Murfreesboro
cNov 11	Departed the Hermitage for Washington, after borrowing money from his friend John Overton for trip
Nov 17	Attended public dinner in Knoxville
Nov 29	Members of the South Carolina legislature endorsed John C. Calhoun for president
Dec 2	James Monroe proclaimed Monroe Doctrine in annual message to Congress
Dec 3	Arrived in Washington
Dec 9	Appointed to Senate committees on foreign relations and military affairs
Dec 11	Georgia senate passed resolution endorsing William H. Crawford for President; house concurred December 13
Dec 17	Resolutions of Alabama legislature proposing Jackson for president were submitted to Governor Israel Pickens, who disapproved them on December 22

Dec 23	"A Visit from St. Nicholas" published anonymously in the Troy (New York) *Sentinel*

1824

Jan 1	Attended general reception hosted by President James Monroe
Jan 8	Accepted gift of pistols formerly belonging to George Washington, a gift to Washington from the Marquis de Lafayette; attended party given by John Q. Adams and a ball hosted by Lewis Carusi
Jan 10	Visited by Major Ridge, Cherokee delegate to Washington
Jan 16	Maine legislature nominated John Q. Adams for president
cJan 18	Nashville pastor William Hume presided over dedication of the newly constructed Hermitage church
Jan 21	Appointed to Senate select committee to consider House resolution regarding visit of the Marquis de Lafayette
Feb 14	Congressional caucus endorsed William H. Crawford for president
Feb 28	*Nashville Republican*, strongly supportive of Jackson's presidential candidacy, commenced publication, replacing the *Constitutional Advocate*
Feb	Sat for portrait by John Vanderlyn
March 2	U.S. Supreme Court ruled in Gibbons v. Ogden that the federal government had exclusive jurisdiction over interstate commerce
March 4	State convention of Pennsylvania Democratic Republicans met at Harrisburg and nominated Jackson for presidency; Ninian Edwards confirmed as minister to Mexico
March 13	Anglo-American convention to suppress the slave trade signed; not ratified
March 15	Hosted birthday dinner in Washington
March 16	Received gold medal voted by Congress for War of 1812 service
March 30–31	Henry Clay used the term "American system" in his speech on the tariff
April 16	House passed the tariff bill
April 17	United States signed treaty with Russia setting southern boundary of Russian territory at 54° 40' north latitude
April 21	Appointed to joint committee to set time for adjournment of Congress
May 13	Senate approved an amended tariff bill, Jackson voting yea

May 19	House and Senate reached agreement on Tariff Act of 1824, which became law on May 22
May 24	Obtained leave of absence for remainder of Senate session
May 25	American Sunday School Union established
May 27	Arrived at Washington, Pennsylvania, en route to Nashville; met with Ninian Edwards who was en route to Washington to testify in the "A.B." matter
June 4	Arrived home at the Hermitage
June 10	Honored at Nashville public dinner
June 17	Bureau of Indian Affairs established within the war department
June 22	Hosted dinner at Hermitage for friends and neighbors
July 3	Attended Independence Day celebration in Nashville
July 6	Attended Independence Day celebration at Fountain of Health near the Hermitage
July 15	Richard Keith Call and Mary Letitia Kirkman married at the Hermitage
Aug 9	Washington *National Journal,* devoted to the interest of John Quincy Adams, commenced publication, replacing the *Washington Republican*
Aug 15	The Marquis de Lafayette arrived in New York to commence national tour
Aug 28	Attended public dinner at Florence, Alabama
cSept 21	Visited Murfreesboro and reached agreement with Bennett Smith on settlement of Smith's lawsuit against John Hutchings's executors
Oct 5	Presided over last meeting as Grand Master of the Grand Lodge of the State of Tennessee Masons; Wilkins Tannehill elected to the position, October 6
Oct 15	Attended Nashville dinner honoring John H. Eaton
Nov 8	Departed Nashville for Washington
Nov 16	Attended ball at Lexington, Kentucky
Dec 1	Presidential electors gave AJ a plurality with ninety-nine electoral votes
Dec 7	Arrived in Washington; took Senate seat
Dec 9	Visited with Secretary of State John Q. Adams
Dec 15	Appointed to Senate select committee to report on president's message about the visit of the Marquis de Lafayette
Dec 31	Kentucky house passed resolution requesting its congressmen to vote for Jackson in the presidential contest

The Papers, 1821–1824

1821

Lingering effects of the Panic of 1819 continued to manifest themselves in late 1820 and early 1821, and Andrew Jackson was duly affected personally and professionally. Loathe to remain in debt to the government, Jackson repeatedly tried to sell his unpaid-for Evans Spring farm in Lauderdale County, Alabama, finally succeeding in September 1821. Professionally, Jackson's position as major general of the army and commander of the Southern Division was also precarious. The federal government's retrenchment policy targeted the army, and in May 1820, the House of Representatives had requested Secretary of War John Caldwell Calhoun (1782–1850; Yale 1804) to draft a plan to reduce army personnel by approximately one-half. Throughout the summer and fall of 1820, the secretary had consulted with leading military figures, including Jackson, about such a plan (see AJ to Calhoun, August 9, 1820, Jackson, *4:385–87).*

As the Congress, which had convened on November 13, 1820, considered the army reduction, rumors reached Washington that Spain had finally ratified the 1819 Adams-Onís Treaty, ceding Florida to the United States and securing the nation's southeastern border. Jackson, who had invaded Florida in 1814 and 1818, supported the treaty because it eliminated foreign influence along the upper Gulf Coast, and as early as 1819, his name had been mentioned as a possible governor of the new territory. Spain's ratification, officially communicated to Washington on February 10, 1821, renewed speculation that Jackson, a possible casualty of retrenchment, might succeed to the governorship.

To James Monroe

Division of the South
Head Quarters,
Nashville Jany. 1. 1821

Sir,

I received with pleasure your letter by Mr. [John S.] Somerville with whom I am much pleased, and doubt not but he will be very beneficial to our college and the youth of our country. It affords us much gratification to hear from you that his demeanour and capacity are good; for it is by procuring such characters in our college that we can at all calculate upon its prosperity or utility.[1]

I am by this day's mail advised that Judge [Dominick Augustin] Hall is no more. From my knowledge of the people of New-Orleans, I know it to be all important that his successor should be a well tried, firm patriot and strongly attached to the American interest, whose knowledge of the people & the laws combined with fitness & legal talent to carry it into effect should enable him to unite the happiness of the people with the security of that country. In Abner L[awson] Duncan Esq. of New Orleans can be found this suitable character. I fully experienced in my defence of New Orleans the energy & capacity of his mind with a great attachment to his country. He was a faithful sentinel, & by his firmness & knowledge of the mixed population rendered his country & myself important services. I am actuated in addressing you on this subject by a sincere regard for the happiness of the people of that country to whom I feel greatly attached & I am confident that by this appointment their happiness & the interest of our common country will be better promoted than by conferring the appointment on any other person. If he is appointed I have no doubt of his accepting the office.[2]

I see by the papers from the City that it is probable our Treaty with Spain is ratified by the King & Cortes. if this should prove to be a fact, and it should be ratified by the Senate, it would afford me much pleasure to have the honor to receive the Barrancas and the Floridas, from the Spanish Authorities.[3]

I have a hope that you are unanimously elected President for the next four years.[4]

I sincerely regret the unpleasant situation in which the House of Representatives have placed the nation by the vote respecting the State of Missouri. Should the House not reconsider the subject I shudder for the consequences. The feelings of the South & West are aroused. The Eastern & Northern people have fully unmasked themselves, & if I can judge correctly Missouri will not retrograde or humble herself. What then will be the consequence? Missouri may seize the public property & funds within her limits. What course will Congress then adopt? I hope the majority will see the evil of this rash despotic act & admit the State and prevent the evil.[5]

Mrs Jackson joins me in requesting to be affectionately remembered to your amiable lady & family.[6] I am with sincere regard Yr. Mo. Ob. Servant

Andrew Jackson

Copy, NjP (8-0034); Extract, NN (8-0036). Monroe (1758–1831) had recently been elected to his second term as president.

1. See Monroe to AJ, December 12, 1820. Somerville, a former tutor of Monroe's family and author of *Somerville's Plume of the Classics, or, Select Classical Pieces, in English Verse* (Washington, 1820), was appointed professor of languages at Cumberland College on January 18. He later taught at other schools in Dickson and Davidson counties.

2. In 1815, Hall (c1765–1820), federal district judge for New Orleans, had fined Jackson $1,000 for contempt of court arising out of Jackson's suspension of the writ of habeas corpus. On December 18, 1820, James Scallan had written Jackson of the illness of Hall and urged the appointment of Duncan as successor. Duncan (c1777–1823), one of Jackson's

volunteer aides during the Battle of New Orleans, was a defense counsel during Jackson's trial before Hall. Duncan did not receive the appointment.

3. Spain ratified the Adams-Onís Treaty on October 24, 1820, and the United States reratified it on February 19, 1821. On March 10, Monroe commissioned Jackson to receive the transfer of Florida and to act as governor. Fort San Carlos de Barrancas, located about 9 miles south-southwest of Pensacola, guarded the entrance of Pensacola Bay.

4. When the electoral votes for president were formally counted on February 14, Monroe received all but one.

5. In March 1820, Congress had authorized Missouri to form a state government, but a clause in the proposed state constitution prohibiting the entrance of free blacks and mulattoes into Missouri rekindled opposition to the territory's admission. On December 13, 1820, the House of Representatives defeated a resolution admitting Missouri into the Union. The ensuing controversy was finally resolved by a second compromise championed by Henry Clay, and Monroe proclaimed the admission of Missouri as a state on August 10 (*Annals of Congress,* 16th Cong., 2nd sess., pp. 390, 440, 453–55, 669–70, 1228, 1238–40, 1784–86).

6. Mrs. Jackson, née Rachel Donelson (c1767–1828). In 1786 Monroe had married Elizabeth Kortright (c1763–1830), the daughter of a New York merchant.

To John Caldwell Calhoun

Division of the South
Head Quarters
Nashville January 4th. 1821

Sir

I have just received your report on the reduction of the Army conformably to a resolve of Congress of May last, accompanied by your polite note of the 16th. ultimo; for which receive my thanks.[1]

I have read your report with great attention and much pleasure, and am happy to find it not only realizing my own expectations and that of your friends; but also those of every description of character here. Since its appearance the enemies of the army are dumb. It has given to the army a character and importance which I have no doubt will convince every mind wishing our prosperity and independence as a nation, that we cannot be secure without an army organized as you have proposed. It is calculated for peace. It is a good basis to build on in war. In it there is system and stability, and in the alternate change from war to peace, the system remains stable and entire. Had such a system existed at the commencement of the late War, thousands of men and millions of treasure would have been saved to the nation. Canada would have been ours, and we would not have met disaster, disgrace and defeat. Our national character would not have been humbled and disgraced by the capture of our Capitol. I think it will silence the *little* members of Congress who have the reduction of the army their *riding horse* for some years[2]

This able system the result of your labour, has raised a debt of gratitude upon your country, which I trust it will soon repay—I have the honor to be Very Respy. Yr. Mo Obt. servant.

(Signed) Andrew Jackson

LC, DLC (63). Published in *Calhoun Papers,* 5:528.

1. Calhoun had forwarded his report of December 12 (*ASP, Military Affairs,* 2:188–98) to Jackson on December 16, 1820.

2. Calhoun's proposal retained the skeletal structure of a larger army by keeping the officer corps intact but cutting enlisted personnel by half, allowing rapid expansion in time of national emergency. Among other "little members," Jackson was probably referring to Newton Cannon (1781–1841), a colonel of the Tennessee Mounted Rifles during the War of 1812 and Jackson's political opponent, who had been attempting to reduce the size of the army since the Fourteenth Congress.

From Robert Butler

Adjutant Generals Office Nashville
January 15th. 1821

Sir.

In the month of September last I forwarded my pay Accounts to the City of Washington for payment embracing therein the months of May, June, July August & September—I resorted to this Measure from the Statement made by Maj. [Cary] Nicholas herewith inclosed and marked A—

I received from the Pay master General the inclosed letter marked B—[1]

You must be sensible Sir, how necessary it is to Officers in our service to receive their pay at early periods and more particularly to those situated as I am with a large family and no other means of support—

I have been patiently waiting (under unpleasant circumstances) the completion of the Arrangement spoken of by the Pay. Mr. General, and I regret to be under the necessity of informing you that Majr. Nicholas does not now expect any funds to be remitted to him, and that out of Eight months estimates he has received but two months funds—

I have due me at the end of the present month nine months pay, except five hundred dollars advanced by the Majr. out of the two months estimate received.

As we are not permitted to send on our accounts—As Majr. Nicholas will not receive any more funds—As there are no other pay masters who could be prepared to pay the Division Staff without having estimated therefor: I feel constrained from a sense of duty as well as personal necessity, to call your attention to the subject—I have the honor to be Very respectfully Yr M. obt. svt.

Robert Butler

ALS, DLC (29). Butler (1786–1860) had married Jackson's niece Rachel Hays (b. 1786) and was adjutant general of the Southern Division.

1. The enclosures, Nicholas to [Butler], September 12, 1820, and Nathan Towson to Butler, October 5, 1820, related to Nicholas paying army officers with local, depreciated bank notes, rather than specie, and Towson's assurance that arrangements had been made to pay officers with money of equal value with specie (DLC-29). Nicholas (1786–1829), a Kentucky native and nephew of Virginia Governor Wilson Cary Nicholas, was battalion paymaster, 1817–21, thereafter moving to Florida where he was postmaster and edited the

Pensaçola *Floridian*. Towson (1784–1854), a War of 1812 veteran, was paymaster general. For the origins of Butler's problem with his army pay, see Nicholas to AJ, September 14, 1820 (*Jackson*, 4:389–90).

The combined effect of the Creek War spoliations of 1813–14, land cessions of 1816–19, encroachments by white settlers, disagreements within the Cherokee nation, and Jackson's own views favoring removal encouraged some of the Cherokees of the Creek Path area in northeastern Alabama to conspire to obtain from the federal government a separate reservation in present-day Marshall, Blount, Saint Clair, and Etowah counties, Alabama, without the approval of the Cherokee national council, and with the implied intent of exchanging that reserve for land in Arkansas. The role of the Cherokee principal chief Pathkiller (d. 1827) in the conspiracy is unclear. When the conspirators presented their plan to Jackson, they suggested Pathkiller's acquiescence, but he later denounced the plot to the Cherokee council, which indicted the leaders for treason in March. Even so, the Creek Path Indians continued their efforts to obtain the reservation as late as November 1822. Jackson, for his part, commended the lower Cherokees' plan to Pathkiller, below, and in another letter of the same date to Secretary of War Calhoun.

To Pathkiller et al.

Division of the South—
Head quarters Nashville
January 18th. 1821

Friends & Brothers

By the hands of <your delegation,> our Brothers George Fields, <the> [Young] Wolf, and Turtle Fields I recd. your letters, one from my old Friend and brother the King of your nation, the Path Killer, dated the 11th. of December 1820—and two from your chiefs, the Speaker, Wausaucy, Archibald Campbell, KnightKiller, James Spencer and John Thompson; which I have read & considered with great attention—and have <heard> received from the mouth of your faithfull friend and agent, Turtle Fields, who has explained to me all your wishes, not expressed in your letters; as it respects the boundary you wish reserved, and the grievances you labour under, from the want of being heard in the council of your nation by your chiefs, heretofore, and your apprehensions of being here after <being> deprived of your country without your consent, as you have been of receiving your proportion of the annuities for the last three years all of which, I think reasonable, and I have no doubt but will be heard, & redressed by your father the President of the U. States.[1]

Friends & Brothers—you have fought with me, I then told you I was your friend, that <the> your father the President of the united States, was not only your friend, but he loved you as children, and he would act allways as your friend—you now ask him through me, to have secured to you a tract of country, small in proportion to what you are entitled to compared with your numbers & compared with the whole country reserved by treaty for the use of the whole cherokee nation <compared with your numbers>, and to have this <secured> allotted to you & your posterity permanantly, so that your nation cannot Sell it without your consent to the u states—Relinquishing all right to any <part of> other land you may be intitled to which has been secured by treaty to the cherokee nation <to the United States> which may of right belong to you as part of that nation—This is so reasonable, that I have no doubt but your father the President of the u. States And Congress assembled will readily grant—<and> The chiefs of the upper part of your nation cannot complain of this, <when> They can procure by proper application the same security This <is> done, you Know that you will rest unmolested in possession of what is thus allotted to you as long as you choose to possess it—and if the upper part of the nation chooses, it can <by the same offer, of Contracting their boundary> obtain the same security you now ask for;[2] <for your part of the nation and which I trust will be granted them as> I hope your request will be granted you—at least I can assure you as a friend and Brother, & as a friend of your whole nation, that as far as I have influence, it shall be exercised to obtain your request from the President & congress of the united States. and for which purpose I have transmitted to your father the President, the three letters recd. by your trusty friends & Brothers adressed to me, as well as your trusty agents Turtle Fields explanation of all your wishes—<all which I hope will be granted you and> so soon as I receive an answer from your father the President of the united States I will forward it to you.[3]

Friends & Brothers I never have flattered or deceived one of my red Brothers—I never tell them lies, I have not the power to say positively that your request will be granted, but I say to you, I think it is reasonable and ought to be granted, and that I will make a faithfull communication of it to your father the President of the United States, and use my influence that the reserve you ask shall be made to you, your happiness and permanant security require it—the Interest of your white Brethern urges it, from which I conclude <in my mind> it will be granted to you. I have directed your delegation to Shake you all by the hand for me as friends & Brothers; and say to you that I wish the happiness of you, <all> & your whole nation—I am your Friend and Brother

Andrew Jackson

ALS draft, DNA-RG 107 (M221-89); Copy, DNA-RG 233 (8-0086). Published in *ASP, Indian Affairs,* 2:505 (from Copy).

1. See Pathkiller to AJ, December 11, 1820; Speaker et al. to AJ, January 3 and 8; and Report of meeting with Cherokee Indians (containing Turtle Fields's explanation), [January 18]. The Fields, George (d. 1849) and Turtle, were mixed-blood brothers, both of whom fought under Jackson in the Creek War. Turtle became an itinerant Methodist

preacher in Alabama and Tennessee before moving to Arkansas in 1839. Of the other Creek Path conspirators, all but Wososey were found in Alabama by the 1835 census. Young Wolf and Speaker, both full blood Cherokees, lived at Turkey Town and in Blount County, respectively. Archibald Campbell (d. 1859), like Turtle a Methodist exhorter, served on the Cherokee executive council in the 1840s. Knight Killer lived at Wills Valley; Spencer, like Campbell, at Creek Path. John Thompson, a white married into the Cherokee Nation, was an interpreter. Wososey and Speaker were considered to be supporters of the so-called "White Path Rebellion," an anti-missionary movement in 1827.

2. The Cherokee nation had been politically split since the 1770s when dissident chiefs who refused to accept peace with the whites founded new towns along the lower Tennessee River valley from Chickamauga to Muscle Shoals. In the early 1800s these lower town Cherokees, to which the Creek Path Indians belonged, were significantly more amenable to removal than the upper town Cherokees of Georgia, the Carolinas, and East Tennessee.

3. See AJ to John C. Calhoun, January 18; no reply has been found.

The probable reduction in the army posed a ticklish political problem for James Monroe. Although Jackson had repeatedly offered to retire, he had not actually done so, and the president was reluctant to dismiss the controversial but popular Hero of New Orleans. Compounding the problem, military practice dictated that Washington retain Major General Jacob Jennings Brown (1775–1828) because of his seniority. Despite Jackson's refusal of the Florida governorship when it was offered during Monroe's western tour in 1819, Monroe again offered the position, and Jackson's acceptance on February 11 resolved the president's difficulty.

From James Monroe

Washington Jany. 24. 1821

Dear Sir—

You will hear from other friends the proceedings of Congress, on the principle of Oconomy, respecting the reduction of the army. On that subject therefore I need say nothing.[1]

We expect daily the treaty from Spain ceding Florida, ratified by her govt. In that event, will you accept the govt. of the territory? The climate will suit you, and it will give me pleasure to place you in that trust. Let me hear from you, as soon as possible, as the arrangment must be made, during the present session of Congress, which will terminate, as you know, on the 3d. of March. You declin'd it when I saw you, but perhaps, further reflection may reconcile the measure to you. with the best regards of my whole family to you & Mrs Jackson I am very sincerely your friend & servant

James Monroe

ALS, DLC (29). Published in Bassett, 3:38.

1. See David Holmes to AJ, January 19, and John C. Calhoun to AJ, January 25. An army reduction bill passed the House of Representatives on January 23 (*Annals of Congress*, 16th Cong., 2nd sess., pp. 933–34, 936–37).

To James Monroe

Hermitage near Nashville
February 11th. 1821

Dear Sir

I have the pleasure to acknowledge the receipt of your letter of the 24th. ulto.[1]

I have read in the last papers a full detail of the proceedings of Congress, and it is with extreme regret that I find (from the *mania* for retrenchment) a majority of the House of Representatives have lost sight of the safety of our country at home, and its character abroad—And if this mania is not restrained by the wisdom and firmness of the Senate, in the event of war, our country must mourn the useless loss of much blood and treasure, as well as great national disgrace. If Congress leaves the nation without complete defence, it at once invites invasion from abroad.[2]

I am pleased to learn that our treaty with Spain is ratified by her Government—This, with proper means, will afford ample security to the lower Country. You ask me, if I will accept the Government of this important Territory? I sincerely thank you for the friendly manner you have regarded me, and the confidence you repose in me by this offer. Actuated from a belief, that my services would not much avail the public good, nor materially benefit your administration, I first determined not to accept it; but from the solictations of my friends at the City as well as here, strongly urging a conviction that my acceptance of the appointment, would quicken the organization of the Government, and tend to draw to that country a respectable population, I have determined to accept it, provided it will answer your views, that I may resign as soon as the Government is organized and in full operation[3]—If the appointment is given me, my private concerns will require this course—My means are not competent to bear the expenses necessary to execute the Government of that Territory for any length of time. My fortune and constitution have already been much impaired in the service of my country, and although a prejudiced world may now say, the Seminole Campaign was but a struggle for the present appointment, yet will I go on, and devote what remains of my strength to its best interests, and in the midst of retirement an unsullied conscience will bid me pray for its happiness, and raise my feeble voice in its behalf—I am Sir, with sincere regard Yr. Mo Obt servant

Andrew Jackson

LS, endorsed by Monroe, and Extract, NN (8-0103, -0109); Copy, NjP (8-0107). Published in Bassett, 3:38–39.

1. See above.

2. Jackson was referring to reports in the Washington *National Intelligencer* of debates on

the army reduction bill. Contrary to the plan for army reduction reported by John C. Calhoun and praised by Jackson (see above, AJ to Calhoun, January 4), Congress passed a bill reducing the number of officers as well as enlisted men (3 *U.S. Statutes at Large* 615–16).

3. For Jackson's continuing vacillation over accepting the Florida governorship, see AJ to John Coffee, March 1, below; and to James C. Bronaugh, February 11.

From Isaac Lewis Baker

Natchez 18th. feby 1821

Dear General,

I did not receive your letter by Miss Sally McConnell untill a few days ago when she sent it to me in New Orleans after keeping it a long while here in Expectation of my arrival.[1] I regret exceedingly to hear that your health has again been seriously assailed but I humbly trust all is yet well with you and that you have constitution enough left after all your sufferings and privations to stand the wear and tear of very many years to come. In my progress thro life I may safely say that after my father[2] I owe you more obligations than to all other men living and you cannot be ignorant, feel great solicitude for any and every thing which regards you. Death and Disease is with us all a common inheritance—but in case the worst befal you—your friends have still the consolation left them that your fame and renown <will> are fixed on a proud basis and will exist as long as History remains to bear testimony of the high deeds of the gallant and virtuous—

I was gratified on reaching this place yesterday to find Mr [Ralph Eleazar Whitesides] Earle in this country. He has done well in exhibiting his full length likeness here as it has gratified the citizens and not been unprofitable to himself. An effort (which will succeed) is making here to raise a thousand Dollars to buy one for this city. When this arrangement is completed which is expected to morrow Mr Earle will go on to New Orleans where I have no doubt he will meet all the patronage he is entitled to receive. I will return as far as Plaquemine on my way home with him and will give him Such letters to my friends in the city as may be of service to him.[3]

I send you with this a pamphlet lately much read and sought after in our State against the [Thomas Bolling] Robertson Dynasty—which has declared open war against all your friends and adherents who dared to oppose their coming into power[4]—They have quarrelled with the French and cannot get on well with only a moiety of the americans to aid them in the extraordinary game they are playing—

My brother-in-Law Mr [Alexander] Porter has been forced on the Robertson administration as judge of the Supreme Court in place of [Pierre Auguste Charles Bourguignon] Derbigny made secretary of State. He gets leave of absence in the spring for Six months to visit his mother & family i*[n Ireland]*[5]

Mr [John] Dick resigned in Oct. last and was *[replaced]* a few days since by J[ohn] W[itherspoon] Smith Esqr. of N. O*[rleans.]* I do no*[t re]*gret this as my affairs are in a predica*[ment]* that made it unadvisable for me to quit

Attakapas—I undertake a Country practise with every chance of Success—tho as to worldly concerns I now feel little interest in them since heaven has been pleased to blast all my fondest earthly expectations—[6]

Please offer my kindest recollections to Mrs Jackson and present me to my old friends Colo. Butler & Capt [Richard Keith] Call.[7] Your friends hope much to see you here in the Spring but by none of them will you be more warmly welcomed than by your faithful servant.

Isaac L Baker

Miss Sally is well pleased with this country and we all hope will not return before June when I will most probably go on to Tennessee myself—

ALS, DLC (29). Published in Bassett, 3:39–40 (extract). Baker (1792–1830), one of Jackson's aides-de-camp after the War of 1812, left the army in 1816 and settled in Louisiana where he was a lawyer, planter, and sometime member of the state legislature.

1. Not found. Sarah (Sally) McConnell (1786–1821) was a cousin of Baker's recently deceased wife Charlotte Lewis Baker (1792–1820), a daughter of William T. Lewis. In April, McConnell died from injuries sustained when the steamboat *General Robertson* exploded on the Cumberland River, near Eddyville, Kentucky.

2. Joshua Baker (1763–1816), a colonel of Louisiana militia during the Battle of New Orleans, had died of influenza while visiting Nashville.

3. Earl (1788–1838), widower of Jackson's niece Jane Caffery (c1801–19), was touring the Gulf Coast and offering for sale his portrait of Jackson surveying the battlefield at New Orleans (now housed at the Tennessee State Museum, Nashville). The Natchez city government was unable to raise the money for the purchase; the New Orleans city council eventually secured a copy of Earl's portrait for $1,000 but its location is unknown. John J. Audubon, present in the Crescent City during Earl's visit, commented upon the portrait of Jackson: "*Great God* forgive Me if my Jugment is Erroneous—I Never Saw A Worst painted Sign *in the Street of Paris*" (Howard Corning, ed., *The Journal of John James Audubon. . .* [Cambridge, Mass., 1929], p. 149).

4. Robertson (1779–1828; William and Mary 1795) was governor of Louisiana, 1820–22. The pamphlet has not been identified. In the Louisiana gubernatorial election of 1820, the traditional American and French factions contested for the post. Each faction, however, had two candidates. Robertson and Jackson's friend Abner L. Duncan campaigned for the American vote.

5. Porter (1785–1844), who had married Isaac's sister Evelina Villars Baker (1797–1819), served as associate justice of the Louisiana state supreme court until 1833, when he became U.S. senator. Derbigny (1767–1829), a native of France, was an associate justice of the state supreme court, 1813–20, secretary of state, 1820–27, and governor, 1828–29. He had been a candidate for governor in 1820. Jane Knox Porter, Alexander's mother, was the widow of the Irish martyr James Porter (1753–98).

6. Dick (1788–1824) had been federal district attorney for Louisiana since 1814. In March he succeeded Dominick A. Hall as federal district judge, serving until 1824. Smith (1778–1829; Princeton 1795), a son of former Princeton president Samuel S. Smith, emigrated to New Orleans by 1804 and served as federal district attorney, 1821–29. Baker's wife had died in September 1820.

7. Call (1792–1862) was Jackson's aide-de-camp, 1818–21.

To John Caldwell Calhoun

(private) Nashville 1st. March 1821

Dear Sir

On the arrival of Capt [Richard Ivy] Easter I made known to him the contents of your letter to me on the subject of his public accounts—After waiting the arrival of letters which he expected from the South, he yesterday made the communication to me, which is herewith enclosed.[1]

Capt Easter is Sensible of the friendship and liberality you have extended towards him, and with his accustomed magnanimity, discloses his unpleasant and unfortunate situation—and is willing to submit to any thing sooner than involve his friends in his misfortunes, and will await in Nashville any process against him on account of the debt due Government. This has been a source of much pain to me, and whatever may have been, Capt Easters imprudence, before he joined my family I can with truth say that the whole tenor of his conduct, that has come within my knowledge, has been that of a high minded honourable man, whoes feelings soar above a base or dishonourable action. That he has been imprudent at some period of his life, is evident, from the fact of his <having> being a public debteor, but I am well assured he has never been dishonourable, and that his misfortunes have arisen from inexperience and the imprudence of youth.[2]

Had I the means, such is my feeling for this young man, I would advance the amount which he owes. but the situation of my finances will with dificulty and not without economy, enable me to meet my own engagements, and, I could not even do this had I not long since <made> determined to keep my wants within my means. I can therefore do no more than to add my solicitude, that he may not be degraded by being stricken from the Rools of the Army, but that if the regulations require that he should leave the service, that his resignation may be accepted.[3]

Capt Easter has talents, I have confidence in his honour, and have no doubt he will, if ever, able, pay this debt I am Sir Very Respectfully your Obt Sert

Andrew Jackson

LS in Richard K. Call's hand and Copy, DNA-RG 107 (M221-89). "(private)" is in AJ's hand.

1. See Calhoun to AJ, January 22, and Easter to AJ, February 28. Easter (d. 1825), a Georgia native and veteran of the War of 1812, served as assistant deputy quartermaster during the Seminole campaign and incurred an arrearage of over $20,000 in his accounts.

2. Easter had joined Jackson's military family in September 1818 as one of Jackson's aides, resigning in September 1820. At that time he went to Washington to arrange for payment of his army account, and Calhoun had permitted him to search in Georgia for missing vouchers and to attempt to secure his debt by indemnity bonds. Easter failed in the attempt,

and resigned from the army on February 28. Subsequently he read law with John Overton and in 1822 formed a partnership with Richard K. Call in Mobile and Pensacola.

3. Easter's resignation became effective April 1. Calhoun delegated the final decision concerning Easter's accounts to the treasury department (see Calhoun to AJ, March 19). For Jackson's subsequent involvement in the settlement of those accounts, see AJ to Easter, May 14, 1822, below.

To John Coffee

Hermitage March 1rst 1821

Dear Genl

I have the pleasure to acknowledge the recept of your letter of the 13th. ult. and am pleased with the course adopted in the suit Bennet Smith against the Executors of John Hutchings—I have but little doubt but the Judgt will be reversed, and should it not, I will be prepared with all the grounds for a bill of Injunction, there, should the Judgt be reversed I will be also prepared to file a bill here to obtain a perpetual injunction in behalf of the child against that demand.[1] I will be able to shew after the debt became due, that his son Joseph [Dickson Smith] Bot. and paid for upwards of $18,000 of merchandize in Nashville and if he had pursued the principle he could have got his debt[2]—his not having done this and his acknowledgement in his letter that he was pressed to bring suit, and his declaration that he never intended to sue his son, combined with other circumstances as I am advised will be sufficient for a court of chancery to decree a perpetual injunction to prevent him from proceeding against the security. I will thank you to say to Colo. [George] Coulter and Major [John] McKinly, to advise me of the decision of the court the moment it is made, that I may be ready to act promptly as the occasion may require—[3]

On the subject of the treaty with Spain the President believes it will be ratified by our goverment, and has wrote to know of me if I will accept the Goverment—I had said to him when in this country I would not, he requests me to reconsider the subject, and the secratary of war has united with the President on this subject—Major [John Henry] Eaton writes me that my friends in congress is determined to have me appointed whether I will accept or not. from which I infer there is some strong political reason <for> operating with my friends for their solicitude upon this occasion[4]—I had determined, and prepared letters to that effect, saying I would not accept the appointment, my friends at Nashville grew impatient at my decision and on their solicitation believing my letters had gone on the preceding mail said to them, if they would apply at the office, if my letters had not gone on, I would say to the President I would accept it, and organize the Goverment, with the understanding that I might resign, as soon thereafter as I thought proper; my letters had not gone on, and thus I have written, to Mr Monroe, if these letters gets on before the President is compelled to make the nomination I will receive the appointment, my hopes are that they letters will not reach there before the 3rd of March, they cannot before the first—for I assure you it will be with great reluctance I will go to that country in the capacity of Governor, a few days will decide this question when you will hear from me—[5]

I am happy to hear of the success of the Florence Tickett—you ought to push the commissioners to a decision, as soon as this is made, the county will acquiesce in their decision and party spirit on this subject will subside—[6]

Our last dates from the city is only to the 7th ult, there is five mails due. I hope tomorrows mail will give us the news to the 15th. on the last dates the land Bill had not finally passed the senate but was expected to pass by a large Majority I have no doubt but it will pass into a law if congress passes any law of a general nature this Session, which is doubtfull[7]—The committee of ways & means have made a report, that the receipts into the Treasury in this year will meet all the expences of the current year, and there is no necessity for loans—This is placing the Secratary of the Treasury and his report of a deficit of 7 Million in rather an awkard situation—three thousand copies of this report is ordered to be printed—down Mr [William Harris] Crawford must go, for one of two things is certain that he is incompetant to the duties of his station or he is desperately wicked, and has made the false report for wicked purposes, his friends have boasted of his talents, and will scarcly say it originates for the want of capacity, they must then admit that he is wicked.[8]

I left a power of attorney with Mr J[ames] Jackson for [James] Gadsden & myself, and hope the commissioners will do something that will give F[lorence] a start—[9]

Mrs J. Joins me in respects to you, Mrs C & family and believe me to be sincerely yrs

Andrew Jackson

ALS, THi (8-0149). Published in Bassett, 3:40–41 (extract). Coffee (1772–1833), comrade-in-arms with Jackson during the Creek War and the Battle of New Orleans, had married Jackson's niece Mary "Polly" Donelson (1793–1871) in 1809. After the war Coffee and his family moved to Alabama where he was surveyor of the northern district, eventually establishing a farm on Coxe's Creek, north of Florence.

1. Letter not found. Smith (c1764–c1848) was a prominent Rutherford County lawyer, brother of South Carolina Senator William Smith, and father-in-law of John Hutchings (c1776–1817), Jackson's nephew and partner in farming in Alabama. In 1819, Bennett Smith had sued the Hutchings estate for recovery of a debt arising from the sale of slaves. Jackson was involved as an executor of the estate and as guardian of Andrew Jackson Hutchings (1811–41), John's only son. For further discussion of the case, see AJ to Coffee, December 13, 1820 (*Jackson*, 4:404–406).

2. Smith (d. c1823) also lived in Rutherford County.

3. Coalter (d. 1849), a lawyer and former Tennessee legislator from Lincoln County, at this time resided in Lauderdale County where he was a militia colonel. Subsequently, he served as judge of the First Circuit Court in Mississippi. McKinley (1780–1852) was a Florence, Alabama, attorney, and later a U.S. senator and justice of the Supreme Court.

4. See above, James Monroe to AJ, January 24; John C. Calhoun to AJ, January 25; and Eaton to AJ, January 27. Eaton (1790–1856) was U.S. senator from Tennessee.

5. See above, AJ to Monroe, February 11. Congress adjourned on March 3, but Monroe gave Jackson a recess appointment as governor.

6. In early February Lauderdale County citizens had elected commissioners pledged to establish the county seat at Florence.

7. The general land relief act of March 2 allowed the relinquishment of a portion of the purchase for the balance due, a substantial discount for prompt payment, remission of accrued interest, and an extension of time for final payment (3 *U.S. Statutes at Large* 612–14).

8. Crawford (1772–1834), Secretary of the Treasury and a Jackson adversary, indicated the deficit in his annual report, December 1, 1820. On February 6, 1821, Samuel Smith of Maryland reported for the House Committee on Ways and Means that the committee anticipated no deficit at all, thereby obviating the need for increased revenues, but Congress ultimately authorized the president to borrow $5 million if necessary (*Annals of Congress*, 16th Cong., 2nd sess., pp. 487–99, 689–92, 1035–41; 3 *U.S. Statutes at Large* 635–36).

9. The power of attorney has not been located. James Jackson (1782–1840) had been a Nashville merchant before relocating to Florence, Alabama, in late 1818. Gadsden (1788–1858), an army topographical engineer and Southern Division inspector general, had joined Jackson and James C. Bronaugh in purchasing several Florence lots in 1818.

From James Jackson

Forks of Cypress March 1st. 1821

Dear Genl.

I duely recd. yours of 18th. ulto. & waited the result of the meeting of the Stock Holders before writing you, they have done every thing that could reasonably be expected, agreed to allow one third of the purchase money for Lots & Land sold in and adjoining Town to be expended in buildings by the purchasers &, to pay for the publick buildings of the County. Tomorrow Genl. Coffee & myself meet the County Commissioners in Florence to conclude the Contract with them, which will beyond doubt be done. Stock Holders acted with great unanimity, the only thing like an exception came from Mathew Barrow, Mr. Pope of Kentucky & Genl. [Walter Irvine] Adiar of Madison County—[1]

I have paid [Richard] Rapier & [John] Simpson their acct. against you & Wm. [White] Crawford & also that against Andrew J Hutchings & [Malachi] Nicholson[2]—I shall have shortly to visit Murfreesborough, will go by way of Limestone, when I'll do myself the pleasure of going to see you, when I'll look at your acct. & will perhaps be enabled to discover how the error has occured of chargeing the $\$83\,^{33\frac{1}{3}}/_{100}$ on your acct. & not being charged in the Books of J[ames] J[ackson] & Co. I am now inclined to think It must have been placed there by me at Nashville after receiving the acct. from Florence, in the way the last $\$83\,^{33\frac{1}{3}}/_{100}$ was charged—all the business I done at Nashville after the store was moved from there was not entered up untill since I seen you last—[3]

I think from the situation of my business I can with conveniance accompany you to Pensacola, In the event you go, & am making my arrangements accordingly—Captn. John Donelson Jr. says He will also go to Pensacola, indeed I could not well do without his presence—[4]

I have overhauled all my papers & have not found any memorandom nor any thing to induce me to believe I paid you for the oxen bought of Captn. Donelson for Mrs [Sarah Jackson] Hanna We have had much wet weather; which has thrown us more backward than we could wish—all well—Mrs. [Sarah Moore McCullough] Jackson[5] joins me in best wishes to yourself & Lady Truly yours

James Jackson

P. S. I regret much to see the Course taken by Mr. Eaton respecting the Land Bill, or Bill for relieving Land purchasers I fear he is willing to gain popula*[rity]* at the expence of sound Policy & by coming in Contact with his old friends, at last his Conduct in the Bubble Bank & on the subject of our Lands look like it & unless I am convinced that my opinion is ill founded, as a political man, he never again meets my support[6] J. J

ALS, DLC (29). Forks of Cypress, James Jackson's plantation, lay due north of Florence, Alabama.

1. Letter not found. The stockholders of the Cypress Land Company were meeting to decide a course of action for developing Florence as the county seat for Lauderdale County. Barrow (1784–1855), a Davidson County citizen, was one of the founders of the Nashville Female Academy. Adair (d. 1835), an army captain during the War of 1812, had been a Kentucky state legislator and militia general. Pope was probably William Pope, Jr. (b. 1775), brother of John, a Louisville businessman who owned lots in Florence.

2. See the Account with Rapier & Simpson, December 21, 1819. Rapier (d. 1826), a merchant and boat owner, had recently moved his businesses to Florence from Nashville. Simpson (1790–1865), a native of Ireland, emigrated to Florence in 1818, associated with Rapier, and later became a substantial planter. Crawford, the son of Jackson's first cousin James Crawford, Jr., had returned as overseer at Jackson's Evans Spring farm after the departure of Nelson P. Jones in late 1820. By 1830 Crawford had moved to Fayette County, Tennessee, where in 1832 he was colonel of militia. Nicholson (d. 1825) was the overseer at Hutchings's farm.

3. Account not found.

4. Jackson's nephew Donelson (1787–1840) and James Jackson were among the eight Jackson associates who had speculated in Pensacola lands during the winter of 1817–18, an enterprise about which opponents raised questions regarding the general's own involvement in 1819 and during the 1824 and 1828 presidential campaigns (see *Jackson,* 4:285, 325–29, 351).

5. Hanna (c1769–1843), James Jackson's sister and a former resident of Nashville, had relocated to Florence, Alabama, after her merchant husband's death. In 1836 the family moved to Thibodeaux Parish, Louisiana, where she died. In 1810, the widow McCullough (1790–1879) had married James Jackson. This Captain Donelson was probably John, Sr. (1755–1830), Jackson's brother-in-law.

6. John H. Eaton had attempted unsuccessfully to confine the relief act to actual settlers, rather than to speculators, and to exclude town sites (see *Annals of Congress,* 16th Cong., 2nd sess., pp. 213–14). Meanwhile, James Jackson held significant tracts beyond his home plantation, and later in 1821, James Jackson, John Coffee, and John McKinley, as trustees of the Cypress Land Company, applied the land relief law to purchasers of lots in Florence and the surrounding area. In 1820, Eaton became a director of the Bank of the State of Tennessee, inspired by the relief movement (see AJ to William B. Lewis, July 16, 1820, *Jackson,* 4:378–81).

To John Caldwell Calhoun

Hear Quarters D. of the South
Nashville 17th. March 1821.

Dr. Sir

On the 12th. Inst: I recd. from Mr. W[illiam] Lee Auditor of the Treasury Department a letter apologizing for an order he had given to the Paymaster General directing a stoppage of my Pay to the amount of $691.73— This letter I answered on the 14th. Inst. and requested Mr. Lee to refer this subject to your decision, taking into view the instructions under which Major [Robert] Searcy made the Payment together with the 9th. Section of the act of April 24th. 1816.[1]

From the apology offered by Mr. Lee in his letter of the 19th. Ult: and regret expressed at the occurrence, I had concluded that this harsh & hasty order for the suspension of my pay had been countermanded by him.

On yesterday Major [Asher] Philips reported himself and exhibited to me his orders to repair to this place and pay the Genl. Staff with directions to Stop $691.73 of my pay—upon reading this order Sir, you can more readily judge of my feelings of indignation than I can express them.[2]

Had it been known to Mr. Lee that I was insolvent and about to abscond from the Country and thereby the Government would loose this amount, his zeal for the public good might have been some apology for this usurped power, so insulting to honorable feelings—when he did know that if an error existed in my accounts it would be promptly corrected and the amount refunded—There has not been a moment since I have held a commission under the Government that I was not able to close my public accounts, nor has there ever been a cent of public money entrusted to my care, applied to any other use, than to that, to which it was specially directed; and really, that on the application of an Auditor of the Treasury Department, the Paymaster Genl. should direct an order to a Paymaster in the Northern Division to suspend my Pay, has the appearance of design in it, to hold me up to the whole army as a public defaulter. If Mr. Lee upon discovering this error, if indeed any existed, had made it known to me, upon an investigation of the subject & being satisfied of the error, the amount should have been immediately refunded—It may be well for Mr. Lee to be more guarded for the future, least those Officers whose feelings are wantonly outraged by his rashness, may become rash in return, and make him atone for his conduct.

It is due to myself to give you from memory a concise history of this payment.

after the declaration of peace, I was pressed with a multiplicity of business, in consequence of which and the bad state of my health, I had never attended to the act of Congress of the 4th. [3rd] of March 1815 fixing the peace establishment—business in the fall of that year called me to the City of Washington—Upon my arrival there, I made a requisition for Quarters & Forage and was informed that by the law of 1815 I was entitled to neither—My expence being great I called on the Paymaster Genl. for my Pay; in making out the account he proposed allowing me for one Servant and twenty Dollars per month for Forage[3]—I replied, that if I was entitled to compensation for one Servant I must be for four, as I knew of no law refered to in the law of the 3rd. March 1815 that had any relation to servants and that I should not receive $20 per month for Forage—I left the City on the 24th. of December under orders to explore the lower Mississippi, but before I left there, the rough draft of the Bill which passed into a law on the 24th. of April 1816, and as explained to me, the 9th. Section of said Bill was intended to revive and give to the Genl. Staff the emoluments they had been entitled to under the war establishment. It was likewise stated to me, that it was in the hurry of business Congress had passed the Bill depriving them of pay & clothing for Servants and full allowance for Forage, that it was a Casus Omissis and Congress would take the earliest moment to restore them their emoluments—In the Month of May 1816 I returned from the lower Country to Nashville, where I found Major Searcy acting as Paymaster—When I called upon him for my pay, he offered to pay me for one Servant and $20 per Month for Forage. I then told him that unless under the 9th. Section of the law of the 24th. April he was authorised to pay for four Servants there was no law to justify him in allowing for either the pay or subsistence of Servants—and if I was entitled to any I was to the whole and I would receive nothing short of it, and should not receive the pittance of twenty Dollars per Month, when my Horses cost me on the late tour upwards of three Hundred Dollars per Month and that if he did not think the law authorised him to pay me for my Servants and Forage agreeably to the allowance during the War I would receive nothing for either, and requested him to write for instructions and an exposition of the 9th. Sec: of the Act of the 24th. of April 1816. he told me he would, and some time afterwards he informed me he was instructed and would pay me for my servants and Forage & made out the accounts accordingly[4]—and I did then & do still think that the exposition of the law was correct and the payment just and legal, as it evidently had not been the intention of Congress to take away this emolument. Be this as it may it was no error of mine, it was the error (if any) of Major Searcy and the Department, and I am perfectly willing to have it investigated & rectified by you. I have recd. from Major Philips pay master my whole pay, not believing that Mr. Lee is cloathed with any power to order a suspension of it & acknowledging no power to exist, competent to suspend it, but the fiat of a Genl. Court Martial—I shall however deposit in the Branch Bank of the State of Tennessee at Nashville the sum of $691.73 until I hear from you on this subject—there is a manifest error in the extract of the account forwarded by Mr. Lee—this may be an error in copying and stand fair on the originial—I have requested him to forward me a duplicate of that Pay Account and will thank you also to give directions to that effect.[5]

As an evidence of the extraordinary conduct of Mr. Lee who I suspect is actuated by motives not altogether the most honorable—I take the liberty of enclosing to you a copy of a letter addressed by him on the 17th. of Feby. to Mr. Stephen Cantrell executor of Major Searcy together with its enclosure from which you will discover that he has passed this very account as paid by Major Searcy and likewise Dr. [James Craine] Bronaughs from which he ordered a stoppage of $82.88—an extract of Mr. Lees Letter to the Paymaster Genl. which was furnished by Major Philips is enclosed. Dr. Bronaugh did not join me until the last of June 1816 and states that he was not paid by Maj: Searcy for one day of the time for which a stoppage of his pay is ordered.[6]

You will oblige me by giving an early answer to this Letter[7]—I have been anxiously waiting to receive your order in relation to the application of the balance of the funds in my hands appropriated for holding the treaty with the Choctaw Indians—It is lying in the B. Bank of the State of Tennessee at Nashville as a special deposit—Mr. W[illiam] Eastin has informed me that Major Eaton had advised him, that in a conversation with you on the subject of an allowance of two Thousand Dollars as a further compensation as contractor for furnishing supplies &c. for the Treaty, in consideration of the reasons set forth in the letter of Genl. Thos: Hinds Doctor Bronaugh and myself[8]—you had said there would be no difficulty in making the allowance and he has several times made application to me to know if I had recd. instructions to pay him that amount—will you have the goodness to give me orders on this subject I remain Sir, with gt. consideration & respect yr. Mo. Obt. St.

Andrew Jackson

Photocopy of LS in James C. Bronaugh's hand, DNA-RG 60 (8-0231).

1. See Lee to AJ, February 19; Lee to Nathan Towson, February 13 (DNA-RG 99); and AJ to Lee, March 14. After the War of 1812, Congress had returned the army to its peacetime strength and cut pay and emoluments, but the act of April 24, 1816, restored some privileges of the general staff (see 3 *U.S. Statutes at Large* 224–25, 297–99). Lee (1772–1840) was second auditor and a sometime contributor to the Washington *National Intelligencer.* Shortly after becoming president, Jackson dismissed Lee for his pro-Adams writing during the 1828 campaign. Searcy (1768–1820), a Nashville lawyer and merchant, served as Jackson's aide-de-camp, 1813–14, and as U.S. army paymaster, 1816–17.

2. Phillips (d. 1843), a native of Ohio, was regimental paymaster with the 3rd Infantry; the order from Paymaster General Nathan Towson to Phillips has not been found.

3. Robert Brent (1764–1819) was paymaster general of the army from 1808 until shortly before his death.

4. See Account for pay and subsistence, October 1, 1815.

5. See AJ to Lee, March 14.

6. See Lee to Cantrell, with its enclosed memorandum of accounts, February 17 (DNA-RG 60), and Lee to Towson, February 13 (DNA-RG 99). Cantrell (1783–1854), a Nashville merchant, banker, and sometime mayor, was dismissed as army pension agent in 1823 for paying pensioners in depreciated banknotes. A Virginia native, Bronaugh (1788–1822)

served as Southern Division surgeon general until the army reduction, thereafter acting as Jackson's secretary during the transfer of Florida.

7. For replies, see Lee to AJ, April 4, and Calhoun to AJ, May 1. Regarding final disposition of the issue, see AJ to James Monroe, October 5, below, and Bronough to AJ, January 30, 1822.

8. Letter not found. Eastin (1784–1829), a Nashville merchant, had married Jackson's niece Rachel Donelson (1791–1822) in 1809. The additional payment to Eastin, one of the contractors for the 1820 Choctaw negotiations, was allowed, leaving a balance of $3,958.93, which was settled in August (see AJ to Lee, April 14 and July 15; AJ to Calhoun, April 14; and Lee to AJ, April 26, May 1, and August 11). Hinds (1780–1840), who served under Jackson at the Battle of New Orleans and was later a Mississippi militia general, had joined Jackson in 1820 as a Choctaw treaty commissioner.

From James Winchester

Cragfont 18th March 1821

Dear Sir

I have had the honor to receive your favour dated at Hermitage the 12th instant covering a note to Mr. C[harles] Cassedy which note has been delivered.[1] I am glad that the proprietors agree on the subject of a division of so much of the [John] Rice tract as is nont attached to the Town of Memphis. But I see not so much dificulty in selecting a fit person to perform for us this service as the Judge seems to see. It would in my humb*[le o]*pinion be quite unnecessary to send a person from here; Because partiality cannot be exercised, if we cast lots for the appropriation of the dividends, evin if there was a disposition to exercise it (which I am sure there will not be) Let Mr. Wm Lawrence who Judge [John] Overton brought up (and an honester man does not live) be appointed to make the division, and return a plat of the courses distances, meets and bounds of each lot which shall be numbered with progressive numbers and drawn for, by ourselves, at home if we please; now Mr. L. is better acquainted with the tract of land than any person sent from here, after a week spent exploring it could be. add to this that he is a correct artist, and surveying his profession, and we could make it worth his time and attention for it is a work which cannot be correctly executed in haste[2] With respect and Esteem Your Obt Servant

J Winchester

Your having given Judge Overton a power of attorney to act for you in this case. I shall address to him a letter containing the same substance of this[3] J. W.

ALS, DLC (30). Winchester (1752–1826), a revolutionary war veteran, had relocated to Tennessee from his native Maryland about 1785, serving in the state legislature and during the War of 1812 as a U.S. brigadier general. Cragfont was his Sumner County plantation.

1. Neither letter found. Cassedy (c1782–1858), a New York native, moved to Tennessee about 1810 and became a writer for hire, penning several defenses of Winchester's War of 1812 conduct.

2. Overton (1766–1833), a former judge of Tennessee's Supreme Court of Errors and

Appeals and Jackson's longtime friend, was a proprietor, along with Jackson and Winchester, of the town development that became Memphis; for a more detailed discussion, see Overton to AJ, December 21, 1818 (*Jackson,* 4:259–61). Lawrence (d. 1830) had surveyed the city limits in 1820. The survey and plats for the portion of the tract formerly held by Rice (d. c1792) were not completed until the following year (see Overton to AJ, March 29, and Deed of partition among Jackson, Overton, and Winchester, December 5, both 1822).

3. Neither the power of attorney nor the letter has been found.

Because almost two years passed after the signing of the Adams-Onís Treaty before Washington received notice of Spain's ratification, while Article 16 of the treaty had provided that ratifications should be exchanged within six months, James Monroe resubmitted the treaty to the Senate, which reaffirmed its acceptance on February 19. On March 10, after Congress had adjourned, Monroe appointed Jackson governor of East and West Florida with the powers of a captain general and intendant of Cuba, and also named him commissioner to receive the transfer of the provinces from Spain.

Spain's delay in ratifying the treaty had stemmed in part from concern over the control of its other American provinces and a desire to retain leverage against United States recognition of the newly declared South American republics. These considerations continued to influence Spanish policy after ratification, as during the interim between ratification and transfer Spain sought to relocate Florida's Indians along the Sabine River frontier, thereby creating a buffer between the United States and Spanish Mexico. When American representative James Grant Forbes (1769–1823), elder brother of John Murray Forbes, carried official notice of the exchange of ratifications to Havana in April, Captain General Nicholas Mahy y Romo (d. 1822) not only delayed Forbes's departure for Pensacola, but also instructed the governors of East and West Florida to procrastinate over the details of the transfer. Although Secretary of State John Quincy Adams (1767–1848; Harvard 1787) precisely anticipated the Spanish position on Florida armaments, his instructions below could neither prevent West Florida Governor José Maria Callava from implementing his government's policy nor ease Jackson's frustration at the resulting delay. Jackson's efforts to speed the transfer ran headlong into Callava's foot-dragging, creating an inevitable tension that set the stage for an incident that Jackson's enemies would not soon forget.

From John Quincy Adams

Department of State
Washington 23 March, 1821.

Sir,

By the second Article of the Florida Treaty, it is stipulated that with the Territories of East and West Florida, the *fortifications* within the same, are ceded and to be delivered to the United States; but no express mention is made of the Cannon, belonging to them.

By the seventh Article of the same Treaty, it is provided that the United States shall furnish the transports and escort necessary to convey the Spanish Officers and troops, and their baggage to the Havanna—But no mention is made of the transportation of Cannon; nor is there any express engagement on the part of the United States, to furnish *provisions,* to the Spanish Officers and Troops on the passage.[1]

It is the opinion of the President, that by a fair and just construction of the Treaty, the Cannon belonging to the fortifications are to be considered as appendages to them, included in the cession; and are therefore to be left with them.

On the same principle he is of opinion, that with the transports and escort to convey the Spanish Officers and troops and their baggage, the provisions necessary for the passage, are also to be furnished at the expence of the United States, although not specially mentioned in the Treaty; and orders have accordingly been given for the supply of provisions.

It is however possible that the Spanish Governors of East and West Florida, may upon a different construction of the Treaty, claim to carry away the Cannon from the fortifications, because they are not expressly named in the Article.[2]

You will in that case claim that they should be left with the fortifications, and insist that upon the principle of the other Construction the United States are not bound to furnish provisions for the passage of the Officers and troops. You will state that the supply has been ordered in the confidence, that the benefit of the same liberal Construction of the Treaty will operate in favour of the United States; and that if it be not extended to them, they will have a just claim to be reimbursed for the expense of supplying the provisions.

You will add that as there is no engagement on their part express or implied, to furnish the means of transporting the Cannon, they have made and can make no provision for that purpose.

Should the Spanish Governors alledge that their orders are express, for having the Cannon carried away, you will leave it to them to make provision for their transportation, and report forthwith the facts to this Department. I am, with Great Respect, Sir, your very humble and Obedt. Servt.

John Quincy Adams

LS and LC, DLC (30, 63); LC and Copies, DNA-RG 59 (8-0261, -0263, -0256); Copy, DNA-RG 46 (8-0254). Published in Bassett, 3:44–45.

1. For the full text of the treaty, see Clive Parry, ed., *The Consolidated Treaty Series* (231 vols., Dobbs Ferry, N.Y., 1969–1981), 70:2–30. Article 7 of the treaty further established a six month deadline for the transfer.

2. The governors of East and West Florida, respectively, were José Coppinger (d. c1825), who subsequently commanded the royalist forces at Vera Cruz, Mexico, and José Maria Callava, Knight of the Royal Military Order of San Hermenigildo and decorated in 1811 for service in the Peninsula War battle of Almonacid.

To Andrew Jackson Donelson

Nashville March 31rst. 1821—

Dear Andrew

I had the pleasure by due course of mail to receive your letter of the 3rd. Instant,[1] and have delayed answering untill I heard with certainty that I should decend the Mississippi this spring, by last mail I received the inteligence that I was appointed to the Goverment of that country, but am still without advice of the kind of Goverment that is to be established there; or any of the officers that are to aid in the administration thereof[2]—It is probable I shall with Mrs. J. & staff set out for that country in two weeks and hope to be Joined by you at Neworleans—Should any alteration of my rout take place, I shall advise you thereof; It afforded us great pleasure to hear of your safe arival & your health, and I have but little doubt but the season is too far advanced for you to progress much in learning the French Language this spring; but having a great desire to see you before you proceed to the east, I cannot advise you to leave Orleans before we arive. By last mail I recd. a letter from my friend Colo. Gadsden, advising that he had passed you on his rout from Mobile Point, but expected to see you in a few days at Orleans, I hope you have met; in him you will find a man of honour in whom you may confide, he is also a man of fine talents, and I am pleased to find has a good standing with the executive—I recd. a letter a few days since from the sec of war speaking in the highest terms of Colo. Gadsden. I have wrote him not to leave that section of Country untill I arive.[3] I have a hope to find you together when I get there

By last Tuesdays mail I recd. a warrent for Daniel [Smith Donelson], he will leave here for west Point about the middle of april, If we can procure eastern funds for him, the regulations are so changed, that the Cadets stand an examination in June for admittance, and in January next when if the Pass the examination <in January> the receive their commission as a Cadet dated back in June—if the student does not pass his examination in January, he is dismissed the school and receives no pay—this makes it necessary that each student should be furnished with the means of support, without the aid of the institution[4]—I sincerely regret that I did not adhere to my first determination not to accept the Goverment of Floridas, your aunt appears very reluctant to go to that climate and really I am wearied with public life. But it is too late to look back, and I will organise the Goverment, and retire to private life—I know even in this I make a great private sacrafice; but my word is out and I must comply at any sacrafice—what may be my compensation I know not but whatever it may be I am determined to spend it, and to live within.[5]

your aunt does not enjoy a good state of health and I have a hope that the Journey may improve it—your friends are all well & Brunaugh &

call, with the rest of your friends, the two little andrews in particular sends their love to you,[6] and your aunt Joins me in prayers for your health, safety, & hapiness & believe me to be your affectionate uncle

Andrew Jackson

P. S. present us affectionately to Mr Duncan & his family <and believe me to> and all & every friends. A. J.

ALS, DLC (8-0274). Published in Bassett, 3:46 (extract). Donelson (1799–1871; Military Academy 1820), Jackson's nephew, was the son of Samuel (c1770–1804) and Mary Ann Michie Smith Donelson (1781–1857), later Sanders.

1. See Donelson to AJ, March 3.

2. Jackson probably received word of his appointment from the Washington *National Intelligencer,* March 10; the *Nashville Whig,* March 28 (from the *National Intelligencer*); or John H. Eaton's letter of March 9.

3. See John C. Calhoun to AJ, March 7. Gadsden's letter and Jackson's response have not been found. Donelson joined Jackson's party at New Orleans in April.

4. Donelson (1801–63; Military Academy 1825) was Andrew J. Donelson's brother.

5. Jackson would receive a yearly salary of $5,000 as governor of Florida, beginning with his retirement from the army (see John Q. Adams to AJ, March 12).

6. Andrew J. Hutchings and the Jacksons' adopted son, Andrew Jackson, Jr. (1808–65).

To John Quincy Adams

Nashville
2nd. April 1821.

Sir

I have the honor to acknowledge the receipt of your letter of the 12th. Ult. together with its enclosures[1] Viz

2 Commissions—
Copy of the Treaty
Do. Law for executing it (in a news paper)
Do. Col: Forbes' Instructions
Do. Royal order for delivery
Do. Do. (translation)
Form of Proclamation.

In pursuance of the instructions of the President as communicated thro' you, I shall proceed as soon as practicable to Montpelier (via) New Orleans, there to await the necessary information from Col. Forbes, and shall immediately upon receiving it take possession of Pensacola and proceed to organize the Government agreeably to the Instructions—I hope to be able to leave this by the 15th. Inst: and to arrive at Montpelier by the 1st. May[2]

I have agreeably to instructions appointed Brevet Major Genl. [Edmund Pendleton] Gaines to receive possession of St. Augustine and by the Southern Mail have forwarded him the necessary instructions for that purpose[3]

There is one subject, which at this early period I wish thro you, to call the attention of the President to, & receive your instructions thereon—It is the situation of that part of the Creek Indians who in the late War abandoned their own Country and fled to the Floridas and continued hostilities against the United States, until conquered in 1818. During that campaign I ordered the conquered Indians above the Florida line, and directed them to settle down within their own limits (the Creek Nation) I have lately however understood that [Peter] McQueen and his adherents have made a settlement at Mickasuckey, and also on the Suwaney river. Are these Indians to be ordered up to the Creek Country, there to settle themselves, or are they to be protected in their new settlement? I have only to remark that the Country set apart for the Creek nation is sufficient for the support of all, & that by removing those within Florida greater security will be given to our frontier, and the Government would more certainly be enabled to prevent smuggleing, which no doubt will be attempted to a considerable extent thro the various inlets in the Country now inhabited by them. Whatever may be the Presidents Instructions upon this subject shall be strictly obeyed and likewise in relation to the Negros who have run away from the States & inhabit this Country and are protected by the Indians.[4] With Sentiments of esteem & regard I have the honor to be Sir your Most Obt. Servt.

Andrew Jackson

LS in James C. Bronaugh's hand and Copies, DNA-RG 59 (M116-5, 8-0281); LC, DLC (63). Published in *ASP, Foreign Relations,* 4:755.

1. See Adams to AJ, March 12.

2. On May 9, Jackson's party reached the abandoned Cantonment Montpelier, located about seven miles northeast of the site of Fort Montgomery, in Baldwin County, Alabama. James G. Forbes had been designated to secure the Florida archives in Cuba.

3. See AJ to Gaines, April 2. Gaines (1777–1849) commanded the eastern section of Jackson's Southern Division.

4. For Jackson's 1818 orders regarding Indian resettlement, see Robert Butler to Gaines, May 5, 1818. President Monroe referred the matter of Creek removal to John C. Calhoun, who deferred a decision pending further information about the number of Indians involved (see Calhoun to AJ, May 1, and Adams to AJ, May 23). On May 26, Jackson acknowledged Calhoun's letter, and from September 18 through September 20 he held a meeting in Pensacola with several Creek chiefs then residing in Florida to determine the Creek population in the territory. Jackson reported the results of his meeting to Calhoun on September 20 and again expressed his preference for removal of the Florida Creeks to the Creek reservation in Georgia and Alabama. McQueen (d. c1820) had been a mixed-blood leader of the hostile Creeks during the Creek War and the 1818 Seminole campaign. In April 1818, Jackson's troops had destroyed Mikasuki, a principle Seminole town west of Lake Miccosukee in northern Florida.

To John Coffee

Hermitage <April> 11th. of April 1821

Dr. Genl

I have no doubt but you have been advised of my having consented to go to Florida and organise the Goverment there, this may astonish you from the firm determination I had taken not to accept it, and my long and a[n]xious desire for retirement, but when I tell you, that the change of this my determination was brought about by the solicitations of the President, the secratary of war, and many of my friends in Congress, and many others, it may absolve me from the appearance of instability in my resolves. Mr James Jackson when you see him will explain to you more fully, the propriety of this change in me. I must confess I enter upon this duty with more reluctance and regret, than any in my life, and the great reluctance of Mrs. J, added to her bad health, increases my regret, she has consented to go with me, but could not consent to leave her son, he goes also. I should have taken with me my little Andrew J. Hutchings, but I am aware if I did, and any accident happen his Grandfather would believe I had destroyed him that his estate should go to his fathers family I have therefore left him at school, and have got Mrs. [Mary Caffery] Knox to remain here and take care of him untill we return which I hope will be in next fall[1]—we set out tomorrow for Nashville and expect to sail on Sunday next for Montpelier via orleans to which point I am first ordered. I shall if possible before I leave Nashville have a bill filed, and leave in the hands of Mr [John Christmas] McLamore, as guardian of little Andrew Hutchings against Bennett Smith. I shall also leave the note of James Jackson & Co, to me as guardian in the hands of Mr McLamore, that (in case Smith should recover) the amount may be collected by you and paid, and you as executor exonerated, but I wish to prosecute this suit to an injunction—[2]

I enclose herewith all the vouchers for mony paid by me as guardian &c &c, except the amount paid & will be transmitted by Mr James Jackson to Mr Nicholson, which when paid I have directed Mr James Jackson to take his recpt in full for his services for the year 1820—I send him one hundred and two dollars which he says is the amount due. I have to ask of you to have an account current made out agreable to the vouchers that I may when I return have a settlement with the court at Huntsville and have the business removed to the county where the childs property is—and preserve the papers carefully for my safety untill I return, and for the safety of my representatives, should I never return—perhaps, should you be at Huntsville at their county court, you could have a settlement made up to the first of the present year for me. I only name this should it meet your convenience, for I am aware how much you are oppressed with business as well as myself—[3]

I shall send a power of attorney to you & James Jackson to transact my land business for me in allabama. I combine you both in the power least business or accident should prevent one from attending to it, when the other can—I was and am still anxious to sell where my Negroes are; to get clear of the encumbrance of that debt to the Goverment, but if this cannot be done, you & Mr Jackson will mannage it in such way as your Judgts may dictate for the best, and with you I thus leave it—I have wrote Capt Crawford, I hope he will do well, at any rate what he makes will be safe[4]—I have to request should he want advice that you will give it to him, and should you be passing call, look, and stimulate him—I have confidence that Nicholson will do well but still I hope you & James will occasionally call & do the like with Nicholson—I have given you & James full powers as guardian to mannage my little Andrew Hutchings land in such way as you may deem best for his interest—I hope to be able to return early in the fall, should I be detained untill congress meets & passes a law for the organization of the Goverment in the Floridas. When I return I return permanantly as a citizen. I will at farthest <and on this event> return in all January, but I may return much sooner. I will do myself the pleasure of writing you often, I am now so pressed with my military, combined with three other commissions in Floridas, that I have not a moment to spare for my friend.[5]

I rejoice to hear that your health is pretty good I would advise you either to vissit me at Pensacola & have the benefit of sea bathing or vissit the Herrodburgh Springs, and bring with you a sufficient supply of the epsom salts to last you for some time—I do think them one of the best medicines for costiveness, and which leaves the bowels in a better state than any other, nothing could afford me more pleasure than to see you at Pensacola, If you should be advised that sea bathing would be beneficial—[6]

How would you like to become the Governor of that place. I ask the question as your friend—I have no doubt but it will be offerred to you on the intimation that you would accept it. and I mean to notify the President that I will hold it no longer than I organise it, and it is in a state of progression under the organization. This is the basis of my acceptance, that after this I resign when I please—and the question is asked of you with heartfelt friendship. I am aware that nothing would induce you to accept it but the benefit of your health—The wellfare of your family and yourself will be allways dear to me, and any act I can do to promote your health or wellfare will afford me pleasure. Mrs. Jackson unites with me in a tender of our best wishes for the wellfare & happiness of you, your lady and family to whom present us affectionately—kiss my son for me,[7] and accept my Dear friend assurances of my sincere friendship and Esteem—

Andrew Jackson

ALS, THi (8-0302). Published in Bassett, 3:47–48 (extract).

1. Jackson was referring to Bennett Smith, Andrew J. Hutchings's maternal grandfather. After her husband John's death about 1815, Mary Caffery Knox (b. c1788), Jackson's niece, continued to live at the Hermitage. Hutchings studied at William McKnight's school (see Account with McKnight, February 5).

2. The note for $36.50 has not been found. Jackson was referring to the lawsuit brought by Smith against John Hutchings's estate. McLemore (1790–1864) had married Jackson's niece Elizabeth Donelson (1796–1836) in 1815.

3. See Malachi Nicholson to AJ, April 5, and Receipt from Nicholson for wages as overseer, April 18.

4. Neither the power of attorney nor the letter to William W. Crawford has been found. For the continuing efforts to sell Jackson's Evans Spring farm, see James Jackson to AJ, May 28, and AJ to Coffee, July 26, both below; and AJ to Coffee, June 27, and Coffee to AJ, July 25.

5. Congress did not organize the Florida Territory until March 1822 (3 *U.S. Statutes at Large* 654–59). Jackson referred to his commissions as receiver of the transfer of Florida and as governor (both March 10) and his commission to exercise special powers in the territory (March 20).

6. The Kentucky Harrodsburg Springs are near the source of the Salt River. In 1825 the proprietors of the Springs claimed: "We are authorized to say that Gen. A. Jackson has, in his own case of dyspepsia or indigestion, given up every other remedy for the use of the salts of this water, from which he has received much relief" (*Nashville Republican,* May 28, 1825).

7. A reference to Andrew Jackson Coffee (1819–91). Coffee's reply, if any, has not been found.

Jackson and his party, including his wife Rachel and their son Andrew, Jr., a niece Narcissa Hays (b. c1795), a nephew Stockley Donelson Hays (1788–1831), and James C. Bronaugh, left Nashville on the evening of April 14 aboard the steamboat Cumberland *en route to New Orleans, and thence via Blakely to Montpelier, Alabama. Mechanical difficulty aboard the boat necessitated their transfer to the* Rapide *on April 21, and the party arrived in the Crescent City the next evening. New Orleans citizens greeted Jackson as a returning hero—toasting him at a public dinner as "General Jackson, our deliverer"—and entertained his party until they departed for Blakely, on the northeast shore of Mobile Bay, on April 27.*

To John Quincy Adams

New Orleans April 24th. 1821

Sir

On the evening of the 22nd. inst. I reached this City on my way to Montpelier, and will if I can procure a transport, proceed on my journey on the 26th. instant.

Immediately on my arrival Mr [Eligius] Frommentin waited upon me, and produced a commission dated in the year 1819, authorising him to receive the Floridas together with the Archives at Pensacola and St Augustine. He appears to be impressed with a belief, that although, that part of his commission to receive the Floridas was superseded, yet as the executive had been silent on the subject of the Archives to be recd. at Pensacola &c., that he with my approval was entitled to the safe keeping of them—From the tenor of my instructions, I do not conceive that I can create any office in the Floridas that does not exist there at present, and that clerks of any kind except those that are contemplated under my instruction to translate and transcribe the Archives for the information of the President, cannot be necessary until the next meeting of Congress—However should the President be of opinion that a safe keeper of the Archives should be necessary, and that Mr Frommentin should be appointed to that trust, and express the same to me with the salary to be annexed, I will immediately notify Mr Frommentin thereof and request his removal to Pensacola—But it does not appear to me that there can arise a necessity for any individual to have a copy of any of the records before the meeting of next Congress. I shall therefore not make any appointment of this kind, until I hear from the President on the subject[1]

I have here met with Majr [Henry] Staunton of the QuarterMasters Department, who advises me that he is without QuarterMaster funds for the purpose of carrying into effect the transportation of the civil and military officers of Spain; from the Florida's as stipulated under the late treaty with Spain, and informs me that it is understood by the QuarMaster Genl., that through me the funds necessary to carry into effect the stipulation for transporting the Spanish Troops are to be obtained—From the perusal of my instructions, it does not appear that I am authorised to draw upon the State Department for Quartermaster funds, but will take upon me the responsibility so to do. I thought it most advisable to endeavour to raise here by a draft upon your Department the sum necessary to meet the expenses of receiving the country and organising the Government, fearing that a draft would not be sold at Mobile or Pensacola, for this purpose I offered for sale a draft, and found I could not obtain United States paper for it without a discount. I therefore directed Majr Staunton to apply to the Branch Bank of the United States, to be informed whether it would advance upon my draft—it refused. I then addressed a note to the Collector Mr [Beverly] Chew, the enclosed is his answer—I also enclose the statement of Majr Staunton, from all which you will discover that without a discount, money cannot be obtained here on drafts upon the government[2]—no delay however shall occur in the transportation of the Spanish Troops from the want of funds, as far as I can command them—nor will I ever consent to sell bills on the government at a discount to any, and more particularly to the Branch Bank of the United States, in which is depositted all the revenue of the Government recd. at this place. I shall endeavour at Mobile or Pensacola to raise the necessary funds on drafts—Should I fail there, I trust upon the receipt of this, the government will instruct the Branch Bank to furnish me with the amount that may be necessary to meet the expenses that may occur in receiving the Floridas and organising the Government thereof[3] I am Sir with great respect Yr. Mo Obt servant.

Andrew Jackson

LS in Andrew J. Donelson's hand and Copy, DNA-RG 59 (M116-5, 8-0361); LC, DLC (63); Copy, DNA-RG 46 (8-0365). Published in Bassett, 3:49–50. Although the letter was dated April 24, internal evidence suggests that it was concluded later. The date was altered to "29" by an unknown hand some time after Adams acknowledged receipt on June 27.

1. Fromentin (d. 1822), a native of France and former Catholic priest, fled the Reign of Terror to America and married into a prominent Maryland family. He subsequently served as U.S. senator from Louisiana, 1813–19. From June through October 1819, Fromentin resided in Pensacola as the American commissioner for the transfer, but he returned to Louisiana when Spain failed to ratify the treaty. Later in 1821, Fromentin was appointed federal district judge for West Florida. No reply regarding a keeper of the archives has been found.

2. For Jackson's instructions, see Adams to AJ, March 12, and, above, March 23. The enclosures were Stanton to AJ, April 25, and Chew to AJ, April 26. AJ's note to Chew has not been found. Stanton (c1786–1856), a Vermont native and veteran of the War of 1812, served in the army quartermaster department from 1818 until his death. Chew (1773–1851), who moved to Louisiana from his native Virginia in 1801, was collector of customs in New Orleans from 1817 until 1830, when Jackson removed him.

3. Securing funds for the transfer of Florida continued to plague Jackson since the government did not authorize funds for his use until early July (see AJ to Adams, May 7, 21, June 8, July 16; Adams to AJ, June 27, July 6; and Ezekiel Salomon to AJ, August 1).

The army reduction act of 1821, the occasion for Jackson's retirement as major general, also particularly affected two of Jackson's favorite officers, Robert Butler and James Gadsden, divisional adjutant and inspector generals, respectively. Major General Jacob J. Brown and Brigadier Generals Winfield Scott (1786–1866) and Edmund P. Gaines, composing a Board of Officers to implement the officer reductions, met in Washington during the spring. After deliberations that later gave rise to charges of favoritism, the board selected Henry Atkinson (1782–1842), who would lose his brigade appointment, as adjutant general, despite his stated desire for a line command. Accordingly, Atkinson declined and was subsequently named colonel of the 6th Infantry. Atkinson's preference, however, displaced all others with less seniority and moved Butler down from colonel of the 4th Infantry (a post that went to Duncan L. Clinch) to lieutenant colonel of the 1st Infantry. Gadsden, originally retained as one of two inspector generals, was then appointed adjutant general, which alienated Butler, leading to his resignation in November, and set the stage for a long and bitter confrontation in the spring of 1822 between President Monroe and the United States Senate (see AJ to Butler, June 13 and July 27, Butler to AJ, September 19, and James C. Bronaugh to AJ, February 8, 1822, all below; and AJ to Butler, August 8, Gadsden to AJ, August 15 and September 14, and Butler to James Monroe, November 16).

From Edmund Pendleton Gaines

Washington city
April 27th. 1821

Dear General,

I have received your letters of the 2nd and 10th. inst. The first enclosing your commission with the other documents refered to authorising me to receive possession of St. Augustine—the last advising me of your having appointed

Colonel Butler to perform this duty—The first having come by the way of Charleston did not reach me until yesterday; when I received the last.[1]

It would have been very agreeable to me to have executed the trust confided by your commission and orders—and I regret that the duty assigned to me at this place should have deprived me of that pleasure. They will however, devolve upon an officer whose discretion and worth will insure their correct execution.

A strong effort has been made to give Colonel Butler the rank and command to which his qualifications and services entitle him. The proceedings of the board of General Officers remain in conclave, but there is doubt that the colonel will at least have the rank in the line which he would have been intitled to had he remained in the line; that of Lieut. Colonel, and the first of that grade, together with his Brevet rank—he will therefore be first for promotion. He will moreover be attached to a Regiment to be stationed either in florida or Louisiana—A Regiment to be commanded by Bt. B. Genl [Moses] Porter—whose ill health & infirmities are such as to leave the Regiment under Colonel Butler, whose brevet will thus entitle him to the rank & pay of a Colonel.[2]

I take great pleasure in assuring you of the gratification I have derived from the many acts of confidence and kindness with which you have honored me; and that since I am to be seperated from your command, (which I should otherwise much regret) you are to be translated to a climate calculated to preserve your health, and to a public sphere likely to be agreeable to your wishes, as it will be benificial to your country—I pray you therefore to be assured of my unalterable respect and friendship, and my best wishes that your future days may be happy, as your past life has been honorable and useful. with my best respects to your lady, I am your most obdt.

Edmund P. Gaines

ALS, DLC (30). Endorsed, "Recd. May 26th 1821."

1. See AJ to Gaines, April 2 and 10.

2. Massachusetts native Porter (d. 1822) was a revolutionary war veteran and a career soldier.

Jackson's April 30 letter to José M. Callava, below, marks the beginning of the actual transfer of Florida to American control, a lengthy and tedious process characterized by delay and a steady deterioration in the relationship between the two. The retiring Spanish governor and his American successor each possessed a well-cultivated sense of the dignity of his person and office, prepossessions that added to the inherent complexities of the transfer. Much of the rancor that developed can be traced directly to what each viewed as a breach of protocol by the other in regard to who ought to make the first visit for an exchange of credentials. Moreover, the reliance upon translators (neither spoke the other's language) also contributed to their mutual misunderstanding (see AJ to Callava, July

15 and 16, both below; and Callava to AJ, July 16). By the time of the transfer of West Florida on July 17, the two governors thoroughly disliked one another. No reservoir of goodwill existed between them, and any spark might set off an explosion. Such an occasion was not long in coming, and by August 22 Governor Jackson had imprisoned former Governor Callava, creating another incident that placed Jackson's actions before the country for public debate.

To José Maria Callava

Montpelier
30th. April 1821

Sir,

I have the honor to inform your excellency, that I have been duly commissioned by the President of the United States, to receive possession of the Floridas, agreeably to the stipulations of the late treaty, between the United States, and His Catholick Majesty. I have also to inform you, that Col James G. Forbes has sailed from New york to Havanna, charged with the Royal order to the Captain Genl, for the delivery of the countries ceded to the United States by the said treaty, and that he is to communicate with me from Pensacola immediately on his arrival, which may be daily expected.

Being desirous, in order to avoid all unnecessary delay, to have in readiness on the arrival of Col Forbes from Cuba, the necessary transports for the civil and military officers, and the troops of his Catholick Majesty, agreeably to the stipulations of the treaty, as well as for their supplies (according to the liberal construction which the President is disposed to give to the treaty,) I have to request you to inform me the numbers of troops to be transported from Pensacola and St. Marks, and also of the number of days in which the passage from Pensacola to Havanna is usually performed—As the transports and supplies, will be procured at New Orleans, you will be pleased to inform me what length of time will be necessary on your part, after the arrival of the order from the Capt Genl., to enable you to make the necessary arrangements to embark—This information is requested in order that I may have every thing in a state of preparation for your transportation the moment you are ready—It is also important to enable me to have the necessary supplies transported to Pensacola and St Marks, and in *depot* for the troops which are to occupy the Floridas.[1]

It being communicated to me, that it is expected from the assurance of his Catholick majesty through his minister at Washington, that no unnecessary delay will take place in delivering possession of the Florida's.[2] I have ordered the supplies of the troops of the United States to be forwarded to Pensacola and St Augustine, and they are Expected to arrive at those points by the fifteenth of the next month. The situation of my troops in the interior, and the difficulty of supplying them there, render this step necessary, and orders have been given to expedite no further supplies to the places which those troops at present occupy. A removal of them at an early day, is therefore rendered necessary, and I have no disposition, unless urged by necessity, to move my troops to any garrison occupied by the troops of his Catholick Majesty, unless the same shall be evacuated, being, I assure you, earnestly desirous that nothing may occur to disturb that harmony and good understanding, which at present so happily exists, between our respective Governments, and the citizens and subjects of each—

From a wish to maintain the most perfect harmony and good understanding between us, during our correspondence, I have charged the beare[r]s of this communication, Doctor J. C Bronough Surgeon General, of the Southern Division, and my friend and one of my private secretaries, Judge [Henry Marie] Breckenridge, to make known to you the sincere desire on my part to carry into effect the stipulations of the treaty and the surrender of the Floridas, in the utmost good faith and amity with the officers of his Catholick Majesty, as well as the promptness with which every thing stipulated under the treaty on the part of the Government of the United States, will be executed agreeably to the most liberal construction of that instrument.[3] God preserve you many years I am with sentiments of respect yr. Most Obt & Humble servant.

(Signed) Andrew Jackson

LC in Andrew J. Donelson's hand, DLC (63); Copies, DNA-RG 59 (M116-6, 8-0394, -0398), DNA-RG 84 (8-0387), DNA-RG 46 (8-0392); Copy in Spanish by Callava, SpSAG (8-0389). Published in Bassett, 3:50–52 (from DNA-RG 59). Contrary to the return address, Jackson did not reach Montpelier until May 9.

1. Fort St. Marks was located six miles above Apalachee Bay, on the Gulf coast. For the reply, see Callava to AJ, May 4; and for further elaboration of the statistics AJ desired, see James C. Bronaugh and Henry M. Brackenridge to AJ, May 7, below.

2. John Q. Adams's letter of March 12 had informed Jackson that the Spanish king Ferdinand VII (1784–1833) had transmitted his order for the delivery of Florida along with the ratification of the Adams-Onís Treaty. The Spanish minister at Washington was Francisco Dionisio Vives (1755–1840), a much decorated general who later served as Captain General of Cuba, 1823–32.

3. Brackenridge (1786–1871), a Pennsylvania native and former Louisiana district judge, had been secretary to the 1817 American mission to South America. Jackson met him aboard the *Rapide* en route to New Orleans and invited him to join his entourage as an interpreter.

To John Coffee

Blakely May the 1rst. 1821—

Dear Genl

We left Nashville on the evening of the 14th. ult. and after a detention of 36 hours in repair of machinary, and changing our Boat we arived at Neworleans on the evening of the 22nd. of april—I remained in Neworleans experiencing the usual attention & hospitality of the place until friday the

27th. & sailed from the Mouth of St Johns at 4. oclock P.M. and reached this place in forty hours—reaching new orleans on sunday <morn> Evening remaining there nearly five days, and ariving at this place on sunday morning 9 oclock a.m.—as soon as it was Known I had arived the corporation met and inviting me to dine with them to day, the corporation of Mobile waited upon me last evening with an invitation to dine with them & partake of a dinner & Ball on thursday next[1]—In the mean time I have dispatched Doctor Brunaugh and Judge Brakenride to Pensacola with a communication to the Governor, to be advised at what time I shall furnish they transports & supplies for carrying the Spanish officers & men to the Havanna—I have recd no information from Colo. Forbes or the Hornet. I expected him from Cuba before this. Capt Call has not arived at Montpelier with our horses, it is supposed his detention is occasioned by the unusual high waters I will therefore have to remain here untill my horses reach me.[2]

If our Mutual friends James Jackson & Capt Donelson has not set out for Pensacola say to them that real property has risen in Pensacola, and if they wish to sell, now is the time[3]—present us affectionately to them both & to all our friends, and to say we will be happy to meet them in this country—They ladies experienced some high waves on their passage and appear to be satisfied with there experience at sea, and Andrew appears to be content to return with his cousin Stockly Hays—[4]

I will be happy to hear from you & your family, and of the progress of the writ of Error[5]—& be informed whether the frosts in april has destroyed the cotton—adress me at Mountpelier Allabama—I am Sir with great respect yr mo. obdt. Servt.

Andrew Jackson

ALS, DLC (8-0412).

1. Bayou St. John, now in New Orleans City Park, emptied into Lake Pontchartrain on its south shore, then approximately six miles from the city. For an account of the receptions at Blakely and Mobile, see *Cahawba Press and Alabama State Intelligencer,* June 2.

2. See above, AJ to José Maria Callava, April 30. The *Hornet* was a 440-ton, 18-gun sloop-of-war, built in 1805 and lost off the coast of Tampico in 1829. Forbes did not arrive from Cuba until June 9. On April 12, while still in Nashville, Jackson had ordered Richard K. Call to Montpelier; he joined Jackson's party at Blakely later on May 1.

3. James Jackson, Sr. and Jr., John Donelson (1787–1840), John McCrea, John C. McLemore, John H. Eaton, Thomas Childress, and John Jackson had speculated in Pensacola land during the winter of 1817–18. In February 1819 a Senate committee chaired by Abner Lacock had suggested that their investment had influenced Jackson's occupation of the town in May 1818, a charge that Jackson vehemently denied (see McCrea to AJ, April 15, 1819, and Affidavit of Childress, January 12, 1820, in *Jackson,* 4: 283–85, 351). James Jackson did not visit Florida, but Donelson joined his uncle later in the summer to inspect his property in Pensacola with which he was "highly pleased" (see AJ to John Donelson, 1755–1830, July 3).

4. On May 18, AJ sent Stockley D. Hays back to Nashville, but Andrew, Jr., did not leave for Tennessee until August.

5. A reference to *Bennett Smith* v. *John Hutchings's Executors.*

From James Craine Bronaugh and Henry Marie Brackenridge

Blakeley 7th. May 1821.

Sir,

In pursuance of your instructions we left this place on Tuesday morning and reached Pensacola about ten O.Clock the Thursday following. The *Hornet* was not there, but from information on which we believe reliance can be placed, she arrived at Havanna on the ninth Ultimo.[1]

We immediately addressed a note (A) to the Governor, enclosing our letter of Introduction, and requesting an interview, as soon as it would be convenient.[2] He sent us a polite answer (B) inviting us to wait on him at the Government House at ten O.Clock the following morning, the 4th Inst.[3] At the hour appointed we waited on him and presented the communication from you of which we were the bearers,[4] and which being explained to him, he observed, that on the subject of the Treaty he was only subordinate to the Captain General of the Island of Cuba, that as nothing had been communicated to him from his superior, he had no authority to enter into any arrangements respecting it; that he could do nothing until he should receive his orders through the regular and proper channel. He declared his wish to avoid all unnecessary delay, and to act with the utmost promptitude the momen[t] he should receive his orders from the Captain General. We observed to him, that this information was requested in order to prevent useless delay, to enable you with greater certainty to provide the Transports and supplies, and offered to shew him the Copy of the Royal Order and other papers in our possession.[5] We reminded him of the situation of the Troops of the United States in the interior, intended to occupy the Posts within the Floridas—the approach of the sickly season—the difficulties of all military movements by Land and Sea, in this climate, after the months of May and June. He repeated that he had no authority whatever to take any step until authorised by the Captain General, declined the perusal of the Royal order, but declared his willingness to communicate fully all the information required by you, the moment of the arrival of the order from Havanna. We then requested him to communicate in writing to you what he had stated to us, which he promised to do. We received his reply (E) in the evening, and the next morning set out for this place where we arrived this morning.[6] Previously to our departure from Pensacola we addressed a letter (C) to the Governor expressing our regret at not being able to obtain the information which we sought, and inclosing a letter (D) to Col: Forbes making known your arrival, and stating your anxiety to obtain possession of the Floridas as speedily as possible.[7]

With respect to the points on which we were instructed to obtain information, the following is the result of our inquiries and observation.

The number of Troops including Officers, and persons connected with the Government who will leave the Country, does not exceed Five Hundred and fifty: two hundred of these are in Pensacola, the remainder at the Barrancas and St. Marks. Every thing seems to indicate the prevailing understanding that they are shortly to quit the Country. The Troops are not regularly drilled, there are no morning or evening parades, the public buildings are entirely neglected, and the Government seems to be carelessly administered. The inhabitants are impatient for the change, and it is said that but few of the Spanish families will leave the place. The Governor, we were told is personally desirous to be gone—he is a frank, candid Soldier, and we have no doubt that any difficulties, or delays, which may occur, will be occasioned by the Captain General.

There are at present, in the Harbour, only a few coasting Vessels; there have been but few arrivals, and we are satisfied from every thing we have observed, that the accounts which we have received respecting the importation of Affricans is not correct. If any such traffic be carried on, it is much more likely to be between Havanna and St. Augustine. On the other subject respecting which we were directed to make enquiry, the injury said to be done by the Soldiery to the untenanted houses belonging to American Citizens, we find, that such injury has been done alike to the buildings of Spanish subjects.[8] Nearly all the houses of this place are in a State of dilapidation, and there are nearly one half unoccupied, few of which can be inhabited without extensive repairs. Nearly every dwelling, however, has been taken by persons who are waiting with impatience the change of Government. Rents have risen astonishingly within a few weeks, and town property is now as high as it probably will be, excepting in particular situations, for some time to come. Nearly all the publick property—the publick squares—the ground around the Block-Houses, estimated at a very large amount, is claimed as private property, it having been sold by the order of the King, as we are informed some years ago; it is a subject, however, very well worth inquiring into. We suspect there is a great deal of very valuable publick property in and about Pensacola.

From the shortness of our stay it was not in our power to obtain information on other subjects, and on those we have noticed, not as full as we have wished. We have the honor to be Sir, With great respect Yr. Mo. Obt. Servt.

J. C. Bronaugh
H: M: Brackenridge

ALS by Bronaugh also signed by Brackenridge and Copies, DNA-RG 59 (M116-5, -6, 8-0447); LC, DLC (63); Copies, DNA-RG 46 (8-0436), DNA-RG 84 (8-0443). AJ addressed the ALS to John Q. Adams, who endorsed it upon receipt. Published in *ASP, Foreign Relations,* 4:758–59.

1. James G. Forbes, aboard the *Hornet* with official notification of the exchange of ratifications, arrived in Havana on April 22.

2. See Bronaugh and Brackenridge to José M. Callava, May 3, DNA-RG 59 (M116-5), enclosing AJ to Callava, April 30.

3. See Callava to Bronaugh and Brackenridge, May 3, DNA-RG 59 (M116-5).

4. See above, AJ to Callava, April 30.

5. See King Ferdinand VII to the Governor of Cuba, October 24, 1820. Adams had forwarded Jackson a copy of the order on March 12.

6. See Callava to AJ, May 4.

7. See Bronaugh and Brackenridge to Callava, and to James G. Forbes, May 4, DNA-RG 59 (M116-5).

8. Rumors of slave smuggling through the Floridas had circulated widely before Jackson's arrival on the scene (see *Niles' Register,* March 17, 24, April 7). On May 1, Jackson had informed John Q. Adams of his investigations of the smuggling rumors and also the alleged property depredations by Spanish troops.

Before leaving for Florida, Jackson had appointed Patrick Henry Darby (1783–1829), brother of the geographer William and later editor of the pro-Jackson Nashville Constitutional Advocate, *as his attorney to superintend the pending* Jackson *v.* Erwin *lawsuit involving the Allison land claims along the Duck River (see Power of attorney to Darby, [April 6], and Agreement among AJ, Jenkin Whiteside, James Jackson, and Darby, April 13; for a discussion of the lawsuit, see AJ to John Overton, December 9, below). Richard I. Easter's letter, below, reveals just how controversial Jackson's choice was, for Darby, an expert in land law, was an aggressive advocate who alienated even Jackson's own associates Felix Grundy and John Overton.*

Jackson's quarrel with Shelbyville businessman Andrew Erwin (1773–1834) had grown beyond the confines of a mere lawsuit, for Erwin, a former Augusta, Georgia, merchant and political devotee of William H. Crawford, was in the forefront of Tennessee's anti-Jackson faction. Already, in 1819, Jackson had warned James Monroe that Erwin and his son James (1796–1851) had been involved with the Creek agent David Brydie Mitchell (1766–1837) in slave smuggling at Amelia Island (see Jackson, *4:329–33). The ensuing scandal and investigation led to Mitchell's dismissal as agent in February 1821, but the Erwin family's influence in Tennessee remained largely unaffected. The elder Erwin won a seat in the Tennessee legislature in 1821. Within three years, James would marry Henry Clay's daughter Anne, and another son, John Patton Erwin (1795–1857) sometime mayor of Nashville and brother-in-law of Jackson's political enemy U.S. Senator John Williams (1778–1837), would assume the editorship of the* Nashville Whig, *turning it into an anti-Jackson paper.*

Given the Erwins' political alliances and Darby's temperament, it is not surprising that Darby and Andrew Erwin would themselves become bitter adversaries and that Jackson *v.* Erwin *would become the subject of newspaper controversy (see AJ to Joseph Norvell and Darby, November 25, 1822, below).*

From Richard Ivy Easter

Nashville 10th May 1821

Dear Genl.

I recd. your letter of the 28th ulto. and the paper you were pleased to send me, and in return I forward you Mr. [George] Wilsons paper of tomorrow morning, there have been no changes in Nashville since your departure nor is there any news—[1]

I saw your Servant Polidore yesterday and made particular Enquiry how your Black family were and how they Conducted, and if he can be relied on, every thing is going on well at your farm—[2]

Majr. Eaton reached home a few days since and is now on a visit to his mother in Franklin he is in good health and will be a candidate again for the Senate, we Know of no opposition as yet Except Judge [Parry Wayne] Humphries—[3]

I feel it my indispensable duty Genl. to explain myself in relation to Mr. Darby, the facts I alluded to in my letter of last week are now Commonly spoken of here And are not pretended to be denied, they are these, last summer at the Robinson Springs a watch was stolen, And was found in the possession of a Mr. [Noah] Outlaw, who alledged he recd. it of a young Mr. [Howel] Lewis, Lewis in Order to Exculpate himself from Censure indicted Outlaw for the theft—I am not positive whether Lewis Employed Darby in his case or not—but the Convesation which he swore to have had with lewis was Confidential as Lawyer—Lewis spoke to Darby to attend to the prosecution sometime last fall, subsequently to which time Darby declared in the presen*[ce]* of [William] Howard Douglass & Mr. [Richmond C.] Tyrie that Outlaw was the thief & he would prosecute him for that he Knew Lewis to be inocent the Case Came on Two weeks ago in Lebanon Darby Changed sides, took a fee from Outlaw and in the Course of the trial offered to give in Evidence against Lewis what he Darby Stated Lewis had Confessd. to him in Confidence as his Council. He insisted on being sworn & deposed positively that Lewis had Confessd. the theft to him when Consulting him as a Lawyer

On his Oath he stated that he had detailed this Confession of Lewises to Mr. Tyrie at a certain place & time, Tyrie was calld in and on his Oath declared he had never held such a Conversation with Mr. Darby at any time or place, Darby then effected to recollect him self And said he remembered distinctly it was not to Mr. Tyrie he made this Communication but to An Other gentleman who he named this gentleman hapening to be present was calld. And on his Oath declared he had never held Any Conversation with Mr. Darby on the subject at Any time or place—Mr Darby then stated that he saw his mistake & that he then distinctly remembered it was not to Either of these Gentleman he made this Communication but to A Mr. [James]

Ball who is Now in Mississippi or Louisianna, And swore positively that if Mr. Ball was there he would depose to these facts, And this he done to put of[f] the suit—Howard Douglass & Mr. Tyrie both swore that Mr. Darby pronounced Outlaw to be the thief in their presence and avowd his determination to prosecute him subsequent to the time which darby states Lewis made the Confession to him; Darby designed to defend outlaw on his own testimony but was prevented by some of the Attys present.[4]

Public sentiment here is Greatly Against him what I have stated are facts detailed to me by some of your best friends & men who have been friendly to Darby—I leave you to draw your own inference. My object is not to leave you in the darke Concerning a man to whom I Know you have Confided much—I am afraid Genl. he has no principles—Indeed I apprehend he is not a proper person to Confide your public papers to & I should have ask'd. him for the Key but feared I might offend you—[5]

I have though it my duty to make this Communication, I have not done so with a wish to injure Mr. D—— but with a view to guard you Augainst Any posible abuse of the trust you have reposed in him—

Govr. [John] Clarke makes hansome mention of you in his Communication to the Legislature of Geo I send you a paper in which you will find it as also Mittchels defince of himself[6]—Eaton tells me the report of the Atty. Genl. on the Subject of the Affricans is Very Voluminous & Conclusive, against Michel & the Erwins I shall write to Col. [George] Gibson to procure me Either Extracts from or a copy of it And if I can procure it, Ervins County men & Country men shall know his perfidy before the August Election, he is a candidate for his County[7]—Cannon has made no defence of himself yet, the publication <I made> of Fiat Justitia has made general impression against him. Several Squibs have come out in Answer to it but they are pitiable & pitifull they are indeed no defence of *his Honor,* but simply idle Efforts to induce the belief it was written for Electioneering purposes. Judge O. did me the honor to say when he saw it that he could not have Changed a word if it had been previously submited to his inspection—[8]

I wish not to trouble you Genl. with my Correspondence such will be the presure of your Engagements I am sure I can not hope to hear from you often, tho no man living would take more delight in hearing of your prosperity & hapiness, I confess I feel here like an object Cast off by the world I once had attachments here but they are now with you I look upon all Around me as objects (with but few Eceptions) to which I am indifferent

I hope Call Joined you in safety Give my love to Mrs. Jackson and the Gentlemen of your family—I am your sincere friend

R. I Easter

P.S. Genl. do not hesitate to Command me in Any thing which you may desire to be done in this Country or at any Other point which I can reach—Yours truly Easter

I have written to Col. Gibson beging him to Cause Fiat Justitia to be republished in the Intiligencer, I have also desired Col. [William] Duane the Editor of the Aurora to give it an insertion[9]—R. I E

ALS, DLC (30). Endorsed by AJ: "Capt R. I. Easters of May 10th. 1821 detailing conduct of P. Darby Esqr to be kept—"

1. Letter and enclosed paper not found. Wilson (1778–1848), a former Tennessee legislator and editor from Knoxville, began the *Nashville Gazette* in 1819. The next issue of the newspaper was dated May 12.

2. In April 1818 near Bowlegs' Town, Jackson had captured and retained in service Polydore (Pallader; Fernando; b. c1784), a runaway slave owned by Charleston's John Satorios. For the details of Jackson's purchase of the slave in 1822, see Catalina M. Satorios to AJ, April 16, 1822, below. Polydore was sent to Mississippi in 1846, and in 1861 was conveyed to Jackson's grandson Samuel (1837–63) in Louisiana.

3. Elizabeth Eaton (c1753–1843) continued to live in Franklin until her death. Humphreys (c1777–1839) was a former congressman and a judge of the Tennessee Superior Court of Errors and Appeals. In September, John H. Eaton was unopposed for reelection.

4. See Easter to AJ, May 3. The theft had occurred in August 1820 and the trial was held at the April term of the Wilson Circuit Court, after a change of venue from Sumner County. For Darby's statement concerning the case, see the Nashville *Constitutional Advocate,* June 17, 1823. Outlaw, Lewis, Douglass (1782–1834), Ball (d. 1830), and tavern-keeper Tyree (d. 1825) were all residents of Sumner County. Robertson Springs is located at the headwaters of the Sulphur Fork in Robertson County, about twenty-four miles north northwest of Nashville.

5. Contrary to Easter's surmise, the trunk that Jackson had deposited with Darby did not contain the general's public papers (see Easter to AJ, June 25).

6. Clark (1766–1832) was the anti-Crawford governor of Georgia. The enclosed newspaper, most likely a copy of the May 1, Milledgeville *Georgia Journal,* contained Clark's April 30 address to the Georgia legislature, lauding Jackson's appointment as governor of Florida, as well as David B. Mitchell's April 27 open letter regarding the dismissal from the Creek agency.

7. For the report of Attorney General William Wirt (1772–1834), made public in May 1822 in response to a resolution by John H. Eaton, see *ASP, Miscellaneous Documents,* 2:957–75. Gibson (1783–1861) was commissary general of subsistence.

8. On May 2, the *Nashville Whig* published an article signed "Fiat Justitia" rebutting Newton Cannon's attacks on the accuracy of John H. Eaton's *Life of Andrew Jackson . . .* (Philadelphia, 1817), particularly regarding the question of the term of service of the Tennessee volunteers during the Creek War (see *Annals of Congress,* 16th Cong., 2nd Sess., pp. 823–41). The *Nashville Clarion* printed one anonymous answer to Easter's article on May 9; two subsequent articles appeared under the pseudonym "Fiat Justitia," also presumably by Easter (*Nashville Whig,* June 6, December 12).

9. Duane (1760–1835) was editor of the Philadelphia *Aurora,* 1798–1822.

To John Coffee

Mountpelier May 11th. 1821

Dear Genl

I reached Blakly on the 29th. ult. and having from thence to communicate with Pensacola, I did not reach this place untill the 9th. instant when I recd your much esteemed favour of the 18th of april[1]—I had wrote you by our mutual friend Mr James Jackson, who I find had not returned when charles called at your house—ere this you have recd it, which will inform you, of the motives and causes that induced me to change what I once thought my fixed determination, and to acept of the commissions to receive, and Govern the Floridas, untill congress meets and passes a law extending a Territorial Goverment over them—as soon as that takes place, I retire to my farm in Tennessee and there spend my latter days.[2]

I have no doubt but the solicitude of the President that I should accept the appointment arose from feelings of friendship, and a desire to give evidence to the world that he fully approved my course on the Seminole campaign—as well as believing that my name would have some weight in establishing the Goverment over the Floridas, he has given me ample power, and Genl Gains & the whole force in the Southern Division is placed under my orders, and if necessary the militia—from which you will discover, that I wield sufficient means, to coerce obedience if it should be necessary at any time to use force. In short my Dear friend Mr Monroe has given me all the means, and placed every thing in my power, necessary to cover my expences as well as to organize the Goverment[3]—and I am free to confess that this added to the multitude of my friends urging me to accept it, and giving reasons which if ever I have the pleasure of seeing you I will give you, changed my determination and induced me to encounter the arduous task—added to this Mrs. J. was in declining health, I was advised it would be the means of restoring not only hers but my own—of the latter I have great doubts, but Mrs. J. health is much improved and I have great hopes that she will be perfectly restored—we all enjoy good health at present, after my arival at Blakly I had a small attack, which has debilitated me very much, but I am now otherwise in good health—I had a hearty welcome at Neworleans and a general Greeting as you will see from the papers—at Mobile and Blakly the citizens of each place gave me a dinner and I am now at this cantoonment awaiting the arival of the hornet, before I can march to Pensacola, and I can form no conjecture of the cause of her detention—she arived at Cuba it is said on the 9th of april and ought to have been here by the first of May at farthest—Rumour says that the commercial interest is combined to induce the Governor Genl of Cuba to withold the possession to the last moment to enable them to throw in a vast quantity of merchandize before the country is surrendered and thereby to evade payment of duties—should Colo. Forbes the commissioner be in this combination there may be some delay—but I will probe the report, and if true expose the charectors—I shall in a day or two adress Colo. Forbes a note to the Havanna,[4] if he does not in that time reach pensacola—

We have experienced a very backward Spring and all the low lands of allabama is now under water—I fear the late frost has ruined our cotton—My Dear Genl write me often—and advise me of your health & family and the prospect of crops—I will see you in the fall or winter—for believe me I never can descend to become a Governor of a Territory—after the offices I have filled—you may therefore rest assured after congress meets I am a private citizen—Mrs. Jackson & the two andrews[5] Join me in affection & good wishes for the health & happiness of you, your lady & Sweet little family—Kiss Andrew [Jackson Coffee] for me & believe me to be your friend sincerely

Andrew Jackson

ALS, THi (8-0472). Published in Bassett, 3:55–56.

1. Coffee's letter has not been found.

2. See above, AJ to Coffee, April 11. Charles (b. c1794) was a Hermitage slave.

3. Elements of the 4th Infantry and the artillery company stationed at Mobile were assigned to occupy Pensacola, and the American garrison at Fort Gadsden (located at Prospect Bluff on the east bank of the Apalachicola River, about sixteen miles above the town of Apalachicola) was to be transferred to St. Marks; while at Montpelier approximately 500 men were under Jackson's immediate command (see Calhoun to AJ, March 22). Jackson's subsequent imprisonment of José M. Callava prompted a majority of James Monroe's cabinet to question the governor's authority over the army; only John Q. Adams supported Jackson's view.

4. No such letter to Forbes has been found.

5. Andrew Jackson, Jr., and Andrew J. Donelson.

To John Quincy Adams

Montpelier May 19th 1821

Sir,

I am still without any information from Col. Forbes, or from the Hornet since her arrival on the 9th ulto at the Havanna, of which you were advised in my last.[1] Her delay is unaccountable and places us in an unpleasant situation—it certainly was, from the treaty, the expectation of both Governments, that we would have been in full possession of the Floridas before the 22nd. inst., the situation of those troops on the Appalachicola in the interior and which are to garrison St Marks, is unpleasant, and the delay will add much to the expense of transporting provisions to them, especially as they are again to be transported to St Marks—[2]

Believing as I do, that as soon as the Spanish agents are notified of the ratification of the treaty and the exchange thereof, there can be no reason for delay; the moment the Hornet arrives, I shall move to Pensacola and having taken possession, shall organise and exercise the Government of the country, as a thing which we have a perfect right to do at any time—The evacuation of the fortifications by the spanish officers and troops and the transporting them to Cuba, is another thing to accomplish which, they have six months if it is not possible to withdraw them sooner

Here, from my instructions, I am to remain until the arrival of Col Forbes;[3] but on his arrival, if any delay is attempted it cannot be attributed to the Government of Spain, but a wanton act of her Officers not warranted by good faith, or by the treaty. In this case, therefore, I have a right to present myself and demand possession—This course I intend to pursue if necessary, and my conjectures that this course may become necessary, grow out of the delay of the arrival of <the Hornet> Col. Forbes—from reading his instructions, I cannot see any real cause for his delay, or how it has occurred—or why he has permitted it[4]—still, I hope he has good reasons to satisfy his Government in this particular I am Sir, with great respect Your Mo Obt servant.

Andrew Jackson

LS (in Andrew J. Donelson's hand with ms insertions by AJ and endorsed by Adams) and Copies, DNA-RG 59 (M116-5, -6, 8-0483); LC, DLC (63); Copy, DNA-RG 46 (8-0482). Published in *ASP, Foreign Relations,* 4:760.

1. See AJ to Adams, May 7.
2. See AJ to José M. Callava, April 30 (above) and May 11.
3. For Jackson's instructions, see John Q. Adams to AJ, March 12.
4. James G. Forbes was to carry the captain general's orders implementing the transfer of Florida (see Adams to Forbes, March 10, DLC-30).

To James Gadsden

Montpelier, 21st May, 1821.

Dear Gadsden,

I received, without date, last night, your letter by Capt. Call. The Shields, as soon as she unloads part of her supply for the troops here, will sail for Pensacola, and be subject to your orders.[1]

On the arrival of the Hornet, you will make the necessary arrangements with the Governor of Pensacola for the occupation of St Marks, and the transportation of the Spanish garrison to Pensacola, and also the delivery of the ceded country to me upon my arrival, in the manner you may judge best to promote the object of a speedy possession by the American Government; for which purpose I enclose you a formal <delivery> authority and power, to appoint an agent to receive St Marks; and receipt for the public property; which authority you can produce, when necessary, to the Governor, (Sr. Callava). You will use the Amelia or Shields for the purpose of forwarding to Major [Alexander Campbell Wilder] Fanning the appointment of commissary to transport his troops, supplies, baggage, &c. &c. and the other for notifying the Spanish Garrison, and transporting it to Pensacola.[2]

As soon as the Hornet arrives, I shall move my troops to the vicinity of Pensacola, and encamp them, until arrangements are made for embarking the officers and troops of Spain. My supplies shall be drawn from the deposit of provisions sent on board the Shields, which belongs to this Regt. We retain here only rations to include the 4th. June, calculating with certainty on the arrival of the Hornet in two or three days.

I must say to you, from reading Col. Forbes' letter, not considering the delay that has taken place, and the information received from Mr. [Gilbert Livingston] Thompson, that Col. Forbes, although 17 days at Cuba before he left him, had not seen the Intendant, would induce me to <believe> conclude that the Governor of Cuba was amusing himself and amusing Col. Forbes, and that delay was intended, were it not for the assurance of Mr Thompson of the positive declarations of the Governor of Cuba, that the Hornet should meet with no delay after the Governor had an interview with this Intendant, which was to take place the day or day after Mr Thompson sailed.[3]

I am happy to find, that the Governour of Pensacola has expressed to me in his answer to my letter by Capt. Call, that frankness which will ensure harmony, and from his character I confidently rely, that no delay will be experienced after the arrival of the Hornet, on his part,[4] and I am also happy to be informed by you that the transports will be in Pensacola harbour in ten days from the date of your letter, from which no delay on my part can arise. Should an opportunity offer, write Majr. Staunton to make all haste with the transports to Pensacola bay. If delay on the part of the Spanish Government unnecessarily takes place, three months having elapsed, at which time it manifestly appears from the 15th. Article of the Treaty, that both Governments expected the U.S. to be in complete possession of the ceded country, it will form a good ground to claim from Spain all damage that may accrue by demurrage on the transport vessels.[5]

It may be proper to name some person with Major Fanning, who in the event of that gentleman's sickness or absence, may act as Commissary and pass receipts on the delivery of the fortification of St. Mark's and the adjacent country. You will enter into an agreement with Govr. Callava, on the form of the receipts to be given, and enclose a form to Majr. Fanning, or the provisional officer appointed under him.[6]

Our situation here although as comfortable as Col. [George Mercer] Brooke and the Officers can make it, is still unpleasant, and a speedy removal, adding much to our comforts, may preserve many lives both to Spain and the U.S., by transporting the officers and men to their respective places of destination, before the sickly season commences.[7] I thank you for your arrangement with Major Staunton as to money matters. Mr Thompson says it may be in his power to oblige me with about $3,000, when I get to Pensacola.

I wish you to arrange every thing, so that you can sail as the messenger from me to St. Augustine, as soon as I receive the government of Pensacola.[8]

You will notify Col. Forbes, on his arrival, that you are appointed by me my agent to make the necessary arrangements for the receipt of the country from the Govr. of Pensacola, and you will push an express to me, or visit me yourself. The latter I would prefer, provided the duty assigned you will permit your leaving Pensacola: this I fear however will not be the case, unless there is great promptitude on the part of the Govr. Yours, respectfully,

(Signed) Andrew Jackson

LC, DLC (63); Copies, DNA-RG 59 (M116-5, -6, 8-0542). Published in Caroline Mays Brevard, *A History of Florida* (Deland, Fla., 1924), pp. 259–60.

1. Letter not found. Gadsden, who had been in New Orleans arranging for supplies, had just reached Pensacola, and Richard K. Call had just returned to Jackson's headquarters at Montpelier from a mission to José M. Callava (see AJ to John Q. Adams, May 7 and 21, and AJ to Call, May 21). The *Thomas Shields,* a New Orleans private transport chartered for government service, had been Isaac McKeever's flagship during the 1818 Florida invasion.

2. Jackson enclosed a commission to receive Fort St. Marks. The *Amelia* was a 32-ton public transport vessel built about 1812; it was sold in 1824. Fanning (c1788–1846; Military Academy 1812) commanded the garrison at Fort Gadsden.

3. See James G. Forbes to AJ, May 7. Thompson, the son of navy secretary Smith Thompson and son-in-law of Vice-President Daniel D. Tompkins, had arrived in Pensacola the previous evening from Havana, where he had accompanied Forbes aboard the *Hornet.* On May 10, attempting to secure the Florida archives in Cuba, Forbes visited Alejandro Ramirez, the intendant of Cuba from 1815 until his death on May 18, 1821, at the village of San Antonio, about 27 miles from Havana.

4. See AJ to Callava, May 11, and Callava to AJ, May 16; see also Call to AJ, May 21.

5. Article 15 of the Adams-Onís Treaty granted tariff concessions, beginning three months after the exchange of ratifications, to Spanish vessels entering Pensacola and St. Augustine.

6. Gadsden subsequently named Call to arrange the transfer of St. Marks, and Fanning received the post on June 27.

7. Brooke (d. 1851), lieutenant colonel of the 4th Infantry, commanded the forces occupying Pensacola after the transfer.

8. On June 26, Jackson appointed Gadsden as courier to St. Augustine.

To John Caldwell Calhoun

Mountpelier May 22nd. 1821

Dear Sir

I had the pleasure to receive your much esteemed favour of the 8th. ult, on the 11th instant, and would have acknowledged it on its recpt, but I had a right hourly to expect information of the arival of Colo Forbes at Pensacola, and had a wish to inform you that I was on my march to receive possession of the country ceded.[1] It is with extreme regret I have to inform you that altho he reached Cuba on the 22nd ult he has not arived at pensacola yet—and from his delay it is impossible for me to conjecture when he may. Mr. Thompson who accompanied him to the Havanna, and left him there on the 7th reached me on the night of the 20th. via Orleans and expected to find him at Pensacola when he reached there—I am fearfull that the Governor Genl of Cuba has discovered in the Colo. too much of the swaviter et modo,[2] and is practising upon him a little of the spanish policy, procrastination and delay for purposes not calculated to promote our interest, but to gain time for his friends to introduce large quantities of merchandize, and africans. This delay is truly irksome, and will produce great inconvenience & expense to the united states by transporting the supplies for the Troops, first to their present stations and then to the places they are to occupy which might have been avoided by a little promptness and [energy] displayed by Colo. Forbes—It is to be regretted that the duty assigned Colo. Forbes had not have been committed to Capt [George Campbell] Reed, if it had we would have been in complete possession of the country by this time—but as it is I fear delay will be experienced, and the occasion of it not result much to the dignity of our country—How Irksome my situation to be compelled to remain here with my arms Folded not able to prevent those illegal practices that from information is daily practicing on the coasts of Florida and to favour which causes this <Govr> delay. But such is my instructions and I must submit to them.[3]

I have my Dr Sir read your letter with great pleasure, the principles you have laid down for your political guide through life will land you in a safe haven, and lead you to a compleat triumph over your Political enemies—and your country to safety and happiness—The course pursued by last congress is universily condemned, whilst your course, & report is approbated by nine tenths of the citizens of the country through which I have passed; indeed it is approved by all except those who, from political and popular views have been with the majority—and finding themselves now in the minority cannot consistantly retreat.

Permit me to make to you a friendly sugestion I say friendly for no man wishes you better than I do, or can have your future wellfare more at heart than I have as I believe your political wellfare to be <it is> intimately connected with the wellfare of our country. I would therefore sugest for your safety a change of <the> adjutant<cy> Genl [Daniel] Parker—he I have no doubt may be a good man—but he lacks both talents and magnanimity—It was alone his report that gave to your envious political enemies, the least shadow of ground to attack you, it was his blunders, occasioned by his indolence & want of capacity that gave [John] Floyd room for his indecorous attack—it was from Genl Parkers want of magnanimity in not stepping forward acknowledging the error to be his own, stating your reliance on his performing his duty correctly, and the frequent calls made upon you that you had not time to examine this report, and the error was to be ascribed to him not to you; this would have <even> made the Doctor to have blushed for his attack. Genl Parker is a weak man, and your safety and ease require a man of capacity possessing high honourable feelings to fill that office, a man of magnanimity industry and pride—you can find this charector in Colo. Gadsden.[4]

Before this reaches you our military relations will have ceased,[5] but my breast will allways cherish with the most lively recollection, that <your efficient conduct> friendly feeling toward you, that your honourable conduct towards me ever since you have been placed in the Department of war was well calculated to inspire, this feeling for you never will cease during life—and in every situation that you may be placed in through life my best wishes for your wellfare & happiness will accompany you It will afford me great pleasure to write you when any thing occurs that I think may be either usefull or amusing to you. permit me through you to make one request for a mutual friend of us both—I should not trouble you was it not that I hold no correspondance with the Sec of the Treasury & and am fully aware how he uses his cunning, in the appointment of the officers in his department—his conduct to Major [Israel] Pickens formerly of No Carolina now of the state of allabama I am no stranger to—I have wrote to Mr Monroe some time since asking for Doctor Brunaugh the office of receiver of public money in west Florida as soon as a land office is opened therein. I have reasons to believe Mr Monroe will give the Doctor this appointment, unless the Sec of the Treasury <should> in the <hurry> crowd of business should play the same game with the Doctor that he did with Major Pickens, My request therefore is that you will remind the President that Doctor Brunaugh has solicited this appointment & continues to be a candidate for it.[6]

I feel grateful to you for your friendly expressions toward me, and the interest you have taken for the preservation of my health—for which receive my gratefull acknowledgements with the assurance of my great respect friendship & esteem, I am Sir yr most obedt Servt,

Andrew Jackson

ALS draft, DLC (30). Published in Bassett, 3:58–60.

1. See Calhoun to AJ, April 8.

2. With charm and moderation.

3. For Jackson's instructions, see John Q. Adams to AJ, March 12. Read (1787–1862), a career naval officer, commanded the *Hornet.*

4. Jackson was referring to Calhoun's January 2 report to the House on the status of military posts throughout the country, which, because of information supplied by Parker (1782–1846; Dartmouth 1801), erroneously included abandoned posts in the roster. Virginia congressman Floyd (1783–1837; Pennsylvania 1806), a War of 1812 army surgeon, referred to the number of posts and to army inefficiency in his January 17 attack upon Calhoun's army reduction plan (see *HRDoc* 41, 16th Cong., 2nd sess., Serial 49; *Annals of Congress,* 16th Cong., 2nd sess., pp. 891–901). As a result of the army reduction, Parker left the adjutant generalcy on June 1 and became paymaster general. In 1822 he was dismissed from the service when Nathan Towson, who was not confirmed in his appointment to a line command, resumed the paymaster generalcy. For the controversy surrounding James Gadsden's appointment as adjutant general, see above, Edmund P. Gaines to AJ, April 27; and James C. Bronaugh to AJ, February 8, 1822, below.

5. Jackson retired as major general on June 1.

6. Letter not found. Pickens (1780–1827), a former North Carolina congressman, apparently felt that he had been promised the register's post at Cahaba by Alexander J. Dallas, Crawford's predecessor, but the post went to another, and Pickens received the appointment at St. Stephens, where he served until 1821, when anti-Crawford forces elected him governor of Alabama.

From James Jackson

Forks of Cypress May 28th. 1821

Dear Genl.

I expected ere this to have been on my road to Pensacola, but found I risked too much by so doing, both on my own acct. & that of my friends. Mr. Crawford has not yet forwarded his instructions under the Law giveing relief to the Purchasers of publick Lands.[1] The arrangement of that business is of most importance to me. I might be too long detained If I went from home. By going in October would have nothing to hurry me—I have sent a power to Doctor Bronaugh to act for me, from his friendship and ability, have no doubt he will do as well for me as I could do for myself—The Genl. [Coffee] & myself have agreed on terms with Genl. [John] Brahan for your Plantation, which are contingent, on his shorty being able to arrange for the payments. The Genl. goes shortly to Huntsville when the matter will be finaly understood, the Terms are much below what we intended to take, but after maturely considering your views & great anxiaty to get clear of any obligations to pay money, We concluded it would be more satisfactory to you. In addition there seems a general disposition not to pay for Lands bought at high prices. In consequence, Certificates can be bought for one half payable in Tennessee money—The bargain with Genl. Brahan is Cost & one thousand dollars for improvements, the Gin reserved, one third on takeing possession the balance in one & two years thereafter in good money. In this transaction have looked as much to your feelings as your interest—[2]

James [Jackson] Hanna brought home one of your fellows a very fine looking fellow & the only one he brought. The other he left authority with a friend to sell as he run, who He expected would get something near his value.[3] It appears this is to be an unfortunate business threwout for your fine Mare is dead, she brought him to Cypress very well & in a day or two after set out for Tennessee & Led him there, but at Granny Whites old place she was taken unwell. He remained all night, & next day got to Nashville where He was aided by [John] Shute, [John] Hardin & others in endeavouring to cure her, but without success, he was recommended to a grat Farryor, who said she had been improperly Treated, for her Complaint was a Chest Cholick & that she in all probability would not recover, which proved but too true—[4]

I won the race at Huntsville, the grey had great superiority of heels. He took the Track & kept it the Sir Archy is rather the best game Horse, but the grey was quite too fat. Campbell was out but did not ride, to please other I permitted a much wors rider & heavyor Boy to ride. Camp lost upwards of $4000 & offered to bet me $6000 in Land Certificates, but I had too many Children for such dashing. The Race is made to be run again in October. I would not take any part being tired of my Company. I have lately been told Camp says his Virginia rider rode Jocky & that he will be sure of his race—[5]

I fear Wm. Crawford will not make you a good Crop. Genl. Coffee & myself were at your Plantation a few days since, did not find things in that order we could have wished. The stand of Cotton generally is not good, most people had to replant, some of mine is good, some middleing & some bad. I have an excellent stand at Limestone. I in part blame the foul state of my Land here for the want of a good stand—

Mr. James G[illespie] Birney of Madison County, who is a very honourable clever fellow has been looking at the Land west of Cypress & was much pleased with your place, want of funds only prevented him from purchasing. He proposed takeing half the Land & to put on 20 Hands & you & He to work it Jointly, He to live on the place and superintend & draw in proportion to the number of hands each had & either to put on as many as He chose, He to be furnished with his meat & Corn for his attention. This is the outline of his proposition, saying if it met Your approbation, there would be no dificulty in details. He the present year made 37.000 lb of Baled Cotton with his 20 Hands, which is a recommendation as a Planter. Doctor Bronaugh is acquainted with Mr. Birney & you & myself played whist with him & a Mr. Davis at Huntsville one evening while the Legislature sat there[6]—From your recent disagreeable experiment in a Partnership, did not encourage the project, but promised to write you on the subject. If the sale to Brahan is not carryed into effect, and no offer from any other person: what would you think of Mr. Birneys proposition—[7]

There is one thing certain to make good Crops you must have a good Overseer, which I expect would be preferable to a partner. I shall hope soon to hear from you & to have the pleasure of seeing you at Pensacola in October next—Will you have the goodness, if necessary, to give Doctor Bronaugh your advice as regards my business—Mrs. Jackson joins me in best wishes to you & Mrs. Jackson believe me sincerely yours

James Jackson

ALS, DLC (30). Published in Bassett, 3:60–61.

1. The land relief bill became law on March 2, but Josiah Meigs, commissioner of the treasury department's general land office, did not issue regulations for administering the law until June 15.

2. Brahan (1774–1834), an army contractor during the Creek War, was receiver of the land office at Huntsville, where he was shortly to be implicated in a scandal involving misuse of government funds. Jackson eventually sold his Evans Spring farm to Richard C. Cross (see AJ to Coffee, July 26, below).

3. In the winter of 1819–20, Hanna (1800–67), the son of James (d. 1817) and Sarah Jackson Hanna, had purchased several slaves in Virginia for Jackson. He returned to the state in February to seek out two who had run away: the recaptured slave was Tom; the still missing slave was Ned. See Hanna to AJ, January 30, 1820 (*Jackson,* 4:353–54), and March 1.

4. Granny White's Tavern, between Nashville and Franklin, was formerly operated by Lucinda White (c1742–1815). Shute (d. 1844) was a Nashville stabler; Harding (1777–1865) was proprietor of Belle Meade. The farrier has not been identified.

5. Camp was probably James W. (1789–1845), a merchant formerly of Nashville and now of Huntsville, where he was a member of the North Alabama Jockey Club and a one-term state legislator. Further details on the horse race have not been found.

6. Birney (1792–1857; Princeton 1810), a native Kentuckian and lawyer, moved to Alabama in 1818 and sat in the first state legislature when, as a supporter of Henry Clay, he refused to vote for a resolution condemning congressional critics of Jackson's 1818 invasion of Florida. A slaveholder in 1821, he later embraced antislavery and became a prominent leader in the movement. Jackson was honored by the legislature when he visited Huntsville in November 1819 after inspecting the military road in northern Alabama. Davis has not been further identified.

7. James Jackson was referring to Jackson's association with Nelson P. Jones for the management of the Evans Spring farm (see *Jackson,* 4:399–400). Jackson's reply, if any, has not been found.

To Robert Butler

Montpelier June 2nd. 1821

Sir

I received your letter of the 4th ulto. Fort Hawkins, some time since and deferred answering, expecting daily to hear of the arrival of the Hornet at Pensacola, until my patience is exhausted;[1] I have not heard from Col Forbes since the 7th of May, at which time he wrote me that he had assurances that he would not be detained more than four days. He had been that at Havanna from the 22nd. of April.[2]

My instructions are, to repair to this place and await the arrival of and report of Col Forbes—How humiliating to the American Government, that it should appoint an agent who would permit himself thus to be trifled with <thus>, and the best interests of his country to be sacrificed by this delay, which can only originate to give scope to the mercenary merchant or inhuman African dealer to evade our laws, and inundate our country with merchandize free of duty. I cannot forsee any other cause for such a shameful delay—that Col Forbes should yield to it, is truly astonishing to me, and that the government should have overlooked this event, and not have provided for it by their instructions, is extraordinary. I reached <this> Blakely on the 29th of April and on that day communicated with this post, expecting that Col Forbe's report was waiting for me[3]—I then dispatched to Pensacola, Doctor Bronough and Judge Breckenridge with a communication to the Governor, informing him of my arrival, and being invested with full powers to receive the country, to which I received for answer, that so soon as he received instructions, he would act promptly, and that no delay should be experienced in his delivery of the country[4]—And here I have been detained awaiting the arrival of Col Forbes, with my transports and provisions all ready to transport the Spanish officers and Troops—and the ambassador Col Forbes amusing himself at the Havanna, writing a history of Florida, as report says[5]

The moment the Hornet arrives, I shall push an express to you with the proclamation et ce. In the mean time notify the Governor of St Augustine of the transports being ready and provisions—stating to him that you are officially informed that the <delivery> Royal order for the delivery of the Floridas was delivered to the Capt Genl and Governor of Cuba by Col Forbes on the 23rd. of April last, and that, from the assurance of the Spanish minister to our Government, you have no doubt that no unnecessary delay in delivering the country should take place, that he has received instructions for the delivery of the country—that the transports being ready, and if detained a heavy expense must accrue for demurrage on those vessels, that as the delay is occasioned by the neglect of the agents of Spain, that the Spanish government must assume the expense occasioned by this delay, or shew that it is not possible to embark their troops, for good reasons not growing out of the neglect of the spanish agents, or you will be compelled to discharge the transports, and report the case to your Government—and be prepared at all events on the 22nd. of August to march in and take possession of St Augustine, and if the Spanish troops are not embarked on the 22nd. of August, discharge the transports, Spain having violated the treaty, and take possession of the country, and if force is opposed to you repel it by force.[6] However, as I have wrote to the President on this subject, I hope I shall be in possession of instructions in due time to communicate to you before the 22nd of August[7]—I am with great regard Yr. Mo Obt servant.

(Signed) Andrew Jackson

LC in Andrew J. Donelson's hand, DLC (63).

1. Letter not found. Butler had passed through Fort Hawkins, established in 1806 at the site of present-day Macon, Georgia, on his way to St. Augustine, Florida, where he arrived on May 24.

2. See James G. Forbes to AJ, May 7.

3. Jackson's letter has not been found.

4. See above, James C. Bronaugh and Henry M. Brackenridge to AJ, May 7.

5. The intelligence concerning Forbes's forthcoming *Sketches Historical and Topographical of the Floridas* (New York, 1821) probably came from Gilbert L. Thompson, who arrived at Jackson's camp on May 20.

6. August 22 was the deadline for the transfer of Florida.

7. Jackson probably was referring to his letter to John Q. Adams, May 30. Adams's June 27 acknowledgement noted that Jackson's letter had been transmitted to the president, but no subsequent response has been found.

To James Craine Bronaugh

Mountpelier June 9th. 1821

Dr. Brunaugh

I recd your letter of the 6th. last evening with the letter inclosed, and the inclosed is an answer which I have to request you to hand to Colo. Jones, that he may deliver it to its adress—say to Colo Jones I regret not having the pleasure of seeing him[1]—I was taken last evening very ill, am under the operation of medicine & better—we recd. the Register last evening, and the appointment of the civil officers in Florida—I have directed Lt Donelson to inclose the National Intelligencer to Capt Call, you will see that not one of those I recommended is appointed, [George] Walten is Sec of the Territory & Colo. Forbes Marshal—had I anticipated this I should have adhered to my first determination not to have accepted the Goverment—but I will close my official duties with the next congress as I am determined, never to be associated with such men as some of those who are appointed[2]—say to my friend Call not to despond—that I am Determined to try my influence in his behalf, next congress—and any thing I have in my power to give him, will be—I would like to see how the Judges will organize their court how a Jury is to be Summoned, and who is to Issue the process to the Marshal[3]—&c &c &c—I am too sick to write more at present, but hope I will be well tomorrow, should I get worse I will send for you—present me to Judge Brakenride & Call—& receive the salutations of the ladies & Gentlemen here—keep me advised of the news at Pensacola—& say to the Judge when I want him to come up I will write him. Gadsden will remain some days with us—

Andrew Jackson

ALS, DLC (30). Published in Bassett, 3:65.

1. Letters not found. Jones has not been identified.

2. The May 18 and 19 issues of the Washington *National Intelligencer* printed the list of Florida appointments, as well as the new army register. Jackson did not receive official notification of the Florida appointments until June 12 (see AJ to James Monroe, June 13). Walton (c1790–1863; Princeton 1812), son of a signer of the Declaration of Independence, was a Georgia legislator before serving as Florida secretary, 1821–26.

3. Richard K. Call had retained his rank as captain in the army rather than receive a Florida appointment. Eligius Fromentin was named federal district judge for West Florida, and William Pope Duval (1784–1854), a former Kentucky congressman, was appointed judge for East Florida.

From José Maria Callava

(Translation) 10th June, 1821.

Most Excellent Sir,

Yesterday evening anchored in this Port the United States Sloop of War Hornet, of which I should have advised Y. E. the very hour of its arrival, had it not been for the assurance made me by Capt. Call that he would do so himself.

By the aforesaid vessel I have received the orders of the Capt. Genl. of Cuba, authorizing me to enter into the necessary arrangements for the evacuation of this Province, its delivery, and the transportation of its garrison, and whatever else conduces & relates to the fulfilment of the stipulations in the Treaty of Amity, Settlement of differences and limits, between H. C. M. and the President of the U. S. concluded at Washington the 22nd day of February, 1819, and ratified on the corresponding day of 1821.[1]

In pursuance of my intimation to Y. E. in my letter of 16th May last,[2] I send you a Statement, marked No 1. of the force composing the Garrison of Fort St Marks of Apalache, which is to be transported here, in order that, united with the Garrison of this place, it may pass to the Havanna, in convoy of the Hornet; No 2 is a statement comprehending the whole number of individuals to be transported from this place, including said Garrison of Apalache; to the number of military officers with their wives, children, and servants. I have deemed it adviseable to subjoin that of the other persons in public employ, their wives, children, and servants, and others of whom you will be informed. No 3. intimates to Y. E. my inability to give a decisive answer to your request of information as to the number of days required for the voyage from Pensacola to the Havanna; my remarks therein may however be found useful in pointing out the most prudent course as regards this matter. The specification which it contains of the mode employed in equipping the S. Troops for transportation, has no other object but the one signified. Nothing now remains but to express to you that I am ready, and that it will afford me the greatest pleasure to satisfy to the utmost extent of my power all the enquiries which may be requisite for the regulation of your proceedings.[3]

Your Excellency having empowered Capt. Call with authority to take any measures which, under the present circumstances he may consider necessary and proper, and the latter having assured me that he is in possession of Y. E.'s orders for the direction of the officer authorized to receive Fort St Marks of Apalache, we are making the necessary preparations for effecting its delivery; I must then flatter myself that Y. E. will be persuaded of my desire to promote your good pleasure, and convinced of the true sentiments of friendship and harmony which animate me.[4]

As Y. E. and myself are the persons authorised on the part of our *[r]*espective governments to carry into effect, as far as relates to the charge committed to me, the terms agreed on in the Treaty, there only remains for us, to preserve in our subsequent transactions that concord which may ensure their mutual success. God preserve you many years.

(Signed) José Callava,
Col. Commt. W. Florida, &c

Translation in Edward A. Rutledge's hand, DLC (63); Translations, DNA-RG 59 (M116-6, 8-0563). Published in Bassett, 3:66–67 (from DNA-RG 59).

1. See James G. Forbes to AJ, June 9, announcing his arrival on the *Hornet.* For the orders of Nicholas Mahy y Romo, May 5 and 27, see *ASP, Foreign Relations,* 4:749.

2. See Callava to AJ, May 16.

3. For the enclosures, all dated June 10, see DLC (63). Jackson later agreed to furnish seventeen days' rations for the Spanish troops (see AJ to Callava, June 20).

4. See AJ to Call, May 11, and to Alexander C. W. Fanning, May 22.

To José Maria Callava

Montpelier—
June 12th. 1821

Sir,

Your communication of the 10th. instant, by Capt Call, was received this morning.[1] I cannot but express my gratification at the order transmitted you from the Capt Genl of the Cubas to evacuate the province of West

Florida, with the authority as commissioner to fulfil on the part of the Spanish nation the stipulations of the Treaty of amity, settlement of differences, and limits as concluded between the Plenipotentaries of his Catholic Majesty, and of the U States, at Washington on the 22nd. of Febuary 1819, and ratified on the corresponding day of 1821—The promptness with which you have complied with my request, after being clothed with authority to act, and the frankness with which you have met my repeated communications, are evidences of those sentiments of harmony and amity which animate you, and which will govern us in our future operations together—

The Documents numbered from 1 to 3, as enclosed in your communication, afford the information required on those subjects as connected with the discharge of the duties of the commission imposed on me. The Transports deemed necessary have been provided, and their arrival in Pensacola may be duly expected. I beg you to be assured that in fulfilling the stipulations of the Treaty, the cumfort and safe conveyance of the Spanish officers and soldiers to their port of destination, will be duly regarded—

Capt Call was authorised by me to make the necessary arrangements for the delivery of the Fortress of St Marks to the American officer designated to receive it.[2] my motives for proposing an immediate evacuation of that post by the Spanish garrison will not be considered premature, or be misunderstood by you—To have the whole of your military command embark at the same period, and under the same escort from Pensacola it was presumed would be gratifying to you; and with a view of complying with so reasonable a wish, the government of the U States will willingly incur the additional transportation of the Garrison of St Marks to Pensacola, in preference to transporting that Garrison direct to Havanna as the stipulations in the 7th article of the treaty might be construed—

Captain Call reports to me that you require in the evacuation of St Marks, a receipt for the cannon and other munitions of War which may be left in said fortress; accompanied with a request that transportation may be furnished for two field pieces with the Troops that may embark from that post for Pensacola.[3]

By reference to the 2nd. Article of the treaty of Amity limits &c, the stipulations of which we are commissioned by our respective governments to execute: It appears that his Catholic Majesty cedes to the U States of America, The provinces of East and West Florida, including the adjacent islands, Lots, Squares, vacant lands, Public edifices, *Fortifications,* barracks, and other buildings which are not private property—It is the opinion of the President of the U States that the cannon belonging to the Fortifications are to be considered as appendages to them, and included in the cession—They constitute a part of the work, for a Fortification deprived of its material of defence, like a ship of war without its armament would lose its character as such—That this fair and just construction of the 2nd. Article of the treaty alluded to, was the one evidently placed upon it by the Spanish Plenipotentiary, Don [Luis de] Onis, who negotiated the same, may be derived in som[e] measure from the stipulation in the 7th Article—In that Article the U States is bound to furnish the transports and necessary escort to convey the Spanish Officers and Troops, and their baggage to the Havanna. no mention is made of cannon, or munitions of War, and there can be little doubt entertained that the Spanish Plenipotentairy believed that he had provided transportation for all the public property which had not been ceded under the treaty, and which could consistantly with the stipulations of that instrument be removed—By the 7th article, to the stipulations of which I would particularly direct the attention of your Excellency; The Spanish Officers, Troop, and their baggage are alone mentioned in the transportation to be furnished—no notice is taken of provisions for the voyage, of the civil department, of the families and servants of the officers, or of the arms and accoutrements &c. of the soldier—yet with as much propriety, and more consistently with the literal construction of the treaty may provisions be denied, and transportation for unenumerated persons, and arms of the soldier be <denied> refused, as a Fortress to be deprived of the Cannon belonging to it, forming its batteries and constituting its principal material of defence—[4]

The stipulations in the 2nd. Article of the Treaty are for the benefit of the U States; those in the 7th Article are for the advantage of Spain; and it is the opinion of the President of the U States as well as his desire, that both should be construed on fair, just, and liberal principles, graduated by the scale of reciprocal benefits—

While therefore I am instructed as commissioner to insist that by the stipulations of the 2nd. article of the treaty, the *cannon* found in the Fortifications, constituting their batteries, are appendages to the same and included in the <same> cession; so am I disposed to give that construction to the stipulations of the 7th article of the same instrument as would comport with the most liberal views; and give satisfaction to that party entitled to its benefits—

Upon a review of the subject a hope is entertained that the difficulties which have occurred in the arranging measures for the early evacuation of St Marks will be removed on your part, and that the cannon constituting the batteries, or the armament generally belonging to that work, will be delivered with the Fort as included in the cession—Capt Call still acts under the authority delegated to him, and will concert with you the necessary arrangements for the evacuation and delivery of St Marks to the officer designated to receive it: He has my instructions with regard to the transportation of 2 pieces of field Artillery requested by you, and be assured that every accomodation consistent with my instructions and which may be calculated to promote the early and harmonious termination of the duties of our respective commissions will be most cheerfully attended to—[5]

I contemplate moving in a few days into the vicinity of Pensacola, with a view of personally arranging those operations, connected with the faithful <discharge> execution of the duties which have been assigned us by our Respective Governments—I have the honor to be Yr. Mo Obt Sert

(Signed[)] Andrew Jackson

LC in Andrew J. Donelson's hand, DLC (63); Copies, DNA-RG 59 (M116-6, -10, 8-0592). Published in Bassett, 3:67–69 (from DNA-RG 59).

1. See above.

2. See AJ to Richard K. Call, May 11; Call to [Alexander C. W. Fanning], June 15, FU; and, above, AJ to James Gadsden, May 21.

3. Call's report has not been found.

4. For AJ's instructions on articles 2 and 7 of the Adams-Onís Treaty, see above, John Q. Adams to AJ, March 23. Onís (c1769–1830; Salamanca) had been Spanish minister to the United States.

5. Callava had also proposed a receipt for the disputed cannon throughout the province, and Jackson authorized Call to agree to the measure "on condition that he likewise receipts for the transportation furnished." The final compromise of this issue left the cannon in place and sent the question of final disposition to the Spanish and American authorities in Washington (see AJ to Call, June 12; AJ to Callava, June 29, below; and Callava to AJ, June 30).

To Robert Butler

Mountpelier June 13th. 1821

Dr. Colo.

Colo. Forbes has at lenght arived at Pensacola, he landed on the Evening of the 9th. and brings with him Don [Pedro de] Alva the bearer of orders for the delivery of West Florida—Mr Forbes in his letter to me of the 9th. represents Don Alva to be commissioner for the Delivery of East & West Florida—from the Govrrs. letter of the 10th I find Don Alva a mere messenger—[1]

It appears from a letter from Colo. Forbes To Mr. Adams Sec of State, that thc nonsuch was to sail from the Havanna the first of June with Don [Juan] Aredondo [y Santelices] Bearer of an order to the Governor of East Florida, and altho Colo. Forbes has represented for some purpose, that Don Alva is the commissioner you will find that the Governor of East Florida is solely authorised to deliver it. Colo. Forbes must have represented himself as the commissioner on behalf of the u states to receive the Floridas as it appears that the first order of date the 5th. of May he is named as the american commissioner to whom the country is to be delivered—and to which the following note is annexed and adressed to the Governor of East Florida

"In the order which I directed to you for the delivery of the province under your command, it is not expressed to whom it is to be made: you will understand that it is to the constituted authorities of the U states who may come forward to require of you its fulfilment May 29th. 1821."[2] When Colo. Forbes & Don Alva reached Pensacola, they still held the Idea out, that East Florida could not be delivered untill they arived at St Augustine—I have however notified Colo. Forbes that I have no further use for him, and as he is appointed Marshal, I presume he will not think so hard of being reduced from ambasedorial robes to that of a civil executive officer.[3]

I move tomorrow for the vicinity of Pensacola to have an interview with the Governor. I had Capt Call in waiting at Pensacola, that on the arival of Colo. Forbes he might make immediate arrangements with the Governor for the removal of the Garrison from St Marks to Pensacola to embark all the Troops under convoy of the Hornet—The Governor appeared to act with promptness, but wanted Capt Call to give a receipt for the ordinance & ordinance stores attached to & belonging to the defence of the fortification—Capt Call promptly told him no—and forthwith reported the same to me—my letter to the Govr and my instructions to Capt Call upon this subject is enclosed to you & which, combined with the instructions of the sec of war, you will take for your guide with the Govr. of East Florida—I have authorised Capt Call to Shew the Govr his instructions, which will bring this matter at once to a close.[4]

There is no way to manage a Spaniard only by energy and promptness—and if the Governor of East Florida will assume the responsibility upon himself to dismantle the fortifications, and claim delay for the want of Transportation for them tell him, that is no cause of delay, that if this was considered a right under the treaty he ought to have been prepared with Transportation—that for such trivial pretexts, the Goverment of the u States cannot be bound to pay demurrage on the transports, for any unnessary delay, and that unless a better reason for delay is furnished, <you will> or the Troops embarked you will be obliged to dismiss the Transports unless the Governor will take upon himself that his Goverment will pay the Demurrage let all your correspondance be in writing—and should the Governor, delay delivering possession and not embark before the 22nd. of august on that day you will dismiss the Transports and take possession of the fortification—as censure might attach, if these Transports were discharged before the 22nd. of August.[5]

The moment I make arrangements with the Governor of Pensacola for the delivery of West Florida, I will send Colo. Gadsden to you with Blank drafts upon the Goverment to be filled for such sum as may meet your wants—If a vessel can be got I shall send him by water if not overland.

we cannot boast of our healths Mrs. J & myself does not enjoy as good health as when I last wrote you[6]—I am advised that you are the Colo. of the 4th. conditionally upon the choice of Genl atkison—This note shews more weakness &c &c than I could have suposed could have existed in such a body[7]—as soon as you receive the country, and the Sec for East Florida arives, you will repair to me at Pensacola & make report how you have executed the <trust> duty with which you have been entrusted—I should have sent an express to you with funds on my arival here, but I knew no bills but that of the u States Bank would answer you there, and I could not sell a draft in orleans for that or orlean notes[8]—I am sir with great respect yr. Most obdt. Servt

Andrew Jackson
Commissioner to receve the country ceded
by the late Spanish Treaty to the u States—

P. S. I keep no copy—the original to be preserved—A. J.

ALS, DNA-RG 59 (M116-5). Endorsed as received on July 9.

1. See James G. Forbes to AJ, June 9; and, above, José M. Callava to AJ, June 10. During the remainder of the month Jackson and Callava debated the role of Alba (c1762–1835), postmaster at Pensacola and comptroller of its military hospital.

2. See Forbes to John Q. Adams, May 30, Order by Nicholas Mahy y Romo, May 5, and Mahy y Romo to José Coppinger, May 29 (*ASP, Foreign Relations*, 4:748–49). Forbes reported Alba's claim to Adams on June 9 (*TPUS*, 22:64–65). The USS *Nonsuch* was a 148-ton schooner with 14 guns, built in 1812 and dropped from the navy list in 1826. Arredondo y Santelices was auditor of war for East Florida.

3. See AJ to Forbes, June 11.

4. The enclosures were AJ to Richard K. Call, June 12, and, above, AJ to Callava, June 12. For the war department's instructions, see John C. Calhoun to AJ, March 22. Instead of the war department instructions, Jackson may have intended reference to Adams's instructions above of March 23.

5. August 22 was the deadline for the transfer.

6. See above, AJ to Butler, June 2.

7. For a discussion of Butler's place in the reduced army, see above, Edmund P. Gaines to AJ, April 27; and Calhoun to AJ, May 19.

8. Regarding Jackson's efforts to obtain funds at New Orleans, see above, AJ to Adams, April 24.

From José Maria Callava

(Translation) Pensacola, 19 June, 1821.

Most excellent Sir,

At this moment I for the first time happily feel myself relieved from the violent and dangerous attack by which my life was threatened, as I informed Y. E. in my note of the 16th inst.[1]

I am still however suffering from the effects of a decided dysentery attended with symptoms of ill omen, but as I ought to prefer the punctual and prompt discharge of all my duties to the preservation of my own existence, it is with much satisfaction I reply to your Excellency's communications which I have on hand.

I have received Y. E.'s note of the 16th. inst. dated at Manuel's house, 15 miles from this place; I am therefore advised of the notice given me by your Exy. of your arrival at that place, and of your being prepared to fulfil the objects of your commission, as sole commissioner named by the Govt of the U. S. to receive possession of E. and W. Florida, according to the stipulations of the Treaty of amity, settlement of differences and limits, concluded by the Plenipotentiaries of Spain and the U. S. on the 22nd February, 1819, and ratified on the same month & day of 1821.[2] In reply, I congratulate Y. E. on your happy arrival in the soil of this Province, and I repeat the assurance I have made you in other communications, of my being furnished with orders under the same treaty to evacuate this Province, and give possession of it to the commissioners or officers of the U. S. lawfully authorised to receive it.[3]

Y. E. expresses also a wish that I would concur in fixing a day as early as possible, and to suit the mutual convenience of both parties, for an interview and exhibition of our credentials, a reciprocal official recognition, and an entrance upon the duties of our respective Commissions: In reply, I have the honour to acquaint Y. E. that in your quality of Commissioner, you may, when it suits your <convenience> pleasure, and in the manner you may deem most expedient, exhibit your credentials to me, as the existing commandant of this Province, and that I have already told your Excellency that I am authorized to enter into arrangements for its being evacuated by his C. Majesty's Troops and delivered to your Excellency agreeably to the stipulations by our respective Governments.

As soon as the first intelligence reached me of Y. E.'s arrival at the abovenamed spot, I should have been very much flattered to have had the pleasure of seeing your Excellency, as the most striking proof of the sentiments of friendship and good intelligence which subsist between us, and which I am particularly desirous of keeping up with y. Exy.; but of that satisfaction I have been deprived by my accidental indisposition. I remain, with the warmest sentiments of friendship, <and> Your Ex.'s most obt Servt

(signed) José Callava, &c. &c.

Translation in Edward A. Rutledge's hand, DLC (63); Translations, DNA-RG 59 (M116-6, 8-0620). Published in Bassett, 3:71 (extract from DNA-RG 59).

1. On June 16 Callava had reported his "severe and sudden indisposition."

2. See AJ to Callava, June 16, transmitted by James Gadsden, Jackson's liaison with Callava. On June 16, Jackson arrived at Manuel Gonzalez's house, fifteen miles northwest of Pensacola at present-day Cantonment, Florida. Gonzalez (d. 1838) was subsequently a justice of the peace; his house was used as the temporary territorial capital during the yellow fever epidemic in 1822.

3. See above, Callava to AJ, June 10.

From José Maria Callava

(Translation) Pensacola, 22d June, 1821.

Most excellent Sir,

I received with the utmost satisfaction yesterday morning your Excellency's communication of the same date, as in it I observe plainly that Y. E. displays your sublime prudence under every aspect: being informed of all the minor points and particulars of your relation, I with pleasure pass on to answer those which require some comments.[1]

I perfectly agree with Y. E. that the exhibition of credentials may be deferred for the present, but I must add that in the single event of my complaint retaining its violence, Y. E. may, at a convenient time, send me, by one of your Aids, the document by which it appears by certificate that Y. E. is the person authorized by your Govt. to receive this province, which H. C. M. has at this time under my charge; because if it contains only that authorization, the original ought to remain in my possession for my own exoneration, and if it should happen to contain any other appointments it will be necessary that four copies of that part of said document relating to the authorization should be taken in the Spanish language, and that Y. E. should attest by your signature the correctness and legality of the same; all of which it will be proper should be done in time to be a suitable evidence of my discharge.[2] Your Exy. must not be surprized or astonished at my refusing to receive the document referred to, at the time you sent it to me by the hands of Dr Bronaugh and Judge Brackenridge, since I had at that epoch (as I apprized Y. E.) no order for entering on, or proceeding to the evacuation and delivery.[3]

It is positively false that the least authorization has devolved on Alva from my govt., as he was only charged with bearing to mc thc orders under cover, and it is an undoubted truth that I am the commander entrusted by Spain with the govt. of West Florida: that without my consent and instrumentality no one could deliver said province to another nation, and that no person has at this time the most distant idea of such an undertaking, either with or without my connivance; and under these circumstances I desire, with the highest sentiments of friendship, fairness, and candour for Y. E., that you would be persuaded of its being altogether unnecessary for you to receive from me the authorizations given me, as the operation demands solely that I should be perfectly assured of the person who is to receive said province.

As soon as the Garrison of Apalache shall be in this place, and the transports shall be ready, I esteem four or six days at the utmost as sufficient for the delivery of it, the embarkation of the equipage, troops, and other individuals; whence Y. E. may now infer thc timc, solicited of me, to be fixed.

I am well apprized of the arrangements relative to the Subsistence agreed upon for the transportation, and acquiesce in them.[4]

I regret particularly the inconveniences with which the U. S. troops have met, in the place where they are located, as well as those attendant upon the conveyance of their provisions: if both of these could be remedied by a nearer approach to this Town, I would with the greatest <pl>eagerness contribute to the better accommodation of both, to the utmost extent of their abilities: Y. E. knows that this is in your power, as also in that of your officers and troops, and that the only obstacle lies in the inconvenience—that the soldiers on either side might be embroiled, which would give rise to unpleasant consequences; Y. E. will follow the dictates of the necessity of the case, your own prudence and good pleasure.

Permit me further, out of your pure goodness, to repeat definitively, that I cannot subject the Artillery and its appendages to any kind of compromise, as I am possessed of no authority to do so, and consequently no other resource remains to me but that which I proposed to Y. E., of which I have already notified H. C. M.'s Plenipotentiary in Washington, as a proof of my good wishes towards you, and of my anxiety about the determination which may or will be agreed upon at that place with the Prest.[5] In the mean while,

I leave a part of it mounted on the fortresses, although this mode of proceeding rests upon my responsibility in a possible though unexpected event, namely that the expense in which the labour necessary to its removal may involve the nation, and which I might have spared by making a seasonable use of the garrison, may be charged to my account; but this mode of proceeding is, in my judgment, consistent with prudence and our better intelligence, considering the above-mentioned perplexity in which we are involved.

I had last night the honour of seeing Lieut. Col. Brooke, to whom I presented my respects for your Exy., and now for the last time I repeat my most effectual thanks for the interest you express in the re-establishment of my health, the return of which I value more particularly from the peculiar satisfaction which it will give me to see Y. E., whom meanwhile I wish every description of happiness. God preserve you many years.

(Signed) José Callava.
Col. Commt of W. Florida, & Commr.
under the Treaty for its cession.

Translation in Edward A. Rutledge's hand, DLC (63); Translations, DNA-RG 59 (M116-6, 8-0647). Published in Bassett, 3:74–76 (from DNA-RG 59).

1. See AJ to Callava, June 20.

2. On June 23, Jackson responded: "I enclose you an attested Copy of my commission: You shall have a view of the original when we meet; and any number of attested copies in English shall be furnished you. The original I deem it proper to retain."

3. See above, James C. Bronaugh and Henry M. Brackenridge to AJ, May 7.

4. On June 20, Jackson had requested a fixed date for the transfer of West Florida and had discussed provisions for the Spanish troops going to Havana.

5. In his letter of June 16, Callava had suggested that Jackson ask the president to consult with the Spanish minister at Washington on the question of artillery in hopes that they could "so arrange the matter as to extricate us both from our embarrassing situation."

To Robert Butler

Manuels 15 Miles from Pensacola
26th of June 1821

Sir,

I have received your letter of the 20th ultimo, and it affords me great pleasure to be informed of your safe arrival at Fernandina and your preparation to visit the Governor of East Florida—[1]

From the date of the sailing of the U States vessel the *NonSuch* from the Havanna to St Augustine, with Don Aredondo bearer of the order of the Captain General and Governor of Cuba to the Governor of East Florida for the delivery of the same—she could not have reached St Augustine before the 13 instant. She was to sail from the Havanna the day after the Hornet sailed from thence to Pensacola and the Hornet only arrived on the evening of the 9th instant, since which I have not lost a moment in preparation for the possession of the country ceded. I would have been in possession by this time had it not have been for the unfortunate loss of one of our Transports, and the unfavorable weather which has detained the vessel since chartered at Orleans and the Transport sent for the garrison of St Marks: as soon as they arrive possession will be had.[2] I hope my two letters by mail have reached you—they will have advised you of the causes and reasons, why I did not communicate to you by express at a more early day than the present.[3]

The want of a vessel to transport Col Gadsden has detained him some time to my great regret[4]—He will give you a copy of my commission authorising me to take possession of the country ceded, with the powers to appoint others under me; this may become necessary, because of Col Forbes having been viewed by the Captain General, the Commissioner to receive East Florida, and from a fear that Genl Gaines may not have committed the copy to you, which was furnished him. From Col Gadsden you will also receive *Blanks* signed by me to be filled with such sums or bills on the Department of State, as may be necessary to cover the expense of taking possession of that part of the country ceded—you will receive the Proclamations necessary to be made public on receiving possession of the country, which you will promulgate as soon as you receive the country, or if in possession as soon as you receive them. I send by Col Gadsden a form of a *Process verbal* which will be proper and necessary to be signed by the commiss<ioner>ary of Spain appointed to deliver the country, and yourself: to which it will be necessary to add after islands "including all the Tortugas," that thereafter no dispute may arise with regard to the right to them—You will receive also the form of an agreement entered into preparatory to the delivery of the country, which if you receive in time will be well for you to adopt, that we may have all things uniform in this transaction.[5]

In my last I informed you that some difficulties had arisen with respect to the Artillery appertaining to the Fortifications ceded—you will receive information of the course pursued by me here, and acceded to by the Governor of Pensacola, which it will be proper for you to adopt if Col Gadsden reaches you in time—[6]

Finding that the President of the United States has appointed a Secretary for East as well as West Florida, (as it appears from instructions) to aid me in the Government of the whole, and to keep up the same distinction which existed under the Spanish Government; I have thought proper by Commission to clothe Mr [William Grafton Dulany] Worthington with all the powers exercised by the Governor of East Florida under the rule of Spain—Col Gadsden is the bearer of this commission and all the necessary instructions to him on this important subject:[7] When you have received the Archives with the possession of the Country and proclaimed the same, you will hand over to Mr Worthington the commission and instructions with the Archives taking his receipt for the same; and charge him with the administration of the Government as confided to him by me[8]—Having performed this with all the other duties confided to you by me—having settled all public accounts and taken duplicate receipts for the same; you will repair to Pensacola in the vessel that carries Col Gadsden to you, or by land, and make a report to me of all the matters and things over which you have had charge; that agreeably to my instructions I may make a report to my Government, and close all accounts that have accrued in taking possession of and occupying the Floridas—I am with great respect your Most Obt servant.

(Signed) Andrew Jackson

note, A few lines relative to Col Butlers furlough, and the situation of his and Genl J's family are not inserted, as they relate not to Col B's instructions or the occupancy of E Florida—

LC in Andrew J. Donelson's hand, DLC (63). Published in *TPUS,* 22:97–99.

1. See Butler to AJ, May 20. Butler arrived in St. Augustine on May 24.

2. The chartered vessel *Cora* was lost off Plaquemines Parish, Louisiana, and the replacement ship, the *Lucy Ann,* did not reach Pensacola until July 2. Another transport, the *Anna Maria,* had arrived in Pensacola sometime before June 20. Richard K. Call, acting under Jackson's authority, had sent transport vessels, probably the *Amelia* and the *Thomas Shields,* to St. Marks to evacuate the Spanish troops at that place, but adverse winds also delayed their return, and they did not arrive at Pensacola until July 9 (see Call to AJ, June 23, and AJ to José M. Callava, July 9).

3. See above, AJ to Butler, June 2 and 13.

4. James Gadsden's departure for St. Augustine was delayed until July 1.

5. Although the final text of the act of cession or process verbal, the legal document effecting the transfer of East Florida to the United States, did not explicitly include the Dry Tortugas, they were ceded and are now part of Monroe County, Florida (see *ASP, Miscellaneous Documents,* 2:890).

6. See above, AJ to Butler, June 13. Gadsden reached St. Augustine on July 10, the day of the transfer. For Butler's arrangement regarding artillery, see Butler to AJ, July 24.

7. See James Monroe to AJ, May 23; AJ to Worthington, June 25; and Commission of Worthington, July 1. Worthington (1785–1856) had served as American agent in South America before accepting the post of secretary of East Florida. He later served in the Maryland legislature.

8. Having received the transfer of East Florida on July 10, Butler left St. Augustine on July 14, over a month previous to Worthington's arrival on August 17. Issues regarding possession of the East Florida archives remained unsettled for several months after the transfer (see John R. Bell to AJ, August 4, and Worthington to AJ, October 6).

To José Maria Callava

Manuels 15 Miles from Pensacola
29th. June 1821

Sir

Your letter of the 28th. inst with its enclosures has been received and after due consideration I hasten to reply to the same.[1]

My letter of the 26th. <Instt> in reply to yours of the 25th Ist.; among other articles approving the heading or prefaratory notice to be attached to the Inventory of Cannon Arms Ordnance Stores &c, was writen and despatched by Col Gadsden some time before your note suggesting and requesting an alteration to be made in the same reached me. Not being able at the time to comprehend the necessity or propriety of the alteration requested, I wrote to Col Gadsden to consult with Your Excellency on the same, which from your note of the 25th. [28th] I found he had attende[d] to—[2]

I now enclose you a copy of the translation I have made from the Heading or prefaratory notice, you wish attached to the Inventory of Cannon, arms, and Ordnance Stores, as expressed in your note of the 28th. Inst. and which I approve. It will be necessary that the Inventory as well as heading &c be made out in English as well as Spanish before signed by us—

You will receive enclosed duplicates of the process Verbal made out in English, leaving a Column for the Spanish, which you will be good enough to have attached; the English will be signed first by me and the Spanish by you, with an interchange of signatures to each—This instrument is substantially the same as that sent me in yours of the 28th. Inst. and will conciquently meet with your approbation.[3] I have charged Maj Staunton of the Quartermasters Department with the commission of examining with any officer appointed by you the Inventory of Artillery, Ordnance Stores &c to be left in my possession conformably to the arrangements concluded between us.[4]

Capt R K Call my Secretary and Aid-De Camp, Doct J C Bronaugh & Judge H. M Brackenridge have likewise been appointed by me, to meet the like number of individuals nominated on your part, to examine and compare the inventory of archives, public papers &c with the documents certifying to their correctness, as well as to certify to the Inventory of Public Edifices &c as exhibited by you.[5]

I have thought it adviseable to make these appointments so that the necessary papers connected with the delivery of the Province of West Florida to me, may all be prepared for Signature by the arrival of the Troops from St Marks, and the expected transport from New Orleans. With sentiments of respect Your Obt Sert

(Signed) Andrew Jackson

LC in Richard K. Call's hand, DLC (63); Copies, DNA-RG 59 (M116-6, 8-0739).

1. See Callava to AJ, June 28.

2. See AJ to Callava, June 26, and Callava to AJ, June 25, 26, and 28. Jackson's letter to Gadsden has not been found.

3. Neither enclosure has been found. On June 30, Callava addressed a confidential note to Jackson requesting that, at the transfer, the commissioners sign four copies of the process verbal, two having the Spanish text in the left column so that he might sign first. Jackson agreed to the request on the following day; for the final text, see the Process Verbal, July 17.

4. Jackson had agreed to the withdrawal of Spanish field artillery, provided that the dis-

puted fortification cannon were not converted to that purpose (see AJ to Henry Stanton, June 23).

5. See the Spanish inventory of public documents, July 4; the inventory of public edifices has not been found. See also Henry M. Brackenridge to AJ, July 4.

To James Craine Bronaugh

Manuels July 3rd. 1821

Dr Brunaugh

by the report of Major Staunton of last evening I learn the other Transport has arived.

I trust a moment will not be lost in having every thing ready for a delivery of the country the moment the amelia arives—I have wrote the Governor, & Major Staunton and urged them both upon this subject.[1]

I am happy to find that Major Staunton has recd. a remittance from Govr. of $10,000 & he advises me that this will enable him to return to me the mony recd from me through Colo. Gadsden, this will enable me to compleat the duty assigned me without drawing any more bills upon the goverment[2]—I now wish the business to be closed with Capt [Daniel E.] Birch—and his duplicate receipts to be taken and my account thereby closed with the Indian department—[3]

My Dr Sir Mrs. J. informs me that our *Bet* has been <putting on> guilty of some improper conduct, say to Mr [Ephraim A.] Blain that it is his duty to controle & chastise her, that I must hold him responsible for the goverment of the servants, as well as the safety & proper use of my supplies, and he must use the cowhide whenever any of them depart from proper conduct, she is capable of being a good & valluable servant, but to have her so, she must be ruled with the cowhide—

My Dr Sir I will thank you to have an eye to the concerns of our house there & have Bet severely chastised on the first impudent or improper conduct.[4] I shall expect to see you tomorrow I am yours respectfully

Andrew Jackson

ALS, DLC (30).

1. See Henry Stanton to AJ, July 2, and AJ to José M. Callava, July 3. AJ's letter to Stanton has not been found.

2. Regarding the debt to James Gadsden, see bills of exchange, June 29 and July 1.

3. Burch (d. 1833), a New Jersey native and veteran of the War of 1812, was an army paymaster. Jackson had been instructed to pay the balance of his 1820 Choctaw treaty account to Burch or to Daniel Randall, another paymaster (see John C. Calhoun to AJ, May 1).

4. Rachel Jackson, who had gone to Pensacola with the rest of Jackson's family on June 28, visited Jackson's camp on July 2 and 3. Jackson was probably referring to the slave Betty (b. c1793), wife of Ned (b. c1798) and mother of Alfred (b. c1817). Blaine, who acted as the Jacksons' steward, has not been identified further. Jackson was more emphatic about the problem with Betty in a letter to Andrew J. Donelson: "It is humiliating to me to have to resort to this, but I have to request of you to observe her conduct and the first disobedience

or impudence order Mr Blain to give her fifty lashes and if he does not perform it, dismiss him, & as soon as I get possession I will order a corporal to give it to her publickly, I am determined to cure her—" (see AJ to Donelson, July 3).

To José Maria Callava

Manuels 5th. July 1821

Sir

I have the pleasure to acknowledge the receipt of your two notes under cover of the 3d. Inst. and am much gratified to find that after making yourself fully acquainted with the contents of my communication of the 1st. Inst. you have approved the same, and that the four documents as specified will be made out and revised by Judge Brackenridge.[1]

I am also much pleased to be informed by you that the addition proposed by me relative to the ceremony of changing flags at Barrancas is approved and that your Picquet will be commanded by a Lieutenant.[2]

I have also the honour to acknowledge the receipt of your Excellencys Letter of the 4th in reply to mine of the 3d. Inst. the assurance you have given of your disposition to act promptly in the delivery of West Florida and its dependencies is perfectly satisfactory. I am well convinced that every thing in your power will be done to facilitate the embarkation of the Spanish Garrison and the delivery of the ceded Territory.[3]

I am advised by Maj Staunton that the weather has been so inclement that the Lucy Ann has not been discharged of her cargo or the Field Artillery put on board the Transports.[4] I hope for better weather and a speedy return of the Vessels from St Marks. I am Sir with great respect your Obt Sert

(Signed) Andrew Jackson

LC in Richard K. Call's hand, DLC (63); Copies, DNA-RG 59 (M116-6, 8-0771).

1. See Callava to AJ, July 3. The specified documents were the four copies of the Process Verbal as proposed in Callava to AJ, June 30, and accepted in AJ to Callava, July 1.

2. See Callava to AJ, July 3.

3. On July 3, Jackson notified Callava of the arrival of the *Lucy Ann* and requested that the available transports be loaded, even though the ships from Fort St. Marks had not reached Pensacola; on the following day, Callava expressed his eagerness to comply.

4. See Henry Stanton to AJ, July 5.

To Henry Marie Brackenridge

Manuels July 8th. 1821

Sir

I have recd. your note of yesterday by Capt Call. The plan of Identifying the records, to be receipted for by me is approved, it was certainly necessary that these should be so identified, so that no fraud should be practised on the honest citizen or subject by the roguish—and altho the record only relates to the transfer of property from one individual to another, still it is a debt due from the Goverment, to protect the h*[o]*nest citizen in his rights—This will do it *[as]* far as we have it in our power.[1]

I am truly astonished to find that the Governor should be out of humour as it respected the process verbal, it was plainly written & in due form, consistant with the custom of all nations in like cases, and by his letters to me fully approved, if his Secratary imposes upon him a false translation that is no fault of mine,[2] and if an attempt is made to impose upon me through such means, I can assure them they will be disappointed. however I am in this case as I was in the dispute about the right to the ordinance, very happy that the Governor now understands it as he advised me by letter he did,[3] and as I allways understood it, and that all things are now harmoniously concluded on—that possession will be had as soon as the amelia arives—as soon as a safe opportunity offers, I will be happy to see the two copies of the process verbal prepared—and on the arival of the amelia I wish to have the earliest notice that I may (if the Governor does not forthwith set a day for embarkation & giving possession[)] write him on the subject, as I am truly wearied with delay. present me to Doctor Brunaugh & tell him I am better, but very much debilitated, that by the advice of *[Dr.]* [Moses H.] Elliot I have commenced this morni*[n]*g his tonic—of its effects I will advise him[4] I am yours verry respectfully

Andrew Jackson

ALS, PPiU (8-0777). Published in William F. Keller, *The Nation's Advocate: Henry Marie Brackenridge and Young America* ([Pittsburgh], 1956), p. 261.

1. See Brackenridge to AJ, July [7]. Brackenridge and James C. Bronaugh had spent some time cataloging the Spanish records to be transferred to the United States.
2. José Ignacio Cruzat was José M. Callava's secretary.
3. See Callava to AJ, July 3.
4. Elliott (d. 1822), a Massachusetts native, was a surgeon with the 4th Infantry.

To José Maria Callava

Manuels July 12th 1821

Sir,

Late last night I received your Excellency's letter of the 11th. dated at 7 in the evening. I had duly received yours of the 10th instant, and considering its tenor and your former pledge, that in four days, or six, at furthest, after the arrival of the transports, you would deliver possession of West Florida and its dependencies: It was with great surprise and astonishment, that I read in your letter of the 11th instant the following paragraph; "From all this I conclude that on Monday or Tuesday the 16th or 17th instant, I can deliver the province of West Florida to your Excellency in the place already designated at 10, O'clock A.M. On Saturday the 14th. I will determine for your Excellency whether the delivery is to be on Monday or Tuesday."[1]

At eleven O'clock A.M. on the 9th inst., the transports with the Garrison of St Marks arrived in the bay of Pensacola—were reported to me, and on the same day the 9th inst I reported the same to you and in the last paragraph of my letter requested <that> you would name a day and hour for the delivery of possession of the Province. In your answer to this letter on the 10th inst, you say, "your Excellency may rest assured that now in the shortest possible time, this province shall be delivered to you, and, that *tomorrow* I will appoint the day according to what I have said to you."[2] In your letter of the 11th inst, you say on the 14th. you will determine whether the delivery shall be made on Monday or Tuesday. I am constrained to say that this is not the candour and promptness, I had a right to expect from your Excellencies former pledges, "that in four, or six days at furthest, after the arrival of the Transports the Province of West Florida should be delivered to me," nor is it in accordance with that frankness which I had a right to look for, from your letter of the 10th inst; the transports (being the last) bringing the garrison of St Marks arrived at 11 O'clock A. M of the 9th inst, the whole time agreeably to your promise of four or six days, in which the Province shall be delivered to me, will have elapsed at 11 O'clock A M. of the 15th inst.

I have used the utmost frankness with your Excellency in all our correspondence—It becomes me now to speak with the same frankness. My government had the most positive assurance from the King your Master, through his minister at Washington, that no unnecessary delay should take place in the delivery of the Floridas. Notwithstanding this, the Hornet was detained at the Havanna upwards of one month—she arrived—I have your pledge that within four or six days at furthest, after the arrival of the transports, possession should be delivered. On Sunday the 15th at 11 oclock A. M. this time expires, and I shall expect the pledge given by you to be exactly performed. I have on a former occasion informed you of the great expense and inconvenience the U States have encountered by the unlooked for delay already experienced; that we are paying heavy demurage on our transports, which cannot be permitted any longer:[3] I therefore consider it my duty explicitly to state to you, that unless your troops are embarked within the time for which I hold your pledge, the Transports will be immediately after discharged from the service of the United States, unless a tender in money be made, of the daily demurrage on the two transports, on which they shall be detained two days and no longer.

The subject of the rations has long since been put to rest. Every thing was offered and done on my part for your accommodation, and as it concerns the ration I have your approbation of the whole, and Majr Staunton has reported to me the full and entire satisfaction on your part.[4] The subject with me is closed. Yesterday Majr Staunton reported to me that every thing on his part was complied with and ready, except the Inventory of the Ordnance, which was to be made out by your Officer, that he went on the 10th inst to the Barrancas for the purpose of completing the same, but found that your officers had made out no Inventory by which he could compare the Ordnance, or ordnance stores, that this was postponed until the inventory should be made, and that on his part he is ready at any moment to complete the business.[5]

I have no powers to treat about deserters; All American deserters have been disgracefully discharged—there are no deserters of yours in my Camp, it is contrary to law to enlist them. No American citizen will be permitted to embark with the Spanish Troops on board the Transports.[6] I hope, Sir, as harmony has accompanied us thus far in the performance of our respective duties, that it may continue to exist between us to the close of our Official transactions, and that you will with that promptness which characterizes the soldier, and agreeably to your letter of the 10th inst. on the receipt of this name a day and hour "within the four or six days, at furthest, after the arrival of the transports," on which you will deliver possession of West Florida and its dependencies. I had hoped after receiving yours of the 10th, that instead of a long letter, nothing more could have been necessary on my part, but a mere acknowledgement of the receipt of yours of the 11th inst. Relying with full confidence on your pledge, I yesterday moved my troops to Galvez Spring, to be in readiness to take possession of Pensacola and the Barrancas, where on this day I shall join them—at that place we will remain until I shall receive your answer[7]—I am Sir, with great respect, Your Excellencies Most Obt & Humble Servant

(Signed) Andrew Jackson

LC in Andrew J. Donelson's hand, DLC (63); Copies, DNA-RG 59 (M116-6, 8-0793). Published in Bassett, 3:92–94 (from DNA-RG 59).

1. See Callava to AJ, July 10 and 11. For the promise to transfer West Florida shortly after the arrival of the Spanish garrison from Fort St. Marks, see above, Callava to AJ, June 22. None of the quotations from Callava's letters match any of the extant translations, but they convey the essential meaning.

2. See AJ to Callava, July 9, and Callava to AJ, July 10.

3. See AJ to Callava, July 3.

4. See AJ to Callava, June 20; Callava to AJ, June 22 (above); and Henry Stanton to AJ, June 27.

5. Stanton's July 11 report has not been found. Jackson and Callava resolved the dispute over the inventory for ordnance on July 14.

6. Adjutant General Daniel Parker's July 25, 1816, order prohibited the enlistment of foreign deserters in the American army. Callava had given refuge to American deserters from Fort Gadsden, but Jackson had earlier determined that even an American prisoner held in Pensacola would not be allowed to leave with the Spanish troops (see AJ to Stanton, July 6).

7. See AJ to George M. Brooke, July 10. Galvez Spring was located at the head of Bayou Chico, two miles west of Pensacola.

To Benjamin Silliman

Pensacola July 14. 1821

Sir

At my instance Mr. Duncan directed Mr. Anthony [Wayne] Butler's return to New Haven where I am extremely solicitous he should be allowed an oportunity of regaining the prospects which his imprudence deprived him of[1]—May I be permitted to request your attention to the very serious effect which the Academic censure laid on him may have on his future life and studies. I hope that on reflection you will consider the act of expulsion as presenting sufficient example to others and punishment to him to need the further Continuance of its effects, with this hope I request that if Consistent with Collegiate discipline he may be restored to Yale and that his offence may be considered so venial as to authorise the faculty to erase the sentence from record. I am Sir very respectfully & with esteem Yr Obedt Servt

Andrew Jackson

LS, CtY (8-0819). Published in *Yale University Library Gazette,* 44(1969):17. Postmarked "New Orleans Aug 5" and endorsed "an Sept 19— 1821." Silliman (1779–1864; Yale 1796) was professor of chemistry and natural history at Yale, 1802–53. Answer not found.

1. On March 4, Caroline S. Bell (d. 1864), Butler's sister, had notified Jackson about Butler's expulsion from Yale. Butler (1803–24; Yale 1823) and his other siblings Edward George Washington (1800–88; Military Academy 1820) and Eliza Eleanor (1791–1850) were children of Jackson's friend Edward Butler (1762–1803). After the elder Butler's death, Jackson became guardian of the children. Abner L. Duncan, present in Pensacola for the transfer, undoubtedly consulted with Jackson about Butler's expulsion. Earlier, Jackson and Duncan had agreed that Duncan would fund Anthony W. Butler's education out of the estate of Richard Butler (d. 1820), Duncan's brother-in-law (see AJ to Anthony W. Butler, January 13, 1823, below).

Jackson's long letter of July 12, above, prompted an even longer response from Governor Callava, defending in minute detail every delay, but setting, at long last, July 17 at 10:00 a.m. as the time for the transfer of West Florida, a date that Jackson quickly accepted (see José M. Callava to AJ, July 13, and AJ to Callava, July 13). Lingering differences over the inventory of ordnance were resolved in a final flurry of letters, and, in the end, the two governors blamed poor translations as the major cause of their misunderstandings and subsequent delay, a formula more diplomatic than accurate.

To José Maria Callava

Galvez Spring, July 15th. 1821.

Sir,

I have this moment, half after one O'clock P. M. received your Excellency's note of this date, and I regret extremely, that I had not received it before I had sent to you my letter of this day, in answer to your two letters of yesterday received as stated in my reply, so that a final close might have been made to the etiquette &ca &ca, as it had been to the substantial part of the duties assigned to us by our respective governments.[1]

I will barely bring to your Excellency's recollection, that the moment I was advised of the arrival of the Hornet, and being informed by you of your powers and orders, I entered the Floridas with a view to the fulfillment of the powers with which my government had intrusted me, and dispatched my friend and one of my staff, Col Gadsden, to your Excellency with my letter of the 16th. of June, in which I said to you, "I have to express a wish that a period, as early as possible may be concluded on to our mutual convenience, when we may meet, exhibit our credentials, officially recognize each other, and enter on the duties of our respective Commissions," and I might have added you as Commissioner to deliver, and I as commissioner to receive the Province. Your Excellency, in your letter of the 22d. of June, after having had the interview with Col. Gadsden which produced his letter to your Excellency of the 18th. of June, and after your letter to me of the 16th. of June, Your Excellency declined the interview proposed by me.[2] Your note received at Manuels, the evening of my arrival, made known to me your indisposition, which with me was a sufficient appology, although a stranger, and my wish was to wave all unnecessary ceremony, and meet you with the feelings and promptness of a soldier, waving all etiquette due to me as a stranger, and to my rank, I was satisfied with your good wishes as expressed, and of your desire to see me as soon as your health was restored.[3] We have conducted the duties assigned us thus far in harmony without ever having had the pleasure of seing each other, or I one of your Officers; my staff, and Officers, have been instructed to shew to you, all the respect due to your rank and situation, and I know them from long experience, never to fail in the execution of my orders, or to be wanting in the respect due to others.

I have therefore to remark, as we have happily and harmoniously brought our duties to a close, and not being a slave to ceremony, I will meet your Excellency on the stairs of the government house at 10 o'clock A. M. on tuesday the 17th. instant, and when conducted into the Hall, I shall take any side of it opposite your Excellency, and fronting you, that your Excellency may think proper, on which my commission shall be read—

authorising me to *take* possession of the Floridas, and present your Excellency with a certified copy of the same, your Excellency will have the royal order read, after this we proceed to sign the various documents prepared for our signatures, on which your Excellency will deliver the keys of the town according to what is set forth in the Process verbal there to be read and signed.

I will have two guards of thirty men each, according to your Excellency's suggestion, detailed for the purpose of relieving your Excellency's guard, and that of the city. I am, Sir, with great respect, Your most Obedt. Servt.

(Signed) Andrew Jackson
Commissioner &ca &ca—

P.S. on the 17th. orders will be given to the Capt. of the Hornet, to take charge of the transports, to sail on the 18th. wind and weather permitting[4]—A. J.

LC, DLC (63); Copies, DNA-RG 59 (M116-6, 8-0825). Published in Bassett, 3:104 (extract from DNA-RG 59).

1. See Callava to AJ, July 14 and 15, and AJ to Callava, July 15.
2. See AJ to Callava, June 16; Callava to AJ, June 16, and, above, June 22; and James Gadsden to Callava, June 18 (DLC-63).
3. See Callava to AJ, June 16.
4. See AJ to George C. Read, July 16. The convoy with the Spanish troops left Pensacola on schedule.

To James Craine Bronaugh

Sunday Evening
July 15th. 1821—

Genl Jackson with compliments to Doctor Brunaugh informs him that the Genl will be in Pensacola to breakfast on tuesday at half after six A. M, and a number of the officers of the army as well as the officers of the navy from the Hornett—will the Doctor have the goodness to aid Lt Donelson in making the necessary preparations for Breakfast, and also dinner—The Scripture says return good for evil, in this feeling I intend asking the Govr & his secrataries to dine with me, he is as I suppose, very sore, and if he was devoid of urbanity I mean to shew him I at least possess magnanimity by which I will heap coals upon his head—had I agreed to the ceremony this day proposed by him we would have had no time for dinner—but as useless ceremony is a great tax upon me, I have waved all that could be dispensed with and I suppose we will get through about eleven oclock & have the Star Spangled banner waving over our dinner—I have been compelled to day to respond to three long letters My answers were short—[1]

If your duties will permit I would be happy to see you some time tomorrow. I would ask you to dine, but it would be a tax upon your appetite. The Genl has not slept much this two nights—he was obliged night before last to write untill after one oclock—& the musquitoes, disturbed him last, this night he expects to sleep as he has a barr,[2] & hopes his correspondence is closed with his Excellency

AL, DLC (30). Published in Bassett, 3:100–101.

1. See Callava to AJ, July 14 and 15; and AJ to Callava, July 15, and July 15, above.
2. Mosquito netting.

To José Maria Callava

Camp Galvez Spring
half past 2 Oclock P M,
July 16th 1821

Sir,

I have this moment received your Excellency's letter of this date[1]—I have not time to respond to it fully—let it suffice, that I do not speak the Spanish language, nor (as I am informed) does your Excellency speak the English; but I am persuaded, that the misunderstanding must have existed from the want of a proper interpretation of our real thoughts as expressed in our correspondence. Let me assure you; long since I should have met you with pleasure in Pensacola, had I not conceived, that it was not your wish—Your letter received at Manuels informing me of your indisposition, determined me to visit you without ceremony in the feelings of the frankness and harmony of a soldier; but your letter of the 19th of June (as translated) altered my determination—for although without ceremony with a soldier, and as I was told you were also; yet when I was induced to believe that an undue condescension was expected, I was compelled to the course which I have pursued—My feelings as a soldier, I suppose, correspond with your's—death before an undue condescension—it is what I ask of no one—it is what I will not render to any.[2]

It will afford me great pleasure to meet you in my camp. I am without a horse, or I should meet and conduct you; but I send my nephew, Lt A J Donelson of the Corps of Engineers and my Aid de Camp, to conduct you to the camp, where you will meet with a cordial welcome, and where I shall be glad to see you should the weather permit; but be assured, I have no wish that you should expose your health if the weather should prove inclement; on this event, I will be in Pensacola early to morrow morning to breakfast with Mrs. Jackson, whom our unfortunate misunderstanding has prevented me from visiting, since she has been in Pensacola—Should I not see you this evening from the inclemency of the weather, will you, with the frankness and friendship of a soldier, breakfast with Mrs J. and myself tomorrow morning at half after six or seven, when I shall have the pleasure of introducing you to my officers, who know well how to appreciate a soldiers merit, and all who have known you appreciate you as such—You will have the goodness to inform me through my nephew, whether or not you will breakfast with me on to morrow at the appointed time, should you not meet me this evening in camp.

Should we not meet each other before 10, O'clock tomorrow on the stair case, I shall then take you by the hand as a soldier and friend, and I am certain after further acquaintance we will know how to appreciate each other[3]—I am Sir, with great repect Yr. Excellancy's mo. Obt servant.

(Signed) Andrew Jackson

LC in Andrew J. Donelson's hand, DLC (63); Copies, DNA-RG 59 (M116-6, 8-0836). Published in Bassett, 3:103–104 (from DNA-RG 59).

1. See Callava to AJ, July 16.
2. See Callava to AJ, June 16, and, above, June 19.
3. Jackson and Callava did not meet until the transfer ceremony at 10:00 a.m.

On June 1, the reduction and reorganization of the army took effect, ending Jackson's military career and leaving only one major general, Jacob J. Brown, to oversee the military establishment. Jackson chose this occasion to prepare a formal farewell to the men of the Southern Division, but the complexities of the Florida transfer, as well as the absence of a printing press at Montpelier and later at Pensacola, delayed the address's release for some two months (see AJ to John C. Calhoun, July 29, below). In the interim, Jackson learned of Brown's criticism of discipline within the Southern Division, prompting the retired general to append a long note, dated July 21, to his valedictory.

To the Officers and Soldiers Composing the Division of the South

Head Quarters D of the South
Montpelier
31st. May 1821

This day, Officers & Soldiers, closes my Military functions, and consequently, dissolves the Military connection, which has hitherto existed between you and myself as the commander of the Southern Division of the army of the United States. Many of us have passed together days of toil & nights of vigilence. Together, we have seen the termination of one British, and of two Indian Wars, in which we have encountered fatigues, privations, and dangers.[1] Attachments, & friendships, formed by associations of this kind, are the most durable, and my feelings will not permit me in retiring from my Military Command, to take a silent leave of my companions in arms.

Justice to you, and to my own feelings, requires that I should place before our Common Country, the testimony of my approbation of your Military Conduct, and the expression of my individual regard. Under the present organization for the reduction of the Army, agreably to the act of Congress, Many valuable officers, who have served with me, have been suddenly deprived of the profession which they had embraced and thrown upon the world,[2] but let this be your consolation that the gratitude of your country still cherishes you as her defenders and deliverers, while wisdom condems the hasty & ill timed policy which has occasioned your disbandment, and that too, while Security was yet to be given to our extensive frontier by the erections of the Necessary fortifications for its defence, greatly extended as that frontier has been by the recent acquisition of the Floridas. But you fellow Soldiers, have that which cannot be taken from you, the consciousness of having done your duty, and with your Brother officers who are retained, <by> of having defended the American Eagle wherever it was endangered.[3]

To you my brother Officers who are retained in the Service of your country, permit me to recommend the Cultivation of that harmony & friendship towards each <officer> other, which will render you a band of brothers; it is your duty so to conduct yourselves on all occasions, as that your enemies Shall have no Just cause for censure. It ought to be borne in mind, that every Captain, should be to his Company as a Father, and should treat it as his family—as his Children; Continue then as heretofore, when under my command, to watch over it with a fathers tenderness & care; treat them like children, admonish them, and if unhappily, admonition will not have the desired effect—Coersion Must. The want of discipline, and Order, will inevitably produce a spirit of insubordination, as destructive to an army, as cowardice, and will as certainly lead to disaster & disgrace in the hour of battle; this, as you regard your Military reputation & your country's good, you must prevent. Imploring from heaven a blessing upon You all, I bid you an affectionate adieu.

Signed Andrew Jackson
Major Genl. Comdg
the Division of the South

21st. July 1821

Note. My official duties having prevented the promulgation of this Order until this time, an opportunity has been afforded of seeing the "General Order" dated ["]Head Quarters of the Army of U. States Washington City, June 1st. 1821" Signed "Jacob Brown." Justice to the Officers of the Southern division, as well as to myself, compels me to offer some remarks upon the following extract from that order.[4]

"The prevalence of desertion has been an evil of Serious Magnitude, and it does not appear to be Justified by a view of the past Condition of the Military establishment. All research in this field for its causes has been unsatisfactory. the character of the Military profession is honorable; the Soldier is as well provided with comforts as the Citizen in common life, and his occupation is neither more offensive nor more laborious. there are restless discontented spirits in every Sphere of life, which no indulgence nor kindness can bind to stability; but these examples do not exist in sufficient number to Justify the range desertion has taken in the army. the evil must be refered, in a degree to an undue severity or to the absence of System in the Conduct of officers towards their men the officer is the depository of the rights of the Soldier, and the obligation of his office, as well as the laws of honor and humanity, claim a faithful execution of the trust; when the soldier ceases to regard the officer as his protector, the authority with which the laws invest the latter loses its efficacy in his estimation the Surest remedy for the evil of desertion is contained in a rigid and steady discipline; to be salutary it must possess both these Qualities, but no violation of law can be deemed essential to its enforcement; its effect upon the Soldier becomes impaired, the moment <that> he feels that the system which governs him is fluctuating in its course or that it violates the principles upon which it is founded—the certainty of laws constitutes their principal efficacy, and, however severe restrictions may be, they are obeyed so long as they are dispensed by the hand of Justice, and not oppression"

This censure is too general to be Just. The time at which it is made, and the course whence it comes, have astonished every generous soldier.

The part which attributes "in a degree to an undue Severity, or to the absence of System in the Conduct of officers towards their men" the unexampled prevalence of desertion in our army, so far as relates to the D. of the South, I do unhesitatingly say, is not founded in fact. It is due to Candor and to truth, to attribute this evil to its real <source> cause; this will be found to exist in the want of adequate punishment for the crime of Desertion. That, prescribed by law, in a State of peace, transcends the offence, & no other Certain punishment is Authorised.[5] While this is the case, desertion will increase, let the conduct of the officers towards their men, be ever so lenient. It is a well Known fact, that more desertions have taken place at recruiting rendezvous, than have Occurred in the Regiments, and at no recruiting rendezvous in the D. of the South has their been, as far as I am informed, any punishment inflicted upon soldiers, excepting by the Civil authority. It is well Known, that in many instances, the soldier has found it a source of speculation to go from rendezvous to rendezvous enlisting, receiving the bounty, and deserting. In some instances, this has been practised from Boston to New Orleans.

The punishment at present inflicted for Desertion, is hard labor with the ball & chain: but this bears more heavily upon the faithful soldier, who is compelled to guard the Convict under a hot sun, with all his accoutrements on, than it does upon him whom it is intended to punish. Every desertion, therefore, but adds to the duties and increases the fatigues of the faithful and trusty soldier. And suppose the convict will not labor, by what means is he to be coerced? Stripes and lashes are prohibited, there are no dungeons, Guard Houses are pleasant places for the lazy worthless soldier, who sleeps & snores, while the faithful Centinel is at his post, on his nightly watch guarding him. Is not this, with the general pardons so frequently extended by the orders of the president, calculated to cause the best Soldiers, who are oppressed with double duty in guarding the worst, to Meditate desertion also?[6]

The government must annex an adequate & certain punishmt <for> to the crime of desertion, and, experience compels me to say it, although at varience with the more refined & sensative feelings of the day—must restore corporeal punishment in the regulations for the government of the army, as it formerly existed, and as it now exists in the navy, or desertion & insubordination will still increase. But it is said to be dishonorable; why should it be more so in the army, than in the Navy? Is it more dishonorable to receive twentyfive stripes and be ordered to immediate duty, than to be manacled with Chains for months & years, an object of disgust to every freeman who sees him, more properly an appendage of ancient despotism, than any thing belonging to republican institutions? Let the deserter in time of peace, for the first offence receive thirty nine stripes, for the second double that number, and for the third let him feel the highest penalty of the law. I will venture to say that a few examples will put an end to that extraordinary frequency of desertion which at present prevails, and the cause of which, has been so unjustly imputed "to an undue severity, or to the absence of system in the conduct of officers towards their men["]—

I sincerely regret the cause which has given rise to these remarks, but the reputation of those officers in common with whom I have encountered so many toils & dangers, is dear to me; and I cannot remain silent when I perceive an unjust attempt to tarnish their well earned fame, let the motives which dictated the objectionable passage in the order be what they may. These remarks my brother officers, flow from a pure source of Justice to you, popularity I have never sought; I have pursued the course which I deemed right, and have done Justice to all according to my best Judgement, this I trust I have rendered to you all during the time I had the honor to command you—and that happiness may attend you all, & that your country may duly appreciate your worth, as her Citizen Soldiers, shall be my last and most sincere prayer.

(Signed) Andrew Jackson

LC and ADS draft, DLC (63, 30). Published as a supplement to the *Baton Rouge Gazette,* August 18 (DLC-70); in the (Frankfort, Kentucky) *Argus of Western America,* September 16 (8-0884), and other contemporary newspapers; and in Bassett, 3:62–65 (from ADS draft).

1. Jackson was referring to the War of 1812, the Creek War, and the Seminole War.
2. The army reduction act of March 2 (3 *U.S. Statutes at Large* 615–16).
3. In using "American Eagle," Jackson was referring to the regimental and army colors.

4. For the full text of Brown's General Order, see *Niles' Register,* June 9.

5. Article 20 of the articles of war prescribed the penalty for desertion as death or other punishment, as the court-martial might inflict.

6. Jackson was perhaps referring to the three general pardons issued by President James Madison (1751–1836; Princeton 1771) during the War of 1812 (see Richardson, *Messages and Papers of the Presidents,* 1:512, 514, 543).

Rachel Jackson to Elizabeth Kingsley

Pensacola, 23d July, 1821.

My Dear Friend:

I have been in this place four weeks. The reason I have denied myself the pleasure of writing you is that I was waiting for the great events which have taken place in this our day. O that I had the pen of a ready writer that I might give you a correct detail of the great transaction, but it is as follows. We having a house prepared and furnished, the General advised me to move down and remain until he could with propriety march in with the fourth regiment.[1]

Three weeks the transports were bringing the Spanish troops from St. Mark's in order that they should all sail to Cuba at the same time. At length they arrived, but during all this time the Governor of this place and the General had daily communications, yet his lordship never waited on the General in person. After the vessels returned from St. Mark's, the General came within two miles of Pensacola. They were then one week finishing the preliminaries and ceremonies to be observed on the day of his entrance into the city. At length, last Tuesday was the day. At seven o'clock, at the precise moment, they hove in view under the American flag and a full band of music. The whole town was in motion. Never did I ever see so many pale faces. I am living on Main street, which gave me an opportunity of seeing a great deal from the upper galleries. They marched by to the government house, where the two Generals met in the manner prescribed, then his Catholic majesty's flag was lowered, and the American hoisted high in air, not less than one hundred feet.

O how they burst into tears to see the last ray of hope departed of their devoted city and country—delivering up the keys of the archives, the vessels lying at anchor, in full view, to waft them to their distant port. Next morning they set sail under convoy of the Hornet, sloop of war, Anne Maria, and the Tom Shields.[2] How did the city sit solitary and mourn. Never did my heart feel more for any people. Being present, I entered immediately into their feelings. Their manners, laws, and customs, all changed, and really a change was necessary. My pen almost drops from my hand, the effort is so far short, so limited to what it might be.

Three Sabbaths I spent in this house before the country was in possession under American government. In all that time I was not an idle spectator. The Sabbath profanely kept; a great deal of noise and swearing in the streets; shops kept open; trade going on, I think, more than on any other day. They were so boisterous on that day I sent Major Stanton to say to them that the approaching Sunday would be differently kept. And must I say the worst people here are the cast-out Americans and negroes? Yesterday I had the happiness of witnessing the truth of what I had said. Great order was observed; the doors kept shut; the gambling houses demolished; fiddling and dancing not heard any more on the Lord's day; cursing not to be heard.[3]

What, what has been done in one week! A province delivered to the American people; the laws of the land we live in they are now under.

You can't conceive what an important, arduous, laborious work it has been and is. I had no idea of it until daily it unfolded the mystery to view. I am convinced that no mortal man could do this and suffer so many privations, unless the God of our salvation was his help in every time of trouble. While the General was in camp, fourteen miles from Pensacola, he was very sick. I went to see him, and to try and persuade him to come to his house. But, no. All his friends tried. He said that when he came in it should be under his own standard, and that would be the third time he had planted that flag on that wall.[4] And he has done so. O how solemn was his pale countenance when he dismounted from his horse. Recollections of perils and scenes of war not to be dissevered presented themselves to view.

There were no shouts of joy or exultation heard; but, on the contrary, we sympathized with these people. Still, I think, the Lord had a controversy with them. They were living far from God. If they would have the gospel of Jesus and his apostles, it would have been otherwise, but they would not. The field is white for harvest, but where are the laborers? Not one. Oh, for one of our faithful ministers to come and impart the word of life to them. I have heard but one gospel sermon since we left home. But I know that my Redeemer liveth. He is my shield. I shall not want. He will not leave me nor forsake me in all my trials through this wilderness. Oh, pray for me; I have need of that aid from my dear Christian friends.

I will give you a faint description of the country and of this place; knowing that my dear friend will throw a veil over my errors and imperfections. 1. Pensacola is a perfect plain; the land nearly as white as flour, yet productive of fine peach trees, oranges in abundance, grapes, figs, pomegranates, etc., etc. Fine flowers growing spontaneously, for they have neglected the gardens, expecting a change of government. The town is immediately on the bay. The most beautiful water prospect I ever saw; and from ten o'clock in the morning until ten at night we have the finest sea breeze. There is something in it so exhilarating, so pure, so wholesome, it enlivens the whole system. All the houses look in ruins, old as time. Many squares of the town appear grown over with the thickest shrubs, weeping willows, and the Pride of China; all look neglected. The inhabitants all speak Spanish and French. Some speak four or five languages. Such a mixed multitude, you, nor any of us, ever had an idea of. There are fewer white people far than any other, mixed with all nations under the canopy of heaven, almost in nature's darkness. But, thanks to the Lord that has put grace in this his servant to issue his proclamation in a language they all understand, I think the sanctuary is about to be purged for a minister of the gospel to come over to the help of the Lord in this dark region.

There is a Catholic church in the place, and the priest seems a divine looking man. He comes to see us. He dined with us yesterday, the Governor, and Secretary, French, Spanish, American ladies, and all. I have as pleasant a house as any in town.[5]

We have a handsome view of the bay on Main street. You will scarcely believe me, but it is a fact, the vessels are daily coming in loaded with people. The place is nearly full; a great many come for their health.[6] It is very healthy—so pure and wholesome. No fields of corn or wheat in all my travels, except one place near Mount Pelier. The growth entirely pine, some live-oak, magnolia, bay, which are all evergreens. The weather is oppressively warm to me, and raining every day. Sometimes the streets are two feet deep in water. But for the sand, we could not live. It has rained three months, almost every day, since we left New Orleans. I have the society of Amanda Grage, and the mother of Mr. Grage, and two more Christian ladies. I fear I shall put your patience to the test. I pray you bear with me a little. I have so many things to write you, and it may be the last opportunity I shall have, and I know I have not half done justice to the picture. I hope you will see it from some able penman. My dear husband is, I think, not any better as to his health. He has indeed performed a great work in his day. Had I heard by the hearing of the ear I could not have believed.

Have we all gone from you so far that no intelligence can reach our place of destination? There is no mail, no post-office here. All these inconveniences will be remedied shortly. Miss Grage received a letter from Mrs. [Mary Craig] Berryhill, wherein she states the illness of Mr. [Allan Ditchfield] Campbell and several others in Nashville, but some pleasing news of the church. Oh, for Zion! I am not at rest, nor can I be, in a heathen land. Say to Captain Kingsley the General sends his best wishes to you both. He will write when he can have a moment. Remember me with much love to all my friends. Say to Mrs. [Jane M.] Foster not to forget me, Mrs. Judge [Harriet Stoddert] Campbell, Miss P. Lewis, Miss Nancy Ayers, Mrs. Somerville, and all and every one. How happy and thankful should you be in a land of gospel light and liberty.[7]

Oh, rejoice and be glad, far more it is to be desired than all the honor and riches in this vain world. Farewell, my dear friend, and should the great Arbiter of fate order his servant not to see her kindred and friends again, I hope to meet you in the realms of everlasting bliss. Then I shall weep no more at parting.

Do not be uneasy for me. "Although the vine yield no fruit, and the olive no oil, yet will I serve the Lord."[8] Adieu, adieu,

Rachel Jackson.

Say to Mr. K. Andrew is learning Spanish.

Printed, Parton, 2:603–606 (8-0893). Fellow Presbyterian Elizabeth Kingsley (b. c1792) was the wife of Alpha Kingsley (1778–1846), former district paymaster in Nashville.

1. The deteriorated condition of Government House, official residence of the governor, led Jackson to rent quarters from Desiderio Lurria from June 5 until October 8. Rachel Jackson had arrived in Pensacola on June 28.

2. Apparently the *Thomas Shields* was substituted for the *Lucy Ann,* originally scheduled to make the voyage to Havana. For other accounts of the transfer ceremony, see *Nashville Whig,* August 15, and *Niles' Register,* August 25.

3. See Ordinance, July 18.

4. Jackson had occupied Pensacola in 1814 and 1818.

5. The Reverend James Coleman, from the Irish College of Nobles at Salamanca, was the parish priest at St. Michael's in Pensacola from 1794 to 1822. The church building, a converted warehouse, was in a state of disrepair.

6. The 1820 Spanish census counted 713 residents in Pensacola, approximately half of whom were black or mixed-blood. The influx of Americans increased the population temporarily to over 3,000 during the next year.

7. Mrs. Berryhill (1789–1857) was the wife of Nashville merchant William McLean Berryhill. Allan Ditchfield Campbell (1791–1861; Pennsylvania), a native of England, served as the pastor of Nashville's Presbyterian Church, 1820–27. Jane M. Foster (c1792–1847) was the wife of Ephraim Hubbard Foster (1794–1854; Cumberland College 1813), later a state legislator and U.S. senator. Harriet Stoddert (1789–1849), a daughter of Maryland's Benjamin Stoddert, first secretary of the navy, married George Washington Campbell (1769–1848) in 1812. Nancy Ayers married John Spence in Nashville in July. Mrs. Somerville was probably the wife of Alexander, a Nashville merchant who was an elder of the Nashville Presbyterian Church. The Grages and Miss Lewis have not been further identified.

8. A paraphrase of Habakkuk 3:17–18.

To John Coffee

Pensacola July 26th. 1821

Dr. Genl

I have recd. your letter of the 22nd ult[1] it came to hand yesterday, my last to you if recd. will have advised you, that I recd possession of west Florida & its dependencies on the 17th. Instant[2]—since which I have been engaged organising the Goverment by Passing such ordinances, for its Goverment as I find absolutely necessary for its peace & good order. Not having any Printing Press, occasions this a great labour, having to copy every ordinance in English & Spanish, & make out many to be stuck up for the general information of the people—[3]

I hope for the wellfare and happiness of Tennessee as well as for its respectability that Colo. [Edward] Ward may be elected, and I still think that there are a majority of honest men in Tennessee, but this election will determine this point.[4] on the subject of the sale of my plantation, you & Mr. James Jackson do as you think best, my letters to you on this subject will give to you my Ideas, and my views, as well as my wish to Sell, and if not sold you will then act under the relief law for me as you may think best—as to little Andrew Hutchings tract, I have no doubt but your sugestion of retaining onehalf of it on which the improvement is made & resigning the other is the proper plan—it can be bought in for a much less sum, and it will meet my approbation It is a course by which the child must be benefitted, and as to him, this is the course I wish pursued—you will therefore adopt it—by retaining one half as above, & relinquishing the other.[5]

It has afforded Mrs. J. & myself great pleasure, in being informed, that you & Polly are blessed with another fine son, on which we heartily congratulate you both—may he be a blessing to you in your old age—[6]

We all enjoy health. I am at present so much engaged, that I must close this letter, with a tender of our best respects to your lady & family, to Mr J. Jackson & Mr [Thomas] childress and their families;[7] & all our friends, and believe me to be very affectionately yours

Andrew Jackson

P.S. In my last I enclosed you a letter & certificate from Mr J. D Smith I will thank you to acknowledge its receipt & give me any intelligence you may possess as to the progress of the Suit.[8] A. J.

ALS, THi (8-0906).

1. Not found.

2. See AJ to Coffee, July 18.

3. Between July 18 and 26, Jackson promulgated seven ordinances for the government of East and West Florida.

4. Ward (d. 1837), Jackson's friend and neighbor, was unsuccessful in his bid for the governorship, losing decisively to William Carroll.

5. On September 20, Coffee and James Jackson concluded an agreement with Richard C. Cross for the sale of Andrew Jackson's Evans Spring farm west of Florence, Alabama. About the same time, Coffee and James Jackson (acting for Andrew J. Hutchings) took advantage of the March land relief law which allowed purchasers to apply the amount paid on the total to a portion of land to be retained (3 *U.S. Statutes at Large* 612–14). Five of Hutchings's tracts were relinquished, and the sums paid upon them applied to two other retained tracts, one of which was shortly thereafter paid off (see Coffee to AJ, July 25; Memorandum relinquishing Alabama land, September 17; and Receipt from James Jackson, [September]).

6. Alexander Donelson Coffee (1821–1901), a lifelong resident of Florence, Alabama, became a planter and manufacturer.

7. Childress (d. 1844), a founder of the Nashville Female Academy before moving to Florence, was one of the group of eight Jackson associates who had invested in Pensacola land during the winter of 1817–18.

8. See AJ to Coffee, July 4. Neither Smith's letter nor his certificate has been found. The suit was *Bennett Smith* v. *John Hutchings's Executors.*

To Robert Butler

Pensacola 27th. July 1821.

Dr Col:

I have just recd. your private letter of the 20th. Ulto.[1] and was mortified to learn that at its date you had received nothing from me since we parted at Nashville.

I dispatched Col: Gadsden from this Port on the 1st. Inst: on board the U. States Sloop Revenge, with letter, and Instructions for you on all points, with a Commission for Mr. W. G. D. Worthington Secy. for East Florida, that you might immediately upon receiving possession hand over the Government to him;[2] in the event of his absence, I also sent a Blank Commission to be filled up with the name of the Commanding Officer, that you might repair hither immediately to enable me to close my whole accounts with the Government before you joined your military command. I find that I acted wisely in providing for the absence of Mr. W. G. D. Worthinton, for since I have commenced this letter I have recd. a letter from him dated Baltimore 30th. June, in which among other things, the want of a Public Transport and the difficulty of getting to St. Augustine, he says "in the present case no urgency exists, I presume, which would require me to charter one for myself alone." from which I suppose it may be doubtful whether Mr. Worthington will reach St. Augustine before Fall.[3] Let this be as it may, If Col: Gadsden has reached you with my dispatches all things will go on there well, as they will here, without the aid of the Officers appointed by the President for the Floridas, none of whom have yet reported themselves, except Judge Fromentin who arrived yesterday.

Col: Gadsden left this with a fine wind which continued for several days and I trust reached you by the 8 or 10th. Inst. The Instructions for yourself & Mr. Worthington were full & ample & if safely recd. all's well. In addition to my anxiety to close my public accounts there are other & weighty considerations which make me desirous to have you here as soon as possible. I send this over land by Capt. [James R.] Hannum—Express who I expect will reach you before your departure from St. Augustine He carries sundry ordinances for the organization of the Government there, which I have found to be absolutely necessary towards the administration of the Government here, and which I trust will prove equally beneficial in preserving order & Health in St. Augustine[4]

I have duly noted the unheard of and unmilitary recommendation of the *learned trio* to the President, which has been given a place in the Register of the Army, as tho' the insult to military feelings by placing meritorious officers at the will & pleasure of one man to be kicked from grade to grade & out of office, was not sufficient to gratify their malignant feelings, but must give the utmost publicity to it, by having it recorded upon the Army Register and those Officers exhibited to the world as being indebted to mere favor for their retention & not to *merit.*[5] How will these men and particularly Genl. Gaines, to whom the Officers of the Southern Division looked for justice account for this unmilitary & outrageous conduct. When it will be asked on the Field of Battle on which Genl. Atkinson has given an evidence of his military prowess and performed those gallant exploits which has given him an exclusive claim of selecting any Office which he might think proper to prefer and that too at the expence of those possessing superior merit & who had rendered important services and suffered the greatest privation and encountered dangers in the very face of the enemy. A comparison will be made, and altho' as you know, I think highly of Genl. Atkinson, he has no one but his friends to blame for creating the necessity for the comparison before the public. More of this when we meet.

If Col: Gadsden is with you present me Affectionately to him, and say, that a few days since I recd. a letter from the Secy. of War enclosing one for him, with instructions to forward it to him, provided he had left me. From my knowledge of his intention of going to the City of Washington, I have enclosed it to him there. It is a notification that the President will appoint him Adj: Genl. if he will accept it (dated 5th. June)[6]

The Ladies are in good health and join me in good wishes to you. Lt. Donelson left this a few days since for Orleans.[7] I obtained formal possession of this place on the 17th. Inst: 10 Oclock A. M. and hoisted the American Colors under the full Band playing "long may it wave o'er the land of the free & the home of the brave." I hope to have the pleasure of seeing you shortly. adieu

Andrew Jackson

LS in James C. Bronaugh's hand and AL draft, DLC (30).

1. Not found.

2. See AJ to James Gadsden, June 26, and Commission of William G. D. Worthington, July 1. The *Revenge,* formerly Gunboat No. 158, was built about 1808.

3. Letter not found. On July 11, Butler had appointed Captain John R. Bell (c1785–1825; Military Academy 1812) of the 4th Artillery as acting governor; Worthington arrived at St. Augustine on August 17.

4. Hanham (d. 1865), a native of England, had served in the American army during the War of 1812 and had been recommended for a Florida position by Vice President Daniel D. Tompkins. Jackson appointed Hanham special messenger and later sheriff at St. Augustine; he subsequently served in the territorial legislative council. Hanham left Pensacola on July 28 carrying ordinances similar to those for Pensacola and also Jackson's July 26 and 27 letters to Worthington; he arrived at St. Augustine on August 13. Butler had left East Florida on July 14 but did not reach Pensacola until August 8.

5. Jackson was referring to military board members Jacob J. Brown, Winfield Scott, and

Edmund P. Gaines and the arrangement regarding Henry Atkinson's place in the reduced army (see above, Edmund P. Gaines to AJ, April 27; and AJ to John C. Calhoun, July 29).

6. None of the letters mentioned have been found. On August 14, Gadsden assumed his duties as adjutant general in Washington (see Gadsden to AJ, August 15).

7. On July 22, Jackson had ordered Andrew J. Donelson to New Orleans on quartermaster business.

To John Caldwell Calhoun

Pensacola July 29th 1821

Dr Sir,

I have the pleasure to acknowledge the receipt of your letter of the 19th ulto, enclosing me a copy of Mr [Jean Augustin] Poniers instructions as Sub-Agent of the Indians in the Floridas.[1] Mr Ponier has not yet reached me, nor have I heard any thing from him, nor has a single officer appointed for West Florida reached me, except Mr Frommentin who arrived day before yesterday, but without his commission and cannot enter upon his Official duties. I was compelled to organise the Government with my old staff in the best manner I could, with the aid of Judge Brackenridge whom I found very useful from his legal knowledge, and his acquaintance with the Spanish language. I have closed its organisation day before yesterday, and have been steady to the existing state of things, the Laws of Spain, new modelling the Government so as to give perfect security to Individual rights, and as far as practicable Keeping up the Spanish mode of trial, excepting only, when it was necessary to secure the individual in a speedy public trial in all civil cases, and in a trial by Jury in all criminal cases. Copies of all ordinances which I have thought necessary for the well being and good order of society here, I have forwarded to the Secretary of State, to which I refer you.[2]

As soon as Mr Ponier arrives, I shall present to him a copy of his instructions, and adopt such measures relative to the Indians as their happiness, and the interest and the welfare of the U States may seem to require. Information received states, that the Indians are preparing to remove up among their brethren in the Creek country above the Florida line, so soon as they can gather their crops—This if true, will promote their security and the tranquillity of the Southern frontier.[3]

I have the pleasure to inform you, that after experiencing every possible delay, first, from the unexpected delay of the Hornet at the Havanna, the loss of the Transport Cora, and lastly the delay, by adverse winds, of the transports from St Marks, 13 days, and an attempt by the Governor for a further delay, which I promptly met and put down; I obtained formal possession of this place, with West Florida and its dependencies on the 17th inst., at 10 O'clock A.M. and on the 27th inst closed its entire organization, and on the 28th started an express to St Augustine with all the ordinances and commissions for the due execution of the Government there; that, perfect order reigns in the city of Pensacola, and if the Board of health which I have established with Doctr Bronough at their head, do their duty, we may maintain health in the city[4]

I have appointed Judge Brackenridge, Alcalde for the city of Pensacola. He is very useful and has given grat satisfaction to the Spanish Population, and nothing but good order reigns.

I have been compelled to Keep Capt Call and my nephew Lt Donelson with me, and have to ask a furlough of three months for Capt Call—he has been doing the duty of Secretary of the Territory pro. temp. I cannot now spare him until the business is closed, and the Secretary appointed by the President arrives, or if he was now here until I get the records up.[5]

My duty has been laborious; being disappointed in a printing press which has long been expected, every ordinance and other act has been copied and promulgated in manuscript—making a task of great labour, and especially so, as many of them had to appear in both the Spanish and English Languages. From all which you will see the necessity of my having a confidential person with me; but as it is, I have no personal acquaintance with any of the Gentlemen appointed to office in the Floridas by the President, and Mr Walton has been represented to me as much in the friendship of Mr Wm H Crawford, a circumstance not very recommendatory to my confidence.

Mr Frommentins character is freely spoken of, and the population are greatly astonished at his receiving the appointment of Judge. It was all important that the Judge should have been a man of good character and of such legal standing as would have given confidence to the people. Mr Frommentin is not that character—the fact is, he has no standing here or at New Orleans, as a Lawyer or as a moral man. It is said here publickly (the reality of it, I will not vouch), but it comes from the most respectable, and men of high standing that he was bred a Priest in France—fled from Bonapartes rule—came to America—married in Maryland—moved to New Orleans—there appointed a Senator in Congress and whilst such, on the restoration of the Bourbons—left his wife—took up with a base woman—travelled with her to Orleans—thence to France, where it is alledged he repaired to regain his Priesthood—disappointed—he returned to America—conceded to his wife and settled in New Orleans[6]—That, when he was here an Agent for the Government under the Treaty with Spain—borrowed money—went off without repaying it—was proceeded against in the Spanish form as an *Outlawry,* and which I am informed by the Keeper of the Records, stands now against him, and when I arrived was posted on the Public Corners. How, I ask, can these people just coming in under our Government have confidence in it; when the Judge who is to watch their morals and civil rights, is thus accused? Or, what claims can Mr Frommentin have upon Our Government that he should be provided for at the expense of the happiness of the people? No people can be happy, unless they have confidence in the laws, and also in the administrators of those laws—In Mr Frommentin, the best informed can have no confidence, and the Judiciary of the Floridas should not only be filled by men of great legal capacity, but by men of unspotted moral character: for how, can it be expected, that an immoral man will execute laws, moralising mankind, while they condemn his own acts.[7]

I have no unpleasant feelings towards Mr Frommentin, for he is seemingly polite and gentlemanly; but to be associated with such a man as he is publickly represented to be, in the administration of the Government; is a thing that I cannot reconcile to my feelings, and I reflect with pleasure that the time is fast approaching when this Government will be in a complete state of operation, when I can retire agreeably to the terms on which I accepted the Government.

I have been so much engaged, that I cannot say what effect the climate might have upon my constitution, but under existing circumstances I am determined to retire on the meeting of Congress I am Sir, with great respect Yr. Mo Obt Sert.

(Signed) Andrew Jackson

LC in Andrew J. Donelson's hand, DLC (63). Published in *Calhoun Papers,* 6:291–94.

1. See Calhoun to AJ, June 19. Pénières (c1766–1821), a French native and a lawyer, had resided in the Alabama and Arkansas territories before his appointment as Indian subagent in Florida.

2. See AJ to John Q. Adams, July 30–August 14; see also Henry M. Brackenridge to AJ, July 26. Eligius Fromentin received his commission on August 11.

3. The source of Jackson's information has not been determined. For more on Florida Indian affairs, see AJ to Calhoun, September 17 and 20, and Report on a talk with Florida Indians, [September 18–20].

4. See Ordinance for the preservation of health in Pensacola and Commission of James C. Bronaugh, both July 19.

5. See AJ to Brackenridge, July 17; for Jackson's later view of Brackenridge, see AJ to William B. Lewis, January 20, 1843. Richard K. Call's furlough was granted. Call had formed a law partnership with Brackenridge, foretelling his resignation from the army, which he submitted in January 1822. Andrew J. Donelson had been posted to Mobile Point, but was subsequently given an extended leave.

6. Fromentin had first come to the United States during the French Reign of Terror, several years before Napoleon Bonaparte (1769–1821) came to power. He married Elizabeth ("Betsy") Polk (d. 1822) of Somerset County, Maryland, in 1800. The "base woman" has not been identified.

7. James Monroe had passed over Jackson's recommendation (not found) of John Haywood for the judgeship and, though aware of the rumors about Fromentin's marital problems, discounted all other reports about Fromentin's character (see Monroe to AJ, September 16; and AJ to James Gadsden, May 2, 1822, below). The papers concerning Fromentin's debt, incurred when he awaited the anticipated transfer in 1819, have not been found. Brackenridge was keeper of the records.

From Samuel Ragland Overton

Nashville, August 1st. 1821.

Dr. General;

I arrived at this place, about a week since; but your polite and friendly letter, dated 14th of April, was not put into my hands, until a day or two ago.[1] I thank you sincerely for this evidence of your friendship, and should have been more than gratified, could I have heard from you occasionally, during my absence. But the circumstance of my communications to you, having always held out the prospect of a speedy return, accounts, in the most satisfactory manner, for the failure.[2] In addition to this, your numerous engagements, afforded the most ample reasons for your exemption from the discharge of such a task.

You inform me, that you have not forgotten my application for the office of "*Register*" in the State of Mississippi. I had previously learned, that you had written to the representation from that state, upon the subject, and that it promises to be productive of the most successful results.[3] Nothing is now wanting but a residence in the country. This difficulty shall certainly be obviated, as I shall remove to the state of Mississippi as soon as I can venture to do so in safety to my health. For your friendly aid on this occasion, be pleased to accept of my grateful acknowledgements. Nothing would give me more satisfaction, than to be enabled, at any future period, to make an adequate return for such distinguished Kindness.

Had I been in this country upon your departure, I would have gladly accepted of any station in your gift, so as to have accompanied you to Pensacola. The trip would have been a very pleasant one to me; particularly so, could I have been persuaded that my services <might> would be useful to you. It might, besides, have partially contributed to the improvement of my health. I would yet join you, were I satisfied that I could render any essential service, in the furtherance and accomplishment of your views, although the time which will intervene between this and my departure for the state of Mississippi is short. Indeed, it will be very little more than sufficient to enable me to visit my friends.

Whilst in the city of Philadelphia, I learned pretty distinctly, that the dominant party in Pennsylvania are determined to run you as a candidate for the next Presidency. I was informed, from a source, which might be considered authentic, that the leading politicians of that state, had been for some time, and were still engaged in collecting materials upon the subject, by which to ascertain the chances of success, and to authorize giving you their decided support. I believe they have become satisfied, that you have more popularity, and greater claims to the office, than any other individual who can be presented to the people of the United States. They have, consequently determined to give you their suffrages at the next election. It was stated to me, that amongst the letters written to different parts of the Union, in order to embody public sentiment upon this subject, one was addressed to Genl. [John] Adair, to which he replied, that you were very popular in Kentucky, and that he was unequivocally friendly to your election.[4] Such circumstances as these, connected with the great augmentation of your popularity, in consequence of the investigation of your military conduct, in Congress, is strongly calculated to induce the belief, that your pretentions to the Presidency, are more imposing and flattering than any of those who are now seeking the patronage of the people for that station. If you are once brought before the people of the United States, in this attitude, and under favorable auspices, I think very little doubt can be reasonably entertained of your election. I think, as little doubt can be entertained too, that you should consent to be considered a candidate for that office. If the people believe that you can render them important services in the capacity of President of the Union, they ought to be gratified, and you should acquiesce in the acceptance of their suffrages. This course would not only be dictated by those obligations which you owe to the people, but also by those due to yourself. I wish you, however, General, not to misunderstand me on this occasion. It is not my wish or aim to perform the office of dictator in this matter; but only desire what I have advanced, to be received as suggestions for consideration. Having accidentally, arrived at a Knowledge of the future operations of your friends at the Eastward, I deemed it my bounden duty to communicate to you the result, to the end that you might anticipate events, and be properly prepared to meet them. I have no doubt your friends calculate with sanguine expectations, that you will yield to their wishes; it is for you, after weighing all the considerations which should enter into the estimate, to decide the question.

My health is greatly improved since I left the state of Tennessee. It is not entirely restored, but promises to be so, by observing a due degree of care and temperance. By adopting this course, I have every prospect of enjoying pretty good health during the ballance of my life. My visit to the Eastward, has resulted as fortunately as I possibly could have anticipated, with respect to the restoration of my health.

Capt. Easter is with us, whom, I regret to say, I found laboring under a pretty severe attack of the rheumatism, upon my reaching the Judges.[5] He is, however, upon the recovery, and I am in hopes will get about in a short time. He desires to be respectfully presented to yourself and family, and promises to write you as soon as he is able.

Be pleased to tender my compliments to Mrs. Jackson, and my much esteemed friends Capt. Call & Lieut Donaldson; also to Doct. Bronaught, and accept for yourself my best wishes. Yr. Sincere frind

Saml. R. Overton.

ALS, DLC (30). Published in Bassett, 3:105–106 (extract). Overton (d. 1827) was the son of Waller and nephew of John Overton.

1. Letter not found. In November 1820, Overton, secretary to the Choctaw treaty commissioners, had gone to Washington with the treaty negotiated by Jackson and Thomas Hinds at Doak's Stand the preceding month.

2. See Samuel R. Overton to AJ, January 30, February 10, and March 11.

3. See AJ to Thomas H. Williams, January 1, and Williams to AJ, January 29. In May 1822, Overton was named a land commissioner for the Territory of Florida, rather than to the Mississippi post.

4. Adair (1757–1840) was at this time governor of Kentucky. He had earlier engaged Jackson in a widely reported controversy regarding the service of Kentucky troops at New Orleans (see *Jackson*, 3:317–21, 4:99–102).

5. John Overton's residence, Travellers' Rest, was south of Nashville.

To James Jackson

Pensacola August 2nd. 1821

Dr. James

I have this moment recd yours of the 16th ult by Mr Gibson[1]—I am really happy to hear that you are all well. My health at present is not good, I have lost a good deal of what little flesh I had acquired in Tennessee, but my labours are very severe, & Having not a great deal of aid, Except my old companions who are all professionally engaged, I have to depend upon myself, and such young men as clerks as I can get—

But I hope as soon as I can get the Govrt. perfectly in motion my report made to Mr Adams, and the officers appointed by the President at their posts, my labours will be less—the sec of west Florida Colo. Walton arived day before yesterday—but as yet has not entered upon his duties[2]—Judge Fromentine is here without his commission—of course he can do nothing except endeavour to pay his old debts and keep himself from being sent to confinement for them—I know none of the officers appointed but suppose they are all broken merchants.

I with great labour got peacable possession of west Florida & its dependencies on the 17th. ult. at 10 A.M. but had like to have some Jarring with the Governor—I had got his pledge to Surrender the country in a certain time after the arival of the Transports from St Marks—as soon as they arived I called upon him to name a day within the time specified he politely answered he would the next day—in his letter of the next day began to prevaricate, and I replied, extracting his Pledges, touched him upon his honour as a soldier, piqued his Castillian honour, but brought him to terms & a day & hour was fixed,[3] had it not been that I had him pledged & knew if I granted him an hour he would prolong it as much longer as he could, I found since that he would trip if he could. These kind of Spanniards, raised in the vortex of corruption, no reliance can be placed in their promises, honours with them, are allways divided, & they play for the odd trick—I have got the Town incorporated, Mayor & Aldermen appointed, and a county court organised which will Commence its first session next Monday—The alcade was the only Judicial officer I found here, his powers were despotic & his will the law, he was a half pay Spanish officer, and of course could not continue. I appointed Judge Brakenridge the Alcade—he is a good lawyer, understand the Spanish language, and gives general satisfaction—The establishing a Mayoralty, and a county court abridges his powers & gives more security to the rights of the citizen, and assimilates the System more to what it must be as soon as congress meets—My ordinances only declare what the Spanish law really is, as far as it can be understood, and giving in criminal cases a trial by Jury—and in all civil a speedy & public trial to confront his Witnesses face to face—Thus you see, I have as far as I had the power exercised it to secure the constitutional rights of the people instead of exercising, those despotic powers delegated to me[4]—If we had a press which we greatly want is shortly expected when you will see & hear from us,[5] I trust you will approve our goverment—

as to all my land matters you must exercise for me your own Judgt. I regret the prospect of my crop, but if Ward is elected Governor for T. & Mr [William H.] Crawford disappointed in keeping out Pickens, I will be content & hope for better times[6]

you will please with Genl Coffee do with little Andrew J. Hutchings land, as you may Judge best for his interest, either by forfeiting half or taking eight years on the whole—I have seen Mr [William H.] Crawfords explanation of the land law I hope he may be merittedly lashed in the papers—[7]

say to William [W.] Crawford I sincerely regret that [Nelson P.] Jones has out cropped him, but that he must make it up by getting his crop out early, and his cotton well handled, clear of all kind of trash[8]—and all his crop up in good time—Mrs Jackson is only in tolerable health—we will all I believe be pleased to return to our own country—n*[ot]*withstanding I have no doubt but in time this will become a very important place from its health & situation—property and rent very high, and titles very doubtfull—

Mrs. J. & myself will accompany you and Doctor Brunaugh if you will be hear & ready to return about the middle of Octbr. This will give us good roads—let me hear from you often—Present Mrs. J. & myself to your lady & sweet little family & all our friends & your neighbours, and accept for yourself our best wishes. Doctor Brunaugh is engaged but sends his best respects to you—Lt Donelson is at orleans expected back in a few days and our little son learning french & sends you how de—for the present adieu.

Andrew Jackson

ALS, NjP (8-0990).

1. Letter not found. Gibson has not been identified.

2. See AJ to John Q. Adams, July 30–August 14. George Walton assumed his duties as secretary of West Florida on August 10.

3. See above, AJ to José M. Callava, July 12.

4. José Noriega (b. c1757), an officer in the Louisiana Regiment, had been the Spanish alcalde. Jackson's ordinances establishing a government for Pensacola and St. Augustine had been drafted by Henry M. Brackenridge and Abner L. Duncan. His promulgation of the "laws" became a major issue in the campaign of 1828. For Jackson's further elaboration on his powers, see Remarks on authority as governor of Florida, [cSeptember 15]; and for the discussion of the promulgation issue, see "Henry," *An Examination of the Civil Administration of Governor Jackson in Florida* . . . (Washington, 1828), reprinting a series of articles that appeared in the Washington *National Intelligencer,* June–September 1828.

5. The first issue of the Pensacola *Floridian,* edited by Cary Nicholas and George Tunstall, appeared on August 18.

6. In the August election for governor of Alabama, Israel Pickens defeated Henry H. Chambers, the Georgia faction candidate, by about 2,000 votes.

7. For the relinquishment of a portion of Andrew J. Hutchings's land, see above, AJ to John Coffee, July 26. Jackson probably was referring to the "Notice to Debtors to the United States for Public Lands," issued for the treasury department by Josiah Meigs, June 15, detailing eligibility and procedures for taking advantage of the law (see Washington *National Intelligencer,* June 23).

8. Jones, a native of South Carolina, had contracted to farm Jackson's Evans Spring plantation in Alabama in December 1819, but Jackson had dismissed him in November 1820.

The harmony between Jackson and José M. Callava after the formal transfer of West Florida on July 17 was more apparent than real. Again, in working out the final details, delay prevailed. Callava and his secretary refused to sign an inventory of the provisions for the return of the Spanish garrison to Havana, although he and Jackson had agreed upon that earlier. In response, Jackson cancelled the receipt for the cannon left in Florida he had signed earlier and informed Callava on August 3 that "this closes my correspondence with Your Excellency on this subject forever."

Such was the situation when Mercedes Vidal Palao, a daughter and an heir of Nicolas Maria Vidal (d. 1806), a former Spanish soldier and auditor of war for West Florida, visited Henry M. Brackenridge soon after his appointment as alcalde and claimed that certain documents necessary to her case against Pensacola merchant John Innerarity (1783–1854), a debtor to the estate, were about to be taken to Havana. The papers were controlled by Callava, who, as judge of the military tribunal, had jurisdiction over legal matters involving Spanish army officers. Domingo García Sousa (b. c1761), a Spanish ensign and secretary to Callava's court, retained physical possession of the documents (see Brackenridge to AJ, August 24).

Brackenridge's investigation of the Vidal estate lawsuit sparked the open conflict that Jackson and Callava had thus far avoided, a conflict that pitted Jackson's power as governor against Callava's possible diplomatic immunity, Innerarity's interest as a prominent Pensacola citizen, and Eligius Fromentin's authority as federal district judge.

From Henry Marie Brackenridge

Pensacola August 21. 1821.

Sir,

I learn from the most satisfactory evidence that a number of documents relating to estates in this place and to suits instituted here are in the possession of an individual of the name of Domingo Sousa. These papers properly belong to this Office, but were not included in the inventory delivered by the late Governor.[1] Some of the circumstances attending the affair are of a peculiar nature, but as the necessity of obtaining possession of the documents is urgent, I must defer making a report respecting them, to some other period—At present I must request Your Excellency to authorize some one to make a regular demand of the said documents and to ascertain precisely what they are.[2] I am Respectfully. Yr most Obdt Servt.

(Signed) H. M. Brackenridge
Alcalde

LC in John C. Connor's hand, DLC (63). Published in *ASP, Miscellaneous Documents,* 2:802.

1. See the Spanish inventory of public documents, July 4. Callava later argued that the documents were excluded from the inventory because they had not fallen under the jurisdiction of the alcalde, whose office handled civilian legal affairs.
2. See AJ to George Walton, Brackenridge, and John Miller, August 21.

Order to Robert Butler and James Craine Bronaugh

[August 22, 1821]

It being made Known to me by the confession of Domingo Sousa that the papers named in the petition of Henry M. Brackenridge Alcalde for the City of Pensacola and which were demanded under my orders as the property of private individuals by Col. George Walton Secretary for West Florida, Col John Miller, Clerk of the County Court of Escambia, and Henry M. Brackenridge Alcalde for the City of Pensacola were after said demand in pursuance of my orders as aforesaid was made; by the said Domingo Sousa and a Negro Man, carried (this day) to the house of the late Governor Don José Callava & delivered the said documents and papers into the possession of his Steward named [Antoine] Fullarat.[1]

Col Robert Butler of the army of the U. S. and Dr. J C. Bronaugh, accompanied by Henry M. Brackenridge Esqr. Alcalde for the City of Pensacola, will wait upon Colo Don José Callava and his Steward *named Fullarat* and demand from them the following papers this day delivered to the said Fullarat at the house of the said Col. Callava, by the said Domingo Sousa, that is to say—First, the documents and papers relating to the Estate of Nicolas Maria Vidal—Second—the documents in the proceedings between Carlos de Ville [de Goutin] and Eugene Sierra—Third, the documents and papers in the case of Manuel Bonfay and Carlos de Ville. Fourth, the documents and papers on the proceedings in the case of Peter Guilkes against Tomas Villaseca, all which documents and papers are acknowledged to be the property of individuals and appertaining to their rights, and which are secured to them by and under the 2nd. Article of the Treaty with Spain, concluded at the City of Washington on the 22nd. day of February 1819 and ratified on the corresponding day of 1821. and must remain for the protection of the rights and property of the said individuals, and no Officer of Spain can rightfully take them away or Keep them from the possession of the duly appointed Alcalde for the City of Pensacola.[2]

It is further ordered that if the said late Governor Don José Callava or his Steward Fullarat, when the above described papers are demanded of them should fail or refuse to deliver the same, that the said Don José Callava and his Steward Fullarat be forthwith brought before me at my Office, then and there to answer such interrogatories as may be put to them of, and concerning the premises, and to abide by and perform such order and decree touching the said documents and papers secured to them as aforesaid and the Justice of the case may demand. Given under my hand at Pensacola this 22nd. day of Augt. 1821.

(Signed) Andrew Jackson
Gov of the Floridas
&c &c &c

LC in John C. Connor's hand, DLC (63); LC, DNA-RG 59 (M116-7). Published in *ASP, Miscellaneous Documents,* 2:805.

1. See above, Brackenridge to AJ, August 21; and AJ to Walton, Brackenridge, and Miller, August 21. See also Walton, Brackenridge, and Miller to AJ; AJ to Butler and Miller; Butler and Miller to AJ; and Minutes of the examination of Domingo G. Sousa, all August 22. The papers related to courts-martial and personal disputes handled by Spanish military tribunals. Miller (c1768–1826) was later mayor of Pensacola and secretary to Brackenridge. Fullarat has not been further identified.

2. Eugenio Antonio Sierra (1761–1849), a surgeon, had made a claim against the estate of de Ville de Goutin (1759–1820), who had been a lieutenant colonel in the Spanish army's Louisiana Regiment; Bonifay (b. c1785) was a farmer who acted as agent for the purchaser of the estate. Guilkes was in the Spanish army. Vilaseca (b. c1755) was a shopkeeper. Anticipating the former governor's refusal, Jackson readied an armed detachment of Lieutenant Colonel George M. Brooke's 4th Infantry (see AJ to Brooke, and AJ to George W. Mountz, both August 22).

When Robert Butler, James C. Bronaugh, Henry M. Brackenridge, and the armed detachment arrived at José M. Callava's house, they discovered that he, John Innerarity, and others were dining at George M. Brooke's residence. Brackenridge went to Brooke's home and con-

veyed Jackson's order to Callava, who protested, claiming diplomatic immunity as the Spanish commissioner. Shortly thereafter Callava returned to his house, where much discussion ensued. After initially agreeing to relinquish the documents upon written request, Callava prepared to flee Pensacola with the requested papers. Upon discovering this, the American force entered Callava's house, where he finally submitted and, with his servant Antoine Fullarat, went to Jackson's office. The interview among Jackson, Callava, and Fullarat quickly degenerated into bilingual shouting, prompting Jackson to jail Callava, Fullarat, and Domingo G. Sousa, the Spanish court secretary (see Butler and Bronaugh to AJ, Minutes of the examinations of Callava and Fullarat, and Orders for imprisonment of Callava, Fullarat, and Sousa, all August 22).

After Callava's imprisonment, Jackson ordered the seizure of the disputed documents. Meanwhile, not knowing that Jackson had already determined to release all the prisoners, several of Callava's friends approached the federal district judge, Eligius Fromentin, asking that he grant a writ of habeas corpus for Callava's release. Fromentin, who had previously joined Callava's circle of friends, issued the writ, transmitting it by Juan Brosnaham (b. c1785), a physician and an alderman of the Pensacola city council. But the March 3 act authorizing the occupation of Florida extended only federal revenue and slave trade laws over the territory, and Jackson argued that this defined the limits of Fromentin's authority. The disagreement over jurisdiction prompted Fromentin's subsequent appeal to Washington (see 3 U.S. Statutes at Large *637–39; Fromentin to John Q. Adams, August 26, September 6–8, in* ASP, Miscellaneous Documents, *2:834–36, 838–41; and AJ to Adams, August 26).*

The controversy surrounding Callava's imprisonment and Jackson's refusal to obey the writ of habeas corpus became the subject of newspaper commentary, prompting an administration review of Jackson's entire conduct as governor. The president commented that Jackson "may have displayed some degree of zeal & warmth, & have executed the Spanish powers, too much in the Spanish way," while the attorney general agreed that "the General certainly takes to this same Spanish power as kindly as if it was natural to him: but you may rely upon it, it will require all his popularity to gild this pill." Throughout that review, only Secretary of State John Q. Adams consistently supported Jackson. After much debate the administration finally adopted Jackson's view of Fromentin's jurisdiction, although suggesting that both the governor and the judge had acted from proper motives (see James Monroe to William Wirt, October 7, Wirt to Monroe, October 11, Adams to Fromentin, October 26, in TPUS, *22:242–43, 250–58, 262–63; Adams to AJ, October 26).*

Order to Eligius Fromentin

[August 23, 1821]

Eligius Fromentin Esqr. will forthwith be and appear before me to shew cause why he has attempted to interfere with my authority as Governor of the Floridas exercising the powers of the Captain General and Intendant of the Island of Cuba over the said Provinces and of the Governors of said Provinces respectively. In my Judicial capacity as Supreme Judge over the same and as Chancellor thereof having committed certain individuals charged with a combination to secrete and of having Attempted to secrete and carry out of the Territories ceded to the United States, the evidence of individual right to property within the said Territories, which has been secured to each individual under the Second article of the Late Treaty with Spain and in open contempt of the orders and decrees made by me and that the said Eligius Fromentin Esqr. be and appear before me at my Office at Five Oclock P. M. in Pensacola, to make Known the above cause and to abide by and perform such order and decree as the undersigned may of right deem proper to make, of and concerning the same.[1] Given under my hand at Pensacola this 23d day of August 1821.

(Signed) Andrew Jackson
Gov of the Floridas
&c. &c. &c.

LC in John C. Connor's hand, DLC (63); Copies, DNA-RG 59 (M116-7, -9). Published in *ASP, Miscellaneous Documents,* 2:822–23.

1. The service of the writ of habeas corpus prompted Jackson to delay the prisoners' release, so that he might compose the above order to Fromentin. The prisoners were released later in the day, and Fromentin's interview with Jackson was delayed until the next afternoon, due to the judge's indisposition (see Philip Wager to AJ, August 24; George W. Mountz to AJ, September 24; George Walton to AJ, August 23; and Fromentin to AJ, August 23).

To John Innerarity

Pensacola August 23rd. 1821.

Sir.

From the report which has been made of the interest manifested by you,[1] and together with your Association with Colo Calava, who has resisted the legal exercise of my Authority under false pretences, and the relation in which you are represented to stand with regard to part of the documents demanded of Colo. Calava on yesterday, and under all these circumstances I have deemed it necessary to inform you, that your Services as a member of the Cabildo are no longer required and that your place will be forthwith filled by some person better disposed to execute the laws and support its dignity—

Andrew Jackson
Govr. of the Floridas &c &c &c &c

LS in Robert Butler's hand, Ms-Ar (8-1091).

1. See Robert Butler and James C. Bronaugh to AJ, August 22.

From Eligius Fromentin

Office of the Executive of Florida
Pensacola Aug. 24th 1821

Present—His Excellency the Governor

Judge Fromentin in obedience to the order of His Excellency appears and acknowledges that he granted the writ of Habeas Corpus without the affidavit of any person and that no affidavit was made before him And that it was granted upon the *verbal* application of a number of individuals who made the application, named [Juan De] La Rua, Innerarity, Brosnaham & Father Coleman[1] and upon being asked to whom he delivered the said writ of habeas corpus to be served upon the officer who had in Custody Col. Callava, he replied that he delivered it to one of the persons who made application for it but to which he does not know.

(Signed) Eligius Fromentin

the word *verbal* interlined in the original by Judge Fromentin[2]

Geo. Walton
Sec. W. Florida

Copy, DNA-RG 59 (M116-7); LC (dated August 25) in John C. Connor's hand, DLC (63); Copy (dated August 25), DNA-RG 59 (M116-9). Published in *ASP, Miscellaneous Documents,* 2:810–11.

1. De la Rua (1790–1832), a Pensacola merchant, later served variously as mayor, member of the territorial legislative council, judge, colonel of militia, and postmaster.

2. Fromentin's original statement failed to specify that the request for the writ of habeas corpus had been verbal. Jackson ordered its return to Fromentin, who altered the text accordingly (see AJ to Fromentin, August 25).

Rachel Jackson to John Donelson (1755–1830)

Pansacola August 25—1821

My Dear Brother

I have often thought I would sit Down & write you a few Lines so maney Comeing in to interrupt me and more then all that a mind never at rest, o what will our poor old sister say when she hers the mealancholey Death of her son He has found a grave in this Land of stangers, he was purfectly in his sences to the last his Lungs wer much affected—Dr Bronough was very attentive to him Andrew waited on him Day and Night indeed all was kind to them[1]—I have not injoyed myself no ways Contented no health but I hope to see you all againe, ther never was a man more Disappointed then he has been in the first place he has not the power to apoint one of his friends which I thought was in part the reason of his Comeing But far has it Exceeded Every Calculation it has almost taken His life—Capt Call says its Equel to the Simenole Campaine, well I knew it would be a ruining Concerne, I shall not pretend to Disscribe the toile fatigue & trouble, those Spaniards had as leve Dye as give up their Country, he has had turrible senes the governer has been put in the Callibous wich is a turrible thing realy I was afraide ther would be a rebelion But the Spanish Troops wer all gon to the Havannah several officers remaining Here yet we have a hope of sitting out the first october for home Little Andrew and Colo Butlar has started for Tennessee[2] he was the most anxious Creature I Ever Saw in my Life theay all begin to think with me that Tennesee is the best Country yet Stockley Hutchings widdow and famaly will return this fall poor thing she Expects her Brother to Come for Her[3] tell our friends and all I hope to see them againe in our own Country and to know it is the best I Ever seen what a pitty that some do not know when theay ar well of in this world theay not only hurt them selves but those that is innocent—But St. P*[aul]* all things worketh togeather for good—[4]

say to sister Mary [Donelson Caffery] I have Herd but one sermon sinc I herd Mr [Samuel] Hoge he promised me to Come to this place in june but no he never Came[5] I have mourned for zion my tears has ran down in the night season—Mr J has been very unwell & no wonder my health is Delicate—the Lord is my help in him will I trust & I will praise him with joyful lips remember me to all my Dear friends the young ones o how I want to hear them tell that Jesus the hope of Glory is formed in them tell Brother Sanday I have maney things to say to him—farwell my Dear Brother & my you say as pious job I know that my redeemer Liveth[6]

Rachel Jackson

ALS, THi (8-1102). Published in Parton, 2:610 (extract).

1. Stockley Donelson Hutchings (1791–1821), son of Rachel's sister Catherine Donelson Hutchings (c1752–1834), had died the previous week. Stockley D. Hutchings had joined the Jacksons on the trip to Pensacola, and Jackson had appointed him with John Garnier auctioneers on July 19.

2. Butler did not leave until August 26.

3. In 1816, Hutchings had married Elizabeth Atwood (c1794–1854). The brother she expected was probably William Atwood (c1781–1836), Huntsville postmaster, 1825–35.

4. A paraphrase of Romans 8:28.

5. Rachel's sister Mary (c1756–1823) had married John Caffery (1756–1811) in 1775. Hodge (1779–1849), a Presbyterian minister since 1805, rode the Middle Tennessee and northern Alabama circuits.

6. Brother Sanday was Alexander Donelson (1751–1834), the eldest son of John (c1718–86) and Rachel Stockley Donelson (c1730–1801). The biblical references are likely paraphrases of Psalm 22:2, Psalm 33:20–21, Psalm 63:5, and Job 19:25.

To Eligius Fromentin

Pensacola September 3d. 1821.

Sir,

I have this moment received your second note of this day; the first, created my astonishment it is true; but the second, my indignation and contempt; for I did not suppose until your note now before me furnished conclusive evidence, that you were capable of stating a wilfull and deliberate falsehood[1]—that you have done so in your note of this evening I do assert, and the enclosed certificates of Dr. J. C. Bronaugh (who was directed by me to pay strict attention to our conversation) and Mr. [Edward Augustus] Rutledge fully prove.[2] That you have the hardihood to deny that when you called at my house, that I did not send for my book to the Office, containing the record of my Commissions and instructions, and that I did not read the whole of them to you, shews that you are regardless of truth, and in this I do pronounce that you have stated another deliberate falsehood.

I have barely to add, that I recommend to you to Keep within your legal jurisdiction and powers; whilst you do this, all your proceedings will be supported and all my aid given, that may be necessary to carry them into effect; but when you attempt to transcend them and interfere with my legitimate powers—recollect the admonition I gave you when before me on the 24th. ultimo—and attend to it, or you will be treated and punished as you may deserve, regardless of your boasts of bloodflowing &c &c which pass by me as the fleeting breeze.[3]

Here Sir (on this subject) our communication closes, as I am too much engaged to read yours. I am Sir Yrs &c &c.

(signed) Andrew Jackson

LC in John C. Connor's hand, DLC (63); Copy in Fromentin's hand and Copy, DNA-RG 59 (M116-7, -9). Published in *ASP, Miscellaneous Documents,* 2:821.

1. See Fromentin to AJ, and AJ to Fromentin, September 3. In his note, Fromentin denied that he had apologized to AJ for alleged errors.

2. See James C. Bronaugh to AJ, and Rutledge to AJ, both September 3. Jackson had employed Rutledge (1802–26), the son of Henry Middleton Rutledge and grandson of a signer of the Declaration of Independence, as a translator.

3. In his second note of September 3, Fromentin denied conceding that he had overstepped his authority and wrote that "my blood recoils at such a statement. It's last drop will flow before I subscribe to it."

From Robert Butler

Wood Lawn September 19th. 1821

D. General.

Andrew and self arrived safely on the evening of the 8th. inst. which you will say did not benefit my horses much—true; they were very much wearied, but have since recruited surprisingly—we found all friends in health and not a little pleased at the prospect of seeing you early in November at your lonesome dwelling—Capt. Donelson no doubt gives you all the information necessary about your farm &c. I sent your letter to Genl. Coffee by mail from Nashville, with directions to the postmaster to sent it to Huntsville should the General have gone there previous to its reaching him—[1]

I find from the papers that Colo: Gadsden has been appointed Adj: General, and I honorably promoted to Lieut. Colo: and not the oldest either—That Gadsden should have accepted it, when he knew my claims, and having read him my letter to Mr. Calhoun on the Subject when at Augustine, surprises me much, but every man for himself and the devil take the hindmost, is the Politics of Washington folks now adays—

I have written to him for a copy of the order making the Appointment, to enable me, "to adopt the Only honorable course left me in a manner called for by the attendant circumstances"[2]

So soon as I can arrange my business I shall then act as becomes me, and turn my attention to that species of labour, which I hope will yield me relief to my wounded feelings, from the most unjust, ungrateful & unmerited treatment which has been heaped upon me—

Mr. Munroes *provision* for me, well comports, with the friendship which he has manifested towards you in the Florida Appointments, and Mr. Calhouns promise to Mr. Eaton *that I should have a regiment* reminds me of the old adage "that promises like Pye Crusts, are made to be broken"—but how far they comport with the dignity of a great statesman can be answered by every *snotty nosed* school boy—As to the recommendation [sett], I can say as our Saviour did "Father forgive them *[for they k]*now not what they do."[3]

When Smugglers and ignorance are associated what can be expected[4]—but the curtain must raise before long, and I venture there will be much tragic before the farce comes on; but I shall have dropt into the pit of forgetfulness doomed to struggle hard with the world to rear my family in decency, and if I can but give my children a good education I shall thank my God for having placed me in the ranks of Independent civil life and think that my Fathers blood was not shed in vain, or the many scenes of blood and hardships which I have witnessed, have not been without their good, howe'er they have been succeeded by cramps & premature grey hairs—[5]

You think I have said enough on this subject—Then our love to the Ladies and my best respects to my friends; and God send you and your family safely and speedily to your peaceful habitation—Yrs. truly.

Butler

ALS, DLC (30). Wood Lawn was Robert Butler's Tennessee plantation.

1. See AJ to John Coffee, August 26.

2. See Butler to John C. Calhoun, June 6 (DNA-RG 94, M566-139), and the Washington *National Intelligencer,* August 14 and 22. Butler's subsequent letter, from which he presumably quoted, has not been found.

3. Regarding John C. Calhoun's promise, see John H. Eaton to AJ, March 9. Butler was quoting Luke 23:34.

4. In referring to the "recommendation [sett]" and to "Smugglers and ignorance," Butler was likely referring to the Crawfordites' efforts to use patronage to boost the candidacy of William H. Crawford for the presidency and to Crawford's ignoring charges of David B. Mitchell's involvement in the Amelia Island slave smuggling business through the Creek Agency.

5. Butler's father, Thomas (1748–1805), one of the famous "fighting Butler brothers" of the Revolution, was wounded at the Battle of Monmouth and twice again during Arthur St. Clair's defeat by Ohio Indians in 1791.

To George Bowie and Henry Marie Brackenridge

West Florida, Pensacola
[September 22, 1821]

Whereas Col. Callava as it is said has proceeded to the City of Washington for the purpose of complaining to the Executive of the U.S. through the Minister Plenipotentiary of H. C. M., and whereas a false and scandalous publication has appeared in the Public Newspapers under the signature of the said Callava, sworn to, as it is therein stated by him and which contains gross mistatements and suppressions of the Truth, and if sworn to before a competent authority, may subject him to a prosecution for perjury[1]—And Whereas it has become necessary that the President and the Government of the U.S. should be furnished with the evidence of all and every person acquainted with the facts and circumstances of the arrest of the said Callava, on the charge of combining with Domingo Sousa and others, to interrupt me in the exercise of my judicial authority and to prevent my orders and decrees, in said capacity from being carried into execution; this is therefore to authorize and require George Bowie, Mayor of the City of Pensacola and H. M. Brackenridge, Alcalde of the said City to cause all such persons to come before them, and them to interrogate on oath touching their Knowledge of the facts and circumstances of the arrest of Callava as aforesaid, and of the facts and circumstances attending or accompanying the same, and all other matters and things to wh. they may be interrogated in relation thereto, taking the same in writing, that it may be forwarded for the information of the Government of the U.S.[2]—Herein fail not, and with your proceedings return this writ. Given under my hand at Pensacola, this 22nd. day of September 1821.

(signed) Andrew Jackson
Gov of the Floridas &c. &c. &c.

LC, DLC (63). A native of Abbeville, South Carolina, Bowie (1772–1864; South Carolina) was a prominent member of that state's bar before moving to southern Alabama. After a brief interlude as mayor of Pensacola, he returned to Alabama in late September, settling finally near Cahaba.

1. José M. Callava left Pensacola for Washington on August 27, stopping at New Orleans where he issued a statement giving his version of the events of late August (see his Protest, [Sept]). Arriving in Washington in late September, Callava accompanied departing Spanish minister Francisco Dionisio Vives to Philadelphia, where an expanded version of the protest was printed (see his second protest, Oct 3). Shortly thereafter, Callava left the United States for Havana.

2. For responses to Jackson's call for testimony, see Deposition of John J. Jackson, September 22; George W. Mountz to AJ, September 24; Francis L. Dade to AJ, September 25; Bowie and Brackenridge to AJ, September 27; Deposition of John Innerarity, [September 27]; and Answer of Innerarity September 29. On September 29, the Spanish officers remaining in Pensacola issued their own statement of the facts regarding Callava's arrest, prompting Jackson's instant retaliation by deporting the officers (see AJ to the Spanish Officers, September 29, below).

To the Spanish Officers

[September 29, 1821]

PROCLAMATION,

By Major General Andrew Jackson, Governor of the Provinces of the Floridas, exercising the powers of the Captain General and of the Intendant of the Island of Cuba, over the said provinces, and of the Governors of said provinces respectively:

WHEREAS, by the seventh article of the treaty concluded between the United States and Spain on the 22nd day of February, 1819, and duly ratified, it was stipulated that the "*Officers* and troops of His Catholic Majesty in the territories hereby ceded to the United States, shall be *withdrawn,* and possession of the places occupied by them, shall be given within six months after the ratification of the treaty, or sooner if possible." And whereas, it has this day been made known to me, that the following officers of His Catholic Majesty, to wit: Marcos de Villiers,

Bernardo Prieto, Louis Gayarre, Civilo Lesassier, Arnaldo Guillimard, Carlos de Villiers, Pedro de Vegas and Mariano Latady,[1] and who according to the said seventh article, ought to have withdrawn from the said ceded territory with the troops of His Catholic Majesty, have without the permission of the existing authorities, contrary to the said seventh article, remained in this city and its vicinity; and whereas it has been made known to me, that the said officers acting in a distinct body, independent of, and disowning even a temporary allegiance to the government of the United States, as existing in the Floridas, have been engaged in stirring up disaffection thereto, and in sowing discontent in the minds of the good people of this said province; and whereas it appears that they are the authors of the following false, scandalous, and indecent publication:

"In speaking of Col. Callava's appearance before General Jackson, H. B. ought to have stated, that none of the interrogatories and highly offensive accusations of the General were faithfully interpreted to Col. Callava, any more than the replies of the latter to the former. It was, therefore, out of the power of our chief, not knowing what was said to him, to make the auditory understand how innocent he was of the foul charges with which his unsullied honor was endeavored to be stained.

Such, in sum, are the observations we had to make on the statement of H. B. and we hope that he and the public will be convinced that we acted from no principle of pusillanimity; that if on the one hand, *we shuddered at the violent proceedings exercised against our superior*—we knew also what was due to a government which is on the most friendly footing with our own. We are, &c.

THE SPANISH OFFICERS,
Resident in this place."[2]

And, whereas, the said publication is calculated to excite resistance to the existing government of the Floridas, and to disturb the harmony, peace, and good order of the same, as well as to weaken the allegiance enjoined by my proclamation, heretofore published,[3] and entirely incompatible with any privileges which could have been extended to the said officers, even if permission had been expressly given them to remain in the said province, and under existing circumstances, a gross abuse of the lenity and indulgence heretofore extended to them.

This is, therefore, to make known to the said officers to withdraw themselves, as they ought heretofore to have done, from the Floridas, agreeably to the said seventh article, on or before the third day of October next; after which day, if they, or any of them, shall be found within the Floridas, all officers, civil and military, are hereby required to arrest and secure them, so that they may be brought before me, to be dealt with according to law, for the contempt and disobedience of this, my proclamation.[4]

Given at Pensacola, this 29th day of September, one thousand eight hundred and twenty-one, and of the Independence of the United States, the forty-sixth.

By the Governor:
GEO. WALTON,
Secretary of West Florida.

ANDREW JACKSON
Governor of the Floridas,
&c. &c. &c

Printed broadside, Ms-Ar (8-1242). Published in many contemporary newspapers and in *ASP, Miscellaneous Documents,* 2:813–14.

1. Marcos de Villiers (1761–1840), a native of New Orleans and John Innerarity's father-in-law, was formerly commandant at Fort St. Marks. Prieto (José M. Callava's aide-de-camp), Luis Gayarré (b. c1778), Cirilo Josef Lesassier (b. c1781), Guillemard, Carlos de Villiers, de Vargas, and Latady were all career Spanish soldiers, serving variously in Louisiana and Florida.

2. Printed in the Pensacola *Floridian,* September 29. The article by "H.B." (probably Henry M. Brackenridge) had appeared in the New Orleans *Louisiana Advertiser,* August 28.

3. See Proclamation announcing the transfer of West Florida, July 17.

4. Before departing Pensacola, the Spanish officers issued a final protest (see Spanish officers to [Cary Nicholas and George Tunstall, October 3], Callava Papers, Ms-Ar). Marcos de Villiers and Guillemard returned in 1822 and were arrested, sparking congressional debate (see *TPUS,* 22:403).

Confusion about Jackson's ancestry and family relationships has plagued genealogists, historians, and editors alike. Once Jackson achieved fame as the Hero of New Orleans, people began claiming, with varying degrees of exactitude, relationship to him. Yet Jackson's own testimony is problematic: in 1819, he denied having any relation in the United States except by marriage, but in 1833 he acknowledged the kinship of Andrew Jackson Crawford (see AJ to William Williams, September 25, 1819, Jackson, *4:325–29, and to Crawford, May 1, 1833).*

In the letter below, one example of many, William McCully outlined his connection with Jackson, one that Jackson apparently gave some credence. McCully's detailed description of family ties, however, fails at critical points, naming Jackson's father as Hugh and his grandfather as Thomas (Jackson's father was Andrew, and his grandfather, Hugh). Whether McCully skipped a generation or whether his genealogy is for one of the other Andrew Jacksons that had gained some prominence in America (specifically in Virginia and Kentucky) is uncertain. Contemporary biographies by John H. Eaton, Henry Lee, and Amos Kendall are silent about relatives remaining in Ireland, and only Kendall mentions Jackson's relation to the Crawfords. In sum, confusion about his family began during Jackson's lifetime, was shared by the general, and remains to the present.

From William McCully

[September 29, 1821]

Honoured Sir

A Gentleman Called Jackson, came here (Parish of Dundonald formerly Kirkdonald, & County of Down) & informed us, that notwithstanding, the Highest Rank you have attained, in the Service of your Country you Gave him strict Orders, to find out your Name, and Relations, in this Parish.[1]

Here follows then, the exact Relationship Stands, with the Jacksons of this Parish, by several of the Oldest & Respectable Inhabitants of this Place—Thomas Jackson, your Grandfather, Inherited a Paternal Estate, of the great*[er]* Part of the Townland of Ballyregan, in Said Parish. Had three Sons, James, Who Succeeded his Father, in the Above-mentioned Estate, was a Clergyman, and Preached Forty years, in the Congregation of Ballibay in the County Monaghan Resigned his Office, came home & Died in the Mansion House Ballyregan—

2d. Hugh Another Son, who Emigrated to America, in his Fathers Life Time, (who, undoubtedly, was your Father,) and a third Died, when he had only obtained his Diploma, from the College for a Clergyman.

James Jackson, your Fathers Brother, Left at his Dicease, one Son, and Four Daughters. Thomas, his only Son, who was Doctor of Medicine, Lived, & Died, in Ballybay, aforesaid, Had only One Son (& no Daugters) Thompson Jackson Esq. of Dublin, unmarried, who now Inherits the Estate in Ballyregan Aforesaid, which may be worth three Hundred Pounds a year—Reverend James Jacksons Eldest Daughter, Martha, was married To Robert Bradford, near Ballybay, who had Issue, (I belive) a Son & Daughter. She was Married the Second Time, & where She and her Husband, now Resides, or what family they have, no one that I know any thing of, has any Knowledge.

2d. Elizabeth Jackson, Married to James McCully—Both Dead a Long Time ago—their Issue, one Son, and three Daughters, now Living—

3d. Mary Jackson, Married to David Dalzell, now a Widow—Their Issue, Living Five Sons and three Daughters—[2]

4th. Jane Jackson, Married to James Burnside, near Fivemiletown County Tyrone. Issue One Son and Two Daughters—

Hond. Sir

I hope this Account of your Relationship, to the Jacksons of Ballyregan, and Parish of Dundonald, in the County of Down, is Hereby Proved, to your Satisfaction, without any manner of Doubt Viz that Hugh Jackson, your Father, was Brother to the Revd. James Jackson, whose Children, and grandchildren, & I enumerated here—

The Bearer, Hereof, James McCully, is only Son of Elizabeth Jackson, second Daughter of the Late Revd. James Jackson, of Ballyregan, & James McCully, Both of whom were of Dundonald Parish, & as I mentioned Before, Long Dead; is a Sober young man, and unprovided for, as yet, & who Having a Spirit of Adventure, Determined, (upon the advice of your elevation To the highest Rank, in the Government of the *United States*) upon Visiting you Immediately, hoping you in your Goodness, & the Love you Seem to have Towards your Relations, & your forefathers Country, will be to him in that Land of Light & Liberty, in Place of his Deceased Parents, & for that Reason, hath Abandoned all his Sisters & Relatives, to throw himself under your Protection[3]

N.B. I, who, wrote this to your Honour, am his Uncle, by the Fathers Side, I knew your Grandfather, who Lived to a very Advanced age—With your Late Uncle, the Revd. James Jackson, I was Personally acquainted, Long Before my Brother was married to his Daughter—I with his Late Son Thomas Jackson, of Ballybay, D.M. I was more acquainted, & Particulary with every one of his Sisters, (the Bearers Aunts) so that I am Perfectly able, in Truth, to ascertain their forefathers and families—I am Sir with every Defference to your exalted Station your Obedient & Humble Servant

William McCully

County of Downe Viz William McCully of Ballymisca, Parish of Dundonald & County of Down, came before me, one of his Majestys Justices of the Peace, in and for said County, and made oath that the aforesaid Letter, to General Jackson of Pensacola, was Written By him & the Revd. James Jacksons family were Personally known to him, & their Marriages & Issues he thinks to be Perfectly Correct & True, as he hath Described, in the Above mentioned Letter.

William McCully

Sworn before me at Comber
This twentyninth September 1821
Geo Birch
Magistrate for the
County of Downe

ALS addressed to AJ in Pensacola and endorsed as received January 8, 1822, DLC (72). William McCully has not been further identified.

1. In her letter of April 6, 1819, Elizabeth Jackson also stated that AJ had made inquiries about relatives in Ireland.

2. Latitia Dalzell Chambers (1795–1852), who emigrated from Ireland with her husband in the the late teens or early twenties and stayed at the Hermitage for a time, may have been a daughter of David. According to family tradition, Jackson gave the couple a farm in Tennessee as a wedding present (see Rachel Jackson to Chambers, August 12, 1824, below; and Chambers to AJ, January 15, 1844).

3. James McCully's ship probably landed first at New Orleans in December, where he discovered that Jackson had returned to Tennessee. Jackson's New Orleans friends immedi-

ately apprised the governor of the young man's arrival (see Abner L. Duncan to AJ, and McCoy & Scallan to AJ, both December 12). McCully went on to Nashville, arriving in early January 1822, and married Jackson's niece, Mary Caffery Knox (b. c1788), widow of John Knox (d. c1815), on November 29 of that year. Subsequently the McCullys settled in Alabama.

To William Grafton Dulany Worthington

Pensacola October 1st. 1821

Sir,

I have the pleasure to acknowlege the receipt of your several letters of the 21st & 28th of August last with their enclosures, which are just at hand, and wishing to answer by the return mail which closes at 12 Oclock I have but a moment to glance over them—[1]

I am fully satisfied with your organisation of the Government—it surely would be viewed a great absurdity to see an American Government executed by Spanish Officers—It could only be intended, that the Spanish Officer might be continued, on his swearing allegiance to the U States, and under its authority, taking the oath of Office. I regret that Mr [John G.] Bird has not reached you, by him I wrote you on this subject. You have fully met my views in the organisation you have given to the Government of East Florida, and the appointments you have made[2]

I feel grateful for your attention to my sollicitude for Majr [Perrin] Willis, he has been left out of Service and is now cast upon the world for a support, when he least expected it—poor and pennyless he will be on as soon as he can travel there from the Bay of St Louis—[3]

The military authority is subordinate to the civil, and bound upon your requisition to furnish any guard or command that may be necessary to carry your orders into full execution, and I am certain from the character of the Officers who command there they will with pleasure yield to your requisition any Troops necessary for carrying into effect the due execution of the laws—I have sent to the commanding officer an order (a copy of which is enclosed) upon this subject—[4]

You, whilst acting as the executive of East Florida, have a right to occupy the Government house, and the military must be supplied with quarters in the Forts or Town, or other Public buildings—It is true I resigned the Government house here to the Officers, because I found it in decay, and that by yielding it to the Officers, and renting for myself, there would be a great saving to the Public.[5]

I cannot too highly approve the propriety of your sentiments expressed on that harmony that ought to exist between the civil and military authorities, and between the military and the citizens of the country, and I trust and hope, that the same harmony which exists here between all the authorities and the citizens may exist with you, should it not, you may rely on all my power and exertions, to restore it when it does not exist, and to remove every thing which can oppose a course as desireable and honorable to military men, as it should be welcome and agreeable to the civil officer and citizen—[6]

On the subject of Indian affairs, I have to refer you to my last letter of Septr 18th, with this remark, that peace must be obtained and maintained with the Indians, and it is best always to speak the plain truth to them, they cannot and must not expect to remain scattered over the Floridas[7]—The old *Red Sticks* must return to the upper Creeks or be collected where the real natives of Florida may be collected by the Government—I learn that the Perrymans on the Appilachicola are removing up to the old nation, with their families—McQueen's and [Josiah] Francis' clans must expect to go back to their old country, or be concentrated with the natives of Florida, already has a robbery been committed on the Appilachicola Bay by the Indians—another such offence, you may say to them, will cause a force to be marched, and punishment inflicted—they must remain peacable, and every suspicious white man you hear of in the nation, must be apprehended and sent out of the nation.[8]

The situation of my family will compel me to remove them to Tennesse, which will occasion my absence from this place awhile—you will continue to communicate to me here, as I shall direct your communications to follow me—The Govt. being now fully organised, no injury can arise from my short absence—whether I will have it in my power to visit St Augustine before the meeting of Congress, I cannot say—I am Sir, With great respect Yr Mo Obt Sert.

(signed) Andrew Jackson

LC in Andrew J. Donelson's hand, DLC (63). Published in *TPUS*, 22:225–26.

1. Only Worthington to AJ, August 28, has been found.

2. See AJ to Worthington, August 13. In his August 28 letter, Worthington detailed his implementation of Jackson's ordinances for St. Augustine and his replacement of St. Augustine's Spanish city council with one loyal to United States' authority. Bird (d. 1821), a Georgian appointed U.S. attorney for East Florida, had been mistakenly directed to Pensacola and did not reach St. Augustine until August 29; he died of yellow fever on December 15.

3. See AJ to Worthington, July 26. Worthington had named Willis (d. 1822), former assistant adjutant general, as clerk of the St. John's County Court.

4. See AJ to [Abram Eustis], October 1.

5. For further discussion of the rental of a house in Pensacola, see above, Rachel Jackson to Elizabeth Kingsley, July 23.

6. See Worthington to AJ, August 28. The tension between civilian and military authorities in St. Augustine regarding the occupancy of public buildings continued throughout the fall.

7. See AJ to Worthington, September 18; see also, AJ to John C. Calhoun, September 17.

8. Francis or Hillis Hadjo, war chief of the Alabama or Holy Ground tribe and a leader of the hostile Creeks during the Creek War, had been executed by Jackson in April 1818 during the Seminole campaign. From September 18 to 20, Jackson had met in Pensacola with three Florida Indian chiefs, John Blount, Neamathla, and the Mulatto King, discussing their tribes' future (see Report on talk with Florida Indians, [September 18–20], and AJ to Calhoun, September 20; see also, AJ to William McIntosh, September 19). The Perrymans were a clan of friendly, mixed-blood Creeks.

To James Monroe

Pensacola October 5th. 1821.

Sir,

Having organised the Government of the Floridas, and it being now in full operation, I have determined to take a little respite from the laborious duties with which I have been surrounded, and leave the charge of the Floridas to the Secretaries appointed for the same—This becomes necessary, as Mrs Jackson is anxious to return home, and the situation of her health requires that she should pass through the newly settled country before the inclement weather sets in—She and my family will leave this on the 7th, and I shall accompany or overtake them with a view to return, should it become necessary for the good order of society here before the meeting of the next Congress.[1]

From the report of Mr Worthington, charged with the Government of East Florida, I have but little doubt that the Govt. of E. Florida will be well and satisfactorily administered.[2]

I should have visitted that section of country, but for the want of transportation, there being no public vessel put under my orders, and a private vessel could not be obtained for charter.

I leave Col Walton in charge of West Florida and all its dependencies, particularly instructed, and from his character and talents, I am confident that the Government will be satisfactorily administered during my absence[3]—Every thing now is progressing with regularity and harmony, and I am happy at so seasonable a time to be able to embrace that relaxation which my enfeebled constitution requires—my labours have indeed been great, and the near approach of Congress fills me with pleasure, as I look to that period when I can resign with propriety, and by Doctr Bronough you will receive my resignation of the Commissions of Governor of the Floridas &c &c—I give you this early information, that you may in the meantime select a fit person to fill this important station—It will require a man of energy to rule these provinces at this time, and Congress ought to provide an energetic code of law for its Government, that may as far as possible dispense with all Spanish customs, and at as early a day as possible, Americanise the Floridas.[4]

I had determined to be silent as to the man whose energy and talents would fit him for this important station; but justice to one, whom I think a much injured man, whose merits as a military man were not inferior to any of his grade, and who by a decision of a Court martial, founded on Testimony, which the Government at this time can duly appreciate, has been degraded and neglected, and if I may be permitted to use the expression, justice requires that he should again be noticed by his government, and placed in some Office by which he and his rising family may be released from the obloquy which the sentence of the court has placed upon them. I have but little doubt, if the same court had the subject now under consideration, and supported by the same evidence, it would pronounce a sentence of acquittal—for these reasons, added to my high opinion of his military merit and his fitness for this office, and the attachment of the people here to him, I bring him to the view of the Government, as a proper person for this appointment—I mean Col Wm King late of the 4 Regt U. S. Infy—A man whose service, whilst under my command, I hold in fresh recollection, and whom I believe innocent of any military offence worthy of the degradation awarded him; and on this belief, for justice and his familie's sake, I now name him, when the opportunity is good, for the Government to restore him to that confidence and standing in society which he is entitled to.[5]

I leave here, with the determination of returning, should Col Walton inform me that such a step may be necessary: But it will be necessary, if possible, to go with my family to Nashville—When I left there, it was on a short notice, and my order positive—I left all my military papers, and had a right to believe that all my military—Public accounts were fully closed—Since reaching this Territory, I am informed that my QuarterM—— account for quarters and fuel whilst in the city of Washington, has been suspended. As I am determined to have these accounts investigated and fully closed by Doctr Bronough it becomes necessary that I should have my papers, that this account may be examined, stated, and forwarded by him[6]—In the mean time, I assure you that nothing relating to my private concerns, shall prevent my return hither should my presence become necessary—Trusting to your goodness to have a successor appointed to relieve me, as soon after the meeting of Congress as your convenience will permit—

Ms J. joins me in a tender of our respects to Ms Monroe & your family, and our best wishes for your health and happiness; And believe me, with sincere respect Yr. Mo Obt sert.

Andrew Jackson

LS in Andrew J. Donelson's hand, NHi (8-1272); Photocopy of LS and LC, DLC (72, 63). Published in Bassett, 3:122–24.

1. Jackson and his suite left Pensacola on October 8.

2. See William G. D. Worthington to AJ, August 28, and above, AJ to Worthington, October 1.

3. See AJ to George Walton, October [5].

4. See AJ to Monroe, November 14. James C. Bronaugh left for Washington from Nashville on November 15.

5. King (d. 1826), whom Jackson had left in command of American forces at Pensacola in 1818, had been court-martialed and convicted in 1819 for shooting deserters and suspended from the army for five years. On June 1, 1820, King had petitioned Monroe for reinstatement in the army but was refused, and on June 1, 1821, he was discharged. Monroe appointed William P. Duval governor of Florida in April 1822. For efforts to promote King's appointment to the post, see Richard K. Call to AJ, October 30; King to AJ, November 23; and AJ to Monroe, November 30.

6. See William Lee to AJ, August 11. On January 12, 1822, Lee informed Jackson that his account had been closed.

The following anonymous letter, first sent to Pensacola, did not reach Jackson until January 6, 1822. When received, it reinforced the General's suspicions about James Monroe's attitude and intentions, pushing him to the verge of an outright break with the president. Monroe's appointments in Florida had disappointed and irritated, if not bewildered, Jackson (see above, AJ to James C. Bronaugh, June 9; and AJ to John Q. Adams, November 13). The letter from "Friend" seemed to supply the missing motive for the president's otherwise inexplicable behavior—jealousy of Jackson's popularity—and suggested an alliance between Monroe and Jackson's enemy, William H. Crawford. Those charges, together with a probable congressional inquiry into the imprisonment of José M. Callava and the dispute with Eligius Fromentin, led Jackson to reconsider his resignation of the governorship (see AJ to Monroe, January 22, 1822). While Jackson regularly saw the conspiring hand of William H. Crawford behind every questioning of his actions, the letter from "Friend" briefly threatened to broaden the general's enemy list to include the president.

From "Friend"

Augusta Geoa. Oct. 29. 1821

It is the curse of our nature that the noble minded frank, and confiding Man should be continually the victim of the designing artful and unprincipled: such in common with other great men has been the fate of Andrew Jackson. The individual who writes you this has motives of no ordinary character to influence him, some are public and some are private; all of them are of elevated character worthy not only of the writer but of him to whom he addresses himself.

My situation during the last winter permitted me to see a part and to hear more of the doings at Washington City in which you were deeply interested. I have long known the President of the U. States, and understood his character—of the latter few have ever formed a just estimate—from nature a dull and stupid man, his mind is incapable of any activity unless where his own immediate interest is in question—cold & selfish, he is governed by no motive, influenced by no Obligation save the motive of personal advantage, and the obligation to take care of himself—besides this he is a man of unbounded pride; <under the> with an exterior of plainness and republican simplicity, he is under the dominion of a pride so inordinate, that nothing short of universal homage can satisfy, and the slightest deduction from which is never forgiven Upon this pride you inflicted a wound, which however innocently done will never be forgiven—You did so when you consented to attend him in his journey through part of his Southern & Western Tour—In that journey Mr. Presidt. intended to play the great man; but the people, stupid as they are said to be by those who calumniate them; very readily distinguished between true greatness, and mere Official rank, and Genl. Jackson therefore, attracted all eyes and secured all respect & Affection, instead of Mr. Monroe doing so[1]—This preference by the people for you was felt—deeply felt, and is not to be forgotten—hence the intrigue to get you from the Army, hence the submissiveness to a dictation from Genl. Brown, Genl. Scott & Mr. Crawford—hence that all your measures are traversed, your recommendations neglected and odium attempted to be excited against you. The President to revenge himself on you for your popularity, has united himself with the bitterest of your enemies, and if you are not crushed it must be because you are strongest. When you were appointed Governor of florida, they told your friends it was to Compliment you—amongst themselves they said it was *to get rid of you*—at the head of the Army you were still formidable—and in a Contest for that station, they felt that their favorite Brown must give way; besides said they as a Govr. of a Territory—a mere colonial prefect without voice or influence in the Government of the Union he will soon be forgotten; or in that unsettled Country he may do some act of violence or irregularity for which we can put him down; they hope that time has now arrived and the War dogs are whetting their fangs, and ready to spring upon their victim when the halloo is given.[2]

At Washington Crawford is against you & Crawford rules the Cabinet. Mr. Monroe secretly abets him, and the Virginia influence of Crawford, Scott, Monroe &ca is all steadily marshalled in opposition to you. Secretary Adams is a poor timid Yankee, who can make no head against a Man of Crawford's energy even if he would attempt it—but the cool and Catching cunning of a Northern Climate, is dominant in his character, and he looks therefore only to himself—and will be sacraficed—he has too little force of Character and too little address to cope with such adversaries as are now arrayed against him, so Crawford is the next Presidt. unless some other Man than Adams is taken up. You must go back to Tennessee, and rouse the Western Country—[George Michael] Troup must not succeed here—if he does Crawford has Georgia, S. Carolina will follow her in such an event and Crawford may succeed.[3]

I shall write you again as I find it advisable to do so—I could now say more, but you may have other Correspondents who will supply my deficiency—In due season you shall know me: it is not for want of confidence in you that I withhold my name; but because the letter may miscarry, and injury be done me not only at Washington thereby, but my means of serving you lessened <but> by cutting me off from information which I might obtain for your benefit.

We have stood side by side in politics, and in arms, and when you know me as you shall do hereafter, you will recognise in me an old and tried

Friend.

ALS and LC in AJ's hand, DLC (72, 63); Copy, DLC (8-1311). The ALS was addressed to AJ in Pensacola and has AJ's endorsement: "recd. on sunday the 6th of January 1822 A.J." The copy, which AJ sent to Monroe, March 19, 1822 (below), contains AJ's ANS regarding receipt and James Monroe's AN: "an anonymous letter from Augusta, Georgia—abusing me." The "Friend" has not been identified. Initially, Jackson suspected the author was a military officer from Virginia, but he later concluded that the letter had been part of William H. Crawford's strategy to drive a wedge between him and the president (see AJ to James C. Bronaugh, January 10, and AJ to James Gadsden, May 2, both 1822, both below).

1. Commencing March 30, 1819, Monroe had undertaken a four-month tour ostensibly to inspect military posts in the South and West. Jackson had accompanied him on a portion of the trip through Tennessee and Kentucky in June and July.

2. Monroe had warned Jackson specifically that his enemies "will watch your mov'ments, hoping to find some inadvertent circumstance, to turn against you. Be therefore on your guard" (see Monroe to AJ, May 23).

3. Troup (1780–1856; Princeton 1797), a Crawford ally and former U.S. senator, lost Georgia's gubernatorial elections to John Clark in 1819 and 1821 but was elected in 1823.

Returning overland to Tennessee, Jackson and party reached the Hermitage on November 4. Fulfilling the promise he had made to himself and his friends, he shortly tendered his resignation of the Florida governorship and on November 15 sent James C. Bronaugh to Washington with it and Jackson's accounts (see AJ to James Monroe, November 13 and 14). Knowing full well that his actions toward José M. Callava and Eligius Fromentin had created a storm of controversy and the likelihood of another congressional inquiry (Fromentin had almost immediately dispatched his version of the story to the administration and the press), Jackson used Bronaugh as his political agent and advisor, and Bronaugh spent much of his time in Washington defending the soon-to-be ex-governor and reporting back to Nashville what he heard and saw.

To Richard Keith Call

Hermitage Novbr. 15th. 1821

Dear Call

I had the pleasure last evening of receiving your two letters of the 14th. ult, nothing can afford Mrs. Jackson and myself more pleasure than in hearing from you often, and particularly that you are well, and doing well.[1] Your gratitude expressed of my friendship towards you, shews the godlike virtue of a heart susceptable of friendship—believe me when I first met with you in the field, your youthfull appearance, your manly and soldier like deportment, attracted my attention—and when mutiny and desertion prevaded my camp, when situated in the howling wilderness surrounded with the savage yell, it was your soldier like and honourable conduct when deserted by your company at this trying moment that drew my particular attention to you, to see a gallant youth of Eighteen abandoned by his captain and company all retiring from the field of Honour, and you left alone, determined to die, rather than tarnish your military fame, by retiring from the post of danger in disgrace. From that moment my opinion was formed of you and I cherished your youthfull merit for your countries good, and aided in promoting your rank as your merit increased, and your Talents were disclosed to me—I regret our seperation but I still more regret, that injustice and inatention of the executive in not having provided for you agreable to his promise and my expectation[2]—But my Dear Call I have been Tossed upon the waves of fortune from youthood, I have experienced prosperity & adversity—It was this that gave me a knowledge of human nature, it was this that <coerced> forced into action, all the energies of my mind, and ultimately caused me to progress through life as I have done—hence this neglect of the goverment may be of service to you, it has & will bring forth, from necessity, the best energies of your mind, & with your application and industry, you will, nay, you must succeed. Permit me to say to you that long experience has made me well acquainted with human nature. It is well to study it as you progress through life—you will find many, professedly, friends, who by, & from their openness of conduct, and specious profession, the inexperienced youth, at once places the utmost reliance—when in many Instances these professions are made with a view to obtain your confidence that it may be betrayed—To guard against such impositions there is but one safe rule—have apparent confidence in all, but never make a confident<ial> of any untill you have proven him worthy of it—and altho you may have good cause to know & believe that great confidence may be placed in him, never, untill you have well tried him, confide to Any a secrete that might be injurious to you if Publickly Known. This I have found a safe rule & have practised upon it.

I met miss mary [Letitia Kirkman], on the road between Mr Simintons and Magees—in company with her *[two?]* uncles & little brother, she is on her way to orleans and will sail from thence to Philadelphia with her uncle; she will rest at the Natchez untill her uncle passes to the Tash and eranges his business on his farm there—On my arival at Judge Overtons, I wrote you which I hope you will receive, since which I have seen major Eaton, who informs me, he has had a long conversation with Miss Mary, that she still bears you in mind as usual—and from which I have no doubt were you now to see her, she would marry—Doctor [Boyd] McNairy has written you as I am Told, his Ideas are certainly correct—you & Miss Mary ought to fo*[r]*get each other, forever, or at once marry your minds must ever be on the torture, the conduct of her mother to her as stated, has been of the most cruel kind—and if your and her ultimate object is to marry—the sooner the better—you have friends who will aid you, in this number include me, and with your own exertions, you have nothing to fear as to a support.[3]

I am happy to hear that all is tranquil in Pensacola—Callava has sailed from Charleston for Cuba—the Eastern climate was too cold for his sickly constitution, and it appears he has retired to Cuba for his health. So Soon as Judge Fromentine is unmasked before the nation, I think he will follow—it is this apostate Priest, that has been circulating secretly these mutulated details of the circumstances; Having enclosed to the president all the documents through the Secratary of State, they will I hope be in that way laid before congress, and the nation—Should it not appear in this way I will under my own name, should Fromentine be nominated to the Senate, bring it before the nation, and fairly shew how the rights of the people have been triffled with by the appointment of an apostate Priest, to execute the laws, and moralise the people[4]—Mrs. Jackson Joins me in prayers for your happiness & wellfare. Easter is with me and well, Doctor Brunaugh has this morning set out for Washington city Mr Saml Overton has Just left me, & Lt Donelson Just gone on a vissit to his mothers, all these Gentlemen request to be affectionately presented to you—Have the goodness to present Mr[s.] J. & myself to Capt [Thomas] Shields & family, Mr [John] Garnier & family, Mr [William] Davidson & family if still with you, to Mr [William Steuben] Smith and Lady to Colo Brook & Lady to Lt [William W.] Lear and his Lady to Mr & Mrs. Austin, to all our French *[&]* Spanish friends.[5]

Mrs. Jackson begs me to remind you of our furniture, to have it forwarded to orleans as soon as possible with instructions to Capt [James] Scallen to have it forwarded to Nashville by the first Steam Boat—our place looks like it had been deserted for a Season, But we have a cheerfull fire for our friends, and a prospect of living at it *[for the balance]* of our lives.[6] I have sent on my resignation by Doctor Brunaugh—I recd. from Mr Monroe last night via Pensacola a letter in which he again presses me to continue as Governor, this I will not do—he intimates that [John] Haywood may be the Federal Judge[7]—as you know I have no thought of continuing, but if I had I should be fearfull of accepting before I saw the Judge to whom I was to be associated least another apostate priest should be found—These perjured immorral Monsters in Society I allways did abhor, they never have or will be my associates—I will be happy to hear from you often—Present us to Cary Nicholas & [George Brook] Tunstall—To all the officers of the army, and say to Capt [Sanders] Donoho that his young widow is in waiting for him, on this subject I will write him the first Leisure moment[8] accept assurances of my friendship & Esteem

Andrew Jackson

ALS, DLC (31). Published in Bassett, 3:129–31.

1. See Call to AJ, October 14.

2. For Jackson's commendation of Call's bravery during the Creek campaign, see AJ to John Armstrong, June 27, 1814 (*Jackson,* 3:83–84), and for Jackson's repeated attempts to have Call appointed to a Florida post, see above, AJ to James C. Bronaugh, June 9; and AJ to Call, October 10. Call had declined Jackson's most recent offer of a recommendation, preferring to practice law in Florida and noting: "*The Husbands of the Sisters of great mens wives, The Sons of those who signed the declaration of Independence, with the Pimps and Panders of Court* are welcome to divide the loavs and fishes of the Government," which referred to Eligius Fromentin and George Walton, respectively (see Call to AJ, October 14).

3. See AJ to Call, November 4. Kirkman (c1801–36), the daughter of Thomas (c1779–1826) and Ellen Jackson Kirkman (1774–1850), married Call on July 15, 1824, at the

Hermitage. Mary L. Kirkman was probably travelling with her uncles James and Washington Jackson (1784–1865), the latter a Philadelphia merchant. Washington Jackson owned a Louisiana plantation in the general vicinity of Bayou Teche, which runs through St. Landry, St. Martin, Iberia, and St. Mary parishes, approximately thirty-five miles west of the Mississippi River. It is unknown which of Kirkman's younger brothers, Hugh, John, or Alexander, accompanied her. McNairy (1785–1859; Pennsylvania 1805), a Nashville physician and brother of Judge John McNairy, later became Jackson's bitter political enemy; McNairy's letter to Call has not been found. Ellen J. Kirkman opposed her daughter's marriage to Call (see AJ to Kirkman, December 16, and to Call, cDecember 16, both 1820, in *Jackson,* 4:406–409). Jackson probably referred to John Simonton (c1772?–1840), a Lawrence County, Tennessee, resident, who was supervisor of a portion of the military road, and Jacob Magee, of Lauderdale County, Alabama.

4. See AJ to John Q. Adams, November 13. For Fromentin's communications regarding the controversy with Jackson, see Fromentin to Adams, August 26, 28, September 6–8, 21, October 28, in *ASP, Miscellaneous Documents,* 2:834–41, 843–48; see also Washington *National Intelligencer,* October 16. Initially reluctant, James Monroe eventually accepted Adams's counsel and submitted the Jackson-Fromentin correspondence to Congress (see Bronaugh to AJ, January 7, 1822, below). Similarly, Adams convinced Monroe not to continue Fromentin in the federal judgeship, once Fromentin's recess appointment expired.

5. Thomas Shields (c1782–1827), formerly a navy purser stationed at New Orleans, had relocated to Pensacola. Garnier, former partner of the late Stockley D. Hutchings, was a merchant and auctioneer at Pensacola and justice of the peace for Escambia County. Davison, a merchant in Pensacola in 1821, became sheriff of Escambia County in 1822. Smith (1787–1850), John Q. Adams's nephew and formerly secretary of legation during his uncle's tenure as minister to Russia, was naval officer at Pensacola; in 1813 he had married Catherine Marie Johnson (d. 1869), sister of Adams's wife, Louisa Catherine (1775–1852). George M. Brooke married Lucy Thomas (c1805–39) of Duxbury, Massachusetts, in 1819. Lear (d. 1846), from Maryland, was a career army officer and at the time assigned to the 4th Infantry stationed in Pensacola. He died from wounds received at Monterey, Mexico. Jackson probably referred to John Austin, a Blakely, Alabama, merchant. The wives of Lear and Austin have not been identified.

6. Scallan (d. 1832), a native of Virginia, had resigned from the army in January 1821, relocating to New Orleans where he formed for a time the merchant and auction firm of McCoy & Scallan. The Jacksons' furniture, shipped from Pensacola in November, arrived at Nashville in January (see Call to AJ, November 19; and Joseph & Robert Woods to AJ, January 19 and 31, 1822).

7. See AJ to Monroe, November 13, and Monroe to AJ, September 16. Haywood (1762–1826), a member of Tennessee's supreme court, was preparing two volumes on the state's history, *The Natural and Aboriginal History of Tennessee* (Nashville, 1823) and *The Civil and Political History of Tennessee* (Knoxville, 1823).

8. Jackson's letter to Donoho has not been found, nor has Donoho's "young widow" been identified. Tunstall (1793–1842), a native of Pittsylvania County, Virginia, was a former publisher of the *Nashville Whig,* 1817–21. He and Cary Nicholas published the Pensacola *Floridian* until June 15, 1822, when Tunstall resigned and moved to Baldwin County, Alabama. Donoho (d. 1826), a North Carolina native, was with the 4th Infantry.

From James Craine Bronaugh

Washington 2nd. Decemr. 1821.

My Dr. Sir,

I arrived here three days since, and had a much more pleasant journey than I could have anticipated at this season of the year—the roads were good & the weather continued fine.

Every thing appears in confusion here—nearly all the Members have arrived and they are continually moving from House to House conversing about the election of *Speaker,* which appears to be the only thing that at present occupies their attention—[John W.] Taylor, I think stands no chance of being re-elected—several are spoken of, but I think it probable that either Hugh Nelson or [Caesar Augustus] Rodney will be elected.[1]

Immediately after my arrival I called at the Presidents but found him engaged with his Cabinet—your letters I delivered to his Secy. and this morng he sent for me He commenced his conversation by expressing his regret at your determination to retire from the Government of the Floridas, and then read to me that part of his Message in relation to the occurrences there, which is in complete approbation of the course pursued by you—regrets the part in relation to Fromentin, enumerates the powers with which you were clothed, shews that he had no authority to issue the Writ of Habius Corpus, but concludes with the opinion that he was actuated by no improper motive—On this part he appeared to entertain some doubt and stated that his correspondence with you was most unaccountable and that he would give it a more attentive perusal before he gave the finishing stroke to his Message He said that if he spoke of him in any other way it would appear like a wish on his part to crush him and might have an unhappy effect. I gave him my opinion very candidly that he had acted corruptly and that I had no doubt when all the circumstances should be made public that it would be the general opinion. I am to have another conversation with him previous to his communicating his Message to congress.[2]

To Mr. Adams I delivered your letters and accounts he enquired after your health in the most friendly manner and expressed his entire approbation of the whole of your conduct—said that some persons who were not acquainted with the extent of your powers had felt disposed to censure you for resisting the authority of the Judge, but that when the facts were known that nothing could be made out of it. The accounts he informed me he would look over the first leisure moment and then turn them over to the proper office.[3]

The evening I arrived, I spent with Mr. Calhoun who enquired very particularly after you, and enquired whether you had recd. letters from him shortly before my leaving you & requested me to present his respects to you & say that he had written three letters.[4] He thinks that the Callava business is now so well understood that it will not be brought before Congress, but in this I differ with him, as I have no doubt some one will be found who to bring himself into notice and justify his malignant feelings towards you, will move the subject. The Newspapers in this section of the country are now perfectly silent on the subject and I have heard no one mention the subject except in approbation—I will write again tomorrow[5]—please present my respects to Mrs. Jackson and Lt. Donelson and believe me with sincere regard Yr. friend &c.

J. C. Bronaugh

ALS, DLC (72).

1. Neither New York's Taylor (1784–1854; Union 1813), a leader of the antislavery forces during the Missouri Compromise debate, nor Virginia's Nelson (1768–1836; William and Mary 1780), nor Delaware's Rodney (1772–1824; Pennsylvania 1789) was elected. On December 4, after twelve ballots, Philip Pendleton Barbour (1783–1841) of Virginia, a William H. Crawford partisan, was elected Speaker.

2. See AJ to James Monroe, November 13 and 14. In 1820, George Hay (1765–1830), Monroe's son-in-law, had become the president's private secretary. For Monroe's fifth annual message to Congress, submitted December 5, see *Annals of Congress,* 17th Cong., 1st sess., pp. 11–21.

3. See AJ to John Q. Adams, November 13 and 14. Adams was referring to the disagreement within the administration over Jackson's powers and actions as governor. Attorney General William Wirt had written that Jackson "knows no law except the law of force; and his want of information, combined with his violence, is perpetually plunging him & his friends into difficulties, from which it is not easy to escape without some loss of lustre. On the present occasion, if even his great popularity saves him from general execration, it will be because one of the sufferers is a Spanish tool & the other a French priest" (see Wirt to Monroe, October 11, in *TPUS,* 22:256). See also, above, AJ to Eligius Fromentin, September 3.

4. See John C. Calhoun to AJ, October 19, 28, and November 16.

5. Probably Bronaugh to AJ, [cDecember 4].

James C. Bronaugh, in Washington obstensibly to close out Jackson's accounts with the government, and Adjutant General James Gadsden were Jackson's chief sources of information about political infighting in the newly assembled Seventeenth Congress, maneuvering directly related to the presidential succession some three years hence. Newspapers were full of comment about the next election, and the allies of William H. Crawford, the leading contender, took aim at his prospective competitors, who included John C. Calhoun, John Q. Adams, Henry Clay (1777–1852), New York Governor DeWitt Clinton (1769–1828), Vice-President Daniel D. Tompkins (1774–1825; Columbia 1795), and Secretary of the Navy Smith Thompson (1768–1843; Princeton 1788).

Although Jackson's name was absent from most lists of likely successors to James Monroe, the congressional inquiry into Jackson's actions as governor of Florida, moved on December 11, made him, perhaps, the most directly targeted rival. But Crawford's other opponents also came under fire. The controversy over the nominations of James Gadsden and Nathan Towson to their respective army posts challenged Calhoun's administration of the war department as did the revelation of his chief clerk's interest in government contracts for the construction of Fortress Monroe at Rip Rap Shoals (see Bronaugh to AJ, February 8, Gadsden to AJ, April 10, AJ to Gadsden, May 2, and AJ to Richard K. Call, June 29, all 1822, all below). Adams's former colleague from the Treaty of Ghent negotiations, Jonathan Russell, attempted to undercut the secretary of state by portraying him as anti-western (see AJ to Andrew J. Donelson, June 28, 1822, below). For reasons unknown, Clay remained unscathed.

But Crawford's adversaries were not idle. Acknowledging his control of the congressional caucus, the traditional nominating forum, advocates of the other presidential aspirants turned to different methods for placing a candidate before the people. On December 18, a caucus of the South Carolina legislature nominated their congressman William Lowndes (1782–1822) for the presidency, and ten days later Calhoun, answering the request of his supporters in Congress, formally entered the contest. As the Washington National Intelligencer *and the* Washington Gazette *became increasingly pro-Crawford, former superintendant of Indian trade Thomas L. McKenney began in August 1822 a new journal, the* Washington Republican and Congressional Examiner, *to trumpet Calhoun's candidacy.*

Nor were the anti-Crawford forces in Congress at rest. In his December 30 letter to Jackson, below, Bronaugh, evidently privy to the plans of Ninian Edwards's son-in-law, Illinois representative Daniel Pope Cook (1794–1827), revealed the prospective investigation into Crawford's appointment of Jesse Burgess Thomas (1777–1853), Illinois senator and rival of Edwards, to inspect federal land offices in the West, which constituted a possible violation of the constitutional provision barring congressmen from holding other federal positions. What began as a potentially embarrassing conflict of interest for Thomas, ultimately led to the sensational "A.B." controversy of 1823–24, calling into question Crawford's competence and honesty in the administration of government funds, and threatening his presidential candidacy.

To James Gadsden

Hermitage Decbr 6th. 1821

Dr. Gadsden

Your congratulatory letter of the 20th ult is Just to hand, and from my own fire side I have the pleasure to respond to it—[1]

I had confidence in the good sense of the honest part of the community, that my proceedings in the case of Callava (which has given so much scope for invective against <my> me, by these restless & unprincipled Editors) would be fully approved by the nation as soon as it was fully disclosed to the public—as I before have stated to you, I proceeded in the case aluded to, with a firm but cautious step—the more I review the case the better I am pleased with myself—and altho I am free to admit, that the approbation of the nation would be gratifying to me, yet would I not change the proceedings if to be acted over again to obtain it. My conscience on this subject is perfectly at rest—I have not seen the advocate of N. Y. But it is the most ludicrous Idea immaginable that he insinuates & intimates—I have never seen Govr. [DeWitt] Clinton—I have never recd but two introductory letters from him, he has never wrote me upon any subject unless that of introducing his friends to me—nor have I ever wrote him but in return and on the subject of his friend, so introduced, and as my recollection at present serves me not more than twice—and then only acknowledging the receipt of his letters, and informing him that there were no offices within my gift that I could bestow *upon* his friend[2]—never did Mr Clinton in his life intimate to me the subject of the presidential election, either by writing, or by verbal communication—nor never has it been heard from my lips that I would support him as such—Therefore on this score Mr Crawford & his friends may have no fear—nor need they expect any other than Mr Adams to be supported in this state unless some Southern candidate should arise—and I am certain no man in the south could concentrate the votes of the south and west but Mr Calhoun—and you are at liberty to say in my name both to my friends and enemies—that I will as far as my influence extends support Mr Adams unless Mr Calhoun should be brought forward—and that I have no doubt but Mr Adams will out pole Mr Crawford in the south and west—should these two run alone—I think highly of Mr Clintons talents and of his great exertions to promote the interest of his state—but his popularity from some cause has greatly declined in the west and if he was to offer could not be elected—you know my private opinion of Mr Adams Talents, virtue, and integrity—and I am free to declare that I have never changed this opinion of Mr Adams since <that opinion> it was first formed, I think him a man of the first rate mind of any in america as a civilian and scholar—and I have never doubted of his attachment to our republican Goverment—you may therefore inform the advocate or his friends that (*as usual*) he is again wrong in his discoveries—and that I never have nor never will form a combination with any man or set of men, to carry any Thing into effect—that I have an opinion of my own on all subjects, and when that opinion is formed I persue it, *publickly,* regardless of who goes with me—that in all things as far as I have control I please myself by doing that which I believe to be right, and this rule I will strictly follow in my choce for the next President[3]—and my dear sir I feel greatly indebted to you for your friendly, defence of my reputation—That man is not on earth, that can with truth say I ever was engaged in a political combination of any kind—or for any purpose—Therefore the advocate and his friends has stated what is not true—present me to Brunaugh & all friends, Mrs. J Joins me in good wishes

Andrew Jackson

P. S. as to Wm H Crawford you know my opinion I would support the Devil first—

ALS draft, DLC (31). Published in Bassett, 3:139–41.

1. See Gadsden to AJ, November 20.

2. Gadsden's letter reported the rumor from the New York *National Advocate* of a secret correspondence between Jackson and DeWitt Clinton to support the latter's presidential aspirations. Only two letters between Jackson and Clinton—both Clinton to AJ, March 1, 1819, and October 2, 1821—have been found. The rumors of a Jackson-Clinton alliance derived from Clinton's opposition to William H. Crawford and from Jackson's toast to the New York governor on February 21, 1819.

3. Mordecai Manuel Noah (1785–1851) edited the anti-Clinton New York *National Advocate*. Later, as editor of the *Morning Courier and New York Enquirer*, Noah supported Jackson's first presidential administration.

When Jackson left Nashville for Pensacola in April, Jackson *v.* Erwin, *his lawsuit over title to lands along Tennessee's Duck River, was entering its seventh year, with no end in sight (for the origins and development of the lawsuit, see* Jackson, *2:62–63, 296–97; 4:315–18). To safeguard his interests and those of his partners, James Jackson and Jenkin Whiteside, Jackson had named Patrick H. Darby to superintend the case. The lands at issue were some 85,000 acres formerly held by David Allison (d. 1798), a North Carolina speculator with extensive land holdings throughout Tennessee, who had died in a Philadelphia debtor's prison. John Overton, like Jackson, had been Allison's creditor, and Allison's bankruptcy and death had left Overton without payment (see* Jackson, *1:104–106, 174–75, 183–84). In April 1800, Overton successfully sued Allison's heirs in the Sumner County Court, and judgment was executed in October 1800 at a sheriff's sale of land once sold by Jackson to Allison; Overton purchased fourteen tracts, one along the Duck River, one along the North Fork of the Deer River, and twelve in the northwestern portion of Tennessee, near the Obion River. Subsequently, Overton learned that Allison had never procured the deeds of conveyance from Jackson, so that Overton's title to the lands was questionable. In August 1808, Overton brought suit in the Mero District Court against Jackson and Allison's heirs for the tracts. Apparently, Jackson did not contest the suit: the bill of complaint was taken as confessed; the case was transferred to the Tennessee Supreme Court of Errors and Appeals; and the final decree, given during the July 1812 term, awarded Overton the fourteen tracts totaling 6,260 acres (see* John Overton *v.* AJ and heirs of David Allison, *July 1812; see also, Patrick H. Darby to AJ, July 4). Overton let the matter rest from 1812 until early December 1821. It is unclear what prompted him to announce his dissatisfaction at this time. As Overton profoundly distrusted Darby, perhaps Darby's involvement with the lawsuit against Andrew Erwin and his consequent research into the Allison land holdings in Tennessee may account for Overton's action. Whatever the cause, Overton's displeasure prompted a hurried effort on Jackson's part to assuage his old friend, take care of the interests of his partners, and keep his lawsuit with Erwin alive.*

To John Overton

Hermitage Decbr 9th. 1821

Dr. Sir

your note of the 5th. Instant is now before me, accompanyed with a copy of your Bill in Chancery vs me and the heirs of Davidson Allison Deceased, and a copy of the Decree there on in the year 1812—[1]

Untill the recpt of your note I had no recollection of your bill in Equity and the decree thereon, I did recollect of your having a suit against the heirs of David Allison in Sumner, and of applying to me for information of the lands I had Sold and Convayed to him the Said David in his life time—and at that time of giving you either the titles made to me, of the lands sold by me to David Allison or a memorandom of various tracts that I had sold to him and I have but little doubt, indeed I have none but those enumerated by you in your bill were amonghst the Number for I have such confidence in your statement, that I am convinced you would make none that were not true—at that time I did not believe there was any course I could pursue to secure my own Debt due from David Allison, and was willing to give you any information I possessed that might enable you to Secure yours—in short sir I had lost all hope of ever recovering any thing from the Estate of David Allison in consequence of the large sum he owed me, I thought him completely insolvant, and viewed my debt as lost—and had it not have been from the unfortunate situation I became placed in by the purchase of five thousand acres under the decree Norton Prior vs the heirs of David Allison I never should have made the attempt, by the situation of the honest Purchasers under me, rendered the attempt Just & necessary for their & my own Security[2]—To enable me to prosecute this suit & meet the payment of the morgage money an article was entered into between James Jackson Jenkins Whiteside & myself—afterwards Mr Whitesides released to me his interest, so far as the morgaged property of David Allison on Duck river extended holding his interest in the ballance.[3] The suit having been much neglected, and to insure the attention of Mr Darby Just before I descended the river last april, Mr Darby was taken in to attend to this suit—for which he was to have an interest in all the land &c not included in the above mentioned morgage for land on Duck river[4]—I have been thus minute to Shew you that at this day, it is impossible for me to make you a general relinquishment for all the land contained in your decree—all the right title and interest I now individual hold, to those tracts enumerated in your bill I am free and willing to relinquish to you—but I have no power since signing the articles of agreement before alluded to, to make a general relinquishment to you—I do not recollect the date of the Deed from Allisons heirs to me, but should your decree vest you with a good tittle, prior to their Deed to me—their

Deed quo ad hoc is void and yours must be a good tittle[5]—I have to repeat as far as I am Justly and legally entitled to relinquish to you, I am free and willing to do so, but I cannot do an act that might involve me with others in a lawsuit, and be considered as to them improper—had I had any recollection of your decree, at the time the articles above named were entered into, I should have excepted the tracts out of it—I did recollect of your Judgt, but the service of your bill upon me and the decree thereon I had forgotten; to prevent lawsuits, with you particularly, I will do any thing I have the power to do, so as not to infringe upon the rights of others and which would involve me in law with those I have entered into covenant with—some of those are determined to hold the land enumerated in your bill, if they can, as to myself I have only to repeat I will relinquish to you all my right—and as to the rest concerned you must take care of yourself[6]—I am sir with great respect your friend & Humble Servt—

Andrew Jackson

P. S. I return the copy of the records herewith, for your use—A. J.

ALS, THi (8-1360).

1. Note not found. Copies of the bill and decree are in the Middle Tennessee Supreme Court Records, T (2-1111).

2. Pryor (d. c1819) was a Philadelphia broker, merchant, and dealer in hides. Jackson was referring to his purchase of Duck River lands at an invalid marshal's sale ordered in 1802 to satisfy Pryor's claim against the Allison estate.

3. A copy of the articles of agreement, January 9, 1813, taken from Deed Book I, TNDa (mAJs), was published in the Nashville *Constitutional Advocate,* December 3, 1822. See also deed of release by Whiteside, and Promissory note by AJ and James Jackson to Whiteside, both March 21, 1820. Whiteside (1772–1822), a Nashville attorney, had acted as Jackson's lawyer in the suit against Andrew Erwin previous to Darby.

4. See Power of attorney to Patrick H. Darby, [April 6], and Agreement among AJ, Whiteside, James Jackson, and Darby, April 13. The agreement with Darby, later a matter of dispute, gave him one-fourth of the individual and joint interests of the other parties to the Allison lands in Tennessee outside the Duck River region. See James Jackson to AJ, October 21, 1823, below.

5. On June 3, 1820, Jackson had acquired from Allison's heirs a duplicate of the lost deed of release, originally given on August 3, 1812. The exact date of Overton's decree is not known. Whether from necessity or from his wish to avoid legal entanglements with Overton, Jackson proceeded as if Overton's decree took precedence. "Quoad hoc" is a Latin phrase meaning "as to this" or "with respect to."

6. For the conclusion of Jackson's arrangement with Overton, see AJ to John C. McLemore, April 11, 1822, below.

From James Craine Bronaugh

Washington 30th. Decr. 1821.

My Dr. Sir

I have this moment recd. your favor of the 6th. Inst. The statement or rather conjecture of the Editor of the Advocate that a secret correspondence was going on between you and Govr. Clinton with a view of electing him to the Presidency was ridiculous in the extreme and was believed by no one, and was promptly contradicted in the Albany Stateman, in which the fact was stated that not more than two letters had ever passed between yourself and Govr. Clinton and that in neither of the letters was the Presidental Election hinted at. That the thing originated with W. H. Crawford I have no doubt—the Advocate is devoted to his views.[1]

It appears to be the general opinion here that Mr. Adams cannot succeed in oppositon to a Southern man—the North will not support him and it is believed that he can not get the Vote of Virginia North Carolina S. Carolina or Kentucky even in opposition to Crawford. It has therefore been determined by those anxious to prevent the election of Crawford to bring forward Mr. Calhoun who it is believed will unite not only the Southern & Western interest, but likewise the North—his popularity is increasing very rapidly and I have no doubt he will make an excellent President I entertain an exalted opinion of his talents and integrity.

Crawford is becoming more contemptible, every day—his appointment of Thomas to examine the land Offices in the Western Country and his deposits of money in local Banks for political purposes must destroy him I shall not be surprised if the President dismisses him before the close of the present Session of Congress. Calhoun entertains the same opinion of Crawford that you do and expresses himself very freely respecting him.[2]

The territorial Govt. for the Floridas has not yet been reported—it is now under the consideration of the committee. Mr. Calhoun has promised to exert his influence for our friends Brackenridge, Call and Overton[3]

I enclose you the papers which were put in my hands by Taylor with the auditors remarks upon them, by which he will see what will be necessary to be done before the money can be paid.[4] With my respects to Mrs. Jackson I remain with sincere regard yrs. truly

J. C. Bronaugh

ALS with AJ endorsement, DLC (72).

1. Letter not found. The Albany *New-York Statesman,* founded on May 6, 1820, ceased publication on January 1, 1822.

2. For resolutions to investigate the land office matter, introduced on January 3, 1822, by Daniel P. Cook, see *Annals of Congress,* 17th Cong., 1st sess., pp. 620–21; and for further discussion of the investigation, see Bronaugh to AJ, January 7 and February 8, both 1822, both below. On John C. Calhoun's views of Crawford, see Calhoun to Virgil Maxcy, December 23 and 31 (*Calhoun Papers,* 6:582–83, 595–97).

3. An act of March 30, 1822, formally organized the Florida Territory (3 *U.S. Statutes at Large,* 654–59). Although Henry M. Brackenridge and Richard K. Call were both named to the territorial legislative council, Brackenridge did not serve, having been subsequently appointed federal district judge for West Florida. Samuel R. Overton was named a land commissioner for the territory.

4. Taylor has not been identified, nor have the papers been found.

For more than a month in late 1821 James Monroe and his cabinet discussed the acceptance of Jackson's resignation as governor of Florida, especially in light of the impending congressional investigation of Jackson's tenure. Although dated December 31, Monroe's letter, below, was not put into final form until early January 1822 and not postmarked until January 9th, after Maine congressman Ezekiel Whitman (1776–1866; Brown 1795), author of the congressional inquiry, had raised obliquely the possibility of Jackson's impeachment (see Annals of Congress, *17th Cong., 1st sess., pp. 534, 558–59, 610–20). Meantime, Jackson, fearing that retirement in the midst of an inquiry would reflect poorly upon his character and having just received his letter from "Friend," sought to delay his resignation (see AJ to Monroe, January 22, 1822). By that time, however, Monroe's letter accepting the resignation was on its way to Nashville. Jackson's acknowledgment noted the discrepancy between the internal date and the postmark, and the obvious political calculations that had informed the president's decision no doubt reinforced Jackson's suspicions about Monroe's friendship and support (see AJ to Monroe, January 29, 1822, below, and Memorandum, [cMarch–April 1822]).*

From James Monroe

Washington December 31. 1821—

Dear Sir

I received some time since, your resignation[1] and should have answered it sooner, had I not wished to retain you in the service of your Country, until a temporary Government Should be organized over the Floridas, and an opportunity be afforded me to appoint your Successor—On great consideration, especially as I know, that it is your fixed purpose to withdraw, I have at length determined to accept it, in which light you will view this letter. The same sentiments which I have heretofore entertained, of your Integrity, Ability & Eminently useful services are still cherished towards you. That you may long live in health & in the affections of your Country is my most earnest desire—With high respect & sincere regard I am Dear Sir Yours

James Monroe—

Copy with endorsement by Monroe, DLC (8-1375); LC, DNA-RG 59 (M40-17). Published in *TPUS*, 22:316 (from LC).

1. See AJ to Monroe, November 13.

1822

To Richard Keith Call

Hermitage Janry. 5, 1822

Dear Call—

on the night before last I returned from Florence where business of a pressing kind had called me, and had the pleasure to receive your two letters of the 19th and 26th. of Novbr,[1] this absence of mine will account to you, for the delay in answering your letters—on my arival at Judge Overtons on my way home from Pensacola I wrote you, I think the 5th. of Novbr. in which I detailed to you the departure of Miss, her probable stay at Natchez and when she would sail from orleans. I have wrote you twice since—the last on 16th. of Decbr last—all of which I hope has reached you in due course of mail—and that you have taken such steps as your Judgt. dictated, and that you have had the good fortune to have had a personal interview with her, and that an end is put to all your doubts, upon that interesting subject to you both—the result of which I anxiously await.[2]

It gives me great pleasure to be informed that Colo. Waltons course has been such as to meet the approbation of all my friends and I hope he will continue this course untill I am relieved from the responsibility of the goverment—I note my friend Carys, rubbing down of the Judge, he has really curryed him, but the Judge must bear it in silence[3]—present me to the major and his family respectfully—to Mr [Thomas] Brown John & all my friends, say to Colo. Miller, that I have recd his letter but the press of business, and bad health at present prevents my answering it at present, say to him that the ladies unite with me in best wishes for his health and happiness[4]—we have had the severest winter I ever experienced in the climate—I had taken a bad cold which fell upon my lungs, and have been for the three last weeks as much worn down with a cough and severe pain on my left side and breast as I was on the Seminole campaign—I have recd two letters from Gadsden and Doctor Brunaugh—Gadsden says since he has seen my correspondence with Judge Fromentine, that he has no doubt but my whole conduct will be fully approved—I enclosed to Colo. Walton, Mr Adams letter to the Judge with his letter to the Spanish Minister with a request that he would shew it to you & Brakenridge, and all my friends, amonghst whom Mr Brownjohn was included[5]—I hope you have seen it—and I have no doubt his honour is on the stool of repentance unless he really has recd. a large fee from his friend Innerarity for his habeas corpus—where is our friend Brakenridge, present me to him affectionately and say to him he writes with such facility, that a line from him ocasionally would be gratefully recd. write me as often as you can, rest assured I will allways respond when health will permit, but at present I must close this scrall, my health will not permit me to write more at present—Mrs. J and Lt Donelson Capt Easter and the two Andrews joins me in best wishes; for the present adieu

Andrew Jackson

ALS, Gallery of History, Inc. (mAJs); Printed, *The Collector* 14 (September 1901):131 (8-1383).

1. See Call to AJ, November 19 and 26, 1821. Jackson had gone to Florence to superintend the transfer of the slaves and stock from his Evans Spring plantation, which he had recently sold, to his Big Spring farm, along the military road in Franklin (now Colbert) County, Alabama. At the same time, he hired Stephen Sharrock, formerly an overseer in Williamson County, Tennessee, to superintend the farm.

2. See AJ to Call, November 4; above, November 15; and December 14, all 1821. As with the letter of November 4, not the 5th, Jackson possibly misstated the date of his letter of December 14. At any rate, no letter to Call of December 16 has been found. For previous discussion of the courtship of Call and Mary L. Kirkman, see AJ to Ellen J. Kirkman, December 16, and AJ to Call, [cDecember 16], both 1820 (*Jackson,* 4:406–409); and Rachel Jackson to Call, December 15, 1821.

3. On November 26, 1821, Call had written Jackson about Cary Nicholas's exposure in the Pensacola *Floridian* of Eligius Fromentin as a fraud (no copy of the relevant issue has been found).

4. See John Miller to AJ, November 26, 1821. Brownjohn was collector of customs in Pensacola.

5. See James Gadsden to AJ, December 3, and, above, James C. Bronaugh to AJ, December 2, 1821. Jackson's enclosures to George Walton were John Q. Adams to Fromentin, October 26 (DLC-31), and Adams to Joaquin de Anduaga, November 2 (DLC-31), both 1821; his covering letter to Walton has not been found. Joaquin de Anduaga was Spanish minister to the United States, 1821–23.

From James Craine Bronaugh

Washington
Jany. 7th. 1822.

My Dr. Sir,

The President will to day communicate to Congress every thing in relation to the Florida transactions. It was the intention of your friends at first to prevent the investigation, as it would consume much time and no good could result from it, and much unpleasant feeling would be produced by it. But upon mature reflection it was conceived best, to permit the call upon the President for information to pass, as by opposing it, your enemies would hold out the idea, that those friendly to you, were affraid to meet the investigation, and that there were some things which could not be justified. I was consulted upon the subject by many of your friends, and gave it as my decided opinion that they ought not to oppose the call for information, as by doing so, those unfriendly to you would be harping upon the subject the whole winter and that as so much had already been said upon the subject, that it was due to you to have all the facts placed before the public. This was also the opinion of Mr. Adams & [Henry] Baldwin. The subject will now undergo a thorough investigation and will terminate in such a way as cannot fail to be completely satisfactory to you, as your conduct will be approbated by more than two thirds of the House and among those all the men of talents & standing. as to such men as Whitman [John] Cocke & Williams, if any act of mine should be approved by them, I should immediately consider that I had acted incorrectly—they are perfectly contemtible.[1]

The Secy. of War after consulting with me has determined to accept the resignation of Col: Butler he will receive his pay as Col: until it is accepte*[d]* He says that by accepting it now, the President will be enabled more certainly to give him a civil appointment. The opposition made by the Senators & Reps. from Miss: & Lua. will prevent his receiving the appointment of Surveyor Genl. in the place of [Thomas] Freeman. He can get the appointment of Surveyor in Florida, a land office or Commissioner for settling land claims: either of those appointments I consider greatly preferable to holding the appointment of Lt. Col: under the circumstances under which he was placed—The appointment of Surveyor Genl. for Florida I think is preferable, and shall therefore make application for him, unless I hear from him on the subject before the appointment is made.[2]

Calhoun is gaining ground rapidly. Crawford must sink. The paper enclosed contains Cookes resolution, & remarks in relation to the land offices.[3] With my respects to Mrs. Jackson I remain with sincere regard Yr. friend &c.

J. C. Bronaugh

ALS, DLC (31).

1. The House did not receive the information regarding the imprisonment of José M. Callava, requested in its January 2 resolution, until January 28 (see Bronaugh to AJ, February 8, below). Baldwin (1780–1844; Yale 1797) represented Pennsylvania in the House of Representatives. In 1830, Jackson appointed him an associate justice of the U.S. Supreme Court. Tennessee congressman Cocke (1772–1854), Jackson's political foe, had commanded the East Tennessee militia during the Creek War.

2. Robert Butler's resignation of November 16, 1821, had been accepted by mid-March, when Congress queried the matter (see AJ to John C. Calhoun, June 28, below; see also James Gadsden to Butler, January 21, DNA-RG 94, M565-6). Louisiana's congressional delegation included senators Henry Johnson (1783–1864) and James Brown (1766–1835) and congressman Josiah Stoddard Johnston (1784–1833; Transylvania 1802). Mississippi's senators were Thomas Hill Williams (1780–1840) and David Holmes (1770–1832); Christopher Rankin (1788–1826) sat in the House of Representatives. Levin Wailes (1768–1847),

not Butler, replaced Freeman (d. 1821) as surveyor south of Tennessee. Butler was appointed surveyor general of Florida in 1824.

3. The enclosure was the January 7 issue of the Washington *National Intelligencer*, which printed Daniel P. Cook's resolution of January 3 and remarks of January 4, complaining of alterations in the system of land office examination instituted about 1818 and alluding to William H. Crawford's employment of Illinois Senator Jesse B. Thomas to conduct such examinations as a possible violation of the constitution.

From George Walton

Pensacola 7 <December> January 1822

My dear General.

I do myself the honor to acknowledge the receipt of your letters of the 17th. November—of the 30th Novr. and of the 6th. December.[1]

Your approval of the course I have pursued affords me the highest gratification, and I take this occasion to express my sincere thanks for the friendly interest you have taken in my behalf with the General Government. Having now removed my family to this Country at great expense, to be disappointed in a continuation of the confidence & friendship of the administration would be a very serious injury to me—I am well aware that I have enemies at Washington, and have but little reliance on the present representation from Georgia; but I confidently rely on the weight of your recommendation to counterbalance these disadvantages—[2]

The notice of Florida affairs in the President's Message, I am sorry to say does not come up to our expectations. The idea of placing Fromentin in competition with you, in any way, is far from flattering; and the ambiguity of expression respecting the different powers, is only matched by the manner in which the compliment to you is introduced, which is very far from being happy. This part of the message is really not what I expected, and I did not read it without feeling indignation, particularly as it did not correspond with the letter to Fromentin from the Secretary of State. Fromentin is about to leave this place; some say he is going to Washington ostensibly as the bearer of a Memorial of the Spanish inhabitants against the annexation to Alabama, and that a purse has been made up to bear his expenses.[3]

A few days ago two of the Spanish Officers, Col: Marcos de Villiers, generally called Col. Coulon, and Arnaldo Guilemard, arrived here in a vessel from Havanna. It was at first intimated to me that they had resigned their commissions in the Spanish Service; but when arrested by my order and brought before me, they declared they had come with the intention of asking permission to attend in person to the settlement of their private affairs, and the removal of their families; they solemnly declared they had not returned in defiance of the Proclamation, which they had promptly obeyed, and that they are ready to submit themselves to any order which should be taken in their case.[4] For the present I ordered them into confinement, but the Calaboze being in no condition to receive them, for, excepting the Officers room it has no fire place, and as Coulon is a very old man, and his wife at this time extremely ill, I thought it best to confine them in their own houses. The situation of old Coulon was such that it would have been cruel to confine him in the dungeon with common malefactors, and I could not with propriety make a distinction with respect to Guilemard. They then presented the enclosed memorial, in which they throw themselves on the mercy of the Government. After these concessions, and the humble manner in which they sue to be permitted to remain, I was well convinced that you would have granted them the indulgence they prayed for. But under my instructions, although, a state of things was presented by the returning sense of propriety on the part of these people, different from what is contemplated in those instructions, yet I did not consider myself authorized to go any further than to continue them in the same confinement until further orders. I was well convinced that while on the one hand, you were determined to cause the Government provisionally established over these Provinces, to be respected, by every one living under it, and as far as you were concerned to cause the stipulation of the Treaty to be enforced, yet, I also Knew, from the magnanimity of your disposition, that you would instantly relent, on the first manifestation of a proper respect to the Government and submission to its determination. This cause, however, was not adopted by me until after consultation with Col's. [John Roger] Fenwick & [Duncan Lamont] Clinch, Major [James Edward] Dinkins and Judge Brackenridge, who all concurred in the opinion that this was, under all the circumstances, the most proper.[5]

The Sixty days in the case of Innerarity having expired, application was made for execution as nothing had been offered by him in the mean time or any claims put in by creditors. He had got the papers on his receipt as had been customary & when called upon, I found he was disposed to try his old tricks, on which I had a notice served on him by the Sheriff to shew cause at Eleven o'clock this day why an attachment should not issue. I had determined to commit him instantly if the papers were not then produced, and to Keep him in prison until they should be forthcoming. He took the hint and left them with Mr [John Coppinger] Connor last night. A long memorial by Mr. [Samuel] Acre was presented praying a review of the whole proceedings; but I shall pay no attention to it, and will now proceed forthwith to compel the payment of the money.[6]

I learn from St Augustine that the "splendid talk" alluded to in my last, has entirely failed, from the unaccountable and singular circumstance of their being no Indians to listen to it, as none attended on the occasion, although a considerable concourse of whites who had assembled in the "beautiful plains of a-la-chu-a," waited impatiently several days for their arrival.[7]

Present me kindly to Mrs Jackson, Miss Hays, & my much *valued* friend Captn. Easter.

I am my dear General, your unalterable friend & grateful servant

Geo Walton

N. B. Besides the documents in the case of the Spanish Officers—you will please find enclosed one private letter.[8]

LS, DLC (31); Extract in AJ's hand and extracts, DNA-RG 59 (M116-10), RG 46 (8-1384). LS endorsed by AJ: "Colo. George Walton letter of the 7th. Janry 1822—to be filed having been answered, and an extract forwarded to the Sec of State with the Judicial proceedg in the case of Colo. Coulon, and Guilemard two Spanish officers—." Published in *ASP, Foreign Relations,* 4:800 (extract).

1. See AJ to Walton, November 17, and December 6, 1821; the November 30 letter has not been found.

2. Walton and his wife, the former Sarah Minge Walker (d. 1861), had two children, Robert Watkins (1812–49) and Octavia (d. 1877); Walton's mother, Dorothy Camber Walton, also resided with them. In April, Walton was appointed permanent secretary of the Florida territory.

3. James Monroe's annual message had suggested that both Jackson and Eligius Fromentin had acted from sincere motives; for John Q. Adams's letter to Fromentin, October 26, 1821, see *TPUS,* 22:262–63. In mid-December, the Alabama legislature had petitioned Congress for the annexation of West Florida to that state, which Pensacola's Spanish residents opposed in a December 29 memorial (see *TPUS,* 22:307–308, 311–16). Fromentin did not travel to Washington, and by April he had returned to New Orleans (see Walton to AJ, January 28).

4. See above, AJ to the Spanish Officers, [September 29, 1821].

5. The enclosures regarding the Spanish officers were Walton to Duncan L. Clinch, to Henry Wilson, and Order of arrest, all January 2; Memorial of de Villiers and Guillemard, January 3; and Walton to de Villiers and Guillemard, January 5 (DNA-RG 59, M116-10). For Walton's instructions, see AJ to Walton, October [5], 1821. Fenwick (1773–1842) was colonel of the 4th Artillery Regiment; Clinch (1787–1849) commanded the 4th Infantry Regiment, in which Dinkins (1775–1822) also served. De Villiers's wife, married in 1784, was Josephine Catherine Griffon d'Anneville.

6. See the judgment against John Innerarity in the Vidal case, October 8, 1821. Both the sheriff, Lexington, Kentucky, native Charles Bradford, and Connor, clerk of the executive court, died later in the year from yellow fever. Acre, a longtime Mobile attorney, represented Innerarity. For Acre's memorial, see Connor to AJ, February 3.

7. On December 17, Walton had informed Jackson about a forthcoming meeting with the Indians of eastern Florida.

8. Letter not identified.

To Edward George Washington Butler

Hermitage, January 8th. 1822.

My Dear Edward,

Your letter of Decembr. 17th. last, reached Nashville during my absence to Florence, on some private business; which circumstances added to my ill state of health, prevented me from answering you until now.[1]

It has ever been with the greatest pleasure, my young friend, that I have tendered you that advice and counsel which my experience has enabled me to give; and especially when I have believed that I could contribute to your future welfare by impressing upon your mind the importance of morality, and by directing your attention to such objects as were most likely to eventuate in your permanent interest; I have done so with the greatest cheerfulness and an eye single to your good—I trust then, that you will view me, when opposing your determination to join the Russian service and abandon that of your country, as influenced by no sinister motive, but alive only to those prospects which may determine your reputation, and the character to which you may attain as a soldier and as a citizen.

You say "that you have spent the best part of your life in a profession which offers no inducements in your own country." Let me ask what is it in the profession of arms, in your country, that is inconsistent with the character which awaits an officer devoted to its service, prepared by science for distinction in that service, and competent to wield, or share in its battles and its dangers? What is it in the character of your country that is unworthy of your efforts to sustain it? What in its national feeling that cannot claim your participation? Where is the country besides your own whose glory is the protection of Liberty and those equal rights which have long since been lost in the despotism and corruption of every European Govt? Where is that love of country, which living even with the chained and shackled Peasants of a monarch, despises all controul? and would you renounce this sacred tie for the Glory to be won in the uncertain career of a foreign Emperor? Could you sacrifice the feelings which should characterise an American Officer to the illusions <of the> which support Royalty, and slander even its corruption? I hope you could not. There are many objections, Edward, to your adopting the course which you have named, but which I shall not now mention, believing that you will unhesitatingly abandon a scheme which you have formed without reflection. It is true that the blind Policy of the last Congress, has limited the prospects of reputation and distinction in our Army, but things will not always be as they are. The Policy must change; and independent of this, what greater incentive do you want, than the persuasion that, by improving the advantages which you now possess, you will be prepared to enter with distinction into the service of your country, when it shall nee*[d]* and will ask for your service and talen*[ts.]* Continue your studies, and your proficiency will be rewarded—Be stu*[dious,]* industrious, and you will never feel the miseries of idleness—[2]

I shall be happy to hear from you at all times, and am very anxious that you should visit me in the course of the winter, in order that you may take charge of your private business—it is growing burthensome to me, and *[it]* is necessary that you should see me, to be acquainted with its exact situation—[3]

Except myself, my family is well—Mrs J. & Andrew send their respects to you, and also Lieut Donelson, who will write you next mail. Your Sincer friend

Andrew Jackson

LS in Andrew J. Donelson's hand, THer (8-1387); Extract, LNT (8-1391). Extract published in Bassett, 3:142–43 (from Charles Gayarré, *A Sketch of General Jackson: By Himself* [New Orleans, 1857], pp. 3–4).

1. See Butler to AJ, December 17, 1821.

2. As a result of the army reduction, Butler had been assigned to the 4th Artillery Regiment as a 2nd lieutenant.

3. Jackson was referring to the management of land in Robertson County inherited from Butler's father Edward, which, after years of litigation and the intervening death of Butler's mother Isabella Butler Vinson (d. 1821), had finally come into the possession of the heirs (see Thomas Johnson to Butler, January 28, LNHiC; and AJ to Anthony W. Butler, June 2, 1823, below).

To James Craine Bronaugh

Hermitage January 10th 1822

My Dr Sir

I have the pleasure to acknowledge the receipt of your letter of the 19th. ult. which reached me last evening for which I thank you.[1]

It is pleasing to me that so large a majority approve my proceedings—but my wish is that the whole proceedings and correspondence be placed before the public—I am then content that the nation may decide—My last, you will be in the recpt of when this comes to hand,[2] I there refer you to an anonimous letter recd, since which, conjecture of the author has arisen; and if correct is a high minded Virginian, and a soldier of your acquaintance, a man of honour and truth—a letter recd. last night from Colo. Walton details the same ideas, notwithstanding all this, I suspend my opinion for the present[3]—but is it possible that Mr Monroe, will permit himself to be branded by an insolent Spanish Minister, the dignity of the nation insulted, and hesitate <forthwith> to notify this insolent Minister of what is due to himself and the Goverment, and if he hesitates, to make the necessary apology, to demand his recall, should he hesitate on this subject, rest assured, that the intelligence given by this high minded annonimous correspondant who tells me he shall be know[n] in due time, is true, and as soon as I hear the stand he takes on this subject, I will prepare to take my own—I hope in god for the sincere friendship I have had for, & the confidence I have had in Mr Monroe, that all these intelligence, and forebodings may prove without foundation, but, if the conjecture of the writer of the alluded to letter is true, there is more truth in the information, than my wishes can accord with.[4]

I am happy that my accounts will be closed, I have but one remark as to my transportation charged to & from the choctaw Treaty—in all the

Treaties I have held with the Indians, I have recd my transportation, and the only mode the Govt. would allow, because they never allowed me to procure transportation, except my own pack horses or my own sansusee[5]—This being the uniform mode, and allways allowed my pay being allways the same I thought it proper to pursue the mode heretofore adopted by the goverment—It is true their was a specific appropriation for this treaty, and it is equally true, that a ballance saved by the commissioners has been turned over by me agreable to the order of the sec of war to the pay department, and all sums previous to that was turned over to the quartermasters department—It is strange indeed that the Goverment in this solitary instance should have changed it former rotine of doing business—and without any notice to me of that change, before I had by the orders of the secratary of war turned over the surplus of the appropriation—I make these remarks barely that you may bring them to the knowledge and view of the secratary of war & of Mr [Peter] Hagner—I really cannot account for this change unless the scriptures are fast a fullfilling, "that all old things are passing away, and all things are to become new"—and as I am determined to have no more public accounts, nor no more Indian treaties, I want my accounts closed. but cannot help remembering that it is the first time such an account of mine has been suspended—I know it will be the *last*—There has been of late so much dificulty in closing my accounts, that I cannot help believing there *must be some lurking cause somewhere.* I have no recollection to what time my accounts were made up nor is it material if I am not paid this way I shall have none[6]

I have Just recd from our friend Judge Brakenridge the letter which I enclose you, you will see his wishes; in my letter to Mr Monroe I named him as I ought. Mr Monroe in his reply mentioned the Judge in the highes terms, of <and> approbation and I have no doubt will be disposed to give him any office he may ask—I have not seen Judge Haywood since my return but have been told, that now, he will not accept of a Judgeship in the Floridas and indeed, after the neglect shewn him by the appointment of Fromentine, was I in his place I should not—you will therefore bring Judge Brakenridge forward in any way you may deem best, assuring the president—<that> of my high Estimation of his integrity and talents, and fitness to preside in any Judiciary or any other office in or over the Fds. but particularly in the Judiciary. I regret Colo. Kings being so unpopular in the senate, there will be a time when such men will be cherished by the Senate—and when *such men alone will* <again> *save the capitol* of our country[7]—But this will be when the feeble course pursued, will again invite us into another war. I hope sincerely my dear friend that you will succeed in your application, that you ought I well know, and I well recollect that Mr Monroe promised you this appointment and I hope he never will violate this promise. I sincerely regret that the appointment of Colo. Butler is opposed and that it should be by the senators in Louisiana is strange to me particularly that Judge [Henry] Johnston should is passing strange to me—the only proper course for a president to pursue is to nominate those he may think well qualified and fit—and leave it to the senate to approve—in doing so he fully discharges his constitutional duties and the Senate does theirs independantly—but this logg roling business between the President & the senate ought to be scouted by every lover of the Existance of our constitutional Goverment—The checks and ballances in this way will be kept alive in their purity—but this Logrolling business—this private consultation between the President & Senate before the nomination is made is a consoladation of the check in this instance secured by the constitution dangerous to the durability of our republic. Now untill you know this from Judge Johnston, I pray you to beware least it is a political hypocritical Juggle between Mr Brown & the P—thereby to serve some humble tool of Mr. Wm H Crawfords. I have confidence in the candeur of Mr Calhoun, but I fear you will find under the rose what Colo. Walton says is now the secrete rumour that Crawford under the rose rules the President, whilst to others of the Cabinet he appears to shew that he has lost confidence in Crawford—This is repeated to me in the annomous letter, and this farce is carried on the more certainly to promote Mr Crawfords views, hence then every man who is opposed to Mr Crawford, why he is to be opposed in the Senate & it will not do to nominate him—look well to this hint—and have a positive promise of Mr Monroe before you leave there. and in the presence of some of your friends who will remain, this can do no harm—and if there are any truth in these secrete rumours of Secrete understanding between Mr M. & Mr W. H. C. you will be safe, or if deceived have proof to dam the conspiracy—I have reasons to think that Judge Johnston would be amonghst the first member in the Senate to approve of Colo. B. nomination—I have no confidence in the stability of Brown—hence I conclude that Mr B. moves the puppet in the shew, ruled by Govr. Robertson of Louisiana to favour Wm. H. C in that state but they are unmasked and the next election will give Mr Brown an Irish hoist

Major Baker has been with me understands all their machinations and the people are prepared to punish these political Jugglers, for their hypocracy—I could write much more to you on this subject—I do not yet wish it made public; My annonimous correspondant does not untill it is ripe for explosition—I make these remarks to put you on your guard that you may silently look at these things without being suspected of having a knowledge of them, that you can the better Judge of them—it is said this Juggle has been going into opperation since the commencement of the congress before this, it is to be continued, in the same secrete way & the appointments all filled with Mr Wm. H. C. Friends without them being known as such—& Brown & Robertson are two of the confidents—silence will if any truth in these things develope it—and if there should be I will come out under my own signature and unrobe them—I have wrote untill I can write no more. I am in bad health, and much debilitated, adieu for the present—let me hear from you as often as you can—present me to Mr [Cadwallader David] Colden[8] respectfully to Gadsden & all my friends

Andrew Jackson

ALS, DLC (72).

1. See Bronaugh to AJ, December 19, 1821.

2. Letter not found.

3. See above, "Friend" to AJ, October 29, 1821. In his letter of December 10, 1821, George Walton suggested, as had "Friend," that William H. Crawford would likely succeed James Monroe as president unless Jackson entered the campaign. It is not known whom Jackson meant by "high minded Virginian."

4. Jackson was referring to the protests of Spanish diplomats Hilario de Rivas y Salmon and Joaquin de Anduaga over the imprisonment of José M. Callava (see John Q. Adams to AJ, October 26, 1821).

5. Jackson's phonetic spelling for an unidentified form of wagon. See Account with David G. Ballard, September 6, and Receipt of Hutchings, October 7, both 1821.

6. In April 1820, Congress had appropriated $20,000 to extinguish Indian land titles in Mississippi (3 *U.S. Statutes at Large* 555–61). For the order regarding disposition of the balance of the Choctaw treaty account, see John C. Calhoun to AJ, and William Lee to AJ, May 1, 1821. Regarding Jackson's general dissatisfaction with the handling of his accounts, see also AJ to Calhoun, March 17, AJ to Bronaugh, July 3, and AJ to Monroe, October 5, all 1821, all above. Jackson's quotation was a paraphrase of 2 Corinthians 5:17. Hagner (1772–1850) was third auditor of the treasury.

7. See AJ to Monroe, August 4, and Monroe to AJ, September 16, both 1821; Henry M. Brackenridge's letter has not been found. In 1821, Jackson had recommended John Haywood for a federal judgeship in Florida and had supported former colonel William King as a possible Florida governor (see above, AJ to Monroe, October 5, 1821; and November 30, 1821).

8. Colden (1769–1834), former mayor of New York City, was serving his only term in Congress.

To Philip Pendleton Barbour

Hermitage Near Nashville
22nd. January 1822

Sir,

I have this day accidentally met with the National Intelligencer of the 2nd Inst in which I have seen a resolution brought forward by Mr Whitman, calling for information from the President of the United States, relative to my acts whilst administering the Government of the Floridas, with the avowed object of impeaching me.[1]

I am at all times desirous that my public acts should be investigated, and on the present occasion I have sought it; being ever disposed to be judged of by my acts, and having perceived that some apprehension is entertained, that, in as much as I had resigned, I could not be impeached; I have to request of you, that, you make it Known to the body over which you preside, that altho' my resignation was forwarded in November, I have received no information of its acceptance, either from the Department of State, or from the President of the United States—I desire it also to be made Known that I have this day written to the President requesting him to withold the acceptance of my resignation, until my conduct as Governor of the Floridas may be fully investigated, if however, unfortunately for me, and contrary to my wish, my resignation should have been accepted by the President before my letter of this date reaches him, I shall nevertheless plead generally to any impeachment that may be preferred against me[2]—This in such an event I have a right to demand. All I ask is, that I may not be condemned unheard, and without testimony; or upon the evidence of Newspaper squibs issuing from certain papers whose condemnation I have ever esteemed the best eulogium upon virtuous action.

These observations have arisen from the language already used in debate, which gives rise to suspicion that some, at least, are more disposed to forestal public opinion, than to enter upon fair investigation. When we advert to the high sounding words of Tyranny, oppression, and usurpation of power not delagated to me, and the still more extravagant assertion that I had exercised the powers of a despot; powers more extensive than any which appertain to the Government of Spain, all which information is acknowledged to have been received from Newspaper report, or from a source more corrupt, we cannot but anticipate that men who are so open to prejudice, are prepared to prosecute the investigation with an avidity and blindness, which will reluctantly yield to the clearest demonstration of Justice and innocence.[3] Knowing as I do that no fact does exist to warrant such charges or such language I would ask how far does such declamation and denunciation, unsupported by proof, comport with the dignity of the Representative character which is recognised by the constitution as the guardian of innocence and truth.

These remarks I have thought were called for upon the present occasion and are respectfully submitted to you, reserving for future expression any thing which the course the investigation shall take, may suggest—I have the honor Sir, to be with sentimts of high respect and esteem Yr. Mot Obt Humble Sert.

(Signd) Andrew Jackson

LC in Andrew J. Donelson's hand, DLC (63).

1. For the January 2 debate on Ezekiel Whitman's resolution, see the Washington *National Intelligencer,* January 3. For the text of Whitman's resolution, submitted on December 11, see *Annals of Congress,* 17th Cong., 1st sess., p. 534.

2. See AJ to James Monroe, November 13, 1821, and January 22, 1822; and, above, Monroe to AJ, December 31, 1821.

3. Jackson was paraphrasing specific allegations made during the congressional debate by Whitman and Virginia's William Segar Archer (1789–1855; William and Mary 1806).

To George Gibson

Hermitage Janry 29th. 1822

My Dear Colo.

your very kind letter of the 7th instant reached me two mails since,[1] but my ill health and other causes combined to pospone my Answer untill now—The stimulant that the second edition of the Seminole campaign will give me, will I hope restore me to health—and as soon as this discussion is over, I trust as a citizen in common with others I have rights, and amonghst those rights secured under the constitution, are the right of investigating the conduct of men and measures—and rest assured I shall exercise it—and If I am not deceived I shall unfold things, that will astonish our republick—

It is truly gratifying to me to learn that the *Secrete combination to destroy me,* allthough powerfull & pretext of friendship (in some) used to deceive me—has not poisoned the minds of the virtuous part of Congress against me, and that from your information and that of my friends Doct. Brunaugh & Gadsden, I will still have with me a large majority.[2] When the time arives that I can explain this letter to you, I know you will be as much astonished as I have been, on the recpt of information that has led to the above remarks—but at present I must be silent—it affords me great pleasure to hear that Mr Calhouns popularity is growing, his offerring will put down that arch fiend Wm H Crawford—It is astonishing to me to see Mr Lownds brought out by the State of South Carolina This will, if presisted in, injure Calhoun & ensure Mr Adams election—I have allways believed Mr Calhoun to be a highminded and honourable man, possessing Independence and virtue—but both him & Lownds continuing their names will defeat them both[3]—I have as far as I know Mr Adams, found him to be a candid independant man and should Mr Crawford be disappointed the nation will be well governed either by Mr Calhoun or Mr Adams, and I hope for the love I bear my country that the people of the united states will make a prudent selection, by which their rights liberties & properties may be long protected, and our republican goverment in its purity agreable to our constitution may be perpetuated

Mrs. J. Joins me in a renewal of our best wishes for your health and happiness and believe me to be with sincere Esteem yr mo. ob. Servt.

Andrew Jackson

It will be viewed by me an act of friendship in you when Leisure will permit, to receive a paper or a line from you A.J—

ALS, PHC (9-0008). Published in *Potter's American Monthly,* 5(1875):823, 826.

1. Not found.

2. For accounts of the pro-Jackson majority in Congress, see above, James C. Bronaugh to AJ, January 7; and James Gadsden to AJ, November 8, 14, 20, and December 3, all 1821.

3. A caucus of the South Carolina legislature had nominated William Lowndes for the presidency on December 18, 1821, and ten days later Secretary of War John C. Calhoun, also from South Carolina, had entered the contest at the request of his supporters in Congress.

To James Monroe

Hermitage near Nashville
January 29th. 1822.

Dear Sir,

Your letter of date the 31st. of December last (Post-marked the 9th. of this present month at the City of Washington), acknowledging the receipt of my resignation as Governor of the Floridas forwarded by Doctor Bronough, has reached and advises me, that the same has been accepted by you.[1]

To be freed from the toil and labour of a Public Office, is what I have long desired, and what indeed, the state of my health and other causes rendered necessary: But as it appears that there is none of my public life but what must be traversed by Congress, and having long since requested Mr. Adams to lay before you the correspondence with Judge Fromentin, from a wish that it might have been submitted to Congress if thought necessary; I did confidently hope, that before the acceptance of my resignation, this correspondence would have been produced,[2] and that with the investigation of all and every part of my conduct, my enemies might have had no grounds to charge me with resigning through fear of impeachment, as Mr Whitman and some other members have illiberally and untruly insinuated on the flloor of Congress on the 2nd Inst., when supporting his resolution for a call for those papers: I therefore sincerely regret that those papers were not laid before Congress agreeably to my request, and before the call made by Mr Whitman;[3]

The moment I saw the Intelligencer of the 2d. Instant, I wrote you to suspend the acceptance of my resignation, until this investigation was complete[4]—Not having at that time any intimation of either its receipt or acceptance, from you or the Secretary of State, and fully believing, that if you found Congress had a wish to investigate my conduct you would have witheld its acceptance under circumstances which were disagreeable to me, and at least, until there was opportunity of meeting the attempts which are made, to stamp my conduct with unworthiness and dishonor.

I addressed a note also to the Speaker of the House of Representatives, stating these facts to him, and requesting him to communicate them to that Body, with assurance on my part, that I was ready and willing to meet and plead generally to any charges that might be brought against me.[5] My wishes and hopes not having been realised, but the acceptance of my resignation having been forwarded by you, seven days after Mr

Whitman's resolution calling for the papers had been passed, leaves but one course for me to pursue, and that is, such course as I may deem, justice to myself, and the American nation, may require under all circumstances.

I have to repeat the request made to the Secretary of State, that my accounts be closed by the Department, information given to what time my Postage and Stationary accounts ought to be made up to, and to whom the ballance of the funds in my hands are to be turned over, and what directions hereafter are to be given to the Public letters addressed to me from the Floridas[6]

I make you a tender of my thanks, for the very flattering manner of approbation, which you have been pleased to express of all my Public acts, and services; and the friendly expressions of solicitude for my individual health and happiness, I sincerely reciprocate I am, Dr Sir yr. Mo Obt Servant

Andrew Jackson

LS, DLC (9-0014); LC, DLC (63). Published in *TPUS*, 22:350–51.

1. See above, Monroe to AJ, December 31, 1821.
2. Jackson had enclosed copies of the correspondence with Eligius Fromentin in his letter to John Q. Adams on November 13 and had informed Monroe of the enclosures on the same date.
3. Monroe submitted the Fromentin correspondence to Congress in his message of January 28 in response to the Whitman resolution (see *Annals of Congress*, 17th Cong., 1st sess., pp. 826–27, 2373–2477).
4. See AJ to Monroe, January 22.
5. See above, AJ to Philip P. Barbour, January 22.
6. For correspondence regarding Jackson's Florida accounts, see AJ to Adams, November 14, and Adams to AJ, December 26, both 1821; AJ to Adams, January 31, and Fontaine Maury to AJ, March 5. Adams finally approved Jackson's accounts on August 16.

As early as January 1822, the Nashville Gazette *had begun to tout Jackson as a possible successor to James Monroe. Although months elapsed before any serious development along those lines, the prospect was surely flattering to the former general, and the possibility of a presidential candidacy informed Jackson's actions toward both friends and enemies. Such was the situation when John Sommerville (1770–1846), a Nashville banker, presented in the letter below the supplication of Thomas Gassaway Watkins (d. 1830), a Maryland native and former Nashville physician. The enmity between Jackson and Watkins began in the aftermath of Jackson's fatal duel with Charles Henry Dickinson (1780–1806) in May 1806, when Jackson received information that Watkins had helped to organize a petition drive that prompted the two Nashville newspapers to publish their June 7, 1806, issues with mourning borders in honor of Dickinson. Although Watkins maintained that he had signed the petition merely out of respect to the Dickinson family, his estrangement from Jackson was completed when Watkins assaulted Jackson's friend Thomas Augustine Claiborne (c1775–1815) on July 2, 1806 (see* Jackson, *2:101–109).*

Watkins's standing in the Nashville community generally eroded later in 1807, when he was charged with forging the will of his patient Polly Herring Davis (d. 1807), naming himself as sole executor with control over the estate's significant assets. The court rejected his version of the Davis will, and sometime later, perhaps as a result of the controversy, Watkins relocated to East Tennessee. He served briefly as a surgeon during the War of 1812, and subsequently moved to Albemarle County, Virginia, where he became the physician of Thomas Jefferson (1743–1826; William and Mary 1762), third president of the United States, and Wilson Cary Nicholas.

Jackson's reconciliation with Watkins was the first of several that the retired general made with his enemies about this time. Temporary truces made in 1823–24 with Andrew Erwin and John Cocke and the reconciliation with his former aide Thomas Hart Benton (1782–1858) were politically fortuitous if not inspired in light of Jackson's presidential prospects (see John H. Eaton to Rachel Jackson, December 18, 1823, below). Moreover, Jackson's renewed friendship with Watkins proved helpful during the 1828 campaign when the doctor defended Jackson against renewed charges concerning the Dickinson duel.

From John Sommerville

Nashville 4th Febry 1822

Dear Sir—

That magnanimity and generosity of soul which has ever characterized you through life will, I am persuaded, pardon the liberty I assume; on this occasion, to produce a friendly reconciliation between you & Dot. Thom: G. Watkins, who has been much injured in your estimation by misconception of his motives and conduct and by the machinations of his enemies.

The Dot. and myself have had a long Conversation on the subject, in which he has convinced me that he never was your enemy nor never wished nor intended you the slightest disrespect whatever, and that nothing was wanting to produce a cordial reconciliation but to bring you together and to a Correct understanding of the motives & Conduct which injured him in your estimation—an injury which he has very sincerely regreted and which he is very desirous to have removed—

The enemies of the Doctor, and he has some very bitter ones, pursue him wherever he goes with slanderous statements of his misconduct, as they term it, in Tennessee & cite the unfortunate misunderstanding with you as proof of his Criminality—and your name, thus used, is calculated to do him very serious injury. The misconduct spoken of relates to the affair of Mrs. Polly Davis's Will, of which you have heard much to his prejudice, but it affords me much gratification to say that he can shew you the most unequivocal proofs of the correctness of his Conduct and the purity of his motives in that affair, in the estimation of disinterested persons, whose standing in Society you respect—These proofs have convinced me of the error which popular clamor had betrayed me into on the occasion, and Completely removed from my mind all prejudice against him[1]

He now resides near Mr. Jefferson, whose family Physician he is when at home, and where your name will do him either much good or much harm. There his enemies have again set the story of Mrs. Davis's Will in agitation against him for the purpose, no doubt, of destroying his popularity as a Physician of the first grade of talents—Allow me then, to solicit you most earnestly to serve a Worthy and deserving man, who has been most falsely traduced—by giving him the hand of friendship and of reconciliation with such letters to your friends Mr. Jefferson & Mr Madison as your feelings will dictate as proper on the occasion[2]—As I have the strongest reasons to believe that this reconciliation is not sought through motives of pecuniary interest in his profession, I can assure you that it is desired to give peace to his wounded feelings, and increase his pleasure in life by being restored to the good opinion of one whose estimation he has ever valued very highly and whose public services has endeared him to the hearts & warmest affections of the American people—With profound respect I have the honor to remain—Your ob. Se & fd.

Jno. Sommerville

ALS, DLC (31). Endorsed by AJ: "Mr John Somervilles letter to A. Jackson on the subject of Doctor Thos. G. Watkins with the copy of A. Jacksons letter to Mr Thos. Jefferson on the subject of Dotr. Watkins—to be preserved—." Published in Bassett, 3:145 (extract).

1. In January 1807, Watkins had attended the pregnant Polly H. Davis. Davis already had an illegitimate daughter, Nancy, and Watkins maintained that he was attempting to help Davis by agreeing to supervise Nancy's education, conditioned on his sole control of the estate. Upon Davis's death in May 1807, he produced a will to that effect. But Davis's stepson, Temple Turner (alias Davis), contested Watkins's document, exhibiting another will omitting Watkins's name as executor. Turner contended that Watkins had exerted undue influence on Davis during the widow's last weeks of life, violating medical ethics (see Nashville *Tennessee Gazette,* May 23, 1807). The exact identity of Watkins's Virginia enemies has not been determined, but Watkins later attributed the attacks upon his professionalism to jealousy (see Watkins to Thomas Jefferson, September 15, DLC-Jefferson Papers). Watkins's "proofs" regarding his conduct have not been found.

2. See below. AJ's letter to James Madison has not been found. John Overton also drafted letters at this time attesting to Watkins's good character (THi).

To Thomas Jefferson

Hermitage
Febry. 6th. 1822

Dr Sir,

While Doctr. Thos. G. Watkins resided in this State, there was a considerable difference between him & myself—which I am informed has operated much to the Docts prejudice—

He calld. on me yesterday at my house for the purpose of reconcilliation He made such explanations as has induced me to restore him to the standing he occupied in my estimation before the unpleasant difference <happened> took place

At his request it affords me pleasure to make this communication—I am happy to learn from the Doctr that you continue to enjoy good health in your old age—

<That your health & life may long be preserved for the benefit of society and the litterary world is the fervent wish of your friend & obt. sert> may this long continue & your life be preserved many years for the benefit of society & the literary world is the fervent wish of your sincere friend & obt svt.

Copy, DLC (31). Published in Bassett, 3:145. No record has been found that Jefferson received the letter.

On January 17, submitting his first officer appointments to the Senate since the army reduction, the president nominated, among others, James Gadsden as adjutant general and Nathan Towson as colonel of the 2nd Artillery. Controversial since their announcement the previous year, these two nominations became an occasion for William H. Crawford's political allies to strike again at John C. Calhoun's war department and the Monroe administration. Upon receipt of the nominations, Tennessee's John Williams, chairman of the Senate Military Affairs Committee, proposed that the committee deliberate in secrecy. On March 13, the committee reported against Towson and Gadsden, and the Senate rejected their appointments on March 16 and March 21, respectively. Faced with a stunning rebuke, James Monroe withdrew the remaining army nominations, promising to resubmit them and the two rejected choices with an exposition of his view of the army reduction act.

Monroe's April 12 message clarified the rationale used in appointing Gadsden and Towson. The president judged the positions of adjutant general and artillery colonel to be new offices, rather than continuations of previous posts; hence, he asserted that he might appoint anyone to those new openings, regardless of seniority. The Senate committee, however, held that the reduction law eliminated only one of two divisional adjutants and that either Robert Butler or Roger Jones (d. 1852), the divisional adjutants, was entitled to appointment as adjutant general of the army, just as Gadsden himself had originally been retained as inspector general. Thus, Gadsden's subsequent nomination as adjutant general violated seniority. Similarly, Towson, a former paymaster general without a line rank, illegally displaced all other officers by his appointment as colonel (for the proceedings and messages, see Annals of Congress, *17th Cong., 1st sess., pp. 470–510).*

Monroe's arguments and resubmission failed to convince the legislators, and on April 29, the Senate rejected Gadsden and Towson by even

greater margins. The next day, the Senate removed the cloak of secrecy from the proceedings, completing the administration's embarrassment, but not ending the controversy, as Monroe refused to fill the posts and Jackson yet nurtured the possibility of saving Gadsden's appointment while appeasing Butler's wounded feelings (see AJ to Calhoun, June 28, below). Jackson's efforts, however, came to naught, and in the end, both Butler and Gadsden failed to win appointments.

From James Craine Bronaugh

Washington
8th. Feby. 1822.

My Dr. Sir

I wrote you a hasty letter yesterday immediatly after waiting upon the President:[1] To day I learn he will have a cabinet council upon the subject mentioned in your letter what the result will be is uncertain and I think not materially important, as you are willing whether your resignation is accepted or not, to answer generally to any articles of impeachment which may be prefered against you.[2] The Speaker has recd. your letter, but has not yet laid it before the House & will wait the decision of the President. When all the documents come out the subject will be so clear, that I doubt much whether any thing will be attempted by those who made the move, for they are I believe completely sick of the subject and regret that they have by the publication of the documents placed you upon such high ground before the public.[3] Those who before en[ter]tained a friendly feeling towards you, from a thorough conviction of the pureness of the motives from which you acted, but considered that some of your proceedings in Florida were rather of too violent a character, have since the publication of the first part of the documents <been> expressed the most decided approbation of your conduct and declare that you are the most astonishing man that the nation has ever produced—that you always act correctly let the situation in which you are placed be ever so difficult. Your friends are devoted—your enemies alarmed at your popularity & standing with the nation—they tremble when they see that they can not bear themselves out, with all their ingenuity, in the measures which their feelings would induce them pursue towards you. Whitman & [William S.] Archer are the only members that have taken a decided stand against you and the latter is cooling off. Williams, Cannon & Cocke are affraid to express any opinion against you, and report says, will vote in your favor should any resolution be offered censuring your conduct. Indeed no man in Congress who is not completely under the influence of W. H. Crawford will be against you. Whitman is his devoted friend & has been exerting all his influence in the State of Maine for the last two years in his favor—he is the violent enemy of Adams—was a Federalist of the Boston stamp—was most violently opposed to the war and altho' not a member of the Hartford convention, yet was its warm supporter.[4] At the course taken by Archer, I have been astonished—he and myself were formerly extremely intimate and I had always considered him a high minded honorable man. We have had some warm discussions on the Florida transactions and he has cooled down much since his arrival here. He declares that he is perfectly satisfied that you acted from the most pure and patriotic motives, but considers that in your imprisonment of Callava and banishment of the Spanish Officers you violated not only the law of nations but the constitution of the U. States. At first he was most violent in relation to your treatment of the Judge, but has now abandoned that ground and says that he is a contemptible scoundrel and had no right to issue the writ of H. Corpus. He pretends not to have a very high opinion of the Secy. of the Treasury but prefers him to the others named for the Presidency. He and Scott were class mates and are upon the most intimate terms, which may have had some influence upon him. But the two Gentlemen in his District to whom he probably owes his seat in Congress and who have always been his warmest supporters are Dr. [Branch Tanner] Archer & Judge [Peter] Randolph who are great admirers of you & are as much devoted to you as any men in Virginia. I am therefore at a loss to account for his opposition unless from Crawford influence.[5]

I enclose you Crawfords report in relation to the examination of Land Offices &c. made in obedience to Cooks resolution. It is a strange production and is made out in the true diplomatic style. It does not contain the information called for and leaves it doubtful whether Mr. Senator Thomas recd. pay or not. The fact however is that he recd. six dollars per day and I believe from the time he left this until his return. Cook has offered another resolution on the subject which will bring out the facts. His friends are much alarmed and attacked Cook most violently in the discussion upon the subject, but he sustained himself well, and the resolution passed almost unanimously. Cook deserves great credit I think for the course which he has taken in this business—he possesses fine talents and is determined to probe it to the quick. He is Son-in-law to Governor [Ninian] Edwards, and your warm friend.[6]

All your acts in relation to the organization of the Government in Florida I understand have been approved by the President & the Scy. of State has written you to that effect. After the receipt of your letter yesterday I called at his house, but he was out.[7] That Mr. Adams en[ter]tains the most friendly feeling towards you, I have no doubt and that he will defend you to the best of his ability I am perfectly satisfied—the more I know of him the more I am satisfied of his perfect sincerity and his devotion to the best interests of his Country. I know no man in the nation so well qualified as he is for the station which he fills. I regret that it is not in my power to give so flattering a picture of the President the more I know of him, the more I am satisfied of his duplicity and his incompetency to fill the office which he holds—the day is not distant when he will be universally despised by the american people or I am a false prophet.

Present my respects to Mr. Overton and tell him that the first leisure moment I will write him—that I think there is no doubt of his being appointed one of the Commissioners in Florida—his recommendation will be so strong that the President can not get over appointing him.[8]

The organization of the Army is making great noise here—I am fearful that our friend Gadsden will be placed in an unpleasant situation—the military committee now have it under consideration Mr. Calhoun has written them a long letter on the subject which you will see in the papers. I think he had better acknowledge that the law was violated and throw the blame where it ou[gh]t to rest—on the board of Genl. Officers. The pruning knife will be applied by Congress to the Army—The Major Genl. or Brigs. the Inspectors & Surg: Genl. I think will go. The military committee have called for Col: Butlers letter of resignation.[9]

The Vice President left this yesterday—I dont think he was perfectly sober during his stay here—He was several times so drunk in the Chair that he could with difficulty put the question. I understand he will never return here.[10]

For foreign news and congressional proceedings I must refer you to the news papers.

My friend B[aptis] Ervine proposes publishing a paper he possesses fine talents and is your devoted friend—He is now preparing several numbers in relation to the Florida transactions. He will send you his paper. I send you three of his subscription papers. If you can place them in the hands of any persons in Ten: or Alabama who will procure subscribers for him you will confer a favor upon a meritorious man and one who from his talents & independence is calculated to do much good.[11] please present my respects to Mrs. Jackson & Lt. Donelson and believe me Sincerely yr. friend &c.

J. C. Bronaugh

ALS, DLC (31). Published in Bassett, 3:145–48 (extract).

1. Not found.

2. Bronaugh was referring to Jackson's letter of January 22 to James Monroe, in which Jackson requested that Monroe delay acceptance of his resignation until the investigation into his conduct as governor of Florida had been completed.

3. See above, AJ to Philip P. Barbour, January 22. Monroe's January 28 special message, responding to Ezekiel Whitman's amended resolution of January 2, conveyed the documents regarding the controversy with José M. Callava and Eligius Fromentin. They were printed in three parts, from February 6 through the 15th.

4. The Hartford Convention, called at the request of the Massachusetts legislature and attended by delegates from five New England states, had convened in secret session in mid-December 1814 to discuss grievances growing out of the War of 1812.

5. William S. Archer and Winfield Scott, who had claimed that Jackson abused his military authority in 1817, had been fellow students at William and Mary; Archer's third congressional district included Amelia, Nottoway, Chesterfield, and Powhatan counties in Vir-

ginia. Branch T. Archer (1790–1856), a distant relative of William S., later emigrated to Texas. Randolph (c1779–1832) was a native of Amelia County, Virginia, and member of that state's court of appeals until 1821, after which he relocated to Wilkinson County, Mississippi. In 1823, Monroe appointed Randolph federal district judge.

6. William H. Crawford's January 28 report praised Jesse B. Thomas's service as land office examiner, but failed to state his exact compensation. On February 2, Daniel P. Cook inquired specifically about Thomas's pay during his western tour, and Crawford answered on February 18. On March 29, a committee headed by Cook exonerated both Thomas and Crawford of any wrongdoing (see *Annals of Congress,* 17th Cong., 1st sess., p. 876; *HRDoc* 44, 17th Cong., 1st sess. [Serial 65]; *HRDoc* 71, 17th Cong., 1st sess. [Serial 67]; and *ASP, Public Lands,* 3:538–44). In the summer of 1821, Cook had married Julia Edwards (d. 1830), eldest daughter of Ninian (1775–1833; Dickinson 1792), governor of Illinois Territory before his election to the Senate in 1818.

7. Neither Jackson's letter to Bronaugh nor John Q. Adams's to Jackson has been found.

8. Samuel R. Overton was appointed a Florida land commissioner on May 8. Among those recommending him for the post were John H. Eaton, John Williams, John Rhea, Thomas H. Williams, David Holmes, Ninian Edwards, Richard M. Johnson, and Henry Johnson.

9. On January 29, John C. Calhoun wrote William Eustis, chairman of the House Military Affairs Committee, which like its Senate counterpart was investigating the army appointments, explaining the administration's position on the appointments. On the same day, Calhoun sent a copy of the letter to John Williams, the Senate committee chairman (see *Washington Gazette,* February 6, and Calhoun to Williams, January 29, DNA-RG 107, M220-1). Eustis requested a copy of Butler's resignation on February 2 (DNA-RG 107, M221-92).

10. Daniel D. Tompkins's habitual intoxication was well known, and he was frequently absent from the Capitol.

11. Irvine, a Scottish immigrant, had worked with William Duane at the Philadelphia *Aurora* before editing the Baltimore *Whig* (1807–13), the New York *Columbian* (1815–16), and, briefly, the *Washington Gazette* (1821). A strong supporter of South American independence, he was the special agent to Venezuela, 1818–19. In August 1822, while a member of a filibustering expedition against Puerto Rico, he was arrested and imprisoned in the Dutch West Indies until 1824. Irvine's newspaper has not been identified.

From John Rhea

Washington 10 February 1822

Dear General,

You received the copy of the Message of the President communicated at the begining of this Session of Congress—<Gener> I have also forwarded to you a copy of the documents accompanying the Message also, a copy of the bill to establish a form of government in the Floridas—and I have forwarded to you a part of a report made in pursuance of Mr Whitmans resolution, and the residue of that report will be Sent to you, if I can procure <one> it and then you will have all the documents on that business.[1]

The Speaker of the House of representatives, received a letter from you—he shewed, it to me—he has written to you respecting it, and I agree with him in opinion, that it is better not to lay it before the House—the last paragraph of it is rather warm & Seems to reflect—if you have a copy of that letter, write all of it except the last paragraph, and then send it to the Speaker of the House, not as a copy but as an original. I now wish that your resignation of the Govt. of Florida, had not been so soon; <or that> however, you may be assured that if any attempt be made to affect you by reason of any of your proceedings in Florida your friends here, and I as one of them, will state that you are <desirous?> ready to meet any charge in the same manner as if you had not resigned. Write to me when you receive this letter, in the manner above alluded to, without expressing any opinion, or reflection in regard to any one directly or indirectly—You are I believe on safe ground; make not any inimical to you.[2] accept my best wishes for your health—Sincerely Yours

John Rhea

ALS, DLC (31). Published in Bassett, 3:148 (extract). Rhea (1753–1832), from Greene County, Tennessee, was serving his last term in Congress.

1. Rhea was referring to Monroe's December 5, 1821, annual message, in part transmitting documents detailing the transfer of Florida, and his special message of January 28, answering Ezekiel Whitman's resolution concerning the Jackson-Fromentin affair. Several bills for the organization of Florida territory were before the House and Senate. The bill introduced in the Senate on February 6 became law on March 30 (3 *U.S. Statutes at Large* 654–59).

2. See above, AJ to Philip P. Barbour, January 22; and Barbour to AJ, February 9. Jackson apparently did not revise and resubmit his letter to Barbour, and no reply to Rhea has been found. Congress shortly dropped its investigation of Jackson's tenure as governor of Florida.

From James Craine Bronaugh

Washington
16th. Feby. 1822

My Dr. Sir

Yours of the 29th Ulto. enclosing extracts from the letters of Brackenridge and Walton has this moment been recd. they confirm the opinion which for some time I have entertained of the Chief of the Qr Mr. Dept. *that he is completely destitute of honor.* He returned here a few days since, but has not [shown?] out—he has but little standing, and Congress will I have no doubt reduce him to a Col:[1]

Yesterday the 3rd. No. of the documents were laid upon the tables of the members. It contains Fromentins correspondence with the Secy. of State and the Secy.'s reply. That you will be astonished at the course of the President I have no doubt, as I know that you have entertained a good opinion of him, but his conduct in this affair must satisfy you that not the least confidence is to be placed in his professions of friendship, that he is a base infamous hypocrite. it consigns him in my estimation to ever lasting infamy. Let us for a moment take a review of his conduct—The Secy. of State lays before him Fromentins letters from the 20th. of August to the 21st. of Sept. in those letters the most billingsgate abuse is lavished upon that man, for whom he has expressed always the most friendly regard, to whom he is indebted for his present elevation & who has rendered his country much more important services than any man now living. What course under those circumstances would a high minded honorable man have pursued. he would have dismissed him from office without a moments delay and directed the Secy of State to inform that he considered him a corrupt scoundrel. But what course did the President pursue? He continued him in Office—in his message to Congress he spoke of him in the same manner that he did of man who had rendered such important services to his country and directed his Secy. of State to inform him that altho' his view was different from that taken by Fromentin yet "that he was persuaded that his motives & intentions were entirely pure."[2] I dont know when my feelings have been as much excited as upon takin[g] a view of the whole conduct of the President upon this subject. The time is not distant when he shall be made to feel, if indeed he has any feelings the dishonorable course which he has pursued in relation to this business. For the present I hope you will take no notice of him—let the decision be made by Congress—you will then have it in your power to make such an appeal to the American people as will satisfy them how much confidence ought to be reposed in the President or his Secy. of the Treasury, by whos advice I am induced to believe he acted on this occasion. I understand that Mr. Adams was decidedly of opinion that the only notice that ought to have been taken of Fromentins communications was "that he was no longer to consider himself a Judge of the U. States." That the President can justify his conduct, is I am satisfied, impossible and the more I consider of it, the more disgraceful it strikes me—

I shall visit Baltimore tomorrow and shall remain there 8 or 9 days and shall immediately upon my return set out for Nashville unless some thing should occur here, which in my opinion may make it necessary for me to remain longer. I am anxious to get back as I am satisfied that I should be enabled to restore you to health, at least, that my presence would have a good effect. I hope that you will take good care of yourself. with my respects to Mrs. J. & Lt. Donelson I remain yr. friend

J. C. Bronaugh

ALS, DLC (31). Published in Bassett, 3:151–52 (extract).

1. Letter not found. The extracts were probably taken from George Walton to AJ, December 10, and Henry M. Brackenridge to AJ, December 22, both 1821. Brigadier General Thomas Sidney Jesup (1788–1860), quartermaster general from 1818 until his death, had just returned from his first inspection tour of the South. While in Pensacola, Jesup reportedly expressed support for William H. Crawford or Henry Clay for president (see Affidavit of Andrew J. Donelson, January 26; and AJ to John C. Calhoun, June 28, below).

2. For the correspondence between Eligius Fromentin and John Q. Adams, see *ASP, Miscellaneous Documents*, 2:833–48. Bronaugh was paraphrasing Adams to Fromentin, October 26, 1821. For James Monroe's annual message, see *Annals of Congress*, 17th Cong., 1st sess., pp. 11–21.

To Francis Preston

Hermitage near Nashville
Feby 19th. 1822

Dr Sir,

The bearer Doctor Thos. G. Watkins who hands you this, was introduced to me in the year 1804 by Mr Willm. B[ranch] Giles of your State, as a young Gentleman of respectable connection, correct and honorable deportment, and of handsome medical talents. I received and cultivated an intimate acquaintance with him as such, until the unhappy affair with Mr Dickinson. On that occasion, the conduct of Doctor Watkins as represented to me, was of such a character as led to a considerable difference between us, which continued until the Doctor on his last visit to this country called on me at my house, and after a full explanation, that friendship and esteem is happily restored which existed prior to the unfortunate difference.[1] Doctor Watkins has intimated a respect for your character, and a desire to become acquainted with you, I have therefore taken the liberty to introduce him to your acquaintance and polite attention. I do this, at this time with the more pleasure, as I discover that Congress is acting over again the *second edition* of the Seminole campaign,[2] and believing that I possess your friendship, and as Doctor Watkins has seen some of the Documents which may not have been communicated, or if communicated, may escape the attention of my friends at first, he can explain and I trust satisfactorily, those parts of my official acts in Florida which my enemies have with the avidity of the War Hawk seized, under a wish to condemn me in the eyes of the Public, or forestall me in Public opinion: But I think without vanity, I can pledge myself to my friends that when all my acts are fairly before the Public, they will all be approved by the virtuous and patriotic part of the community—

Mrs Jackson joins me in a tender of affectionate regard to your lady[3] and amiable family, and accept the assurance of my individual respect and esteem

Andrew Jackson

LS, NHi (9-0029); Photocopy of LS, DLC (72). The LS was endorsed by Thomas G. Watkins: "Genl. Jackson was in bad health and kept a private secretary who wrote the above letter as Dictated by the general verbatim—the Genl. signed it with his own hand TGW." Preston (1765–1835; William and Mary 1787), who had served with Jackson in the 4th Congress, resided in Abingdon, Virginia.

1. Giles (1762–1830; Princeton 1781) was a former Virginia congressman. For Jackson's reconciliation with Watkins, see above, John Sommerville to AJ, February 4, and AJ to Thomas Jefferson, February 6.

2. Jackson was comparing the inquiry regarding his confrontation with José M. Callava with the 1819 congressional investigation of his invasion of Florida.

3. In 1793, Preston had married Sarah Buchanan Campbell (1778–1846), Patrick Henry's niece.

From James Craine Bronaugh

Washington
23rd. Febry. 1822

My Dr. Sir,

The weather has been so bad since I wrote you last,[1] that I have been prevented from visiting Baltimore as I then intended and I was so disgusted with the conduct of the President that I had determined not to call upon him again: last night however I went with Mr. Hay (his son-in-law) at a Ball who entered into a long discussion of every thing connected with the Florida transactions and he came out so warmly in your defence, that I candidly stated to him my difficulty in relation to the conduct of the President and my opinion that it could not fail to produce in your mind unpleasant feelings towards the President. He expressed his regret at the circumstance and said that he had for some time been fearful of that result—that he was satisfied of the Presidents high regard and friendly feeling for you and appeared I thought to attribute his course to timidity. He declared that he very seldom conversed with the President on subjects connected with the Govrt. that in consequence of the free manner in which he was in the habit of expressing his opinions of men and measures when those subjects had been introduced that the President very rarely broached them in his presence but that he had taken the liberty on several occasions to give him the opinion which he entertained both of you and Fromentin and that in strong language. And declared that altho' he could not boast your acquaintance, that there was no man in existance for whom he entertained so exalted an opinion. This morning the President sent for me—he appears uneasy—made a long speech on the subject of the important services which you have rendered your country and the obligations which he considers himself under to you—hoped that you never could for a moment have doubted his friendship for you—declared that it had never Known any diminution, that he considered your glory as intimately connected with that of the country and that his object had always been to place you on the highest possible ground. That in the approval of the motives &c. of Fromentin it was only in relation to <the> his issuing the writ of H. Corpus and that it would give him extreme pain if he supposed it could possibly be construed into any kind of sanction of the improper language used by him in relation to you, that he thought it best not to appear to crush him as by a contrary course he would be enabled to come out more strongly in your favor and have it in his power to cover the whole ground—desired that I would explain this to you—that he was so conscious his motives and conduct towards you had always been pure and friendly that he could not for a moment suffer himself to think that they could be doubted by you and that for him to enter into a vindication of them to you would appear awkard and unpleasant. He then informed me that on Friday he should give the Spanish minister a Dinner and invited me to attend

I dont think Congress will do any thing on the subject—the number opposed to you is very small and but little talents among them—you need give yourself no uneasiness, if a discussion should take place, you will be ably defended. I hope for the present you will remain perfectly silent. I think it will be best for you not even to express your opinion to the President on the subject—his friends will be compelled to defend you. Now is not the time to act. Perhaps after the adjournment of Congress it may be necessary to come out—more of this when we meet Yr. friend

J. C. Bronaugh

ALS, DLC (31). Published in Bassett, 3:152–53.
1. See above, Bronaugh to AJ, February 16.

To John Coffee

Hermitage Febry 25th. 1822

Dear Genl

I recd. your letter of the 13th. Instant,[1] and answer it in due time to meet your return from Huntsville, on the 13th. Instant Mr Guilbert [Gray] Washington set out for the purpose of having the bill filed against Bennet Smith, and on yesterday I recd. the letter from Mr Thomas Washington, a copy of which is enclosed, which I have answered stating to Mr Thos Washington, that as the first object is to secure you as executor, and the second to secure the orphant from injury, or his Estate from being injured by that debt, and his property prevented from being sacraficed at Sheriffs sale, I leave it to the discretion of him and Mr Whitesides, to determine where the Bill will be filed—at Nashville, or at Florence—In Tennessee, or allabama—If it can be safely done here I would prefer it, and on that event, instead of you being a party I suppose it is intended to make you a witness in the case. I have been confined to my house ever since you left me. I did go to Nashville to swear to the Bill—but the least exposure renews my cough. I write to Mr Thos. Washington this day for advice where it is concluded to file the bill & when it will be necessary for me to go to see him & Mr Whiteside on the subject—as soon this is determined on, I shall advise you.[2]

I have heard not a word from William Crawford since I left him, the cause of this I cannot conjecture—I have a horse I wish to send to my overseer, and expected William in by whom I intend sending him—I learn casually that the cotton is all taken out of the field, and Ginned & Bailed, if this is the fact, I cannot see what has prevented him from coming in—I would be much gratified to hear how my new overseer is progressing—I am waiting for some information from the city, on the progress of the 2d

Edition of the Seminole Campaign—but my enemies it is said, appear silent since the papers were communicated to congress, as yet, or I mean at the date of last advices, they had taken no step in the business—they are at a loss what to do their precipitancy, and relying on news paper information and Mr. Fromentine, they find does not correspond with the proof—To <pass> move for a vote of thanks to me, would be too magnanimous a course & a direct censure upon Fromentine—what course they will adopt I know not, I will be silent untill they unmask themselves, when I intend speaking out.

Present Mrs. J & myself affectionately to Polly and the children & believe to be your friend

Andrew Jackson

ALS, THi (9-0035). Published in Bassett, 3:153 (extract).

1. Not found.

2. See Thomas Washington to AJ, February 23; neither Jackson's response to Washington nor his affidavit has been found. Thomas (1788–1863) and Gilbert Gray Washington (d. c1847), brothers from Brunswick County, Virginia, were prominent Davidson County attorneys. For a discussion of the lawsuit, *Bennett Smith* v. *John Hutchings's Executors,* see above, AJ to Coffee, March 1, 1821.

To Horace Holley

Hermitage Near Nashville
Feb'y. 27th. 1822

Dr. Sir,

This note will be handed you by my adopted Son, A. J. Donelson, whom I have taken the liberty of introducing to your acquaintance. He visits Lexington, for the purpose of studying law, and attending the lectures delivered on that branch of science in the Transylvania University.[1] I have another adopted son, and a nephew whose education I am superintending, and am desirous of sending to the school over which you preside, as soon as they finish the course of study in which they are now engaged, preparatory to the University.[2] Any attentions which you have it in your power to bestow upon Lieut. Donelson, will be thankfully acknowledged by your friend & mo. Obt Sevt.

Andrew Jackson

LS, TU (9-0038). Holley (1781–1827; Yale 1803), a Unitarian minister, was president of Transylvania University, 1818–27.

1. Donelson's resignation from the army was accepted on February 1.

2. Jackson was referring to Andrew Jackson, Jr., and Andrew J. Hutchings. Both later attended the University of Nashville (formerly Cumberland College).

From Thomas Gassaway Watkins

Jonesboro'. E. T. March 13. 22

Dear General,

On my return to this place I had the happiness to find Mrs. Watkins and all Mr. [Samuel Dorsey] Jacksons family in good health, and they have all expressed much gratification that we have agreed to obliterate the circumstances that interrupted our old friendship, and they give it in charge to me while writing, to reciprocate cordially the kind remembrance of Mrs. Jackson & yourself.[1] Acting under the influence of the false impressions made upon me by the misrepresentations of others, I at the commencement of our differences indiscreetly rejected the proffer you made for a meeting to explain before the estrangement between us had gone too far. From the moment I fairly discovered my error in this, it has been my wish and determination, when I cou'd do it upon proper grounds, to propose myself an explanation, and if a reciprocal disposition was manifested on your part—to tear from my feelings all remains of hostility, and cherish a recollection, only, of the former kind & friendly intercourse which subsisted between us—and I assure you it adds much to my happiness to be able to say with a sincerity of heart, that, *all this I have truly done.*

On my return here I found several letters awaiting me from Virginia, two or three from Characters intimately acquainted and connected with some of the leaders of our Virginia policy—The next presidential election is a subject which occupies a prominent part in some of these, and I learn from them, that there the public mind seems as yet entirely unsettled, the question is considered premature, and there appears to be an unwillingness on the part of the state to stir a question, from which so much discord and diversity of opinion is likely to arise, the candidates are so numerous, and no one standing preeminently superior to the rest, that, as yet the public opinion can scarcely be said to be directed to any definite point. Some, perhaps, unfriendly to the present incumbent, say, that these numerous candidates are encouraged to get the nation so completely bewildered, that they will agree to his reelection as the only means of allaying the ferment—& that this is his expectation—Be this as it may, I believe, that the reelection for a second term has become so completely a part of the constitution from custom & public opinion, that no one <in future> will dare in future to suffer himself to be named for a third; and if he were <in Virginia> I am sure he wou'd be rejected with disdain. I am satisfied that in the presence instance Virginia wou'd not for that reason (if no other existed) support the present incumbent upon a new nomination[2]—besides this, however, there is in his native state, a powerful party as yet without a head, or in array—silently but decidedly disapproving, the aberration (from the old republican principles) which has manifested itself for the last five or six years—The excessive accumulation of offices, profuse expenditure of public money & annual increase of the national debt. The affectation of european & princely etiquette, where the president if he chooses can so decidedly give a tone to manners—the lust of office and the pride of power, about the seat of the General government, so utterly repugnant to the true genius & spirit of our institutions, have Sunk deep into the minds of both federalists and republicans of greater original simplicity of manners & principles—any circumstance which wou'd embody and array this party—wou'd call forth & display an opposition, as powerful as it wou'd be unexpected. it composes the soul & body of the State. If we wou'd preserve the original simplicity of our institutions and perpetuate this grand republic—we wou'd choose our presidents not for the splendour of their manners—but their simplicity & plainness—not for the eloquence of their haranguing—but the soundness of their judgment & their decision of character, not for their pliancy and amiable accommodation of the ten thousand particular wills and wishes that assail them on every side, but a firm, dignified and commanding resistance of every thing not founded in *right,* & plain solid *republican utility.*[3]

I trust that the people on this momentous subject will take the business into their own consideration, & transact it among themselves. On such occasions if they do not learn to think and *act for themselves* they will be betrayed. but my enthusiastic nature & feelings have hurried me on farther than I had at first intended to have obtruded my thoughts on this interesting subject upon you.

The servant man I had thought of selling you I find we cannot dispose of untill we get back to Virginia—where his mistress is willing that I shou'd sell him—then I cou'd also furnish you a likely young woman slave 16 years old also, and if you cannot more readily supply yourself with the whole number you want—I wou'd engage to purchase them for you carefully in my neighbourhood & upon the best terms they cou'd be had—and deliver them to your agent & order without any charge but their original cost—in this way you might procure tho*[se]* known to be good and upon much better terms than of the traders—Waggo*[ns re]*turning from Baltimore might take them to Knoxville. It will gi*[ve me much]* pleasure if I can serve you in it. If your agent chooses to take the *[servant?]* offered you can have him for the 500 dolls. Tennessee money still—off which *[if I]* sell him in Virginia to you his expences out to Knoxville shall be taken. I sh*[all]* be happy to hear from you at "*Milton Albemarle Co. Virginia*"[4] with my friendly respects to Mrs. Jackson I am with great respect Yr. friend & Obdt. Servt.

Th G Watkins

ALS, DLC (31). Endorsed by AJ as answered May 19; answer not found. Published in Bassett, 3:153–55 (extract).

1. On the reconciliation between AJ and Watkins, see above, John Sommerville to AJ, February 4, and AJ to Thomas Jefferson, February 6. Susannah (usually Susan) Woodrow Watkins (1788–c1873), Thomas G.'s wife, was the daughter of Samuel D. Jackson (1755–1836), a former Philadelphia merchant, who like his son-in-law had been involved in the Jackson-Dickinson affair. It is not known when the reconciliation between AJ and Samuel D. Jackson occurred.

2. As early as October 1821, some politicians suggested that James Monroe seek a third term in order to spare the nation from political division. Thomas Ritchie, editor of the *Richmond Enquirer,* rejected the idea, calling it "odious" and warning against the prospect of a "President for life" (*Richmond Enquirer*, October 23, 1821).

3. Elements of the Virginia Republican Party, counting among their number Ritchie, John Randolph, and, to a lesser extent, Jefferson himself, had expressed concern about the amalgamation of old-line Republicans and former Federalists, Monroe's personal and official formality, and the expense of refurbishing the White House after its burning in 1814. These Republicans generally became the "radical" wing of the party and supported native Virginian William H. Crawford.

4. Jackson was probably interested in purchasing slaves for his Big Spring, Alabama, plantation. See, for example, AJ to Andrew J. Donelson, March 21, below. Milton was at "the Shallows" on the Rivanna River near Charlottesville, where Watkins owned a plantation, "Glenmore."

To John Coffee

Hermitage March 14th—1822—

Dr. Genl

I have this evening recd your letter of the 10th. instant by the hands of Mr Crawford I have duly observed its contents, and with the advice of Mr James Jackson have employed Mr Egbert Harris, to proceed forthwith and take charge of my hands & farm[1]—Mr Harris, made the proposition—saying he had nothing to support on now, but his labour and he was determined to persue any Employment that would yield him a support—Mr Jackson says he is a good farmer & industrious—and has no doubt but he will do well—I could not get [Benjamin P.] Parsons and from the letter from Sharrock handed me by Mr Crawford, I find he will wantonly lie[2]—he says my negroes were & have been all sick with the Epidemic Pleurecies, bad colds &c &c—and that he found them naked & bare footed—this last I know to be fales, & is stated to form an excuse, and to raise an account for new shoes—he still has his stud there contrary to my express orders—this must take a hand, or if he attends to him my business is neglected When an overseer begins so early to lie—to deceive, it is time to drive him off—he has Just turned out as Mr [Robert P.] Curren of Franklin wrote me he would—I have wrote him and left it open for you & Mr J. Jackson to read, you must turn him out & give Mr Harris possession—I enclose you his receipt for the negroes Toolls, stock &c &c &c[3]—you will see that they together with the pork and Beacon are delivered to Mr Harris—I have (to prevent Mr Harris from any contracts for tools or any thing else) <have,> directed him to call upon you & if any are wanted you will have them got for me—I have got Mr Jackson to lay in for me one hundred yards of Linnen for the negroes Summer cloathing—you will direct Mr Nicholson to deliver to Mr Harris the little bed two chairs & the table, and such table furniture as Mr Crawford left there and have a pair of Blanketts bought for the bed—Mr Crawford having taken the blanketts I think by keeping Mr Harris from any trading he will do well—he says he will plant the old ground in cotton—and from Eighty to one hundred acres in corn—& put up my ginn house if I can get the loggs hewed—Mr Crawford has agreed to do this & to hew the whole timber for the press as soon as he is done survaying—I am determined to have my ginn up this fall—for should I fail herein I fear I will not afterwards be able—I have directed Mr Jackson to have the timber for the running gear, and boxes Sawed at Mr [John H.] Cloppers mill, I wish Mr [Francis] Kemper to give the bill and direct that it be sawed out of good post oak timber, will you have the goodness when you see Mr Kemper to get him to make out the bill, and let him know that I rely on him to have my running Gear for mill & Ginn ready by the first of October—I rely on him cutting the mill stones—I am determined to push that farm for a livelihood—[4]

Say to Polly that Capt Crawford will pack out her feathers on the horse I send to Mr Nicholson—[5]

I have had a hard time, but Mrs. J. Donelson Sent me over the other day a bottle of syrrup (I know not the composition) that is checking the cough very much and gives me hopes I may still get clear of it.[6] Should I, I will try to go out in april or first of May

My Dr. Genl I am really sorry in your press of business, to have to trouble you with my business, but I cannot venture out yet—and Sharrock must be removed or I am ruined—present Mrs. J. & myself affectionately to Polly & the children, & accept for yourself our best wishes

Andrew Jackson

ALS, THi (9-0048). Published in Bassett, 3:155–56 (extract).

1. Letter not found. Harris, a resident of Madison County, Alabama, remained overseer at Big Spring only until November, when Jackson dismissed him for failure to carry out directives on schedule.

2. The letter from Stephen Sharrock, whom Harris replaced, has not been found. Person (Parson), a Davidson County resident who had served in Coffee's brigade during the War of 1812, later replaced Harris as overseer at the Big Spring farm. Following the sale of the Alabama farm, Person supervised the resettlement of Jackson's slaves to the Hermitage, where he remained as overseer until late 1826.

3. Currin (d. 1857), an early settler of Williamson County, was a merchant who, in 1818, had joined with William B. Lewis to secure a lease of the Chickasaw salt lick reserve. Currin's letter, Jackson's reply to Sharrock, and the receipt have not been found.

4. Clopton and Camper (d. c1850), a native of Botetourt County, Virginia, worked periodically for Jackson over the next ten years. The receipt has not been found.

5. For Jackson's offer of the feathers, see AJ to Mary Donelson Coffee, March 20.

6. Mary Purnell Donelson (1763–1848) was the wife of John Donelson (1755–1830).

To William Berkeley Lewis

Hermitage March 19th 1822

Dr. Major

I recd. last evening your note of the 16th. with the copy of the letter enclosed,[1] the alterrations you have made after mature consideration are approved, and no alteration will be made in it; but leaving out one sentence in the conclusion beginning "you are Sir &c &["] and ending ["]knowingly injure," which I have thought upon mature reflection was superfluous, and ading a few words to a sentence where it speaks of his fromentines Jurisdiction being exercised by him believing it was his legitimate powers &c &—I have barely added his acknowledgement of his having no Jurisdiction except growing out of the two acts of Congress extended over the Floridas, of course he was assuming powers he knew he did not possess.[2] Since I have had the pleasure of seeing you I have recd two letters from Doctor Brunaugh he informs me, that being about to leave the City for Baltimore, the night before he was to set out, he was at a ball and fell in with Mr Hay who introduced the subject of the affairs of the Floridas, and spoke in the highest terms of me and approved all my acts—The Doctor spoke very freely to him of Mr Monroes' communication to Congress, and the manner which he had introduced that subject—On the next day Mr Monroe sent for Doctor Brunaugh and had a long *talk* with him on the subject many professions of friendship &c &c, & regret &c &c[3]—now my Dear Sir I see something in this ill timed, regrets, &c &c—that I do not like it comes at a time when he thinks, that an overwhelming majority of the nation and congress will approve my acts—and all this at a time when he suspected to be severely lashed through the medium of the Baltimore paper[4]—There has been a debate of great heat on the petition of the two spanish officers—Doctor Brunaugh describes Mr. [George] McDuffee in the most eloquent manner & with great point and severity, lashing Mr [John] Randolp[h], untill in his Mr Randolphs reply, he was as calm & moderate as a christian, and bestowed upon myself many & great ulogiums winding up with an expression that he had but little doubt that I would be the next president—If this was not intended as a piece of Irony by Mr R. Mr McDuffee has wrought, as great a miracle upon him as was wrought upon paul of old, and perhaps with as deep repentence[5]—The Doctor requests me to be silent for the present—I shall be so, except so far as to enclose Mr Monroe a copy of the annonimous letter, under cover of the one prepared—[6]

It will afford me great pleasure to hear of you from Knoxville, and as you progress—Mrs. J. Joins me in prayers for your safety & happiness, and may you obtain your wishes, and may that lead to a promotion of your happiness through life is the wish of your sincere friend—[7]

Andrew Jackson

ALS, NN (9-0056). Lewis (1784–1866), Jackson's longtime friend and confidant, served during Jackson's presidency as a member of the "Kitchen Cabinet" and as an auditor in the treasury department.

1. Neither the note nor the enclosure, a draft of AJ to James Monroe, March 19, below, has been found. Jackson had sent the draft to Lewis on March 15 for criticism and revision.

2. See AJ to Monroe, March 19, below; see also the Memoranda on Florida controversies, [cMarch–April], probably part of Jackson's process of composition. Jackson was referring to the acts "to authorize the President . . . to . . . establish a temporary government" in Florida, March 3, 1819, and "for carrying into execution the treaty between the United States and Spain," March 3, 1821 (3 *U.S. Statutes at Large* 523–24, 637–39). Both acts retained the Spanish governmental powers, vested in such officers as the president should designate, until the end of the first session of the following Congress unless Congress passed legislation sooner. For a discussion of Eligius Fromentin's jurisdiction as federal judge for West Florida, see above, Order to Fromentin, August 23, 1821.

3. See above, James C. Bronaugh to AJ, February 23; the second letter from Bronaugh has not been found.

4. The Baltimore paper to which Jackson referred has not been established.

5. Bronaugh's letter has not been found. The debate between South Carolina representative McDuffie (1790–1851; South Carolina 1813) and his Virginia colleague Randolph (1773–1833) occurred during the House of Representatives' consideration of the petition of the "two spanish officers," Marcos de Villiers and Arnaldo Guillemard, requesting Congress to reverse acting Governor George Walton's order for their imprisonment. Randolph had urged the petition's acceptance, while McDuffie opposed congressional intervention. On March 2, the House tabled the petition, but Monroe had already ordered the officers released (see above, Walton to AJ, January 7; see also *Annals of Congress,* 17th Cong., 1st sess., pp. 1104, 1139–49, 1172; *TPUS,* 22:369). Jackson's allusion was to the conversion of the apostle Paul by "a light from heaven," as described in Acts 9.

6. Jackson enclosed a copy of the letter from "Friend," October 29, 1821 (above), to Monroe in his letter of March 19, below.

7. Lewis had just embarked on a trip to North Carolina where, in May, he married Mary Adelaide Stokes Chambers (c1791–1823), the daughter of U.S. Senator Montfort Stokes (1762–1842). In later life, Lewis recalled that during the trip he had attempted to win Stokes's support for a presidential bid by Jackson, but that the senator declined because of a previous commitment to John C. Calhoun. Upon Calhoun's withdrawal in 1824, however, Stokes supported Jackson.

To James Monroe

Hermitage March 19th. 1822

Sir

I received a few days ago, the documents that accompanied your communictation to Congress on the 28th. of January last agreable to Mr Whitmans Resolution of the 2nd. of the same month, which were transmitted to me by Mr Adams.[1] After a full and dispasionate examination of those documents, and particularly those from the pen of Judge Fromentine, being the first opportunity I have had of seeing them, I cannot withold an expression of my surprise at the manner in which you introduced that subject to Congress in your Message at the commencement of the Session.

I would not be exercising that candor towards you which a long and stedfast friendship, on my part, dictates, were I to withold from you the state of my feelings on comparing those documents with that part of your Message which relates to this particular transaction.

I had a right to believe, and did believe, before I saw those singular productions of Judge Fromentines, that you were in possession of testimony of a very differrent description, which had induced you to express yourself in the way you did, when you supposed that both of us had been actuated by equally "pure motives." From our long acquaintance, and the friendship that has allways existed between us, I had supposed that you were sensible that I would not make <a> any statements that were not founded in fact: but if any doubt<s> had existed on your mind, from an apprehension that my communications had been written while under the influence of great excitement, I should have supposed the evidence by which those statements were substantiated, would have satisfied you as to their correctness.[2]

If on this subject, it was thought to be necessary to express an opinion in your Message, Justice, to all concerned required that it should have conformed to the facts which had been established. Here I must be permitted to say, that from the base falshoods, slander, and distorted facts contained in those communications of Judge Fromentines—his continued attempt to exercise other powers than those delegated to him, as defined by you and explained by me—his abandoning the charector of Judge and taking upon himself that of a lawyer, and his reiterated charges that I had *usurped* powers not delegated to me by you—and this too after you had defined his Jurisdiction, and your approbation had been given to my official acts[3]—he must have been actuated by other motives, than what he conceived, an *honest desire* of discharging the legitimate functions of his office; This must manifestly appear, when the proof is adverted to, of his acknowledgement, "that he (after seeing my powers & instructions) had no Jurisdiction except such as grew out of the two acts of Congress extended over the Floridas, and that he might as well return to Neworleans."[4] I am free to declare to you, that I think much injustice has been done to me in that part of your Message alluded to; and when it was written, Justice, as well as friendship to me, required that the facts upon which your opinion was founded should have been stated, and the documents have accompanied the message; or if this course was not deemed proper, the expression of an opinion, as to mine, and Judge Fromentines motives, should have been witheld altogether, from Congress and the nation. I feel satisfied in my own mind, that the manner in which your communication to Congress was written, made an impression, in part, on the public mind, unfavourable to me, and such as was not authorised by the facts in the case; I doubt not however, that the publication of those documents, now, will remove in a great degree, those impressions—The manner however in which this transaction was presented to the nation, has furnished, and still will furnish, my enemies, and those who are determined not to be satisfied, with a pretext to abuse me. I have adopted as a rule, through life, never to abandon my friend, unless he first abandons me; and never to believe that my friend acts unjustly, towards me, or intends to do me an injury, untill an opportunity is afforded for explanation—It is in this spirit, that this letter is written; and with a view also of aferding an opportunity for explanation, should it comport with your wishes to give it. In the meantime my friendly course towards you, will, as heretofore, be continued, untill I hear from you upon this subject, or ample time be afforded for that purpose. as an evidence of my still entertaining the same friendship for you, as I allways did, I herewith enclose a copy of an anonimous letter recd on the 6th. of January last.[5] It had been sent to Pensacola, and from thence to Nashville, where I recd. it, at the time before stated. I have forwarded it, to you, that you may Judge for yourself, of the views, and motives of the writer; The circumstance of my enclosing it to you, is sufficient proof that I have no confidence in the statement it contains. I never could suspect you, whom I have allways considered one of the most sincere, candid, Just and impartial men, guilty of such duplicity and hypocrisy. Could I for a moment entertain such an opinion, I should deem you unworthy of the high & dignified station you fill. That you might be enabled to Judge whether your enemies are within the range of your Cabinet, or else where; and that you might be advised of the conduct and motives of some of them, friendship has dictated to me the propriety of sending you a copy of this anonimous letter; and particularly under existing circumstances. Justice to Mr Adams and Mr Calhoun requires that I should explicitly state that, no suspicion ought to attach to either of them, of having written, or of having *any knowledge or agency* in writing it. Their acts so far as I have any Knowledge of them, will not authorise the belief that they could be capable of such duplicity and treachery to any one. In their official acts with me they have at all times, and on all occasions manifested a manly, energetic, dignified and honourable course—in all respects worthy of themselves—worthy of great and enlightened statesmen, and worthy of the confidence reposed in them. If in this letter, I shall have used any expressions, that may be calculated to wound your feelings, I hope you will do me the Justice to believe they were not intended. I have allways since our first acquaintance commenced, been in the practice of speaking to you in the language of freedom, and sincerity and hope that I may be permitted to continue in that practice, so long as our friendship shall exist. I will not then, disguise the fact, that my feelings have been excited on this occasion. Both my Judgement and my conscience, after a deliberate review of my whole proceedings in Florida, approve my acts while Governor of that Territory—and all I ask is, that, that Justice may be meted to me which I am entitled to, and facts warrent. With sentiments of Esteem I am Sir your Obt. Hbl. Servt.

Andrew Jackson

ALS, DLC (9-0059); ALS copy, DLC (63). ALS endorsed by Monroe: "with anonymous—abusive of me—His remarks on my message, relative to his affr with Judge Fromentine."

1. See John Q. Adams to AJ, February 22.

2. See AJ to Adams, November 13 and 22, 1821; see also, above, James C. Bronaugh to AJ, February 16.

3. For the charges against Jackson, see Eligius Fromentin to Adams, August 23, September 6, October 28, and December 2 and 9, all 1821 (*ASP, Miscellaneous Documents,* 2:837–41, 844, 868–73). For comments on Fromentin's "Jurisdiction," see Adams to AJ, October 26, 1821. For Monroe's written approval of AJ's conduct in Florida, see Monroe to AJ, September 16, 1821.

4. Jackson here paraphrased Fromentin's alleged statement made shortly after his arrival in Pensacola on July 26, 1821 (see AJ to Fromentin, September 3, 1821). The episode was also recounted in Andrew J. Donelson's affidavit, November 12, 1821.

5. See above, "Friend" to AJ, October 29, 1821; and Monroe to AJ, May 30, below.

To Andrew Jackson Donelson

Hermitage March 21rst. 1822

Dear Andrew

I have the pleasure to acknowledge the recpt of your letter of the 12th. Instant.[1] My letter to you will have advised you of the safe return of George[2]—I am happy you have commenced your course of study with Mr [William Taylor] Berry and that you are comfortably situated in lodgings well adapted for study and retirement—Having a good library, you will loose nothing by the vacation of lectures, your mind will be better prepared when they commence to be benefitted by them—you can amuse yourself occasionally with history—amonghst which if to be had, I would recommend to you the history of the Scottish chiefs—I have allways thought, that Sir William Wallauce, as a virtuous patriott, & warrior was the best model, for a young man[3]—In him we find a stuborn virtue, which was never overcome by vice, it was too pure for corruption—we find in him the truly undaunted courage, allways ready to brave any dangers, for the relief of his country or his friend—In him we find true greatness of soul capable of true friendship, and in his enemies, a lesson from the want of it, necessary for every virtuous high minded youth to be acquainted with, that he may be guarded against that vile hypocrisy, & deceipt, that often lurks beneath a fair exterior which is cloathed with power—and my young friend let me now tell you, that in our republican Goverment <you> (where it ought not to exist, and nothing but integrity & virtue in its officers be found) you will find, hypocrisy, duplicity, and the lowest kind of intrigue, practised by those in power to agrandise themselves, those who think the object is worthy of the means to obtain it, let those means be ever so Treacherous or base—hence then the propriety, of young Gentlemen coming into public life, to study mankind, and to view them as they are, not what they ought to be in a republican Goverment—In the history of Sir William Wallace you will See the great contrast between virtue & vice, between the high Minded honourable man, & the base treacherous deceiver—from which, as you progress thro life, you may greatly profit by Knowing that in all whom that have fair exteriors you ought not to confide.

In your next let me know at what time it will be necessary to make you a remittance—and the amount that I may make the necessary erangements for it—will you have the goodness to make inquiry, whether three or four likely negro girls from 15 to 20 can be bought in the neighbourhood of Lexington, or one or two boys, from 12 to 18 years old, and at what such negroes can be bought at—If you can make the engagement, at an average of four hundred and fifty dollars, or at five hundred in Kentuckey paper, I would thank you to do so for me, and I will send for them—but as they are for my own use, I want none but those of good charector, likely and healthy, and none else will I purchase—If an engagement cannot be made, you can make inquiry at what prices such can be bought for in Kentucky & advise me. Major Levy has said to me that he will aid in this inquiry[4]

My cough is abating—I hope with the warm weather it will cease, and once more I will be relieved from it—I hav*[e]* recd. several letters from Doctor Brunaugh[5]—he is still in the city will be with me by the 1rst of april he writes[6]—you will see they have had warm sparing in Congress on the subject of the spanish officers—I have recd a letter from Mr. Adams in which he promises me his final answer to the spanish minister so soon as it is made[7]—your aunt & the two little Andrews Join me in love to you, & believe me to be afectionately yrs—

Andrew Jackson

ALS, DLC (9-0070). Published in Bassett, 3:156–57 (extract).

1. Letter not found.

2. See AJ to Donelson, March 15. George was a Hermitage slave.

3. Barry (1785–1835; William and Mary 1803), a former Kentucky senator and lieutenant governor, taught law at Transylvania University. In 1297–98, Wallace (d. 1305) had led an unsuccessful rebellion against the English King Edward I.

4. Probably William Leavy (d. 1831), a Lexington merchant who had relocated from Pennsylvania in the late 1780s.

5. See above, James C. Bronaugh to AJ, February 8, 16, and 23.

6. Letter not found. Bronaugh did not arrive in Nashville until early May.

7. See John Q. Adams to AJ, February 22; for the promised transmission of Adams's reply to the Spanish minister, see Daniel Brent to AJ, April 18. Regarding the congressional debate on the Spanish officers, see above, AJ to William B. Lewis, March 19.

To Richard Keith Call

Hermitage March 25th. 1822

Dear Call

By last mail I had the pleasure to receive your letter of the 24th. ult. and am pleased to learn that Mr Brakenridge had shewn you my letter[1]—upon great consideration, on the recpt of the documents, and a sight of Fromentines Letters to the sec of state (for baseness, falshood & impudence has not their parralel, and which the Judge never expected to be before the public) I adressed a letter to Mr Monroe, calling on him for an explanation in a friendly way, of the "*good cause he had to believe,*" that Fromentine & myself thought we were both acting agreable to our respective powers; as he has expressed in his communication to Congress on the 5th. of Decbr last.[2] and to be consistant, and not to depart from my friend untill I had a full explanation with him, or untill I had satisfactory proof that he had departed from me, I enclosed him a copy of the enonimous letter, dated at Augusta Georgia the 29th. of Octbr last[3]—a copy of this letter I will send you by Doctor Brunaugh, let it have been wrote by whom it may, what he has informed me was in contemplation, has thus far taken place, and the time & manner of my resignation being [accepted] is well calculated to confirm a belief that Mr Monroe is, & has been acting the double part by me, my resignation is excepted the 31rst. of Decbr and Mr Whitmans resolutions the 2nd of January & it is postmarked the 9th. of January, seven days after Mr Whitmans resolutions, and in which debate it was intimated that I had resigned to prevent an impeachment; however I was fortunate; for before I recd Mr Monroes' letter of acceptance, I had seen the resolutions in the National Intelligencer, and wrote by the next mail, both to the President & the Speaker of the house of Representatives to the first to withold the acceptance of my resignation, and to the latter to assure congress, if my Resignation was accepted of before my letter reached the President, that I stood ready to meet any charge that might be brought against me and would plead generally as tho I had not resigned.[4] The Speaker has not laid my letter before congress—nor has Mr Monroe made any communication to the house—I will await his answer to my late letter[5]—if he chooses to explain, & that explanation is satisfactory, I will be silent, but should he not answer my letter, or if he answers & that should not be satisfactory, I have determined on my course—and when I state the facts to the nation—If I mistake not the public, will Judge rightly—and Mr Monroe will go out of office with less popularity than any President that has preceded him—I have been perfectly silent, and mean to maintain that course untill congress, disposes of the Florida business—I have not even wrote to one member of Congress, nor do I mean to do so—but I trust when it is over I shall speak, and that with effect. When my friends at Pensacola reads Mr Fromentines letters to the secratary of state, I expect he will find hotweather there—and I think when my friend Duncan gets a sight of them, he will have a warm & hot bed in Neworleans, his language as it respects Mr Duncan is of such a kind, (if F was worth notice[)] th*[e man's]* ears might be in danger. I have no do*[ubt]* but he dreams of horsewhips & cowskins every night of his life—& when you read these letters you will be still more surprised how Mr Monroe could consistant with Justice to me, introduce the thing to Congress in the manner he has done—Mr F. has introduced Mr Brakenridge as a channel through which he has recd some information he details[6]—where is the Judge, present me to him if with you—Mrs. J. desires to be presented to you affectionately—Lt Donelson is at Lexington studying law, & the two andrews request to be remembered to you. present me affectionately to the officers of the army, and all friends, and believe me to be as usual your sincere friend

Andrew Jackson

P.S. My health is slowly improving.

ALS, TU (9-0074).

1. Neither Call's letter to Jackson nor Jackson's letter to Henry M. Brackenridge has been found.

2. See above, AJ to James Monroe, March 19. The quoted phrase came from Monroe's fifth annual message to Congress, December 5, 1821.

3. See above, "Friend" to AJ, October 29, 1821.

4. See above, AJ to Philip P. Barbour, January 22; and AJ to Monroe, January 22. For the acceptance of AJ's resignation, see above, Monroe to AJ, December 31, 1821.

5. See above, AJ to Monroe, March 19; and Monroe to AJ, May 30, below.

6. Eligius Fromentin's October 28, 1821, letter to John Q. Adams characterized Abner L. Duncan as "the friend and adviser of all the tyrants, be they who they may. . . . who . . . was pre-eminently entitled to become, in 1821, the adviser of the unconstitutional, iniquitous, and tyrannical measures but too faithfully pursued since by General Jackson." Fromentin also claimed that Brackenridge had related that Jackson "was raving" when he first learned of Monroe's appointments in Florida (*ASP, Miscellaneous Documents*, 2:844).

From [James Gadsden]

Washington
10 April 1822

My Dear General

Absence from the City prevented my receiving your letter of the 15th Ulto, untill yesterday[1]—The letter enclosed for Mr Monroe was delivered by Mr Calhoun, The President will I presume correspond with you on the subject; & with the same frankness which characterised your communication[2]—The aspect given in the Message to Fromentins transaction could not have been dictated by any other than pure motives—In ascribing to a weakness of the head, what seemed to you to be the corruption of the heart; could not have been from any disposition to resist your opinions, or from disrespect to you—I have good reason to believe The President entertains the highest respect mingled with a large share of personal attachment for you—He evidences it in all his communications & he permits no opportunity to escape of publickly expressing the debt the country owe you—In his report on Fortifications, an able document honorable mention is made of your services; and in a communication now preparing for the Senate, on the subject of my appointment &c he will pay a high tribute to you[3]—The Country is at present in an agitated state: The Radicals are active in exciting dissentions; & overanxious to seperate all the influential men of our country from the present Executive—Mr Monroes administration is as well known to you as myself: & although there has been possibly in many cases too great a disposition to temporise; yet I believe you will approbate the general policy recommended—That it has not been pursued is to be ascribed to the opposition of the Radical party[4]—A party if permitted to triumph would entail on this nation evils that would take a century to remove—These remarks are made merely to place you on your guard, that party stick at nothing; & will make use of every little act to disgust you with the executive—They cannot hope to gain you on their side, but if they can make you inactive; or impress the community with a belief that you disapprove of the policy of the present administration, they will strengthen their own side as much as they will weaken their own—

It is time for all honest men to step forward in support of a liberal & independent policy—A policy which looks to building up: & consolidating the government, not to pulling down & distracting—On you & your exertions much reliance is placed; & a happy triumph is yet anticipated—

Mr Monroe will send on to day or tomorrow a spirited communication on the subject of my rejection; accompanied with a renomination explaining the motives which induced him originally to select me; & exposing my claims to such distinction—This spirited rept has alarmed many who voted against me—The motive was political & the blow aimed at Calhoun—They had been busy in impressing the <senate> community with a belief that my nomination was by the influence of Calhoun: & forced upon the Executive—If the Executive had tamely submitted to the nonconfirmation; a triumph to the radicals would have been afforded by impressing the community still further with a belief of a seperation between the Executive & C—— thus making the latter responsible for what they termed an undue exercise of authority—The Radicals will however be discomforted & still further with the fact that my nomination was a selection by the Board <of army> General Officers

As Congress will not adjourn untill the middle of May; it will not be in Mr C—— power to make the contemplated Tour west[5]—As you are anxious this summer to seek a restoration of your helth, I wish you could make it convenient to visit the East—If you will & will meet me in this City Early in June I will accompany you to Saratoga, the falls of the Niagara, descend the St Laurence to Quebeck & visit Boston &c Your friends in the East have long expected & would be greatly gratified with a visit—We would travel alone; & in the unostentatious style most agreeable to yourself—Let me controul the expences & I assure you the cost would be inconsiderable—Let me beg you to take it into serious consideration & accede to my proposition—You know you have long promised me such an excursion & no season can be more favourable than the present—You may take the Stage from Nashville & the public means of transportation hence is excellent—If you will consent the Sec of War will nominate you as one of the Visitors to West Point during the annual examination, which takes place on the 1[s]t of July—Let me hear from you on the subject soon that I may make arrangements accordingly—[6]

Say to [Samuel] Houston his accounts have been allowed; but that the Auditors will only pay me the balance; deducting the amount reported for suit against him[7]—I will write him tomorrow on the subject

I send you a Pennsylvania Paper—In which Mr C—— is mentioned—[8]

AL, DLC (31).

1. Not found.

2. See above, AJ to James Monroe, March 19. Most likely Jackson held his March 15 letter to Gadsden until he received William B. Lewis's comments on the draft of the letter to Monroe (see AJ to Lewis, March 15, and, above, March 19).

3. For Monroe's March 26 message to Congress regarding fortifications, see *Annals of Congress,* 17th Cong., 1st sess., pp. 345–51. In his April 12 message to the Senate, Monroe characterized Jackson as "the very gallant and patriotic defender of New Orleans" (*ibid.,* p. 482).

4. The term "Radical party" was commonly used to refer to the supporters of William H. Crawford.

5. Congress adjourned on May 8. For John C. Calhoun's proposed tour of Michigan Territory and the West, see *Calhoun Papers,* 6:701; 7:24, 52.

6. See Jackson's reply, May 2, below. Jackson was not appointed to the Board of Visitors.

7. Houston (1793–1863), major general of the West Tennessee militia, claimed pay as U.S. Army 1st lieutenant from October 1817 to March 1818, a period in which he was also Cherokee sub-agent (see Houston to AJ, March 11; AJ to Gadsden, March 13; Calhoun to AJ, April 6; and *Calhoun Papers,* 7:144–45, 202).

8. The newspaper may have been the Philadelphia *Franklin Gazette,* which supported Calhoun's presidential candidacy.

After John Overton had raised his competing claim to Allison land along the Obion River in West Tennessee, Jackson began negotiations for a compromise settlement that would placate his old friend (see above, AJ to Overton, December 9, 1821). But the entangled claims of Jackson's partners, James Jackson, Jenkin Whiteside, and Patrick H. Darby, and Overton's partner, former U.S. Senator Jesse Wharton (1782–1833), made a fair settlement difficult. Further complicating the matter was Overton's growing disenchantment with Darby and Whiteside, who were bringing harassment suits on defective land titles. On the other hand, Overton offered to sign over his judgment against the Allison estate to Jackson, thereby buttressing Jackson's case in his lawsuit against Andrew Erwin (see Overton to AJ, March 29 and April 5, and Darby to AJ, April 7). The complicated settlement, outlined below, involved reciprocal cessions between Overton and Jackson, giving Overton undisputed title to more than 2,000 acres. Jackson then immediately conveyed to James Jackson what Overton had just ceded (some 1,650 acres) and relinquished his remaining claims to Allison lands except those along the Duck River (see Deed from Overton and Wharton, April 17; Deeds to Overton, April 19; and Deeds to James Jackson, April 20).

To John Christmas McLemore

Nashville April 11th. 1822—

Sir

When Mr P. Darby returns to Nashville you will have the goodness, to make Division of the land Between Mr James Jackson, Jenkin Whitesides, and Patrick Darby, and myself—of the obion Lands, including five hundred acres of the 1000 acres patented in the name of William Terrell Lewis—in the Division, if it can be so eranged, it will be well, to give me the 500 acres out of the Lewis tract of 1000 as I am to convey my interest to Judge Overton—and as I am informed, that there is an adverse claim to this tract—set up by Ephraim [B.] Davidson[1]—and the ballance of my part, out of one of the Tracts, that adjoins one of Judge Overtons on the obion connection—as soon as this is done, I wish Mr. Darby for himself Jenkin Whitesides and James Jackson to execute the enclosed release and when I make the convayence of my part to Judge Overton I will execute to him a similar release[2]—Deeds to be made mutually from Judge Overton to us, agreable to allotment, and from us to him agreable to allotment without responsibility on either part—Mr Darby says in his letter to me that the one half of the part surrendered by Mr Wharton shall be mine—If this is done—it will be well, and will enable me to comply fully with Judge Overton in the Terms of the agreement—but I am intitled to but the one fourth and so have stated to the Judge[3]—I have laboured hard to bring about this compromise, without any view to my own interest, but at a sacrafice of all interest to that of feeling, and of friendship, and I wish this business speedily closed, when the division is made, and the release executed say to Mr Darby I wish to see him, and I will be responsible that the mutual Deed shall be made by Judge Overton as agreed on between him & my self—When the partition aforesaid is made by you, I wish it reduced to writing & signed by Mr Darby for himself Mr Whitesides & Mr James Jackson and by you for me and as being mutually chosen by all for the purpose of making Division—The papers herewith enclosed you will please retain, and return to me;[4] I am yours respectfully

Andrew Jackson

Photocopy of ALS copy, TU (mAJs); Copy, THi (9-0106).

1. On March 11, 1796, Lewis (1757–1813) had conveyed to Jackson patent 155 for 1,000 acres along the North fork of the Deer River. Davidson (d. c1825) was a resident of Stewart County.

2. The various deeds of release mentioned above were signed on April 17 and 19.

3. See Patrick H. Darby to AJ, April 7.

4. Enclosures not identified.

To Egbert Harris

Hermitage april 13th. 1822

Dr. Sir

I recd. your letter of the 2nd Instant on last evening,[1] which I have read with great attention I have full confidence you will do every thing that was left in your power from the latness of the Season when you commenced—and I have no doubt from your experience, but your plan of planting the crop is well Judged of, and will be the best, that could have been adopted.

I sincerely regret the bad conduct of the negroes in running away Guilbert is not heard of here; nor do I expect that he would attempt to come this way, never having been here; If he has left the neighbourhood of his wife he has attempted to go back to Carolina or Virginia, from whence he was brought[2]—should he not have been heard of, when this letter reaches you, have him advertised, in the Florence Gazzett, and get Genl Coffee to forward one to Huntsville there to be published, and the Editor of the Gazzet to forward one to the Knoxville Gazzett—and say to him to forward one to me, and I will have it inserted in the Nashville papers—I still hope he is lurking about his wife house—I have wrote to Mr James Jackson Who I know will have him examined for in that neighbourhood,[3] and if he can be got, I wish him well secured with irons, untill an opportunity may offer to send him down the river, as I will not Keep a negro in the habit of running away

should you want more horses advise me and I will have them sent out—The plan you have adopted with the Bull is a good one, and I think I will try to adopt it with mine here—

I will certainly see your friend Mr Saunders & your sister, and give them the information desired[4]—I have but little doubt but Mr Sanders will go out to Huntsville to court—I will endeavour, my health permitting, to go out & see you in the month of May next—My Dear Sir, altho you will find some of my negroes, <there> at first hard to mannage—still I hope you will be able to govern them without much dificulty. I have only to say, you know my disposition, and as far as lenity can be extended to these unfortunate creatures, I wish you to do so; subordination must be obtained first, and then good treatment—I am in haste your friend

Andrew Jackson

ALS, THi (9-0114). Published in Bassett, 3:158.

1. Not found.

2. On the night of March 25, Gilbert (c1787–1827), likely one of the slaves James J. Hanna purchased during trips to Virginia in 1820 and 1821, ran away from Jackson's Big Spring farm. Harris requested John Coffee's assistance in recapturing Gilbert, and Coffee

placed a notice in the newspapers. Gilbert was later apprehended and moved to the Hermitage, from whence in 1824 and 1827 he again ran away. After his final recapture, Gilbert was killed by Jackson's overseer, Ira Walton, when he resisted efforts to whip him (see Harris to Coffee, April 22, A-Ar; Advertisements for Gilbert, April 24, 1822, and [September] 1824; and AJ to William B. Lewis, September 1, 1827). During the 1828 presidential campaign, Gilbert's death prompted charges of Jackson's cruelty to his slaves. Gilbert's wife has not been identified.

3. The letter to James Jackson has not been found. The editor of the *Florence Gazette,* established in 1820, was Pierre (Peter) Bertrand.

4. Neither identified.

From James Gadsden

Washington
April 13 1822

My Dear General

I write in haste to acknowledge the receipt of your favr of the 25 Ulto— You may rest satisfied that Pensylvania is committed; Dr B—— who leaves this in a few days will give you every information on this subject—[1]

I write to repeat the proposition of your joining me this summer Either in this City or N York; with a view to an excursion to the <Spring> Saratoga Springs & from thence on a visit to Canada & New England— You have long promised your Eastern friends such a visit; & you know you once made a conditional arrangement with me to accompany you—I would now wish to exact the fulfilment of that arrangement—The excursion would be gratifying to me & would I feel persuaded <and> contribute largely to the restoration of your health—[2]

I would advise your taking the Steam boat to New Orleans & a water conveyance from thence to New York or Philadelphia—thus avoiding the <cost> fatiguing Stage ride from Nashville to Washington—Let me know as soon as possible your determination, that I may be prepared to meet you accordingly—Dr Bronough thinks it would be of great service to your health—It would be as salutary no doubt to your constitution; as the visit would be gratifying to those who appreciate your public & private virtues—

I have another request to make you—You know you promised me as an inheritance your public papers books documents &c—These though valuable may not contain all the matter relating to your campaigns which live only in your recollection—I wish you therefore at Every leisure moment to throw together in a book, it matters not as to arrangement; your recollection of all important events of your life public & private—Your Early career, the difficulties you had to struggle with in the world—Facts relating to the Early settlement of Tennessee <whether> Indian hostilities &c—The important events of Your creek & Orleans campaigns; the difficulties encountered in both—your plans how far executed; & your views generally which must have been known solely to yourself, of the operations undertaken & your confidence in success—It is impossible to enumerate all that I could wish; write therefore every thing in this great depository whether of private or public nature which you think would be interresting—Fail not to mention what you know of [Aaron] Burs operations—&c &c &c &c—[3]

I am anxious to travel with you this summer partially on the above account: that I may occasionally put questions to you on subjects which it would be valuable to preserve—I do not calculate myself to become <your> the Historian of your Campaigns but would feel pleased to have the documents which relate to them placed in able hands—To you we are indebted for the most brilliant part of our National history; & it may be said that your victories were as fruitful in beneficial consequences as Laurels—The Western World was saved by the one; an important state was added to the union by the other of your campaigns—[4]

I regret the fate of my colt; but <it> You know I am always prepared for events which are unavoidable—

To Mrs. J—& Andrew present my best respects & believe me Your friend

Gadsden

ALS, DLC (31). Published in Bassett, 3:158–59 (extract).

1. Letter not found. In his reference to Pennsylvania, Gadsden was probably predicting that the state would not be counted for William H. Crawford in the presidential contest.

2. See above, Gadsden to AJ, April 10.

3. It is not known if Jackson ever furnished Gadsden with notes or accounts of his life, although he promised materials in his letter of May 2, below. Gadsden published *Sketches of the Life and Public Services of Gen. Andrew Jackson* (Charleston, S.C.) in 1824. For documents relating to Jackson's putative involvement with Burr (1756–1836; Princeton 1772), see *Jackson,* 2:59–177, *passim.* Gadsden's *Sketch* did not contain a discussion of Burr's venture.

4. Gadsden was referring to Jackson's victory at New Orleans in 1815 and to the 1818 Seminole campaign, which many felt had led to the acquisition of Florida.

From James Craine Bronaugh

Washington
16th. April 1822

My Dr. Genl.

You will no doubt be surprised when you receive this to find that I am still here. I left this nearly three weeks since upon a visit to my friends, intending in a few days after to set out for Nashville, but returned here on Saturday, in consequence of information which I recd. that it was probable the President might not nominate Brackenridge as one of the Judges, which I find was but too true, for yesterday he sent in his nomination and has omitted both Call & Brackenridge For District Attorneys he has nominated [Alexander] Hamilton [Jr.] of New York who married a near relation of Mrs. Monroes & a young man from Va. by the name of

[Tipton B.] Harrison who is not more than 21 years old[1] & for Judges [John] Branch of N. Ca. and Col: [Joseph Lee] Smith late of the army who was cashiered on disgraceful charges about 12 months since. He has been guilty of the most disgraceful acts since he entered the Army in 1812 he has speculated on his Soldiers, converted public property to his own use, signed false certificates and many other such acts which are all matters of record and which were well known to the President, yet not withstanding all this, strange as it may appear, he has nominated him as a judge. I have placed the facts before the Judiciary committee of the Senate and have no doubt he will be rejected[2]—I have no confidence in the President—I have not been near him since my return, have spoken my sentiments very freely respecting him & shall before I leave this recall all letters of recommendation which have been addressed to him in my favor. I much fear that Overton will not receive the appointment of Commissioner. Duvall is the Governor & Walton Secy. F*[or]*bes is nominated as Marshall but *[will]* be violently opposed in the Senate.[3] I will be in Nashville in four or five days after you receive this Sincerely yr. friend &c.

J. C. Bronaugh

ALS, DLC (31).

1. Hamilton (1786–1875; Columbia 1804), a son of Alexander (1757–1804) and a War of 1812 veteran, had married Elizabeth K. Monroe's niece, a daughter of New York City merchant Thomas and Maria Kortright Knox. Appointed district attorney for East Florida, Hamilton later served briefly as a Florida land commissioner. Harrison, a resident of Lynchburg, Virginia, died at Pensacola later in the year.

2. Former North Carolina governor Branch (1782–1863; North Carolina 1801) declined the appointment as district judge for West Florida and later in the year was elected to the U.S. Senate. In 1829, Jackson appointed him secretary of the navy. Smith (1779–1846), a Connecticut native, was a veteran of the War of 1812. Smith's 1820 court-martial had stemmed from a feud with Alexander Macomb, and although convicted, he was granted clemency and honorably discharged, June 1, 1821. Smith was confirmed as federal district judge for East Florida and served until 1832. In December, James Monroe nominated Henry M. Brackenridge to the vacant West Florida judgeship.

2. Samuel R. Overton was appointed one of the Florida land commissioners, and Bronaugh was named to the territory's legislative council. James G. Forbes's nomination was withdrawn.

From Catalina Mir Satorios

Charleston 16th. April 1822—

Dear Sir,

I have before me your valuable letter of the 28th of February, & noticing the contents, I beg leave to say to you, that I am afflicted to hear of your indisposition, but hope in God, that you are at this time perfectly reestablished—[1]

If my husband, did not present himself (at the time) to lay claim to his slave, as you say he should have done, it was from his having been quite unable to undergo the least fatigue, & he consequently took the liberty of writing to you mentioning his indisposition, & not meaning any offence—His letters were written by the hand of Judge Mitchell, & the unhappy man did not live to receive an answer, which he so much desired—I did not write to you myself, hoping to have the pleasure of presenting myself personally to you at St. Augustine, where from the publick papers, I was induced to <think> Suppose, you would have fixed your seat of Govərnt. But I had not that pleasure as you went to Pensacola, However it was a great consolation to me to have received your letters.[2]

I am bound to believe, that your not having taken away the life of this ungratefull negro, (as he deserved) was the effect of the divine will, that inspired you with mercy towards him, out of compassion to me, that I might not in my misfortunes, be deprived of his value.[3]

I enclose to you, the Bill of the purchase, & the Bill of Sale as you required, which I hope may be agreable to your wishes—[4]

I also enclose a paper, that you may see, whether you can send me the money in the form that I request. It is a favor that I ask of you—[5]

I shall always pray, that no accident <shall> may befall you & I shall ever remain your very humble Servant, I kiss your hands,

(signed) Catharine Satorios

P.S. I will esteem it a favor if you will send your answer to the care of Messrs. [Andrew] McDowall & [Alexander] Black, that it may come more safely[6]—I kiss your hands (Signed) Catharine Satorios

Translation by Henry M. Rutledge and ALS, DLC (31). Satorios was the widow of Charleston merchant John (d. c1819). For a transcription of the Spanish ALS, see Appendix I.

1. See AJ to Catalina M. Satorios, [February 28].

2. The correspondence between Jackson and John Satorios has not been found, but for Jackson's earlier effort to identify and locate Polydore's owner, see Gabriel W. Perpall to AJ, June 16, 1818. The judge was possibly John Hinckley Mitchell (d. 1832), a Charleston magistrate.

3. In 1813, Polydore escaped from St. Augustine, joining the bands of British provocateurs Edward Nicolls, and later George Woodbine and Robert Christie Ambrister. An armed insurgent, Polydore was subject to execution when Jackson apprehended him near Bowlegs' Town in April 1818, but upon learning of his ownership, Jackson retained the slave in his service pending arrangements for Polydore's return. By 1822, Polydore had married Sally (b. c1804), one of Jackson's slaves, prompting Jackson's purchase (see Satorios to Fernando [Polydore], June 14, DLC-31).

4. See Bill of sale from Satorios, April 12.

5. See the undated note from Satorios, DLC (9-0117).

6. McDowall and Black were Charleston merchants. For the conclusion of the sale of Polydore (for whom Jackson paid $500), see AJ to Satorios, May 16 and 22; Bill of Sale, June 25; and Satorios to AJ, June 7 and July 8.

From John Sommerville

Branch Bank &c at Nashville
17h. April 1822

My dear Sir—

The remittance intended to close your account with the U:S. is not yet to your Credit for the reasons which the inclosed Copies of letters will shew, but as I have it now on the way to the treasurer himself in a channel that Cannot fail, we will Soon receive the necessary vouchers therefor.[1] On the extraordinary Conduct of the Branch of the U:S. Bank at N Orleans I will forbear to Comment further than to Say, that it certainly was not within the views of government or of Congress in creating the B.U:S. to put it in the power of its branches thus to fleece & put to trouble and great inconvenience, expense & hazard those who have public money to refund to government in closing their public accounts—It would seem that the office at N Orleans has become a complete shaving Mill. Such Conduct was very unexpected and unlooked for—[2]

Since sending my letter to the office for the U:S. Treasurer, it has occurred to me that your name does not stand upon his Books—you will therefore be pleased to write immediately to him to apply the Check remitted to him for your use with government—[3]

I most sincerely hope this will find your health much restored, again, and with the most respectful esteem I remain yr frd

Jno. Sommerville C[ashie]r

ALS, DNA-RG 59 (M116-10).

1. The enclosures, Sommerville to Joseph Woods, March 18, Woods to Sommerville, April 3, and Sommerville to Thomas T. Tucker, April 15 (all DNA-RG 59, M116-10), discussed Jackson's attempt to close his accounts as governor of Florida.

2. Charles S. West, the cashier at the New Orleans branch of the Bank of the United States, first refused a certificate of deposit for $662.37½ on Sommerville's bank. After Sommerville shipped the specie to New Orleans, West issued a certificate of deposit on the Bank's main Philadelphia branch only after charging a ½ percent premium, and the ensuing delay prevented the closing of Jackson's account until August (see AJ to Fontaine Maury, May 19; Maury to AJ, June 5; Warrant for transfer of funds, June 30; and Joseph I. Anderson to AJ, August 20).

3. Jackson made the request in a letter to John Q. Adams, April 23. Thomas Tudor Tucker (1745–1828) was treasurer of the United States.

To Andrew Jackson Donelson

Hermitage April 26th. 1822

Dr. Andrew

your letter by Mr C. J Brown was handed to me by that Gentleman on last evening.[1] I thank you my young friend for this introduction, from the short stay he has made with us, I have formed of him, a good opinion, and think he merits, all you have said of him, in short sir I am happy to find he is one of your associates—he appears to possess that kind of mind improved by education, that his society is well calculated, to improve, & enlighten that society with whom he mixes, such companions, alone ought to be sought for by young Gentleman, preparing themselves for the theatre of publick life—all others ought to be treated with politeness, but not as associates—

I expected you would find yourself a little lost, on your first settlement in Lexington—there you had to form a new circle of acquaintances—and in that, great care and circumspection, was to be used, to prevent yourself from being imposed upon by impostors, wearing the <appearance> exterior of finished gentleman, when in fact, you would find some in that Garb devoid of all the necessary qualifications, that compose one—hence there was the necessity of the excercise of great prudence—& circumspection, to prevent yourself from forming an intimacy with those who did not deserve your confidence or society—

I am happy to learn from Mr Brown that you are reconciled with your situation and I hope, it, may reallise those benefits to you, in the finish of your education that I anticipated before you left me. I well wayed the subject—it was with great regret I parted with you at the time I did, or that I could bring my mind to consent that you should be so far from me—but I could see no beneficial prospect for your study of the law here, or at Nashville—In short there was no legal charector of sufficient standing in morality & law knowledge, who was in the habit of taking in legal students, under whom I could have placed you, to have received those benefits I wish—I hate a quack of any kind—and another thing, the scriptures tell us, "a prophet has no honour in his own country."[2] These ideas, with the information I had of that institution, determined me to send you there—I still flatter myself it was a prudent choice.

I wish you to advise me when it will be least injurious to your study, to vissit me & I will send you a boy & horses—we will be happy to see you, but not thereby to injure your study, as I hope in Eighteen months, you can return, to enter into your profession, and remain with us—I have a great desire that you should turn your attention to writing on various subjects, nothing tends more to expand the mind, and improve the intellect, than writing & investigating various subjects; it gives to thought a wide range, and when your mind is habituated to writing when young, you acquire a facility in managing a subject, that is hard to acquire when of Mature age, or the meridian of life. writing is a good deal machanical, and is only to be acquired by habit at an early age.

I would also recommend to you to Join freely into the debating society, or the mote court, it will give you a habit of public speaking that you will find very beneficial when you come into public life, this like writing with facility, is only to be acquired by habit, which introduces system into the mind, and gives a fitness in the erangement of the subject, not to be acquired by any other mode but by habit & reflection—& when once acquired, gives ease, and grace to the Speaker, or writer in the management of all subjects.

My health is improving, but I find it very dificult to get clear of the cough, every change of weather gives me a new cold & excites my cough—I have found some dificulty in keeping my bowells open—when my bowells are open, the cough measurably subsides It is probable I shall vissit the Herrodburgh Springs this summer, should I, I will send for you there or see you in Lexington[3]—your aunt & the little Andrews Join me in affectionate respects I expect D. Brunaugh daily, have not heard from him in some time. your affectionate uncle

Andrew Jackson

P.S. I have not heard from Danl since I wrote you, but from his last letter have full confidence that he will do well.[4] I wish you to write him often & encourage him to application, and a strict attention to the obedience of all legal, and usual orders in the rotine of dicipline there—I shall do likewise—I have a great desire that his education should be compleat A.J—

ALS, DLC (9-0137). Published in Bassett, 3:159 (extract).

1. Letter not found. Brown has not been further identified.
2. A reference to John 4:44.
3. Jackson did not visit the Harrodsburg Springs during the year.
4. See AJ to Donelson, April 22. Daniel S. Donelson's letter has not been found.

To Andrew Jackson Donelson

Hermitage May 2nd. 1822.

Dr. Andrew

I recd your letter of the 23rd ult. and hasten to remit you one hundred dollars, in a bill No. 1, letter A payable at the Branch Bank Columbia to J McGuire or bearer dated Knoxville July 1rst 1818—signed Hu[gh] L[awson] White prest. Luke Lea cashr. which I wish safe to hand[1]—I have hastely glanced my eye over the fees and expences of the University and will endeavour to be prepared to meet them when they become due. I have only to remark that whatever may be thought of the pretensions of Mr Clay to the Presidency, by the Kentuckians, he has no prospect of being elected, Virginia as I am advised will not support him—But my young friend Keep yourself from the political vortex of contending parties for the present, and Look forward to a period of life, when your age & experience will Justify your country in calling you to that station, let this be a stimulant to your application to your studies, that at a short day you may prepare yourself for the bar, and to meet with credit to yourself, and benefit to your client, even Mr Clay in Forensic debate.

I cannot say whether there is any differrence or cause of differrence between Colo. Butler and Gadsden—In a letter to me Gadsden has alledged against Butler an interferrence with the Senate that gave rise to his rejection—his observations are ill natured as it respects Butler—I have not shewn the letter to Colo. Butler; but I have asked him if he ever had written to any of the Senators on the subject, he replied he had not, and that I might give to Gadsden the answer that it was a damd. lie—I hope nothing may grow out of it—but I know if I had shew Colo. Butler the letter he would have answered it with great bitterness—Butler is very firm when he takes a stand—Gadsden wrote under feelings excited, and has ascribed things to Butler not true, when he answers my letter I expect he will reflect and calmly do Butler Justice—[2]

In my last I advised you that if you had not made engagements for the negroes not to make any[3]—the Kentucky paper is so fast depreciating that I expect shortly to hear that it is worth nothing and has ceased to be received by any one it is impossible ever to restore its credit the people having lost all confidence in it, its credit cannot be revived.

I have been lately taken with a violent Lax, what ultimate effect it is to produce upon my health I cannot say—when a vacation happens and you can vissit us without injury to your study notify me & I will send for you—

your aunt & the little Andrews unite with me in good wishes toward you—Doctor B has not yet returned, your affectionate uncle.

Andrew Jackson

P.S. acknowledge the recpt of this letter on its recept as I have kept the marks nos. & date of the bill if it should be taken out, the thief can be detected[4] A. J—

ALS, DLC (9-0142).

1. Neither found. White (1773–1840), president of the Bank of the State of Tennessee, had been appointed one of the claims commissioners under the Adams-Onís Treaty. In 1825, he succeeded to Jackson's U.S. Senate seat. Lea (1783–1851), cashier at White's bank, had served under Jackson during the 1818 invasion of Florida and later was elected to Congress. McGuire has not been further identified.

2. The letters exchanged between Jackson and Gadsden have not been found.

3. See AJ to Donelson, April 22.

4. No reply has been found.

To James Gadsden

Hermitage May the 2nd. 1822

Dr. Gadsden

On yesterday I had the pleasure <of> to receive<ing> your two letters of the 10th. & 13th. ult.[1] It affords me sincere pleasure to find that Mr Monroe has renominated you, and has with that firmness & energy, due to himself, the nation, and the army explained to the Senate the causes that lead to your appointment—<as adjutant Genl—>your renomination with the reasons assigned will convince the Senate, that the President is determined, to support his own constitutional powers, and will not be awed to the silent acquiescence, of a faction, whose object has long been to demolish the army regardless of the injury which <will> must inevitably result to the nation thereby—It will afford me great pleasure to read the Presidents communication on this subject—and I shall anxiously await the arival of the news of your confirmation by the Senate.

I am happy to learn that my letter to Mr Monroe of the 19th of March last under cover to you, has been delivered to him, from the friendship that <heretofore> existed between us; upon mature reflection, I did believe the course I have adopted, was the only magnanimous one that I could pursue, <with propriety,> consistant with that friendship I allways had for Mr Monroe, and I am happy to learn from your letter, that he will answer it with that Frankness that I have exercised toward him.[2] When I first received the anonymous letter I had <some> doubts as to who was the writer or from what source it could originate—my belief <has been> is and I have but little doubt now but <I had no doubt, nor have I now>—that <the anonymous letter> it was written by the conivance of William H. Crawford or some of his parasites, because it details some facts that could <not> only be known to <any, unless> myself & family; or Mr Monroe & his Cabinett.[3] <and> This trick is in unison with the information given in 1818 to the Editor of the Georgia Journal, "that the Cabinet was divided on the subject of my arrest" which Mr Monroe told me (when I produced to him the letter of my friend from Georgia inclosing Doctor [Thomas] Moors (brotherinlaw of the editor) certificate that Grantland the Editor told him that he recd. the information from Mr Crawfor[d] or Mr [Thomas Willis] Cobb, but he believed from the former) was as positive a falshood as ever was fabricated, is pretty much of a peace with the anonymous letter—and affords strong presumptive evidence, of it originating from Mr Crawfords fertile genius at intrigue—[4]<altho> I know he is incapable of writing such a letter, still I believe it was written through his agency—If it had been as it states from a friend of mine, he would have come out and produced proof of the hypocrisy & wickedness of those professing to be my friends; & whose views was to destroy me—

I am free to confess to you, that there are misteries in these things that I cannot fathom <in this thing>, when I view Judge Fromentines communications, <and> he being selected as a Judge devoid as he was known to be of legal Knowledge, as well as moral principle in preferrence to Judge Haywood who was recommended by me & not an officer appointed that I had recommended or could have confidence in for the want of a knowledge of him and the attachment that is alledged to exist between Mr Monroe and Mr Crawford—after Mr Monroes knowledge of the baseness of this man; and the willfull lie he propagated in 1818 to injure me by forstalling public opinion in <the> which if it had been true he violated that pledge of secrecy as one of the Cabinet, for which, <even, if it had been true,> Mr Monroe ought in Justice to himself to me & the nation to *[have removed him]* from his cabinett, as an unworthy member; however I have never let those things take deep root in my breast, still hoping that Mr Monroe would be able to explain satisfactory to me those things that have tended to my injury, and of the injustice of which, I had a right to complain, I therefore suspend any opinion for the present & await his answer. There is no <danger> fear ought to be entertained that I shall ever be led astray from the support of Mr Monroes administration, as long as he persues principle; I love my friend & will support him, as far as he pursues the principles of our constitution, and acts Justly to all with <a> the sole view to the public good—and I never can believe without <positive> good proof that my friend will abandon principle, for the base & unworthy motives of self agrandizement but I would abandon any man who for selfish motives <of popularity,> would act unjustly <to the republic> abandon principle, <for the agrandisement of himself, or> with a view to enhance his own popularity or his own views, that were seperate from the public good—I hope & trust Mr Monroe never has or will <never> do this, and as long as he <continues to> takes Justice for his guide, public good his end, I will, as I have heretofore continue to support his administration.

Dear Gadsden I would to god my health and other circumstances combined would permit me to take with you the proposed Tour to the North & East[5] The pleasure of travelling with you would be a sufficient inducement, but there are many opposing obstacles—first, my present strength would not Justify the attempt at such a Journey—My private concerns require my attention, when my health will permit it—being much deranged from my long absence—The state of our paper money would preclude the posibility of procuring Eastern funds *[without a]* great sacrafice—I have my little sons including Lyncoya, at *[school,]* and their education has been greatly neglected in my absence.[6] Justice to them, require my attention when I have health to give it, in short Sir I must <have> take rest or my stay here on Earth cannot be long—for four months I have been oppressed with a violent cough—and costiveness, which had determined me as I wrote you to spend a few weeks at the (Herrodburgh) springs in the month of July next[7]—I have been recently vissitted by my <usual> old bowell complaint, which has weakened me very much, having a constant flow; in the last twelve hours, upwards of Twenty passages—my cough has nearly subsided, altho I continue to throw up great quanties of fleme. If I can moderately check this last—I am still in hopes of getting my health again, and be relieved from the cough—to these I might add other cogent reasons <cogent> but those I trust already named will suffice Present my thanks to Mr Calhoun for his friendly offer.[8] My public papers I have long since given to you, I will have them carefully colated & Boxed for you, and if health permits will make a memorandom of those things requested, there is no man, I have more confidence in than you & I resign to you my papers with great pleasure; with this request that they be preserved & returned to my adopted son when you are done with them, that he may peruse them when of mature age—[9]

In my last I named to you that I had not shewn your letter to Colo. Butler—I have since seeing him determined that I will not—Colo. Butler assures me in the most positive manner that he never wrote but the one letter to the military committee of the house of representatives, that he has never written to any member of the Senate upon that subject and requests me to say to you, if such a statement has been made to you, that it is a positive falshood—I have no doubt but he despises both Benton & Williams as much as any other man.[10]

I am much pleased that Genl Houstons account has been allowed, it is Just, & well supported by law[11]—<The Genl was of the opinion that Colo Williams of the Senate had an agency in preventing his account to be allowed, that he might appear as a public defaulter> Houston is a noble minded fellow & should he be returned for congress at our next election, of which there is but little doubt, I expect him & Colo Williams will see each other—The latter has shunned him it is said for some years.

Your mare will soon bring you another Pacolet or Pacolets, her appearance would evidence the latter, & I hope you will have better luck with them[12]—contemplating a vissit from you this spring I was looking out to be prepared with a good horse for you—I have not seen Colo Hays since I recd your letter—he is to be in here in a few days, he has moved to the forked Deer—I will endeavour to have the business eranged for you with him[13]—I am so weak I must close for the present—Mrs J. Joins me in best wishes for your prosperity & happiness—believe me your friend.

A. Jackson—

ALS draft, DLC (31). Published in Bassett, 3:159–62.

1. See above, Gadsden to AJ, April 10 and 13.

2. See above, AJ to Monroe, March 19, and Gadsden to AJ, April 10. Jackson's covering letter of March 15 to Gadsden has not been found.

3. See above, "Friend" to AJ, October 29, 1821.

4. Jackson here conflated his warnings about William H. Crawford. On August 25, 1818, the Milledgeville *Georgia Journal* had revealed the Monroe administration's division over Jackson's invasion of Pensacola, and while in Washington in early 1819, Jackson had

warned Monroe that Crawford was untrustworthy. Jackson undoubtedly repeated his admonition when Monroe visited the Hermitage in June 1819, showing the president John Clark's letter of May 24, 1819, which discussed the reported cabinet division and named either Crawford or Georgia congressman Cobb (1784–1830) as the source of the rumor. Jackson, however, did not forward information about Thomas Moore, probably a resident of Dublin in Laurens County, Georgia, or Moore's statement, until later in 1819 (see AJ to Monroe, November 22, 1819; and AJ to John Clark, January 6, 1820, *Jackson,* 4:349–51. Fleming Grantland (c1790–1819) and his brother Seaton (1782–1864) edited the Milledgeville *Georgia Journal.*

5. See above, Gadsden to AJ, April 10 and 13.

6. Lyncoya (c1812–28), a Creek Indian orphan found on the site of the Battle of Tallushatchee, grew up at the Hermitage. For the education expenses incurred by Jackson, see the Account with William Chandler, January 24.

7. Letter not found.

8. John C. Calhoun had offered to appoint Jackson to the Board of Visitors for West Point to facilitate AJ's trip north.

9. For Gadsden's interest in publishing a biography of Jackson based on primary materials, see above, Gadsden to AJ, April 13.

10. On January 17, Robert Butler had written the Chairman of the House Military Affairs Committee, William Eustis, complaining of his arrangement as lieutenant colonel (DNA-RG 233). Thomas H. Benton and John Williams led the opposition to Gadsden's nomination as adjutant general. Neither Jackson's previous letter nor Gadsden's letter to which it referred has been found.

11. See above, Gadsden to AJ, April 10.

12. Gadsden's mare has not been identified; Jackson had owned the famous racehorse Pacolet (c1808–25) from about 1813 until 1816.

13. Stockley D. Hays had established a law practice at Alexandria in Madison County, near present Jackson, Tennessee.

To Richard Ivy Easter

Hermitage, *May* 14, 1822.

Dr. Sir:

Our mutual friend Doctor Bronaugh left us this morning for Pensacola, & expects to sail in the Genl. Green tomorrow for Orleans—by whom I send this letter, and to whom I refer you for the congressional news.[1]

I have just received the final answer given by the Secretary of State to Don Duagua—on the subject of the officers in Florida—it is an able State paper, & puts my enemies, and newspaper scribblers to shame & to silence—had I a spare copy I would send it to you—but I hope it will reach you through the newspapers.[2]

Doctor Bronaugh is candidate for Delegate to Congress from the Floridas. It is all important that he should be elected for the welfare of that country—he has a general acquaintance amongst the members of Congress, and must therefore have more influence than any other member that could be chosen, and it is important to the happiness and prosperity of the Floridas that all the vacant land within them should be brought in to market at as early a day as possible, to give to you a stable, as well as an extensive population to enable you to become a member

State of the Union, which you will do shortly, provided you select a confidential member, who will look to the interest of your country.

Doctor Bronaugh informs me that Mr. [Henry] Crabb, who is now on a tour to the city of Washington and whom he saw there, says he is entrusted to push the Judgt. against you—I will attend to this and advise you thereof—Should he do it, you will have to return to Nashville.[3]

My health is slowly improving—the unfavorableness of the weather has been very injurious to my speedy recovery—I intend to travel a little as soon as the weather becomes more settled.

You have no doubt seen in the papers that our friend Gadsden's appointment as Adgt. Genl. has been rejected in the Senate, this has filled me with great regret—The President has again nominated him to the Senate, I fear from the Signs of the times, that the Senate will not approve and Mr. Monroe will not have firmness to renominate him until the senate be compelled to approve or give the nation their reasons for that disapproval.[4]

Let me hear from you occasionally I am very loansome, entirely without any of my military family & army companions.

Mrs. J. joins me in our best wishes for your health & happiness. Your friend,

Andrew Jackson.

Printed, *The Collector* 17(February 1904):37–38 (9-0160).

1. The *General Green*, a 300-ton steam boat constructed about 1820 at Cincinnati, Ohio, was based at Columbia, Tennessee.

2. See Daniel Brent to AJ, April 18.

3. Early in 1821, Easter's delinquent accounts as an assistant paymaster had been turned over to the treasury department for disposition. Later that year, Crabb (1793–1827), U.S. district attorney for West Tennessee, instituted proceedings and won a judgment against Easter for $26,990.60, including costs. Jackson and John Overton became sureties for Easter's bonds, prompting a suit against them for recovery of the amount, but the intervention of the treasury department relieved them of the debt (see above, AJ to John C. Calhoun, March 1, 1821; AJ to Overton, December 21, 1823, and January 10, 1825; and *U.S. v. John Overton and AJ, bail of Richard I. Easter*, May 27, 1824.

4. For a discussion of James Gadsden's nomination, see above, James C. Bronaugh to AJ, February 8.

To Richard Keith Call

Hermitage May 20th. 1822

Dear Call

Yesterdays mail brought me your letter of the 14th. of April—I recd. one from Capt Easter via Neworleans of the 6th. instant—I name this to shew you the delays of the post rout from Pensacola direct over land.[1]

I sincerely regret that I had not recd your letter before Doctor Brunaugh left here—his friends at the city, amonghst whom I include Govr. Duval had induced him to offer for delegate, and I should regret very much that you and him should oppose each other as I think it might be the means of Shutting you both out, and opening a door for someone to come in who would not be disposed to pursue a course that would promote the real interests of that country. as to Colo Walton he is provided for, and I am induced to believe that he owes his being preferred to Mr Worthington to the differrence that was likely to arise yet unsettled, as I am awaiting his answer to my letter with which I forwarded hi*[m a copy]* of t*[he anony]*mous letter, &c &c &c between Mr Monroe and myself, and Mr Monroe finding I viewed things that were past as they ought—and in my last letter to Mr Adams, had recommended Colo Walton warmly, and as I believe Mr Monroe had no wish *now* to break with me, this I think with other Views, determined his selection of Walton[2]—Therefore Colo. Walton is out of the way—I have no doubt but your popularity is more extensive than any others in that country and I will with the Candeur of a father and a friend give you my advice on the present important occasion—I say *important*—it is so, both to your Country and yourself To your Country, as I do know its future greatne*[ss]* will much depend, on having all fraudulen*[t]* grants put down, the valid ones speedily establ*[ish]*ed and the vacant lands brought into markett at an early day, which will give speedily to your country great wealth and a stable population, untill this is done, men of Capital will not emigrate to your Country and become Squatters—added to this the Indians in the Floridas must be concentrated, or sent up to the Creek Nation—These things alone can be brought about by the energy & attention of your Delegate, <to your interest> as the present executive will not risque his popularity by urging any thing that may be opposed by the Eastern people; therefore these things I repeat are to be brought about by the exertions of the Delegate—These objects I have no doubt, <you> (if choosen) would be brought about if in your power; But the delegate will have a delicate situation—<and> all these things will be calculated on and expected to be done by him, and if he fails in any, his political opponents, will seize on it as a theme, to pull him down, and destroy his popularity for the future—you are Just entering into your pr*[o]*fession, have laid a foundation for an independant fortune, by its pursuit; and, (if you were to become a Delegate) it might <not> throw you out of your practice as a lawyer which you have obtained, and will maintain, if you pursue it, ought to be well weighed in your Situation, for let me tell you, without an independance within yourself, you never will obtain it <from> by serving the public[3]—and if reduced to poverty, your friends altho now numerous will become few, and if ever you should (by entering into public life) loose your practice it will be dificult again to regain it, as you may calculate on an augmentation, both as to numbers, and talents, to your bar, and the confidence that is now placed in you might be transferred to others by your being absent—from all which, I would recommend to you, to view these things in all their bearings, before you determine on entering into a political life. But on the other hand; society has claims on every individual who compose it—and if your Country calls on you to represent <Florida?

Public?> her as a delegate, you are bound to obay that call; the services of every man belongs to the country, when that country requires it—and upon that principle I have commenced and will end my life; I never was a candidate for any office I have filled.

My Dear young friend, it would afford me great pleasure to see you on the floor of Congress, my own interest would point out to me, to recommend it to you, to offer as a Delegate, finding that you could be elected, <when> then I could have a friend on the floor with sufficient energy—to call up Mr Whitemans & Archers resolutions, that has been permitted to sleep upon the table—& the last and final answer of Mr Adams to the spanish minister has never been ordered to be printed by the house of representatives, or a motion by one for that purpose, fearfull least (as I suppose) it would shew to the american nation, my Justification, & their condemnation[4]—But Sir I could not recommend to you Just entering into life, in a lucrative practice, in a new country, to abandon that practice (that might not be regained) to become Delegate by offering for it, and foregoing on the electioneering scenes to obtain it—If it *[is]* voluntarily offerred and your services required by your Country, you must accept, your Country has a right to demand it—and if you did not yield it—When your circumstances become independant, and you might wish to be in public life, and offerred yourself for the suffrages of the people, your refusal would be wielded to your injury—again, if it is thought by your friends in that country that your services is more important (in their opinion) than any other, and they press you to hold a poll for Delegate; if they are a majority of your inte*[llige]*nt friends, it will be your duty to yield your consent; but you are not bound even to do this, at the sacrafice of your private interes*[t]* because it is not certain, that it is the wish of your Country untill it is Tested by a vote, but still if the sacrafice of private interest is not too great, I would recommend your acquiescence—I do believe it will be necessary for the benefit of your Country that you or Doctor Brunaugh should be selected—but you must not both offer in opposition; let your friends decide, if it is both your wishes to offer—I am clearly & decidedly of opinion that one of you are the only individuals that can effect much for you Country but would sincerely regret hearing that you <should be> were in opposition to each other. I approve in all young men enterprise, and aspiring views, without them, no young man ever did become conspicuous—and I must confess I approve of your views; the very moment that your private interest will permit of you persuing a political life, and you can be serviceable to your country, you are right in pushing your fortune by offerring your service to the Public; without enterprise you never can be known, with it, and industry, you are sure to succeed—But as you are in a lucrative practise, would it not be better to pursue it for the present—and be ready when you become a state, to represent it in <Congress> the house of Representatives, or the senate—If it should be the fact that Doctor Brunaugh cannot be elected, I would rejoice that you could, offer, if not at too great a sacrafice of *present interest,* and *future* *prospects.* I wish one or the other in our next congress, the good of your Country require it—but I do not wish you to oppose each other—but I wish you to let your friends decide if both of you are up.

I foresee with great pleasure that you will become one of the most prominant charectors of that Country, and to do this, and place yourself permanantly in the affections of the people, is to pursue, a steady independant course, pursuing your own Judgt. giving Conscience fair play, and never upon no occasion where national principles are involved <ever?> to abandon it—Keep it ever before you, as your polar star, and you wi*[ll]* ultimately succeed; This has been my universal guide, and altho <often> my official acts have been araigned by many, still upon investigation, all my acts have been approved by the Govr and the nation.

I wrote you on the subject of Doctor Brunaughs offerring by yesterday mail—to which I refer you, not expecting that you would be up for delegate at the time I wrote, and which of you may be first before the public I do not know—if both are up, let your friends decide who will hold the poll—it will not do for a house to divide against itself[5]—Present me to Colo. Walton, and say to him for the present I have not time to write him.

By last nights mail I recd transmitted to me by Major Eaton the proceedings of the senate the injunction of Secrecy being removed on the recommendations of the President, & nominations for office by him[6]—I sincerely regret the fate of our friend Colo. Gadsden, he is rejected with Towson on the renomination of the President—The military committee has made a report embracing a view of the late reduction, in which they have been severe upon the President, and board of officers, which you will see—and Indeed I think very merittedly in some instances—and Genl Scott and his Book is brought before the nation in ruther suspicious coulors—and I do suppose the 14th. & 75 sections will be repealed—Major Eaton says that Parker, Fenwick, & [William] Linday he presumes will be rejected[7]—The two latter I regret—but I wrote Mr Monroe & Mr Calhoun as soon as I saw that unmilitary recommendation upon the Register my opinion of matters & things, they have found them realised—in fact I never knew wise men get into such errors before, and the Testimony of Genl Parker & a document published signed by J. Bro*[wn,]* President of the Board, really places the bo*[ard]* in the contemtable light, of being a boar*[d of]* general favouratism, than any thou*[ght it]* & the recommendation of Colo. Smith *[by]* Genl Brown as Govr. of the Floridas, & Mr Monroe nominating him as Judge of East Florida placing both the President & Genl Brown in an awkard situation—Whenever men deviate from the broad path of Justice, or pursue a course for popularity, they are sure to fall into the pitt they dig for others—[8]

I named to you in my letter of yesterday that I had <followed?> sent to Major Nicholas a paper containing Mr Adams final answer to the Spanish Minister—with a request to shew it to you.[9]

Present me to all friends & accept for yourself, Mrs. J. & my sincere prayers for your wellfare & happiness they two Andrews greet you affectionately, your friend

Andrew Jackson

P.S. present Mrs. J. & myself to Capt Easter—I rejoice to learn that Dinkin & [James] Ramage[10] are frien*[ds]* present me to them both affectionately A. J.

ALS draft and Typed copy, DLC (31).

1. Neither letter found.

2. See above, AJ to Monroe, March 19. For Jackson's endorsement of Walton, see AJ to John Q. Adams, January 31. William G. D. Worthington and Walton had served as secretaries of East and West Florida respectively, but President Monroe appointed Walton secretary for the united territory.

3. Shortly after the transfer of Florida in July 1821, Call had formed a law partnership with Henry M. Brackenridge.

4. Ezekiel Whitman's February 28 resolutions, calling for further investigation into the Callava and Fromentin controversies, were tabled after a brief debate, and William S. Archer's March 5 resolutions condemning generally the appointment of a Florida governor with supreme powers and specifically Jackson's arrest of José M. Callava and citation of Eligius Fromentin for contempt were never debated. Adams's letter of April 15 to Joaquin de Anduaga, sent to the House on April 19, was also tabled, but it was ordered printed in the Senate (see *Annals of Congress,* 17th Cong., 1st sess., pp. 1157–64, 1195–96, 1619, 2040–54).

5. Letter not found. The house divided allusion was to Mark 3:25.

6. Eaton's letter has not been found. On April 30, the Senate made public its proceedings regarding the James Gadsden and Nathan Towson nominations (see *Annals of Congress,* 17th Cong., 1st sess., pp. 470–510).

7. Jackson was referring to section 14 of the army reduction law, which enacted Winfield Scott's "General Regulations for the Army," and article 75 of those regulations, governing transfers (3 *U.S. Statutes at Large* 616; *ASP, Military Affairs,* 2:201–266). In its April 25 report, the Senate military affairs committee had noted a discrepancy between the war department's text of article 75 and that enacted by Congress in 1821 (*Annals of Congress,* 17th Cong., 1st sess., pp. 489–502). Daniel Parker was displaced by Towson's reappointment as paymaster general; John R. Fenwick was confirmed as colonel of the 4th Artillery; Lindsay (d. 1838), who had been assigned to the 7th Infantry Regiment on June 1, 1821, was transferred back to the 3rd Artillery Regiment, where he was lieutenant colonel.

8. See AJ to John C. Calhoun, July 29, and to James Monroe, August 4, both 1821. Parker's April 23 deposition, and Jacob J. Brown's April 13, 1821, letter to Henry Atkinson, detailed the maneuvers that led to Atkinson's line command (*Annals of Congress,* 17th Cong., 1st sess., pp. 502–503, 505). For Brown's recommendation of Joseph L. Smith, see his letter to Monroe, February 12 (DNA-RG 59, M439-15).

9. The letter to Cary Nicholas has not been found. Adams's April 15 letter to Joaquin de Anduaga (dated April 5) appeared in the Pensacola *Floridian,* June 15.

10. Ramage, a naval lieutenant cashiered in 1831, commanded the *Porpoise,* a 198-ton, 12-gun schooner built in 1820.

To Andrew Jackson Donelson

Hermitage May 20th. 1822

Dr. Andrew

yours of May 10th. & 14th. reached me last evening,[1] and I am happy to learn that my letter of the 2nd Instant enclosing to you one hundred dollars had reached you—[2]

I was fearfull that it had miscarried, or had been purloined on its passage as I did not receive by due course of mail, your acknowledgement.

I wrote you on the 19th. by Mr [Frederic] Harris from Alabama who was to leave Nashville this morning for Lexington to enter the University at Lexington, he appears a good young man, and is well spoken of by Mr Wm Sanders my neighbour, you will therefore, treat him with that attention due to him[3]—<My> one of my objects in placing you at Lexington was that you might become acquainted with the young gentlemen from various parts of the south & west—that when you enter in to professional life, which may be a prelude to political; you may be known—for I will not disguise, I look forward, if you live, to the time when you will be selected to preside over the destinies of america—I therefore wish you for the present to steer clear of all political broils—I do not mean that you should be silent on political subjects, but when you speak on them do it with reflection, embracing general remarks unless where it may become necessary to give an opinion, then, if necessary give it agreable to your opinion of the subject before you, agreable to your ideas of right, and Justice, reguardless of consequences, allways keeping in view principles, not men, the public good, seperate from individual agrandizement—constitutional & legal rights—seperate from individual views—in short, *measures* that will promote the public good, reguardless, of individual views, or the agrandizement of party <views> purposes.

by this mail I send you two news papers, the Nashville Gazzett containing Mr Adams last & final answer to the Minister of Spain, with a short comment by the Editor; which I wish you to have published in the papers of Lexington—The other the National Intelligencer giving the proceedings of the Senate & President on the subject of the reduction of the army on which I shall at present make no comment, as I wish to have your opinion on those proceedings, as well on the message of the President, as on the report of the military committee[4]—I will barely remark, that you must recollect, that in my letters to Mr Monroe & Mr Calhoun from Pensacola, I brought to their view the dificulties with which they are now surrounded—[5]

your aunt & the little Andrews *[are]* in good health & send their respects to you I should have set out for Alabama, but I am waiting for the act of Congress if finally passed (of which I am not informed) allowing the claim of Thos. Carr and others which I mentioned to you in my last, that I may when out, enter your & Danls. interest & that of your aunt Cafferys—where she may have a home for her & her desolate daughters & their children.[6] I am your affectionate uncle

Andrew Jackson

P.S. I never authorised my subscription to the L. reporter—[William W.] worsly was my bitter enemy, and about that time, heaping all scurulous abuse upon me—however as he says Major Baker did it, it was right to pay the mony—when I see Major Baker I shall make the inquiry—so for the present let it rest,[7] A.J—

ALS and Extract, DLC (9-0167, -0171). Published in Bassett, 3:162 (extract).

1. Letters not found.

2. See above, AJ to Donelson, May 2.

3. See AJ to Donelson, May 19. Harris (d. 1829) was from Limestone County. Saunders (c1776–1846) operated the Fountain of Health spa, about one mile from the Hermitage, frequented by Jackson and his family.

4. The enclosed issue of the *Nashville Gazette* is not extant. The Washington *National Intelligencer,* May 4, covered the Senate proceedings regarding the nominations of James Gadsden and Nathan Towson. Neither the Lexington *Kentucky Reporter* nor the *Kentucky Gazette* republished the articles.

5. See AJ to John C. Calhoun, July 29, and AJ to James Monroe, August 4, both 1821; see also, AJ to Calhoun, January 5.

6. See AJ to Donelson, May 19. Despite Jackson's optimism, Congress did not compensate the heirs of John Donelson (c1718–86) and Thomas Carr, surveyors of the "Big Bend" of the Tennessee River, until May 1824, when it awarded 5,000 acres in Alabama or Mississippi (6 *U.S. Statutes at Large* 313). Jackson was referring to his sister-in-law Mary Donelson Caffery, her widowed daughters Mary Caffery Knox and Catharine Caffery Walker (b. c1797), and their children Sarah (Sally) Knox (c1807–91), William Lucky Knox (1814–81), Rachael Walker, and George Wythe Walker.

7. Jackson was referring to a bill for a subscription to the Lexington *Kentucky Reporter.* Worsley (d. 1852) and his brother-in-law Thomas Smith had edited the newspaper until March 1819, when Smith became sole proprietor, and Worsley continued as a bookseller. Jackson had clearly subscribed to the paper at one time, for in late 1814 Jackson's aide Thomas L. Butler wrote Worsley asking that Jackson's paper be forwarded to the Gulf area (October 15, Draper Papers, WHi). Whether Isaac L. Baker renewed the subscription in 1816 is unknown. For Jackson's disagreement with Worsley, see AJ to Worsley & Smith, March 11, 1817 (*Jackson,* 4:99–102).

From James Monroe

Washington May 30. 1822.

Dear Sir

I have been much hurt to find complaints in your late letters, that I had not done you justice, in the views which I presented to Congress, of proceedings in Florida, or at least that I had done more than justice, to another, in a concern which had relation to you.[1] I am utterly incapable of doing injustice to any one, intentionally, and certainly if it were otherwise, an injury to you, would be among the last acts of which I could be capable, in any form whatever. All those acting under the Executive, have a claim to its protection, & to a liberal view of their conduct, and nothing more was shewn, to the person in question, in what was said, of the act alluded to.[2] I will only remark, that had the defense and support of you, been the sole object, I could not have taken a course better adapted to the end. But that was not the sole object, nor ought it to have been. I have however no hesitation to say, that it was one, which I never lost sight of, in any act during the Session, nor indeed on any occasion, when I have been called on to speak of your conduct. Had I acted otherwise, I should have done great violence alike to my feelings and judgment, which have always impelled me, in a very different direction.

I was exposed in the course of the last session, to much embarrassment. The lessons of the late war, seem to have been forgotten, and the efforts, since made, to put the country in a better state of defense, for another, happen when it may, have been tortur'd into crimes, and those who have been most active, treated as the greatest criminals. Every little transaction, has been sifted into, in many instances, under the instigation of anonymous writers, on false or prejudic'd views, and the great effort seems to have been, to pull down institutions and characters, rather than to rear them up, for the support and honor of the country. It is due to Congress to observe, that this effort has been confin'd, to a small portion of its members, only, by far the greater number, having been spectators of the scene, believing also, as I presume, that less injury would be done, by suffering the calls & scrutiny to be made, than by opposing them. The inquiry turned out always differently, from what the promoters of it, expected, for I do not recollect, a single instance, in which, that was not the result. I mention these things confidentially, for altho' they must have attracted your attention, yet it is not proper for me to say, any thing harsh of Congress, or of any part of it. It becomes me more to hold up the body, and to put the best face on our affairs, in support of our institutions. There are enough to do what is right, in respect to those in the public service, by keeping the people well informed, and stimulating them to do their duty.

I send you my message, respecting the right of congress to adopt & execute a system of internal improv'ment, and on the subject generally. I shall be glad to have your sentiments, on that subject.[3] I have heard with pleasure that your health hath improvd, & that Mrs Jackson has entirely recover'd hers. Our best regards to you both—with great respect &ca.

J. M—

ALS copy, DLC (9-0175). Published in Stanislaus Murray Hamilton, ed., *The Writings of James Monroe* (7 vols.; New York, 1898–1903), 6:291–93.

1. See above, AJ to Monroe, January 29 and March 19.

2. A reference to Eligius Fromentin.
3. On May 4, Monroe had vetoed a bill providing for the repair of the Cumberland Road and to supplement the veto had also transmitted to Congress a discourse regarding internal improvements (see *Annals of Congress*, 17th Cong., 1st sess., pp. 1803–05, 1809–63). For Jackson's response, see AJ to Monroe, July 26, below.

To Andrew Jackson Donelson

Hermitage June 2nd. 1822

Dr. Andrew

I have not recd any letters from you for some mails. I should have set out for Florence this morning but the inclemency of the day prevents me, it has rained here for a month every other day. I do not recollect, that we have had two whole days of sun, for that period—our cotton crops are much injured by the wet weather, & cut worms. I shall set out the first clear day.

you named to me that you had written Colo. Gadsden about your pay accounts several times, without any answer being recd from him, this, (if your letters reached him) is what I did not expect, as in all his letters to me he desires to be remembered to you in the most affectionate manner.

If you should be without advice as to your pay accounts, if you will enclose duplicates to me, I will have them attended to, as I will adress a letter enclosing them direct to the sec of war.[1] do this to meet my return to Nashville, which will be about 12 days after I set out—you will have seen, that Towson and Gadsdens' renominations, has been rejected—Gadsden is gone to Charleston S. Carolina, and says to me he will be in this country during this summer. I suspect he is gone as the friend of Mr McDuffee, in the affair of honor, with Colo. [William] Cummin of augusta Georgia.[2] There is a firm division, between the President & Senate—The President, has not made any nomination to fill the adjut Genls. office—and we are without a paymaster Genl; how this differrence may end between these two Depts. of our Goverment; I cannot say—I have no doubt but the design is to effect the popularity of Calhoune, and if possible thereby to elevate Wm H. Crawford—for if the Majority of the Senate had been actuated from the pure principles of Justice, and a regard for the constitution, and the laws, they would have rejected all officers Razeed, there being no law, or military usage, that Justifies, or countenances such a procedure.[3] In the organization they began wrong, and never can get right, without reorganising the army. I have said began wrong—for to make way for Genl [Alexander] McComb, and get him out of the way of Scott—[Walker Keith] Armstead was transferred from the Corps of Engineers (who by the law was retained as it then was, & not the subject of reduction or erangement) to the artillery and pushed out of service those officers, who were the subjects of erangement, by the act of Congress—having commenced wrong—Injustice of course was done, and the law not executed agreable to its intension—This I early foresaw, & as you may remember wrote the President & Mr Calhoune from Pensacola. I sincerely hope Mr Calhoune may escape without injury to his popularity but I expect these things will be renewed next Congress—with a view to his injury—[4]

your aunt & the little Andrews are well and sends their love to you, all friends are well—I am your affectionate Uncle

Andrew Jackson

ALS, DLC (9-0184).

1. It is not known whether Jackson ever wrote to John C. Calhoun on the subject. Donelson's letters to James Gadsden have not been found. Donelson's accounts were settled later in the year.

2. Jackson was referring to the widely publicized upcoming duel between George McDuffie, a Calhoun supporter from South Carolina, and Cumming (d. 1863), a Crawfordite from Georgia and former army quartermaster general. Their duel, in which Benjamin T. Elmore, not Gadsden, served as McDuffie's second, was fought in South Carolina on June 8. In the duel, McDuffie was seriously, though not fatally, wounded. Gadsden's letter to Jackson has not been found.

3. The principle of razee, first adopted during the 1815 army reduction, allowed the retention of some officers by lowering their ranks, thereby displacing downward less senior officers. Henry Atkinson, Alexander Macomb, William Bradford, and James Dalliba were razeed and confirmed in their lower ranks.

4. Macomb (1782–1841), a career soldier who had been awarded a congressional medal for the 1814 defeat of the British at Plattsburgh, New York, was a more senior brigadier than Winfield Scott. Nonetheless, Macomb was lowered in rank to colonel and made chief of the Corps of Engineers, succeeding Armistead (c1785–1845; Military Academy 1803), who was designated colonel of the 3rd Artillery Regiment. In 1828, Macomb succeeded Jacob J. Brown as the army's commanding general. For Jackson's letters from Pensacola, see AJ to Calhoun, July 29, and AJ to James Monroe, August 4, both 1821.

To John Caldwell Calhoun

(private) June 28th. 1822—

Dr. Sir

Being absent vissitting my little farm near Florence, when your letter of the 16th. of May reached Nashville—I did not receive it untill the 22nd. Instant the day of my return, and will account to you for the delay of my acknowledging its receipt—[1]

It will at all times afford me sincere pleasure to interchange with you my sentiments on any, and all subjects that may be interesting to you—or in which the interest of our common Country may be involved—There is no one's welfare & prosperity, I have more at heart than yours, <and> This was the reason, <why> I have wrote you with the Frankness I have done, and hastened as soon as advised to lay before you, the conduct of Genl Jessup at Pensacola—I believed you, like myself, to have held in estimation the Genl free from duplicity or dishonourable conduct—<but as to myself> from information recd, some time since I was fully convinced of my Error <some time before I was advised of his conduct at Pensacola> and

I am happy you are now guarded with respect to him—he is unworthy of confidence, & capable in my opinion of betraying it. As to our mutual friend Gadsden, you may rely on it, there is neither deception or duplicity in his composition, <and> the longer you are acquainted with him, the more you will be convinced, <of> that I have formed a Just Estimate of him.[2]

It is certainly true, that the Military committee of the Senate <are> have and <have been> will be wielded by the <Senate> present Secratary of the Treasury; Mr. Monroe <cannot but have long> must have long since Known of his intrigue, and I do assure you his best friends ha<s>ve viewed <it> with regret and astonishment, that he still retains him in his Cabinet—Mr Crawford if I mistake not, has not abandoned his intrigue and it is probable, the military Committee may at the next session of Congress renew their attack against Mr Monroe Their object <is> to effect you, and draw the attention of the nation from <the> his corruption, and intrigue, <of Crawford,> his friends well know they can neither Justify or defend him, and it is plain that this is their course from the game that is played <off> by the red Jacketts through the city Gazzett—[3]

The right mode is to meet an enemy with his own weapons—and if Mr. Cook could meet with that support that virtue ought to elicit and at the next session call up the report of the committee on the subject of the employment of <Mr> Senator Thomas, unfold Mr Crawfords conduct fully, and his false statement to the Chairman of that Committee, on which the chairman founded his eroneous report—it will put the Sec and his friend down forever.[4] Mr Crawford <cannot> will not in my opinion get a vote in this state—I have said that I am induced to believe, that Crawford, through the military committee of the Senate, will at the next Session of Congress, make another effort against the Executive, to injure you. Colo. Benton will wield Williams <like a shewman> and Crawford will wield them both like a shewman does his puppets—I know they men well, and from a front view can well Judge of their <views> interior—Benton has laid a resolution on the table calling for information whether Colo Butler has resigned <or not> &c &c—This is not acted on, <it> but is left for further operations, at the next Session[5]—If these men expect any thing from Colo. Butler to aid their views they are widely mistaken—he is too honourable a man to have any thing to do with such men—I must be frank, it behoves you and Mr Monroe to act with great caution, and give to those men no opportunity of advantage by any act that you may do, that relates to the army—you have no adjutant Genl, this will <involve> create for you great labour—Should you detail one to perform the duties, and allow him compensation they will endeavour to assail you for having applied the public money, <to uses?> not appropriated by law—alledging that the fault was with the President in leaving the office unfilled, and if Colo Gadsden should be detailed it will be handled by them as a contemptuous conduct of the President to the Senate, that body having rejected his renomination—Permit me to remark Colo. Gadsden is too valuable to the army & his Country for his services to be lost, <to

it—> permit me to sugest a course, that will disappoint your enemies, silence them and bring Colo. Gadsden into the adjutant generals office, his feelings untouched, and the President free from blame—let it be remembered, that the military committee contend, that the adjt. Genl office of right ought to have been filled by Jones or Butler[6]—Butler has tendered his resignation, which as yet has not been accepted, <of,> he is under permission by Genl Gains to remain in Tennessee or untill he receives information whether his resignation is accepted of or not—<There is no public order [dischargin? dismissin?]g him from the Public> in point of law he is still in the army <?>—& the P. in pursuing the intimation of the military committee by reappointing Towson paymaster has shewn an inclination to adopt the course pointed <to him by the committee—> out by them—Let Butler then be ordered to the city as adjt. Genl, <let him> he will obay the order, and continue to perform the duties to the next meeting of Congress with an understanding that he is permitted then to resign, and that Colo. Gadsden <will> be nominated by the President to the Senate to fill the office of adjutant Genl—this will <stop the mouths of the babbles of Crawford Williams & Benton> silence the opposition of the military committee and ensure Gadsden an unanimous confirmation by the Senate—I well know that Colo. Butler will make this sacrafice of absence from his family, to secure his friend Gadsden the appointment & his country his services—and to relieve the administration from the present embarrassment believing as he does that Mr Monroe will provide for him by giving him the appointment of <adjt> Surveyor Genl. of the Floridas when that appointment is made—Major Eaton reached me last night this sugestions I have made to him which he approves[7]—Colo. Butlers accounts goes on by this days mail, addressed to Maj. [Christopher] Vandeventer should these sugestions be approved and adopted his account <for?> can be suspended I <will> pledge myself, for Colo. Butlers complience with <any> the erangement above sugested—present me to Mr Monroe and say to him I have recd his letter with the enclosure which shall be answered so soon as I have time to peruse with attention the enclosure[8] in haste I am Sir with great respect yr mo obd Servt

A. J.

ALS draft, DLC (31). Published in Bassett, 3:164–66.

1. Letter not found.

2. See Henry M. Brackenridge to AJ, December 22, 1821; Affidavit of Andrew J. Donelson, January 26; and, above, James C. Bronaugh to AJ, February 16. Only an extract of Jackson's letter of January 26 to Calhoun has been found.

3. Jackson was referring to attacks by the *Washington Gazette* on Calhoun's involvement with the Rip Rap Shoals scandal. For discussion of the scandal, see AJ to Richard K. Call, June 29, below. In using "red Jacketts," Jackson perhaps was alluding to the English (redcoat?) origin of Jonathan Elliot (1784–1846), editor of the *Washington Gazette*, a newspaper rumored to be controlled by treasury department clerks, or to the Seneca Indian chief Red Jacket (c1758–1830), noted for political trickery and intrigue.

4. For discussion of the investigation of Crawford's appointment of Jesse B. Thomas to

inspect western land offices, see above, Bronaugh to AJ, December 30, 1821, and February 8, 1822.

5. Thomas H. Benton had submitted his resolution on March 22 (*Annals of Congress*, 17th Cong., 1st sess., p. 478). On March 23, Calhoun informed John Williams, chairman of the Senate Military Affairs Committee, that Robert Butler's resignation had been accepted (*Calhoun Papers*, 6:757).

6. Charles J. Nourse (d. 1851) was acting adjutant general, May 7, 1822, to March 7, 1825. Roger Jones, adjutant general of the northern division before the army reorganization, became captain of the 3rd Artillery. In March 1825, John Q. Adams appointed him to the then long-vacant adjutant generalcy.

7. On January 19, 1823, Butler wrote to Calhoun denying knowledge of Jackson's scheme (DNA-RG 107, M221-95; see also, Eaton to AJ, February 23, 1823, below). In opposing the nominations of Nathan Towson and James Gadsden, the Senate Military Affairs Committee had insisted that they intended no deprecation of the merits of the two officers and suggested that the 1821 reduction act had intended their continuations as paymaster general and inspector general respectively (*Annals of Congress*, 17th Cong., 1st sess., p. 501). Following the rejection of the nominations on April 29, James Monroe, on May 4, nominated Towson as paymaster general.

8. See above, Monroe to AJ, May 30; and AJ to Monroe, July 26, below. The phrase "addressed to Maj. Vandeventer" is in another hand. Vandeventer (1789–1838; Military Academy 1809) was chief clerk of the war department, 1817–27.

To Andrew Jackson Donelson

Hermitage June 28th. 1822

Dr. Andrew

I returned from alabama on the 22nd. instant and recd. your several letters up to the 13th instant[1]—I should have wrote you sooner after my return, but I have had a great deal of company, and the Journey with the extreme heat & constant rain, has fatigued me very much, from the experiment I have made I have declined the contemplated vissit to the Springs, believing that the fatigue of the Journey would counterballance any prospect of benefit to be received from the water.

My cough has considerably abated, but I afflicted still with the pain in my left shoulder and neck, with the oppression of the cough in the morning—The weather has been so wet and atmosphere so damp, that I am allways afflicted with a stoppage in my head as tho afflicted with a cold—

I found my business in alabama not so flattering as I expected, I have a tolerable prospect of Cotton, but from the cause of the absence of my negroes, four having ran away, I found but a poor prospect of corn—I was fortunate in regaining my negroes, and although I hate chains, was compelled to place two of them in irons, for safe-keeping untill an opportunity offers to sell or exchange them—so soon as I have leisure I shall give you my ideas on the subject submitted to you for your opinion It is certainly true, that the senate in part has given a Just decision—and if it had been uniform, and rejected all that were razeed as well as those brought into the army improperly It would have commanded my full approbation—I wish you to state to me candidly the state of your health—in one of your letters you slighty advert to your side—should any appearence of a permanant seat of complaint shew itself in your side, you must desist from close study—and relax—on this event I will send for you—your aunt and the Andrews enjoy good health—I cannot boast of mine—we all unite in good wishes for your health & happiness. I am your affectionate Uncle

Andrew Jackson

P.S. present me to Mr [Joseph] Ficklin, say to him I have recd his letter, and will reply when Leisure permits[2]—I have been engaged in answering letters recd from Mr Monroe & Mr Calhoune & Mr Adams—[3]

Have you seen Jonathan Russells letter on the subject of the negotiation at Ghent—and the meritted chastisement and Lashing, given him by Mr Adams[4]—What an accomplished Villain this J*[o]*nathan must be—a fit subject *[to]* be turned to the Trade of making wooden Nutmegs, to impose upon the world with[5]—This exposure <of> by Mr Adams, of Mr Russell Touches more than *Jonathan,* and has done Mr Adam much credit, and instead of destroying his popularity in the south & west has increased it—Mr A—— strictures upon Russells letter I recommend to your attention A.J.

ALS, DLC (9-0191). Published in Bassett, 3:166–67 (extract).

1. Only Donelson's June 5 letter has been found.

2. Neither the letter from Ficklin (c1802–50), editor of the Lexington *Kentucky Gazette* and postmaster at that place, nor Jackson's response has been found.

3. See above, James Monroe to AJ, May 30, AJ to John C. Calhoun, June 28; and AJ to Monroe, July 26, below. Other letters not found.

4. Russell (1771–1832; Brown 1791), a Henry Clay supporter from Massachusetts serving his only term in Congress, had been chargé d'affaires at London in 1814 when he joined John Q. Adams and Clay as American peace commissioners at the Ghent treaty negotiations. Early in 1822 John Floyd attempted to portray Adams as anti-western by requesting a copy of Russell's February 1815 letter to then Secretary of State Monroe, which had protested a proposed exchange of British navigation on the Mississippi River for American rights in the northeastern fisheries. In April, Russell supplied the state department with a "duplicate" of the heretofore missing letter, which cast Adams in an especially bad light. Adams then retrieved the original letter from Monroe's private papers and, discovering significant textual variations between it and the copy, wrote an extensive commentary exonerating himself. Adams submitted his report to Congress, which adjourned before printing it, but it appeared in the Washington *National Intelligencer,* May 21–23. Subsequently, Adams issued an even longer defense, *The Duplicate Letters, the Fisheries and the Mississippi. . .* (Washington, 1822).

5. The phrase "wooden nutmeg" was a pejorative reference to New Englanders' alleged misrepresentation of goods.

By mid-1822, Jackson's name was being mentioned more frequently as a possible successor to James Monroe. Reflecting the growing sentiment against the Crawford-controlled congressional caucus, former congressman and then Davidson County representative Felix Grundy (1777–1840) informed Jackson on June 27 that a group of Tennessee legislators was planning to nominate the former general for the presidency when the legislature assembled the following month. Jackson's first recorded reaction, below, struck the pose that he maintained throughout the campaign—he would serve if called, but he would not actively seek the office. Accordingly, a caucus of the Tennessee House of Representatives met on July 27 and unanimously recommended Jackson for the presidency; a Senate caucus followed suit on August 3. From that time until March 1837, Jackson was either a candidate for or serving in the presidency, a remarkable turn of events for someone who, only six months before, had been the target of a possible impeachment.

To Richard Keith Call

Hermitage June 29th. 1822

Dear Call

I have Just recd yours of the 2nd Instant and am happy to find for the present you have declined holding a poll for delegate—you have got into a handsome practice—the moment you would enter Congress some person would supplant you in the practice, and as your population is growing fast, by intrigue, might supplant you in your popularity—first I would recommend you to stick to the law, untill you are perfectly independant in your circumstances—preparing the way in the mean time, for your future views; and by the time you come into the union your circumstances, and popularity will be such, that with it, you may come into congress—you have now a practice, as long as you remain at the bar, which cannot be taken from you—but which would soon leave you after going into congress, which would be hard to regain.[1]

I have read with attention your remarks on Mr Monroes conduct in the appointment of officers for the Floridas—I sincerely regret with the course he has pursued, it has lost him the Esteem of his friends, and has giving ample scope for his political enemies to assail him. In short Sir his popularity is fleeting from him—and if he does not alter his course, he will go out of office with less popularity tha*[n]* any of his predecessors—he has lost his popularity by seeking it—and making appointments that he conceived would augment it—never looking to the wellfare of the republic in making them—by which he has disgusted his friends, sacraficed the interest of his Country—and politically damd himself—what must be the feelings of the Floridians at the appointment of Smith as one of the Judges to administer the laws over them—it is equal to the appointment of Fromentine—a man who by a <board> court of his brother officers has been found guilty of cheating at cards, making a false statement on oath, and cheating his soldiers, for which the court decreed him to be cashiered. This to be sure was disapproved of by the President, & his sword returned to him—But a Judge ought to be like Cesars wife, "not only chaste, but unsuspected."[2] as to my self I have no confidence in his promises, I am determined never to recommend anothe*[r]* to office as long as he is President—all his Cabinet is by the ears, all up for the Presidency, and he sits and looks on viewing scenes that will and must disgrace us in the eyes of Urope—was I President I would Remove all who have come out as candidates for the Presidency—and fill my Cabinet with those whose whole time could be devoted to the duties of their office, and not to intrigue for the Presidency. It is passing strange that he sticks fast to Crawford—as far as I know Mr Adams, he steers a strait-forward, correct course—attends to the duties of his office well—I believe Mr Calhoune does the same, but his friends has injured him—and it will be by great prudence that he can absolve himself from Injury—The reduction of the army has brought upon him the influence of Crawfords friends, and the course pursued, has given them strong grounds—they have, & will make the best of it—The [Elijah] Mix contract, has given them a hold, that they stick to, with great glea, and will operate against Calhoune with some—and Keep the eyes of the people closed to the intrigue & corruption of Crawford; whilst him & his friends are silently continuing their intrigue to the best advantage—The attempt made against Mr Adams, by the letter of Russell, detailing the proceedings at Ghent was a wicked thing—Mr Adams has turned the Tables upon clay & Crawford, and has given Russell as severe a drubbing as any Rascal ought to receive—it has placed Mr Adams on high ground, extended his popularity, and forever damd. Russell and all concerned in the vilanous scene[3]

Major Eaton was with me last evening on his return—he informs me that the Judge appointed for west Florida has refused to accept the appointment—Mr Monroe on this event was under promise to Doctr Brunaugh to appoint our friend Judge Brakenridge, but I have no confidence in his promises—and I have no doubt as he calculates on the friendship of Judge Brakinridge, if he can find another that he thinks by the appointment he can make his friend, he will give it to him—present me to the Judge, say to him I have recd his letter & will answer it shortly—and that I still have a hope that he will receive the appointment of Judge for west Florida[4]—on the subject of The ordinance which Congress has thought proper to repeal, I have only to remark, that wisdom & prudence dictated their adoption—nothing but folly could dictate their repeal—and experience, has taught me how necessary, such an ordinance is on a frontier sea port Town Just ceded to us. My situation at orleans give this experience—The inhabitants ceded with the Territory have the right to become citizens of the u States if they choose, now where is the evidence of their election—no where—These ordinances were necessarily introduced to form a record of this election, which would be evidence of the fact—prevent imposition and on cases of emergency compell all who had by election become citizens, to defend their country when invaded—what was my situation for the want of such a record at orleans, my defence endeavoured to be destroyed by the perfidy of the French consul Col. [Louis de] Tousard giving certificates of French citizenship, to every individual who would apply and give him five dollars for it, whether the applicant had ever been in France or not—I did my duty with an eye single to the public good—and I am content—I have never been able in the public prints to see one sentiment on this subject—nor has ever the bill been yet published—But I think it will be well for the Legislative council of Florida to give this subject an investigation, and severe comment—The best interest and security of your Country require it[5]—I have no doubt but it was intended silently to effect my standing—This they cannot do; I am Silent, but the papers are not—the voice of the people I am told would bring me to the Presidential chair, and it is probable, some of the Legislatures may bring my name before the Public—but I have long since determined to be perfectly Silent—I never have been a candidate for office, I never will. The people have a right to call for any mans services in a republican goverment—and when they do, it is the duty of the individual, to yield his services to that call. I will be silent—neither sayi*[ng]* aye, or nay, altho I have been often solicite*[d]*

Present me to my friend Easter—say to him, that from debility my eyes have become so weak that with dificulty I see to write—however I shall write him and Brakenridge shortly—I have been pressed with a numerous correspondence lately—which I shall soon get through, when I will attend to my friends—<and> I have been lately absent at my farm in alabama and my letters have accumulated in my absence. In the mean time I shall expect him to write me. Mrs. J. has recd his letter & will shortly answer[6]—Present me to Walton, [David] Shannon, Connor, & Rutledge—To all my military friends, and to my friend Dinkin my best congratulations for his & his partners happiness—it is a happy union & much happiness must grow out of it[7]—Present me to my friend Shields—& Miller, Garnier & all other friends—Mrs. Jackson—and the little Andrews Join me in best wishes—and believe me yr friend.

Andrew Jackson

P.S. Present me to Brunaugh & Overton if they have reached you—say to them that all friends are well & I expect to hear from them.[8] A.J.

ALS, IaDaM (9-0195).

1. Letter not found. On June 15, Call dissolved his partnership with Henry M. Brackenridge, and a month later he began a new practice with Richard I. Easter, specializing in land claims arising out of the Florida transfer (see Easter to John Overton, August 4, THi).

2. Jackson was referring to the 1820 court-martial of Joseph L. Smith. Quotation after Plutarch, *Lives,* Caesar, section 10.

3. Jackson was referring to the Rip Rap Shoals scandal, brought to public attention in April by Tennessee congressman John Cocke. In 1818, Mix, a former navy master and brother-in-law of war department chief clerk Christopher Vandeventer, contracted to supply stone for the construction of Fortress Monroe at Old Point Comfort and the Rip Rap Shoals in Virginia. In 1819, with John C. Calhoun's knowledge but against his advice, Vandeventer purchased a half-interest in Mix's contract, selling it in 1820 to other relatives after Mix regained financial stability. A dispute over payment to Vandeventer ensued, however, and Vandeventer's and Calhoun's apparent impropriety, once disclosed, prompted a congressional investigation and critical newspaper reaction. The inquiry cleared both of any

wrongdoing, but the clerk lost his post in 1827 when the issue resurfaced, even though a second investigation again exonerated both him and Calhoun (see *ASP, Military Affairs,* 2:431–49, and *HRRep* 79, 19th Cong., 2nd sess., Serial 159). For the John Q. Adams–Jonathan Russell controversy, see above, AJ to Andrew J. Donelson, June 28.

4. Letter not found. Brackenridge received the appointment.

5. On May 7, Congress repealed, without published debate, Jackson's July 21, 1821, ordinance regulating the naturalization of aliens in Florida (see *Annals of Congress,* 17th Cong., 1st sess., pp. 431, 440, 442, 1888; 3 *U.S. Statutes at Large* 685–86). Tousard (1749–1817), French consul at New Orleans during the 1815 British invasion, had issued certificates of citizenship to Frenchmen wishing release from the Louisiana militia (see *Jackson,* 3:294). Jackson also cited his Louisiana experience in his letter to Adams, July 30–August 14, 1821.

6. Letters not found.

7. Jackson had appointed Shannon (d. 1822), a lawyer from Lexington, Kentucky, presiding judge of the Escambia County Court. He died during the yellow fever outbreak, as did Ellen Turman Dinkins, wife of James E.

8. James C. Bronaugh and Samuel R. Overton arrived in Pensacola on June 3.

To John M. A. Hamblen

Hermitage June 29th. 1822.

Dear Sir

Having taken a travel to my small farm in Alabama, where I was on the arival of your letter, and from whence I have Just returned, will account to you for the delay of acknowledging your letter of the 18th. ult.[1]

your friend Mrs. Jackson on the recpt of your letter vissitted your little Mary [Eliza Overton Hamblen], and presented her with that kiss from you, enjoined on me to give, she Just returned from the vissit as I reached home, your Dear little chattering Mary is well (and grows finely)—as well as Mrs. Donelson and the family—you will be much pleased with her, she is the perfect image of her mother—you must come and see her and let her know you—She is taught to expect you, and makes many inquiries about her papa—cannot you spend the next winter with us.[2]

I thank you for your good wishes for the restoration of my health, it has improved with the warm season, but I am still much afflicted with a pain under my left should, and back of my neck—and in the morning with a cough—I throw up a great deal of stuff—I apprehend, that I will never regain my health—My constitution has recd so many severe trials—that it is too much weakened, ever to be regained, or my health—however I reconcile myself to my fate, and cry out that the lords will be done. he giveth life, he supports it, & health, and his will, will, be done—Mrs. J. & myself will be happy to see you in this country—and when health and circumstances will permit, will with great pleasure vissit your sweet little daughter advise me what time you think you will vissit this country, and accept assurances of my Esteem & regard—Mrs. J. requests to be presented to you. yours

Andrew Jackson

P.S. I will thank you for the promised paper[3] A. J. The information requested to be given to Mr Earle shall be given so soon as I see him—A. J.

ALS, THer (9-0202). In 1818 Hamblen, a physician, had married Mary C. Donelson (1799–1819), a daughter of Jackson's brother-in-law, William Donelson (1758–1820), who died after giving birth to their daughter Mary Eliza Overton (b. 1819). Thereafter Hamblen settled in Monroe, Ouachita Parish, Louisiana, and subsequently served in the state legislature.

1. Not found.

2. After her mother's death, Mary E. O. Hamblen had lived with her grandmother, Charity Dickinson Donelson (1778–1827).

3. Not identified.

To William Berkeley Lewis

July 1rst 1822

Genl A. Jackson with compliments to Major Wm B Lewis regrets to hear of the indisposition of Mrs. Lewis; Mrs. J. presents her compliments to Mrs. & Mr Lewis, and requests to be advised of Mrs. L's health—Mrs J. would have been down to vissit Mrs. L. but really the Genl's crop is so full of weeds & grass, that her Carriage horses ha<s>ve been compelled to be turned into the plow—she will do herself that pleasure the moment this press of labour, and the Sacrament is over—[1]

The Genl has recd a note from Govr. [William] Carroll informing him that the sword voted by the Legislature in 1819, is recd. and requesting to be informed whether it will meet <my> his approbation to receive it in Nashville 4th. of July—the Genl has answered in the affirmative[2]—Therefore the Genl will spend the evening of the third with his friend Major L. & hopes to see him at home—The Govr. tells <me> him there is an address to accompany the delivery of the sword—of course it is expected that there should be a response, and the Major knows that the Genl is not well versed in flatterry—& will be awkward in the reply—and will require an eye to strike out any thing too Blunt—or that might be construed into disrespect—for although the thing is very late—still it ought not to be treated in such away as might be construed into offence—The Genl requests his respects to Mrs. L. & the young Ladies.[3]

AL, NN (9-0206). Published in *NYPLB*, 4(1900):192.

1. Lewis and his new wife Mary had returned from North Carolina about June 1.

2. Notes not found. Carroll (1788–1844) was serving his first of six terms as governor of Tennessee. On November 22, 1819, the Tennessee legislature had voted swords to both Jackson and Edmund P. Gaines for their services during the 1818 Seminole campaign. Jackson's sword, forged by Nathan Starr of Middletown, Connecticut, had been exhibited in Washington in early May before being carried to Nashville by Congressman Newton Cannon. For the presentation, see Carroll to AJ, and AJ to Carroll, both July 4. In his will, Jackson left the sword to Andrew J. Donelson.

3. The young ladies were probably Lewis's sister, Elizabeth Berkeley (c1795–1877), his daughter Mary Ann (c1814–1866), and his niece, Mary E. T. Claiborne (c1805–52), the daughter of Sarah T. Lewis and Thomas A. Claiborne.

To James Craine Bronaugh

Hermitage July 18th. 1822.

Dr. Bronaugh

I have had the pleasure to receive your letter of the 17th. of June which reached me by due course of mail & also yours of the 24th. which is Just to hand.[1]

I delayed answering your letter of the 17th. with a hope that I would have had it in my power to have seen Doctor [Alexander] McCall [IV] who had a few days before its recpt, went to alabama—I saw his father yesterday who says he expects his return daily, when he will call upon me, and I shall endeavour to hasten his Journey to you & by him (if he goes) send <you> your horse.[2] I sincerely regret the disagreable situation of the Territory from the absence of the officers appointed to carry the organization into effect given to the Territory by the late act of Congress; but one thing is certain, that the existing authority continues, untill the officers appointed under the late regulations arive and are sworn into office, and the idea of an interregnum which I see afloat in your country is entirely ideal—The conduct of Mr Monroe in appointing councillors, not inhabitants of the Floridas at the time of the appointment is inconsistant with (my recollection of) the act of Congress, for that act if I mistake not confines the selection of the council from amonghst the then citizens or residents of Florida[3]—It is very strange that he has not filled the vacancy in the Judiciary of *West* Florida by the nonexceptance of Mr Branch—but not more strange than his appointing him when he knew he would not accept the appointment; I am of the opinion he does not intend to appoint our mutual friend Brakenridge if he can get any body in North Carolina to accept it—for my part I cannot understand him, he has wrote me a very cautious, and studied answer in which he takes no particular notice of the anonymous Letter; I have not replied to it as yet—[4]

It affords me much pleasure to hear that the Govr has reached you, and that he has been well received by the people, this augurs well—but I know the people there, and you may look out for feuds, and party—and unless the Govr shapes his course at first, and firmly pursues an undeviating policy, he will get himself in dificulty, the council (if united) will be his eficient prop; but Colo. [William] Barnett, will raise a party in opposition <of> to the views of the Governor; except he goes with Barnett which I am certain he will not—nay that he cannot, if he pursues a course, to produce the best results to the interest & prosperity of the country—and say to Govr. Duval to have his eye upon the Colo. he is arch, and cunning, and if he can, will intrigue. By pursuing an enererjectic, steady, course the Governor will succeed in keeping down party spirit, and administring the Goverment, both, to the happiness, & harmony, of the people, as well as to the benefit of the country—but to effect this he must at once take his course with energy, and convince those spirits of party, that he cannot be shaken. I have not the act of congress before me, but I am of the opinion the Legislative Council can by law point out & establish the mode of electing the delegate, and if it is found from the lateness of the season, that a law authorising the election of the delegate by the people, cannot be passed and promulgated in due time for an election before Congress meets, it strikes me, that the council can, temporarily, appoint the delegate untill an election by the people can take place <to>—but not having the law before me, I cannot, nor do I, pretend to give a deliberate opinion upon this subject.[5]

I hope you will have nothing to fear from the opposition of Colo. Barnett—Should not Mr. Worthington of East Florida be a candidate, I will write him, and I expect he will support you. Should he, with the interest of the Govr. you will have but little to apprehend—from Mr W. farewell adress, I was apprehensive he was preparing the way for some favour from the people.[6]

I am happy to find from letters from Capts Call & Easter that all my old friends will support you. I knew Major Bowie was a sneak in the grass—he is opposed to you. <and> I hope Mr Austin will support you—Say to Colo. Walto*[n]* I cherish for him the sincere feelings of friendship, he has my best wishes—I would write him but I am really oppressed with answering letters in the last quarter my postage amounted to $54 this is equal to my cotton crop, give my good wishes to all my friends—I shall write Overton Call & Easter & Brakenridge tomorrow[7]—Mrs. J. & the andrews Join me in good wishes, you will see from the papers that my name has been brought forward[8]—every application to me, I give the same answer—that I have never been a candidate for any office. I never will—But the people have a right to choose whom the will to perform their constitutional duties—and when the people call, the Citizen is bound to render the service required—I think Crawford is lost sight of, and his friends are about to bring forward Mr Clay—Calhoune (Eaton says) at Congress is the strongest man—I am told Mr Adams at present the strongest in this state <at present>—accept my Dear Sir, of my best wishes, adieu for the present.

Andrew Jackson

ALS, DLC (31). Published in Heiskell (2nd edition), 3:156–58.

1. Not found.

2. A North Carolina native, McCall (1797–1869) was a Nashville physician and businessman. His father has not been identified.

3. See section 5 of the Florida territory act (3 *U.S. Statutes at Large* 655–56). The territorial council (which included Bronaugh and Richard K. Call) assembled on July 22, when it elected Bronaugh as its president.

4. See above, "Friend" to AJ, October 29, 1821, James Monroe to AJ, May 30, 1822; and AJ to Monroe, July 26, below.

5. See section 14 of the Florida territory act (3 *U.S. Statutes at Large* 659). Governor William P. Duval arrived in Pensacola on June 20. Barnett (1761–1832), a cousin of William

H. Crawford and former Georgia congressman and Creek boundary commissioner, opposed Bronaugh in the ensuing campaign for Florida territorial delegate.

6. On May 27, William G. D. Worthington issued a farewell address to the citizens of East Florida, but a week later he announced his candidacy for territorial delegate. He subsequently withdrew from the race. No letter from Jackson to Worthington on the election has been found.

7. None of the letters have been found. Both Richard K. Call and Richard I. Easter subsequently gave lukewarm support to Bronaugh's election as territorial delegate (see AJ to Bronaugh, August 27). On July 17, Jackson paid $19.12 for an account with Nashville postmaster Robert Brownlee Currey (1774–1848) for postage from February 1. At the end of the year, Jackson sold his Hermitage cotton crop for 8 1/2 cents per pound, totalling $1,386.42 (see Account with James Stewart & Co., December 31).

8. The July 13 *Nashville Gazette* and the July 18 Nashville *Clarion* (neither extant) carried an article supporting Jackson for the presidency (see *Richmond Enquirer* and *Washington Gazette*, both July 30).

From James Jackson

Forks of Cypress July 24th. 1822

Dear Genl.

I duely recd. yours of 27th. ulto.[1] & would much sooner have written you, but my new business added to my other conserns has pestered me much, and perhaps leaves every thing badly done, of all the business I ever was engaged in, being a Candidate is the most disgusting, most of those who wishes a man to become a Candidate, think they have done him a great favour—every scrub in the Country considers himself entitled to take what liberty He pleases & those opposed will manufacture little insignificant stories, unworthy of notice but still calculated to have an injurious effect. A man who is determined to be a successful Candidate, must be all things to all men, never express his opinion freely & learn the nack of geting round every subject that presents it self. The popular opinion, no matter how wrong, is not to be met by a candidate. There is so much in this business to disgust & so little that gratifies that I think my first effort will be my least & to mend the matter, there is some probability that I'll either be beaten by or associated with a Hog Thief—I still think I'll be Elected, should that be the case & I find Mr. King to be the man He has been represented to you, He'll not visit Washington City as Senator with my consent, If better can be done[2] I have not yet had any posative information of my Negroes, but am inclined to the opinion that they aimed for Nashville. I wrote Mr. Thomas Martin to have one hundred Copies of my advertisement striken off & forwarded from Nashville in every direction—[3]

On the subject of the expences of your Mare, I contemplated, that I was not only to pay the season but the Expences and according to my understanding all things are now correct—[4]

I turned my Colt into the Corn Field & have got him to thriving handsomely—my three year old Pacolet is improving very fast & from his form and action have strong expectations that He'll make a good race Horse

Our Crops are rather much improved, tho we had rather too much rain, my Limestone Crop is of the very first rate & should the season be favourable may not be able to get it out—'Tis probable I'll make 300,00 lb seed Cotton on that Plantation—Genl. Coffee informs me you have some Idea of joining him & me in the purchase of Hopkins's Negroes, It will entirely meet my approbation—from all information the purchase will be a good one.[5]

I have been informed there is a probability of Major [John Williams] Walkor resigning his seat in the senit If so, We'll have a chance of selecting those who will not be so subserviant to Mr. Crawfords views—[6]

All friends here are in good health and nothing very new amongst us—

Mrs. Jackson joins me in best wishes to you & your good Lady believe me sincerely yours

James Jackson

ALS, DLC (31). ALS endorsed by AJ as answered on August 1. Answer not found. Published in Bassett, 3:170–71 (extract).

1. Letter not found.

2. James Jackson was a candidate for the Alabama House of Representatives. Mr. King was either former 4th Infantry Colonel William King or the incumbent senator William Rufus deVane King (1786–1853). James Jackson initially supported John McKee in the Senate race, but later switched his vote to William R. deV. King, who won reelection.

3. James Jackson offered an $80 reward for the return of the slaves Claiborn and his wife Charity, purchased the preceding year from James G. Martin and Thomas Martin, respectively (see *Nashville Whig,* July 3). Thomas Martin (c1781–1835), the son-in-law of Joseph Philips, had purchased James Jackson's plantation near Nashville when the latter relocated to Alabama.

4. See the Receipt for season of mares, March 4.

5. The exact location and extent of James Jackson's Limestone County, Alabama, plantation has not been determined. No evidence of a purchase of slaves from Hopkins, possibly Arthur Francis Hopkins (1794–1865), who represented Lawrence County in the Alabama state senate and who was later that state's chief justice, has been found.

6. Although aligned with the Georgia faction, Walker (1783–1823) had maintained good relations with Jackson. In November, ill health prompted Walker's resignation from the U.S. Senate, giving the Alabama legislature the opportunity to elect a second senator. Walker was replaced by the anti-Crawford William Kelly (1786–1834), but James Jackson voted for the Georgia faction's John McKinley, his partner in the Cypress Land Company, whom Martin Van Buren appointed to the Supreme Court in April 1837.

To Andrew Jackson Donelson

Hermitage July 25th. 1822

Dr Andrew

I have Just recd your letter of the 13th. instant in the close of which you advise me that you are about to remove to the country,[1] you say nothing about your health—I am fearfull that it is not good—if so let me know it—and if you could with benefit to yourself read at home here, I will send for you at any time—Speak freely to me, recollect that health is the greatest blessing we can enjoy, and whilst young we ought to be carefull to preserve it—if once lost it is hard to regain, if your health is bad or if you think a little relaxation from your study would be beneficial or gratefull to you I will, on it being intimated by you to me, send for you, I have my grays in tolerable order they will travel to & from in ten days.

My health will not permit me at present to write you fully on the subject that at present distracts Kentucky—The party who advocates the omnipotent power of the Legislature, and call the Legislature the people, forget that the people in their sovereign capacity have formed a constitution for their own Goverment, and that, as all power are inherent in the people, those powers not delegated, to the differrent functionaries of the Goverment by that constitution remains with the people. The people by the constitution have divided their goverment into three departments, the Legislative executive & Judiciary, seperate & independant of each other—now if either of these departments, exercise powers not granted by the constitution the act is void, for the want of power & authority to do <it?> that act—the Legislature by the constitution is to enact laws, the Judiciary to enforce them & the executive to see that the are executed &c &c—Now there is nothing plainer than the constitution is the supreme law of the land, and if the Legislature pass a law in violation of that constitu[ti]on, that it becomes the imperious duty of the court to declare it so, and not carry it into effect—The Legislature are not the people, they are the creatures of the people, created by & under the constitution, made by the people, giving them certain powers, so long as the keep within the pale of those powers granted them, their act is binding on the people, the moment the transcend them, their acts are without authority and void—The Judiciary are bound to declare every act done by the Legislature contrary to the constitution void—This is the valuable check—and the only mode by which the rights secured by the people under the constitution—and rights not delegated but reserved to the people can be maintained to them unimpaired—and the Judiciary being a creature of the constitution are as much the people as the Legislature, & are more apt to be free from party Spirit or the influence of vociferous & designing demagogues than the other departments of the goverment—from this concise hint you will easily see, how these Demagogues in Kentucky are trampling upon the rights of the people, destroying the constituted goverment, and boldly asserting in the very teeth of the people that these Demagogues, the aristocracy of the country, *because Legislatures,* are they people and that their will is the constitutions this directly leads to the prostration of all constitutional goverments, and leads directly to despotism, and if the people do not stop these demagogues in their mad carreer, and on their native dunghills set them down, t*[he]* people when too late, will find, they have lost their Liberty, and to regain it, they must again bleed, fight, & conquer, the[i]r independence from these Despots.[2]

My health is not good—your aunt and the andrews unite in love to you—I am your affectionate uncle

Andrew Jackson

ALS, T (9-0224).

1. Not found.

2. In mid-May, Kentucky circuit court judge James Clark (1770–1839) had declared unconstitutional the state's 1820 replevin law that allowed debtors to delay payments for up to two years. Meeting in special session later that month, the relief-faction-dominated Kentucky legislature had failed narrowly to remove the judge. When the state court of appeals subsequently upheld Clark's ruling, the legislature retaliated by abolishing that court and creating an entirely new, pro-relief body, fomenting a constitutional crisis in Kentucky that lasted until 1826.

To James Monroe

Hermitage July 26th. 1822

Dear Sir

Your letter of the 30th of May reached Nashville by due course of mail, being absent on a short Tour to my farm in alabama, I did not receive it untill late in June, and have been prevented by various causes (ill health included) from answering untill now.

Nothing could be more painfull to me, than to have cause to complain of the conduct of one, I considered my friend, the principles upon which I have allways acted toward my friends, induced me to write to you with the candeur of one, when the occurrence happened, which induced the belief that the act was not only injurious, but unfriendly to me, and not warrented from the facts of the case, or the rules of general Justice to all. My letter to you was dictated by these considerations, and whether an injury has accrued to me by the communication as made to congress, as you now tell me in your letter (& which I had allways believed) that "you were utterly incapable of doing injustice to any one intentionally," this suffices.[1]

The thing being done without the intention of producing injury, if injury hath acrued, the intention being absent, no breach of friendship can be ascribed with Justice. I have seen with great regret the emberasments with which you were surrounded during the last session of Congress, some of which (but I confess not the whole) I anticipated from the moment I saw placed on the army Register the recommendation of the board of Genl officers. This I well knew would give to a certain party, an opportunity to bring the army in review, before congress, and if possible destroy its usefullness to the country by reducing it, and from matter growing out of this investigation strike (if possible) a blow at the rising popularity of the secratary of war, it was this view of the subject that induced me to write you from Pensacola, with the freedom and candeur that I did.[2]

The indecorous phraseology of the report of the military committee of the Senate too plainly marked the intention of its promoters, and has destroyed that effect upon the Public mind, it was expected, and must recoil upon the makers of the report.[3]

I have read with great attention, & interest your message to congress on the subject of the constitutional right to adopt, & execute a system of internal improvements. your reasoning I think Just, and the conclusions well drawn, and <I think> must be satisfactory to the nation.[4]

My opinion has allways been that the Federal goverment did not possess that constitutional power—That it was retained to the States respectively, and with great wisdom. My health is not good, nor have I much hope of regaining it, retirement & ease may prolong my life, but I fear never can restore health. Mrs. J. requests to be kindly presented to you, your lady, & every branch of your family, to whom I pray you to present me respectfully & believe me to be with great respect yr mo obdt. Servt.

Andrew Jackson

ALS, NN (9-0228); ALS draft, DLC (31). Published in Bassett, 3:171–72 (from ALS draft).

1. See above, AJ to Monroe, March 19, and Monroe to AJ, May 30.
2. See AJ to Monroe, August 4, 1821.
3. For the report of the Senate Committee on Military Affairs, see *Annals of Congress,* 17th Cong., 1st sess., pp. 489–502.
4. Jackson was referring to Monroe's May 4 veto of the Cumberland Road bill and to the treatise he sent along with the veto.

From Egbert Harris

Franklin, *July th 27, 1822*

Dr *Genrall.*

On my return from Huntsville I receaved yours dated th 15.[1] In answer I can say to you, that I left your farm on the 16th. & returned to my Business on the 26th. which I had entrusted to the care of our mutual friend Mr. John Cafferry, and feel highly gratifyed in saying that during my absence he conducted the Business much to my satisfaction all thing's going on smothly, as it respects the farm. I am sorry that the Old man Mr. [Stephen] Upchurch, as I am informed, is unable to worke.[2] I immediately gave Mr. Crafford, fore hands for the purpose of finishing the logs for the Gin House, as we requiered 8 more to have engouh. he is employed in getting them at this time, and will I hope compleate them in a shorte time. I have seaded your turnip patch, beging seed, from my Acquaintances as there was not half enough provided by your friend I should be glad to seed eight or ten Acres more if seeed can be procured. I have my strong hands employed in getting logs for the crib and gin House the Weomen Grubing aroun the Houses as you requested for turnips and tatos I can say I beleave this is tantermount of my Business & I beleave it is disposing of the hands as you requiered. I shall detain the Horses which I had preaviously determined to send for purpose of getting the timbers together, so soon as I can spare them I shall starte squre up with them. Speaking of Capt. Kemper I can say nothing as I have not seen him in purson. I called at Col. Jones's for that purpose but was informed that he was on the Opposite side of the River.[3] Mr. Crafford I beleave has seen him but unfortunate for me, in conversation on such subjects as appears to have been entrusted to his direction I can, learn but little, & as it appears to have been made a seperate [apartement], I feell some delicacy. I have haed no positive Instructions about engageing the reasidue of the plank, & I know not whether it is engaged or not, Mr. Crafford if I understood him, said he would engage it, if so I presume it is safe, Mr. [G. Frederick] Hover, has not delivered the [stuf?] for the [wheal], at the river but I presume he will when requiered.[4] I have been informed that Kemper, finds considerable fault of the logs stateing that they should not have been Boiled this was the positive instruction of Genrall Coffee, when he delivered your note's which Instructions I have Obsearved dilligently & beleaved it the most Expeditious mode of cureing them, as I had but little time to season the logs and I feare they will not be perfectly seasoned. his Objections are maney and I fear from reporte he is not desposed to do your worke. Should you discover from your friends that this is his determination I am resolved that you shall not be diappointed, provided you say to me, in proper authority that you wish your jin up & runing say when you can be able to pay for the runing gear, provided it is done in Workeman like manner. I hope you are aware that I will if it is left to me, make myself responsible, for it's preformance, but I hope you will not throw any responsibillity on me for that parte managed by Others. I feell no hesitation in saying when I am Autherised to build your jin, that I can have it compleate by the firs[t] day of October, or before. Use your pleasure I will follow your Instructions if I am able, but trust you will not involve my situation as it respects my Crop. I Know if it is left to my own management I can compleate the work with ease, say that an insermountable obsticle should be removed. By my conduct to you as my first friend I expect to stand or fall, I hope you will answer this as I conceave it all important. I would not say that these things could be effected without. I am positive I presume my crop will pay for Gin provided we have men that will worke. I will deliver the Oxen to your Order, & pursue the Instructions—

My Friend as it respects my Family, I have seen my darling Babes and will wit[h] your consent Bring them down, so soon as I can. Mrs. [Sally G. Wall] Harris says she is not disposed to live with as man & Wife, & I am determined to use no coersive measures.[5]

Present my Respects to Mrs. Jackson, in the most feeling language. I Remain yours, with Gratitude,

Egbert Harris

PS. since the sealing of my letter the wagon has returned without corne, or so little it is no worth mentioning. the Boy states there is no more there for me save too loads for meal Please to say what is to be done. I must have corne or my Oxen and Horses will perish. yours & E Harris

ALS, DLC (31). Published in Bassett, 3:172–73.

1. Letter not found.

2. Caffery (b. c1795), Jackson's nephew, was the son of John (1756–1811) and Mary Donelson Caffery. Upchurch has not been further identified.

3. Squire (b. c1799) was born at the Hermitage and served as a slave foreman in the 1840s. Jones has not been further identified.

4. Huber was a carpenter.

5. In 1815, Harris had married Sally G. Wall, but his declining fortune strained the marriage. In 1828, she left her husband (reportedly moving to Tennessee), whereupon he filed for divorce.

To James Craine Bronaugh

Hermitage August 1rst. 1822

Dr. Doctor

Doctor McCall returned from alaba on yesterday and vissitted me last night, he is gratefull to you for your profered friendship, and will set out to Join you at Pensacola, so soon as he can erange his private concerns, which he thinks will detain him Seven days, you may calculate on his Joining you about the 28th instant—the Doctor will ride your horse, he is in good order and I have no doubt will reach you in good condition.

I see you have an opponant in Colo Barnett—This I expected as I well knew he was unfriendly to me. I expect he will be supported by Major Bowie—I allways viewed him from the time of my Colision with the Spanish officers, as innimical to me, and I could see a great intimacy between him & Barnett—and although Barnett was not open in his opposition, I knew he was secretely my enemy—and I had no confidence in the Major from the Period spoken of, the are both weak men, and full of duplicity—I name this to you that you may be on your guard—for a secrete enemy can do more injury than two open ones—I have Just recd a letter from Governor Duval,[1] he expresses towards you the most sincere friendship—and I expect his influence in east Florida, will give you a majority there if prudently wielded.

The news papers will give you the Political news of this quarter, our Legislature is in session and I am told has passed a resolution by a unanimous vote in the house of representatives on the Presidential election. I have not seen it. I therefore must refer you to the news paper containing their proceedings[2]—I have not vissitted the assembly—I had intended it—but my health was not good, and hearing accidentally that something of the kind was intended, I instantly declined going there—I knew it would have been said that I was there electioneering—as I never have, nor do not intend—I shall remain at home. I never have been an applicant for office I never will—The people have a right to do as they please—in this instance as you are well advised I mean to be silent. I have no desire, nor do I expect ever to be called to fill the Presidential chair—but should this be the case, contrary to my wishes & expectations, I am determined it shall be without any exertion on my part—and on this unexpected event, all that can be expected of me, is to obay the call of the people, and execute the duties, to the best of my matured Judgt.

I am very solicitous about your success. I am sure you will meet with the support of all the enlightened & honest class—and I think if you manage Doctor Brosinham well, he can wield the Spanish interest regardless of the wields of Annirarety who I have no doubt was one of Colo. Barnetts solicitous friends, that caused him to come out—

Let me hear from you, and your prospects. I have not seen Doctor [Samuel] Hogg since you left me—Shall write him shortly on your business, should I not meet with him.[3]

Mrs. J. Joins me in good wishes for your success, and believe me to be your friend sincerely

Andrew Jackson

P.S. present me to the Governor respectfully. A.J.
P.S. give my compliments to all friends, particularly to Call, Easter, Rutledge, Walton, Miller, Brakenridge &c &c &c & to Carry—

ALS, DLC (31). Published in Heiskell (2nd edition), 3:158–59.

1. Not found.

2. The *Nashville Whig*, July 31, carried a report of Jackson's nomination for the presidency by a caucus of the Tennessee House of Representatives on July 27.

3. Hogg (1783–1842), a former congressman, was from Lebanon, Tennessee. In 1819, Hogg and Bronaugh established a joint medical practice in Nashville. If Jackson wrote to Hogg, the letter has not been found.

From Samuel Houston

Murfreesboro—3d. Aug 1822

Dear Genl.

On this day a resolution has passed the Senate (unanimously) recommending you as a person the most worthy, & suitable to be the next President of our union.[1] The expression <to you> cannot be esteemed by you any thing less than a grateful a honorable expression of the feelings of your fellow Citizens.

I am aware of your sensibility on such occasions; but the crisis requires that something shou'd be done! The Canker worms have been (already too long) gnawing at the very core & vitals of our Government & corruption stalks abroad; without obstruction, or reprehension.

You are sensible how long I have been faithless in the Heads of Department; It was at a time <that> when you hoped better things than corruption. You had confidence in *men,* perhaps you have yet: But if you will allow me to Divine any thing, I will assure you that you have no friendship to expect from "The Gentlemen of Washington." Whilst it was probable that you coul'd, or wou'd throw any thing in the scale of either Champion; hope of that influence & advantage, wou'd readily induce the friendship of either—

You are now before the eyes of a nation; You have nothing to fear, but every thing to expect. The hopes of men in Washington will be *frost biten* by the bare mention of your name! Then can it be expected that every effort will not be used to Guard against; the *rule,* of Justice & Truth? They will strike like the wounded viper; fall victims of their own poison, rather than see Integrity; (the great enemy of corruption,) triumph.

In calculating the result of the next election; I reflect thus. You have been your countrys Great Centinel; at a time when her watchmen, had been caught slumbering on post—Her Capitol had been reduced to ashes. You have been her faithful guardian; her well tried servant! This admited will not the nation looke to you again? will it not regard your interests, when they are connected with your <own> countrys future welfare. There will be no *caucus* at the next congress! The next President will be the "Peoples Choice."

These matters considered, I have very little to dread of the result. As to my own wishes they are only for the best interests & honor of my country.

You have friends throughout America: each has his sphere, & each will feel & act, from the best motives—

Some one or two Gentlemen quit the house on the occasion; They will repent it![2]

Please present my best respects to Mrs Jackson. I have the honor to be Your most obt sevt & friend

Sam Houston

ALS, DLC (72). Published in Bassett, 6:478.

1. After the vote, state senator Thomas Lanier Williams (1786–1856; North Carolina 1808), a brother of U.S. Senator John Williams, insisted that the clerk of the senate strike the word "unanimous" from the vote recommending Jackson (see *Knoxville Intelligencer,* May 12, 1823).

2. The identity of those who "quit the house" has not been established. This, too, was possibly a reference to Thomas L. Williams, who may have been reacting to the rumor that Jackson's nomination was a maneuver to block John Williams's return to the U.S. Senate in 1823 by making support of Jackson's candidacy a *sine qua non* for election.

To Andrew Jackson Donelson

Nashville August 6th. 1822

Dr Andrew

Since my last respects to you, I have the pleasure to acknowledge your two letters of the 22nd & 29th. ult. which are now before me.[1]

I did not vissit Murfreesborough as was anticipated, nor do I intend;

casually, it being hinted to me, that it was intended by some of my friends to bring my name before the nation, as a fit person to fill the presidential chair, by a resolution of the Legislature, I declined going to the Legislature at all, well knowing if I did, that it would be said by my enemies, that such a resolution was produced by my procurement—<and> never having been a aplicant for any office I have filled, and having long since determined that I never would, I intend in the presence instance to pursue the same independant, republican course. They people have the right to elect whom they think proper—and every individual composing the republic, when they people require his services, is bound to render it, regardless of his own opinion, of his unfitness for the office he is called to fill—I have recd many letters from every quarter of the united states on this subject; I have answered none, nor do I intend to answer any.[2] I shall leave the people free to adopt such course as they may think proper, & elect whom they choose, to fill the Presidential chair, without any influence of mine exercised by me; I have only one wish on this subject, that they people of the united states may in their selection of an individual to fill the Presidential chair, do it with an eye solely to the prosperity of the union, the perpetuation of their own happiness, and the durability of their republican form of goverment, unbiased by the intrigues of designing Demagogues, if left free, to decide for themselves, uninfluenced by congressional caucuses, I have no doubt but they will make a happy choice; If they should permit themselves to be dictated to by a congressional caucus, then, as great a scounderal as William H Crawford might be elevated to the executive chair—contrary to the wish of a great majority of the people—Believe me my Dr Andrew that I never had a wish to be elevated to that station if I could, my sole ambition is to pass to my grave in retirement, But as the Legislature of my state has thought proper to bring my name forward without consulting me, I mean to be silent—and let the people do as it seemeth good unto them—My enemies had at the city of washington circulated the report that I had no popularity in my own state, the resolution of the Legislature, will inform the nation with how much truth this has been circulated—and I suppose this, with other reasons, prompted the move to bring it forward, and has determined me to be silent—I have no business with it, it is now the province of the people to pronounce upon it—and this they shall do without any agency of mine.

I have no doubt but it has alarmed some of the Kentuckians; and some of their great men, in their nightly dreams see the gosts of [Alexander] arbuthnot & [Robert Christie] Ambrister—and are frequently alarmed by the Indian prophets—& exclaim "save them their religion, save them their prophets," and preserve to me the Presidential chair for which I have been intriguing, for many years—and when these Demagogues see the Public Journals throughout the union their fears and alarms will doubly increase, whilst I am, perfectly at ease, regardless how they people may decide—having but one wish that, that decision, may prove beneficial to their own happiness—I am fast going out of life, but my fervent prayers are that our republican goverment may be perpetual, <and> the people alone by their Virtue, and independant exercise of their free suffrage can make it perpetual.[3]

Present me affectionately to [Robert F.] Crittenden & [Anthony] Butler, and when you receive the letter from him it will give me pleasure to be informed of the arkansa publication, you remember Call wrote to Crittendon on the subject of a scurrilous publication in the arkansa Gazzett—I never heard of the result.[4]

Altho nothing would give me more pleasure than to see you, still I am so anxious for you to finish your education with benefit to yourself, (and <which> if you are blessed with health & long life) which may prove beneficial to your country; as long as you enjoy health I shall not interrupt your studies by sending for you—should any thing occur, that I may want your aid, I shall send for you, and I hope you will speak freely to me as to your health—should you want funds let me know it. If your wants should not press you before I can get my cotton in markett, I can supply them with convenience, but keep me advised when your board & tuition becomes due, you gave me this information but I have mislaid the letter—[5]

I have recd a letter from Danl. he is well. I intend in my answer to scold him a little—he is doing well, and I have no doubt but next examination, he will stand well.[6]

I approve of your retirement, both as to your health & study—both I hope will be benefitted by it—and your study will not be so often interrupted by company—my health has been very much checkered of late, but I think upon the whole I have acquired strenght—Genl Coffee & his family <h>is now with us, the Genl wishes to be kindly presented to you—all friends are well, your aunt wishes me to send for you, she is anxious about your health and anxious to see you—The little Andrews are in good health, their education in books, has been interrupted by going to a dancing school, but has improved much thereby[7]—receive our best salutations—and believe me to be your affectionate uncle

Andrew Jackson

P.S. I write with candlelight, and see so badly that I am doubtfull whether you can read it, and without correction A.J.

ALS, DLC (9-0239). Published in Bassett, 3:173–74 (extract).

1. Letters not found.

2. Most correspondence of this description is no longer extant.

3. Jackson had court-martialed and executed British subjects Arbuthnot (c1748–1818) and Ambrister (c1785–1818) for aiding the Seminole Indians during the 1818 invasion of Florida. In his January 20, 1819, House speech condemning the invasion and the 1814 Treaty of Fort Jackson, Henry Clay had opposed the forced conversion to Christianity of Indian tribes, exclaiming "But sir, spare them their prophets! . . . Spare them even their religion, such as it is, from open and cruel violence" (*Annals of Congress,* 15th Cong., 2nd sess., p. 635).

4. Letter not found. The 1820 Choctaw treaty, negotiated by Jackson and Thomas Hinds, had elicited considerable opposition in Arkansas because of its cession to the Indians of lands that whites had begun to settle. In January 1821, a letter by "Helvidius" in the *Arkansas Gazette* severely attacked the treaty and Jackson's character, prompting an anonymous writer from Tennessee (undoubtedly Richard K. Call) to inquire about the identity of Helvidius. The editors refused to disclose the information and renewed the attack upon Jackson, who had, by that time, left Nashville for Florida (see *Arkansas Gazette*, January 27 and May 12, 1821; and AJ to Donelson, September 6, below). Crittenden (1797–1834), a brother of John J. and a member of Jackson's personal guard during the 1818 invasion of Florida, was secretary of Arkansas Territory; he had returned to visit Kentucky earlier in the summer. At this time South Carolina native Butler (1787–1849), a War of 1812 veteran and former Kentucky legislator and gubernatorial candidate, maintained plantations in both Kentucky and Mississippi. In 1829, Jackson appointed him chargé d'affaires to Mexico and authorized him to purchase Texas. Failing in the attempt, Butler settled in Texas.

5. Letter not found.

6. Neither Daniel S. Donelson's letter nor Jackson's reply has been found.

7. On August 5, John Darrac had opened a dance school in Nashville; Jackson's accounts list a $10 payment for Andrew J. Hutchings's dance lessons (see Memorandum book of accounts, September).

To James Gadsden

Hermitage August 9th. 1822

Dear Gadsden

I have had the pleasure to receive your letters of the 16th. & 17th. ult. with the enclosure of the 17th. and on yesterday laid your letter before <me> Colo. Butler, the enclosed note from Colo Butler will inform you of <the Colos.> his feelings and wishes on this subject;[1] his letter I have therefore committed to the flames, <and> I feel happy on this <event as that friendship> termination of those unpleasant feelings which had been excited by groundless reports between two friends which I had a right to <suppose> believe cherished for each others, that pure friendship, which prevades none but the real virtuous <heart> breast—The late <liberal> conduct of Colo. Butler <towards you you> when I sent for, <to come> to make known to him the project proposed to the Secratary of war, the object of which was to enable the Executive to bring you again into the Adjt Genl office, when disclosed, <to you> will convince you <not only> of his friendship for you, you say to me in yours of the 16th. that Mr Calhoun has not recd the letter I advert to—This to me is unacountable, I wrote him on the 28th. of June the same day I wrote you, and enclosed the one to you under cover to him (& as I believe under the same cover) Colo. Butlers letters were placed in the Post office <at> on the same <time> day by me, with those to you & Mr Calhoun but for reasons after the mail had closed—the one to you & Colo. Bs. to the Department referred to in mine were recd, it is strange that mine to Mr Calhoun miscarried, it was a private letter & marked private, and I believe under the same envelope that enclosed mine of the 28th. to you—when I have the pleasure of seeing you, we will converse this thing over between ourselves—[2]

On taking a full view of the report of the military committee<s report>, seeing, <that> it contends<ed> that Butler or Jones <still> were Legally entitled to fill the adjutant Genl office & on this ground you were rejected—that Colo. Towson had been as well as yourself rejected—and the President had given evidence of his intention of yielding to the wishes of the Senate, by bringing Colo. Towson into the pay department again, a way was opened as I believed for the Executive, to bring you into that office by the unanimous vote of the Senate—and to have destroyed the intention of his enemies by their own weapons—Colo. Butler had tendered his resignation, which had not been accepted, he was by the report of the Senates committee Legally adjt Genl, it was only necessary therefore to have ordered Colo. Butler to the city as adjt Genl—at next session of Congress, <his Name> this *erangement* to have been laid before the Senate, <as such>—Their own report debared them from raising any objections to it <to the> confirmation was certain—so soon as that was done, Colo. Butler had the right to have resigned, as soon as he pleased—(which he certainly would have done) and the Executive had the right to bring you before the Senate to fill the vacancy occasioned by B. resignation—under these circumstances those who had objected to your nomination upon legal grounds before, would have been under this circumstance <to> compelled to approve, and having in the case of Colo. Towson Yielded to the wishes of the Senate as expressed in the report—I could see no impropriety in Mr Monroes yielding to it in the case of the adjt Genl; <when> It appeared to be the wish of Mr Calhoune & Mr Monroe to continue you in that appointment, I therefore after consulting Major Eaton & he approving, and Colo. B giving me assurance that he would conform to my wishes—I adressed the project to the Sec of war, with the assurance that Colo. Butler would if ordered obay—it being understood that he should be permitted to resign as soon after the meeting of the next Congress as it could be convenient for him under existing circumstances to do so.

<Whether Mr Calhoun has or has not recd this letter, the situation in which Colo. Butler is now placed by the letters Just recd would prevent him from accepting if ordered, but I have no doubt myself, but it has been recd but for reasons to themselves only known—the project proposed is not agreable, therefore as it is a private letter will not be answered—This is my opinion and for your own ear> I had written a letter recapitulating <the substance of> my letter of the 28th of June, which on the recpt of the answer to the letters by Colo. B. I destroyed & would not forward believing that the project had been recd & not approved—<My Dear young friend,> I wish to see you, when I will fully unboosom myself to you, indeed I cannot understand, the modern course pursued by the Executive—<I will as a friend when we meet unboosom myself to you> I cannot foresee any plan but the one I proposed by which you can be brought into the office of adjt. Genl—and I am aware that Benton & Williams intend re-

newing the investigation at the next meeting of Congress their object to injure Calhoun—I enclose <this under cover> to the care of Genl Gains at Louisville Kentuckey, & hope to see you shortly[3]—<I am Sir> Mrs J &c &c & believe me to be with great respect your real friend

Andrew Jackson

ALS draft endorsed by AJ, DLC (31). Published in Bassett, 3:174–76.

1. Only Gadsden's July 16 letter has been found.

2. See above, AJ to John C. Calhoun, June 28; the other letters have not been found. Gadsden did not arrive in Nashville until October.

3. No letter to Edmund P. Gaines has been found. For the report of the Senate Military Affairs Committee, see *Annals of Congress,* 17th Cong., 1st sess., pp. 489–502.

To Andrew Jackson Donelson

Hermitage Sept. 6th. 1822

Dr. Andrew

Last evening I recd your two letters of the 27th & 28th. ult and am happy to learn that the $200 I sent you is safe to hand.[1]

I recd. on last evening the enclosed letter with the checks therein mentioned to me, the one for $149 50/100 I herewith enclose to you, the other I retain untill I return from Alabama to which place I set out on Monday next—you can exchange this check for at least three hundred dollars Kentucky paper, if that will answer your purpose where you are, and it is fair, and Just, that you exchange it for as much as the markett will offer—Having sent you the memorandom of your accounts, I hasten to write you, that you may not forward them for payment—& send this by a boy, that it may go by this days mail from Nashville.[2]

My last letter will have afforded you all the information on the subject of the payment to Mr Rutledge in my recollection. I have wrote Doctor Bronaugh on this subject—I have no doubt but it is paid, and when you receive my letter you may have some recollection of having given Doctor B. the mony to pay Call, Brakenridge, & Rutledge, however if it is not paid the debt is due by me and not you[3]—My Dr. Andrew be assured that it will allways afford me great pleasure to remit to you any sum that you may stand in need of, and within my power to command—The settlement of my accounts, has for the present left me destitute of funds, but my credit remains unimpaired, but a person who has credit ought to be carefull never to contract debts that the could not meet, or their credit will be lost & then they will be poor indeed—I am happy to find that you will graduate next spring—and that you have a proper Idea of oeconomy, parsimony ought to be avoided as much as extravagance—but no person can get well through life without a proper regard to oeconomy—& a proper distinction ought to be drew between parsimony and oeconomy—

I thank you for the enclosed copy of Mr Crittendons letter to you[4]—it is the first & only information on the subject I have recd after I left Nashville in 1821—If Capt Call recd the papers aluded to he never communicated them to me, [Joseph] Selden must be a perfect, scounderal, he like Mr Clay, has allways professed a great friendship for me, and at Richmond entered into a personal quarrel with Mr [Benjamin Watkins] Leagh, as the reputed author of the virulent peaces that appeared in the Enquirer—[David] Brearly is a very contemtable fellow, in short I suppose they are worthy companions & as such they ought to repose. Should I meet either I will take ocasion merely to let them know, I am aprised of their cowardly conduct—present my thanks to Capt Crittenden for his friendship in this instance.[5]

have the goodness to advise me of the recpt of this letter that I may know that the check has reached you in safety—& let me know the exchange you made of it—Our Andrew has recd your letter & will answer it—I hope it may be a stimulant but he is very idle—he was to have answered it on Saturday but his mother sent him for Peggy allen[6]—your aunt Joins me in love to you & believe me to be your affectionate uncle

Andrew Jackson

ALS, DLC (9-0263).

1. See AJ to Donelson, August 19, and Donelson to AJ, August 27. Donelson's letter of the 28th has not been found.

2. Neither the enclosure, John L. Smith to AJ, August 16, nor the memorandum of Donelson's accounts has been found. The checks were for Donelson's back military pay.

3. See AJ to Donelson, August 28, and AJ to James C. Bronaugh, August 27. Edward A. Rutledge's claim was for services as translator at Pensacola. Jackson paid Rutledge $250 for his account on November 25 (see Account of Rutledge, May 12, 1821).

4. Not found.

5. For a discussion of controversy in Arkansas, see above, AJ to Donelson, August 6. In 1820, Virginia native Selden (1787–1824), a former army officer and War of 1812 veteran, had been appointed federal district judge for Arkansas Territory. In late 1818 and early 1819, Leigh (1781–1849), Selden's cousin, had authored the anonymous "Algernon Sidney" attacks upon the invasion of Florida that had appeared in the *Richmond Enquirer*. Brearley (1786–1837) had been colonel of the 7th Infantry Regiment until he resigned in 1820 to become Cherokee and Quapaw agent in Arkansas Territory. In 1819, Jackson had sought Brearley's testimony implicating David B. Mitchell in slave smuggling activities in Georgia, but Jackson found Brearley's affidavit evasive, and he later turned against the colonel after Brearley brought military charges against Edmund P. Gaines (see Brearley to AJ, October 20, and AJ to John C. Calhoun, November 15, both 1819). Apparently, Crittenden had implicated both Selden and Brearley in the Helvidius incident.

6. Letters not found. In December 1814, Margaret Watkins, Jackson's former ward, had married John Allen, who kept a dry goods store near Stones River.

To John Coffee

Hermitage Sept. 29th. 1822

Dr. Genl

I reached home on the night of the 25th. instant, on the eve of Mr. Wm. Donelsons mariage, we have been in a constant bustle ever since, and this morning the young people have left us, and I send John on who will hand you this. William has nothing now to do but to attend to finishing his house & picking his cotton, all friends here are well—as I expected my poor negro Jack died a few days after I left him—[1]

The news from Pensacola are shocking to humanity, my friend Bronaugh has fell a victim to his exertions to arrest the progress of the fever, he died the 2nd instant—all the Phicians are dead—and the distressed inhabitants who cannot get away left to its ravages without medical aid—at the last dates not a single american who was taken with it, had survived—Call & Easter has escaped, they are out of Town—Mr S. R. Overton is up the Bay with the other commissioners—& the council sits at Manuels 15 mile this side of Pensacola I fear the diseas has been admitted into the town by too Lax a police—[2]

It is Rumored that McDuffee & Colo Cummings has determined their dispute, the latter shot through the heart who instantly died McDuffee shot through the lungs, the wound supposed to be mortal—a subsequent rumor is, that they have not fought that Colo. Cumming was arrested by the civil authority on his way—the first report most credited.[3]

Present me to Mr J. Jackson & family—Mrs J. Joins me in good wishes for your, your Lady & sweet little families welfare and happiness—I am your friend sincerely—

Andrew Jackson

P.S. Please do not forget to send me in your affidavit when Leisure will permit, keeping a copy for yourself & the papers I gave you the memorandom for.[4] A. J.

ALS, THi (9-0277). Endorsed "Answered"; reply not found.

1. Jackson had been to Alabama to check on his and Andrew J. Hutchings's farms. William Donelson (1795–1864), son of John (1755–1830) and Mary Purnell Donelson, married his first cousin Rachel Donelson (1803–24), daughter of Severn (1773–1818) and Elizabeth Rucker Donelson (1782–1828). Jackson's messenger may have been John Fulton (b. c1810), a mulatto slave owned by Rebecca Nowland of Florence, Alabama, and purchased by Jackson in December. Fulton remained on the Hermitage slave rolls until at least 1825. Jack has not been further identified.

2. For the mid-August outbreak of yellow fever in Pensacola and the death of James C. Bronaugh, see Edward A. Rutledge to AJ, August 24–26; Samuel R. Overton to AJ, September 2; and George Walton to AJ, October 10. Jackson and Walton shared the administra-

tion of Bronaugh's estate. Jackson remembered Bronaugh as "my bosom friend, he was every way worthy of that confidence I reposed in him, he was incapable of violating confidence, or departing from the true principles of friendship" (see AJ to Walton, November 26, and Noncupative will of Bronaugh, September 20). Overton and the other land commissioners had moved to Juan de la Rua's home, about eight miles from Pensacola, not the house of Manuel Gonzalez, where Jackson had stayed in 1821.

3. William Cumming had been arrested by North Carolina authorities, temporarily preventing a second duel with George McDuffie. The second duel finally occurred on November 8. For the origin of the McDuffie-Cumming duels, see above, AJ to Andrew J. Donelson, June 2.

4. See Deposition of Coffee regarding the lawsuit by Bennett Smith, August 5; other papers not found.

To Andrew Jackson Donelson

Hermitage Octbr 11th. 1822.

Dr. Andrew

On my return from Florence I wrote advising you thereof, and acknowledging the receipt of your letters which had arived in my absence. I have recd yours advising of Colo. J. Gadsden being with you, he is now here. Mr Baker & his sister left us yesterday after spending a day & a night with us.[1]

I should have sent you the phamphlets desired by you had an opportunity of private convayence offerred—they are too bulky to be sent by mail.[2]

Before this reaches you, you will have recd. the intelligence that our friend Doctor Bronaugh is no more—he had not one of his old acquaintances round him. Mr Wm Davidson whom you recollect spent last summer was a year ago with us in Pensacola writes me he stayed with him to the last—closed his eyes & followed him alone to his grave—the Doctor lay at Colo Waltons. Mrs. Walton & child was down and I have no doubt every attention was paid to him that was in the power of Colo. Walton—Mr Davidson writes me that the Doctor became religious in his last, was perfectly sensible of his death and met it with resignation and fortitude & requested Colo. Walton thus to inform me. I sincerely regret his death—I had wrote him on the subject of Mr Rutledges account—I have recd no answer. I have wrote Mr Rutledge by this days mail, stating to him that if Doctor Bronaugh has not paid him that the mony is still due & to draw on me for the amount—all friends are well. I have wrote to Danl. and am gratified to learn that he is doing so well[3]—I hope your Lectures have commenced, I would like to learn the mode of Lecturing—from which I could form an opinion of their usefullness—I have no doubt the Litchfield institution, from the age, & great experience of its professors, and the mode of Lecturing, is superior to yours,[4] but as you are there, and I wish you to be with me in the spring & next summer I wish you there to continue untill the present session is complete—I am sure you can with due diligence & application improve yourself much—Mr Barry and [Jesse] Bledsoe are both men of talents—it is true they both have been taken with the Bank mania, which has realised the adage that there are no great men without their weaknesses—But as lawyers, unconnected with politicks, they are both men of great talents—It is their Legal know[l]edge, abstracted from politicks, that I wish you to learn—not the absurd doctrine that the Legislature is the people, when every child in politicks does know, that the Legislature is as much the agents of the people, as the executive & Judiciary—The Legislature are created by the constitution, their powers defined by it, & whenever it transcends its powers expressly given, its acts are void—The Judiciary being the check, their duty becomes imperious as the faithfull agents of the people, so to declare it—<&> The Legislature are no more the people, than any other department of the Goverment established by the people, by the constit*[ution]* for the benefit of the people, to do their *[b]*usiness agreable to their letter of attorny, *to* it, *the constitution*—But notwithstanding all this as lawyers, I think them men of great talents[5]

The boy is waiting & this is mail day—your affectionate uncle

Andrew Jackson

ALS, DLC (9-0285). Published in Bassett, 3:178–79 (extract).

1. See AJ to Donelson, September 27; Donelson's letters have not been found. It is unknown which of Isaac L. Baker's four surviving sisters accompanied him to the Hermitage.

2. The pamphlets have not been identified.

3. See AJ to James C. Bronaugh, August 27; the other letters have not been found.

4. The Litchfield (Connecticut) Law School, the first independent law school in the United States, was established in 1784 by Tapping Reeve (1774–1823) and, after 1820, administered by James Gould (1770–1838).

5. Bledsoe (1776–1836), a former U.S. Senator from Kentucky, was judge of the Lexington circuit court, as well as professor of common and statute law at Transylvania University. For more on Jackson's views on the controversy in Kentucky, see above, AJ to Donelson, July 25, and December 23, below.

To Andrew Jackson Donelson

Hermitage Octbr. 23rd 1822

Dr. Andrew

I received by due course of mail your letter of the 5th. instant,[1] on Tuesday of last week, being engaged at home with company which I could not leave, I did not get to Nashville untill last Thursday evening, when to my great regret I was informed that Mr [Martin Adrien] Durald had left the Town about two hours before I arived, had I have heard of his & his families arival I should have forthwith have repaired to Nashville to have invited, and brought them to my house—but from the date of your letter advising me of Mr. D. leaving Lexington, I was of the belief that my vissit to Nashville on last thursday would have been sufficiently early to have meet them there, however I was disappointed which I sincerely regret—we have had much company this fall that has confined us at home—at present & for some days past, we have had Madam Chotard & daughter with us—[2]

My business calls me out to Florence. My manager there wishes to be relieved, & I have no wish to detain him—I have been compelled at a high premium to get a Mr Parsons—with whom on the 27th. instant I set out, to place him in possession of my farm—erange all my business and return before the cold weather sets in. My health has much improved, but every change of weather I find renews my cough—I had a bid for my place out there and would have sold it, but I did not like to sacrafice it for a less sum than I knew it was really worth—and from its situation it must become very Valuable—I therefore declined for the present—& have determined to make another effort to make it productive—it has hitherto been a source of expence, & great trouble—[3]

I am happy to learn that your Lectures will soon commence—I wish you to take a part in the debates in the moote court—and in your Legislative exercises—it is all important that you should familiarise yourself to public speaking, when you commence the practice it will relieve you from that emberassment, that all those experience on their first essay before the public. I shall prepare to send for you in march next, unless before that period you may advise me, that your benefits there, are not equal to your expectations, or worthy of the expence you have to encounter.

I ought to have sent you the amount of the check I retained before now, but really I had to use it—and did expect to have been able to collect it before now, in which I was disappointed, and believing that the funds forwarded would be adequate to your wants untill you were about to leave there, I did not like to go into Bank for that sum—I have therefore awaited the sales of my cotton, and have to request, if you should want it, before I sell, that you will advise me, and it shall be remitted.[4]

I have recd a letter from Mr Saml Overton in which he begs to be presented to you[5]—Colo Gadsden has Just recd your letter, he accompanies me to alabama whether he will return with me or not I cannot say.[6] I am informed that young Mr Rutledge will be here in all this month—I had not heard from our departed friend Doctor Bronaugh on the subject of the payment to young Mr Rutledge—I suppose he was dead before my letter reached him—I on the information of the death of Doctr B. wrote Mr Rutledge, which I hope *[he]* will receive before he leaves the lower country—[7]

your aunt and they Andrews unite in love to you & believe me to be your affectionate uncle

Andrew Jackson

ALS, DLC (9-0297).

1. Not found.

2. A New Orleans resident, Duralde (1785–1848) had married Henry Clay's daughter, Susan Hart (1805–25), in April. Sarah F. Chotard (1777–1825) of Alabama, the widowed stepmother of Henry Chotard (1787–1870) who had been on Jackson's staff at New Orleans, had come to Nashville to inquire regarding lands that had belonged to her father

James Williams. Her daughter was Eliza Williams Chotard (1798–1878), who subsequently married William Proctor Gould.

3. For Jackson's earlier attempt to hire Benjamin P. Person, see above, AJ to John Coffee, March 14. The offer to buy the Big Spring farm was probably from Anthony Winston, Jr. For discussion of the subsequent sale, see AJ to Richard K. Call, November 27, below.

4. Regarding the retained check, which was for $80, see above, AJ to Donelson, September 6.

5. Probably Samuel R. Overton to AJ, September 22.

6. Donelson's letter to James Gadsden has not been found.

7. See AJ to James C. Bronaugh, August 27; AJ to Edward A. Rutledge not found. Rutledge returned to Nashville in early November with Bronaugh's slaves and horses, which Jackson took charge of as an administrator of the estate (see AJ to George Walton, November 26).

From James Gadsden

Florence Alabama
20 Novr 1822

My Dear General

Since you left this place, I have received a letter from my Brother, stating that a copy of the record in the case of Griffith & Fraser, had, agreeably to your request, been transmitted to Nashville—The Clerk who transcribed the papers refused to make any charge against you—With the documents now in your possession, and the diligence of Darby, I hope that a speedy issue will be brought to a vexatious suit which has been so long pending in the Tennessee Courts—[1]

Pro Patria has again made his appearance in the columns of the National Intelligencer, will you be good enough to have the article republished in all the Nashville papers; It is a well written, temperate document—I shrewdly suspect a return of sober reason on the subject; at least for the first time the Editors of the National Intelligencer draw the attention of the community to it, with a remark on its general interest & the little notice it has hitherto attracted—[2]

Nothing of moment has transpired since you left this place—I shall depart myself day after tomorrow on my contemplated excursion[3]—Let me hear from you frequently & command my services as you may wish them in this quarter—To Mrs Jackson & your family in general I beg you to present my best regards Your friend

Gadsden

ALS, DLC (31). ALS endorsed by AJ: "answered Novbr 27 1822." Answer not found.

1. See Thomas Gadsden to AJ, October 29. In his January 23, 1821, amended answer in the *Jackson* v. *Erwin* lawsuit, Andrew Erwin sought to strengthen his case by adding the claim of former South Carolina Senator Pierce Butler (1744–1822) against the David Allison estate. In 1814, however, the United States Supreme Court had affirmed a South Carolina circuit court decision in *Griffith* v. *Frazier* denying Butler's claim (8 Cranch 1–30). In the December 17 issue of the Nashville *Constitutional Advocate,* Patrick H. Darby used the case record to rebut Erwin's claim. Thomas Gadsden has not been further identified. Jackson left Florence, Alabama, about November 17 and reached the Hermitage on November 24.

2. For the articles by "Pro Patria" criticizing the Senate's opposition to the appointments of Gadsden and Nathan Towson, see the Washington *National Intelligencer,* August 21, September 18, and November 2; the latter two articles were republished in the Nashville *Constitutional Advocate,* October 15 and November 26. Joseph Gales (1761–1841) and William Winston Seaton (1785–1866) edited the Washington *National Intelligencer.*

3. Gadsden toured Alabama south of the Tennessee River before returning to Florence in mid-December; in January 1823 he joined Jackson in Tennessee.

Patrick H. Darby, Jackson's counsel in the long-pending Jackson *v.* Erwin *lawsuit, had in the summer of 1822 purchased the Nashville* Clarion, *renaming it the* Constitutional Advocate. *Editor Darby supported Jackson's presidential candidacy, but also used the newspaper to attack professional and political enemies. Beginning in August, Darby linked Bedford County legislator Andrew Erwin with some of Jackson's most important allies as principals in the passage of the 1821 champerty law, which prohibited lawyers from receiving contingent fees from litigated lands (Tennessee,* Acts of a General or Public Nature. . . *[n.p., 1821], pp. 71–75). Erwin, who had been in Mexico City as agent for a group of Tennessee and Kentucky investors who would form the Robertson Colony in Texas, returned to Tennessee, announced for Congress in October, and responded to Darby's charges in early November. Exchanges between the two, which also appeared in the* Nashville Whig, *continued through December. In his letter, below, Jackson sought to distance himself from Darby's newspaper war, reinforcing another statement denying Jackson's involvement, published by "A.B." in the* Nashville Whig, *November 20. Jackson's letter was not published.*

To Joseph Norvell and Patrick Henry Darby

Hermitage, Novbr. 25th, 1822

To the Editors of the Whig & constitutional advocate—

Upon reading the news papers since returning from my plantation in Alabama, it was perceived that Mr Darby, the Editor of the constitutional advocate, and Mr Erwin, were discussing the merits of a lawsuit depending in court, in which Mr James Jackson of Alabama and myself, only, are interested. Mr. Darby has no interest in this suit, other than as counsel employed by Mr James Jackson & myself—The Editor of the advocate in his paper of the 19th. instant, with truth, observes, that I had neither connection in, nor any influence as to his publications—otherwise, it would have been exerted, so as to exclude newspaper discussions of lawsuits, so highly reprobated by the laws—as well as similar enquiries into the motives of men. The tendency of the Public acts of public men in civil society, is, in decorous language, apropriate to public enquiry[1]

Andrew Jackson

ALS, DLC (9-0316). Norvell (1793–1847), with his brother Moses, had founded the *Nashville Whig* in 1812, and had published the newspaper until 1817; Joseph resumed ownership in 1819 and continued publication until January 1826, when he sold the paper to Andrew Erwin's son James (1796–1851), brother of then editor John P. Erwin.

1. See Agreement among AJ, Jenkin Whiteside, James Jackson, and Patrick H. Darby, April 13, 1821; and the Nashville *Constitutional Advocate,* November 19. English practice dating at least to 1742 held that a court has a right to safeguard its proceedings and litigants by citing for contempt those responsible for discussion of pending lawsuits in the newspapers (see 2 *Atkyns Report,* 469–73). In 1824, Darby was disbarred for publishing commentary on another pending lawsuit (*Nashville Whig,* August 9, 1824). Darby's "interest in this suit" became a matter of dispute among Andrew Jackson, James Jackson, and Darby (see James Jackson to AJ, October 28, 1823; AJ to John C. McLemore, January 30, 1824; AJ to John Coffee, February 15, March 4, and March 28, 1824, all below).

To Richard Keith Call

Hermitage Novbr. 27th. 1822

My Dear Call

On my return from my farm in alabama where I had been for the last month, I had the pleasure to receive your letter of the 15th. of October,[1] which informed me that you, Brakenridge, Easter & my friend Cary Nicolas still survived, the desolating fury of that dreadfull disease, that has depopulated Pensacola, and has swept from existance so many of my friends & acquaintances—

How I deplore the Loss of my friend Bronaugh, I shall never cease to mourne his premature death, & suffering. I deeply deplore the loss of our mutual friend Major Dinkin, he is a serious loss to his friends, his country, & particularly the army, his activity, industry, and military skill gave life & Vigor to his Regt. in short he might be called the soul of his Regt. But the scripture tells us, mourne not for the dead but the living.[2] I rejoice that a few of my friends there still live, present me to Brakenridge, Walton, Easter & Nicholas, with the prayers of your friend Mrs J. for all your happiness & continued health.

I have noted the vote for Colo Barnett. Should he leave the Floridas, it will be but little injury to its future benefit & prosperity.[3]

I had a long personal conversation with Mr James Jackson before he left home on the subject of Colo. King Mr. Jackson will persue any Just plan to defeat the machinations of Crawfords friends, and will support Colo. King provided he finds the Colo. can succeed, but on the event it is found he cannot be elected, he will unite in the support of some charector from the lower, or middle part of the state who can be elected and who is positively known to be opposed to the Crawford interest—Mr James Jackson will do right. I gave him a letter to Major Montgomery believing the Major was a true friend of Colo Kings' with whom Mr Jackson will freely converse.[4] I have nothing new, the news papers of the east will shew you, that the presidential question is still agitated, and agitating throughout the Eastern & middle sections of the union—they papers ask the question

¿what has Mr Crawford done to entitle him to the presidential chair! This is a *hard* question for his friends to answer.

My health is greatly restored—and I have sold out my farm in alabama intending to house myself this Winter[5]—I see my friend Capt Hugh young is no more, I sincerely regret his untimely end—Has he left any Estate, or pay due him. He is in debt to me one hundred & fifty dollars, one hundred of this, for a horse Bot of Doctor Bronaugh & fifty loaned mony. I had wrote him on the subject, but finding that he was not in funds I did not press the subject—If he h*[as]* left any funds it would be a convenience for me to receive it, as, in winding up my accounts, I find my funds reduced much Lower, than I expected. Will you make inquiry, and if this debt can be collected out of his funds I will be glad to receive it—if not I will cheerfully resign it.[6] I wish you to make search & inquiry about my manuscri*[pt]* Book, it is probable in Doctor Bronaughs liberary, or got with Colo Brooks Books at Montpelier—perhaps it might have been left at Mr Austins, at Blakely, do my Dr Sir make the necessary inquiry and if it can be found send it to me—you recollect it is in the appearence of a large Pockett Book, tied with a string, with Pocketts at each side containing my Public receipts and vouchers it is covered with rough brown leather like my other record Books.

I care not for the vouchers as all my Public accounts are finally closed but contains my correspondence with W. H. Crawford which I want.[7] accept assurance of my friendship & Esteem yr friend

Andrew Jackson

ALS, DLC (9-0322).

1. Not found.

2. Apparently after Luke 23:28. Jackson often quoted the phrase "Mourn not for the dead, but for the living" (alternatively, "Weep not for the dead, but for the living"), but neither version appears in the King James Bible.

3. The outbreak of yellow fever in West Florida and resulting chaos helped bring about the election of St. Augustine's Joseph Marion Hernandez (1793–1857) as territorial delegate over William Barnett. In June 1823, Call succeeded Hernandez, and Barnett thereafter returned to Alabama.

4. The letter, possibly to Alabama state representative Woodson C. Montgomery (d. 1824) of Limestone County, has not been found. The Alabama legislature convened on November 18 at Cahaba; for the election of Alabama's U.S. senators, see above, James Jackson to AJ, July 24.

5. Jackson had accepted an offer from Anthony Winston, Jr., and sold the improved half of the Big Spring farm for an undetermined amount.

6. See AJ to Hugh Young, February 26, 1821; the debt was not recovered. Young, a topographical engineer from Tennessee, had also died during the yellow fever outbreak in Pensacola.

7. Jackson's letterbook for February 1816 through September 1818, which encompassed much of William H. Crawford's tenure as Secretary of War, has not been found.

To George Nashee

Hermitage near Nashville. T.
Decbr 17th. 1822

Dear Sir

I have Just recd your letter of the 29th ult. Informing me, for the first time, that I was a subscriber to your paper, and enclosing me your account as a subscriber to the Supporter from the month of august 1813 to February 1821—and to subscription to Supporter & Sciota Gazette from February 1821 to February 1823; advising me that this paper was directed to be sent me by an officer of the army whose name you have forgotten, then serving in the Northwestern army.[1]

Permit me to assure you, that I have no recollection of ever requesting or authorising any one to subscribe for your paper. Nor do I ever recollect to have recd it untill my return to Nashville in May 1815—when it was sent to me with other papers by the Postmaster, calling upon me for the postage[2]

I then supposed that it was sent me, as many others are, and have been; as a compliment, for which I could not do less than pay the postage, and gratefully receive them. Should I be called upon for the subscriptions of all news papers sent me, for which I have never been a subscriber—it would require more funds to meet this demand, than all the neat proceeds of my estate—you will therefore be pleased to discontinue sending me your paper.

If I had, had the most distant intimation that your paper was sent me as a subscriber I should on its receipt have desired you, as I now do, to have it discontinued, not having authorised any one as I believe to <have> place<d> me as a subscriber to your valuable paper.

<In 1813 in the fall I entered the savage wilds of the south, and was immersed in them the most of 1814, where I had no opportunity of receiving any news papers—and if I had received them, I had no leisure to peruse them—and when I recd your paper in 1815 I did believe it had been sent me as many others were, & now are, to which I am not, nor ever have been, a Subscriber>

My funds are <not able> In[su]fficient to meet such heavy contributions, as to pay for all the news papers that are voluntarily sent me—and I have ever kept my wants within my means. I am sir—with due respect, yr mo obdt. servt.

Andrew Jackson

ALS draft, DLC (31). Published in *Cincinnati Commercial*, January 8, 1881. In 1807, Nashee (c1786–1827) had moved to Ohio from his native Massachusetts. A year later he founded the Chillicothe *Supporter*, which in 1821 merged with the *Scioto Gazette*.

1. See Nashee to AJ, November 29.
2. See Robert B. Currey to AJ, June 24, 1815.

To John Coffee

Hermitage Decbr 21rst 1822

Dear Genl

By Colo Ward on the 19th. I recd yours of the 10th. instant.[1] am happy to hear of your good health, and am happy that I have it in my power to say to you that all your friends here are well The little infant is growing finely—and Mrs. D. watches over it, and the ballance of the little orphants, with that tender care that displays so much benevolence & goodness of heart—and how much she feels the loss of her daughter. I have been this cloudy and inclement weather afflicted with pains I have not been out, but have communicated to Capt Donelson & his family the recpt of your letter, your compliments and health—[2]

This will be handed to you by Mr [Alexander] Barksdale he was prepared to set out to reach you by Christmas the time I expected your old overseer to leave you—he goes to try to get employ, if he should not, I have told him to return & I will give him a Job of Carpenters work on my Ginn house—He is an excellent young man, industrious, sober and honest, and I suppose as good an overseer as any of his age; he can make any thing in wood, wanted on a farm—you will oblige me by aiding him to get a good Berth for the present year.[3]

I have noted your remarks as to the lease to Mr McKean—I have directed Colo Gadsden to decline giving him a lease—I have wrote Mr Jos. [W.] McKean today on that subject—I have had several offers to purchase—& Colo Ward has named to me his wish to exchange—I was to have spent this day with him, but the inclemency of the weather has prevented. I fear we will not agree, as the part he proposes has no timber, and he wishes to split the spring—this latter would be but little objection if the line on the branch is left so that it could be enclosed for stock water however I will see his proposals the first clear day, and let you know the result.[4]

What do you do with your cotton this year, do you ship it—should I not sell, will you have <yours> mine shipped with yours—I have said to Mr Parsons when the cotton is Bailed advise you, & you will order what is to be done with it—I have wrote some time since to [Isaac L.] McCoy & Scallen, but have recd no answer yet—If I can sell below for eleven cents, I will ship—exchange at Nashville is rising—the holders of our raggs will have to bid up or they will get no Cotton—I do not believe we ought to take less than 12 cents in these raggs that are depreciating daily—however I shall write you shortly, on this and other subject*[s]* in the mean time if Mr Parsons gets the Cotton ready, and is about to move in make him deliver at the river in some ware house—and deposit on the Bank under cover—what will Rapier & Simpson give—inquire & write me—say to them I have requested the question to be asked.[5]

Present Mrs J. & myself respectfully to Mrs C. & the children, and receive for yourself our best wishes, present us to Capt Jack & say to him we expect him soon—your friend

Andrew Jackso*[n]*

P. S Mr Easton has been with me. I have had much conversation with him. I think he will act with energy and some enterprise—if he can get time I have no doubt but he will wind up *well*[6]

ALS, THi (9-0364). Published in Bassett, 3:181 (extract).

1. Letter not found.

2. On November 20, in Franklin, Tennessee, Rachel Donelson Eastin died following the birth of her daughter, Rachel Jackson. Returning to Nashville from Alabama, Jackson arrived at the scene shortly after his niece's death. Mary P. Donelson cared for her surviving Eastin grandchildren, Mary Ann (1810–47), Susanna (1812–24), Elizabeth Donelson (1817–39), and John Donelson (b. 1820).

3. In late November Jackson had engaged Barksdale (c1798–1850), then resident in Davidson County, as Coffee's overseer; Barksdale remained in Lauderdale County, Alabama, until the late 1830s, when he moved to Yalobusha County, Mississippi, where he became a planter. Coffee's previous overseer has not been identified.

4. Letters not found. The proposed exchange of land did not occur, but was possibly for a portion of Hunters Hill in Davidson County, purchased in 1804 by Edward Ward from Jackson. A native of Nashville, Joseph W. McKean (1799–1851) lived near Jackson's Big Spring, Alabama, plantation; he soon moved to Hardeman County, Tennessee, where he was a justice of the peace. He eventually settled in Sevier County, Arkansas. The other McKean has not been identified.

5. See McCoy & Company to AJ, December 13, which answered AJ to McCoy & Scallan, November 27 (not found), by advising Jackson of the demise of the former partnership. McCoy was a New Orleans merchant. Coffee's reply has not been found.

6. William Eastin owed significant sums to the Franklin, Tennessee, bank and to unnamed Philadelphia merchants. His Donelson relatives rallied round with loans and other support, but some debts remained unsettled when he died in 1829 (see John C. McLemore to Coffee, October 13, 1822, and March 4, 1824, THi; and P. F. Pearson to Coffee, August 31, 1829, NcU).

To Andrew Jackson Donelson

Hermitage Decbr 23rd. 1822

Dear Andrew

I have the pleasure to acknowledge the receipt of yours of the 14th. instant accompanied with Mr Bledsoes introductory lecture, which I have perused with attention and satisfaction[1]

In this introduction he has displayed considerable research, and Genius, and I hope from a continuation of his Lectures they law students will experience much benefit—It is gratifying to me to find that you are both pleased, and edified, by the proceedings of the Moote court—and it affords me considerable gratification to be informed that you have been successfull in your first suit—and from which I infer, that you must have displayed in the argument considerable ingenuity, to convince the court that state paper was *mony* and that an action of debt was the proper remedy on the contract stated—when the constitution of the U states has declared "that no state shall coin money, emit bills of credit, or make any thing but gold & silver a tender in the payment of debts,"[2] all the states have adopted this constitution, and of course cannot make *paper, mo[ny]* of course commonwealths paper not legally *mony* of such certainty as an action of debt would be for the recovery thereof—But an action of covenant (if the instrument was under seal)—if not, an action on the case—I make these remarks, that you may in answer, give me the substance of your argument, and th<at>e <of> reason assigned by the Judges on which their opinion was founded. I would barely add that dollars and cents are the legal <coin> mony of the united states—paper is not—and an action of debt when brought, If brought on an instrument for any other coin, than that of the united states, must state of the vallue of so many dollars, & cents—by what certain rule <of reason> did the*[y e]*stimate the common wealth paper to be worth so many dollars and cents. This rule, must be some known, established, legal, & certain rule—for if it lacks certainty, it must require a Jury to assess the damage, and of course an action of debt cannot be maintained. I regret I have not time to look into some authorities on this subject, I write in haste for tomorrows mail, and drop these hasty hints, to draw from you the arguments on both sides, and the reasons of the Judge—I hope with a continuation of your application, you will soon be gratified with being an actor on the public stage.

you will find by my last letter to you that Daniel has become much dissatis*[fied with]* the military school, and has tendered his *[resi]*gnation which has not been accepted, awaiting my approbation—I have not answered his letter, nor will I, untill I hear from you. I enclosed his letter to his Grandmother for her opinion & Mr [James] Sanders, I have as yet recd no reply. Should you recommend me to give my approbation to his resignation I will do so, and raise & send on the funds to bring him home.[3]

I have to request that you will give me notice when & how much mony you will need—I expect to sell my cotton shortly[4] & I am to receive a payment for the land I sold in alabama on the 15th. of February next but if your wants are pressing, I will raise it by a note in Bank—I mean to send for you in March next, as I learn your Lectures close in that month—

your aunt & the Andrews, with your cousin Saml [Jackson] Hays tender to you their respects[5]—and believe me to be yo*[ur]* affectionate uncle

Andrew Jack*[son]*

ALS, THer (9-0368).

1. See Donelson to AJ, December 14. The enclosure was Jesse Bledsoe, *An Introductory Lecture on the Study of Law, Delivered in the Chapel of Transylvania University, on Monday, November 4, 1822* (Lexington, Ky., 1822).

2. Jackson was paraphrasing Article I, section 10, of the federal constitution. For more

on Jackson's views of paper currency, see AJ to William B. Lewis, July 16, 1820 (*Jackson*, 4:378–81); and AJ to Donelson, February 8, 1823.

3. See AJ to Andrew J. Donelson, December 16; Daniel S. Donelson to AJ, November 20; and Andrew J. Donelson to AJ, [cDecember 30]. Jackson's letter to Donelson's maternal grandmother, Sarah Michie Smith (c1755–1834), has not been found. Sanders (1764–1836) had married Donelson's mother, Mary Ann Michie Smith Donelson in 1806. Daniel S. Donelson graduated from the Military Academy in 1825.

4. James Stewart & Co. had tendered an offer for Jackson's Alabama and Tennessee crops, and on December 24 Jackson agreed to sell the company his Tennessee crop (see Stewart & Co. to AJ, December 17 and 25; Account with Stewart & Co., December 31).

5. Hays (1800–66) was the son of Robert (1758–1819) and Jane Donelson Hays (1766–1834).

To John Coffee

Hermitage Decbr. 27th. 1822

Dr. Genl

I wrote you by Mr Barksdale, but a letter this moment recd from Mr Parsons asking me what he will do with the Cotton when Bailed, induces me to write you again—[1]

I find from Mr Parsons account of the cotton, Mr Harris must have very much deceived me. Harris stated that there were thirty thousand in the house—This I did not believe, but I supposed there was Twenty thousand and thirty in the field—Mr Parson sa*[ys]* he has all ginned and Bailed *[what]* has been picked, in all seven*[teen]* Bales, which cannot amount *[to more]* than seven thousand, which w*[ould]* be in the seed about twenty five *[thousand.]* I do not suppose, <they> will get out more than six or Eight Bales. I have wrote Mr Parsons to apply to you for instructions what to do with it when Bailed—I may sell, if I can get ten cents for it—I wish you however to ship it with Little Andrew J. Hutchings, if an opportunity offers, unless you should receive further advice from me, before an opportunity of shipping offers, and instruct the house to whom you ship (I suppose [John Robertson] Bedford) to sell the first markett that offers at ten cents advising him that it is Andrew J Hutchings and to do the best for him I believe I can get ten cents here for it, giving to the first of June next—advise me whether I ought to take it, by the next mail after the recpt of this.[2] your friends are all well—Mrs J Donelson, last Monday got an unfortunate fall, sprained her ancle *[w]*hich has confined her, she has suffered *[so]*me pain with it, but I hope will *[so]*on recover from it—Mr Easton *[li]*ttle ones, are well, the infant growing finely—Mrs. J. and myself tenders to you Polly, & the family, the Joys of the season, with our best wishes—your friend

Andrew Jackson

P.S. We are looking for the Capt hourly—They Miss Lukes left their compliments for him[3]—A.J.

ALS, THi (9-0374). Published in Bassett, 3:182 (lacking postscript).

1. See above, AJ to Coffee, December 21; Benjamin P. Person's letter has not been found.

2. Letters not found. For the disposition of Andrew J. Hutchings's cotton crop, see AJ to Coffee, January 10, 1823, below. Bedford (1782–1827), formerly a Rutherford County doctor, was now a merchant in Alabama and New Orleans, associated with James Mackey.

3. The "Miss Lukes" have not been identified. The "Capt." was John Donelson (1787–1840).

ANDREW JACKSON

Henry Marie Brackenridge

George Walton

George Mercer Brooke

James Gadsden

Nathan Towson

Henry Atkinson

Richard Ivy Easter

Samuel Houston

James Jackson

George Wilson

Patrick Henry Darby

John Donelson

Josiah Nichol

Original sketch of
Genl Jackson. taken
immediately after the
battle of New Orleans. T Sully

Andrew Jackson

Henry Clay

John Caldwell Calhoun

John Quincy Adams

William Harris Crawford

THE LETTERS

OF

WYOMING,

TO THE

PEOPLE OF THE UNITED STATES,

ON THE

Presidential Election,

AND

IN FAVOUR OF ANDREW JACKSON.

ORIGINALLY PUBLISHED IN

THE COLUMBIAN OBSERVER.

'Midst the battle's commotion he rose on the view
Of his Country—to shield her, or perish there too.

"JACKSON, all hail! our Country's pride and boast,
Whose mind's a Council, and whose arm's a host!
Welcome blest chief! Accept our grateful lays,
Unbidden homage of our grateful praise.
Remembrance long shall keep alive thy fame,
And future ages venerate thy name."

Life of Jackson.

PHILADELPHIA:

PUBLISHED BY S. SIMPSON & J. CONRAD.

1824.

THE LETTERS OF WYOMING

James Monroe

George Hay

William Drayton

DeWitt Clinton

Ezekiel Whitman

NATIONAL NOMINATION.

THE PEOPLE'S TICKET.

Gratitude, Glory, Patriotism!

FOR PRESIDENT,

ANDREW JACKSON.

Recommended to the People of the United States, by his Pure Democratic Principles, Stern Integrity, Long Experience, Eminent Talents, and Transcendent Services to his Country.

"Freemen, cheer the Hickory Tree,
In storms its boughs have shelter'd thee;
O'er Freedom's Land its branches wave,
'Twas planted on the LION'S GRAVE."

FOR VICE PRESIDENT,

JOHN C. CALHOUN.

THE PEOPLE'S TICKET

Daniel Pope Cook

Ninian Edwards

Oh my honour
It serves you right, you stupid NINNY AN' so it does, for trying to stop him
That inner track fellow goes so well that I think he must have got the better of the bots
Like enough; but betwixt you & I — I dont think he'll ever get the better of the QUINSY
Blast my eyes if I dont venter a small horn of rotgut on that bald filly in the middle
D—n my wig if I dont bet you
PRESIDENTS HOUSE
PRESIDENTIAL CHAIR
Ah hah! Now Neddy I tink dat kick on de back of you side is worse den have no dinner de fourt of july
The fore most fellow shows fine bottom
Ay, but the hind most has the best bone
CAPITOL
You need'nt be so CLA-morous there — your old Kentuck's come to a stand still
D— me if he once gets upon ALL FOURS, he'll
take the lead of the whole pack
Well dont distress yourself — there'll be some scrubbing by & by & then you'll have a chance
D—n it I cant save my distance — so I may as well draw up

A Foot-Race

Rachel Jackson

Andrew Jackson

1823

To John Coffee

Hermitage January 10th. 1823

Dear Genl

I have Just recd your letter of the 1rst. instant[1] and regret to learn that your two youngest has the whooping cough, but as it appears here of a mild kin*[d]* trust in god that they will spedily recover from it—permit me to recommend a free use of cotton seed tea—it is the most sovereign and safe remedy that can be applied—I never knew it to fail of a happy effect when applied, the seed must be put in a bag to prevent a mixtur*[e]* of the lint with the tea, a little bruised, and w*[ell]* boiled. I regret much the delay of Parson and the hands there, they are much wanted her*[e]* to prepare for another crop, particul*[arly]* as all there cabins will have to be m*[a]*de after they come in, as I find it as much as my hands does here to get firewood, feed the stock & Bale the cotton. I would thank you to write a line to Mr Parsons to leave the crop if it is not housed before this reaches you, as I wrote him to let Mr [Anthony] Winston [Jr.] have it on the shares for picking out—which I suppose his overseer would not agree to take or he would have advised me of his being on the way.[2] I want him here as I cannot attend to the hands in inclement weather—

I cannot sell my cotton there to any merchant here on terms that I think would be doing Justice to my little ward, have made an agreement with Major George [Washington] Martin—that he is to have the cotton, or the proceeds thereof, at orleans, he being accountable for the exchange at the time the cotton is sold, or at such exchange as you & him may think is equitable in the month of March next[3]—it is now in Nashville at 25 pr cent premium—Should cotton rise in price exchange will decline, if cotton declines, exchange will still rise—My object is to contract with the Major on fair terms, so that he *[w]*ill loose nothing and Justice will be done to my little ward Hutchings.

I feel a desire from a full exposure of his situation, and that of his mother & Brother, to let him have the use of the proceeds of this cotton to the first of June next, and still longer should it be in my power to let him have it longer, it will be the means to establish his credit in Philadelphia for punctuality, and enable him to progress with his mecantile Views with safety and advantage[4]—I leave it with you & him to determine to whom to ship it at Neworleans—I should prefer to have it sold from on Board the Boat as the drayage, warfage & storage is a very great deduction from the present prices I leave this to you and him to eran*[ge]* as the more it neats the better for him as well as me. and the sooner he can use the proceeds the better for him—The Major will secure the payment—

you have not said whether your assembly has risen—if it has, Colo Winston is at home, and will I suppose be prepared to deliver the negroes, and in due time take up his notes—The negroes *[I]* have determined to deliver over to M*[r]* Nicholson for A. J. Hutchings, you w*[ill]* please to have them Vallued by such men as will be satisfactory to those I have to account.[5] I will risque the suit of old Bennett—and endeavour to be prepared to purchase in the land when sold that has been forfeited[6]—I hope Colo. Winston will be punctual as part of the mony I will need to finally close my accounts here. I will be happy to hear from you as soon as you hear from Colo. Winston—and can advise m*[e]* of the prospects of the payments by him—I write in haste—will write yo*[u]* again shortly—Major Martin will be out in a few days—I hope my cotton will be all ready by the time he reaches you Mrs J. & myself respectfully present our best wishes to you Polly & the little ones with our prayers for their speedy recovery, and future health—I have been spending the 8th by invitation with our friends in Nashville—the papers & Major Martin will advise you of these proceedings—[7]

I note your postscript—I am happy that Mr Crawford has but few friends in alabama—him & Clay as I believe is trying their individual strength, and the weakest will yield to the strongest—Mr Adams & Mr Clay as you will have seen is about to enter upon a public contest—Adams will lay him as low as he had done Jonathan Russell[8]—I cannot believe that either Crawford[9] can be brought into the presidential chair—and if so I am content—and the nation will have nothing to fear from faction & Intrigue. I am sir your friend

Andrew Jackson

ALS, THi (9-0397). Published in Bassett, 3:183–84 (extract).

1. Not found.

2. Jackson's letter to Benjamin P. Person has not been found. Jackson was closing out his Big Spring farm and had sold half of it to Winston (1782–1839) in the fall of 1822. Previously a resident of Davidson County, Winston became a large purchaser of Franklin (now Colbert) County, Alabama, lands and represented the county in the state legislature at this time.

3. Jackson's agreement with Martin (1792–1854), a stepson of Stockley Donelson (c1759–1805), has not been found. Martin, a major in Coffee's cavalry during the Creek and New Orleans campaigns, was at this time in a mercantile partnership in Nashville with Willoughby Williams.

4. Elizabeth Glasgow Martin Donelson Anderson (1772–1847), George W.'s mother, had been widowed for the third time by the death of John Anderson in 1818. His brother,

James Glasgow Martin (1791–1849), had married Jackson's niece Catherine Donelson (1799–1836) in 1815. The Martin family was financially strapped by the legal costs of James G.'s suit against Richard G. Waterhouse, and George W. had probably approached Jackson for aid (see George W. Martin to James G. Martin, December 19, 1822, THi).

5. See bill of sale from Anthony Winston, Jr., February 18.

6. For Bennett Smith's suit against the executors of John Hutchings, see above, AJ to Coffee, March 1, 1821. Jackson apparently intended to repurchase at least a portion of Hutchings's plantation relinquished under the land relief act of 1821 and perhaps lands relinquished by other owners (see AJ to Coffee, October 24, below).

7. For an account of the January 8 celebration honoring Jackson, see the *Nashville Whig*, January 15.

8. The Washington *National Intelligencer* of December 17, 1822, published a letter from Henry Clay of November 15 pointing out "errors" in John Q. Adams's pamphlet regarding his controversy with Russell (see above AJ to Andrew J. Donelson, June 28, 1822). A reply by Adams appeared in the *Intelligencer* of December 19, 1822.

9. Jackson probably meant to write "either Clay or Crawford."

From John Henry Eaton

Washington City
Jany 11. Jany 1823

Dr Genl

Occasionally I have written you without being able to say more than that I was well: it has been my lot to write in a hurry, tho the barreness of my letters may be rather traced to want of matter; for apart from the busy hum of noisy politicians seeking thro noiseless intrigue to prescribe to the people whom they shall patronise: we have little to think of, or to talk about. Most of our politicians however who are here observe a marked silence in relation to the Presidential contest: many from honest motives are unwilling to be placed in a situation, by which to feel themselves committed, while another class, governed by the principles of self, would rather stand aloof untill he who shall seem to be the strongest before the people may be pretty accurately ascertained; and hence is it, that it is quite as difficult <here> to conjecture here in the centre of our political circle who stands most prominent, as it would be on the lap of the Alleghany mountains: all is doubt and uncertainty. The people however are beginning to think of the matter, and if left to themselves, undisturbed by selfish & designing men, will I have full confidence settle down correctly. It is a misfortune tho, that however the Constitution has vested with the people the proud privilege of selecting a chief magistrate for themselves, they do not, do it, and while nominally the power is theirs, they are but instruments in the hands of those who are commonly termed the *leading men* of the Country Upon this subject the members of Congress have heretofore, and may too hereafter be expected to do much in producing impressions thro the country as to the relative merits of the different Candidates. If this state of things is to exist, how unfortunate is it that the incumbents of Departments should be ever found urging their pretensions. We have seen enough of the ills resulting from this condition of things to desire a change; and were it not, that the respect & reverence of posterity for our Constitution must diminish in proportion as alterations & change are made in it, I would gladly see some experiment ventured to heal this defect. It has been told, & plausibly too, that rivalry and contest for office with the heads of Departments, was the primary cause which induced the capture of our city, and the burning of our Capitol, & which worse than all left a stigma on our national character and it is this same evil which at this moment causes the President to be without an Executive council: for how can it be otherwise, when his secretaries are each in quest of his own interest and promotion—each acting from motive, must and will hazzard and advocate opinions, calculated to further his own views: & thus necessarily <results> to produce discordance & want of harmony. A state of things like this exists, and must continue to exist while secretaries of Departments shall be found urging their pretensions to the Executive chair. There was a time when, for this office men thought not of themselves, but wished the free declaration of the people to be drawn to them resulting from great fidelity in public trusts, but now *To Puff* is the style—the fashion of the day, and persons are not wanting who can bow and court and intrigue for a high station to which they are not entitled either from merit possessed, or any particular service rendered to the Country. But enough of evils, which time & the good sense of the nation can alone correct.

Mr. Adams is again at War: he & Genl [Alexander] Smyth as you will see by the Intelligencer is waging a personal paper contest covering a field of 30 years of our history. Adams surely, confides rather much in the seeming strength of his pen, & the vanity of that feeling leads him into error: for there is such a thing as a mans rendering himself cheap, & falling gradually and insensibly in the estimation of the people, by too frequently appearing before them; more especially when [in] that appearance matters of self are involved. Is it his province to come forth in a long appeal to the public, whenever any person shall question his infalibility, or suggest objections to him? certainly not! and prudence if consulted would say not. It must operate injuriously from the mere circumstance of the motive to which it will be ascribed; but worse than all, this latter contest involves principles which rendered the father odious; and which, by now being brought up, will give birth to recollection of the fathers deeds, calculated to raise up irreconcileable prejudices against the son. I do not say 'tis right, but we have scripture for it, and its' verity is shewn by the willingness which mankind always manifest to visit on the child the misdeed of the son. This controversy was therefore imprudent for many reasons that might be suggested. Whether Mr. A will now quit it, or go on I can't say; he certainly ought never to have commenced it.[1]

I enclose you an extract of a letter written to a member from Pensyla. and which with his leave I have copied: you will percieve that the people of that State are starting forth in *propria persona,* and pointing to yourself as the one in whom they most confide. The writer is an intelligent member of the Legislature.[2] Some of our *Noves homines* (mushroom men) are beginning to manifest a fear and trembling at the new denouncemant in the political camp. While the Legislatures should nominate, there was a hope that impressions so slight might be changed, as often policy might suggest, but when the people are found stepping out in support of their rights & privileges, and openly proclaiming the man who rests strong in their affections, alarm is produced, from an apprehension that such a spark, may presently be fanned into a flame; & such indeed will be the case. Congress caucusses are objected to; and indeed none of our secretaries are so prominently before the Country, for faithfull service and known & long tried integrity as to be able to fasten upon its notice & favour: the people hence are beginning, and that sentiment will increase, to look to one who has the ordeal of difficulty & trial. It is incumbent on you therefore to act with the caution that belongs to you, when your own prudence shall suggest prudence to be necessary: Commit not your opinions; nor let malevolence, whatever insinuating shape it may assume, drag you into any *news paper* controversy. Already are Mr. Crawfords folks seeking to convey the idea that you have not consented to be placed before the nation as a candidate and that you have disavowed any such intention. The inquiry has several times been made of me, & I have generally replied, that the statement was not correct, & that you would not decline any call of your Country where it might be thought you could be useful to her; that such a sentiment you had thro life acted upon, & was one which I had frequently heard you express. Should any man of standing & character (so known to you) address you on the subject, I suggest whether you had not better reply to him in sentiment & language like this "That you had at no period of your life sought for, or inquired after Office, but had ever felt it your duty to act, where by the voice & wishes of your Country, you had been called to do so: that altho you had now retired from that bustle & public service in which for the last nine years you had been actively engaged; yet if your Country should think it in your power to aid her views & promote her happiness, it would be a departure from the uniform course of your life should you manifest an unwillingness to obey that call" Something like this should it become necessary might be well. From what is buzzing about it seems quite probable Pensyla may settle down on yourself, & if so I am persuaded the matter is settled.[3]

I again suggest that any thing & every thing like certainty seems floating on the breese; were I to hazzard an opinion from every thing seen & heard here, I would say Mr Crawford is the strongest of the Sectys at present. Virga will certainly sustain him, for he was *born there.* [Martin] Van Buren Senator and a leading man in New York is thought to be seeking to aid him, far as he can at present amidst so great uncertainty go.[4] Adams is rather it would seem going back, & Calhoun not advancing.

The policy & feelings of both these will be I have no doubt, to retire & throw far as practicable their strength on you, should your prospects of success seem the most prominent

Crawford & Clay are each of the Radical party; & will be pressed as one or the other shall appear strongest. Your appearance tho on the stage of action has & will greatly frus[t]rate the Latter: already he appears on the wane. The same sort of policy should prevail on the other side, [To] Press you, Adams or Calhoun as success may promise. Enough now—

The President early to day addressed me a note & desired to see me. I called I want says he as a further evidence of my regard for genl. Jackson to appoint him minister to Mexico but desired to see you first. He has been nominated for President, and you know he has my good wishes for any thing the Country can give him. I'm afraid it may be thought & said, if nominated that it is done with a view to get him out of the way. I answered some might say so. I was sure tho that the genl would impute nothing of the sort; not knowing tho how far such a thing might be acceptable to genl Jackson I could not then suggest any thing to him; but would confer with one or two of the genls friends & see him again day after tomorrow; & he agreed to defer the nomination untill then.[5] Here is the result of my conference—I shall so say to the President—

Nominate Genl J. If you accept well & good; if not, no diservice will be produced as regards any other matter; but a benefit. The offer is spontaneous—not asked for; & the office one of the first that can be presented with the President it flows I am sure from kindness & good will & from nothing else—Day after tomorrow I will again see him & then again write you. The Secty of Legation I will seek to have defered, & will suggest it, that your wishes may be consulted[6]

News today says the French Cordon on the confines of Spain are ordered to advance into Spain, for what purpose is not known. The same a/c says War is inevitable twixt Fr & Spain. I have not yet seen the information but only heard it spoken of—Confusion th[is] being true is to be looked for in Europe. The a/c receives credence [here].[7]

The Bill for Donnelson & Carr &c has passed the Senate: about this & Gadsden more in a day or two[8] my kind remembrances if you please to Mrs Jackson yr friend

J. H Eaton

The President U S desires me to present him affectionately to you[9]

ALS, DLC (72).

1. Eaton was referring to two articles, "National Politics and History," in the *National Intelligencer,* January 7 and 11. The first reprinted a letter of December 3, 1822, from Smyth (1765–1830) to his Virginia constituents promising that he would oppose John Q. Adams should the presidential election go to the House of Representatives and Adams's reply of December 30. The second article featured Smyth's response to Adams, in which he referred

to the tutelage of John Q. Adams by his father John (1735–1826) of Alien and Sedition Act fame. John Q. Adams apparently chose not to respond to Smyth's second circular. For the probable scriptural allusion, see Exodus 20:5.

2. The extract, likely discussing Jackson's nomination by a meeting of Westmoreland County Democrats at Greensburg, Pennsylvania, on December 28, 1822, has not been found, and the letter's recipient has not been identified. Eaton forgot to enclose the extract, detailing one of Jackson's earliest nominations in Pennsylvania, with this letter, but forwarded it on January 15. The *National Intelligencer* of January 11 noted the meeting and its deliberations.

3. For Jackson's close adherence to Eaton's advice, see AJ to H. W. Peterson, February 23, below.

4. Van Buren (1782–1862) supported William H. Crawford throughout the campaign.

5. Among those Eaton consulted was John C. Calhoun, who advised against acceptance, arguing that Jackson could be more useful at home in the current "political peril" (see Eaton to AJ, January 15).

6. James Monroe nominated Jackson as minister to Mexico on January 21, and, on the same day, nominated John Mason, Jr., of the District of Columbia, as secretary to the legation.

7. At the Congress of Verona in October 1822 the European powers had authorized France to take action against Spanish revolutionaries who had seized control in 1820 and forced Ferdinand VII to restore the liberal constitution of 1812. Reports reaching Washington at this time dated from about December 1, 1822, long before the French invasion of Spain, which took place on April 7.

8. The bill to compensate the heirs of John Donelson (c1718–86) and others for survey work performed for Georgia passed the Senate on January 10, but failed in the House. In his letter of January 15, Eaton expanded his comments on the Donelson bill and noted continued deadlock between Monroe and the Senate regarding the confirmation of James Gadsden as adjutant general.

9. Inscribed on the letter's cover.

To Anthony Wayne Butler

Hermitage January 13th. 182*[3]*

My young friend

I have Just recd your letter of the 9th ult.[1] I have perused it with attention and pleasure, but cannot approve your fondness for the Classics, and your neglect of Mathematics. I wish you not only to become a Classical, but a mathematical scholar, well versed in every branch of science, without this, altho you may become a pretty writer, a fluent speaker, you never can arive to the degree of a systimatic reasoner; it is a thorough knowledge of the sciences, that opens and expands the mind, and gives a proper erangement and system to argument. I therefore as your friend advise you not to abandon the study of Mathematic'; nor never think of leaving Yale College untill you are a thorough schollar.

Your deceased friend Richard Butler by agreement with me was to finish your education and altho it is said his last will that made this provision cannot be found—still your friend Mr Abner L Duncan and myself made the erangement with Capt [Samuel] McCutchen & Captain [Moses] Hook, that you should be educated out of his estate.[2] you have made such progress in your education, that your own Judgt. and pride ought to stimulate you not to abandon your studies untill your education is perfected. The moment you leave Yale College you will be deprived <from> of all aid from the Estate of your deceased friend, and I need not apprise you, of what you already know, that most of your friends are in straightened circumstances They have nothing in their power, however friendly they might be toward you. Therefore my advice is to remain where you are, untill you acquire a perfect education, this you can do in the space of another year with proper application.

I approve of the society of which you speak, and of which you say you are a member; if well regulated much improvement may be obtained, both in speaking and in facility in writing, both of which is highly important in the advocate and statesman. I would therefore recommend you to continue as a member as long as it is conducted with order & decorum.[3]

I sincerely regret to learn from you that your health is not good, that healthy climate ought with care, to insure health, and you ought to be guarded against exposure; it is in the youthfull habits, that health, or disease is laid up for the meridian of our days, by proper precaution in youth our health is preserved, our constitution invigorated and matured, by exposure & evil habits, disease is contracted, and the constitution destroyed before the years of manhood. I therefore caution you against all exposure, or evil habits, that contract disease & destroy your constitution & your health—You say "your constitution is shattered["]? By nature it was good, by what exposure has it become debilitated, for you are too young for it to be shattered—you are free from excess of drink, & I hope equally free from other evil habits that bring on disease that *shatter* the constitution.

I am happy Edward called to see you, and tarried with you some time—he is a model for you & all youths, his modesty & gentlemany Conduct has gained for him the Esteem of his brother officers and the approbation of his friends, he is Just such a man as I wish you to be; still I anticipate more briliancy of talents from you, particularly if your turn your attention to the study of the sciences, and become as good a mathematician as he is.

It is true my friends Bronaugh and young are no more, they are numbered amonghst the dead, their course is finished, no man mourns their loss more than I do—none knew their merrits better, but we are instructed to mourn not for the dead but the living, we ought to live, allways prepared to die, or in other words *[we]* ought to live, to, learn how to die.

*[Y]*our sister Caroline was not in good health last summer—she has recovered. you*[r sister]* Eliza is now in Nashville, and at present *[in]* good health we expect her with us shortly.

It will give Mrs. J. & myself great pleasure to see you, I have your prosperity much at heart—and as such recommend you to remain at Yale College untill your education is perfect, you will find in your travel through life my advice proper, and if not now attended to, you like myself will regret it when it is too late, and cannot be regained. Mrs. Joins me in prayers and good wishes for your health and happiness & prosperity through life, and believe me your sincere friend

Andrew Jackson

ALS, LNHiC (9-0403). Endorsed as answered on March 15.

1. Not found.

2. McCutchon (1773–1840) and Hooke (1777–1821) were married to Richard Butler's sisters Rebecca (1782–1844) and Harriet (1787–1830).

3. The literary society to which Butler belonged at Yale has not been established.

From Samuel Houston

Nashville
19th Jany 1823

D Sir

From a friend in Alabama, I had the pleasure to receive a letter of the 6th Inst. he is the partner of Wm Kelly Esqr Senator, & from an extract of his Letter to me you will discover Mr Crawford is not the favorite of Alabama, as has been stated. I well Know that my friend, & Kelly accord in sentiment.[1]

"Every possible plan had been laid, & every exertion made to have the representation prepared for Walkers resignation, so as to put in McKinley. Two weeks of the session had expired before Kelly heard of the resignation, and at the eleventh hour without having had a previous idea of it, & without having endeavored to conciliate a friend, he resolved to go down, and combat the matter, with the big man of the north. He got there three days, before the day of election and whiped out foremost. From what I understand, you will shortly join him at the Capital;[2] Let me charge you, that if Old Hickory cant be President, to go for H Clay. At all events save us from *Crawford*, & Georgia politics!" From this paragraph I infer that McKinly must have been for Crawford, by the understanding between him & Crawfords friends—You will see the politics of Mr Crawford are not hoped for, by honest men. I do not agree with my friend about Mr Clay, but I see, it is more *his* invetracy to Crawford, than his love to Clay. I told him in a letter of yesterday my notions on the subject. I have no doubt, myself, but what, Mr Adams will lay out Mr Clay a fit subject for *political burial*! Mr Hutchinson in conclusion says "*Crawford* will stand no chance in Alabama. H. Clay, and our noble old Chieftain, are the preeminent characters!"

T[homas] G[amaliel] Bradford, has arrived here from the City, and I discover some change has taken place in our Gov's sentiments. Crawford, or John Williams must have sent their compliments to him, or Mr Clay must have neglected writing to him for some time[3]—I will be up on next satureday to see you <& th> and Mrs Jackson unless an accident. Please do me the honor to make my best respects to Mrs Jackson, also Col Gadsden & Mr Earl. I send you the last Gazette. I like the remarks on "Indian Treaties."[4] I have the honor to be Your Most Obt. & friend

Sam Houston

ALS, DLC (72). Published in Bassett, 6:479.

1. On December 12, 1822, the Alabama legislature elected Kelly to fill the unexpired Senate term of John W. Walker. Houston's correspondent was probably Anderson Hutchinson (1798–1853), a Huntsville lawyer who later achieved notoriety as codifier of Mississippi laws and as a Texas district judge.

2. Houston, a candidate for representative from Tennessee, was elected in August 1823.

3. Bradford, the former editor of the Nashville *Clarion*, may have brought reports from Washington that William H. Crawford would carry Tennessee. No evidence has been found that William Carroll wavered in his support of Henry Clay at this time. See, for example, Carroll to Clay, February 1, 1823 (*Clay Papers*, 3:360–62).

4. Houston was likely forwarding the *Nashville Gazette* (issue not found).

To John Henry Eaton

—Copy—

Hermitage
21. Janry. 1823

Dear Sir

Since writing you the early part of the present session of Congress; an idea has suggested itself to me by which the present most unpleasant difference between the Executive and Senate may be reconciled without the sacrifice of principle or prerogative on either side; and in a manner calculated to do justice to the *only two officers* who have been seriously affected by the late organisation of the Military Peace Establishment[1]—I do not advert in this letter to what I conceive, as expressed to you in a previous communication, is the undoubted right of the Executive in his nominations to office; or to the dangers to the institutions of our country from any unfortunate collisions between the Senate & Executive on this subject—Where these differences exist however; some effort should at least be made to a perfect understanding with a view to a restoration of the harmonious cooperation of these two distinguished branches of our National Government. To my mind nothing is easier in the present case, and therefore I have taken the liberty of suggesting the following to you; with the permission to make such use of it, as in your opinion, may be best calculated to produce the much desired result—However the constructions placed on the law for the reduction of the Army by the Executive and Senate may differ in their details; it is not to be questioned that both Departments were operated on by the same motives; *The good of the Military service* and *justice to the meritorious officer*; on one point certainly the difference of opinion does not appear so wide as to prohibit on principle a happy union—

The power of judging of relative merit the Senate acknowledge rests with the Executive; but that the law confined the selection to each grade—Butler, and Gadsden were, though attached to the Staff, by law Colonels in the Army, and agreeably to the very construction insisted on by the Senate, might have been arranged to any Colonelcy in the reduced Military Establishment that the Executive might have selected. Col Butler for whose rights the Senate are now contending, has always insisted on the correctness of these principles; and has never denied the propriety of Col Gadsdens arrangement to the Adjutant Generalcy as conformable to the law, military principle & usage. He contends however, and with great propriety that the President with his undoubted right to judge of comparative merit might arrange him to any station in the army conformable to his grade; and the exceptions taken by him to the late organisation <of the were> were against the provisional order reducing him to a Lt Colonel, when he had been regularly & justly arranged to the head of a Regiment—He was a Colonel and he claims only a situation, if retained at all, of the same grade in the Army without specifying which—

Col Gadsden & Butler have never disagreed therefore as to the principles which should have governed in the arrangement of officers from the old to the new Establishment—They were both Colonels and without obtruding their claims on the Executive & Senate they only expected, if retained, They would be retained with their respective grades: they neither sought elevation, or could they submit to reduction—There are two Colonelcies now vacant, the one in the Staff the other in the line, and the idea I would suggest is that Butler & Gadsden by an understanding with the Executive should be arranged to those two stations—They are both entitled, if retained at all, to Colonels situations, and as the Senate conceive that the one, and the Executive the other has been injured; by arranging both as suggested the Two Departments would most unquestionably meet on principles reconcileable to the objects, and powers of each—In what manner the arrangement of each officer should be made is not material; but it is proper. I should repeat to you that a short time before the Execution of the law for the reduction of the Army; that with a view to the good of the service from the known merits of Butler & Gadsden I did recommend the former to be placed at the head of a Regiment, and the latter in the station of Adt General[2]—My impression was that such an arrangement would be sanctioned in the change from the old to the new establishment, and it was further more Butlers wish preferring a Regiment, and thereby relinquishing any peculiar claim which the Senate may consider he had to the Adjutant Generalcy—

I have viewed with pain the present unhappy difference between the Senate & Executive & have reason to believe the same feeling general—To what possible consequences its continuance may lead I presume not to say; it is certain but one feeling would pervade all parties on a harmonious reconciliation involving neither principle or prerogative—I have suggested the mode which in my opinion should produce that desired object; and have only to add a hope that the Executive & Senate concurring in opinion with me, may unite on that ground—

You are at liberty to shew this to Mr [Rufus] King, [John] Gaillard and such others as you think proper—I have mentioned those two Senators particularly from my knowledge of their character, their long services in the Senate, and their known experience on political affairs and knowledge of constitutional law involving the best interests of our common country—If they feel, as I have no doubt they do, with me on this subject, they cannot but most cheerfully unite on principles which will restore at once the harmony between two important branches of our Government; and promote the best interests of our Institutions—[3]

Let Butler & Gadsden be arranged as suggested and while it will produce this desired result, the Executive & Senate may rest assured it will give general satisfaction to the Army, and promote the good of the public service—

Should this arrangement not meet with the approbation of the Executive & Senate; it may be well to reflect seriously on the possible consequences of a continuance of the existing differences—

(Signed) Andrew Jackson

Copy in James Gadsden's hand, NN (9-0413). Jackson sent the copy with a note to James Monroe, [January 21], hoping for his "approbation."

1. Letter not found.

2. See AJ to John C. Calhoun, February 18, 1821, and above, May 22, 1821.

3. King (1755–1827; Harvard 1777) and Gaillard (1765–1826) were senators from New York and South Carolina, respectively. King initially supported the nomination of James Gadsden for adjutant general, but after the Senate rejected the appointment in March 1822, he opposed the renomination in April. Gaillard voted against Gadsden's confirmation on both occasions.

To John Coffee

Hermitage Jany 24th 1823

Dr. Genl

I enclose you the papers & vouchers of Sundry accounts settled by Mr Nicholson as pr general statement on the other leaf [1]—and have drew on you in his behalf to close the same for twelve dollars he has paid out of his own funds the Ballance for Ferriages at the military ferry which you will please pay to him out of the mony you may receive from Colo. Antony Winston.[2] The Colo. writes me by Mr Crawford "that he will meet the payment for the land agreable to contract, which he will with the negroes pay over to you; They cattle, pork, corn, he must give his note bearing interest as he has been much disappointed."[3] Mr Crawford informs me that he sent you by Capt Donelson, the receipt for the corn—I herewith send you the receipt for the pork & stock Hoggs—I left with you the receipt for the Cattle—for all which I will thank you to take Colo. Winston note with Interest—There was some fodder that the Colo. will render you an account of—Should the Colo. meet his contract for the land it will enable me to clear myself of all encumbrance—I thought what I brought in would have done this—But my Pensacola Trip hangs on me like a mountain, still producing accounts, which I cannot refuse payment & of which I know nothing—there amount is known, and I hope the amount due me from the Colo. in Tennessee mony will close every debt I now owe any, & every where, I therefore rely on the Colos. punctuality—

I have waited with anxiety to hear from your sweet little ones, how they were with the cough, I hope they are out of danger. When you pay Mr Nicholson—Take his recpt & include in it the sum paid by me to Mr Cross which you will see stated in Crosses account[4]—we have had a very wet winter my Negroes have got in safe & are nearly housed and ready for work—I shall write you in a few days & give the political news of the north & East. I have recd a letter from Mr Baldwin of Pittsburgh formerly of Congress—stating that If I will say that if elected I will serve the state of Pensylvania will go with me, as he believes & particularly the west unanimously—I have answered this letter with caution & care, Giving my political creed "that every mans services is his countries when that country requires it—that I never have nor never will solicit office—but I never have nor will refuse my service when my country demands it," &c This for yourself for the present—[5]

Present Mrs J. & my self to your lady & sweet little ones, & believe me your friend

Andrew Jackson

Accounts for sundries Bought for the use of the Farm of A. J. Hutchings & settled by Mr Malachi Nicholson out of the proceeds of the farm—viz

To O[lsimus] Kendrick[6] as pr account & receipt No 1 Dated the 29th. of Decbr 1821— $2.50

Ferriages at M. Ferry as pr account & receipt Novbr. 12th. 1822—for $16.25—four dollars paid by Mr Nicholson twelve dollars in cash—for which A. Jackson gave Mr Nicholson an order on Genl John Coffee *recpt* No 2. 4.

Mr Cross acpt for Halling Cotton five days $15—out of which Mr Nicholson paid $8.37½—the Ballance by A. Jackson as pr Recpt & account Decbr. 6th. 1822 No 3— 8.37½

To this sum paid by Mr Nicholson for Loom as pr account & Recpt Decbr 25th. 1822 & No 4— 8.00—

This sum paid by Mr Nicholson to Mrs James Jackson for wool as pr account & Recpt Decbr. 28th. 1822 & No 5— 20.—

This sum paid by Mr Nicholson to Mr Hover[7] for plank & Scantlen as pr account & Recpt Dated day of 1823— 29.15

as pr account rendered This 27th. of January 1823— 72.02 $^{1}/_{2}$

Andrew Jackson
Guardian—

ALS, DLC (9-0428).

1. The enclosures have not been found.
2. See AJ to Coffee, January 27.
3. Anthony Winston's letter regarding payment for his purchase of part of Jackson's Big Spring plantation has not been found.
4. Probably Richard C. Cross (c1800–23), a former Nashville resident who had purchased Jackson's Lauderdale County plantation in 1821.
5. See Henry Baldwin to AJ, January 2, and AJ to Baldwin, January 24.
6. Originally from North Carolina, Kendrick (1780–1845) moved from Maury County, Tennessee, to Lauderdale County, Alabama, before 1820 and remained at least until 1830 before moving to Tallahatchie County, Mississippi.
7. G. Frederick Huber.

To Robert Butler, John Donelson (1755–1830), and Francis Saunders

[January 31, 1823]

To the commissioners appointed by the worshipfull court of Davidson to apportion & divide the Estate of Severn Donelson deceased amonghst his heirs[1]—My desire is that Andrew Jackson, my adopted son should not be considered in the Division of the Estate as one of the heirs of the said deceased—Mrs. J. & my self having adopted him as our son, we intend to educate and provide for him, I therefore obligate myself to give him as much property as will fall to the share of any of the Legatees of the said S. Donelson deceased, and to secure him this I hereby bind Myself my heirs Executors &c &c under my hand & Seal. This 31rst day of Janry 1823—

Andrew Jackson (seal)

Test
Robert Butler
Francis Saunders } Commissioners
John Donelson Senr

ADS, Anonymous (9-0441). Jackson's neighbor Francis Saunders (d. 1826) was brother-in-law of North Carolina congressman Romulus M. Saunders.

1. Donelson (1773–1818), Jackson's brother-in-law, was the biological father of Andrew Jackson, Jr.

From Isaac Lewis Baker

New Orleans. 14. feby 1823

Dear general,

Mr. Clays friends a few days since made a most desperate effort to have him nominated as president of the U. S. by our Legislature. Notice was formally given that on a particular day a motion for a recess would be made with a view to nominate a successor to James Monroe. Your friends—who are quite numerous & very respectable prevented any thing from being done—for the mover when the day came only found three or four of his own way of thinking and declined the affair entirely.[1] Your friends for the present will not advocate a caucus. Before the People of this state you have nothing to fear from the result should you continue a candidate and for the present the opinions of the present members are so difficult to get at, that we think it rather unwise to risque a cau[c]us untill we see our way more clearly. Mr. Clay's friends are in despair & talk with less confidence than two weeks ago—

The governor is very unpopular and can be of no use to any one he advocates—It is supposed he would prefer Crawford who has not the slightest chance of getting a vote in the state—

I send you along with this some newspapers which contain some few of the publications which have appeared here the subject of the Presidential Election. You will see from a piece signed Fair Play in the Louisiana Advertiser that they lay Mr. Clay's Failure here to my charge and they are continually croaking in the streets about my being the most desperate of Intriguers.[2] They could with much greater justice attribute their failure to public sentiment.

All kinds of Produce sell low in this market Tennessee cotton is from 9. to 10. cents. Louisiana commands 12. to 16½ tho very little sells above 14 cents.

Our winter has been wet & unpleasant & this city thro the carnival rather dull. There are great complaints about scarcity of money.

Mr Ritchie about whom you wrote to [Auguste Geneviève Valentin] Davezac & myself was pardoned a few days since & released from prison.[3]

Please offer my best respects to Mrs. Jackson & Colo. Gadsden—very sincerely dear general, I remain your friend & grateful hl. Servant

Isaac L Baker

P.S. Colonels Fenwick, Clinch, Brooke & others are here now on their way to Batton Rouge to try Colonel [Mathew] Arbuckle & other officers—[4]

ALS, DLC (32). Published in Bassett, 3:187 (extract).

1. Without identifying either Baker or Jackson, the *Nashville Gazette* published the pre-

ceding, deleting the discussion of Jackson's friends and changing "for" to "but" (see *Nashville Whig*, March 12).

2. The article has not been found.

3. Jackson's letters have not been found, nor has Ritchie been identified. Davezac (1780–1851), the brother-in-law of Edward Livingston, was a New Orleans lawyer who had served as judge advocate under Jackson during the New Orleans campaign. Jackson later appointed him to diplomatic posts.

4. The trial of Arbuckle (1776–1851), a career army officer who had served during Jackson's Gulf and Seminole campaigns, was scheduled to commence at Baton Rouge on February 20, but the court-martial did not convene until March 8. Arbuckle was found not guilty of charges brought by Major David E. Twiggs and army surgeon Thomas Lawson.

To John Coffee

Hermitage Febry 17th. 1823.

Dr. Genl

Being absent (at Gallatine on an arbitration) when Capt Donelson arived I did not receive your letter by him or that by Mr Eastin untill last evening & will account to you for my delay in answering[1]

I thank you for the attention to my business but regret that you are encumbered with it, as I am fully aware of the multiplicity of your own—The sale to Major Martin I fully approve it may be beneficial to him, and I am content both as to my own interest and that of my ward, A. J. Hutchings, and believe both will be benefitted by this erangement—[2]

I hope Colo. Winston will not disappoint me in the receipt of the mony agreable to his Obligations—had it not have been from his declarations of punctuality, and expressed wish to be clear of debt, and his determination to pay when due, I should not have made other engagements on his assurances, but have made them agreable to other resources only—hence is my present dificulty—I should not have bought two negroes that I have done the one from Mr [David] Fulton & the other (a half Blacksmith) from Mrs. [Elizabeth Rucker] Donelson nor should I engaged to have Bought Capt J Donelsons Cotton, and would have been enabled with my means thus applied to have met the other calls upon me from Pensacola &c &c—without being pressed—It was his determination expressed, that he would not submit to the payment of Interest that lead me into my present dificulty, and you will please say to him he must by the payment of the sums thus relied on take me out—I still rely on his punctuality, and hope there will be no delay, in all this month I am to pay Capt Donelson, and at all Sacrafice, I will not disappoint him. I therefore wish on the receipt of this you will advise me of the prospects from Colo Winston, that I may provide for Capt Donelson.[3]

I rejoice at the pleasing intelligence that your sweet little ones have recovered from the Hoopencough—but regret that you have lost any of your negro children—The present severity of the weather here has never been experienced & no doubt nearly as cold with you—This is unfortunate for the children, but Mrs J. tells me that Capt Donelson has discovered that the Herrodsburgh salts is a specific for the complaint, and that from an experiment made with Mrs. Eastons little inphant & the other children that they have all reco*[vered]* without sufferring any—This may be a f*[or]*tunate discovery and I therefore name it that your black family may profit by it—I have noted your remark with respect to our mutual friend, of a suspicion of some friend confidentially communicated, rest assured I have, nor never had any such a suspicion, the course he pursued was a friendly & prudent course, and as to his vote for Major McKinly I can easily account for, altho our friend is mistaken in the man[4]—The course of Doctor [Thomas] Fearn I cannot account for—it cannot be solved by me—Clay is connected with the Shelbys, and Nearly so with Mrs Governor Shelby—This may have reached Doctor Fearn—But I cannot believe that Doctor J[ohn] Shelby nor Genl [Robert] Deshea could be brought on that side whatever others might[5]—There is one thing (*well*) believed, that Clay & Crawford understand each other, and so does their confidential friends—that is to try the strength of both & support the strongest—finding Crawford on the *hip* under the blind, that they will not support Crawford they are eranging their forces under which is the erangement as believed made by Clay & Crawford & their friends—you have here a clue both to Major McKinly & Doctor Fearn, the latter wielded by the former—and these things will be all seen through, and you will find that all the former friends of Mr Crawford will rally around Clay. This is not a thing of the moment, it has been in operation since last fall—it is a child of Colo. Bentons & Colo Williams begot in the city last year when Clay was on and accounts for B. using his influence with the Misouri Legislature[6]—They people begin to see this Deep intrigue, and when fully discovered they will leave all concerned on their native Dunghills—but the friendship of James Jackson I could never doubt—he has no duplicity, but he has been deceived by McKinly who my friend at the city long since told me was the most prominant man in allabama and Colo. A. Butler in Louisiana, wh*[o]* under Ideas of Hostility to Crawford w*[ishes?]* to bring Clay into notice in the two states[7]—I have long knew this—but determined to take no part; untill now; I have not lisped it—note I have been silent untill Mr Baldwin of Pensylvania wrote with great Frankness to know if elected as president would I serve—I answered that I never had been an applicant for office that I never would—that I had never [declined] rendering service to my country when required by the unsolicited voice of my Country & that I never would whatever might be my own opinion of my deficiency in qualifications—the people having Judged—on this principle I had allways acted, and from which I never would depart[8]—when called on from any other quarter, the same reply will be made and I will not speak untill applied to—you now have my views & course you can use it as you please—my paper is written over, if any other explanation is wanted, any of my friends can have it when applied for in the way expressed.

Mrs. J. & my self Joins in good wishes and prayers for the health happiness & prosperi*[ty]* of you, Polly, the children, & family & believe me your friend

Andrew Jackson

P S. enclosed I send you the Bill of sale to Mr [William] Griffin as you sugested, it is without witness, knowing that my hand is well known at Florence, & can be proven in court & recorded[9] A. J

ALS, THi (9-0451).

1. Letters not found. Jackson had gone to Gallatin to act as an arbiter of a mercantile dispute involving Samuel K. Blythe, Hardy M. Cryer, and Samuel Gwin (see Jackson's deposition regarding the arbitration, May 10, 1825).

2. Jackson was referring to arrangements for the sale of Andrew J. Hutchings's 1822 cotton crop (see above, AJ to Coffee, January 10).

3. Jackson was referring to the purchase of John Fulton through David Fulton, and Aaron (b. c1793) from Donelson. David Fulton was a Gallatin banker, the father of William S., Jackson's former private secretary.

4. The "mutual friend" was probably James Jackson, who represented Lauderdale County in the Alabama House where he voted to elect John McKinley senator; the other friend has not been identified.

5. Fearn (1789–1863), a surgeon with Jackson during the Creek War, represented Madison County in the Alabama House and voted for McKinley. In June 1824 he was named as a Crawford elector. He later served in the Confederate Congress. Susannah Hart Shelby (1764–1833), wife of former Kentucky governor Isaac (1750–1826), was a first cousin of Lucretia Hart Clay, Henry's wife. John Shelby (1786–1859), a Nashville and Sumner County physician who had served as a surgeon with Jackson's troops during the Creek War, was Isaac Shelby's cousin and Fearn's brother-in-law. Desha (1791–1849) of Sumner County, who was a captain in the 24th Infantry during the War of 1812 and was commissioned in 1823 as brigadier general of the Tennessee militia, was John Shelby's brother-in-law.

6. A March 1821 verdict of the United States Supreme Court adverse to Kentucky's occupying claimant laws had led the state legislature in December 1821 to designate Henry Clay and George M. Bibb as commissioners to negotiate the subject with Virginia and to reargue the case before the court. Clay arrived in Washington in mid-January, went to Richmond and addressed the Virginia legislature on February 7, and returned to Washington to reargue *Green* v. *Biddle* in early March, before going to Kentucky by late April 1822. On November 7, 1822, a caucus of Missouri legislators nominated Clay for president.

7. Anthony Butler had written in 1815 to encourage Jackson to become a presidential candidate, but for the 1824 campaign he was supporting Clay.

8. See Henry Baldwin to AJ, January 2; and AJ to Baldwin, January 24.

9. The bill of sale has not been found, but AJ's memorandum book of accounts, September 1822–August 31, 1825, indicates that he sold Griffin a slave, George. Griffin (c1780–c1839), who moved to Fayette County, Tennessee, in 1826, was probably the individual who had done occasional work on Andrew J. Hutchings's Alabama farm since 1820.

To James Monroe

Hermitage Febry 19th. 1823

Dear Sir

I have the pleasure to acknowledge the recpt. of your letter of the 30th. ult. which has Just reached me, advising <me> of my nomination to, and confirmation by the Senate of the United States, as envo*[y]* extraordinary, & minister plenipotentiary to Mexico.[1] I shall allways view this as an aditional proof of your friendship towards me, and as a further proof of my countries confidence in my integrity as a public officer, and as such I duly appreciate it, altho I cannot accept of the appointment conferred for several reasons, some of which I will state. Under the present revolutionary State of Mexico, caused by the Despotic acts of [Agustín de] Iturbide [y Aramburu], whose tyranic yoke the republicans under [Guadalupe] Victoria are endeav*[oring]* to shake off, it appears to me that the app*[earance]* of a minister from the united states at *[Mexico]* would prove detrimental to the caus*[e of]* freedom in that country, and might a*[id the]* Tyrant Iterbide in rivetting the chai*[ns of]* Despotism upon his country.[2] I never ca*[n be]*come the instrument, however innocently, *[to aid]* Tyranny to oppress a people who of right oug*[ht]* to be free, and whose freedom is so importan*[t]* to the united states—was I to go there my feelings would be so differrent from the Emperors, that it would be impossible for our sentiments to accord, and evil instead of benefit to my country might grow out of it, and I have made it a uniform rule of my conduct never to accept a public station where it did appear to me I could render no benefit to my country—added to this Mrs. Jackson could not be prevailed upon to go to that country; to seperate again from her for two, or more years, when the interest of my country does not imperiously call upon me to make this sacrafice, when this trust can as well, if not better, be performed by another, all which will I hope be considered by you & my country <a> sufficient reasons for declining it.

Under all circumstances, it is no small gratification to me, to find from your letter that there is no obligation on me to accept, otherwise than may be alltogether in accordance with my own views, and wishes, the appointment being made without consulting me.

Major Eaton had advised me of your consultation with him on the subject of nominating me to the Senate, and your friendly views; My answer to him will have shewn, *[t]*hat I fully appreciate your friendly intentio*[ns a]*ltho I could not accept the appointment, *[wh]*ich he will have made known to you.[3]

I have recd a letter from Mr [Joel Roberts] Poinsette *[giv]*ing his views of the present disturbed *[sta]*te of Mexico, which fully confirms other *[ac]*counts from there; and shews the propriety of the view I have taken of it, and confirms me in the idea that it might prove detrimentall to the republican interest by sending out a minister under existing circumstance—and Mr Poinsetts ideas, I think, well worthy of your mature deliberation.[4]

Mrs. Jackson begs through you, to present to Mrs Monroe, & Mrs [Eliza Monroe] Hay, her affectionate reguard,[5] and believe me to be with sincere friendship and respect, yr most, obdt. servt.

Andrew Jackson

ALS, NN (9-0459); Copy, DLC (72). Published in Bassett, 3:188–89. Where the ALS has been torn, characters were supplied from the copy.

1. See Monroe to AJ, January 30.

2. Iturbide (1783–1824), a leader of the forces that expelled Spanish authority from Mexico in 1821, had been crowned emperor in July 1822. Victoria (1785–1842), an old revolutionary who was among the coalition opposing Iturbide's rule, became the first president of the Mexican Republic in 1824.

3. See above, John H. Eaton to AJ, January 11; Jackson's reply, dated February 5, has not been found.

4. See Poinsett to AJ, January 31. Poinsett (1779–1851), a South Carolina congressman, had just returned from a special mission to Mexico.

5. Monroe's daughter Eliza (1786–1835) married George Hay in 1808.

No state outside of Tennessee was more important to Jackson's presidential candidacy than Pennsylvania, where early support from papers such as the Philadelphia Columbian Observer, *the Meadville* Crawford Messenger, *and the Harrisburg* Commonwealth *aided Jackson's cause. One of Jackson's Nashville friends responded to the December 28, 1822, Westmoreland County endorsement of Jackson with an encouraging letter on February 1, and Jackson himself responded to a letter from Henry Baldwin of Pittsburgh by indicating his willingness to serve (see Greensburg* Westmoreland Republican, *February 28; Baldwin to AJ, January 2; and AJ to Baldwin, January 24). Soon thereafter, Jackson's reply below to an endorsement by a meeting of Dauphin County citizens on January 21 was published in a slightly revised form by the editor of the Harrisburg* Commonwealth. *Widely republished, Jackson's reply became the effective announcement of his candidacy. In keeping with his stance as a man apart from the corruption of office-seeking that characterized other candidates, Jackson announced not an active candidacy but a willingness to be drafted.*

To H. W. Peterson

Nashville
23 Feb 1823

Sir

Your letter of the 3d instant, with the Harrisburgh paper entitled the Commonwealth, containing the address you have alluded to, has been this day received—The complimentary manner in which my fellow citizens of Pensylvania have been pleased to notice my military services, & their voluntary expressions of respect & confidence in me, has excited on my part a proper sense of gratitude—[1]

As a member of a Committee appointed to draft an address to the People of the U S on the subject of the next Presidential election, *and by the request of that Committee* you ask to be informed "Whether I can or do approve of my name being used at this time as a candidate for the Presidency of the U States"—[2]

I shd have consulted my own feelings by continuing to avoid speaking on the subject but the respectable source from whence the inquiry emenates, prohibits any but a candid notice of your communication—

My undeviating rule of conduct through life, and which I have & shall ever deem as congenial with the true Republican principles of our government; has been neither to seek, or decline public invitations to office—For the services which I may have rendered & which have, it is hoped, proved in a degree beneficial to my country I have nothing to ask—They are richly repaid with the confidence & good opinion of the virtuous and well deserving part of the community—I have only essayed to discharge a debt which every man owes his country when her rights are invaded, and if twelve years exposure to fatigue & numerous privations can warrant the expression: I may venture to assert that my portion of public service has been performed & that with this impression I had retired from the busy scenes of public life with a desire to be a spectator merely of passing events

The office of Chief Magistrate of the Union is one of great responsibility; as it should not be sought by any Individual of the Republic: so it cannot with propriety be declined when offered by those who have the power of selection[3]—It is interresting to the American People alone & in the election they should exercise their free & unbiased judgement—It was with these impressions I presume & without any consultation with me, that the members of the Legislature of the state of Tennessee as an additional testimony of their confidence in me: thought proper to present my name to the consideration of the American community—My political creed prompts me to leave the affair uninfluenced by any expression on my part; & to the free will of those who have alone the right to decide Yrs

A Jackson

Copy in James Gadsden's hand, DLC (32); Printed, Washington *National Intelligencer,* March 24, 1823 (9-0466). Published in Bassett, 3:189–90. Peterson was a tavern keeper and perhaps also the itinerant journalist who edited *Die Freyheits-Fahne* at Carlisle, 1814–17; *Perry Forester* in Perry County, 1820–21; *Lebanon Telescope and United Republican* in Lebanon County, 1821; and *Der Unabhaengige Beobachter* at Harrisburg in 1823.

1. See Peterson to AJ, February 3. At the January 21 Dauphin County meeting, Peterson and four others had been appointed to draft an address recommending Jackson for president. The address was submitted on January 28, and 10,000 copies were ordered printed. The publication in the Harrisburg *Commonwealth,* enclosed by Peterson, has not been found, but for the text of the address, see *Harrisburg Chronicle,* February 3.

2. When the letter was published, the editor altered this paragraph slightly to address the committee as a whole and not Peterson individually (see John McFarland to AJ, August 14, 1824, below).

3. Jackson's declaration echoed John H. Eaton's recommendation of January 11, above, and the well-publicized sentiments expressed by William Lowndes in response to his December 1821 nomination by a caucus of the South Carolina legislature: "The Presidency of the United States is not, in my opinion, an office to be either solicited or declined" (Washington *National Intelligencer,* January 19, 1822).

From John Henry Eaton

Washington
23 Feby 23—

Dr Genl

To day brought me your Letter of the 5th. and as had been calculated upon, your annunciation that the trip to Mexico was declined.[1] I am glad of it, tho I did not feel disposed to hazard any thing like opinion; but to leave it altogether with yourself. Great solicitude, & numerous inquiries have been made, whether or not you would accept; & generally a desire has been, not only manifested, but expressed that you should agree to act: my own opinion constantly declared when asked about it, was that you would not go. At present there are weightier matters to be attended to at home, than abroad.

I thank you much for the seeming compliment paid me, that the duties of this mission might be well discharged by me; there is no doubt with me, (vanity all aside) that it would be in my power to get along in profound diplomacy well as C. A. Rod——y—& Hymen Allen, one of whom is known to me, & the other not spoken even tolerably of;[2] but then my dear Genl there is this difficulty in the way. My state has confided to me, when a great many others better merited it, a highly honorable station; and one which in regard to the state, and duty to myself, should not be exchanged for any other offer. My opinion has been often given, that members of Congress should not be appointed to office; they should consider their stations superior to any thing the Executive could offer; and without such an impression, it is not to be hoped that the Legislature can be kept at that high state of Independence, which they should maintain. The Man who looks to office with concern, as matter of importance to him, will presently loose his independence, & do as he may be bid to obtain it. These however are mere speculations, for I dare say my chance for *White House* favours are as limited as any, and that there will never arise any necessity for putting my *utopian* notions to the test; if there should, there is no reasonable ground to apprehend, that I more than others would adopt the rigid Catonic virtue, here preached up, and which indeed is oftener preached than practiced The truth is I dislike the appointing of members of Congress to office; and altho opposed to medling with the Constitution fearful that to mend it, may presently become too common, it would still afford me great pleasure if in the good sense of the Executive such a practice could have a beginning: much good would in the end flow from it; & soon tho not so much courted, would he be highly esteemed for his orthodox course

The difference between the Executive & Senate I regret to say cannot be adjusted. Your letter gave me an opportunity to converse freely with the President. I stated to him that you had sent me, a copy of a Letter address'd to him.[3] He desired me to call & see him with a view to conversation & I did; since then I have sought to ascertain, if in the Senate there was such a change of opinion as could lead to a hope, the disagreement might be settled; but there is none! If Butler is gotten clear of, the answer is Jones is entitled: & it is only in the event of both Butler & Jones being disposed of, that the opponnest say, the injunctions of the act of 1821 are gotten clear of, and the President left to select <else> at pleasure: with him on the other hand, feelings of the warmest kind exist; & he will do nothing which may be construed a surrender of his Constitutional rights. Upon this subject the old man feels all the warmth & feeling which youth might be supposed to have: his notion seems to be "not a cent for tribute." As regards the Adj Genl. appointment, all is still; but the next Session will probably raise again a breese, by a demand why it has been kept vacant; & as *Caucuses* will be then the rage, should the Radicals not feel secure they will seek to make the most of it. At present however the Radical Candidate seems on the wane I am sorry this difference cannot be settled, but such is in truth the fact[4]

Of news I can give you none; the papers will tell you all, about the noise of Congress—suppressed Documents and such like trifles, about which much has here been said—A B. in the Washington Republican is said to be govr. Edwards, such is the town talk.[5] Mr. C[6] had a grand party on Friday, & so crowded that no one had more than six Inches to move on; what may be the effect I can not say; perhaps to call back some doubting friends, & to secure firm ones more firmly; for it is hard, very hard you know that any mans wine & cordials should be drank; & his Ice creams fed upon and still to say or think ought against him: no reasonable man could be guilty of such an act of thoughtless meaness. Secty Adams however has one on Tuesday where again the same obligation will arise. Oh! it is too abominably bad, to see gentlemen electioneering for this high office; & seeking by parade & kindness to win for themselves patronage & favour Time was when the virtue of the people would have laughed to scorn such attempts; & contemned the man who would have practiced them; but times alas are altered; & now in the 47 year of the exercise of a govmt, which claimed for its duration naught but the virtue of its people are we confronted with the sad, melancholy & deplorable picture of four gentlemen intriguing managing & seeking by little pretences to worm themselves into the favour of the folks of Congress; & by their endorsement to be made before the people, to palm upon the Country, Intrigue for Intelligence—management for good sense, and the subserving their own interest, for a devotion to their Country. But the people will not awake from their slumbers. they quietly sit still, and leave with the few, the pretended patriots of the land, to dictate to them what is best, and hence it is, with the exception of the first chief magistrate, perhaps one other might be also excepted, the people have had nothing to do with the filling this high office.

Judge [William] Smith you will perceive by the National Intelligencer, grumbling and sad because he lost his election, is coming out in numbers to prove his course in politicks correct: to his last number I take exception, he is without the line of prudence to speak of Gadsden in the way he does; he could praise others without attempting improper comparisons and indeed where is the necessity of thus forcing into public discussion a man to whom he seems disposed to allow no claim for merit whatever, when he & those going with him have all along avowed that it was principle alone by which they had been influenced, & nothing of personal pique or prejudice. Gadsden's friends were indeed against him in So Carolina, but for this they not he, are responsible: I regret that the Judge has permitted his feelings so to run ahead of his judgment: age & experience should have prompted to a different course.[7]

Accts from Europe leave things as they were the Spring from every appearance must bring important results to view, which may put the Continent again in confusion

I rejoice that you are determined to forbear news paper discussions in any shape. Let no circumstance or provocation of any sort lead you before the public at a moment like the present: perfect silence is the true & correct system which prudence at this moment demands

Tender my kind regard to Mrs Jackson & should Col Gadsden be with you, say to him I've recvd his letter & will shortly reply to him Truly yours

J H Eaton

ALS, DLC (72).

1. Letter not found.

2. Caesar A. Rodney was nominated as minister at Buenos Aires on January 13; Heman Allen (1779–1852), a former congressman from Vermont, was nominated as minister to Chile on January 21.

3. See above, AJ to Eaton, January 21; and AJ to Monroe, January 21.

4. For the controversy regarding the adjutant general appointment, see above, James C. Bronaugh to AJ, February 8, AJ to John C. Calhoun, June 28, and AJ to James Gadsden, August 9, all 1822. Eaton quoted from a toast offered by Robert Goodloe Harper at a banquet given by Congress, June 18, 1798, for John Marshall, one of the commissioners to France who broke off negotiations of a treaty of amity and commerce rather than honor the French demands for a bribe, an episode which became known as the XYZ Affair.

5. A series of letters signed "A.B.," appearing in the *Washington Republican and Congressional Examiner* from January 20 through April 9, charged that the printing of a treasury department report to the House of Representatives had suppressed documents showing William H. Crawford's mismanagement of department dealings with western banks. A House select committee report on the suppression, January 30, exonerated the public print-

ers but failed to establish responsibility for all the deletions from documents in the treasury department report. A second committee was authorized, but its report on February 27 did not advance matters. Neither report addressed the question of mismanagement. Edwards finally confirmed his rumored authorship of the A.B. letters in a communication to the House on April 6, 1824.

6. William H. Crawford.

7. Eaton was referring to the second of Smith's letters "To The Good People of South Carolina," which appeared in the Washington *National Intelligencer,* February 19. In that circular, Smith had defended his vote against the nominations of Gadsden and Nathan Towson and touted the claims of Robert Butler as superior to those of Gadsden. Smith (c1762–1840), said to have been a classmate of Jackson's in the Waxhaws, had failed to obtain reelection as senator from South Carolina. While president, Jackson twice offered him appointment as associate justice of the Supreme Court.

To John Coffee

Hermitage March 10th. 1823

Dr. Genl

Your letter by Mr Smith enclosing to me two thousand dollars and of date the 23rd. ult reached me last evening, and for your attention to this business receive my thanks, it came in good time.[1] I had got Colo. Gadsden to set out to you for it on Saturday last, he met your letter at Nashville, & returned last evening. This morning I started a boy & horses, with the means to bring my young friend A. J. Donelson home from Lexington Kentucky

Present me to Colo. Winston when you see him, & assure him I have full confidence in his punctuality—I am certain he will pay the ballance as soon as he can with convenience—assure him that I am well satisfied with the negroes, and the prices at which you recd them—from your description, they are such as will be both valuable & beneficial to the child, and I approve highly of your receiving them without Valuation—he has shewn a high sense, of an honourable complience with his contract, agreable to his promise, and under such circumstances fifty dollars was no object—The childs interest was promoted, and that is fully satisfactory to me, and the Colo gratified at there being recd without valuation, this is all, as it should be.[2]

In my last to you, I gave you all the information I could with regard to the account of [Charles] Buckhannon & [John] Johnston to which I refer you—& to the books of Rapier & Simpson—If Mr James Jackson has not paid for the cordage it still remains due & ought to be paid, on the subject of the other items, viz, the iron & salt I can afford you no other information than given you in my last; I enclose this account, & the one for ferriages—you will please make the necessary inquiry of Messrs. R. & S. and Mr James Jackson, and do what is Just & right—It is much regretted by me, that these accpts had not been presented to me whilst there; by which you would have been saved this trouble, <which> I could have closed them myself—it is to me a very unpleasant business to have so many overhauling of accounts, I had applied to Messrs. Rapier & Simpson to furnish all the articles wanted to both farms to prevent multiplicity of accounts, & when I closed & paid up their account, I had aright to suppose (having none any where else) that my accounts were paid, and in short I never even looked over their account, & if I had, seeing a Barrell of salt charged, & twelve or thirteen dollars (for articles not named) by Sharrock, I would have been certain that the iron, & salt, was all paid for: and I was as certain that the cordage with which my cotton crop of 1821 was bailed with & sold to Mr J. was also paid for, when Mr Jackson & myself had the settlement at your house last June, as he had paid for me R & Simpsons account.[3]

I find from a letter recd from our friend Mr James Jackson, that he begins to see the combination of parties, between Mr Crawford & Clay[4]—the latter, through his friends made great exertions to obtain a nomination by the Louisiana Legislature, my friend writes me, when the day came there was but three could be mustered in his favour, and posponed the meeting—my friend also writes me, that Governor Carroll has been writing to some members there, that Clay will get a unanimous vote in Tennessee.[5] I mean the first opportunity to shew the Governor this letter, which is all the notice I <will> mean to take of him—his friends shall also see it—& I suppose the Individuals of Tennessee will inquire by what right he attempts to give the lye, to the expression of the Legislature of the state[6]—should the people take up the subject in the south, & west, as they have in Pensylvania; they will soon undeceive Mr Clays friends—if the people of Alabama, Mississippi, & Louisiana, follow the example of Pensylvania, they will place Clay & Crawford where they ultimately will be; *Dehors the political combat*—but their intrigues are united, and their friends are industrious.

It is true I was appointed Envoy extraordinary & minister to Mexico—but it is equally true that I declined excepting it—In the present revolutiary state of Mexico, no good *[c]*ould be brought about for my country—an american minister going there & presenting his Credentials to Iturbide at present, might add much to his strength & enable him to rivet the chains of Despotism upon that part of the country, and I hate bowing to a Tyrant—again I am not desirous to treat with Ghosts—and I hope ere this Iturbide has lost his head—for these & other reasons which I named to Mr Monroe I declined—[7]

We all enjoy as good health as the late cold weather, & the sudden change, to heat, will permit—I was at Capt Donelsons today, they are all well, the old lady able to go to the garden[8]

Present Mrs J. & myself to Mrs. C. & the little ones & accept for yourself our good wishes

Andrew Jackson

ALS, THi (9-0486). Published in Bassett, 3:192 (extract).

1. Letter not found. The carrier was possibly William Hunter Smith (1797–1871), son of Bennett and lifelong resident of Rutherford County.

2. See bill of sale from Anthony Winston, Jr., February 18.

3. See AJ to Coffee, March 1. The account of Florence merchants Buchanan & Johnston has not been found. The ferriage account may have been Jackson's account with Walden Fuller & Co., January 8–December 15, 1822, which has an undated receipt showing payment by Coffee. For Coffee's report regarding settlement of Jackson's accounts, see Coffee to AJ, April 6–11.

4. Letter not found.

5. See Isaac L. Baker to AJ, February 14 (above) and 26. When these reports resurfaced in 1826, the governor explicitly denied having written any such letter (see William Carroll to Robert C. Thompson, October 24, 1826, in *National Banner & Nashville Whig*, October 28, 1826).

6. Jackson was referring to his nomination for president by caucuses of the Tennessee House, July 27, and Senate, August 3, 1822.

7. See James Monroe to AJ, January 30; and, above, AJ to Monroe, February 19.

8. Probably a reference to Mary Purnell Donelson.

From Alfred Balch

Nashville 12th March 1823.

Dear Sir,

I have consumed several days in a very careful examination of your original and amended Bill against Erwin and others the answers & proofs in the cause and the law arising thereon. As I have lately been employed in the case—as I have hitherto partook so little in the excitement which it has created, that I did not even know the prominent facts of it—I think my judgment upon it is impartial. It is my habit to write out every case in our Supreme Court in which I am employed and to set down the law which applies to it much at large. In a few weeks I will have made a copious brief of your cause which I will send to you and the outline of which is already half finished.[1]

For myself I have not a single doubt of your success. If every fact in the answers were true there is still no good defence against a decree: and I do beleive that if the controversy concerned two or three hundred acres of land instead of 85,000 acres there would not be an objection made to a recovery

It is very clear that the Federal court had no jurisdiction, of course *its decree is as tho it had never been.*

It is equally clear that the defence must be founded in the participation of yourself [Joseph Inslee] Anderson & Pryor in the agreement to procure a foreclosure to be made.[2] Take it for granted that you did participate in it as agent and as counsel—in order that we may examine the cause in the very way that the defts desire tht it shall be examined. That agreement was founded upon no valuable consideration passing between the parties—it cannot be considered as an agreement to speculate on the *lands,* because it was an agreement to procure the money due and if it was intended to be any thing else a court of equity will not carry that intention into effect. An agreement between a Lawyer & his Client that the Lawyer shall procure a foreclosure of a mortgage & buy 10,000 acres of land & give his client half & take half himself cannot be pleaded by the client in Bar to the claims of the Lawyer to the property purchased, if that foreclosure was never made & there was not in fact, tho there was ostensibly, a sale of the land—More especially if the subsequent claim of the lawyer is founded in a good consideration & in a deed from those having the equity of redemption & who by reason of the nullity of the pretended decree have never been before the court and have never had their rights in any degree affected. The client can get his mortgage money & nothing more.

The relation of Lawyer & client or agent & principle stands on a very different footing. Neither Anderson nor those acting under him could take advantage of their situations to affect Norton Pryors rights to his *mortgage money*. And if it had been agreed tht on a sale made tht <Pryor> Anderson should give <Anderson> Pryor one half the lands & Anderson had taken the deeds to himself & refused to convey and there had been a *valid decree* & a *valid sale* and a *valid deed* from the Marshal then Pryor might have gotten the half promised him, because this would have been a fraud on Pryors rights which rights were never cognizable in Law or equity, till an actual valid sale under a valid decree of a competent court. The right of Pryor lay in his legal title which legal title he had himself chosen to subject to the equitable title of Allison. Unless this equitable title was destroyed, by a *legal* proceeding, it stood in its original integrity to be affected only by a *legal* proceeding—And the most that can be said of the Agreement of Anderson and Pryor is, that when the attempt to foreclose proved to be abortive, Anderson got no land, and Pryor got neither land nor his money. If strangers had come in and purchased these lands, under such a decree as was rendered they would have acquired no rights and Pryor must have had his mortgage money by a subsequent *legal* decree and Allisons heirs would on payt of the money have had their lands. If strangers then could not affect Pryors rights by purchasing at such a sale, it proves tht Pryor having purchased himself under a void decree could acquire no rights additional to the right created by the mortgage deed itself.

The whole proceeding was a nullity. Pryor had never changed his original situation. And as on the one side Anderson got nothing for his trouble because he got no title, so Pryor on the other escaped expence & still stood secure in his $21,800. The law of principal & agent is that the agent can do nothing *unfair* to affect the legal or equitable *rights* of his principal—But there must be such *rights* to be affected—This is a sine qua non—Pryor & Anderson agreed to make a speculation—The instrument was the *right* of Pryor as mortgagee—The end in view was to procure the lands—nothing has been done to affect the right as mortgagee, of Pryor, the plan to effect the sale failed—Pryor is in his original situation & Erwin stands in his shoes with his Pryors claim to the money in his possession[3]—The ends intended to have been effected by the decree having wholly failed and as tho it had never been so was the *agreement* to procure that decree, because the agreement gave no remedies by either party against the other until a right was created by the effectuation of the purpose of that agreement. The validity & efficacy of the agreement are not found in itself, but its validity & efficacy depend on the rights which might flow from its *completion. Such* rights would be cognizable both in Law & Equity—An agreement to make a prospective speculation binds none of the parties unless it is actually & legally made From this opinion this conclusion inevitably results, that if the decree was a nullity all parties were remitted to their original situations Pryor had the right to sue again Anderson & all others finding the rights of Allisons heirs unaffected had the right to buy of them & there were no obligations subsisting under the agreement relied on, on the part of any one concerned.

From This opinion another conclusion inevitably results that you & Erwin are in a court of Equity total strangers to one another & all notices & conversations &c &c charged denied & retorted have but little to do with the cause, because the efficacy of all these matters depends on their effect upon clear unequivocal rights possessed by those who plead them—either as evidences of fraud or in bar of a decree—As to the statute of limitations if the decree was void the deed founded thereon could give no title—[4]

If the mortgage deed is relied on it shows an equity of redemption & of course speaks for itself—

I deem it to be matter of importance that the true points of this cause should be understood and have thought it might be well to present to you my opinions of your prospects of a recovery—The defence has made a great many questions, but they are made more to sustain the sinking hopes of the defts than <for> with any confident <hope> reliance that they will avail much—

When Mr James Jackson arrives I should like to see you and him together as I wish to converse privately with you concerning the organization of a court to try the cause—[5]

Where six or seven hundred thousand dollars are depending it is necessary that every step should be taken after long reflection and very minute & *private* enquiry Respectfully your obt Servt

Alfred Balch—

ALS, DLC (32). Balch (1785–1853; Princeton 1805), a Nashville lawyer, served briefly as a Florida federal judge after an appointment by Martin Van Buren in March 1840.

1. See case file in *Jackson* v. *Erwin,* July 8, 1814, for the original bill of complaint, July 8, 1814 (9-0946), and the amended bill, June 12, 1819 (9-0956). Balch's brief has not been found.

2. In 1800 Norton Pryor had employed Anderson (1757–1837), then U.S. senator from Tennessee and at this time comptroller of the U.S. treasury, to foreclose Pryor's mortgage against David Allison, and Anderson had asked Jackson to handle the matter. Jackson then engaged John Overton to prosecute, and Overton obtained the decree for a sale, later ruled invalid. See Joseph Anderson to AJ, March 20, 1802, *Jackson,* 1:283–84.

3. According to Andrew Erwin's statement of January 23, 1821 (9-1032), he obtained a

conveyance of Pryor's entire interest in the Allison lands in October 1813. Balch argued that this gave Erwin no claim to the land, but only a right to sue for payment of the mortgage.

4. The Tennessee law of 1797 had barred legal claims made after seven years against anyone in "peaceable possession of any land, by virtue of a grant or deed of conveyance founded upon a grant" (Edward Scott, *Laws of the State of Tennessee, Including Those of North Carolina Now in Force in This State. From the Year 1715 to the Year 1820, Inclusive,* 2 vols., Knoxville, 1821, 1:613). Balch argued that the settlers claiming under Erwin could claim no such deed. The 1819 law extending the same security to peaceable possession under any "assurance purporting to convey an estate in fee simple" could not affect Jackson's case, which was already in litigation (*ibid.,* 2:482).

5. For Balch's ideas on the "organization of a court," see below.

From Alfred Balch

Nashville 20th March 1823.

Dear Sir,

I deemed it necessary to commence thus early an examination of your suit not only on account of the great value of the property in dispute; but that I might contribute my feeble aid in preparing for the final disposition of it in such way as would be fair and just—I send you my views of the subject which *you* can examine and Mr James Jackson like wise if he desires to do so—When convenient you can return the manuscript to me—[1]

After all, it will be found that the defence will be rested on your agency under Anderson & at the sale—I have very little doubt that the defts when they purchased disregarded the decree of the Federal court—They calculated that the mortgage money was already of great amount—They saw that the lands were good—They thought that even if Blount had a claim it might be bought up—that the heirs were poor & at a distance—that after a while the mortgage money would reach such a sum that no one in the country would attempt to raise it or if they did that matters might be adjusted—one thing was certain—by the purchase for $25,000 the handsome sum of $20,000 was made at once in the way of the interest already accrued—This course of reasoning is strongly supported by the very clear and satisfactory testimony of Mr Whiteside & the statement of Mr [John] Childress.[2]

Were the case mine, I should hesitate to leave it in the first instance, to such a court of last resort as could *now* be procured—I feel confident that Judge [Jacob] Peck must decide the cause in your favour.[3] There would then be a decree for an account—This would open the eyes of the tenants—when they saw commissioners upon their lands taking an account of the rents & profits & improvements. If the cause were taken before a special court, this acct wd have to be taken—That court might be dissolved other Judges might come into it—Another struggle might be made & more delay produced—But, if a decree is rendered by Judge Peck rely upon it, there will not be much difficulty with the principal part of the claimants afterwards. They will soon make their peace by purchases—

This is my view of the subject with a good deal of knowledge how the tenants feel in Bedford.

Perhaps a better plan can be suggested—It will be necessary for the legislature to authorize Judge Peck by a special act, to sit in October.[4] To this course I presume no one will object. very respectfully yr obt Servt

Alfred Balch.

ALS, DLC (32).

1. Manuscript not found.

2. See case file in *Jackson* v. *Erwin,* July 8, 1814, for Jenkin Whiteside's deposition, May 17, 1820 (10-0134), and testimony, April 23–May 12, 1821 (10-0153); Childress's statement does not appear in the file. However, Balch may have referred to statements by Childress and Whiteside that had been published in the *Nashville Whig,* September 4, 1819. Childress (d. 1819), a Nashville resident, was marshal of West Tennessee, 1803–19. David Allison had been deeply in debt to John G. (1752–1833) and Thomas Blount (1759–1812) at his death. Andrew Erwin stated that in July 1813 he purchased the judgment of more than $30,000 against the Allison estate obtained by John G. Blount in the Knox County Court in May 1800.

3. Peck (1779–1869) was elected to the Tennessee Supreme Court in 1822 and served until 1834.

4. The matter of the passage of the law became immaterial when Jackson and Erwin agreed to a settlement on September 19.

To John Caldwell Calhoun

Hermitage March 23rd. 1823

Dr Sir

I have lately seen Mr Smiths adress to the citizens of So. Carolina—the manner in which he has introduced the name of that high minded meritorious officer Colo. Gadsden before the public, is as wicked as the production is weak.[1] I have thought that Justice to Colo. Gadsden might require that the public should know the estimation in which I held Colo Gadsdens military merits whilst serving with me—and that it was I that urged his claims to the adjutant Genls office—without his knowledge or approbation commencing from the moment I was advised by you that Colo Butler (agreable to his wishes) would be provided for in the line of the army. My letters will shew, that I did this from a convition of his talents & military merit—with an eye single to the public good the wellfare of the army, and thereby to promote the public service.[2]

It being intimated to me that Mr McDuffie intends to reply to Mr. Smith, I would sugest the propriety, that he <might> be furnished with extracts from my letters to you that bear upon the above points—They would be furnished by me, but the enemies of Colo Gadsden might say that they were furnished (by me) for the occasion—coming from your Department with their dates & time of receipt, will foreclose such intimations as those, & they will be duly appreciated by the public. You will see

Colo Gadsden reply to Mr S. in the Nashville Gazzett of the 21st instant—This reply must make him feel—and bring to his view the adage of, "O that mine enemy might write a Book."[3] accept assurances of my friendship & Esteem

Andrew Jackson

ALS draft, DLC (32). Endorsed "Substance of a letter wrote to J. C. Calhoune 23rd. of March 1823—" Published in *Calhoun Papers,* 7:539–40.

1. For William Smith's address, see Washington *National Intelligencer,* February 19.

2. Calhoun notified Jackson of Robert Butler's appointment to command the Fourth Infantry in a letter of May 19, 1821. Jackson suggested James Gadsden's appointment as adjutant general on May 22, 1821, before receipt of Calhoun's letter.

3. George McDuffie's reply to Smith, March 24, appeared in the *Columbia Telescope* on April 1. Gadsden's response, "To my Fellow-Citizens of South-Carolina," defended his appointment as adjutant general, publishing among his evidence Jackson's letter of March 1. On the dispute, see also Smith's rejoinder, "To the Good People of South Carolina," in Washington *National Intelligencer,* December 9. Jackson's quotation was apparently a reference to Job 31:35.

To Edward Livingston

Hermitage March 24th 1823

My Dear Sir

On the receipt of your letter of the 25th ult, I had only time by the return mail to acknowledge its receipt, and say to you, that on the subject of the Mission to Mexico I had not been consulted, and that I had declined accepting of this Mission.[1]

It was a Just deduction of my friends, to conclude that I had been consulted before my nomination to the Senate, and of course that I would accept the appointment, and many of them, under this impression, may conclude that I am very fickle when they learn that I have declined; for this reason, I have thought it due to you, that you should be informed truly on this subject, & also my reasons for declining.

The first I heard of the intentions of the President was in a letter from Major Eaton our senator who advised me that Mr Monroe had sent for & consulted him upon this subject enquiring his opinion whether I would accept; to which the Major replied that he could form no opinion on the subject—Mr Monroe expressing a wish that he would assure me of his friendly views in making this nomination—I immediately answered that I would not accept, & a few days after this answer to Major Eaton I recd Mr Monroes letter advising me of his nomination and the approval of the Senate of the u. States, to which I replied that I could not accept for the reasons following in substance[2] The present unhappy revolutionary state of Mexico with an oppressed people struggling for their liberty against an Emperor whom they have branded with the Epithets of *usurper & Ty-*

rant, convinces me that no minister from the u. States could at this period effect any beneficial Treaty for his country: and of the impolicy of a Republican Representative at a court which might be construed as countenancing the empire in opposition to a republic—The people of Mexico in their honest efforts for freedom command my warmest sympathies, and their success is intimately connected with the ultimate & general triumph of those liberal principles for which our Revolutionary worthies fought & bled, and which now form the pride & boast of united america. with these feelings & wishes which I believe to be general & in unison with my fellow citizens I did believe my situation at Mexico would be embarrassing to me, independant of the conviction that I was rendering no service to my country, when by appearing at that court it might strengthen the totering crown of Iturbide and enable the Tyrant to rivet the chains of despotism upon his country—To render service to my country could alone constitute any motive for again acting in a public capacity—you will find from my reasons stated that in consulting my own feelings I have not been unmindfull of, or uninfluenced by considerations connected with the best interests of my country, which I trust has heretofore, & shall allways govern my conduct. Had the situation of Mexico been differrently situated, had the free voice of the people governed; my conclusion would have been differrent—for I believe it the true principles of our Goverment, that every mans services belongs to the nation when it is required by the unsolicited voice of his country—and the appointment being made without consulting me embraced what I believe ought to be the govrning rule of the President in making his nominations. Had I accepted of this Mission, it would have been amonghst the first of my wishes to have had you with me—should I ever be again brought by the unsolicited call of my country on the public or political theatre, I shall calculate to have you near me—but on such an event I do not calculate—I am no intriguer, I would not act in one single instance that charector for all the public favour that could be bestowed—My country has brought my name before the american nation and the people must decide—The Presidential chair is a situation which ought not to be sought for, nor ought it to be declined when offerred by the unsolicited voice of the people; to their choice the constitution has left it, and happy for the permanancy of the constitutional Goverment & the perpetuation of our union if designing Demagogues will let the people exercise this their constitutional privilege without attempting to athwart it by subtle intrigue, & management.

on the recept of this if Leisure perm*[its]* I would thank you for your views of the correctness of my decision, and the ground I have assumed & on which I have allways practised, and I would add; I have grown too old in the practice, ever to change.

Present Mrs. J. & myself respectfully to your Lady & daughter,[3] & to Major Davazac, and accept assurances of my friendship & esteem

Andrew Jackson

P.S. I have not had Leisure to read your report through—as far as I have gone I approve it fully—If the Penitentiary system can be established to meet your views it will be a happy amendment to the criminal code & the name of E. L. will be handed down to posterity as the brightest luminary of his day[4] A J.

ALS, NjP (mAJs). Published in Charles Haven Hunt, *Life of Edward Livingston* (New York, 1864), pp. 313–16. Livingston (1764–1836), who had served as one of Jackson's volunteer aides during the New Orleans campaign, was a newly elected congressman from Louisiana. He later served as Jackson's secretary of state.

1. See AJ to Livingston, March 14. Livingston's letter has not been found.

2. See above, John H. Eaton to AJ, January 11, and AJ to James Monroe, February 19; and Monroe to AJ, January 30. Jackson's reply to Eaton has not been found.

3. Louise Moreau de Lassy (1786–1860), the sister of Auguste G. V. Davezac and the widow of a French officer, had married Livingston in 1805. Their daughter Cora Livingston (1806–73) married Thomas P. Barton of Philadelphia in 1833.

4. In February 1821 the Louisiana legislature had selected Livingston to prepare a criminal code for the state. He had completed a preliminary *Report Made to the General Assembly of the State of Louisiana, on the Plan of a Penal Code for the Said State* (New Orleans, 1822) and had apparently forwarded a copy to Jackson. A copy of the preliminary *Report* remains in the Jackson library at the Hermitage.

From John Caldwell Calhoun

Washington
30th March 1823

My dear Sir,

Incessant application to official duties since the commencement of the late session of Congress compelled me to suspend wholly my private correspondence, which I hope you will accept as an apology for not acknowledging your favour of the 12th Decr. last, at an earlier period.[1]

I find few with whom, I accord so fully in relation to political subjects, as yourself. I have a thorough conviction, that the noble maxim of your's, to do right and fear not is the very basis, not only of Republicanism, according to its true acceptation, but of all political virtue; and, that he who acts on it, must in the end prevail. The political gamblers will fail. The cause of the Georgian[2] is, if I mistake not, rapidly declining. It has no foundation in truth, and can only be proped by false pretexts. Should he fail in New York, as I think he must, he will have not the least prospect of success.

Mr Clay, I think, is not advancing on this side of the mountains, tho' his friends speak confidently of his strength to the West. They expect him to be nominated in Louisiana, during this session.

Our news from Europe has been interesting, and I expect will be still more so by the next arrival. It is not improbable, that a mighty contest has commenced there not for commerce or territory, but to crush any vestige of liberty on the continent of Europe. In its progress, it will probably approach our shores, as Cuba will be involved in all likelyhood in the course of events. That England looks to that Island; and will be ready to seize on it, if a favourable opportunity offers, can hardly be doubted, and that such an event would be full of danger to this union, is not less clear. I deem the moment important, and do think the country ought to be prepared for the worst. Without Cuba our confederacy is not complete; and with it in the hands of the English, the best line of communication between the entrance ports, would be intercepted.

Say to Col Gadsden if you please, that I will write him in a few days; and that the President has selected him to treat with the Indians in Florida, which I hope he may find convenient to accept. I think his chance of being confirmed as adjutant genl at the next session is good.[3] With sincere respect & esteem

J. C. Calhoun

ALS, DLC (32). Published in Bassett, 3:193–94.

1. Not found.

2. William H. Crawford.

3. Calhoun offered James Gadsden the treaty appointment on April 7, and Gadsden, who had arrived at Washington, accepted on April 9. James Monroe chose to submit no further nominations for adjutant general. Upon taking office in 1825, John Q. Adams filled the post with Roger Jones.

To William Savin Fulton

Hermitage, *April* 4, 1823.

Dear Fulton—

I received your letter of the 26th last evening.[1] Our friend Gardner[2] left me on the 22d ult., *via* Washington, D. C., for Charleston, S. C. I hope he will return shortly & settle with us. Mrs. J. and myself regretted much that we had not the pleasure of seeing you and Mrs. F. at our house; you will always find us friends without disguise.[3] My counsel is always at your command, and on your change of life particularly you ought to have no fear of well-doing. The industry and economy of Mrs. F., in aid of your own exertions, will lead to wealth, or at least to independent competency, which is all that ought to be desired, it being all that is necessary or desirable. There is but one rule which every one ought to adopt and pursue to make him independent; this I adopted when I first had a family, and have pursued it through life. It is, shortly, this: to learn to live within your means. A man can be as independent on $100 dollars as on $5,000. Our real wants are very few, our imaginary wants numerous, which will daily increase if we feed or cherish them.

It requires some energy to adopt this rule—fashion, a habit,[4] has introduced many ideal wants which our pride, if left to rule, would lead us to keep up. It requires some little exertion to keep down these feelings that habit has formed on us, but when once the resolution is formed, the propriety of the course examined and approved, you go on triumphant in your laudable course, and competency, happiness and independence follows in its train. I have benefited by this course.[5] It is the one friendship and mature judgment recommends to you, which, if you adopt, your success through life is certain.

Your talents, with industry, will, without doubt, afford you a competency. You never ought to despond; if you do, you lose that energy of application,[6] that makes talent profitable. When you look around and see men, with half the information you possess, succeeding,[7] it ought to give spur to your energy, that will insure success. You have many friends who will aid you, but in passing through life, you will find greatest aid when you are getting on well yourself. I have no doubt—never had—of your succeeding well. You can calculate on my friendship. Present Mrs. Jackson and myself affectionately to your lady. It is probable we shall be out in July next, when we shall certainly visit you.

I have read the Florence *Gazette,* and read the piece you alluded to in your letter.[8] It is well written, but you have erred in calling the "court" a court-martial. This court was a "*special court*" of inquiry, and so called in the order convoking[9] it, for investigating the charges against Arbuthnot and Ambrister. The order closes thus: "The court will record all the documents and testimony on the several cases, and their opinion of the guilt or innocence of the prisoners,[10] and what punishment, if any, should be inflicted."[11] Its jurisdiction was created by the order creating the court, and the court had no jurisdiction to award punishment. Its power was to inquire into the guilt or innocence, and give their *opinion* thereon.

This was a court similar to the special court ordered by [George] Washington in the case of [John] Andre.[12] It neither enlarged nor contracted[13] my powers as commanding general, as in all such cases, I had the right by the law of nations to retaliate or punish; nor could the organization of the court deprive me of this power. To give my full views on this subject, I have inclosed an extract from my memorial to congress on the subject, and will send you by the first opportunity the vindication of the president, and his commanding general on this subject. From both of these you will see my justification complete, and unanswerable, and it will enable you to amuse the readers of the Florence *Gazette* and inform them.[14] It would be gratifying to me to learn from what quarter the late censure of my conduct has arisen, for having Arbuthnot and Ambrister punished agreeable to the laws of nations and of war. They cannot be Georgians or Alabamians, for it was this energy and decision that rescued[15] all ages and sexes on the frontier of both States from the tomahawk and scalping-knife of the ruthless savage, excited by the wily arts of Arbuthnot and Ambrister, the parents and progenitors of the revolting[16] war. Every Christian and philanthropist must approve of their execution, as promoting the objects of humanity. I would, when your leisure occurs, like to know from what source this has arisen.

I will like to hear of the result of your county meeting;[17] there can be no doubt this is the only way the voice of the people can be heard. Intrigue is the order of the day, and unless the people assert[18] their rights, it will be lost to them. The election of the president by the people, will be a mere name; he will be elected by intrigue and management without the voice of the people being heard. Should you see General Coffee and Mr. James Jackson present me to them—the latter I have expected on for some time. I shall write to the general shortly.

I am, sir, with esteem and respect, your friend.

Andrew Jackson.

P.S. Judge Fulton can use the inclosed as he thinks proper. If published, he can prepare[19] it as he thinks proper,[20] but not as furnished by me. A.J.

Printed, John Hallum, *Biographical and Pictorial History of Arkansas* (2 vols., Albany, 1887), 2:186–88 (mAJs); Copy, KyLoF (9-0509). Significant variations between the two texts have been noted below. Fulton (1795–1844; Baltimore 1813), Jackson's former private secretary, was a Lauderdale County, Alabama, judge.

1. Not found.

2. The copy renders the name as Gadsden, which in context appears to be correct.

3. On February 9, Matilda Frances Nowland (d. 1879) and Fulton had married at Florence.

4. The copy reads "fashion & habit."

5. The copy shows the text as "This is the course I have benefitted by pursuing" for this sentence.

6. The copy at this point reads "you looze that energy of application of your talents."

7. The copy reads "getting on well without half the information & talents you possess."

8. Article not identified.

9. The copy reads "convening." For the order, See General order by Robert Butler, April 26, 1818. In the aftermath of the trial, Jackson's critics had challenged the court's jurisdiction, leading his defenders to distinguish a "special court" from a court-martial.

10. The copy reads "persons."

11. In the copy, the remainder of the paragraph reads: "and details Lt. J M Cassell [Glassell] recorder its was by the order investing the court, & the court had no power to award a punishment—its powers was to inquire into the guilt or innocence, give their opinion thereon, and what punishment should be inflicted."

12. In September 1780, André (1751–80), a British adjutant general, was captured while carrying correspondence between the British commander and Benedict Arnold. Washington (1732–99) ordered a board of general officers to examine him and "report a precise state of his case, together with your opinion of the light, in which he ought to be considered, and the punishment, that ought to be inflicted" (John C. Fitzpatrick, ed., *The Writings of George Washington from the Original Manuscript Sources 1745–1799,* 39 vols., Washington, 1931–1944, 20:101). His execution followed the recommendation of the board.

13. The copy reads "it could neither enlarge or contract."

14. See *ASP, Military Affairs,* 1:754–69, and [John Overton], *A Vindication of the Measures of the President and His Commanding Generals, in the Commencement & Termination of the Seminole War* (Nashville, 1819).

15. The copy reads "arrested."

16. The copy reads "existing."

17. Perhaps Fulton had reported plans to hold a public meeting to nominate a presidential candidate. The meeting, held at Florence on May 31, resolved to support Jackson.
18. The copy reads "exact."
19. The copy reads "preface."
20. The copy reads "best."

To John Coffee

Hermitage April 15th 1823

Dr. Genl

I expected to have wrote you by our mutual friend Capt. Jack Donelson, whilst I was engaged at the Grand Lodge he took his departure without me seeing him—I regret this as by him I intended to have convayed to my friend Fulton a Book which I have promised & which I will send him by the first safe hand.[1]

Inclosed I send you a production sent from the neighbourhood of Mobile to a friend of mine in this state who has inclosed it to me with a view to its insertion in a Nashville paper—I think it better calculated for the meridian of Alabama—and if you think proper you can hand it to Mr Fulton for his inspection & publication if thought worthy of a place in the Florence Gazzett[2]—The Eastern papers team with the Presidential question and Pensylvania has taken her course—The public Journals their stand, & disect, disapprove, & approve of the charector & conduct of the differrent candidates at pleasure, & with great freedom—Virginia as yet has not declared for any—a new paper has been established in Richmond in opposition to the inquirer & in opposition to Mr Crawford[3]—Virginia will not support Clay & if he cannot get Newyork or Pensylvania to support him he <will> must withdraw—Pensylvania will not—and Newyork it is said will follow in her wake, some say she will support Mr Adams, this I think the most probable—I have been expecting Mr James Jackson for a long time—I have a great desire to see him on our private business—Darby has, & is still using his quill with much severity—he has brought down the anger of many in Nashville, but stands well with the people—some, (I know not who) has brought him out before the people for the assembly[4]—This has alarmed some—and put Judge Overton in a great state of fretfulness—I have heretofore witheld Darbys pen from the abuse of the Judge, nevertheless he said the other day it was thought by the people that I was patronising him, that I had lost Grundys friendship, or at least Grundy would be silent—in the mean time Judge Grundy is professing great friendship to me, and proposing great plans to which I gave no countenance[5]—I mean therefore to say to Darby I have nothing to do with you, in either controling your pen, or advising you <any> how or what way to pursue your <own> course, that my name is not to be coupled with any of your investigations & abuse—and let them & Darby manage their business in their own way—& I do expect Darby will Dam the whole—he has got hold of some things that is well qualified to injure the Judge and to identify him with a verry corrupt combination to destroy Darby and change the uniform decision of the supreme court on the subject of the Statute of Limitations[6]—This I have had influence enough over Darby to have laid to sleep heretofore but Darby having as he says got fresh proof & the Judge as he says continuing his secrete plans to injure him, that unless the Judge does desist from interfeering with him he will expose him in the papers—therefore I have determined hereafter to let each take their own course—I have given the Judge the advice of a sincere friend he may adopt it or not as he pleases & I am done—he cannot suppose that Darby will tamely lay himself down for a few to trample upon without resistance—& the Judge will find that the people will support Darby, if he confines himself to facts, and makes out his case—Darby says that he has advice that the Judge drew the law at Nashville enclosed it to Mr [Pleasant Moorman] Miller at Knoxville before the meeting of the Legislature[7]—*[Ha]*ywood writes a member that the Judges must be put down (that is those who decided contrary to him, Judge [Robert] White & [Thomas] Emerson) or that they would put down the people—the law is passed Judges are selected & to be catichised to know how they will decide before voted for—If he proves this combination, he will make them all wish they had let these things alone—I have heard of packing Juries before, but an attempt by few to inveigle a Legislature to pack a court, I never heard before—such are the features of matters here—[8]

Mrs J. unites with me in good wishes to you, Mrs C, & the sweet little ones—& believe me to be your friend

Andrew Jackson

ALS, THi (9-0524). Published in Bassett, 3:194–95 (extract).

1. As Grand Master, Jackson presided over a special meeting of the Masonic Grand Lodge of the State of Tennessee, held at Nashville, April 7–11. The book was probably the *Vindication* promised in AJ to William S. Fulton, April 4, above.

2. Enclosure not found.

3. The *Virginia Times*, supporting John C. Calhoun, commenced publication on February 14, but ceased around the end of August.

4. Patrick H. Darby later claimed that the first announcement of his candidacy to represent Davidson County in the Tennessee House, a letter signed "Many Voters" in the *Nashville Gazette* of April 4, was written by one of his enemies. He, however, accepted the candidacy in a subsequent letter to the *Gazette*. On his candidacy, see the Nashville *Constitutional Advocate*, August 19.

5. Felix Grundy, previously a judge of the Kentucky Supreme Court, was a frequent target of Darby's attacks in the *Constitutional Advocate*. He held the seat for which Darby became a candidate.

6. Darby argued that, with the exceptions of John Overton and John Haywood, Tennessee justices had uniformly extended the protection of the 1797 statute of limitations on challenges to deeds only to cases where the deed could be connected to the grant upon which it was founded. After an 1819 law was passed to codify the wider protection espoused by Haywood and Overton, Darby argued, Pleasant M. Miller, Felix Grundy, and others had conspired to pass the 1822 judiciary act, providing for a fourth supreme court judge, in order to pack the court with judges who would find the revision constitutional. In addition,

he charged, the conspirators had passed the 1821 champerty law specifically to embarrass him because of his opposing view of the limitations statute (see above, Alfred Balch to AJ, March 12; Nashville *Constitutional Advocate,* August 20, October 15 and 22, and November 26, 1822).

7. Miller (1773–1849), a former congressman, represented Knox County in the Tennessee House, 1817–23. Jackson carried Darby's information to Overton, who denied authorship of the 1821 champerty law and asked Miller to testify on the subject (see Overton to Miller, April 13, THi). Miller then wrote Jackson on July 1, claiming authorship of the law.

8. Haywood, Whyte (1767–1844), and Emmerson (1773–1837) had served as the Tennessee Supreme Court from 1819 until Emmerson's retirement in 1822.

To John Coffee

Hermitage april 28th. 1823

Dr. Genl

I have recd by mail your letter of the 6th. instant intended to have been sent by Mr James Jackson with the Recpts of the acpts you were kind anough to settle for me together with the fifty dollars you enclosed.[1] I regret that you did not retain the full amount you had disbursed for me, for although the amount is small, still it is anough that ones friend is put to the trouble I have done you, in settling those accounts instead of being in advance for me—I am glad they are closed—nothing gives me more pain than dificulty in settling accounts—& particularly when I expected, & had a right so to do, that all my acpts had been closed by my friends Rapier & Simpson—My friend James after looking over his & my settlement at your house says the account is now Justly closed by you—and I am happy that it is so, and tender you my thanks for your attention to this business.

I must refer you to Mr Jackson for the news of this country—there is not much very interesting, still the political parties of our county may be somewhat amusing—Mr Jackson got his runaways & sold them to Mr James Martin who has this moment left us with his whole family to settle in Rhea County for a while, the better to attend to his notional suit, in which there are flattering prospect of his succeeding—Genl [George W.] Gibbs & Mr Darby both say there is no doubt but he will recover—indeed I learn that all holding under [Richard Green] Waterhouse has abandoned all hope & several has proposed to purchase from him—This will free him from all embarrasment, and give him independence[2] The Nashville Gazzetts will give you the politics of the north & East—Crawford is believed to be Dehors the political contest, & I think Clay is on the wane, his intrigue & that of his friends has destroyed him as is believed, the attempt to have him nominated at orleans, & having to submit to the humiliating alternative of producing it by a subscription, with a preamble so flattering to myself, has & will recoil upon him with double force, the people of Louisiana will I am told come out but the Louisiana maneuvre was intended to operate favourably to the East & north, where Mr Clay is now personally making his last effort, should he fail in bringing over Newyork, he is gone, without it, or Pensylvania, he cannot be elected, and from appearrences, his Vissit there & the public dinner given him by a few Philadelphians & a number of Kentuckians does not augur much in his favour there[3] & his own state will withdraw from him as soon as it is found that Newyork or Pensylvania will not support him—I never did believe Clay could be elected, and I still think he has no chance, but I do believe the moment it is found that Clay cannot succeed, his, & Crawfords friends, will make a great effort to resussitate Crawfords popularity—Crawfords friends altho at present silent are not sleeping—it is fully assertained that Clay will not get one Vote in Virginia & there it will be, that Crawfords friends will make the stand, with a hope that it will draw North Carolina, Georgia, alabama &c &c after it. These are the speculations of the day, which a few months will fully develope.

I am much gratified to learn that you have got your office at Florence,[4] this must be a great convenience to you, as well as to your family, and will afford you more time at home—we are happy to hear that your health is so good, o[u]r prayers is for its continuance we do not believe that a man of your industry will ever become so corpulent as to be an inconvenience to you—present Mrs J. & myself affectionately to Polly & the sweet little children—& believe me your friend.

Andrew Jackson

ALS, DLC (9-0533).

1. See Coffee to AJ, April 6–11.

2. Gibbs (1785–1870), a Nashville lawyer, was adjutant general of Tennessee at this time. In 1807 Littlepage Sims, acting as attorney for Stockley Donelson's widow Elizabeth and her father James Glasgow, sold 19,000 acres granted to Donelson in Rhea County to Waterhouse (1775–1827). The Martins, Elizabeth's sons by a previous marriage, repudiated the deed, claiming Sims had exceeded his authority, and attempted to dispossess those claiming under Waterhouse. Martin won initial victories, but Waterhouse eventually succeeded in establishing title. For details of the case, see *Waterhouse* v. *Martin*, in *Tennessee Reports*, 7:413–36, and Patrick H. Darby, *The Opinion of Judges Haywood and Peck, of the Supreme Court of Errors and Appeals, in the Case of* R. G. *Waterhouse vs. Martin and Others, Lessee, Delivered at Knoxville, May Term, 1824; with a Commentary* (Knoxville, 1824). James Jackson's captured slaves were probably Claiborn and Charity (see above, James Jackson to AJ, July 24, 1822).

3. For Henry Clay's "Louisiana maneuvre," see above, Isaac L. Baker to AJ, February 14, and May 3, below. For an account of the Clay dinner at the Western Hotel in Philadelphia on March 29, see the Washington *National Intelligencer*, April 8.

4. After he was reappointed surveyor of the public lands in January, Coffee moved his office from Huntsville to Florence.

From Isaac Lewis Baker

St Martinsville Loua. 3d. May 1823.

Dear General,

A great press of private affairs to regulate, large sums of Money to raise in times when that article is most difficult of attainment—and an almost constant attendance in courts the spring term of which begun the first Monday of April are all scarcely sufficient to excuse my delay in writing to you since my return from New Orleans. The news papers have given you some vague accounts of the transactions of our Legislature for the last few days of its session with regard to the question of the presidency. I wrote to you from Natchez that all was safe and so it was as far as a poor set of poor devils could be relied on.[1] The day after my return to the Legislature notice of another caucus for the next day was given. [John Holmes] Overton Davezac & myself turned out at once & counted noses.[2] We could not have asked a more favorable result for it appeared out of about sixty members we had at least forty with us. Next morning to our great surprize we found two or three who had always been with us had gone over to the Enemy's Camp. We then made a severer scrutiny and found our majority still large. at night when we met things had changed a little tho we were still strongest by ten or twelve. [Étienne] Mazereau and all your Enemies had been hard at work all day.[3] Many of them spoke the language of a large majority of the members perfectly. Knew better how to opperate on them & did all they could. Davezac in a most able speech opposed the Caucus. He spoke in English & was followed by Mazereau on the other side in French. I rose to answer him, but the instant I got up the opposition started their resolutions round the Tables to get signatures & by dint of persuasion & persecution got some twenty odd <signatures> signers. In the preamble to the Resolutions in favour of Clay there was a vast deal in your praise with the view solely of deceiving your friends. This trick got them some support. For two or three days after they made every exertion in their power to get more signatures & at last wonderful to relate they got thirty four. These names are sent forth upon the world as the deliberations of members in caucus. They were no such thing. In the caucus if a vote had been taken in the usual manner Mr Clay would not have been nominated. They broke up the meeting of their own accord and no vote was taken notwithstanding the pompous signatures of their president and secretary. It was all a trick.[4] Overton told me he had long since written a letter to his father (or some other friend in Nashville) giving an account of the whole which I hope was published. Overton & I made some publications in the Orleans Gazette which was sent which placed the transactions in their proper light.[5] In this state it makes no impression. The people know nothing of Mr Clay & are not for him. Of twenty seven Americans in the Legislature there are only six or seven who were prevailed on to sign his resolutions. It is hard to say how the French will go but the Americans are decidedly against Mr Clay.

[Joseph] Rouffignac (by Duralde's influence) is for Clay—but he is your friend & after Clay will be warm for you.[6] Duncan Livingston & [John Randolph] Grymes did nothing in your favour. It was not right in them—but as it was they did not choose to act. Duncan's brother in Law [George] Mather signed Clay's resolutions. Davezac is true & the only one of the French members who sticks to you thro good & evil Report, if we except [Pierre Adolphe] Rost a fine young man from Nackitosh who was not present at the caucus.[7] General Overton ought to be proud of his son John. He is a man of fine genius—as yet a little too wild—but one who will come out exceedingly well in the end. He was *[a]*s true as steel to you throughout the whole year.

In this poor state of Louisiana we have so many rascally adventurers who will do any thing for office that they only look to who is strongest to declare themselves. Should Clay & Crawford compromise as you think Crawford cannot get any vote here. I do not believe twenty men can be fou*[n]*d in the state favorable to him. He is generally & justly detested.

I certainly heard it said often before the caucus as coming from Governor Carroll that Clay would get the vote of Tennessee. Those who reported it may have done so for electioneering purposes but when I recollected the old John R. Bedford business I was strongly inclined to put faith in it.[8]

Should Pennsylvania declare for you you will stand the best chance for if there is a chance of success; the people are so strongly against you that all the west will be yours & most of the south.

For the part I have taken in this state I have been much assailed in public & private—but it matters not. I glory in such calumny. You have been a warm & useful friend to me & as long as I can serve you you shall not find me seeking shelter under the standard of your Enemies as some others do who have perhaps more regard to their interest than reputation.

Do me the favour to write to me often. Since I begun this I have been so often interrupted that I have delayed till the post is starting without touching on many points Events justify the view you took of Mexican affairs. The republicans have prevailed & Iturbide is a prisoner. The american people may thank you that our government never paid court to the scoundrel.[9]

I have only time & space to add my respects to Mrs Jackson & Colo Gadsden & to subscribe myself Your grateful friend & Servt

Isaac L Baker

ALS, DLC (32). Published in Bassett, 3:195–97 (extract). Extracts also published, with an added sentence, "They are for Jackson," in the *Nashville Gazette,* June 6, as a letter from a member of the Louisiana legislature to a friend in Nashville.

1. See Baker to AJ, February 26.

2. The Louisiana caucus was held on March 15. Overton (1797–1883) was a son of Jackson's neighbor and friend Thomas Overton (1753–1825).

3. Mazureau (1772–1849) had been in the Louisiana legislature in December 1814 when a dispute arose over Jackson's closing of the legislature. In March 1815, as the newly appointed Louisiana attorney general, he assisted with the prosecution of contempt charges against Jackson.

4. For the Louisiana resolutions, see *Niles' Register*, May 3, 1823. Presiding was Philemon Thomas (1763–1847), a major general of Louisiana militia during the New Orleans campaign and unsuccessful gubernatorial candidate in 1824 who served in Congress, 1831–35. The secretary was Jean F. Canonge (1785–1848), clerk of the House, a lawyer and later judge.

5. Neither Overton's letter nor the articles in the *Orleans Gazette* have been identified.

6. Roffignac (1766–1846) was mayor of New Orleans. Henry Clay's son-in-law Martin A. Duralde was at this time register of mortgages in New Orleans. Clay's brother John, also of New Orleans, was married to Duralde's sister Julie.

7. Grymes (1786–1854), a New Orleans lawyer, had served as a Jackson aide during the New Orleans campaign. Mather (1783–1837), a planter, was the brother of Abner L. Duncan's wife, Sophia. Rost (1797–1868), at this time a Natchitoches lawyer, later served on the Louisiana Supreme Court and as Confederate commissioner to France and Spain.

8. Bedford and William Carroll had apparently circulated a rumor in late 1815 charging fraudulent practices by Jackson and John Coffee in regard to Alabama land sales (see Coffee to AJ, December 27, 1815; and AJ to Coffee, February 2, 1816, *Jackson,* 4:6–8). In September 1822 and again in January and February 1823, Carroll had written Clay that he could count on Tennessee's support if Jackson withdrew. When Clay disseminated this information, he sometimes wrote that Carroll promised Tennessee support "when" rather than "if" Jackson withdrew, making Carroll's assurances even more positive (see Clay to Langdon Cheves, October 5, 1822, and Carroll to Clay, February 1, 1823, *Clay Papers,* 3:291–93, 360–62).

9. Iturbide abdicated his throne in letters of March 19 and 20, and opposition troops entered Mexico City on March 27. He then remained in loose custody until his departure from Mexico on May 11.

To John Coffee

Hermitage May 24th. 1823

Dear Genl

I recd. by the hands of our mutual friend Capt [Samuel] Savage your letter of the 7th. instant enclosing four hundred dollars in united state notes and four hundred in Tennessee notes the amount paid you by Colo. Winston on my account for which receive my thanks.[1]

I had sat down to write you about two weeks ago—I commenced my letter with the information of my fine prospect of my cotton crop, this was on Saturday—whilst writing I was interrupted by company who remained with me untill Tuesday, which days were cool & cloudy—I reasumed my letter on Tuesday, but thought before I would conclude my flattering prospects of a cotton crop I would view it—and I never saw such ravages committed as had been on my cotton for those three days—I cast my letter into the fire with a determination not to write untill I could see the real stand, Mr Parson has got over the greatest part of my cotton the second time, it has Just began to grow, the most part from six to Eight leaves, and I believe I may now Venture to say that I will have a tolerable stand, part stands well—and some is thin I think that now the worms will cease & the cotton quit dying, if so, I may with a favourable season, hope for a good crop—my corn is good, Mr Parson has gone over twice with the plows & hoes, *the old ground*—the new ground not planted, but all ready, once coaltered, & twice plowed, this is intended for a pumkin crop, as well as Corn—my plantation is in good order 160 acres of corn mostly knee high, not as good a stand as I could wish, the crows squirrells & pigeons has been very bad.

I must say that I think Parsons one of the best managers I ever saw—he has more system & gets on with more care than any overseer I ever had, I am happy to hear that the weather with you is good, & your hopes of good crops, flatering—My health has not been so good for about a fortnight, I am better, but I have had to loose a good deal of blood, & to take Herrodsburgh salts every other day for a fortnight, my cough has abated but I am a good deal pestured with it yet—the paign in my breast, side & left shoulder was unusually severe—I intend to Vissit you in July with Mrs J. & spend a few days with you—the travel may be beneficial.

I could not detain my friend Savage but one night—I gave him a letter to our friend Simpson Harris, with a request that he would introduce him to his daughter Mrs. DuPriest—he appeared to express a desire to become acquainted with her—and it gave me great pleasure to be the instrument of making her acquainted with so good a man—I think our friend has some thought of changing his situation—[2]

The pension business has created considerable feeling (I am told) about Nashville & through the country—I have very little doubt but it will be the means of electing Darby to the Legislature—his enemies could not have added more to his popularity than by the measures and ways they have adopted—another piece against him in the wig containing another anonymous Letter would send him to congress, or make him Governor of the state; This with Mr Grundy on the court of inquiry has roused public sentiment—believing there is a combination between the secratary, Bank directors, & pension agent, to put him down—it matters not whether this is true or not, it is anough—that they people think so.[3]

It was unfortunate for Mr Grundy that he had any thing to do in it; it will loose him Votes, & that many.

Mrs. J. with our little ones & Mr Donelson Join me in our best salutations to you, your lady, & amiable family, to whom present us; & believe me your friend

Andrew Jackson

P.S. Present us *[to ou]*r friends Mr J. Jackson & lady, & say to James *[I wil]*l write him shortly. A.J.

ALS, THi (9-0569). Published in Bassett, 3:197–98 (lacking postscript).

1. Letter not found. Savage (d. 1837), a supporter of Jackson's presidential candidacy, was from Lauderdale County.

2. Harris (1768–1833) had married Coffee's sister Mary (1774–1839) in 1792. His daughter Eliza G. was the widow of Horatio DePriest (d. 1820), a Maury County doctor. In June 1824, Savage married Anne Fitzgerald.

3. In the February 11 and subsequent issues of the Nashville *Constitutional Advocate,* Patrick H. Darby had accused Stephen Cantrell, the pension agent at Nashville, of corruption, most notably in receiving funds in United States notes or specie and paying pensioners in depreciated Tennessee and Kentucky bank notes. In April Secretary of War John C. Calhoun appointed Felix Grundy and Robert Armstrong to investigate the charges, and the two met as court of inquiry in Nashville commencing about May 13. Although Darby strongly criticized Grundy's acceptance of the position, claiming his enmity to Darby would bias the court's judgment (*Constitutional Advocate,* June 3), the court's report led Calhoun to dismiss Cantrell (see Calhoun to Cantrell, July 30, *Calhoun Papers,* 8:187–94). Grundy and William Lytle were elected in August as Davidson County representatives in the Tennessee House, defeating Darby and Thomas Claiborne.

To Willie Blount

Hermitage May 29th. 1823

Dear Sir

I recd your letter by due course of mail and would have replied sooner, but have been prevented by indisposition from coold which occasioned a return of my cough, from which I am measurably relieved.[1]

Before the receipt of your letter I had been aprised of our mutual friend Colo. [John] McKee, having become a candidate for congress, and had taken an early opportunity of writing a letter, in which I did his patriotism, & services rendered, in the late war, Justice. This was a debt due, which I trust I have duly paid to his merit, both as a man, & an officer, and which I hope will be duly appreciated by the freemen of his District in Alabama when they come to the poles on the day of election. My letter was written for the purpose of appearing in print whenever the Colo. might think proper, and will foreclose the necessity of publishing the extract of your letter—The last account from Alabama give a favourable account of his success—Colo. McKee resides at the Town of Tuskaloosa on the Black Warior, at which place there is a post office.[2]

It will afford me & Mrs J great pleasure to see you at the Hermitage & particularly if you could bring up Mrs B. with you[3]—I hope your health will Justify your contemplated ride to Nashville when we shall count with certainty on a vissit from you, it will afford us much pleasure, and we live close to the fountain of health, where a swelling in the *leggs* might be easily cured—we will expect to see you at the Hermitage if you come to Nashville.

You will find from the papers, that the Tyrant Iturbide has fallen, he is a state prisoner This to me is pleasant news, I hope the next arival will bring us the news of the spanish General [Francisco Espoz y] Mina, marching under the banner of the tricoulered flag to put Napoleon the 2nd. on the Throne of france, This will make the *unholy* alience of Despots leagued against the rights of man, tremble for the safety of their own thrones—and I hope it will be the commencement of freedom to the world.[4] Should the combination succeed against spain, we may begin to prepare for another struggle for the liberty we enjoy, and the rights of freemen.

Mrs J. present has come to hand, it is a superior piece of <workmanship> mawnism, the performance of two little girls, under twelve years of age—it would gratify us very much to have your personal observation on its merits—it is real american, the grass grew upon our own soil, and the girls are natives of our own country—I hope to see before I die, our country independant of urope, by all our fabricks being manufactured at home.[5]

be pleased to present Mrs J. & myself to your lady & accept for yourself our good wishes—your friend

Andrew Jackson

ALS, T (9-0578). Blount (1768–1835), governor of Tennessee, 1809–15, had retired to his Montgomery County plantation. He became a Jackson elector in 1824.

1. Letter not found.

2. See AJ to McKee, April 14. As Choctaw agent, McKee (1771–1832) had raised Indian allies for Jackson during the Creek War and Gulf campaigns. He was elected to Congress in 1823. McKee's supporters apparently first published Jackson's letter in the Tuscaloosa, Alabama, *American Mirror*. Other newspapers copied the publication, and in 1827 critics of Jackson's presidential ambitions republished it as evidence of the general's improper interference in a congressional election.

3. Mary White (1782–1824), widow of Hugh White of Knoxville, had married Blount in 1813.

4. The Holy Alliance, signed September 26, 1815, by Austria, Russia, and Prussia, and ultimately joined by all of Europe except Great Britain, Turkey, and the papal states, was an innocuous declaration of Christian principles, but it came to symbolize the reactionary cooperation of the three eastern powers. After France invaded Spain in April with the approval of the allied powers, Mina (1781–1836) led armies that continued a guerrilla resistance until his surrender in November. Napoleon II (1811–32), son of Napoleon Bonaparte and Marie Louise of Austria, was the Bonapartist candidate for the throne of France after 1815, but he remained a virtual prisoner in Austria until his death.

5. The grass bonnet made by Miss Pike and Miss Andrews of New York and presented by Robert Patterson, one of Jackson's supporters in Philadelphia, elicited a widely published letter from the general favoring the encouragement of domestic industry (see Patterson to AJ and to Rachel Jackson, March 20; AJ to Patterson, May 17; and Rachel Jackson to Patterson, May 18).

To Anthony Wayne Butler

Hermitage June 2nd. 1823

Dear Antony

I have Just recd yours of the 9th. of May mine in answer to your previous letter will have informed you of my pecuniary situation at present, and authorising you to draw upon me in favour of your friend, accompanied with his note that he has advanced for you the amount to clear you of the costs of the suit & damages recovered against you[1]—My last will have informed you of the letter recd from Mr Duncan on the subject of the representatives of our deceased friend Colo Richard Butler obligation to furnish the funds for the completion of your education after you graduate at college, from which you will have discovered that they were to furnish you with $750 pr year untill you gradu[a]ted at college, when this obligation ceased.[2]

you ought my young friend to have confined your wants within the above sum—at present it is wholy out of my power to command $100 in u states mony—the outfit of my young friend Saml. J. Hays who left me last monday for the military academy exausted all my resources—I have no means but my farm from which I can draw any resources—my crop measurably failed last year—This with the expence of my differrent young friends at school has exhausted my funds—but still on the receipt of your draft in favour of friend for one hundred dollars, I will make some erangements to meet it, by the sacrafice of some property.[3]

I hope & trust that your present difficulty will bring you to reflect upon the difficulty of raising mony, and of the great necessity of every person to bring their wants within their means—when you reflect that it takes one of our best farms to neat seven hundred & fifty dollars a year—it surely will induce you to oeconomise, and on your mature reflection, calculate, if you cannot live upon seven hundred & fifty dollars a year, how is it possible for me, to support my family & four student when my farm last year did not produce me that sum—you are now coming into life when you will discover that it is easy to spend mony, but dificult to make it honestly, that at the rate of seven hundred & fifty dollars a year your education thus far, has cost a great sum, and when you reflect that this was the boon of your deceased friend your heart ought to be filled with gratitude to his memory—and if you could not bring your wants within $750 a year, what is now to be your condition when this sum will be witholden from you entirely as appears from Mr Duncans letter to me an extract of which I have heretofore forwarded to you[4]—There is nothing now left for you & your brother but your land in Robertson, which at present could not be sold for near its Vallue—that this might be preserved to you, was the basis of the erangement between Colo. R. Butler & myself, that he should educate you, & I Edward out of the personal Estate of your deceased father, which then remained unexausted in your & Edwards education it at first was only fourteen hundred dollars—had it under my direction cost $750 pr year, this would have been exausted in one year[5]—I only name this to bring you to reflect upon the necessity there is for you to oeconomise—and had you sufficiently oeconomised, that you could have saved out of this $750 a year sufficient to have finished your legal study.

expecting you to graduate next month and believing that your friends below will furnish you the means to return we will be happy to see you—

and as far as I have the means will, with pleasure, afford you present relief & aid you in your study of your profession but I must repeat again the necessity of your mature reflection, how hard it is to make mony honestly—& how necessary it is for every one to bring their wants within their means, or their feelings will be allways liable to be hurt—mony never ought to be borrowed from a friend without a positive certainty of being able to return it at the time appointed, and your friends to relieve you, might place their feelings precisely in the situation in which your is now. reflect on these things seriously my young friend, you will find this the best advice that can be given you—follow it my dear young friend or more unpleasant situations may befal you—your friends here all enjoy health & request to be remembered to you & believe me your friend

Andrew Jackson

ALS, LNHiC (9-0582).

1. Butler's letter of March 15 had requested $100 to pay a portion of the court costs and fine assessed for whipping a man who had insulted him. Jackson's reply of April 17 and Butler's letter of May 9 have not been found.

2. See AJ to Butler, May 18.

3. In addition to assisting Butler and outfitting Hays, Jackson was also supporting Daniel S. Donelson's education at the Military Academy and Andrew J. Donelson's legal education. Jackson may also have had in mind his earlier contributions to the support of Edward G. W. Butler and Andrew J. Donelson at West Point.

4. Abner L. Duncan's letter of May 2 has not been found; for the extract, see AJ to Butler, May 18.

5. The Butler family retained Robertson County lands until the 1830s, but the specific property, at least part of which Jackson had leased to James Benton, has not been identified. For an accounting of Jackson's administration of the Edward Butler legacy, see Memorandum of accounts, January 18, 1813 (DLC-6).

To Pleasant Moorman Miller

(private) Hermitage June 9th. 1823

Dr. Sir

I have recd your note, I am aware of what you remark upon the Views of the beligerants a friend of mine, & a citizen of your County made the proposition[1]—I answered, the war was made upon me without cause, & secretely when I had a right to expect the warmest friendship from Colo Williams, that the last time I have ever seen him was at Ft Jackson, when at his request I obtained an order from Genl [Thomas] Pinckney, in favour of the Colo to superintend the recruiting service at Knoxville[2]—on my part we parted friendly, on his every declaration that friendship could produce, was declared, the next news a s[e]crete combination against me to destroy me, to arrest me, and to dam me—& that has been his secrete course ever since, witness his [conduct] in the Senate on the Seminole question by his Vote Mr [John Wayles] Epes, was chosen to fill the place of Mr [John] Forsyth, with a full knowledge that he would agree to Mr. [Abner] Lacocks report &c &c &c—and has been, & now is engaged with Mr Cocke (if letters from my friends in Philadelphia is entitled to credit) in difusing the intelligence that the State of Tennessee will not ultimately support me.[3] I am but little known to those who suppose, that I would under all these circumstances when he has endeavoured to injure me under the rose in the most secrete <&> cowardly, and assasin like manner have any friendly intercourse with him—and that at this late period when he finds he could not injure me, but that his base conduct is about to recoil upon his own head, no, no, things must go on as the have, no alience or Treaty upon this subject—he must as a preliminary, acknowledge his base conduct to the whole nation before this can take place—I feared his enmity as little, as I esteem his friendship—to be sure I have been silent as to him—I knew the course he was pursuing would recoil upon his own head, and that him and his friend Wm. H. C. both would politically die shortly and be forgotton when I would still live in the memory of my country—I was therefore silent as to a knowledge of his secrete enmity to me, & I intend to continue so—I think him too insignificant to notice publicly—and particularly under existing circumstances—but be assured I make no treaty with my enemies—and I intend to pursue, the cou[r]se I have hitherto done with regard to the Presidential question—to be silent—& let the nation decide—if others intrigue for the office it is no excus*[e]* for me—The public Journals will *[do]* all that is necessary & I suppose M*[r.]* Williams conduct before the election will be by them fully brought before his country—This is what ought to be—I will be glad to receive the paper spoken of, it will be attended to—I expect you will see Genl H. shortly in the N. Gazze putting some interrogatories to the Colo.—& I have no doubt that Colo [Samuel] Bunch & Houston can tell the position of the Colo. at the horse shoe as well as any others—& when this declaration of Mr Thomas Williams is seen, it is probable those Gentlemen who were there, will say whether it contains the real facts, or not.[4] I am yrs respectfully

Andrew Jackson

ALS, DLC (9-0590).

1. Note not found. The proposition discussed was apparently one of several efforts to reconcile Jackson with John Williams (see AJ to John Brown [1779–1843], October 8, 1819, *Jackson,* 4:335–36; and AJ to John McNairy, [September 6], below), but the friend making the overture has not been identified.

2. Pinckney (1750–1828), of South Carolina, was the major general of United States troops in overall command of the Creek campaign of 1813–14. While Jackson, John Williams, and Pinckney were at Fort Jackson (at the confluence of the Coosa and Tallapoosa rivers in Alabama) following the Creek campaign, Jackson wrote Pinckney on April 21, 1814, to recommend that Williams be detached on recruiting duties, and Pinckney agreed on April 22.

3. When Forsyth (1780–1841; Princeton 1799) of Georgia resigned the Senate in 1819 to accept the appointment as minister to Spain, Eppes (1773–1823; Hampden-Sydney 1786) of Virginia replaced him on the Senate committee that investigated Jackson's 1818 invasion

of Florida and issued a critical report. Lacock (1770–1837) of Pennsylvania chaired the committee. The letters from Philadelphia have not been found.

4. Bunch (1786–1849), at this time a state senator from Grainger County, had been a colonel of the East Tennessee militia during the Creek War. Jackson's victory at the Battle of Horseshoe Bend on March 27, 1814, broke the power of the Creek confederacy and effectively ended the Creek War. Jackson's report of the battle to Pinckney, March 28, 1814, praised the "skillful & intrepid" leadership of Williams (*Jackson,* 3:52–53), but his views had changed as the two men became political enemies. Samuel Houston's interrogatories to John Williams and the declaration of Thomas Williams—perhaps John's brother Thomas L.—have not been found.

From Charles Pendleton Tutt

Locust Hill near Leesburg Loudoun County
Virginia June 24th 1823

Dr. Sir

I arrived safely at home about the middle of April and should have much earlier apprised you of the safe arrival of Doctr. Bronaughs property but have been prevented heretofore from doing so by a variety of circumstances, having now however a leisure moment, I avail myself of it to give you the necessary information. I directed Dick to proceed from Lebanon to Beans Station—the small bay & riding horse I took with me through Kentuckey, on my arrival at Beans Station I found that Dick had not arrived, although he ought to have been there several days before, he however arrived that night—he then informed me that he could not possibly travel more than twenty miles a day—my anxiety to reach home would not permit me to travel at that rate, I therefore employed a waggoner to take charge of them and deliver them in Winchester which he did from whence they got safely home.[1]

the cariole gave out entirely shortly after they entered Virginia. the balance of the money in my hands after defraying the expenses, to wit, about $174 & some cents which as Mrs. Bronaughs rect. is not before me, I cannot exactly state, was paid to her order.

Our Congressional Elections here have terminated very much as I expected with the exception of Genl. Alexdr. Smyth, whom I had no doubt would have been left at home. from all I can see & learn it appears to me that Virginia will support Mr. Crawford for the next Presidency—not from any great love or regard they have for him but because he has pleased in some way her delegation in Congress. as to yourself My Dear Sir I need not say that you are universally esteemed by the people and if the election was by districts the result would be different. your enemies too are very industrious, they have labored hard to produce an impression, that you were a man governed alone by Passion & impulse. cannot something be done to counteract their views—your personal acquaintances and friends do all they can but they are not sufficient in number to turn the scale—

Be pleased to remember me most affectionately to my friend Genl. Houston

Accept my thanks for your civility and kindness when at your house. With best respects to Mrs. Jackson I am most Respectfully Yr. Obt Servt—

Chas. Penn. T*[utt]*

ALS, DLC (32). Published in Bassett, 3:199. Endorsed, "To be answered agreable to the with memorandum <by> & ready for A J signature." Neither the memorandum, nor an answer, has been found. Tutt (1780–1832) was a Virginia planter; Locust Hill was his plantation.

1. Jackson was serving as co-administrator of the estate of his friend James C. Bronaugh, who died in Pensacola in September 1822. Tutt was transporting Bronaugh's personal servant Dick from Tennessee to Bronaugh's mother, Rebecca, in Virginia. In 1830, Jackson purchased Dick and his family from the Bronaughs. Bean's Station was a village in Grainger County, Tennessee, about thirty miles northeast of Knoxville.

To Hardy Murfree Cryer

Hermitage July 12th. 1823

Dear Sir

Mrs. J. & myself returned from our visit to Murfreesborough yesterday, when I recd your note by Cyrus. and on inquiry found that Cyrus had delivered this note to Mr Parsons who had ordered him to go to the shop and attend to his work—but instead of obaying this order he went & got his cloaths, passed the shop, threw the key to Aron, and bid him farewell & went off—I am Just informed that he is in Nashville Jail & Mr Parsons is about to go for him.[1]

I learn from Mr Parsons, that the cause of his flogging him (which was quite moderate) was owing to this, I had from the conduct of Genl overtons Ben, placed Aron & Cyrus under the charge of Mr Parsons with directions that neither should be absent from the plantation without his or my knowledge, in order that every morning he might see them he ordered that they should make a fire in the Kitchen, on monday morning Cyrus was absent when he come Mr Parsons asked him where he had been, he replied he had overslept himself without giving a direct answer to the question, Mr Parsons being in the act of going to the river, ordered him to the shop, and on his return, ordered him to strip himself, or to cross his hands to be tied, this Cyrus was unwilling to do, Mr Parsons ordered Sampson to seize & hold him untill he would tie him, this was done, & Mr Parsons gave him about fifteen cuts upon his breach, Cyrus went to his work, & after he had recd this flogging I was in the shop & Cyrus said nothing to me about it—in the Evening Sampson passing by the shop Cyrus began a quarrell with him, which was told Mr Parsons, he immediately called up Cyrus, and began to question him about it—Cyrus began gradually to retreat, Mr Parsons says he saw from his conduct he meant to run & thought he would seize him, made the attemp, Cyrus avaded his grasp & runaway Mr Parsons assures me he had nothing more in view than to let him know he must obay—this he must be taught to, or he is worth nothing to you, & still less to me, & it is such an example as cannot be tolerated by me, it would ruin all my negroes; but one thing you may rest assured of, Cyrus shall not be abused, but he must be taught subordination & this Mr Parsons will do—unless he is more ungovernable than most negroes, Mr Parsons is sure to bring him to this—Be not uneasy—he has runaway without cause, and I have but little doubt but Mr Parsons will entirely cure him without injury.[2] I am Dear sir respectfully yr friend

Andrew Jackson

ALS, John P. Mullins (mAJs). Cryer (1792–1846), of Sumner County, was a Methodist minister and horse-breeder, an interest he shared with Jackson.

1. Note not found. The Jacksons had gone to Murfreesboro to attend a public dinner in Jackson's honor on July 10. Cryer had sent his slave Cyrus to Jackson on June 10 as a trial for possible purchase. Aaron was probably the "half blacksmith" slave recently purchased from Elizabeth R. Donelson, but Jackson also owned Aaron (c1785–1878), a blacksmith purchased in 1791.

2. Nothing further is known of the conduct of Thomas Overton's slave Ben, a blacksmith hired by Jackson. Sampson was probably Big Sampson (c1788–1833), but Jackson also owned Old Sampson at this time. The fate of Cyrus is unknown; he does not appear on any of Jackson's surviving slave inventories.

From James Gadsden

St Augustine
30 July 1823

Dear General

I have just received your letter of the 9th ulto—I have previously tendered you my acknowledgements for the copies of your Indian talks &c forwarded me[1]—They will prove no doubt influential at the approaching meeting—I agree with you perfectly as to the only course to be persued to ensure success—& am resolved myself to urge it: if however opposed by the other Commissioners let the failure be on their heads—I anticipate however no such difference: Govr Duval has been recently associated with us: & he has concurred with me on all points[2]—We have only to dictate & the Indians must & will no doubt obey—Recognise the right of their refusing: or assenting and Indian like they will rise in their demands: and nothing will be done—Our order is to concentrate them on the Peninsula; but to obviate some of your objections to such a location I propose a central situation; reserving to ourselves all south of Charlotts Harbor: & ten miles on the sea coast East & west otherwise—[3]

I am happy to hear of the prospects in the Political world; though I do not rely so much on the influence of newspaper articles as you appear to do—The men most assailed and with most justice often succeed best politically—It arrises either from the effect of political excitement which blinds the judgement & induces a population to follow their leader right or wrong; or from a total absence of virtue & patriotism in the community. Those under the latter denomination have been appropriately designated as Radicals—men who are for themselves: who fight under no banner: who regard not the good of their country but only look to their individual agrandisement—To such Mr C——d has appealed and with effect; for there is no man who in any way contributes to his elevation that does not expect an equivalent in return—His friends, with all the disclosures which have been made, are still confident; vigilant & active—They have in view their single object: their party is well organised & they move in concert—There is no doubt that the party opposed to Mr Crawford could triumph if they were united: but we find them divided between yourself: Calhoun & Adams—There ought therefore to be an understanding between the friends of you three so as ultimately to unite on the one whose election can be secured—You are gaining strength daly: and could the appeal be brought directly to the People I entertain no doubts of your election—The Politicians however are not so friendly & for the obvious reason you have made them no promises—There is a want of virtue among these men; I know not however that is peculiar to our country we find it every where & has been the cause hitherto of the destruction of governments—

We need a little regeneration & this can only be done by elevating those who have the patriotic virtues & independence of soul to enforce them—Where the head is corrupt it will affect the whole frame: We should be vigilant—& active therefore to defeat the pretensions of the Radical Candidate—

You have no doubt the last intelligence from this quarter—Our Legislative Council has adjourned: & Call is elected to Congress by a respectable Majority

To Mrs Jackson & friends generally present my regards—Say to Andrew I wish he would write me often Your friend

Gadsden

ALS, DLC (32). Published in Bassett, 3:200–201 (extract).

1. See Gadsden to AJ, June 12. On April 30, Jackson had forwarded a copy of his talk with the Florida Indians of September [18–20], 1821, and a new talk to be read at the 1823 negotiations (not found). Jackson's letters have not been found.

2. Gadsden and Bernardo Segui of St. Augustine had been commissioned in April to negotiate with Florida Indians, and on June 30 William P. Duval was ordered to join them. They met with the chiefs on September 1 and negotiated the Treaty of Moultrie Creek, signed on September 18.

3. For John C. Calhoun's instructions to the commissioners, April 7, see *TPUS*, 22:659–61. Jackson evidently preferred that the Indians be concentrated along the Apalachicola River rather than within the Florida Peninsula (see AJ to Calhoun, July 14).

To John Caldwell Calhoun

[cAugust 12, 1823]

Dear Sir

I have had the pleasure to receive yr letter of the 31rst. Ult. from which I am happy to find you have given to the Commissioners appointed to Treat with the Florida Indians all necessary means that was in the power of the Goverment to insure success, <you may be assured that the confidence reposed in my recommendations, as far as my Judgt> This I hope may enable them to concentrate & locate the F Indians at such a point as will promote their happiness & prosperity and at the same time, afford to that Territory a dense population between them & the ocean which will afford protection & peace to all.[1] The result of the investigation in Mr Cantrells case has terminated as I expected from the facts disclosed, and alltho I sincerely regret, <that society> that any man in Mr Cantrells situation should so far forget <virtue truth &> the golden rule to do unto others, as he would the should do unto the him, I am happy we have an administration, that where its <disbursing> officers act improperly <& dishonestly> it will apply a corrective—our society has been much demoralised, by our paper banking system, and its corrupting influence has been no where felt more seriously & banefully than in this Country, the result of this inquiry will be beneficially felt in a moral point of view, Mr [Thomas] Crutcher is a very honest man, and the only reason why I did not sugest his appointment was, that he was Treasurer of the State, & our constitution declares, that no individual shall hold two lucrative offices at one & the same time; and I did believe if the letter of our state constitution, in his appointment & acceptance was not violated, the spirit was infringed, I therefore sugested the appointment of Mr [Michael C.] Dun knowing him to be an honest man and in no wise connected with banks, he lives about <one> mile or a mile & half from Nashville, acted for many years sheriff & has allways settled his publick acccounts promptly.[2]

I much regret to see the Gloom that hangs over the affairs of Spain, but I trust her leaders may be faithfull to the constitution, & if so, all the bribery of the holy alliance cannot put out the spark of freedom there lighted, <out> The Castilian spirit will shortly electrify the whole nation and unite them, if this happens, from Mina position, the French army must be destroyed—I rejoice to see the independant spirit that prevades the Cortes, should they be able to keep up the spirit of resistance three months longer, the Spanish nation will be safe, the Tyranny & oppession of its enemies will unite them, and rouse the spirit of the nation to a successfull resistance[3]—but should I be mistaken, should the Spanish nation succumb to the will of its invaders we must prepare for defence, we will not be left in the peacefull & undisturbed enjoyment of our liberties;

america has given birth to civil liberty, and from it, the whole Globe will ere long be electrified, unless the combined efforts of the Despots in Urope can extinguish it in america, as well as else where. The King & nobility of England in heart & wishes unite with the other despots, and will only give aid to Spain when coerced by the strong current of Public oppion there—should Spain be prostrated it is not Cuba alone but south & north america, that will be placed in a critical situation and we ought to prepare for defence, Cuba should not be permitted to fall into the hands of any uropean power—our aid can prevent it, and we ought not to hesitate on this subject it is too closely allied to our own safety & prosperity as a nation—

The view I gave you of the understanding of Mr Clay & Mr Crawfords friends, I thought was correct, but the former will not openly now withdraw in favour of Mr Crawford, and if he was, he could not strengthen the latter in the west, Mr Crawford can have no hope of success but in a congressional caucus, and even then the western people could not be brought to act in concert with it, I do believe that a congressional caucus would destroy the election of any man whose name is before the nation Mr Clay has no chance of being elected as it is believed by the best informed, and Mr Crawford has no interest that can benefit him, <in the> west of the mountain.

I have great relience on the good sense & virtue of the people, and I hope with yourself that coalition intrigue & management will never place a citizen in the highest office in the gift of the people to bestow <but from the late example in the county in which I live I have seen it lately employed> But from the exertions that has been & are still making in favour of Mr C. we have aright to believe that coalition & intrigue is staking abroad through our land, with manly strides & the whole exertions of the virtuous portion of the people will be required to put it down, in their exertions I have full confidence at present, and therefore feel satisfied that Mr C. with all his intrigue & patronage that the Treasury has aforded him cannot succeed—and it will be a happy result for the nation. But altho I have great confidence in the virtue of the people, still from local precedants we have aright to fear that the people in some parts have become degenerate & demoralised, in the county in which I live one of the most flagitious charectors of his day has been returned to represent us in the State Legislature, once a fugitive from Justice—This was owing to his wealth & to the Bank influence; arguing from thence, what might not the influence of the Patronage of the Treasury produce—[4]

A straightforward course, taking virtue <for> & independence for our guide, leaving the people to themselves, uninfluenced by any thing but their own reason & they will allways decide right—I hope they will in the next Presidential election—I am very respectfully yr friend

A. J

ALS draft, DLC (9-0625). Published in Bassett, 3:202–204.

1. In his letter of July 31, Calhoun had responded to Jackson's recommendations of July 14 regarding the upcoming treaty with Florida Indians.

2. Calhoun had removed Stephen Cantrell from his position as pension agent for West Tennessee following investigation of charges that he had paid pensioners in devalued bank notes. Crutcher (1759–1844), an early settler of Davidson County, had served as state treasurer since 1803. Jackson was referring to article 1, section 23, of the 1796 Tennessee constitution. His recommendation of Dunn (d. 1853), Davidson County sheriff, 1808–15, has not been found.

3. News from Spain was contradictory, but Jackson apparently credited reports of a continuing spirit of resistance in the Spanish Cortes, such as appeared in the articles "France and Spain" and "Spain" in the Washington *National Intelligencer,* July 25 and 30. Francisco Espoz y Mina commanded troops in Catalonia.

4. Jackson was referring to the election of William Lytle, whom Jackson suspected of involvement in the Glasgow land frauds (see AJ to John Coffee, August 15, below). Patrick H. Darby, one of Lytle's unsuccessful opponents, had attempted to make the management of Nashville banks an issue in the campaign (see "To the People of Davidson County," Nashville *Constitutional Advocate,* July 15 and August 19).

To John Coffee

Hermitage August 15th. 1823

Dr. Genl

I reached home on last Saturday morning, and found Mrs. J. & all friends well[1]—I have been surrounded with company, that untill now I had not a moment to write you—on Saturday I examined my Cotton, it is a very fine crop indeed, I have seen no crop this year its superior—& if we have a dry fall I have no doubt it will produce 1200 to the acre, its branches are large & all bending & breaking with the weight of the bowls—My corn has improved after the fall of the rain very much but I fear has been injured much by a wind that has threw much of it down my new ground very fine.

Our election had closed before I reached Nashville—strange to tell Wm Lytle the associate of Wm Tyrel in all kind of frauds forgeries & Villainy is elected highest poll, & still more strange to me is that Judge Overton Voted for & supported him—Judge [John] McNairy &c &c &c—when men standing high in society with a full knowledge of the Villainy of another supports him—They participate in his crimes by supporting him, and loose their charector for honesty—they by this act disgrace their county, and inflict a wound in the breast of every honest man in the county, and establish a precedent that strikes at the root of morality, religion, & Virtue, by holding to the View of the rising generations, that it matters not what crime you commit, how you acquire property, proved they do, and ravel in their ill gotten wealth, they are the proper subjects for preferment to office of honour & trust—& to pass laws for the regulation of society—The time will shortly arive when men Thus acting in support of Villains will meet with the indignant frowns of every honest man—It is stated, that three houses, (grogshops) were opened in Nashville for Lytle & Grundy with labels on the door—it is stated on this ground their election will be contested; & if proven, it being positively forbidden by the constitution, they will be prohibitted from a seat for two years.[2]

I have turned to Gadsden papers, and found the ten shares of Florence stock—& amonghst my own papers have found Mr James Jackson receipt for the *[same?]* which I will destroy—I will send *[the]* stock by Capt J. Donelson with o*[ther]* papers necessary.[3]

Present Mrs. J. & myself to Polly *[and]* the children & accept for yourself our best wishes.

Andrew Jackson

ALS, THi (9-0637).

1. Jackson had gone to Florence, Alabama, to attend a sale of town lots by the Cypress Land Company, commencing July 24, and to raise funds to assist Anthony W. Butler.

2. The election was held August 8–9. Lytle (c1779–1839) represented Davidson County in the Tennessee House, 1823–27, and the Tennessee Senate, 1827–33. Terrell (Tyrrell) was a leading figure in the Glasgow land frauds involving North Carolina military warrants, which were uncovered by Jackson in 1797. Lytle held military warrants in connection with which he had dealings with Terrell and with Thomas and John Gray Blount, also accused of fraud, but he was not named as a leading figure in the 1799 North Carolina report on the frauds (see *Jackson,* 1:157–58). McNairy (1762–1837) was federal district judge for Tennessee. Jackson was referring to article 9, section 3, of the 1796 Tennessee constitution, which provided penalties for "any person who shall directly or indirectly give, promise or bestow" any "gift or reward . . . in meat, drink, money or otherwise" for votes to be elected.

3. On June 8 James Gadsden had requested that Jackson try to sell Gadsden's Florence stock and lots. Jackson's endorsement on Gadsden's letter indicates that he replied on August 15 (not found), announcing a $1,500 offer and asking instructions.

Jackson and his neighbor Edward Ward were the leading figures supporting construction of a church on Jackson's property at the Hermitage in 1823–24 and attempting to find a minister for the congregation, as evidenced in the letter below from Ward, an elder of the church. The general's efforts did not go unnoticed during the presidential campaign. A published letter from a Nashville pastor (probably Allan D. Campbell or William Hume) to a New York clergyman, August 13, 1824, mentioned Jackson's role in the affair and declared that "One reason why I wish to see him President is, because he will come out more decidedly in favour of religion than any other of the candidates" (Hagerstown, Md., Torch Light and Public Advertiser, *December 14).*

From Edward Ward

Nashville
Augt 25th. 1823—

Dear Sir.

I have just this moment receved your Letter by Genl Houston. I am very sorry I missd of an opportunity of conversing with you relative to the propriety of Parson Hodges's return. I had just as I left home received a Letter from the Parson, in answer to one I some time ago wrote to him on that subject—I wrote to him that I thought he ought to return, that our neighbours in general wishd it, & that I was of opinion, that a more liberal spirit, for the support of the preaching the Gospel, prevailed with us now, than did when he left us. I shall again write to him as soon as I reach my Farm to the same effect.[1] I feel much at a loss what to say about the best mode of raising a Salery for our minister—I fear we should make but a small progress that way by selling Seats—I cannot think of more than 12 or fifteen persons that would purchace Seats, & from the very good neighbourhood feelings that prevail with us, there would be no competition excited in the sale of them—The consequence would be that the Seats would sell, just for as little as each person would think proper to bid for them. I am fearful that a plan of this sort is not well calculated for the Country, particularly in a thinly populated neighbourhood like ours; furthermore I should fear that it would not be generally pleasing, & might frequently operate against the attendance of persons, not immediately interested in, or connected with the Church. I on the whole am of opinion that it will be best, to pay our parson thro private subscripton—A Church being built, & a parson engaged regularly to preach in it, will draw from our neighbours a liberal contribution. whatever plans may be adopted by the neighbourhood for the support of the preaching of the Gospel, I will with promptitude subscribe to—As to the Rye you want, with pleasure I will furnish you, & wish you to be at no trouble to procure it by way of retu[r]ning that quantity will produce no inconvenience with me—I know not whether any is thrashd out; but it will be prepared for you when calld for. Inclosed is a note to my Overseer on the subject.[2] With great respect & friendship your Ob Servant

Edw Ward

ALS, DLC (32). Published in Bassett, 3:204–205.

1. Letters not found. Jackson had also written Samuel Hodge, at this time living near Tuscaloosa, Alabama, expressing a desire that he return to serve as pastor of the church (see Hodge to John Coffee, March 28, THi).

2. Note not found.

To John McNairy

[September 6, 1823]

Dear Sir,

By the hands of Governor Edwards this morning I received your kind & friendly letter of the 3d inst and regret that I have not more leisure to reply to it.[1]

Blessed is the peacemaker, *saith the Holy scriptures,*[2] & I feel grateful to the memory of our deceased friend for his & your attempt on a former occasion to produce harmony & peace to society in a certain quarter; and, altho from my acquaintance with men & human nature I was aware that it would prove abortive as it did, still I have the same feelings of gratitude for the actors as tho their efforts had proved effectual—[3]

Unanimity I grant is all important to the well being of all societies, and particularly to the perpetuation of our Republican govt; but I fear there is too little virtue & morality in ours to <produce> and maintain this blessing. Demagogues pursue a course of self aggrandizement regardless of public good, without cause have in many cases attempted to prostrate the character of those, who, by pursuing an independent course with an eye single to <the public goo> their country's interest, have obtained the approbation of their fellow citizens; lest they might obstruct or retard their own progress to prefermant—This is the fact as I suppose in the case alluded to. I parted with Col Williams in perfect friendship at Fort Jackson; <(whom I have not seen since) in perfect friendship> (since then have not seen him) and my last friendly act was at his request, the obtaining of an order from Genl Pinckey for him to repair to Knoxville where his family was, to superintend the recruiting service of his Regt. The next information I received was through the Knoxville Gazette after I had reached Mobile in 1814 stating that I was to be arrested upon charges emanating as private advice detailed from Col Williams & the Officers of his Regt. Feeling myself free from any charges that truth <could> would support, I felt no alarm at what falsehood or calumy could raise. Afterwards in the early part of 1815 at Orleans, I was advised by a friend that charges had been sent on signed by all the officers of the 39th Regt. This only raised in my breast contempt for the movers, and a withdrawal of friendship from those capable of such assasinlike cowardly conduct, unworthy of [any] man who had *ever worn* a epulet & who could under the appearance of friendship [act?] in the work.[4] Upon my return to Nashville I met with my friend H L White, to whom & the whole of his family I have been warmly attached in friendship—We had a long conversation on this subject. The Judge assured me that Col W could not be as he believed guilty of the acts alleged against him; to which I replied, if he were not I had no wish to criminate him, and would with pleasure have an interview with him on my way to the city of Washington in 1815 When I passed Knoxville at which place I remained two or three days, <I was> as I have been advised <that> Col Williams had left Knoxville the morning of the day of my arrival for a part of the county that he was not in the habit of visiting. Suffice it to say that I did not see him. The Col arrived at the City, as I was informed after my arrival there. I was confined by sickness, he did not call to see me.[5] His conduct and expressions on the Seminole question—His false<hoods &> assertions to the members of Congress that I had no standing in my own state—His charges of speculation in Florida lands, & salt works; have convinced me that he is amongst the most unprincipled men I ever knew:[6] Therefore believing this, and being <well> advised of his mean, hidden & ungentlemanly conduct behind my back; *I have forgive <but> I cannot forget.* But ought confidence to be reposed in any man who has without any cause become my enemy, has endeavourd to secretly stab me on the Seminole question by falsehood & insinuations of speculation in Florida lands <& in salt works> [& &c&c], has applied to me motives as base as they were unfounded; And all this after he had as I believed, intentionally evaded an interview with me for explanation, and never has made a personal advance to make an atonement for <the> these repeated injuries which it is alleged that he both originated & propagated? His <friendship> Enmity I was regardless of—In his friendship now I could not confide.

I never have interfered in any election, as yet; I do not know that I will: but until he makes personal advances for the purpose of reconciliation, we cannot be further reconciled than we are—<(should he do this & be able to give me any satisfactory reason for his attempts to injure & lessen me in the estimation of the world, I cannot take him by the hand in friendship)>.[7] The conduct of the Col has not nor never <will> shall lessen my friendship and esteem for Judge White & his family, and that of his deceased father—[8]

On the other subject you know my detestation for law suits. Col. Erwin knows whenever he makes propositions I will hear them, but situated as I am now & my express declarations to him in your presence & in the other gentlemen if propositions are made, the propositions must come from him, and if they are such as in justice to others I can accede to; I assure you it will give me great pleasure to accept of them, and get clear of Law. It is the only suit but one I have ever had in my own name and I hope it will be the last.[9] I have lost all views of accumulating wealth, & I wish peace & tranquillity if I can fairly obtain them. I have but one grand view, and that is to promote as far as I have influence a proper respect for character, religion & morality, and thereby lay a solid foundation for the perpetuity of our happy form of Govt. Whenever these are lost sight of party views substituted in their stead, our Goverment will be changed—it cannot stand, virtue being the only prop which sustains it.

My Dear Sir, I acknowledge the truth of your remark "we are getting old," time rolls on apace, we shall soon cease, and I flatter myself we shall descend to our graves in friendship & in peace. From what I have expressed as my views & duty, I can see nothing that can or ought to interrupt our friendship here, for I am aware you can have no view other than my own, which is, the prosperity of our country, & the happiness of society—

With my thanks for your friendly expressions which I sincerely reciprocate, I am yr. friend

Draft in Andrew J. Donelson's hand, revised and endorsed by AJ, "Judge McNairys Confidential Letter with copy of answer 6th. Septbr 1823 to be carefully filed," DLC (32). Published in Bassett, 3:207–209 (last paragraph misattributed as McNairy to AJ). The draft was inscribed on pages containing the date and first line of a draft of a letter of August 31 to DeWitt Clinton. For clarity, these lines have been omitted from the transcription.

1. See McNairy to AJ, September 3. John Williams suspected that Ninian Edwards had been sent by the Monroe administration to assist in defeating him. See Williams to Jesse B. Thomas, November 2, IHi; and to Rufus King, November 19, NHi.

2. Matthew 5:9.

3. Nothing more is known of McNairy's previous attempt to reconcile Jackson with Williams. The deceased friend was Joseph Philips (1763–1822), father-in-law of former state representative William Williams and former congressman Jesse Wharton, who had owned a large plantation about six miles north of Nashville along the Dickerson Pike.

4. See above, AJ to Pleasant M. Miller, June 9. No issues of the *Knoxville Gazette* or *Wilson's Knoxville Gazette* for 1814 have been found.

5. Jackson arrived in Knoxville on October 17, 1815, and left on the morning of October 19. Later when Williams took his Senate seat on December 4, Jackson was in Washington conferring with the president and the war department. Some time between December 7 and 11, Jackson suffered a serious infection of his wounded arm and was bedridden, from which he recovered around December 16.

6. For a brief review of Williams's charges about the salt lick reservation in the 1818 Chickasaw treaty, see AJ to Joseph McMinn, September 13, 1819 (*Jackson,* 4:320–21). Jackson also blamed Williams for the implication in the 1819 Lacock committee report that involvement in Pensacola land speculation had influenced Jackson's 1818 Seminole campaign. See AJ to Thomas McCorry, March 8, 1819 (*Jackson,* 4:275–76).

7. In the left margin at this point is the comment, "(ought it not to be left out)." What may be Jackson's reply appears upside down at the bottom of the page: "not be as good here as else where, This is a question no one can decide for you as well as yourself." At the top of the verso are the following lines in Donelson's hand, also crossed out:

"All Philosophers who find
Some favourite system to their mind,
In every point to make it fit
Will force all nature to submit."

8. Williams had married Hugh L. White's sister Malinda (1789–1838); James (1747–1821), the father of Hugh L. and Malinda, had been a brigadier general of East Tennessee militia during the Creek War.

9. Jackson and Andrew Erwin signed an agreement to settle their suit on September 19. McNairy, who witnessed the agreement, had perhaps arbitrated the dispute. The other lawsuit referred to by Jackson has not been identified. Tennessee court records show many suits filed in his name (see, for example, the decisions in *AJ* v. *William Bush,* July 24, 1812, *AJ* v. *William B. Vinson, William P. Anderson, and John Gordon,* January 18, 1813, and *AJ* v. *Alexander Outlaw and Patton Anderson,* August 1814).

With enemies spreading rumors that Jackson's presidential candidacy lacked the full support of Tennessee, the reelection of Senator John Williams, who had been critical of Jackson as the 1818 Chickasaw treaty negotiator and as governor of Florida, could have been a serious blow. Partly to silence eastern reports of weakness, the general's supporters had orchestrated a drumbeat of county meetings to endorse his candidacy in the spring and summer of 1823. Commencing with an April 29 meeting at Nashville, Tennessee papers reported Jackson meetings at Blountville, May 21; Pulaski, May 24; Rogersville, May 28; Carthage, May 29; Lawrenceburg and Maryville, late May or early June; Columbia, June 23; Reynoldsburg, June 28; Lincoln County, Charlotte, Lebanon, and Jacksborough, July 4; Knoxville, July 7; Franklin and Gallatin, July 12; Jackson and Clinton, July 15; Jonesborough, July 19; and Roane County, July 28. Some adopted resolutions that no candidate should be elected who had not pledged to support Jackson's election bid.

Jackson's candidacy in general and the citizens' meetings in particular created a problem for the otherwise popular Williams. On July 23, Thomas H. Benton, who had been travelling around the state for two months, reported to Henry Clay that "Col. Williams will be very hard pressed for the Senate, and cannot possibly be elected unless he gives in *for Jackson" (*Clay Papers, *3:460). Some of Williams's friends attempted to forge a reconciliation, but without success (see above, AJ to Pleasant M. Miller, June 9, and to John McNairy, [September 6]).*

*When the Tennessee legislature convened in Murfreesboro on September 15, Jackson supporters such as Samuel Houston and Thomas Claiborne lobbied actively for Williams's opponents, but Williams, who had pledges from many legislators, the active support of his brother-in-law Hugh L. White, and hope for assistance from John Overton (who had married White's sister), remained confident of victory (see Thomas L. Williams to Overton, September 20, THi; John Williams to Jesse B. Thomas, November 2, IHi; and John Williams to Rufus King, November 19, NHi). On September 18, Felix Grundy, whose relations with Jackson had been strained by Patrick H. Darby's candidacy in opposition to Grundy's reelection to the legislature (see above, AJ to John Coffee, April 15, May 24, and August 15), introduced a resolution that strongly condemned congressional nominations as "a violation of the spirit of the constitution" and instructed Tennessee senators and requested Tennesseee representatives to oppose any congressional caucus nomination for president. While consonant with the Jacksonians' expressed views on the caucus system, the resolution, some warned, could strengthen Williams by making the question of his support of Jackson less directly relevant. The resolution lay on the table until October 2, the day after the senatorial election was decided, when the House passed it unanimously (*Journal of the House of Representatives of the First Session of the Fifteenth General Assembly of the State of Tennessee . . . *[Murfreesborough, 1823], pp. 79–84). The Senate concurred in the resolution on November 15.*

From William Brady and Thomas Williamson

Murfreesboro' 20th September 1823

Sir

It would be gratifying to many of your friends at this place to see you amongst us. There is much commotion here among certain persons about the Senatorial election. Plans and schemes of opperation by foreigners not of the Legislature, to effect the election of their choice. To twhart them, will be our especial care, tho' their *case* is skilfully organized. That *Grundy* is opposed to the best wishes of Tennessee is but too apparent; his manuvering with the enemy alone; their leading orator on the floor of the Legislature—and lately the introducer of a string of reslotion, going to excuse our representatives in Congress from a participation in r[e]commending yourself to the people of the U.S.[1] The direct object of this proceeding could not be misunderstood; most evidently to promote the interest of *Williams,* and draw the attention of the Legislature from an enquiry into the course he would pursue with regard to yourself should he be ultimately elected. As the representatives of the people, as well as in our individual character, we hold ourselves bound to give no vote on this subject, but which shall accord with the unanimous consent heretofore expressed by the people of Tennessee. On this subject we hold it a maxim not to be departed from; that the representative obey the voice of his constituents on all subjects when fully and fairly expressed. Public opinion on no subject has in our opinions ever been so generally acquiesed in as that you are the choice of Tennessee to be our next President. We can answer for our constituents and for our own feelings and wishes on this all important matter. And further Sir we have too long known your high claims upon this republic, to give our support to a man, and place him in the highest station in the gift of Tennessee, who will not readily and openly express her sentiments. Believing as we do that attempts have been made by certain individuals high in trust from Tennessee, to have it whispered at Washington City, that you were not seriously talked of as our next president, requires that we should well weigh the character and conduct of the aspirants now before us, before we surrender out of our hands this great constitutional trust.

We do not expect that you would if here take an active or open part or stand in this election; but we know that your presence would disperse some of the small atoms now floating in our atmostphere to the obstruction of the formation of correct opinions. Much is said that *Williams* is not your enemy, on the contrary your friend—That if difficulties has heretofore existed between *you,* it has recently been removed—and therefore would be your supporter at the city. In matters of election we well know from experience, that a luke warm supporter, will do more mischief than an open enemy—and that you shall ever receive the hearty and open support of this *man* is what we cannot believe

As we have been your companions in arms, we are your supporters here—Accept our hearty wishes for your good health and ultimate success

William Brady
Thomas Williamson

LS with docketting endorsement by AJ, DLC (32). Published in Bassett, 3:209–10. Brady (d. 1835), who had served as adjutant to the First Regiment of Tennessee Volunteer Militia in the Seminole campaign, represented Rutherford County in the Tennessee House. Williamson (1767–1825), who had served as an officer of Tennessee Volunteers in the Creek War, Gulf, and Seminole campaigns, represented Madison and other counties in the Tennessee Senate.

1. Brady and Williamson were apparently referring to Grundy's resolution opposing caucus nominations.

Despite the pressure exerted to force any Tennessee candidate to endorse Jackson, John Williams remained a formidable contender for reelection. At first Jackson hoped that John Rhea could defeat Williams, but when it became clear that neither Rhea nor Pleasant M. Miller could muster the necessary votes, John H. Eaton and William B. Lewis, in Murfreesboro to monitor the election for the Jacksonians, brought the general's name forward (see Lewis to Lewis Cass, July 1844, NN). On being informed of this development, Jackson himself journeyed to Murfreesboro, where legislators were now scrambling to adjust to the new situation. A resolution to postpone the election for two days passed the Senate but failed in the House, and on the evening of October 1, Hawkins County Representative William Young (1777–1826) formally nominated Jackson at the joint session held in the House chambers.

Though he achieved his primary objective by defeating Williams, Jackson worried that his election to the Senate might be perceived as evidence of political ambition, blurring the distinction between the people's candidate and those cabinet officers who were actively intriguing for election. Jackson's exchange with Abram Maury, below, was widely published to demonstrate that the general finally came forward from a sense of duty, not ambition.

From Abram Maury

Murfreesboro.' Sept. 20, 1823.

Dear Genl.

I am particularly requested, by many friends of yours, to enquire if you are willing to serve in the Senate of the United States. The general wish here, is, that you may assent to what your friends earnestly desire, and enter upon a service, which, tho' at war with your individual interest, is yet one, which it is hoped you will not decline. Indeed, looking to the declaration made by you, to the committee of the State of Pennsylvania, "that office should be neither sought for nor declined,"[1] a strong disposition was entertained to venture your name for the proposed appointment, without enquiring of you ought about it; but considering that you are at convenient distance, I have thought proper at the desire of several of the members, to propose it in confidence to you. If you shall consent to let your name be used, it is probable that the three gentlemen, who are at present before the Legislature fo[r] the appointment, will decline; if this however should not be the case, even then although some of the members have become pledged and although the sectional division of East Tennesse[e] rights may somewhat operate,[2] still I feel authorised to say, and entertain no doubt of the fact, that you will be supported by a large majority of the Legislature. All we want, is, a belief that you will permit your name to be used.

I am, with very great respect, your most obt.

ABRAM MAURY.

Printed, Nashville *Constitutional Advocate,* October 18 (mAJs); *Niles' Register,* November 8 (9-0672); and other papers. Maury (1766–1825), the planter father-in-law of Jackson's biographer and former aide John Reid, represented Williamson County in the Tennessee House of Representatives.

1. See above, AJ to H. W. Peterson, February 23.

2. Tradition dictated that Tennessee's senators be divided between East and West Tennessee. As John H. Eaton resided in West Tennessee, the three candidates for the other Senate seat were all East Tennesseans.

To Abram Maury

Hermitage, 21st *Sept.* 1823.

Dear Sir,

Your letter of yesterday has reached me, stating it to be the desire of many members of the Legislature that my name may be proposed for the appointment of Senator to Congress.[1] It is very true, as you remark, that I have not only said, but have, I believe, through lif[e,] acted upon the principle, that office in a Republican Government, like ours, should not be solicited, nor yet when conferred, declined; [s]till I would suggest to my friends, whether they ought not to excuse me from accepting the appointment they have proposed. There are many better qualified to meet the fatigues of journey than myself, and on whose services, a reliance for a time to come, with a prospect of becoming better as they advance, might be safely reposed; whereas from health impaired, and advancing age, neither the one nor the other could be calculated on from me; and besides, it might be thought—nay would be said, that my state had conferred it upon me, and that it ha[d] been sought for too by me, with a view to other objects, and for other purposes which are at present pending before the nation. I have therefore earnestly to request of my friends, an[d] beg of you, not to press me to an acceptance of the appointment. If appointed, I could not decline; and yet in accepting, I should do great violence to my wishes, and to my fee[l]ings. The length of time I have pa[s]sed in public service, authorises m[e] to make this request, which with m[y] friends, I trust, will be considere[d] reasonable and proper. With great regard, I am, very repectfully, Yours,

ANDREW JACKSON.

Printed, Nashville *Constitutional Advocate,* October 18 (mAJs); *Knoxville Register,* October 24 (9-0673); and other papers.

1. See above.

To William Brady and Thomas Williamson

Septbr. 27 1823.

Your letter of the 20th inst did not reach me until late this evening; I am therefore the more hastened to give you a reply.[1]

My Political view as stated in my answer to the Com of Pansylvania, upon which I have acted thro life, and from which I would not now deviate, does not under present circumstances sanction the pleasure which a visit to my friends at Murfreesborough would afford me.[2] At this period it would be called an overture of self interest, and would be used as a handle by my enemies abroad—it would, Gentlemen, be said that I came for electioneering purposes—<at> unwilling, therefore to favor the malice of party, at a proper time I will visit the Legislature & pay my respects to my friends in whom I have every confidence.

I am aware of the plans of——[3] not of the Legislature, and schemers of the opposition with Mr G as their head & spokesman; <but> And I admire your independent course, it is that of freemen determined to carry into effect the will of <the> a majority of the people when that will has been emphatically expressed, and displays a proper disgust for those who attempt to interfere with your constitutional duties. Personality far from my view, has not this state expressed its attachment to the administration of Mr Monroe, and will its representatives acknowledge the uniform declaration of the people, by electing a man who has been the open & avowed enemy of that administration, who has united with the Radicals to prostrate <Monroe's> its popularity and elevate Crawford upon <h> its ruins? I answer no. In their county meetings the people have been impelled by a regard for principle, and they will spurn the election of the man false to that principle, false to their feelings & wishes, and false to the construction of the general good. There is but one mode by which the Legislature can comply with their instructions, and that is, by a resolution calling upon the candidates for their declaration at the bar of the house—If Col W can make the required one, I would not believe him, tho' it may be an excuse for those who choose to vote for him.

As to the remark "much is said that Williams is not your enemy"—This can only be since <his friends> he finds it necessary to obtain his election. To prove this it is only necessary to take up the report of the comittee of the senate of the US upon the Seminole question.[4] His enmity to me there fully appears, and his conduct in endeavoring to impress upon the members of Congress that I had no standing in my own state, which circumstance gave rise to the County meetings, still more evinces it. I parted with him at Fort Jackson, friendly—I have never seen him since; and be assured let him profess what he may, I have no confidence in that profession.

Could not a union of interest elect Mr Rhea—*He is faithfull—he is honest.* This would leave the two belligerent candidates to fight out their quarrels leisurely at home—it would too, I think meet the full approbation of the state under existing circumstances resptfully

A. J.

LS draft, DLC (32). The body of the letter is in Andrew J. Donelson's hand; the dateline, the complimentary close, and the signature are in AJ's hand.

1. See above.
2. See above, AJ to H. W. Peterson, February 23.
3. Inserted here in another unidentified hand are the words, "Your foreigners."
4. See *ASP, Military Affairs,* 1:739–54.

To [John Caldwell Calhoun?]

Hermitage 4th day of October 1823—

Dear Sir,

<I have had the pleasure by due course of mail to receive yours of the 8th ulto> I received by due course of mail your's of the 8th ulto, and permit me to express the pleasure which I feel on finding an accordance of opinion & sentiment upon <those great political> the general principles spoken of[1]—no one can be insensible to the favorable opinion of the people when obtained by the pursuit of <an> independent, virtuous conduct. The popularity which is eye single to the public good, has for its basis the best moral qualities of human nature; is grateful to the possessor, and is durable beyond the fortuitous history of <factions and> intrigues. Intrigue may assail it, and may even prosper for a time, but <when unmasked will fall prostrate before an indignant people> its own career unmasks its ugly [face] and it cannot but fall prostrate before the indignation of the people who have been abused & trampled upon. <Thus> in this state the voice of a large majority, it was believed from the East to

the West had been declared; yet an intrigue as secret as it was systematic & corrupt had <addressed> answered with such art this voice of the state, as almost to have drawn from it the election of Col Williams—to counteract which, and the idea <abroad> that <had> would hence have gone abroad, viz. that Crawfords popularity was resuscitating here; I <have thought> felt it my duty to <the> yield to the wishes of my friends, and have accepted the appointment in the midst of the inauspicious circumstances under which it <was made> will go to the <public> world. I have been elected by a majority of ten votes, <35–25> in opposition to all the crawford interest, aided by the secret pledges <of> obtained by Williams as the supporter & advocate of my election to the Presidency.[2] These pledges were obtained, before it was understood that my name would be taken up, and under the idea no doubt that no circumstance could force me from my Hermitage. <My name> <But> Until after it was found that neither Mr Miller or Mr Rhea (4 days before the election) could succeed, especially as Mr Williams professed the same feelings as to Presidency & Policy—my friends did not announce my name, it was then done without any consultation with me, and indeed in opposition to my expressed feelings & wishes. With the pledges that had been give to Mr Williams <by> as the preferable candidate to Miller or Rhea by many of the deluded members of the Legislature, and fully aware of the principle which I had declared to the committee from Pensylvania, my friends took me up, and elected me 35 for 25 against me[2]

Thus you see me a Senator contrary to my wishes, my feelings & my interests, to gratify the state in prostrating Crawfordism & the intrigues—

It has been confidently affirmed to me that Senator Benton passed several weeks in our state aiding the election of certain candidates for our Assembly from whom he had obtained secret pledges for Williams if elected—this was never suspected until after the Legislature met; and its developement with much other corruption was one reason among others given me by my friends for hazarding my name at so late a period, in the midst of pledges, <to> and so contrary to my wishes & feelings; this measure it was believed will give the united efforts of the state against a Caucus system—As to pelf they knew that I would not be seated in the Presidential chair except by the free & unbiassed voice of the People

I heartily rejoice to find that you perfectly coincide with me on this subject, and let things ultimate as they may, I am confident those good & friendly feelings that have always existed between us, cannot in the least be interrupted: on my part I am sure, they will not, nay, cannot, for I know your honorable course, and nothing can lead to a departure from it—

My young friend Genl H is elected to Congress for his enmity to Col W. He has had some unfriendly feeling towards you, but from several conversations I have had with him, I find he has no wish to cherish them. My sincere desire is that you & the Genl may meet as friends, and when you know each other you will continue so—[3]

Thus in this state the Crawfordites are prostrated, and I trust will become so in every state of the union:

Draft in Andrew J. Donelson's hand, DLC (72).

1. Letter not found.

2. John Williams himself estimated that at least forty of the sixty legislators had supported his candidacy previous to Jackson's entry into the race (see Williams to Jesse B. Thomas, November 2, IHi).

3. Samuel Houston had been upset by Calhoun's treatment of him when he had accompanied a Cherokee delegation to Washington in the winter of 1817–18. Those feelings were exacerbated by Houston's later difficulties with the war department about his accounts, which caused Houston to accuse Calhoun of inflicting "unprovoked injuries," "personal bad treatment," and "official injustice" (see Houston to Calhoun, July 6, 1822, in *Writings of Sam Houston,* 1:12).

To John Coffee

Hermitage Octbr. 5th. 1823

Dear General

I recd your letter of the 26th. ult; advising me of your having recd. mine of the 12th. & in pursuance of my request, that you have recd from Mr [Robert] Black the ten pieces of Scotch Bagging as pr my order recd by direction of Doctor J. R. Bedford, a bill of which you have inclosed amounting in all to 611 yds.[1]

I hope it will be in the power of Mr Black to have it sent into Nashville shortly, if not please to advise me.

It will, I have no doubt have astonishd you to hear that I have been elected Senator, but I can assure you it has astonished me as *much* and a circumstance which I regret more than any other of my life, on several accounts—not having anticipated such an event I am unprepared to leave home—and my feelings & wishes all conspired to remain at home—but it was thought expedient by my friends that my name should be brought out—the vote stood 35 for, 25 against me—every intrigue that could exist, & indeed corruption was resorted to—my name was brought forward 4 days before the election, & this after all the pledges by Williams friends could be obtained in his favour against Mr Rhea & Miller, & after it was found neither could be elected—bringing my name forward under such circumstances was hazarding much, still it succeeded—& I am a senator against my wishes & feelings—but from my political creed as promulgated to the committee of Pensylvania I am compelled to accept.[2] My friends sent for me three times—the last messenger was general [Blackman] Coleman with whom I went & reached there in the night preceding the election, but I neither Vissitted or conversed with a member except when Vissited & the conversation introduced by them They whole Crawford interest was there convened from every quarter of the state with Colo. Cannon &c &c &c at their head—many members voted against me who openly declared, they would have voted for me before they became Pledged by promise to Colo Williams, poor [Robert] Getun was threatened to be burned in efigy—[Robert] Weakly also—but I prevailed upon the leading charectors to put a stop to it.[3]

How cruel it was for Colo. Williams finding his friends thus situated, & a vote for him contrary to the<ir> instructions of their constituents would politically prostrate them, that he did not like Mr Rhea withdraw, how much more magnanimity would have been shewn by him, to have withdrawn than to urge his friends to prostrate their own political standing to elevate his—now his & theirs are all prostrated—present me to Mr James Jackson & family, inform him I will write him shortly.

Mrs. Severn Donelsons family has been very sick are recovering, all the rest of our friends are well—Mrs. J. Joins me in good wishes to you Mrs. C. & family with our prayers for Mrs. C. safe delivery[4] & believe me your friend

Andrew Jackson

P.S. Parsons is getting out my cotton pretty well, but have been much hindred by getting my Gin house, gin, & press compleat, my gin is ready, & press, except the digging the pitt. & the leaver to put on—I think my Cotton will produce an average of at least 8.00 to the acre—it is whispered that Capt Jack & Eliza is to be maried shortly[5] A. J

ALS, THi (9-0680). Published in Bassett, 3:210–11 (extract).

1. See AJ to Coffee, September 12. Coffee's letter and the bill have not been found, but AJ's account with Bedford & Mackey, January 30, 1824, gives an invoice of the bagging shipment. Black was a Florence, Alabama, merchant.

2. See above, AJ to H. W. Peterson, February 23.

3. Coleman (d. 1840), who served as a captain in Coffee's cavalry during the Creek War, was Rutherford County Court clerk, 1813–24, before moving to Haywood County where he was chosen as a Jackson elector in 1832. For his account of Jackson's election, see Coleman to Coffee, October 24, A-Ar (extract in Bassett, 3:210). Jetton (1781–1840), who had served under Jackson in the Creek War and Seminole campaigns, represented Rutherford County in the Tennessee Senate, and Weakley (1764–1845), a former congressman, was speaker of the Senate, where he represented Davidson, Dickson, and Williamson counties. Weakley ran a poor third in his campaign for reelection in 1825, a result that Jackson's supporters attributed to his vote for Williams. Jetton was also defeated in 1825.

4. Coffee's daughter Rachel Jackson (1823–92) was born on November 3.

5. John Donelson (1787–1840) and Eliza Eleanor Butler married on November 6.

To James Monroe

Hermitage Octbr 10th. 1823

Dear Sir

The first intimation I have had of the late act of Congress, was derived from the extract of a letter from Judge Brakenridge from Pensacola of date 12th of Septbr 1823, & herewith inclosed.[1]

If the claims are for cattle taken or used by my army either in 1814, or 1818, they are groundless & fraudulent, which is easily to be established by proof—They are such as ought not to be admitted or paid without an opportunity on behalf of the united states to be heard. They accounts admitted by the Department produced by the cherokees, & incorporated into the cherokee Treaty which has been shewn to have originated in fraud certainly ought to have put congress on its guard, and have prevented such a law as alluded to by Judge Brakenridge from having been passed.[2] If the claims are dated in 1814, it will be easy to shew, that the cattle seized by my Troops were trailed from allabama, to the Perdido & there overtaken, all of which were claimed by our citizens, as stolen from them by the Indians at the instigation of the spaniards, Antwine Collins then spanish contractor, & Capt [Thomas H.] Boyles were seized on suspicion & held in custody, untill I marched on Pensacola and found the cattle by Colo. [Robert] Henry Dyer with a detachment as before stated—a few of these cattle were slaughtered on our return march their marks & brands preserved, and the <quartermaster> contractor ordered to pay the Individuals for the Cattle Thus slaughtered & for which he recd abstracts for Issues <ordered to pay for out of the contractors funds for [B . . . & reserve] rations for the [. . .]>. This was reported to me to have been done & the Ballance by orders to the quartermaster delivered to the <american citizens> owners <by orders to the quartermaster> who attended, & proved their property in the Cattle.[3] On my march in 1818 from Ft Gadsden to Pensacola, on the East Bank of the Escambia, two spaniards who was met at the head of the Bay by that name collected us a few cattle, which was slaughtered by orders to the quartermaster, & paid for[4]—On the East side of the Escambia, we were met with supplies, & Colo. George Gibson Joined me, who can vouch for the payment of every particle of supplies obtained whilst in Florida. It is passing strange that where claims are exhibitted by our own citizens with what Just scrutiny they are investigated, but when exhibitted by *Indians,* or *spaniards,* admitted without an opportunity of investigation by those concerned, & the united states thereby defrauded out of thousands. The object of this hasty letter is to request that you notify the secratary of the Treasury, of the frauds upon which these accounts are founded, that they may be suspended untill a full inquiry shall be had into the Justness of these claims. I am determined that an inquiry shall be had—I bestowed much Labour to investigate the <flagrant> frauds committed by the cherokees in the accounts incorporated in the Treaty, had them forwarded with a request that the Testimony should be laid before congress, without avail.[5] Colo. Gibson is in the city Colo. Gadsdens Testimony with Captn. <Butler> King, Williamson [George] Elliott Dyer, Brady & [William] Mitchell with many others can be procured, I enclose a certificate of Colo. Robert Butler.[6] I am Sir with great respect yr Mo. obdt. Servt.

Andrew Jackson

ALS draft, DLC (32). Published in Bassett, 3:211–12.

1. Letter not found. The act of March 3 (3 *U.S. Statutes at Large* 768) provided for adjudication of claims arising under the ninth article of the Adams-Onís Treaty.

2. Jackson had vehemently objected to Cherokee damage claims under article 5 of the Cherokee treaty of March 22, 1816 (see AJ to William H. Crawford, June 16, 1816, and to Isaac Thomas, July 24, 1816, *Jackson*, 4:45–47, 53–55).

3. Antoine Collins (b. c1788), a Pensacola rancher, gave information about British strength in August 1814. Boyles (d. 1821), who lived north of Pensacola, served as an American spy. In 1816 Congress voted to compensate Boyles for his services and damages incurred as a result, including cattle seized when he was arrested by the British (see File 3181, Settled Accounts and Claims, Records of the Third Auditor, DNA-RG 217). Dyer (c1744–1826), of Rutherford County, commanded Tennessee volunteers in both the Creek War and Seminole campaigns. Orders not found.

4. Orders not found, but see Robert Butler to John Maul, June 3, 1818, DNA-RG 98, ordering the settlement of all outstanding claims contracted by the quartermaster department under Jackson's command.

5. See AJ to Crawford, November 12, 1816.

6. All the cited individuals served as officers in the Seminole campaign. Elliott (c1781–1861), of Sumner County, and Mitchell were the lieutenant colonels of the two Tennessee volunteer regiments. Butler's certificate has not been found.

To George Washington Martin

Copy. Hermitage Oct 15th. 1823

Dr. Major

When last at Nashville I had a hope to have seen you, but you not having returned from East Tennessee was disappointed—The unexpected and I may say the unwished for election as senator to Congress has damaged all my business, I was looking only to the active means that would meet my expenses to the close of the present year, this would have been but small & which I had in hand—The expense of my visiting Murfreesborough, at the election at once consumed this, but has left me without a cent—the preparation for my journey will add greatly to my wants of money, and I am compelled to look to your house for the means of outfit and travelling expenses—This call being unexpected I am afraid will put you to inconvenience which I would gladly have prevented if I could. But I have no other source; from which at present I can obtain the necessary means; but from you—I believe I gave you the amount of the cotton delivered you, but least I have not I send you the amount—you have rec'd from me as guardian of A. J. Hutching

10854 lb. in 27 Bales at ten cents pr lb.	$1085.40
My own—11233 lb. in 28 Bales at D. D.	1123.30
	$2208.70
Of this sum I have rec'd as per memorandum about $1800.	2208.70
	1800
	$408.70

—There will be a ballance of current notes about this sum.

In U. states notes borrowed as per note 13th of March 1823—$400.[1]

The object of this note is to apprise you of my situation & wants that you may inform me how far you will be able to advance to my necessity—I have to go to Murfreesborough & have not one dollar, indeed when last in town I had to apply to your Mr [Willoughby] Williams for ten dollars[2]—I shall be down on tomorrow if the weather is good or on saturday when I shall see you on this subject—

I hope you have been successfull in your suits—I heard you were about compromising, which I recommended to your brother strongly whenever the tennants show a disposition.[3]

Thirty thousand dollars at a short day would be more profitable to you than $60,000 at a distant day. I therefore recommended to him to compromise as soon as liberal terms was proposed to him. I am with great respect your friend

(signed) Andrew Jackson

Photocopy of Copy, MsSM (9-0699). Published in Bassett, 3:212–13.

1. Jackson enclosed the note (not found) to Martin, October 30, below.

2. Williams (1798–1882), Martin's cousin, had associated with him in the mercantile firm of Martin, Williams & Co. The purpose of Jackson's trip to Murfreesboro has not been established.

3. The Martins had won initial judgements in Bledsoe and Anderson county suits against those claiming land through Richard G. Waterhouse. Martin wrote his brother James G. on October 15 regarding compromise (THi), but the Martins eventually lost on appeal.

From Richard Gilliam Dunlap

Knoxville Tennessee
Octr. 16th. 1823

Dear Sir

The object of this letter is to ascertain, at what time you will be at this place, on your way to Washington—Your *friends* are anxious to know the time, and I hope you will give them the satisfaction, so that they may be ready to see you.[1] The election for senator produced a momentary agitation, with some of the *elect,* who believed that they were only to be saved, by the wisdom, goodness and power of the fallen Colonel[2]—But the change of Masters has satisfied them, that if they can be saved, it will be by placing their faith on another Saviour—their faith has received a schock, and time only will prove the result—The union of parties to thee, is the most probable. Your friend

R. G. Dunlap

ALS, DLC (32). Dunlap (c1795–1841), a Knoxville lawyer, had captained a company of Tennessee volunteers in the Seminole campaign. He later served as minister to the United States from Texas.

1. Citizens of Knoxville hosted a public dinner in Jackson's honor on November 17.

2. John Williams.

On September 19, following a trip by Jackson to attend Andrew Erwin's taking of depositions in the neighborhood of the Old Stone Fort in Franklin County, Jackson and Erwin suddenly agreed to a settlement of Jackson's long-standing lawsuit against Erwin. The exact impetus to agreement was disputed in the 1828 presidential campaign, with Jackson's partisans claiming that a tearful plea by Erwin's wife had moved the general to soften a previous offer by foregoing any personal profit, while Erwin denied his wife's involvement and claimed that Jackson had initiated the settlement. In any case, whether Jackson was moved by a woman's tears, whether he doubted his lawyers' assurances of ultimate success, or whether he simply wished to conclude an irritating and potentially embarrassing legal dispute before the impending presidential campaign, Jackson clearly decided to relinquish the possibility of a speculative profit in order to obtain a settlement.

According to the agreement, Jackson and his partner James Jackson were to give deeds of release to those claiming land under Erwin and to pay their own court costs. In return Erwin agreed to clear title for those who had purchased from the general by giving a quitclaim for the 10,000 acres originally awarded to Jackson in 1802 and settling two lawsuits involving tracts Jackson sold later. In addition, Erwin was to pay $10,000 to James Jackson as consideration for the Jacksons' abandonment of their claim.

Although he gained little, Jackson expressed only relief and pleasure at the settlement. James Jackson and Patrick H. Darby, however, were less satisfied, and Darby would later claim that the general had entered into a "combination" with Darby's enemies requiring that Darby be "sacrificed in character and fortune" to secure the support of Felix Grundy for Jackson's Senate bid (Darby to James G. Dana, December 26, 1827, in Trenton True American, *January 19, 1828). Tensions about the settlement and disputes about the payment of court costs helped to erode the close relationship between the two Jacksons and perhaps contributed to the political break that occurred in 1824.*

From James Jackson

Florence October 21st. 1823

Dear Genl.

I this day received your favour of the 17th. Inst. & Note it's contents.[1] I must beg your refering to my letter of 19th. Inst. on the subject of the compromise[2]—In my letter to Mr. Darby of the same date, after explaining every thing to him so far as my recollection enabled me, enclosed him a Note to Judge McNairy, requesting that Mr. D should have the examination of the articles of agreement with Erwin, & told Mr. D. that He should have one half of what was coming to me on the compromise, after paying my half of the Note to Whiteside & my part of the Costs, or If He did not like that—I was willing to get clear of the compromise If to be done on *honourable terms.*[3] I will write again to Mr. Darby to day enclosing the paper you sent me & refering him to you for further information. This acceptance of the terms of compromise are not agreeable to the Articles in as much as the acceptance & promise to pay, provides for paying in current Bank Notes, which in my opinion would If we thout proper rel[e]ase us from that engagement—*obligations payable in Current Bank Notes I would not receive,* even If we wish to confirm the Compromise. This no doubt would not be a stumbeling block with them.[4] If we do not choose to avail ourselves of it My wish is to satisfy Mr. Darby. I feel mortified to think that the Article which secured his interest was in my possession & that I should have failed, from forgetfullness, to consult him before compromising & indeed to leave him entirely out of view. I have however in my opinion done towards him every thing that could be reasonably expected to attone for that neglect—You seem to apprehend that I was not entirely satisfied with the compromise when we made it. I must confess I felt some reluctance in leting such a man as Erwin off so easily, after his having made use of every foul means, not only to defend himself but injure you & every person who was interested with you, but on the other hand, I was gratified at releasing you from a business disagreeable in the extreme & in persuit of property which your situation in life did not leave you in want of. I also felt Relieved on my own account. The Idea of being involved in Law for many years, even in persuit of a large property, was an unpleasant feeling, whether It would have been better or wors for my Children, I have not foresight enough to determin; I was however perfectly satisfied so far as regards myself & my interest. Tho the Costs on our part are so large we should have compeled the adverse party to pay them. However as matters now stands I'll be perfectly satisfied with any thing you & Mr. Darby may think best with this reservation, that obligations for current Bank Notes are not to be taken, the money *must be,* really *money &* I must be perfectly satisfied that the persons who gives the Notes ar perfectly good; this is the conditions of the Compromise. I expect those persons whoes names I have are good, but my knowledge of them at present would not enable me to determin nor would It be necessary before the first week of the Court in January—

Altho I should regret much to have heard of John Williams being elected to Congress, I still regret more the necessity your friends put you under of becomeing a senator in Congress, what effect it may have on wishes as regards you in an other respect, time alone will determin, had you been permitted to remain at home, your personal comfort would have been much greater & your feelings on an other subject would have been beyond the r[e]ach of Malice—I shewed your letter to Genl. Coffee—He has not yet increased his family—all friends are well with my best wishes to Mrs. Jackson believe me sincerely yours

James Jackson

ALS, DLC (32). Endorsed by AJ as answered on October 25; answer not found.

1. Not found.

2. See James Jackson to AJ, October 19.

3. The agreement of September 19 provided that Erwin execute $10,000 in bonds to James Jackson. James argued that the agreement of AJ, Jenkin Whiteside, and James Jackson with Patrick H. Darby, April 13, 1821, gave Darby a quarter interest in the settlement, but Andrew contended that Darby's interest applied only to the Allison lands not involved in his suit with Erwin. See also the memorandum of AJ to James Jackson, October 23, 1823, and John C. McLemore to AJ, January 13, 1824.

4. The Jacksons' agreement with Erwin provided that the settlement would be voided if Erwin and his fellow defendants refused to "accede" to the $10,000 payment. James Jackson apparently objected here to the terms of Erwin's accession, which has not been found.

To John Coffee

Hermitage October 24th. 1823

Dear General

I have duly received your letter of the 19th instant, on my return from Murfreesborough on yesterday; for your kind attention to my business in transmitting the Cotton Bagging which is recd in good order, receive my thanks.[1]

Your views of my election to the senate, without my approbation or consent are certainly correct, and leaves me no alternative but to obay the will of the majority—I will set out on the 9th. 10th. or 11th proximo—I leave home with more reluctance than on any former occasion, the notice being so short, & not having anticipated any thing of the kind, puts it out of my power to take Mrs. Jackson with me, & to leave her, for four, or five months, fills me, as well as her, with much regret—I had hoped that I had filled my measure of public service, & would have been permitted to have spent some time in retirement—in this I am disappointed—to become conspicuous as a public man, is inconsistant with private ease, or happiness, at least it has this effect with me.

With what feelings of gratitude do I read that generous & friendly offer you have made of a supply of horses to me, had I have been taking on Mrs. J. I should have accepted your friendly & kind offer, but as I mean to travel part of the way in the stage, I shall take such horses as I intend selling for what they will bring, at the point where I may take the stage, but next summer if your grays will work & you can spare them, I will give you a liberal price for them, to carry on Mrs Jackson—Mr William Donelson has long since parted with his gray—My Dear Genl—this liberal & friendly offer will be long cherished with gratitude by me.

When I was in Florence Major [David] Hubbard named to me that he had got into his hands Nicholson note for a horse $90—I told him as soon as any mony of mine could be collected it should be paid, your calling on Capt Garner is right, and take in the note when due, and place it to my Credit with the Estate of my little ward Hutchings[2]

My unexpected Journey, will make it imperious to call on my friends Antony Winston, & Mr Griffin, & the ballance from Garner by the first day of January next will you please if convenient notify them that about christmas & Newyear I have made some engagements, to return some mony I have borrowed for expence of my Journey, the current notes due will be wanted about that time, & I will direct Capt A. J. Donelson to go out for it, should you advise him that it will be paid at that time.[3]

I have made an engagement <of> with Mr William Eastons for his three mules for A. J. Hutchings farm, you are to place the price on them, & give him a receipt for the amount, which will be good against his note—he is to deliver them as soon as they can be spared from his farm. I sincerely regret to hear that you have been indisposed, but rejoice to learn that your health is restored. I am pleased with your prospect of a crop of cotton, 800 is a good average crop & the price promises to be good this season & the fall very fine—my negroes has been un[u]sually sickly this fall, this with my buildings, Gin house, press &c &c, has impeded parsons in getting out his crop—he has housed about 50,000 lb. he thinks my crop will average from 800 to 1000 to the acre—& make about 80 Bales he started the gin on yesterday, she runs well but I think too fast, he thinks not—I give way to his Judgt, she is completely fixed, and makes good cotton—the flue 8 feet long

Will you & your family be in this fall¿ how much pleasure it will give Mrs Jackson to see you, Polly & your sweet little family this fall—we rejoice at the good health of your family, may it continue, & every blessing in life attend you & them is our sincere prayers. we hope to hear of the safe delivery of Polly, and that she has added a fine son or daughter to your lovely family.

Capt Jack is not yet maried, it is expected as soon as he returns, & Judge McNairy gets home from Knoxville.

On my return from Murfreesborough in the night I was taken with a palpitation of heart with great fluttering, I ro*[de]* home about 23 miles, it continued with an occasional bli[n]dness—I took on wednesday night a dose of salts, it continuing I had one quart of blood taken, it has measurably subsided, in other respects perfect health except a slight pain in my side & breast.

I shall write you again before I leave home, & whilst at the city will be glad to hear from you when leisure will permit, I shall write you occasionally—Present us affectionately to Polly & the sweet children & for yourself receive our best wishes, your friend

Andrew Jackson

P.S. Mr F Sanders having proposed to sell & I fearf*[ull]* of a bad neighbour I have bought & paid hi*[m]* for his plantation, I have transferred him [Richard C.] Cross Bonds & Thomas childress—I am now out of danger of being interrupted by a bad neighbour—& makes my situation here quite comfortable as it respects land[4]—will my 320 near the big spring sell for $12 pr acre in land office mony—Colo. McDaniel wanted it very much—suppose you sound Colo Antony Winston on the subject, I have promised to let him have the refusal—you can say to him I have bought here, & am now inclined to sell there—If he will give $12 pr acre in silver or u states notes let him have it[5]—I am looking forward to prepare for the expence of next year & to purchase Hutchings forfeighted lands—I wish you to ship his cotton to Doctor Bedford & direct the Doctor to transmit the amount of sales to you with the amt of the sales of your own—I shall if I can purchase the quarter northeast of the we*[ll]* the 2 forfeited quarters & it is agreed between *[m]*e and Capt Jack Donelson to split the 2 quarte*[rs so]*uth, east & west this will make him a fin*[e tr]*act, this done & I am satisfied as it respects *[my]* little ward—I have some hope of settling the suit with B Smith[6]—your friend A Jackson

ALS, THi (9-0709). Published in Bassett, 3:213–15.

1. See Coffee to AJ, October 19.

2. Hubbard (1792–1874), Samuel Houston's cousin, was a lawyer in Florence, Alabama, at this time. He held the note as agent for Samuel P. Black of Murfreesboro. Coffee's neighbor Garner, possibly Lewis who was appointed a captain of the Sixteenth Regiment of Alabama militia in 1818, owed Jackson $320 for a stud horse.

3. In August Jackson had left with Coffee two of Anthony Winston's notes, for $337 in United States money and for $454.25 in Tennessee bank notes, received as part of Winston's purchase of half of Jackson's Big Spring plantation, and William Griffin's note for the purchase of George, a slave (see Memorandum book of accounts, September 1822–August 31, 1825).

4. In October 1824 Francis Saunders transferred 348¼ acres purchased by Jackson to Andrew J. Donelson. The property, a wedding gift to Donelson and his wife Emily Tennessee Donelson (1807–36), became part of Donelson's Poplar Grove (now Tulip Grove) plantation (see Deed of partition between AJ and Andrew J. Donelson, October 11, 1824; and John Donelson to Coffee, August 15, 1825, Coffee Papers, THi). Cross had given three notes totaling $7,500 for the purchase of Jackson's Lauderdale County plantation in 1821 and still owed $5,000 in 1823. Before Cross's death on June 16, his attorney gave Childress $623 to be applied against the outstanding debt (see Bolling Gordon to AJ, June 1, and AJ to Gordon, June 12). If Jackson was referring to a debt in Childress's own name and not to some connection with the Cross notes, the debt has not been identified.

5. McDaniel has not been identified. Jackson apparently sold the remainder of his Big Spring plantation to Winston, who later asserted that he had purchased all of Jackson's land at Big Spring for $6,976 (see Huntsville, Alabama, *Southern Advocate,* June 6, 1828).

6. In accordance with the land relief act of 1821, Jackson had relinquished from Andrew J. Hutchings's Lauderdale County plantation, the southwest and southeast quarters of section 15, township 3, range 12 west; the land was not reacquired until 1830. Jackson reached a settlement with Bennett Smith in 1824 (see AJ to Coffee, September 23, 1824, below).

To George Walton

Hermitage October 28th. 1823

My Dear Col.

Your letter of 24th ult is before me, and I take great pleasure in acknowledging its recipt—Your remarks respecting the succession to Mr

Duval had been anticipated, and were, some time since, substantially presented to Mr Monroe, with such considerations as were in my power in favor of your claims. No doubt much *sinister manoevure* has been used; but opposed to the evidences of integrity & talent furnished by your past services, I trust that the President will not give the victory to inferior pretensions—[1]

The favorable location of the Indians was necessary to the establishment of Harmony between the two sections of your Territory[2]—If this be secured, the channels to improved government, agriculture & commerce are unobstructed, and Florida, flourishing & powerful, will yet prove how necessary she was to the best interests of the Union, especially to its military protection.

You are aware of my appointment to the senate of the US by the legislature of this state; a measure adopted without my approbation. I accepted the appointment, because of the general obligation which binds every citizen to the service of his country. For, certainly, he who enjoys the blessings of our free and happy institutions should not shrink from the responsibilities of such service; when the citizens of other forms, aristocratic, & even despotic, <hold> recognise the principle, accounting it the sacred tie between the government & the governed—The only question with me, after my name had been put in nomination, was, whether from my age & the impaired state of my health, there were not others better qualified for the station. These considerations however, not prevailing with the Legislature, I am elected, and I commit myself to the same Providence that has directed my past destinies—

I should write you more in detail, but that I am much hastened with business, intending to leave this for Washington on the 10th proximo—Mrs Jackson unites with me in best wishes to your aged mother & to Mrs Walton—We also beg to be presented to Mr Overton—yr. sincere friend

Andrew Jackson

LS in Andrew J. Donelson's hand, FU (9-0718). Published in *FHQ*, 34(1955):28–29.

1. See AJ to James Monroe, September 25. Walton's letter has not been found. The anticipated resignation of Florida Governor William P. Duval did not occur at this time.

2. Jackson was referring to the treaty of September 18 with Florida Indians.

From James Jackson

Forks of Cypress October 28th. 1823

Dear Genl.

I this day recd. your favours of 23rd. 24th. & 25th. Inst. & duely note their contents.[1] enclosed you will receive a copy of the agreement made with Mr. Darby by yourself, Jenkin Whiteside and myself—which appears clearly to me to vest Mr Darby with one fourth of the entire interest of the Lands for which we are contending with Erwin and others, my recollection is not good enough to depend on, but It was my impression that such was the intention of our agreement.[2] I have never seen any of the papers you alude to, viz the compromise with overton & Wharton & the conveyance of all your interest in Allisons Estate, except the Norton Pryor Lands, nor do I recollect hearing of any more being said on that subject than your having made a conveyance of the remainder of Allisons Estate to me for the benefit of Darby Genl. Coffee & myself & also making some reservation for the security of Mr. McLemore & that those papers were left with Mr. Darby in order to be recorded[3]—why Mr. Darby wrote me on the subject of the compromise with Erwin & not to you also, He alone can give the reason. I know of none, It would at first view appear strange that Mr. Whiteside should have signed the agreement with us after conveying to us his interest in the Lands claimed by Erwin & others under Norton Pryor, but still it is not inconsistant for him to have done so, for the agreement only binds him as far as his interest—It really seems to me that we acted strangely to have signed the agreement giving Mr. Darby one fourth the Estate of David Allison decd. in the state of Tennessee, reserving only that which was claimed by individuals under yourself, If we had not intended at the time to convey him one fourth of our entire interest. I do not recollect having any conversation with Mr. Darby since that agreement was entered into, with regard to his precise & particular interest—when you examine the agreement will be glad to hear from you, you are a much better Judge of such papers than I am & by compareing those deeds you speak of with the agreement, It will probably shew exactly how matters stand & If Mr. Darby is not entitled to one fourth part. I can assure you I am not disposed to give money away for nothing, however as you say, there is no occation for any unpleasant feelings on the subject It is only necessary to ascertain what is right & let that be done, As regards myself I have no wish to evade the compromise If Erwin fully complys with his part of it, I have no great rellish for a long Law suit, and If it is to be continued I have no objection to come to any explicit understandings that may be necessary—I presume you will have conversed with Mr. Darby on this subject ere this reaches you & you will discover from my last letter that I had written to him,[4] therefore precludes the necesity of my attending to the request in one of your letters to do so—I am extremely sorry to hear of your indisposition It is a kind of complaint I never before heared you complain of & hope you have got entirely clear of it—I will set out for Cahaba on 8th. of next month & expect to be home at furtherst in the first week in January,[5] will get to Nashville on the first week of the Court to attend to your Power of Atty. authorising me to close the suit with Erwin,[6] It shall be strictly attended to & I can assure you both on your account and my own would be pleased to see an end put to it—I set out for Limestone in the morning & expect to get back on saturday or sunday next—all well Mrs. Jackson joins me in best wishes to you & Mrs. Jackson. believe me sincerely yours

James Jackson

ALS, DLC (32). Endorsed by AJ as answered November 1; answer not found.

1. Letters not found, but Jackson endorsed the substance of his October 23 letter on James Jackson to AJ, October 19.

2. See Agreement, April 13, 1821.

3. For discussion of the compromise, see above, AJ to John C. McLemore, April 11, 1822. For Jackson's conveyance of his interest in the Allison estate, see deeds to John Overton, April 19, and to James Jackson, April 20, both 1822.

4. See above, James Jackson to AJ, October 21.

5. James Jackson had been elected as a Lauderdale County representative to the Alabama House, which convened at Cahaba (on the Alabama River southeast of Selma in Dallas County) on November 17.

6. See Power of attorney, November 6, 1823.

To George Washington Martin

Hermitage Octbr. 30th. 1823

Dr Sir

I intended to have Vissitted you to day, but Mrs J. is not willing, thinking I am a little indisposed—I enclose by my Nephew A. J. Donelson the cotton notes, and also the note for $400. loaned mony, for settlement[1]—I shall want three hundred dollars of the Eastern funds—one hundred & seventy dollars, to be paid in current notes to Mr Somerville, in 30 or forty days—to be to <discharge> the credit of Mr F. Sanders note & mine in Bank as pr my letter to Mr Sommerville—which I wish your firm to give a memorandom to Mr Sommerville for—& take & send to me his acknowledgement[2]—fifteen dollars to be paid to Alexander Porter & Son, for articles got by Mr [Thomas] Weston[3]—My account with Mr Vanleer for iron, which I wish you to assume, & send me a receipt for[4]—your account closed in full, including the cloak I ordered the other day[5]—& if convenient the ballance in current notes before I set out which will be the 9th instant. I regret the necessity for this call on you, but my Dear George—I find many little debts pressing, which I suppose would not, if I had not to leave home, which I want to close before I do, please send me a statement of your account, the accounts I have requested you to assume, and the Ballance that may be coming to me from the cotton & mony loaned—do yourself Justice, as to the weight of the cotton I know nothing of it only as the enclosed papers shew[6]—I will be to see you before I set out—procure for me a good pair of winter overshews or socks, & charge them on the Bill—when able I will be happy to serve you your friend.

Andrew Jackson

P.S I have said I could do with 300 u states or Eastern funds, If when the accounts within are assumed by you, there should be more of a ballance than one hundred dollars current notes & $300 Eastern funds, if it will be any convenience to you, I can let the Ballance remain in your hands untill christmas, as I can borrow *$150* from Judge Overto untill that time[7]—send me a full statement of our account[8]—your friend Andrew Jackson

Photocopy of ALS, MsSM (9-0723).

1. For further discussion of the notes (not found) and loan, see above, AJ to Martin, October 15.

2. Jackson's letter, the notes, and John Sommerville's receipt have not been found. This payment was probably related to Jackson's purchase of Francis Saunders's plantation adjacent to the Hermitage.

3. Porter (d. 1833), an uncle of Louisiana senator Alexander Porter (1785–1844), was a prominent Nashville merchant. Weston (c1782–1830) was painting and papering at the Hermitage.

4. Either Bernard (c1778–1833) or Anthony Wayne Vanleer (1783–1863), both of whom supplied iron to Jackson. Receipt not found.

5. Probably a reference to the coat Jackson had ordered for his slave George (b. c1807), whom Jackson took with him to Washington (see AJ to Martin, October 18).

6. Not found.

7. See AJ to John Overton, October 24.

8. No record of Jackson's account with Martin, Williams & Co. at this time has been found.

To Unknown

Hermitage, Nov. 4. 1823.

Dear Sir—

I have the pleasure to acknowledge the receipt of your friendly letter of Oct. 10, and altho' not in the habit of answering letters on the subject of the Pres[i]dential election, from the proper view you have taken of my feelings, and as I trust of my universal conduct, I cannot refrain from acknowledging its receipt, reviving as it does the pleasure of the small acquaintance I have had with you, a citizen of my native state, and one whose opinions seem so congenial with those which I have always endeavored to possess, and which I trust I shall cherish whilst the pulsation of life lasts.[1]

The letter, in answer to the Pennsylvania committee, was a just exposition of my feelings and my views.[2] My name, unsolicited by me, has been brought before the American people, & although I have the highest esteem and regard for Mr. Calhoun, and some others, whose names are before the people, I shall not interfere in any way. It is a question with the people whether or not they choose to drop me; but should they do so, I have no power to transfer political influence; and notwithstanding the high opinion I entertain of Mr. Calhoun, my political creed would prevent any attempt to exercise a power which does not legitimately belong to me. Believe me, Dear Sir, with great respect, Your ob't Servant,

Andrew Jackson.

Printed, *Richmond Enquirer,* November 26, 1824 (9-0732); first publication in a Charleston paper, not identified. The newspaper indicated that the addressee was a resident of Edgefield County, S.C.

1. Letter not found.

2. See above, AJ to H. W. Peterson, February 23.

To John Overton

N*[ov 8t]*h 1823

Dear Sir

I have this mome*[n]*t recd your l*[etter of]* this day by your Nephew Mr John [Waller] Ove*[rton.]* I have only to reply that it will afford me much pleasure to use my influence in any way that may be in my power to place Mr John Overton in a situation that may unite the two brothers as citizens together in Florida Mr John Overton has only to point out in *[w]*hat way I can serve him & be assured it will be attended to.[1]

Mrs J. is more disconsolate than I ever knew her before, & I do assure you I leave home with more reluctance than I ever did in my life—it was so unlooked for, unwished for, & so inconsistant with my feelings—But I have no doubt but providence will protect her & myself as well absent as present, we are travelling our Journey through life, when our time is fulfilled here below we will *rest,* providence will continue us here untill <for> we fulfill those purposes that his goodness has designed, & we ought allways to be ready to say the lords will be done—Present Mrs. J. & myself to your Lady & family & for yourself receive our best wishes[2]—may you & yours be happy is the prayer of yr friend

Andrew Jackson

ALS, THi (9-0744). Published in *THQ,* 6(1947):162–63. Date supplied from endorsement.

1. Letter not found. Jackson recommended John W. Overton (c1791–1853), brother of Samuel R., for district attorney of West Florida, but he did not receive the appointment (see Richard M. Johnson to James Monroe, April 22, DNA-RG 59, M439-12). During Jackson's presidency, Overton obtained positions as clerk in the post office department and as commissioner to negotiate a treaty with the Two Sicilies.

2. Overton's wife, whom he married in 1820, was Mary McConnell White May (1782–1862), sister of Hugh L. White and widow of Dr. Francis May.

To John Coffee

Hermitage Novbr. 9th. 1823

Dear Genl

I wrote you last night, I expected Eaton here, but not having arived, I will remain at home to day & tommorrow set out—[1]

I informed you in my letter of yesterday that I had referred the suit as guardian of A. J. Hutchings vs Bennett Smith to arbritration This gives time, & I hope will release the estate & if any thing is allowed Smith it will be from Washington who has Joined in the refferrence—If therefore it is needed, the debt due from Mr James Jackson to me as guardian, which on the 18th of Decbr next, principle & Interest at 8 pct will amount to $2078.65, can be used for the childs benefit—I name this to you least you may not be in funds at the sale of the forfeighted lands & I wish Bought in for the child, the 2 forfeited quarters, the quarter north East of the well & half the two quarters south of A. J. Hutchings Tract, these two quarters are to be Bought in by Capt Jack & divided between him & Hutchings the north half of the two quarters to be Hutchings, he paying for the same Nicholsons wages will be due, you will have to pay this to him out of the proceeds of the cotton or by a call on Mr Jackson

Tell Mr Nicholson to push the crop as early as possible for markett & to write me to Washington how he gets on,[2] I will have to trouble you to have & eye to that farm, & give directions as you may Judge best—my young friend Capt A. J. Donelson will vissit you in next month—about the 20th. so as to return by the 1st. of January—I hope such collections may be made as will relieve me from the failure of Martin & Williams, to pay me the mony loaned them last march[3]—This done, it has opened my eyes as to loaning mony to relieve others; & leave myself in distress—with our prayers for the health, happiness, & prosperity of you, & your family, adieu your friend

Andrew Jackson

ALS, DLC (9-0747).

1. See AJ to Coffee, November 8.
2. No letter from Malachi Nicholson at this time has been found.
3. On the $400 loan, see above, AJ to George W. Martin, October 15 and 30.

To Anthony Wayne Butler

Hermitage Novbr. 10th. 1823

Dear Sir

I recd your letter of the 5th of Octbr in answer to mine of the 14th. of August[1]—In my letter to you I developed fully my situation as it respected my pecuniary matters, telling you if your necessities still existed, & the funds furnished you from Neworleans were not sufficient to meet your real wants, that you could draw upon me for one hundred dollars payable at Nashville in the current notes of that place—I did suppose when I had thus candidly exposed to you my real situation, informing you that my means would not Justify me doing more, that <still> you would have drawn upon me for a larger sum—To place my feelings in such a delicate situation, and your credit in drawing for a sum that you were not authorised (but expressly told not to exceed one hundred dollars) in the situation that my want of funds, has compelled me to do, by not accepting your draft; it was presented to me on last Thursday in Nashville when I was without mony—I told the holder I had authorised you to draw on me for one hundred dollars, which at every sacrafice I would raise & pay—and in order to save your credit & feelings I would pay the other fifty on the sale of my cotton, he replied that he would consider of it, I went and obtained the hundred dollars at a sacrafice of 30 pct, offerred to him, & offerred if he would take the ballance in cotton I would take up the draft—this he refused, I offerred him the hundred dollars & requested him to endorse it on the draft this he would not do—the next morning I called & offerred to give him the hundred dollars, & pay him the ballance in cotton at a fair markett price in cash as soon as it could be bailed—This was refused, and I then told him I had made all the propositions I could within my means and bid him goodby—I therefore suppose the bill is sent Back protested for non acceptance, and I hope through life will be a lesson to you never to draw upon your friend for a sum you are notified before hand that he has not in his power to meet[2]—This circumstance has sorely wounded my feelings—I cannot coin mony, you knew I had no means but my farm to produce mony—that my expences were large—and advised not to draw for more than $100—did you suppose I was acting with duplicity with you—I hope it will have the effect to make you reflect how hard it is to make mony honestly—and to support as many youths at school as I have under my care—The means procured for your education has been double, to that, of others, & still you have been pressed for funds—you are now entering on life where you will have to procure your own support, & you will learn the dificulties you will have to encounter with all industry & oeconomy, to keep clear of debt, & meet your own real wants—and I have to admonish you as a friend—to enter life with a determination to keep your wants within your own means, and contract no debts but what you have the means to pay. I have delayed writing you to the moment of my setting out for the City of Washington, in hopes that you would have arived, as from your letter I had a right to expect by this time[3]—I set out on borrowed funds—leaving my family without funds, relying on my crop of cotton, to meet there wants, and my small debts—when my crop is sold, or had I met you, the hundred dollars *[will be]* freely yielded to you—when this is done it is all I am able to do—and I am getting too old & infirm to struggle in this world any more—the young must pursue my example—and use industry & oeconomy and depend, as I have done, on their own exertions for a lively hood.

accept of my best wishes for your prosperity through life and I pray you to abstain from extravagance, and debts which plunges so many young men into ruin. I am with sincere respect your friend

Andrew Jackson

ALS, LNHiC (9-0751).

1. See AJ to Butler, August 14. Butler's letter has not been found.

2. The presenter of Butler's note has not been identified. In December the New Haven firm of Hull & Townsend protested to Jackson at Washington regarding Butler's nonpayment of the $150 draft, and he sent them $100 in Tennessee money, all he could raise at that time. When the firm applied a 35 percent discount to convert Jackson's funds to eastern money, Butler and Jackson argued that the draft was payable in Nashville bank notes. Shortly before his death in 1824, Butler acknowledged Hull & Townsend's claim and promised to request that Jackson send $100 to New Haven, but no record of his request or of any payment by Jackson has been found (Butler to Hull & Townsend, August 29, 1824, LNHiC).

3. Jackson left this letter at Nashville, where he expected Butler's imminent arrival. When Butler did not appear, Andrew J. Donelson forwarded the letter to Louisiana (see Donelson to Butler, December 15, LNHiC).

To Andrew Jackson Donelson

Kingstons Novbr. 16th. 1823

Dr Andrew

I have but a moment to write you & that by candlelight in the morning—we were met 12 miles in advance by a committee & invited to dine on the 17th. at this place—This I could not comply with—it being anticipated another comittee was sent on with an invitation to dine with the citizens & its vicinity in the evening; this we complied with, & sat down by candle light to a sumptuous repast, with a large & respectable collection of citizens—This as I suppose is to counteract some reports attempted to be circulated, that my election has been badly received by the citizens of East Tennessee—This repot you will find is not true—I can say no more at present when time will permit I shall write you fully—write me to the city, take care of your aunt, & say to the overseer <with respect> take care to my horned stock this cold weather, & believe me to be your friend sincerely

Andrew Jackson

ALS, DLC (32).

To Rachel Jackson

Staunton Novbr. 28th. 1823

My Love

I reached here at 11 oclock last night in the mail stage in my usual health, I rest here today for my friend Major Eaton who I left yesterday morning he is on horseback, & will take the stage with me here, Genl Call & Colo. Owing is with me[1]—If we can procure private Hacks we will go on tomorrow morning—if not we will leave here on sunday in the mail stage for Fredricksburgh where we will take the steam Boat, two days travel will now take us to the steam Boat—& in 14 hours after we will reach the city, I can now say that my fatigue of the Journey is nearly over—we have been blessed with fine weather on our Journey—we have experienced but one inclement day—to avoid which I took the stage & Major Eaton came on horseback.

I have been greeted by the people wherever I have halted, to avoid much of this was one reason why I took the stage, & even then in many places, on the way side were collections who hailed & stopped the stage to shake me by the hand, This through Virginia I did not calculate on—altho tiresome & troublesome still it is gratifying to find that I have triumphed over the machinations of my enemies, & still possess the confidence of the people—were you only with me I could be satisfied—But should providence once more permit us to meet, I am solemny resolved, with the permission of heaven, never to seperate, or be seperated from you in this world. Present me to Capt A. J. Donelson say to him I will write him so soon as I reach the city—say to my son & my little ward Hutchings that I expect them to be obedient & attentive to you, bless them for me, & accept of my prayers for your health & happiness untill I return, & believe me to be your affectionate Husband

Andrew Jackson

P.S. Genl Call writes you & Andrew J. D. from here.[2] A.J.

ALS, CSmH (9-0766). Published in *Huntington Library Bulletin,* 3(1933):118–19.

1. Probably George Washington Owen (1796–1837; Cumberland College 1815), representative from Alabama.

2. Letters not found.

To John Overton

City of Washington
Dcbr. 5th. 1823

Dear Sir

I reached here the morning of the 3rd instant, the President had delivered his message on the 2nd. Major Eaton & myself half after 12 oclock P.M. appeared in the Senate, but the Senate had met at 12 and adjourned untill to day, to attend the funeral of the Prusian Minister[1]—I should enclose one to you but as yet have not been furnished, when I attend the house today & take my seat I will do myself the pleasure to enclose you a copy—you will find from the Message that the President takes a proper ground as it respects south america—If they Holy alience will maintain their nutrality as it regards south america, we will also, If they aid spain—we will interpose in behalf of the colonies.[2]

Having one hundred & fifty dollars on hand of Tennessee mony, I herewith enclose it to you. If my friend Capt A. J. Donelson has collected & paid you this sum borrowed, you will please hand it over to him—If not you will retain it, & destroy or hand over to him the due Bill which I gave you, accept my Dr Sir my thanks for this act of friendship & present me affectionately to your Lady—[3]

I have maintained my health upon the Journey pretty well, was greeted by the people on the whole rout—indeed I had set out with the determination not to participate in their hospitality any where—I could not get by Kingston & Knoxville without dining by candle light with them—at Rogersville Blountsville, Staunton & Fredericksburgh I was invited to tarry & dine with them, this I declined, & altho I reached Fredericksburgh in the stage at three in the evening and proceeded on at half after 4, I was escorted out of Town by the aged & the young accompanied with two companies of their independant corps of Infantry—knowing you to be my friend I name these circumstances to you believing it will be gratifying to you to hear that your native country treated your friend with these attentions—when I take Lodgings, for I am now in a tavern, I will have more Leisure & occasionally write you—I am informed by Major Eaton that it is probable a law will be passed by Congress this session creating a circuit of Tennessee & Alabama—will you say to me confidentially whether you would accept of the appointment of Judge for that cirquit—This is all Major Eaton and myself wish to know of you & that before the bill passes[4] I am your friend

Andrew Jackson

ALS, THi (9-0783). Published in *THQ*, 6(1947):164.

1. The Prussian minister Frederick de Greuhm (c1770–1823) died on December 1.

2. After the restoration in Spain, fears that the European powers would intervene to recover former Spanish colonies in Latin America led the president to issue what has come to be known as the Monroe Doctrine in his annual message to Congress (*Annals of Congress*, 18th Cong., 1st sess., pp. 12–24).

3. Jackson was repaying money loaned to finance his trip to Washington. See above, AJ to George W. Martin, October 30.

4. On December 10, Richard M. Johnson submitted a resolution for the Senate Committee on the Judiciary to inquire into the expediency of creating three additional circuits in the West, the first composed of Tennessee and Alabama. The resolution passed, but the circuit court bill became entangled with questions about the relationship between the Supreme Court and district courts, preventing its passage in the current session of Congress.

To Rachel Jackson

City of Washington
Decbr. 7th. 1823

My Love

I wrote you on my arival here on the morning of the 3rd. instant[1]—The weather has continued good & my health improving from rest—altho I cannot say that of this I have had much—there being a continued scene of Vissits to me, and of course on my part a return of them—Today being sunday I have spent at Church where I was edified with a very sensible discourse from a young presbeterian preacher. Since my arival many inquiries have been made after your health by your acquaintances here, & I am charged by Mrs Wilson & Doctor Tucker, when I write, to present you with their respectfull compliments & also by Mrs. [Elizabeth Courts Love] Watson, Miss Jones, & all the family.[2] I have taken lodgings at Mr. [William] Oneals Major Eaton & Call make my mess, we are private & comfortably accomodated in a worthy family[3]—how my constitution may bear the winter should it prove very inclement I cannot say—I shall endevour to take care of myself. I had a hope by this days mail to have recd a letter from you or Capt A. J. Donelson <still> in this I have been disappointed, still hope I shall receive one soon—This seperation has been more severe to me than any other, it being one that my mind was not prepared for, nor can I see any necessity for—still my country [did]; & no alternative was left for me but to obay—If providence permits us <to> again to unite, we must travel together, & live together whilst permitted to remain Tennants here below—before I leave this I shall engage rooms for your reception next fall. I shall expect you to write me as often as you can—It will be pleasing to me to receive from Mr Parsons a statement of the amount of my crop as soon as it is housed—and say to Mr Donelson I shall expect him to write me very often.

I would be delighted to receive a letter from our son, little Hutchings, & even Lyncoya—the latter I would like to exhibit to Mr Monroe & the Secratary of War, as I mean to try to have him recd. at the military school, as early as I can, I shall examine the college here with a View if I like it,

& its moral Goverment, to bring they two Andrews here next fall & leave them here—I am told it is superintended by a worthy Baptist Clergyman of great celebrity—[4]

When you see parson Campbell present me affectionately to him & family also to Mr [Richard] Dabbs[5]—should my friend parson Hodge have returned present me kindly to him, say to Colo Butler I shall write him as early as I can have an interview with Mr Monroe, which will be as soon as the days of ceremony are over—there is nothing done here but Vissitting & *carding each other.* you know how much I was disgusted with those scenes when you & I were here, it has increased instead of diminishing—

present me to Capt John Donelson *[&]* family, & all my good neighbours affectionately—and accept my continued prays for your health & that of my little Andrews—present me to Capt A. J. Donelson & believe me your affectionate Husband

Andrew Jackson

ALS, DLC (32). Published in Bassett, 3:215–16.

1. See AJ to Rachel Jackson, December 3.

2. Mrs. Wilson was probably Sarah (1755–1825), who operated a boarding house at Seven Buildings in Washington. The Jacksons had stayed with her in 1815. Watson (c1778–1853) was the sister of Charles J. Love, who had moved to the Nashville area from Fairfax County, Virginia, around 1820. Miss Jones and the preacher have not been identified.

3. O'Neale (d. 1837), former owner of the well-known Franklin House, now took Jackson, John H. Eaton, and Richard K. Call as boarders at his wife's house across from the West Market near John Gadsby's Hotel.

4. Lyncoya wrote Jackson on December 29. William Staughton (1770–1829) served as president of Columbian College (later George Washington University), 1822–27.

5. Dabbs (d. 1825), a Virginian who had been installed as first pastor of the Nashville Baptist church in December 1822, was a Masonic brother.

To William Berkeley Lewis

City of Washington
Decbr 7th. 1823

Dear Major

We reached this place on the morning of the 3rd instant—our health as good as when we left you—nothing but *carding* & Vissitting done here as yet—I would enclose you the Presidents message, but five thousand having been sent off the morning We arived, unless the weight has broke down the stages on the road it would be too late to be acceptable—The Message is a good one, and I have no doubt but Congress will prepare to meet the crisses—I have no doubt but the holy alience will make the attempt to restore south america to spain—This must be prevented—or our goverment will be Jeopardized—and we will have a bloody contest with the combined despotism of urope—for my part I think it best to prevent them gaining a foothold upon the Terra firma of the american continant least when they might be in possession of Mexico, their foreign Bayonets might make an attempt to pierce us in the south & west.[1]

I will be glad occasionally to hear from you—and I hope you and the young Ladies will Vissit Mrs. Jackson in my absence as often as it may be convenient.

as to the Presidential election I leave others to detail to you the rumors of the day—I was greeted by the citizens as I passed to this place kindly and I really think from what I hear that the sec of the Treasury is fast declining—a nomination by a congressional caucus would dam politically any man it might name.

with my best respects to your family & my friend Mr Crutcher I am your friend

Andrew Jackson

ALS, NN (9-0790). Published in *NYPLB,* 4(1900):193.

1. For James Monroe's message of December 2, see *Annals of Congress,* 18th Cong., 1st sess., pp. 12–24.

To Rachel Jackson

city of Washington
Decbr. 11th. 1823

My Dear wife

I recd. your kind & affectionate letter of the 23rd. ult. in the Senate Chamber & barely acknowledged its receipt[1]—I now lift my pen to answer it. I have to repeat the pleasure its receipt afforded me, when it informed me you were well—I have to thank my god my health has improved and I trust that with care I may continue to enjoy health—The weather is cold, we had a fall of snow night before last, to day the weather is quite moderate but the climate is so changeable, that Tomorrow may be intensly cold—when we Trust in providence, it is well placed and under every circumstance in life as you will observe, in him alone we ought to trust, he is the fountain of all good, he giveth life & health, and at pleasure taketh it away, and we ought so to conduct in all things, that we ought allways to be prepared to say his will be done Therefore I am sure that in this Variable climate if it is his will I shall enjoy as much health here as at home—provided I can bring my mind to be calm under our seperation—This, being informed of your health, I shall endeavour to do. I am happy to hear that all the family are well—and that they hands are getting out my crop so well, I hope Mr Parson will in all things do what you desire, I have confidence in him, & I am sure he will obay you in all things you may require—I do not wish my hands laboured too hard—& if you think they are, I know when you name it to him he will moderate—I wish them well fed, & warmly cloathed and they will be then contented & happy This is my wish—I do not want them in any way oppressed, and if they behave well I am sure Mr Parsons knowing my wishes, will treat them well—It gives me much pleasure to hear that my two little andrews are well and behave well—Tell them to continue this good conduct and I will be delighted to meet them again—I shall expect them both to have improved much, and also Lyncoya—I shall expect our son to answer the letter I have wrote him—I wrote to A. J. Donelson by this mail[2]—present me affectionately to Colo. Butler I truly appreciate his goodness—he is aware of my friendship—I shall write him as early as I can discover fairly how the land lies, I shall either get him into the army again or a civil appointment. I shall write you as often as I can, I shall see Mrs Watson on sunday morning & go with her to church, when I shall remember you to her—Capt Call & Major Eaton lives with me, are both well & desires to be affectionately presented to you.

May the blessing of heaven rest with you the Andrews & the family untill I return is the prayer of your loving husband

Andrew Jackson

P.S. present me to my friend Capt J. Donelson &c &c Mrs. E. Donelson & &c & all friends—& to Colo. & Mrs Butler

ALS, CSmH (9-0798). Published in *Huntington Library Bulletin,* 3(1933):121–22.

1. See AJ to Rachel Jackson, December 10. Her letter has not been found.

2. See AJ to Andrew Jackson, Jr., [cDecember 11], below; the letter to Andrew J. Donelson has not been found.

From Winfield Scott

[Hiel] Peck's, Geo. Town, D.C. Dec. 11th, 1823.

Sir:

One portion of the American community has long attributed to you the most distinguished magnanimity, & another portion the greatest desperation in your resentments. Am I to conclude that both are equally in error? I allude to circumstances which have transpired between us (& which need not here be recapitulated) & to the fact, that I have now been six days in your immediate vicinity without having attracted your notice.[1]

As this is the first time in my life that I have been within a hundred miles of you, & as it is barely possible that you may be ignorant of my presence, I beg leave to state that I shall not leave the District before the morning of the 14th instant. I have the honour to be, sir, your most Obt. Servant

Winfield Scott.

ALS, DLC (32); Copies, CSmH (9-0801) and NjHi (mAJs). Published in Bassett, 3:216. Peck, formerly of Rossburgh, near Bladensburg, Maryland, acquired the Union Tavern of

Georgetown in 1822. He later operated a boarding house at the corner of 15th and Pennsylvania in Washington.

1. Scott was referring to the controversy regarding Jackson's division order of April 22, 1817 (see *Jackson,* 4:112–14, 133–34, 142–44, 156–58).

To Winfield Scott

Mr. Oneals Decbr. 11th. 1823

Sir

Your letter of to day has been received[1]—whether the world are correct, or in error, as regards my "magnanimity," is for the world to decide: I am satisfied of one fact, that when you shall know me better, you will not be disposed to harbour the opinion, that any thing like "desperation in resentment" attaches to me.

Your letter is ambiguous; but concluding from occurrencies heretofore, that it was written with friendly views, I take the liberty of saying to you, that whenever you shall feel <that> disposed to meet me on friendly terms, that disposition will not be met by any other than a correspondent feeling on my part. I have the honor to be Sir your most obdt. Servant

a copy Signed Andrew Jackson
Test. J. H Eaton

ALS copy certified by John H. Eaton, DLC (32); Copies, CtY (9-0803) and NjHi (mAJs). Published in Bassett, 3:217.

1. See above.

To Andrew Jackson, Jr.

[cDecember 11, 1823]

My Dear son Andrew.

Being a long distance from you & your mother, and being very solicitous for your wellfare, & that of little A J Hutching I write you—I bear in mind the promise you made me when leaving you, that you would be attentive to your education & carefully attend to the wants & wishes of your mother, that you would not leave her on any occasion without her consent & knowledge, have you my dear son complied with this promise to me, I hope you have, for nothing would be so painfull to your papa, as to believe you would <forfeit> break your promise on any occasion. never promise to do any thing without due reflection & when you make a promise never fail to execute it—never on any occasion whatever depart from the truth, be Just to all, learn your Book, become well informed, and you will be esteemed by all—many inquiries have been made after you here Mr [Benjamin Williams] Crowningshield and his daughters are hear, do you recollect them, they have inquired affectionately after you & your mother, & request to be affectionately presented to you both[1]—I have said to them I will bring you on here if I can next fall, I hope you will therefore be attentive to your Book, & progress in your studies, that you can stand an examination as well as any of your age—Tell my dear little Hutchings that this letter & the advice given is intended for him as well as yourself, & I hope you both will attend to & pursue it—I wish you to answer this letter—present me affectionately to your mother & <Cap> your cousin A. Donelson—Tell him I have not recd any letter from him yet—& tell Hutchings I wish him to write me also—I am your affectionate papa,

Andrew Jackson

ALS, DLC (60; 9-0927).

1. Crowninshield (1772–1851) represented Massachusetts in the House. During Jackson's visit to Washington in 1815, he, Rachel, and Andrew, Jr., had stayed at the same boarding house as then Secretary of the Navy Crowninshield, his wife Mary Boardman, and their two eldest daughters, Elizabeth and Mary.

John Henry Eaton to Rachel Jackson

Washington City
Dec. 18— 1823

Dear Madm.

The general is in very fine health, and in just as good spirits. He has so many visits however to make as well amongst the Ladies as the gentlemen that it is quite probable he is not a punctual correspondent, & therefore is it that I write to you. He is constantly in motion to some Dinner party or other, and to night stands engaged at a large Dancing party at Genl Browns; but whether or not he will become one of the Dancers shall become the subject of some future letter. I assure you he is in most excellent health, much better than he has been in a long time—the journey was of great service to him, and since arriving here is in just as comfortable quarters as he could have

It will afford you great pleasure I know, to be informed that all his old quarrels have been settled. The General is at peace & in friendship with Genl. Scott, Gen Cocke—Mr Clay & what you would never have expected Col Benton: he is in harmony & good understanding with every body, a thing I know you will be happy to hear[1]

I am quite in a hurry with great respect—

J H Eaton

P.S. the enclosed information is all true but highly coloured as it respects the dining & vissits—too much of that is true, & as yet I cannot free myself from them, It is a pleasing subject to me that I am now at peace with all the world, The kindness and attention of my friend Major Eaton on the Journey, & here, has added much to my comfort & health, I shall write you soon, hope to hear that your health is good, accept of my prayers for it & believe me your affectionate Husband.

A Jackson

ALS with ANS postscript by AJ, DLC (32). Published in Bassett, 3:217.

1. On December 14, Richard K. Call described the reconciliations for John Coffee. "You will perhaps be surprised to learn," he wrote, "that with the exception of Crawford & Benton Jackson has buried the Tom-Hawk with all his enemies. Yesterday Genl Cocke and Col Erwine dined with him, and he is to dine with them day after tomorrow. Genl Scott has waited on him, indeed they have exchanged visites mutually, and are on the most friendly terms. he has had a friendly interview with Clay, and every thing is go*[ing]* on as smothly as you could wish" (Coffee Papers, THi). For a discussion of Jackson's relations with Benton, see AJ to Andrew J. Donelson, January 14, 1824, below.

To William Savin Fulton

Washington Decbr. 21rst 1823

My Dear Sir

I have recd your letter of the 30th. ult. and will aid with great pleasure in furnishing you with all the political information in my power[1]—have obtained a promise from our mutual friend Genl Call to aid me—for the truth is, with the recpt of letters, the frequent calls on me by my friends, leave me but little Leisure, add to this that I intermix but little amonghst the political circles, which prevent me from obtaining either as early, or as perfect a knowledge of the passing scenes as those in the situation of Genl Call—I have directed him to forward weekly to you the Columbian observer which he has promised to do.[2] I shall obtain from Genl Houston a similar promise—

The caucus mongers has tried their strength but as yet, I am told, it is too feeble to m*[ake]* a movement—I am told they cannot muster more than the number of Votes given for Mr Barber as Speaker this was I believe 42[3]—I am told they are decreasing in number whether this be the fact I cannot say—I touch not, handle not of this unclean thing—& I hope they people will assume their rights & maintain them, & shew the designing Demagogues of the day that the will not be intrigued out of their direct right of electing the President of the u. states on the subject of the Presidential election I can say nothing but my friends here tell me I am gaining fast—Pensylvania is fixed, Maryland it is said will follow her—Newyork will unmask herself shortly—& if Crawfords friends does not find their strength equal to getting up a caucus he will be withdrawn is my opinion, in that case it is thought I will get Georgia & South Carolina certain if Mr Calhoun is withdrawn It does not appear that Mr Clay has gained any ground since he came here, should he not obtain Newyork or Virginia he will be withdrawn, and Kentucky Elinoi & Misouri will, it is said & thought by some will be friendly to my election—The State of ohio it is thought will not support Mr Clay—it certainly will not unless he obtains more than his present strength, on that event unless Mr Clinton comes out it will be divided between Mr Adams & myself[4]—you are to receive this as mere rumor a few months will develope these things—The american people have become alive to this question, and they will I hope elect the President, & should the choice fall upon another it will leave no heart burnings in my breast—it is probable that if the state of Newyork elect their electors by the people that a part of that state will be for me & ohio will be divided, a few months nay I may say weeks will unmask the whole movements, and a Judgt. may be correctly formed—as it occurs you will be furnished with it—I am happy you have read [Barry Edward] omearas works, the world generally had take up false ideas of Napoleon—much prejudice had been raised against him I never had a doubt but he was a great & good man—his attack upon spain was the only evidence of ambition—[5]

you will have seen the Presidents message it is *strong* & such as it should be.[6]

I am invited to a Ball given by Mr & Mrs Adams on the 8th. of January next[7]—The executive candidates are vying with each other—I stand alone, & my friends have pursued a prudent course by supporting me on my own merits & not by destroying the charector of others I hope they will pursue this course to the end—altho the Sec of the Treasury is Vulnerable still per*[s]*ecution would be th*[e]* cry—it would injure more than benefit—When the other candidates quarrel, when any is withdrawn it is human nature not to unite with an enemy where there are others to unite with—I shall write you as leisure & matter may ocur—recollect this is for yourself not for the Public—

Present me to Genl Coffee tell him I will write him shortly present me to your lady & believe me to be your friend

Andrew Jackson

ALS, KyLoF (9-0817). Published in John Hallum, *Biographical and Pictorial History of Arkansas* (2 vols., Albany, 1887), 2:188–91.

1. Not found.

2. The Philadelphia *Columbian Observer*, edited by Stephen Simpson, was one of the earliest papers to support Jackson in Pennsylvania.

3. On December 1, Henry Clay defeated Philip P. Barbour, a Crawford supporter, in his bid for reelection as Speaker of the House, 139 votes to 42.

4. News had reached Washington of a meeting at Steubenville, Ohio, on December 2, at which the citizens recommended DeWitt Clinton for president and Jackson for vice-president.

Clinton supporters called a number of other meetings, but by March 1824 the Clinton movement in Ohio had virtually collapsed.

5. O'Meara (1786–1836), surgeon to Napoleon Bonaparte, produced several books on the emperor. Jackson was probably referring to *Napoleon in Exile; or a Voice from St. Helena,* which appeared in many American editions including an 1823 Lexington, Ky., printing, or to the *Historical Memoirs of Napoleon,* translated by O'Meara. Editions of both works (New York and Philadelphia, 1823, and Philadelphia, 1820) remain in Jackson's library at the Hermitage.

6. See *Annals of Congress,* 18th Cong., 1st sess., pp. 12–24.

7. Jackson accepted the Adams's invitation on December 20.

To Rachel Jackson

Washington Decbr. 21rst 1823

My Dear wife

I have received to day your kind letter of the 5th. instant,[1] and am rejoiced to be informed that you are in good health—I can say with truth that my health is improved—The kind attention of my friend Eaton has been great, and to him I feel truly indebted for the comfortable quarters we occupy—we are in the family of Mr Oneal whose amiable pious wife & two daughters, one maried the other single, take every pains in there power to make us comfortable and agreable, Mr Oneal himself is an agreable man this family has been wealthy but by misfortune & endorsments for others, has been reduced to the necessity of keeping a boarding house,[2] I can with truth say I never was in a more agreable & worthy family—When we have a leisure hour in the evening we spend it with the family—Mrs. Timberlake the maryed daughter whose husband belongs to our navy, plays on the piano delightfully, & every Sunday evening entertains her pious mother with sacred music—to which we are invited, & the single daughter who is also pious & sings well unites in the music[3]—I am thus particular in giving you a narative of our situation with which I know you will be pleased—every Sunday we spend at church—This family belong to the Methodist society—on last sunday as I named to you I went with Mrs Watson to her church.[4] she belongs to the Presbetarians, to day I went to hear a Baptist whose church is near us, & was edified by a good concise discourse, so my dear you see, that notwithstanding I am in the midst of intrigue, gaity & bustle, I spend my Sundays & leisure hours agreably, & I hope profitably—as to Leisure, I have but little, and could I get clear of the dining parties, I think with care, I can maintain my health—but under existing circumstances, I cannot yet, (untill I go the rounds) refuse; the President is very kind to me; indeed amidst the intrigue for the next Presidency here, I get on pretty well, as I touch not, handle not of that unclean procedure; I keep myself entirely aloof from the intriguers, and caucus mongers—with a determination that if I am brought into that office it shall be by the free unsolicited Voice of the people. I trust that the god of Isaac & of Jacob will protect you, & give you health in my absence, in him alone we ought to trust, he alone can preserve, & guide us through this troublesome world—& I am sure he will hear your prayers—we are told that the prayers of the righteous prevaileth much[5]—and I add mine for your health & preservation untill we again meet—Major [William] Davenport is now with us with his young & amiable wife that he has lately maried in Philadelphia,[6] he has given this family your charector, and Mrs Timberlake (from what she has heard of you from Major Eaton & Major Davenport) has requested me to present you with her respects, when you come here I am convinced you will be much pleased with this family—The only consolation to friends who are seperated, is the pleasure of communicating with each other by writing—how gratefull this converse between husband & wife—I will therefore, as you have requested me, endeavour to content myself through this winters absence, endeavouring by occasionally writing you, to console myself—& expecting often to hear from you—I have recd the letter from my son, I have read it with great pleasure & have answered it, which I enclose[7]—I hope in the next to see his handwriting improve—I feel gratefull to our cousin Milbury for her staying with you[8]—and the other ladies for Vissitting you, I hope their cheerfull dispositions will keep your spirits up. I am much pleased with the information of my crop & the forwardness with which Mr Parsons has got it—I hope before the cold weather sets in he will have it housed, & ready for markett The weather here has been very fine for the season altho very variable. Capt A. J. Donelson writes me often—present me to him affectionately & to the Andrews & Miss Milbury if with you & all friends—I have wrote Colo Butler today & regret much that he has been unwell I hope he has recovered, I have recd from my friend Parson [William] Hume, a kind letter; in my answer, I have requested him to Vissit you[9]—in your next advise me how the church progresses, I hope it is finished, present me to Col Ward & family, & say to him I expect he will attend to it, that it must be finished if him & myself pay for it. it is late & I must close this letter, accept of my prayers for your happiness & preservation untill we again shall meet, & believe me to be your affectionate Husband

Andrew Jackson

ALS, DLC (32). Published in Bassett, 3:217–19.

1. Not found.

2. Among others, O'Neale had endorsed notes for Benjamin G. Orr, who had suffered financial collapse. John H. Eaton had helped the O'Neales through financial difficulties, assuming their debts in exchange for their property, then deeding the property back to the family, and building the house for Mrs. O'Neale on land owned by her husband.

3. Rhoda Howell (c1771–1860), a sister of New Jersey governor Richard Howell, married William O'Neale in 1798. Her daughter Margaret (1796/99?–1879), who married John Bowie Timberlake (d. 1828), a naval purser, in 1816 and had a son and two daughters, became better known as Peggy Eaton after she married Eaton in 1829. The single daughter was probably Mary B., who married Philip Grymes Randolph in October 1824, rather than Georgianna C. (d. 1836), who married French S. Evans in 1829.

4. See above, AJ to Rachel Jackson, December 11.
5. An allusion to James 5:16.
6. Davenport (d. 1858), a brevet major of the 7th Infantry, had married Hannah Israel of Philadelphia on December 1.
7. Letters not found.
8. Milbery M. Donelson (1806–36), daughter of William (1758–1820) and Charity Dickinson Donelson, was Jackson's niece, not cousin.
9. Letters not found. Hume (1770–1833) came from Scotland as a missionary, arriving in Nashville in 1801. His church of Scottish seceders joined with the First Presbyterian Church of Nashville in 1818.

To Thomas Martin Maund

City of Washington Decbr. 27th. 1823

Sir

yours of the 26th. Inst. has been this day recd.[1] The letter of which you speak was published with the documents communicated to congress by the President of the united states in 1819 when the subject of the Campaign against the Seminole Indians was under discussion before that body, by refferring to those documents, you will have a full view of all communications made to Genl Gains, and all other communications to, & from me, relative to my operations & transactions in Florida.[2]

My whole public life is before the nation, I have not, & never had any political secrete, I dread not investigation, I fear not any exposure that my enemies can make either of my public, or private life.

accept a tender of my thanks for your friendly intentions, and believe me to be very respectfully your most obt. Servt.

Andrew Jackson

ALS, MdHi (9-0851). Published in *Maryland Historical Magazine,* 20(1925):135. Maund (1794–1838) was proprietor of the Baltimore *Morning Chronicle and Daily Advertiser,* which supported Jackson in the presidential campaign.

1. Not found.
2. The letter requested has not been identified. Most of the documents before Congress in 1819 were transmitted in presidential messages of December 3 and 28, 1818 (*HRDocs* 14 and 65, 15th Cong., 2nd sess., Serials 17 and 20).

To John Coffee

Washington Decbr. 31rst 1823

Dear General

Since my arival here I have had but little leisure, many letters on business which I was obliged to answer, which left but little time for friendship, and of course this is the first time I have taken up my pen to write you

Indeed congress has done but little yet, and untill the holidays are over, little is expected to be done—whether the Presidential question may not intermix itself with the business of Congress, so as to retard Legislation, I cannot say but I would presume from what I am informed that this will be the case—I intermix with none of those who are engaged in the intrigue of caucus, or president makers, nor do I intend, I have taken my course long since, from which no earthly consideration shall turn me, & should the choice of the people fall upon another it will give me no pain—I have but one feeling, & that is that the people make a good choice, when I say this, I have to add, that I think it would be a great curse to the nation if the choice fell upon Wm. H. C. It is strange, but it appears nevertheless true that his name & intrigue are intermixed where ever any election is on hand, this remark is brought to me mind from a letter from Georgia detailing the circumstances of the late election for Governor there, where it is stated that four Votes pledged for Mr [Matthew] Talbot was Bot. over for Crawford, it is said that a pamphlet is preparing on this & other subjects[1]—If then corruption is used to bring him into office, how far would it spread to retain him—I however from present appearences I have but little fear on this head—should he loose the support of Newyork, he will be, as I suppose, withdrawn from the contest, but Virginia & part of Carolina will make a struggle to buoy him up—every nerve has been tried on Pensylvania but it is said she is immovable—

My health has improved, but of late I have taken cold, & how I cannot tell, I Vissit little, still my cough has shewn symtoms of return—I will be happy to hear from you, & receive the news of your country & the health of your family & also how Mr Nicholson is progressing I have requested him to write me as soon as his crop is housed—as soon as the cotton is ready for markett I would suppose it ought to shipped with orders to sell so soon as it reached there if the price continues up—This hint is not to control your instructions but merely as a hint if 14 cents can be obtained for it it ought to be sold.

give my respects to your lady & family, to Capt Jack & Eliza, tell Elisa that he[r] brother Edward is well he has Just left me for Newyork with Genl Gains. write me when you have leisure & believe me yr friend

Andrew Jackson

ALS, THi (9-0868). Published in Bassett, 3:220–21.

1. The Georgia legislature on November 6 elected George M. Troup, a Crawford supporter, as governor over Talbot (1767–1827) by a vote of 85 to 81. Neither the letter nor the proposed pamphlet has been found.

1824

To George Washington Martin

Copy. Washington City. July [January] 2nd. 1824.

Dear George

Your letter of the 18th. ult. is just rec'd.[1]

I kindly thank you for the information given of Mrs J. and her good health; under existing circumstances and the courses that lead to our seperation, the anxiety on my mind, that my absence from her at a time when it was so necessary to her health that hers should be kept at ease, might prove injurious to her health; hence the gratification I feel on hearing that she enjoys good health. I rejoice to hear that a court is appointed in your case, my prayers are that you may have a speedy trial, & success—[2]

I am greatly incumbered with numerous letters, visiting etc. etc., my health thus far is pretty good; if I could have three months ease I would, I believe, regain my health.

There has been a good deal said of a congressional caucas, but if I was to judge from the appearance today of the treasurer's friends; I would suppose he was politically (as he notably is) sick.[3]

Virginia by her legislature has not come forth, as was expected, by the friends of a caucus, North Carolina has split, Mr. Vanburen can not *manage* New York, and it is my opinion, that Virginia will not seperate, from Penn. & New York; She will unite with one of them at least;[4] however I know but little upon the subject, as I neither met with the politicians, or conversed on the Presidential question—But is my opinion that Mr Crawford will be withdrawn from the contest so soon as New York unmasks herself, provided he does not get her support.

I have become friendly with all here & Genl Scott and myself met before *[he]* left the city & parted friendly—This has destroyed the stronghold of my enemies who denounced me as a man of revengefull Temper and of great rashness. I am told the opinion of those whose minds were prepared to see me with a Tomahawk in one hand, & a scalping knife in the other has greatly changed—and I am getting on very smoothly.

Present me to your mother & family kindly & to all my friends in Nashville adeiu,

(signed) Andrew Jackson

[P]. S. I write Mrs Jackson weekly. *[Sh]*ould you meet with her present my love to her & tell her I am well & tell the two Andrews I send my love to them & I expect every fortnight to receive a letter from them—Present me to Capt A. J. Donelson, [Joel] Parish [Jr.] Armstrongs & Marshall, your Brother & family & my friend McLemore & his family—you are the only one who has wrote me except Capt A. J. D. I have recd Mrs J. letters[5] signed A. J.

Copy, MsSM (9-0883). Published in Bassett, 3:221–22 (lacking postscript). The bracketted date is from Bassett.

1. Not found.

2. Jackson was probably referring to *Martin* v. *Waterhouse*. By an act of November 28, 1823, the Tennessee legislature had provided for the appointment of a special court to try appeals in cases for which judges of the state supreme court were disqualified. The Martins' attorneys argued that the law applied to the *Waterhouse* case, but the supreme court justices ruled otherwise, and the case was heard by two of the justices in regular session (see *Acts Passed at the First Session of the Fifteenth General Assembly of the State of Tennessee* [Murfreesboro, 1823], pp. 74–75; *Tennessee Reports*, 7:394–412).

3. William H. Crawford had suffered a possible stroke in September. With his illness complicated further by his medication, he was unable to attend cabinet meetings from December 1823 through April 1824. The precarious state of his health weakened his presidential prospects.

4. The Tennessee legislature's resolutions opposing caucus nominations (see above, William Brady and Thomas Williamson to AJ, September 20, 1823) included a call for submission to the other state legislatures. In Virginia, they were referred to a committee headed by John Tyler, who reported on December 23, 1823, a preamble and resolutions condemning them and endorsing the congressional caucus as "the only practicable mode whereby the wishes of a majority of the nation, are likely to be attained." When the Tyler resolution was taken up on December 30, opponents succeeded in postponing action by a vote of 77 to 76. The triumph of anti-caucus forces in Virginia was short-lived, however. On the evening of January 5, a caucus of 157 members of the Virginia House and Senate approved resolutions endorsing the sentiments supportive of the congressional caucus passed by a New York caucus in April 1823 (see *Richmond Enquirer*, December 27, 1823, January 1 and 6). In North Carolina, when Governor Gabriel Holmes submitted the Tennessee resolutions with his endorsement on December 27, the House voted to print his message, but the Senate, with the speaker casting the deciding ballot, voted to postpone indefinitely the House motion (see Raleigh *Star, and North-Carolina State Gazette*, January 2). New York did not act until later. Resolutions rejecting the Tennessee motion and again supporting the congressional caucus were introduced in the Senate on January 8 and passed soon thereafter (see Washington *National Intelligencer*, January 16 and 22).

5. Parrish (d. 1834), a veteran of the Battle of Horseshoe Bend, served for a time as Jackson's secretary and was brigade inspector for John Coffee's mounted gunmen during the Gulf campaign, when Martin was Coffee's aide. Probably Robert Armstrong (1792–1854), a veteran of the Creek War and New Orleans campaigns whom Jackson appointed as Nashville postmaster in 1829, and Samuel B. Marshall, a volunteer aide for Jackson during the Seminole campaign whom Jackson appointed as marshal of West Tennessee in 1831. Rachel Jackson's letters have not been found.

To Andrew Jackson Donelson

City of Washington
Janry 14th. 1824

Dear Andrew

I have this day recd yours of the 29th & 30th ult. with Genl Coffees & my little ward Hutchings enclose'd.[1]

your several letters aluded to has come to hand—The answer of Mr [Ezra Stiles] Ely, I enclosed under cover to your aunt, noting it to you, that you might see it. you will receive other business from Philadelphia, and attention will acquire you much more.[2]

My former letters will have advised you that I am at peace here with all[3]—Colo Benton has, on the committee of military affairs; & some select committees of which we are members; treated me with marked politeness: <but as I know the man,> I return it civilly and we meet friendly—I pursue the advice I so often have given you; it is the best rule in life. The Public Journals will afford you all the Political news of this, & the adjoining countries: They people begin to speak a language that will be heard. Newyork will in a few weeks unfold her views. If that state passes a law giving to the people the right to elect the electors; the Radical candidate will be withdrawn. whether Calhouns friends will still Push him I cannot say; or whether Mr Clinton will be taken up by Newyork is doubtfull—If the latter, it will be to put down for the present, other pretentions; and the people lastly to decide; you recollect what Doctor Dolivan said: I have reasons to believe that is true.[4]

I have recd from your aunt her letter of the 29th. ult with my sons enclosed—I answer your aunts by this mail.[5] I have but little time to spare to my friends; the numbers of letters recd, added to the calls of my friends; and the official business of my station is truly laborious—my friend Eaton does much for me; I will, I trust get on, without any discreted either to myself or station

you must write as often as you can—but cannot expect me to answer all—

you will see from the papers, that I have been honoured by the present of the Pistols of Genl Washington presented to him by Lafayett—the adress upon the occasion & my answer &c &c[6]—I have read Genl Coffees letter, I hope you will collect as much as will meet the debts due—I am glad to learn that the mony I remitted ($150) to Judge Overton has reached him, altho you do not name it, I infer it; from your remark, that you have taken his acknowledgement for it.[7] I am pleased that your aunt enjoys health & all things are doing well—

say to little Hutchings I will write him—Lyncoyas letter Major Eaton asked me for, I have given it him[8]—its now eleven P.M. with compliments to all adieu—your affectionate uncle

Andrew Jackso*[n]*

ALS, DLC (32).

1. Letters not found.
2. See AJ to Rachel Jackson, January 10. Ely (1786–1861; Yale 1803) was a Presbyterian minister in Philadelphia. His letter, which has not been found, responded to Jackson's urging that Ely again bring an appeal of Thomas B. Craighead's suspension before the General Assembly of the Presbyterian Church, where consideration had been postponed in 1823.
3. Not found.
4. Possibly Benjamin Delavan (d. 1827), an army surgeon originally from New York. New York politicians opposed to Martin Van Buren's Albany Regency had organized as a People's Party and campaigned for popular election of presidential electors instead of legislative selection. Despite considerable success in the 1823 elections, they were unable to pass their bill in the legislative session that began on January 6.
5. See AJ to Rachel Jackson, January 15, below. The letters to Jackson have not been found.
6. See Charles F. Mercer to AJ, and AJ to Mercer, January 8.
7. See AJ to John Overton and to Donelson, December 5, 1823. John Coffee's letter has not been found.
8. See Lyncoya to AJ, December 29, 1823. Jackson's letter to Andrew J. Hutchings has not been found.

To Rachel Jackson

City Janry 15th. 1824

My Dear wife

I have recd your kind & affectionate letter of the 28th December with one from our son enclosed.[1] I am rejoiced to hear of your health & spirits and pray that they may continue untill I return. I have been kept too busy since my arival to adopt your advice of retiring early; you know my habits when at home; when I am without company I retire at 9: when I have company, at 10–11. as the company desire; but here when the early part of the evening is spent with my friends who visit me the latter must be spent in attention to duty and to business; one thing I can assure you, that I take as much care of my health as I can, and am happy to say to you, it has improved & is as good as I have any right to expect it. I thank you for your prayers, mine is offerred up for a continuation of your health, may the be heard. say to Colo. Butler all things progress slowly, as usual, fair promises, without acts. I have the Presidents positive promise that something shall be done for him, but what that may be I cannot say, the Survayor District in Florida if the law passes[2]—Present me to all friends & delivered the enclosed letter to my son,[3] and believe me to be your affectionate Husband

Andrew Jackson

ALS, DLC (32). Published in Bassett, 3:223.

1. Letters not found.
2. The act of March 3, 1823, regarding the settlement of private land claims in Florida, had stipulated that a surveyor be appointed after those claims were settled. The act of May 24, 1824, setting aside land for a seat of government, repealed that provision, thus allowing

immediate appointment of a surveyor, for which Robert Butler was confirmed on May 24 (see 3 *U.S. Statutes at Large* 755, and 4 *ibid.* 31).

3. Letter not found.

The first stirrings of controversy regarding Jackson's correspondence with James Monroe in 1816 and 1817 appeared when the Philadelphia Democratic Press *of January 14 reported Jackson had recommended that Monroe appoint two Federalists and two Democrats to the cabinet, a charge with some credibility as Jackson had recommended one Federalist, William Drayton, for secretary of war and approved Monroe's choice of John Q. Adams, arguably a second Federalist, for secretary of state (see* Washington Gazette, *January 17). When the news reached Washington, Jackson prepared to respond, but neither he nor Monroe exhibited any detailed memory of their correspondence. Mistakenly believing that he had recommended Adams and Drayton in a single letter, Jackson initially requested a copy of his letter of March 18, 1817 (*Jackson, *4:102–103), in response to Monroe's of March 1, 1817. Monroe's reply, below, apparently referred to Jackson's letter of November 12 (*Jackson, *4:73–75) and Monroe's of December 14, 1816. Monroe's initial denial of the* Press's *report (see AJ to Andrew J. Donelson, January 18, below) did not quiet the controversy, which continued even after publication of the correspondence in May, with anti-Jackson newspapers implying that Jackson had advocated a balance of Republicans and Federalists in the cabinet and pro-Jackson papers stressing that the general had merely recommended a nonpartisan appointment of one highly qualified individual.*

To James Monroe

city of Washington
Janry 16th. 1824

Sir

Having wrote a letter in answer to one recd from you (I think early in 1817) giving my opinion of Certain charectors which you had therein named; & who had been recommended to you for your Executive council & heads of Departments: and not having a Copy here, will you have the goodness to furnish me a coopy of that letter—should that be inconvenient, please send me this Evening the original which shall be returned so soon as a coopy is taken—your complience will oblige. Believe me to be very respectfully your friend

Andrew Jackson

ALS, DLC (9-0937). Published in Washington *National Intelligencer,* May 8.

From James Monroe

Washington, Jan. 16, 1824.

Dear Sir:

Since the receipt of yours of this day,[1] asking for your letter addressed to me, about the time I came into this office, I have been engaged in searching for it among my papers, but have not yet found it. I very well recollect the letter, as well as my answer to it, and well know that I have both, and that the difficulty experienced in finding them proceeds from my having taken too good care of them. I will continue my search to-morrow, and I hope with better success, unless I may have left them in the country. Your letter did you honor. It expressed noble and manly sentiments, having for their object the preservation of our Republican Government, by a generous exercise of power, by the Republican party, in a way to inspire general confidence, and draw the Union together. I hope, however, to find your letter to morrow, and in which event I will send it to you. With great respect and sincere regard, yours

JAMES MONROE.

Printed, Washington *National Intelligencer,* May 8 (mAJs), *Jackson Gazette,* June 5 (9-0939), and other papers.

1. See above.

To Andrew Jackson Donelson

City Janry 18th. 1824

Dr. Andrew

I wrote you yesterday requesting you to search for, & send me, a copy of my letter written to Mr Monroe in the latter part of the year 1816. or early in 1817. & a copy of Mr Monroes letter to me on the subject of his Executive council or heads of Departments—My letter to him which I want is the one in which I bring to his View, & recommend to him Colo. [William] Drayton of Charleston So. Carolina as a fit person as sec. of war. I wish you to send copies attested & keep the originals least they may be taken out of the mail; and adress them to Major Eaton. If you have time; send duplicates; one to Major Eaton, & the other adressed to me. read over Mr Monroes letters of that date, & send me copies of all you <th> find on the Subject of officers & appointments, and copies of my letters that contain recommendations of date 1816 or 1817.[1] I expect the object is, by the publication at this moment to produce an effect upon Pensylvania who is about to form an electoral Tickett to support me. But this will not take as I believe; Mr [George] Kreamer a member from

Pensylvania, the moment he saw it, went direct to the President and asked him, if there was any truth in the publication; & received for answer: "that there was not," he immediately wrote to [John] Binns the Editor in Philadelphia a letter giving the declaration of Mr Monroe, & requesting him to publish it—which if he does not; Mr Kreamer (who is my warm friend) intends to have it published here. This will dam the contriver; and make the Calumny recoil on the author.[2] If it was intended to irratate me, they have missed their mark—I laugh at it. Present me to Mrs. Jackson affectionately—to they Andrews & Lyncoya, & to all friends—I have only to add, that intrigue is the order of the day here. I steer clear of all that I suspect of it, I abhor it, and its actors, & would not be placed in the Presidential chair by it. present me affectionately to Miss. E. to my old friend Capt J. D. & to all friends.[3] your affectionate uncle.

Andrew Jackson

P.S. I have heard from Mr Monroe this evening & he has not yet found it—This makes it necessary for you if you can find it to forward it at as early a day as possible.[4] A. J.

I am informed, South Carolina, Alab. Mississpi, Louisiana, Tennnessee Kentucky, <&> Ohio, & Maryland, will all come out in my favour—North Carolina & Newyork are divided, this make the present effort necessary to endeavour to divide if possible the great leading state Pensylvania. There is a great stir in Virginia: & Georgia if she gives up her candidate; is said will support me—whether one half of the above information is true I cannot say; I give it as I have heard it, for yourself only. I am told Missouri is coming out also—but as I know nothing only what others tell me, I let it pass for mere rumor—as you know the Hermitage is my delight, and my only ambition to dwell on it: adieu A. J.

ALS, DLC (32). Published in Bassett, 3:223–24.

1. See AJ to Donelson, January 16. Drayton (1776–1846) had been commissioned colonel of the 18th Infantry, but had seen no action, finishing the war as inspector general. As president in 1831, Jackson again considered him for secretary of war following John H. Eaton's resignation. Jackson had recommended Drayton to James Monroe in letters of October 23 and November 12, 1816 (*Jackson,* 4:69–71, 73–75).

2. The January 17 letter from Kremer (1775–1854) to Binns (1772–1860), editor of the Philadelphia *Democratic Press,* was published in the Washington *National Intelligencer,* January 26. According to Kremer, Monroe denied that Jackson had urged appointment of two Federalists and stated that Jackson had made only one recommendation for office (a reference to Drayton).

3. Emily Tennessee Donelson and her father John Donelson (1755–1830).

4. No letter from Monroe of this date has been found.

To Edward George Washington Butler

City W. Janry 20th. 1824.

Dear Edward,

your friendly letter of the 9th. instant, giving me an account of the celebration of the 8th., came to hand by due course of mail.[1]

It cannot but be gratifying to me to see this day commemorated by the american people; and particularly for the praise-worthy object of raising funds to aid the oppressed, but gallant Greeks: It must be gratifying to every bosom, that cherishes, as it ought, warm feelings for the liberty of mankind, & a Just abhorrence of the cruelties that have been inflicted on the oppressed Greeks; and the patriots of spain. It will have another good effect; It will keep in the recollection of this nation, what gallant men can do, when united; and act as a stimulant to others, to gallant deeds, should our country again be invaded by a foreign enemy.[2]

The party at *[M]*rs. Adams was the largest I ever witnessed at a private house; every room was crowded; you have a good description of it in the papers.[3] The present made me by Mr. [George Washington Parke] Custis was truly grateful. I view it as the highest honor that could be paid to me, to be considered worthy, by the representatives of that *immortal man,* the father of his country; to be a fit repository for the implements used by him in the procurement, & Establishment of our national independence, & liberty. It is more gratifying to my feelings than all the honours my country has hitherto bestowed upon me. you have, no doubt, ere this, seen the account of the Pistols, presented by Lafayette to Genl. Washington, being presented to me, on the 8th. by Colo. [Charles Fenton] Mercer, at the request of Colo. [William] Robertson, one of the Genls. Legatees[4]

I shall, at as early a day as I can, wait upon Mrs. [Eleanor Parke Custis] Lewis & pay my respects personally to her, and to Mr Custis. I do intend to write her before I leave the city.[5]

It will afford me much pleasure to hear occasionally from Genl. Gains; to whom & his lady, present me respectfully.[6]

I have but little time to write to a friend; I am constantly engaged, and on business, & the question that now appears to agitate the public mind; I receive about ten letters pr. mail; I answer none but on business—except those from men, who ask to be informed as to facts, to correct errors—you, therefore, cannot expect me to write you often: still it will afford me great pleasure to hear from you, when you have leisure from your official duty. I write *[no]*w in haste & for your own eye; and tender to you my warmest affection & good wishes, & believe me yr friend.

Andrew Jackson

ALS, MnHi (10-0381); Extract, LNT (10-0384). Published in St. Louis *Missouri Republican,* August 7, 1883, and other papers (extract).

1. Not found.

2. On the evening of January 8, the anniversary of the Battle of New Orleans, a grand military ball was held at New York City's Park Theatre to raise funds to support Greece's recently declared independence, at this time jeopardized by an invading Turkish force.

3. The *Washington Republican, and Congressional Examiner,* January 9, and New York *Statesman,* January 16, both carried descriptions of the Adams's party, also held on January 8.

4. Custis (1781–1857), the son of George Washington's stepson John Parke Custis, presented Jackson with a pocket spyglass used by Washington during the revolutionary war. Mercer (1778–1858; Princeton 1797), a Virginia congressman, presented the Marie Joseph Paul Yves Roch Gilbert du Motier, Marquis de Lafayette (1757–1834) pistols as a gift from Robinson (1782–1857) of Sudley plantation along Bull Run in Loudoun and Fairfax counties. Robinson, the husband of Anne Aylette Washington (1783–1804), a daughter of George Washington's nephew William Augustine Washington, was later selected as a Fairfax County delegate to the June 28 Jackson convention in Fredericksburg. The spyglass was destroyed in the 1834 Hermitage fire; Jackson bequeathed the pistols to Lafayette's son, George Washington Lafayette.

5. Lewis (1779–1852), John P. Custis's daughter and wife of Washington's nephew Lawrence Lewis (1767–1839), had presented Jackson with a china plate used by Washington at birthday feasts. See AJ to Rachel Jackson, December 28, 1823. Jackson's letter to her has not been found.

6. In 1815, Edmund P. Gaines married Barbara Grainger Blount (c1792–1836), a daughter of Southwest Territory Governor William Blount.

To Chandler Price

Washington City
Janry. 20th 1824

Dr Sir

I thank you for the friendly letters you have written me; two have lately been recd., one yesterday. Your request relative to the appointing of Judges arived too late, they appointments had been made & the Gentleman highly spoken of by several Gentlemen of the Senate who were acquainted with them.[1]

In answer to your inquiry about publishing the letter I wrote you; it might be sufficient to propose to leave that altogether to your Judgt. & discretion.[2] I beg leave however to suggest to you, that any thing from me on such a subject might & probably would be interpreted as aiming at *electioneering*. That I was pressing my letters thro the country with a view to my own advancement. Such an interpretation altho remote from truth, I should regret to see made, & yet such an imputation might & probably would be made, on the publication of a letter from me on that subject. This is the only objection I could have, & even this is only thrown out by the way of suggestion to you; for I write no letter, the sentiments of which I would ever desire to conceal; and this I assure you is true, notwithstanding that Mr. Binns has positively pledged himself to my having written a letter to Mr Monroe in 1816, urging as necessary & proper that his Cabinet should be so made up as that two Federalists, & two Republicans should form it. Mr. Binns can produce no such letter, & has my free consent to publish it forthwith; for by my opinions, & my acts would I be Judged; leaving with the people of the united states to decide as I myself should, in favour of no man whose sentiments & conduct, are not practically in conformity to those principles, on which are based the republican institutions of our country.

I know the importance & value of health too well, not to regret to hear that yours is bad; let me advise you to keep clear of the Doctors, preserve your mind tranquil, & practice temperance in living, for these are the great, the important Phicians, that have raised me again to pretty good health, & which, if attended to, will soon restore you. I am with great respect your Mo obdt. Servt.

Andrew Jackson

ALS, PHC (10-0385). Published in *Potter's American Monthly,* 5 (1875):826. Price (c1766–1827), a Philadelphia merchant, presided at a December 20, 1823, meeting that supported Jackson for president, at which he was appointed to the committee of correspondence and as a delegate to a proposed convention to select Jackson electors for Pennsylvania. At the Harrisburg convention in March, he introduced a resolution that only electors pledged to Jackson be nominated.

1. Letters not found; the nature of Price's request about the "appointing of Judges" has not been established.

2. In his letter of January 6, Jackson stated that he would "be content to leave" the presidential choice to the American people "without any, the least interference of mine." Excerpts from both letters to Price, January 6 and 20, were first published in the Philadelphia *Aurora,* February 2 (not found), and republished in other papers.

To Andrew Jackson Donelson

Washington City Janry 21rst 1824

Dear Andrew

your letter of the 6th instant is Just recd[1] I am glad to learn that my cotton in part will be shipped so early in this present month—I wish to have the debt due my friend Mr [Josiah] Nichols paid. I hope you have made the necessary erangements with him for this purpose—by directing the amount of sales of the cotton when made to be remmitted to him, or direct to you at Nashville. The amount of sales over the account of Mr Nichols I wish retained its being u states notes, will be usefull on our Journey here next fall: I was charged 33 pct advance on my Tennessee funds on my way hither at Abington.[2]

The Public lands in Alabama will not be sold this year, Therefore Mr Crawford will not be able to redeem his Pledge to his friends, but it is my opinion the ought, the delay is injurious both to the country & to those who are waiting to purchase for settlement, as well as the Goverment.[3]

The Intrigue is still going on here; but it will not avail, a letter from a gentleman of N. Carolina of the first respectability was shewn me to day, who says if Pensylvania declares for me N Carolina is certain—This days mail brings intelligence of a meeting held at Philadelphia on Saturday last, where there were five standards hoisted, one bearing the name of each candidate, Mr C. Price writes me they were all deserted but one & that bore the insignia of Jackson[4]—This being a trial at the place where the other candidates expected to make an impression on Pensylvania, and at a time when all were invited to attend has cast the die, and has fixed Pensylvania—& of course N Carolina—if Judge [Archibald De Bow] Murphys information is true.[5] I found many gloomy faces to day in the Senate Hall—It is said There is to be a *caucus*, This I cannot believe—but it is the last hope of the friends of Mr Crawford, and I have no doubt it will be attempted—with what success time will determine. But it appears to me that such is the feelings of the nation that a recommendation by a congressional caucus would politically Dam any name put forth by it. write me often & my Dr young friend be attentive to your aunt & write me often—I wrote you for copies of the Presidents letters to me on the subject of his cabinett in 1816. or early in 1817. & copies of my answers or letters to him recommending Colo Drayton of Charleston & Mr Adams send me copies of all[6]—your friend & affectionate uncle

Andrew Jackson

ALS, DLC (32). Published in Bassett, 3:224–25.

1. See Donelson to AJ, [January 6].

2. Jackson kept a running account with Nichol (1772–1833), a Nashville merchant, premised on advances for his cotton sales. While en route to Washington, he instructed Rachel, "I hope you will not permit yourself to want for any thing, apply to Mr Josiah Nichols, and he will furnish you with any thing you may want" (November 23, 1823). His account for this period has not been found, but Jackson had written Donelson on December 5, 1823, that he would like to pay Nichol $400 by Christmas. Donelson's endorsement on Jackson's account with Bedford & Mackey, January 30, states that he paid the $400 debt on March 27, banking the remaining $2,015 balance from Jackson's cotton sale.

3. Jackson was probably referring to the sale of northern Alabama lands relinquished under the 1821 relief act. On January 6 James Monroe had proclaimed sales of relinquished land in southern Alabama for June at Cahaba and St. Stephens, but the northern Alabama sale was not set until July 14, when Monroe proclaimed a sale at Huntsville in March 1825. In December, the Huntsville sale was postponed further.

4. Chandler Price's letter has not been found.

5. Jackson had probably seen Murphey's letter of January 16 to John H. Eaton (THi). Murphey (1777?–1832; North Carolina 1799) served on the North Carolina superior court, 1818–20. He reported strong support for Jackson among the people of North Carolina, although the political leaders tended to support William H. Crawford or John C. Calhoun, and stated that if Pennsylvania "should come out openly for Genl. Jackson, his Friends here will feel confident of his success, and a vigorous effort will be made for him."

6. See AJ to Donelson, January 16 and, above, 18.

To Rachel Jackson

Washington City Janry 21rst 1824

My Dear wife

I have this day recd. your affectionate letter of the 4th. Instant,[1] and sincerely regret that you are indisposed: but I trust that kind providence will soon relieve you from the pain that the inflamation of your eye must inflict—with what pleasure would I apply the *cooling wash* was I with you; & how painfull it is to me to hear of the least affliction in my absence; but I trust & hope, that we will again meet, when we will here below travel together while life lasts.

My health is good, altho I am much pressed with business, and with Company—The attentions I have recd. loose all their relish I assure you, whilst you are absent; still it is gratifying that after all the shafts of envy & malice that has been levelled at me by my enemies; that my country approve my Public conduct; & that too amidst the combined intrigue & efforts of those who would by falshood the most *vile* deprive me of public confidence if they could. But that providence who will allways protect those who take virtue for their guide, has protected me, & will shield me from the efforts of my enemies; in him I allways have put my trust & he has & will protect me. My love, remember you have promised me that you would bear up under my absence—recollect that your health much depend upon your keeping your mind calm & at ease, & I pray you to do so. I am gratefull to your nieces for staying with you, present me affectionately to them I am pleased to learn that Eliza is with you, I hope her spirits are good, & that she will keep yours up while she tarrys with you; present me affectionately to her, & tell her I have Just recd a letter from Edward from Newyork, that he is well & doing well—he spent some weeks in the city after my arival—he requests me in his letter to present him respectfully to you—he is a fine young man, & is much respected in the army. I have just heard from Danl & Samuel—they are doing well at the M. accademy—give this intelligence to all their friends.[2] I am much gratified to hear that my two little Andrews are so obedient to, & stay with you; I hope they learn their Books *well*; say to them that I would be sorry when I bring them here, that they boys of their age should laugh at their ignorance, tell my son I recollect his expressions in his letter "that he hopes he will be able to hold up his head when he comes here—amonghst they boys of his age, and be able to compare with them in point of education & good deportment," This is what his papa wishes & for which he has sent him to school, and hopes him & Hutchings will reallise.[3]

I am glad to learn that all things on the farm goes on well, this is what I expected under the management of Mr Parsons—present me to him, he has my confidence.

Present me to Colo. Butler & family: say to him I will write him, so soon as a Bill that is now on its passage, directing the lands in Florida to be survayed is passed into a law; finding all things uncertain *here*, I will not write him untill I can do so with some certainty.[4]

I write by this mail to Capt A. J. Donelson,[5] & will be happy to hear from you as often as it is convenient for you to write—with my respects to all friends believe me to be your affectionate Husband

Andrew Jackson

P S. Major Eaton & Call send their kind respects to you Major Eaton wrote some mails <ago> past.[6]

ALS, CSmH (10-0388). Published in *Huntington Library Bulletin,* 3(1933):122–24.

1. Not found.
2. The letters from Edward G. W. Butler, Daniel S. Donelson, and Samuel J. Hays have not been found.
3. Quoted letter not found.
4. For a brief discussion of the Florida bill, reported to the House on January 20, see above, AJ to Rachel Jackson, January 15.
5. See above, AJ to Andrew J. Donelson, January 21.
6. John H. Eaton's letter not found.

To John Geddes

Washington City, Jan. 27th, 1824.

Sir—

The Resolution of the City Council of Charleston, communicated by you through Major [James] Hamilton [Jr.] and Mr. Poinsett of the House of Representatives, requesting that my Portrait may be taken by Mr. [John] Vanderlyn, is with pleasure acceded to.[1] It will subject me to no inconvenience I assure you; and if it did, that would form no consideration. It is matter of pleasure and satisfaction to me, that my native State can think so favourably of me, as to desire to procure a resemblance, and hence to retain a remembrance of me. I therefore cheerfully comply with the request made through you, on behalf of the City Council. I view it in no other light, than a testimonial of respect and regard from those who are of the State that gave me birth, and where many of the pleasurable days of my youth were spent.

Accept my best wishes for the kind expressions you are pleased to offer me, and receive mine for your health and happiness; and be pleased to tender me most respectfully to the City Council. I have the honor to be, respectfully, your most obedient servant.

ANDREW JACKSON.

Printed, Charleston *City Gazette and Commercial Daily Advertiser,* February 12 (mAJs), *Sparta Review,* March 24 (10-0400), and other papers. Geddes (1777–1828), a former governor of South Carolina, was Intendant of Charleston.

1. See Geddes to AJ, January 17. Vanderlyn (1775–1852), a noted New York portraitist, visited Washington in February. His full-length painting of Jackson remains in the Charleston City Hall collection; for a reproduction of the painting, see *Jackson,* 2:332. Hamilton (1786–1857), of Charleston, represented South Carolina in Congress, 1822–29.

To Francis Preston

City of Washington
Janry 27th. 1824

Genl

I am glad to find you are so young and active as at so inclement a season to be found so far from home. I have Just recd your letter of the 25th. instant,[1] and assure you, that nothing but want of time, and the fatigue of a long & troublesome Journey prompted me to pass Abingdon without calling at your house. on my return should I come by Abingdon your polite request to call & see you will not I assure you be neglected.

your other request to vissit Richmond, cannot be complied with: and when it is recollected, that such a vissit would be atributed to any thing than the real and true cause, I am persuaded you would by no means desire me to do so. My course is that which my feelings dictate, to practice nothing, and to take no step, which may have imputed to it, a disposition to recommend myself to anyone. Not to decline or seek office is my maxim: & to do any act which may present me in a different charecter, even in the opinion of any Person would produce to me a most unpleasant reflection. I cannot therefore now vissit Richmond, altho it would under other circumstances afford me pleasure to do so.

you are right in your opinion; many do indeed believe me unfit for civil life; and many here, strangers to me, had expected, I understand, to see a most uncivilised, unchristian man when they beheld me. They had derived their opinions from some of those dificult situations in which heretofore it was my good or bad fortune to be placed; and forming their conclusions from them I most usually have been pronounced a rash & inconsiderate man. I am content they should continue to think so; premising to you, however, that those who do think so know but little about me. If to do my duty & to follow the dictates of my Judgtment when running counter to the opinion of others, be rashness, I indeed have sometimes been rash; but permit me to assure you, that however in times of toil & trouble, this charecter may have been imputed to me; now in these our times of peace there are some of the politicians of the country who in their construction of constitutional power go greatly a head of where I should dare to venture.

Peace with all the world, suffering insult & indignity from none, would be the amount of my prudence & of my rashness: & if this be wrong, my country should be cautious how they ventured to confide her rights & her interests into my hands. I hope to see our Republican principles & institutions long preserved; & this being attained, I shall go down to my grave I assure you, contented & quiet.

I write you quite in haste, & beg you to accept my best wishes; & when you shall reach home, to present me kindly to Mrs Preston, & the family. I am Dr Sir with great respect yr mo ob servt,

Andrew Jackson

ALS, CSmH (10-0402). Published in *Huntington Library Bulletin*, 3(1933):124–25.
1. Not found.

The letter below, now available only in fragmentary form, was apparently intact as late as 1922, when Andrew Jackson IV and Frank J. Klingberg published extracts in the South Atlantic Quarterly. *The comparison of overlapping texts in the surviving extract, a catalog listing for a currently unlocated fragment, and the 1922 publication makes possible a near-total reconstruction of the letter.*

To Rachel Jackson

City of Washington
Janry 29th. 1824

My Dear wife

I had the pleasure to receive your kind an affectionate letter of the 12th. instant on yesterday and presented your respects to the pious old lady & her daughters with whom we live, and they beg of me to reciprocate their kind wishes—[1]

It is true when I have leisure, my time passes agreably with this family; but of Leisure I have but little; every mail brings me at least one dozzen of letters, most of which are on business, & requires answering. This occasions me much labour, which added to my congressional duties, is really oppressive; however I am blessed with better health than when I left you; and learning from your letter, that you are blessed with health; will add greatly to mine. I am not surprised that your *[. . . .]* I trust in providence that this fine weather may continue; and that health may be maintained every where; but This cannot be expected

I have no doubt you have seen in the papers that there are now two commets that are seen nightly—This I have but little doubt has an effect upon the season, and produces this very extraordinary winter; I believe this is a phenomna, not before recorded in history, I have no recollection of hearing of two commets being seen at once in any country before the present.

I am truly happy to hear that our church is about to be finished, and that pious good man Mr Hume, is to dedicate it—If such a mans prayers cannot obtain a blessing upon the neighbourhood, I would despair of the efficacy of prayer from any other; but we are taught to believe, that the prayers of the righteous prevaileth much,[2] & I trust his will procure a blessing to the neighbourhood & that the church will be of great benefit in christianisin[g] the people in our settlement.

AL fragment, THer (10-0415).

1. Letter not found.
2. Probably an allusion to James 5:16.

I feel grateful to the members of the church and my neighbors for giving the name of the church to me. I regret to think I am unworthy of it, but still hope thru the influence of the Devine Spirit to become worthy to be a member. . . . It was my desire to retire to private life & live free from the bustle of public life & the scenes of intrigue and corruption that appear to be the order of the day as practiced in this great city. There is one consolation left for me & that is, that I mingle not in it; I pursue my old course of doing that which my Judgt dictates & fearing no consequences, thus my conscience is left free from remorse,

Extract, Kingston Galleries, Inc., Catalog 26 (c1970), Item 129 (9-0876).

[which is better] than what, all earthly things can bestow.

I am pleased that every thing appertaining to my farm goes on well—& that you have resolved to be contented in my absence—Thi*[s]* is truly a consolation to me, & I trust in that kind & overruling providence that he wi*[ll]* bless you with health & that he will permit *[us]* once more to have a happy meet*[ing.]*

I write you often & hope my letter*[s reach]* you; say to my friend Colo. Butler, *[that]* Mr Monroe has said to me, he wi*[ll as soon]* as the law passes give him the *[appointment]* of survayor in Florida. I have re*[cd. my son's]* letter,[3] but have not time now to *[answer it. Say]* to him he must write me often *[and must try to]* improve his handwriting, & his *[diction. I am pleased with his letter bu]*t wish *[him to improve by writing me often. . . . Give my love to the Andrews, Eliza and what young ladies may be with you. . . . believe me to be your affectionate husband*

Andrew Jackson]

AL fragment, THer (10-0415); bracketed and italicized material from *South Atlantic Quarterly,* 21(April 1922):134–35.

3. Not found.

To John Christmas McLemore

Washington City
Janry 30th. 1824

Dear Sir

I have Just recd your friendly letter of the 13th. Instant;[1] It affords me sincere pleasure to be informed of your success in the sales of your land, and that you now see your way through those dificulties brought on by your liberality to your friends: I now trust you will see the propriety of adopting my course; that is, endorse for no one, unless you are confident that the paper will be taken up without application to you; If your friend is in distress, & if you have the means to spare, in property or otherwise, *give it*; & if it is lost it does not carry with it, either the evils or sacrafices occasioned by endorsements; which are never provided for, allways calculating that the bills will be punctually met & taken up; I thank you for the information you have given me as it respects Mr. Darbys late claim. In your office we had the last conversation, Mr Darby had drew an instrument relating to the transfer of the right of property I was to sign on the compromise with Judge Overton; this Instrument I objected to in its then form to sign, as it was not specific anough on the right retained, and you & Mr Darby & perhaps Mr [Jesse] Blackfan, had another drew in which it is positively stated that the right tittle & interest in the land claimed in suit myself vs A. Erwin & others is retained in James Jackson & myself & no others—These papers were left with Mr Darby, to be recorded in Davidson for my safety & in the county, where the land relinquished by Overton &c &c, for the safety of those to whom the were convayed. I will thank you to give to Mr James Jackson all the information on this subject that is within your recollection, & please to examine whether they papers executed in your presence & to which you are a witness has been recorded by Mr Darby in Davidson, If they are, the record will shew, that Mr Darby acknowledged he had no interest in the suit pending; as I have left with Mr James Jackson a power of attorny to close & settle all & every thing about that disagreable suit, I will thank you to give him such information on this subject in writing as your recollection & referrence to the papers will furnish, keeping a copy of your statement to him.[2]

We are doing little business here; The intrigues & management, of, & concerning the Presidential question will prevent much being done this congress: whether the friends of the Treasury will be able to get up a caucus is unknown to me but if they do, they cannot muster more than 70; this would not have any weight with the nation, & I suppose hearring nothing of it for some days, their effort has failed.

The Radicals so called, are making their last effort in new york, should the friends of Crawford fail there, he is gone—should new york support him, his friends will continue the struggle—& Virginia may unite—from information from Newyork if the people are left to elect, the Electors, Mr Crawford will get <none> few, if any, in the state—North Carolina from late accounts will unite with Pensylvania, & on that event So Carolina & Georgia with the western states will unite This is the opinion as communicated to me, by those who have correspondence on the subject; as to myself I write not, nor mix with intriguers—I pursue my old course, *[from]* which I will not depart—I am greatly pestered with letters on business from all quarters and keeps me busy. Present me to Mrs. McL Mrs Anderson & all friends, and accept assurances of my friendship & Esteem

Andrew Jackson

P.S. I thank you for the intelligence of Mrs J health.

ALS, TMPPM (10-0417).

1. See McLemore to AJ, January 13.

2. See power of attorney to James Jackson, November 6, 1823. Jackson was referring to his negotiations with McLemore, John Overton, Jesse Wharton, and Patrick H. Darby in 1822 to settle conflicts over the Allison land claims (see above, AJ to McLemore, April 11, 1822). Neither the instrument drawn by Darby nor the subsequent agreement recollected by Jackson has been found; and McLemore's reply, if any, to this letter is also not found. Blackfan, originally from Bucks County, Pennsylvania, was an attorney in Nashville by 1813.

To Rachel Jackson

City of Washington
Febry 6th. 1824

My Dear wife

I have this evening recd your kind and affectionate letter of the 19th. January:[1] It gives me great pleasure to learn that the church is finished, and that good man Mr Hume has dedicated it; I hope it will be a means of uniting the neighbourhood in the bonds of christian benevolence, and friendship, and that we may obtain a pastor, imbued with all the christian Virtues, who will shew us by his walks, & conversation; that the welfare of the little flock is his chief care: then truly the labourer will be worthy of his hire; & I trust as good christians, we will freely yield it to him. It is pleasing to me that my friend Eatons letter has reached you[2]—rely on it, he is amonghst the most worthy, of the humane race—Our friend Call, Eaton, & myself are the only occupants, of one half the house of our worthy and amiable Hostess Mrs. Oneals, & her charming family; I say Hostess, because the house is kept under her name, from the pecuniary losses of her husband Mr Oneal, who is a very good & worthy man—we are as comfortable as we could be under my seperation from you.

My health continues good, I have abstained from parties, except Mrs Adams, Mrs [Floride Colhoun] Calhouns, & Mrs. [Elizabeth Washington

Gamble] Wirts, these latter; I was obliged to go to, as I had attended Mrs Adams party on the 8th. of Janry.[3] I have not yet vissited Mrs. Monroes drawing room, this I intend once, and that the first good evening on which it happens: The various attentions & presents from the Legatees & representatives of the *best* of *men, the mighty chieftain, the father* of *his country, the immortal Washington;* is the most acceptable gifts I could receive;[4] I lay them up as precious relex, worthy to be preserved; I know you will think me Vain—but I assure you Vanity has no seat in my boosom; but to be thought worthy of this deposit, has confirmed me, that the independant course I have pursued, following the dictates of that Judgtment that the wise creator has endued me with, has been right when approved by those whose approbation I ought most to esteem, & is the greatest gratification I could enjoy, by any expression of any portion of my country. It is, under the influence & intrigues of this city, a triump over my enemies, of honest worth, over corruption, & will save the nation from the rule of Demagogus, who by intrigue are, & have been attempting to cheat the people out of their constitutional rights, by a caucus of congressional members. I have recd a letter from our young friend Capt A. J. Donelson,[5] he has detailed to me the progress of my business, I beg of you to take your ease, keep your mind composed, preserve your health, and I pray god for its continuance untill we meet again which I trust a kind providence will grant.

It is late at night, I must close this hasty scrall written for your own eye; please say to my friend Genl Overton, I have not time to write him at present, I have recd twenty letters to day, most of which is on business; My friends must excuse me from writing to them—give my compliments to your brother John & family, & all friends; say to my dear little Andrews that I rejoice to hear of their good conduct that I hope to find them much improved in their education, I shall write you again shortly when I will have more leisure. I shall write Capt A. J. D. tomorrow.[6] accept my prayers for your health & happiness & believe me to be your affectionate husband.

Andrew Jackson

P.S. If Mr Hodge is with you present me to him—present me to Mr Hume & *[to]* Mr Cambell, Colo Butler & family *[& to]* Mrs. F.[7] & William Sanders & there families & to the young ladies that may be with you & to Mrs. E. Donelson & her family.

ALS, CSmH (10-0436). Published in *Huntington Library Bulletin,* 3(1933):125–27.

1. Not found.

2. Not found.

3. Floride Colhoun (1792–1866) married John C. Calhoun in 1811. Elizabeth Washington Gamble (1784–1857) married William Wirt in 1802. For an account of the Calhouns' party on January 13, see the New York *Statesman,* January 20.

4. See above, AJ to Edward G. W. Butler, January 20, for discussion of the George Washington relics.
5. Not found.
6. Letter not found.
7. Possibly Alethia Saunders Saunders, wife of Francis Saunders.

John Henry Eaton to Rachel Jackson

Washington City
8. Feby 1824.

My dear Madam

I have lately recvd. a letter from you,[1] and now reply because I am unwilling at any time to be a debtor and more particularly where the obligation is to a lady. But then my head is so full just now of politics bills laws and such like trash as to be wholly unable to work my fancy up to any point that can give interest to a letter. Well this makes no difference, for inasmuch as there is a very strong probability that ere long you may be required to come into our political Corps and join with us in the great affairs of the nation, it would not be a misplaced att*[em]*pt even were I to tell you, all about the little workings, management & intrigue that passes on here amidst our learned band of Congressmen. would you believe it we are so depraved as scarcely even to go to church, unless to the Capitol where visits are made rather for the purpose of shewing ones self, than that any pious feeling prompts; and then it has such an air of fashion, and shew to go there; more like going into a theatre than to the house of worship. Oh we are truly a wonderous set; not much inferior to the good people of Sodom & Gomorrah spoken of in olden time, who perished, not on account of their virtues. In this list the Genl is not included, for every Sunday he takes himself to some one of the churches, and returns again about 1 Oclock. Now while writing to you, he is off, attending to the admonitory voice of some good Divine

Genl. Jacksons health is most excellent. The climate agrees well with him, and he seems in better health than he has been since the war. Mrs Adams and Mrs Calhouns partys over he has declined altogether going out of evenings; and will only go out once again to Mrs. Monroes drawing room. The first good evening he will attend on that duly, and then will have ended all his night visits. He has most delightful comfortable quarters, and is subject to no exposure except in passing to the Capitol which we do every day in a warm comfortable close carriage

If the Genl had remained at home, I am satisfied he would not have enjoyed such health. His farm would have annoyed him—business would have s*[oon cal]*led him to alabama or Nashville, exposure & wet would have been met with: but here nothing of that is found. Gowing and returning from the Capitol is ample exercise; and when at home the reading & replying to letters, and sitting with a round of pleasant company that is perputally calling to see him, keeps his mind employed and his spirits cheerful. 'Tis very well he came here. Call & myself are all that live with him, and we are quite comfortable & happy I assure you with very great respect yours

J. H Eaton

Having returned from church, our friend handed me this letter to put a P.S. to; I have only to say that it is true, <as> my letter of yesterday will have advised you[2]—Mr & Mrs Monroe, & Mrs Watson & family, who I have Just seen, begs me to present to you their kind respects. A. J.

ALS with ANS by AJ, DLC (32). Published in Bassett, 3:225–26.

1. Not found.

2. Probably, above, AJ to Rachel Jackson, February 6.

To John Donelson (1755–1830)

City of Washington
Febry. 9th 1824

Dear Sir

your letter of the 22nd ult, which is Just recd afforded me much pleasure:[1] The account you give me of my overseer, & the progress of my farm & Domestic concerns is gratefying—I feel gratefull to my young female friends for their attention to Mrs. J. that her spirits should be kept up is alltogether important to her healt; and nothing as likely to obtain this, as the company of her young female friends. The View you have taken of our relations with urope; and the intention of the combination of the Holy alience, are well founded. I have no confidence in England, nothing but her interest will induce her to take a stand against the combination of Europe, but this may; her own situation is not without its perils, Rusia has been endeavouring to shut her fabrics from her dominion, south america has opened to her View a profitable commerce, & a markett for her manufactures, this may induce England to act in behalf of south america; and her interest will induce her; If it does; with the stand the u states has, & will take, the despots of Europe will pause before they attempt to interfere with south america.

The presidential question begin to agitate the minds of the people much; the attempt of a small minority of the members of Congress to get up a caucus & force public opinion to take up a particular candidate will still agitate it more; & I trust will eventuate in prostrating the caucus system alltogether; should the people suffer themselves to be dictated to by designing demagouges, who carry on every thing by intrigue, & management, they cannot expect to see their present happy Goverment perpetuated; it must sink under the scenes of Corruption that will be practiced under such a system; and in time open bribery may, & I have no doubt will be resorted to, to obtain a seat in the presidencial chair, if the people do not assume their rights of choosing a president themselves.

In this contest I take no part; I have long since prepared my mind to say with heartfelt submission, may the lords will be done; If it is intended by providence that I should fill the presidential chair, I will submit to it with all humility, & endeavour to labour four years with an eye single to the public good, imploring the guidance of providence in all things; but be assured, it will be an event that I never wished, nor expected. My only ambition was to spend the remainder of my days in domestic retirement, with my little family; it has turned out otherwise to my great annoyance; still I submit with proper resignation.

I thank you for your kind attention to Mrs J. be good anough to continue your attention to her, present me respectfully to your good lady, Emily & little family & believe me your friend,

Andrew Jackson

P.S. present me to my Mrs. J. say I wrote her two days ago.[2]

ALS, THi (10-0440). Published in Bassett, 3:226–27 (extract).

1. Not found.

2. Jackson was probably referring to his letter of February 6, above.

To Andrew Jackson Donelson

City. Febry 12th. 1824

Dear Andrew

I recd your letter of the 28th ult. and noted with some anxiety the protest of the Bill drew by D. [William Edward] & Colo Butler, & endorsed by me for non acceptance.[1]

This was a business I did not like when I did it; I told the Doctor so, but on his pledge that he would take care that I should never hear of it again, & it being entirely for his benefit, I endorsed it. However this is the second time; I shall beware of the third. I still think the Doctor will take it up, if he does not it will place me in a situation I would not be for all his property. your precaution in giving the order to Dr. Butler on Bedford & Mackey is approved.[2] I hope no accident may happen the Doctor on his passage to orleans, or his property; should any, it will place me in an unpleasant situation. This has been an unfortunate speculation to the Doctor; it originates from his purchase of scrip from Genl Parker, which took place several years since & to enable him to meet this Debt, in Judgt. the Bill was drew.[3] I would not have my bill protested for all the property I possess; I hope the Doctor will prevent it. I write weekly to your aunt; I write by this mail, I am fearfull her health is not good, her last letter enclosed in yours, displayed a gloom of mind not very usual for her to express, I pray you cheer her as much as you can.[4]

you will have seen from the papers & my last letter that there are to be a caucus of a small minority on the 14th. instant; 181 against going into caucus; from which it is evident that this minority are determined as far as their influence will go, to coerce public opinion, not as usual for caucus to follow it: no doubt remains with me but they will prostrate both their candidate & themselves in public opinion.[5]

Pensylvania, is said to be firm, Newyork will not it is believed support the caucus candidate Maryland & North Carolina will go with Pensylvania, Newjersy, <North &> So. Carolina will follow in her train, if this Happens, Virginia will not, *dare not,* seperate from Pensylvania, and the western states will unite. I give the above, as the information derived from those who are in correspondence with the influential charectors in the differrent states—But there are now here charectors from all parts of the union, intriguing on this subject; and if intrigue, management & Corruption can avail, the Treasury candidate[6] may (altho at present politically dead) be resussatad; and become the strongest; nothing but the Virtue of the people can prevent this; and to them, & them alone I look for a proper stand, such as will put down this system of intrigue, & restore the election of President to the people

I will be happy to hear from you often I have wrote you many letters that I find has not at the date of your last reached you. Present me to Major Lewis tell him I have no time to write any one except on business; and he will see from the papers all the Political news I could give him

Present me to all my Nashville friends, & those of my neighbourhood, & believe me to be your affectionate uncle

Andrew Jackson

ALS, DLC (10-0449). Published in Bassett, 3:227–28 (extract).

1. Letter not found. For the protest, see Greenbury R. Stringer to AJ, January 9. Doctor William E. Butler (1790–1882; Transylvania 1812), Robert's brother, was married to a niece of the Jacksons, Martha Thompson ("Patsy") Hays.

2. John R. Bedford had joined with James Mackey (d. 1824), formerly of Huntsville, in a New Orleans mercantile firm, through which Jackson disposed of his and Andrew J. Hutchings's cotton in 1824. Donelson had arranged to make $1,008 of Jackson's cotton proceeds available for William E. Butler to pay the protested note. See Donelson to Bedford & Mackey, January 23, DLC (32).

3. For Daniel Parker's judgment against the Butlers, June 12, 1823, see Minute Books of the U.S. Circuit Court for West Tennessee, 1803–1839, 2:372, DNA-RG 21 (M1214-1).

4. See AJ to Rachel Jackson, February 12; Rachel's letter has not been found.

5. Jackson's letter to Donelson, probably dated February 7, has not been found. In an undated document published in the *Washington Republican and Congressional Examiner* and the Washington *National Intelligencer* on February 12, Richard M. Johnson, John H. Eaton, and twenty-two other members of congress asserted that they had obtained information of 181 members who deemed a congressional caucus "inexpedient, under existing circumstances" (Richard M. Johnson et al. to [AJ?], cFeb 11).

6. Secretary of the Treasury William H. Crawford.

To John Coffee

City of Washington
Febry 15th. 1824

Dear Genl

It is some time since I wrote you; The Florida Bill spoken of in my last has not passed into a law: I believe if it does it will be laid out into two survayors District.[1]

I have had a long conversation with Mr [George] Graham who is much your friend: He is of the opinion that the business of the survayor Genl of your District cannot be closed in less than three years; from this calculation, and from the anxiety of many to have the lands in Florida survayed, & pushed in to Markett; I have doubts whether adding part of Florida to your District would be advantageous; It would add Labour without benefit, as it appears to me; four years more would be as long as your activity would desire a labourious office; I have therefore resolved not to do any thing in the business untill I hear from you. Write me freely on this subject.[2] I do assure you the applications for office here are many & I am so much disgusted with the want of energy in *some* of the *Departments*—that I hate to press any man in whose independence & Virtue I have confidence, finding as I have, that every thing is carried by intrigue, & management, promises are made often & not complied with; and this gives rise to murmurs, & dissatisfaction—In short sir all things here appear to bend to the approaching Presidential election—It is now a contest between a few demagogues and the people and it is to be seen whether a minority less than one fourth of the whole members of Congress, can coerce the people to follow them; or whether they people will assume their constitutional rights and put down these Demagogues; who say our course is necessary, for if you leave the election to the people: They will elect a certain Individual who is obnoxious to us. This my dear Sir is as much as to say they people are incapable of self goverment; and yet they call themselves Democratic Republicans. You will see the Resolutions of the Citizens of Baltimore on the 13th. the evening before the caucus was to be held here; they are strong & speak the language of freemen; who are Determined to maintain their rights, & perpetuate their republican form of Goverment.[3]

The caucus was held last night, they whole number who attended was sixty six, Crawford got sixty two Votes present, and two by proxy; both sick absent, and one perhaps dead. Having been six times interrupted since I commenced writing, has detained this letter untill the extra sheet of the Washington Republican has reached me—I enclose it for you & Mr James Jackson.[4]

I intended this day to have written Mr J. Jackson but from the Various calls of gentlemen I have been prevented, I shall write him the first leisure. I have not heard whether the suit, myself vs Andrew Erwin & others, have been compromised agreable to the articles entered into; I learn that Mr Darby has not returned to Tennessee, I enclose to you a letter I have recd from Mr McLomore I wish you to shew it to Mr James Jackson & then preserve it untill I see you; I wish you to do this, that Mr James Jackson may believe that my recollection, altho impaired, still, on important subjects, serves me pretty well; and when the papers aluded to are seen, they will fully shew that Mr Darby there fully and expressly acknowledges that no person but James & myself have any interest in the suit pending. I hope the suit is settled, if it is, I am sure it will be a lesson to me; & keep me from law the ballance of my life. If settled I hope Mr James Jackson has acted Liberally with Mr Darby, this I requested—but one thing is certain if the suit is not at an end, Mr Darby, from what I learn, will not return to Tennessee; of course we will not have his services in the prosecution: I therefore wish it at an end.[5]

I do assure you I am wearied already with the life of a Legislature: but would you believe it, that I have become a perfect Philosopher: It is true when I see the scenes of Intrigue & management that is going on here; my honest indignation arises within me—I look forward, & heave a sigh for the Liberties of my country, which must be destroyed by a continuation of such a course. I have still confidence in they people that they will preserve their Liberty by exercising their constitutional rights.

The 4th. of next month the delegation chosen to meet in convention to make an electorial tickett in Pensylvania, will unmask her strength; Maryland, Newjersy, North & South Carolina, ohio, will follow her; & it is believed by many; Virginia will not *dare* to seperate from her, time will unfold the verity of this.

present me affectionately to Polly and your sweet little children, to Mr & Mrs Jackson & the family, to Capt Jack & Eliza, to Captain Savage & his family & to all my friends in your neighbourhood & in Florence & believe me your friend

Andrew Jackson

P.S. Say to Judge Fulton to use his pen in opposition of this usurpation of the rights of the people. It is a fine theme, & it ought to be assailed from one end of the union to the other—This course will prostrate These Demagogues—and ever hereafter secure to the people their rights—This will be the last of King caucus—its Funeral Knell well will be sounded throughout the union.

ALS, THi (10-0457). Published in Bassett, 3:228–29 (extract).

1. See AJ to Coffee, January 5.

2. Graham (1772–1830; Columbia 1790), formerly a war department clerk and acting secretary of war, became commissioner of the General Land Office in December 1823. He had written Coffee, cNovember 18, 1823 (A-Ar), suggesting that Coffee might wish to apply through Jackson for the surveyorship of Florida Territory, and Coffee had asked Jack-

son to investigate (see AJ to Coffee, January 5). No response from Coffee has been found, but evidently he did not apply for the Florida position.

3. The meeting of Baltimore citizens disapproved of a caucus nomination as "an unjustifiable attempt to influence unduly, and to impede the free exercise of the most important privilege of freemen, and as tending to establish a practice at variance with the principles of the Constitution of the United States" (*Washington Republican and Congressional Examiner*, February 14).

4. The congressional caucus, which met in the House chamber about seven in the evening, gave William H. Crawford 64 votes, John Q. Adams 2 votes, Jackson 1 vote, and Nathaniel Macon 1 vote. The two proxy votes were William L. Ball of Virginia and Edward F. Tattnall of Georgia. Ball died on February 28. Enclosure not found.

5. See John C. McLemore to AJ, January 13. The compromise of Jackson's suit with Andrew Erwin, per the agreement of September 19, 1823, had just been executed (see deed to land in Bedford County, February 11). No letter to James Jackson near this date has been found. Patrick H. Darby had moved to Kentucky by the fall of 1824.

To Rachel Jackson

City of Washington
Febry 20th 1824

My Dear wife

I have to day received your kind letter of the 5th. Instant acknowledging mine of the 5th & 10th ult. to hear that you are in good health is a great pleasure to me: I am gratified that your niece Milbury is with you, she will keep your spirits up.[1]

How gratifying must your Vissit to your old friends have been to you, I rejoice to hear that they are in good health—and my old friend Mr [Thomas B.] Craighead is in good spirits; but you have not said any thing as to his sight, whether he obtained relief by his Vissit to Kentuckey or not—I should have been pleased to have been informed on this subject—say to my son I shall (as he has promised) look for his letter next mail—I recd one from A. J. Donelson to day.[2]

I am pleased to learn that Mr Parsons is progressing well, I have no fears but he will continue to do well, and I hope he will consult your ease & wishes & do them—This part of his duty will be as pleasing to me as any other & I hope he will perform it above any other; give to him my respects. To hear that all my neighbours are well & doing well is a great gratification to me. I recd to day a letter from Mr [William] McKnight, he gives the progress of the church & I am pleased you have a place of worship & I hope you will have a good pastor shortly, he writes that Mr Hodge is expected, but whether on a Vissit he does not say, present me to him affectionately.[3] You ask me to inform you when congress will rise? I would to god I could answer that question, we have done but little, and there are much to do. I have a hope we will adjourn by the middle of april some say not before the middle of may & others the middle of June. Believe me I shall not stay here a moment longer than I can leave it with propriety—the moment I can determine when this time will be, I shall advise you. I shall return the most expeditious rout, and that I expect will be by Pittsburgh & take the steam Boat to Louisville, but in due time you shall be advised of the time I leave here & my rout—be assured my love I shall not detain a moment longer than I can help; I am & will be as anxious to reach you, as you can be to see me.

say to the little Andrews I am anxious for their wellfare, & I wish them to learn their Books & be obedient to you, when you have company, do keep them with it, that they may learn to behave well; & be easy amid company. Say to Colo. Butler our Bill progresses slowly—when it passes, if it does pass, he will hear from me.[4] My health is good, I have a little cough but as the spring approaches I hope it will leave me. It is late & I must close this letter, I will write you shortly again—I shall see Mrs. Watson on tomorrow & Mrs. Wilson when I shall present you to them. your friends Eaton, Call, & Houston all send their respects to you, they are all as kind as they were my children—Colo Gibson begs me to reciprocate your good wishes—present me to all friends and may the god of Abraham, Isaac, & Jacob take you & our little ones, & all the family in his holy keeping untill I return is the prayer of your affectionate husband

Andrew Jackson

P.S. present me to Milbury tell her for her kindness in staying with you I shall allways remember her with kindness & gratitude—present me to Genl Overton & Mrs [Penelope Holmes] Overton, The Judge writes me often & says the Genl is low in health—It may be I may not see him again—[5]

ALS, THer (37-0417).

1. See AJ to Rachel Jackson, January 5 and 10. Rachel's letter has not been found.

2. Letters not found. Craighead (1750–1825; Princeton 1775) was a Presbyterian preacher at Nashville. In 1810 he was suspended by the Presbytery of Transylvania and the Synod of Kentucky for advocating a Pelagian concept of grace. His efforts to gain reinstatement received Jackson's support in 1823, but the Presbyterian General Assembly in Philadelphia had postponed action until 1824, pending information from the Kentucky synod on the case (see AJ to Ezra S. Ely, April 21, 1823, and, above, to Andrew J. Donelson, January 14). Subsequently, the 1824 General Assembly pronounced the proceedings in his suspension irregular and referred the matter to the Presbytery of West Tennessee, which reinstated Craighead's ministry.

3. Letter not found. McKnight, a local schoolteacher who had tutored Andrew Jackson, Jr., Andrew J. Hutchings, and Lyncoya, was an elder of the new Hermitage church.

4. Probably a reference to the bill regarding Florida land surveys (see above, AJ to Rachel Jackson, January 15 and 21).

5. John Overton's letters have not been found. Penelope Holmes (1765–1843) married Thomas Overton in 1795.

The Jackson campaign in Pennsylvania gained momentum as the state's acrimonious 1823 gubernatorial campaign ended. On November 14 a meeting of Allegheny County Democrats in Pittsburgh called for a pro-Jackson convention to meet at Huntingdon in March (later changed to

May) to select an electoral slate. The call was taken up elsewhere, most notably at a Philadelphia meeting on December 20, with the result that by January 20, 1824, eleven counties plus Philadelphia had arranged to attend the Huntingdon convention.

A different convention proposal came from state legislators, most of whom supported John C. Calhoun or William H. Crawford. Meeting in caucus on January 10, they urged that "unity and harmony" be preserved and state influence be maximized by the selection of a single electoral ticket at a convention in Harrisburg on March 4. Suspicious of a Calhoun-Crawford plot to join forces against the growing pro-Jackson movement and especially resistant to the legislators' proposal that any district or county failing to elect a convention delegate "be considered as authorizing" their Democratic senators and representatives to act as delegates, Jackson's supporters were initially inclined to oppose the Harrisburg call. By early February, however, they had determined to elect Jackson delegates to Harrisburg. In Philadelphia, where Jacksonians were victorious in ten of fourteen wards, Calhoun supporter George M. Dallas recognized their dominance and, at a citywide meeting on February 18, offered a resolution recommending Jackson's election.

Although made without consulting Calhoun, Dallas's decision (as reported below) in effect withdrew the South Carolinian from the presidential race, and it transformed the Pennsylvania contest into a Jackson landslide. Jackson's near unanimous nomination on March 4 radically altered his stature as a candidate. Shortly after receiving the news, John H. Eaton wrote John Overton on March 12 to obtain information for a possible defense of Jackson's marriage, noting, "heretofore the Radicals have not dreaded him; but now seemingly a most prominent rival, they are bringing all their batteries to bear against him."

To John Coffee

(Private)

Washington city
Febry 22nd 1824

Dear Genl

I have Just recd your letter of the 1rst instant and I am truly gratified that you & your amiable family enjoy health.[1]

I wrote you a few days since which will have advised you of the interview I have had with Mr Graham. I have no doubt but he is your friend, and amonghst they few here that in this respect can be relied on. I assure you, your former letter was precisely as you have recollected it: it was the evidence of your usual feeling for others, and of your liberality in like cases allways displayed.[2]

Should the law pass as Mr Graham <expected> wished part will be thrown in to your District, but this I do not expect—Therefore was my inquiry as to the time your present office would cease, calculating no aditional Territory to be annexed. It is the belief that it cannot be closed in less than three years, say in 1827. This I did suppose would be as long perhaps as you would wish to be employed in active office; you may rely on one thing that every care will be taken of your interest; extending to those worthy & in need a due attention—

I found shortly after my arival here that the survayor Genls office for the Floridas was intended for Colo. [James Patton] Preston late Governor of Virginia, he had been appointed commissioner of land claims held it nearly two years, recd the emoluments, & never went ther I had, in Justice to Colo. Butler, to interpose his claim, & bring to Mr Monroes recollection his promise to do something for Butler, and I have obtained his promise that he shall be provided for in florida—& Mr Preston provided for otherwise[3]—from the circumstance of the officers appointed for Florida not going & residing there, a bill has been brought in for the purpose of compelling all officers appointed for, to reside in Florida, This, unless part can be thrown into your District, would compell you to reside in Florida, <if> which you do not wish. Suffice it for the present to add; that Mr Graham and myself will erange all things as far as we have the power for the best, I have no friend on earth who possesses more of my affection than you, Mrs. J. only excepted.

I thank you for the attention you have paid to the interest of my dear little Hutchings when the crop is disposed of please give me information of the amount: They fifty five Bales is a good crop I should suppose—I hope Mr. Nicholson will continue, as he has done, to do his duty. It would afford me pleasure to hear how you have progressed with your mill; the amount of cotton you have raised &c &c. It is true I am much oppressed with business & with company—I had once a hope of ease & retirement in my old age: but I fear that hope was Vain, I admire your determination never to embark into a political life—in which I can assure you there is no pleasure for me; to be seperated from ones family, at my age, is a sacrafice too great to be made by me. Into this, I have been forced by my country without my wishes; and my name by that country has been brought before the nation equally opposed to my wishes, and I am placed in a situation that I cannot use my free will in withdrawing from the political contest, and its is now probable that I will be made a slave to the public for six years to come.

It is now announced by Mr Calhouns friends in Pensylvania that he is withdrawn & the whole weight of that state will support me, This to my friends is gratifying, but to you as my boosom friend I can say with truth, that altho I feel gratefull to my country for this act of confidence, still to be a slave to office in my declining years has no charms for me. But should I be elected *serve I must*; and will devote my best Judgt to the good of my country—But why should I give way to these gloomy thoughts—th*[ey are]* for your own eye, and I suppress them

I must refer you to the Public Journals for the current news.

Present me affectionately to your Lady & family & all my friends in your neighbourhood—say to my friend James Jackson that I have not recd a line from him. accept assurance of my friendship & Esteem.

Andrew Jackson

P.S. present me to Capt Jack & Elisa, say to them Lt E. W. Butler is well.

ALS, THi (10-0464). Published in Bassett, 3:229–30 (extract).

1. Letter not found.

2. See above, AJ to Coffee, February 15. Coffee's "former letter" has not been identified.

3. Preston (1774–1843), brother of Francis, served as governor of Virginia, 1816–19. He was appointed a Florida land claim commissioner, May 24, 1822, and resigned, February 20, 1824. In September he was appointed postmaster at Richmond, Virginia.

To William Berkeley Lewis

City of Washington
Febry 22nd. 1824

Dear Major

your letter of the 7th instant was this morning recd.[1] The vacancy in the Senate by the death of one of the Clerks (who was sick when I arived) has been filled by the Secratary of the Senate who, by law, has the appointment of his subordinate clerks;[2] your friend has not presented me your letter, when he does, it will be duly attended to.[3]

I have duly noted your remarks on the subject of your Politics, in Nashville, &c &c &c.

Mr. Crawfords friends <are> have become desperate and will do any thing—their motto, the end, is worthy of the means. Their minority caucus has recoiled upon their own heads, and the unanimity of Pensylvania has defeated all their plans.[4] I refer you to the news papers for the current news of the day. Wonder not if you see the attempt made to make me a Federalist—

The proof, a letter I wrote Mr Monroe in 1816, or –17—you no doubt recollect it—It was copied by you; wro*[te]* to bring into the War Department Colo Drayton who served throughout the late war—*by some means,* Mr Monroes letter in answer to mine <& my answer> has got into their hands; Mr Monroe says by stealth—& I have no doubt but all my private letters are also in their hands. But one thing I know, that the opinions expressed are the true Republican course—and men, call them what you will, who risk life, health, and their all, in defence of their country are its real support, & are entitled to share the offices of the Goverment. Colo.

Drayton was said to be a Federalist before the war—I can say truly of such; that we are all Federalists, we are all Republicans. and I would to god we had less professions and more acts of real patriotism.[5]

I am truly crowded with various business; I beg you to tender me affectionately to your sister, Miss Claibourn, your daughter, and kiss the babes for me.[6]

I had not influence anough to obtain the mission to Mexico for our friend Genl Stokes—as soon as I found we could not succeed with Genl Crabb, I threw my weight in the Genls scale—I am disgusted with the manner, & means all things are caried on here. When I was told that Genl Stokes could not be appointed because he dissipated some times at a card table—I then tried Mr Baldwin, with as little effect as any other—Govr Edwards of Elanois is before the Senate.[7] I write in haste & for your own eye. your friend,

Andrew Jackson

ALS, NN (10-0471). Published in *NYPLB,* 4(1900):194–95.

1. Not found.

2. The secretary of the Senate, Charles Cutts (1769–1846; Harvard 1789), elevated John G. McDonald to replace chief clerk Samuel Turner, who died on February 1, and appointed William Hickey to replace McDonald.

3. Neither Lewis's friend nor the letter has been identified.

4. A reference to news that supporters of John C. Calhoun in Philadelphia had agreed to support Jackson.

5. See AJ to James Monroe, November 12, 1816 (*Jackson,* 4:73–75), and Monroe to AJ, December 14, 1816.

6. The "babes" were William Henry (1823–42) and Margaret Adelaide Lewis (1823–c1845).

7. Jackson twice recommended Montfort Stokes, father of Lewis's deceased second wife, for ambassador to Mexico (see AJ to James Monroe, December 30, 1823, and January 15). His recommendations of Henry Crabb and Henry Baldwin have not been found. Ninian Edwards was nominated on February 18 and confirmed for the appointment on March 4.

Following George Kremer's challenge to his assertions that Jackson had recommended the appointment of federalists to James Monroe's cabinet (see above, AJ to Monroe, January 16; Monroe to AJ, January 16; and AJ to Andrew J. Donelson, January 18), John Binns claimed in the Democratic Press *of January 20 that Monroe had shown such a letter to Pennsylvania senators William Findlay (1768–1846) and Walter Lowrie (1784–1868) in the winter of 1821–22. When Findlay denied the report, the burden of sustaining Binns's charge fell on Lowrie. On February 21, Lowrie informed Monroe (DLC-32) that an anonymous Richmond correspondent had just sent him a copy of Monroe's reply to Jackson's recommendation. When George Hay showed Lowrie's note to Jackson, he admitted lacking "a distinct recollection of the substance of your several letters" (AJ to Monroe, February 22) and requested the date of the letter obtained by Lowrie, sparking the response below. When Lowrie finally released the document to Monroe in May, it proved to be a copy, partly in Monroe's hand, of Monroe's December 14, 1816, letter (see John H. Eaton to Monroe, May 8; Lowrie to Monroe, May 18; and Monroe to Samuel L. Gouverneur, May 19, all DLC-Monroe Papers).*

From James Monroe

Washington, Feb. 22, 1824.

Dear Sir:

I have no knowledge of the date of the letter to which Mr. Lowrie refers, nor can I imagine in what manner any letter of mine to you or other friend should have got into the possession of any one. At the time that I was about to form an administration, I communicated freely with some members of Congress, who had co-operated with me in the war, and in whom I had perfect confidence. I also corresponded with some other friends at a distance. It was natural, at that time, that I should communicate to those near me the opinions of distinguished characters at a distance, as having weight in my decision, as to the arrangement. But I have no recollection of giving any copy of my views on the subject to any one. The copy in question, if correct, must be resorted to, for unfriendly purposes, and in breach of confidence, and has probably been purloined. I recollect writing you a letter, in answer to yours recommending Colonel Drayton, in which, I concurred with you in the great result, that the President ought to be the head of this nation, rather than of a party, but thought that that result could only be brought about by time, considering the circumstances in which we were then placed. By perusing your letters, I find that you essentially concurred with me in that sentiment, although you inclined to the opinion that such men as Col. Drayton, who had given such proofs of patriotism and devotion to the cause of his country, ought to be considered as having a just claim to the confidence of the Government, and, in fact, to be considered as Republicans. The copy of this letter I have not been able to find, nor do I recollect ever seeing it, or your letters, till within a few days past, since the year 1817.

To Mr Lowrie's note I have given no answer, nor shall I. Let him take his course; we stand where we did. If my confidence, given at the time referred to, has been, in any manner abused, or the letter been purloined, that is an incident which must dishonor the party guilty of such acts. I do not think that there is any thing in your letters which can injure you, nor in mine, in reply to them; but the contrary. Defiance, by reserve, and silence, is what the transaction, and all connected with the present movement, merit.

I have done what I could to moderate and put down party spirit, believing that, by so doing, I gave the best support in my power to our republican government. It can only be put down by the republican party, and, while that party is in power, by a magnanimous policy[.] Persecution would keep the federal party, which, at one time, was, in certain members of it, a monarchical one, alive, and give it force. With sincere regard, I am, dear sir, yours,

James Monroe.

Printed, Washington *National Intelligencer,* May 8 (mAJs), *Niles' Register,* May 15 (10-0477), and other papers.

To Andrew Jackson Donelson

(Private)

Washington
Febry 26th. 1824

Dear Andrew

I recd your letter with the wished for enclosures on yesterday; the other two letters, I have obtained copies of, you for the present may cease your search.[1] I am now prepared to stand upon the defensive should an attack be made; I am sure it was intended; but it may be seen by those who intended it, that I am prepared, should it be made, to make it recoil upon them. providence has been kind to me. I did suppose I had been sufficiently guarded, reposing confidence only where I had a right to think it was well placed, and where it would not be Violated: however with all my experience of man, I have been deceved, but without injury I hope; be you my son on your guard, & profit by my admonition formerly given you, & now repeated. I would not wish you to take up an idea from this; that I believe it proceded (in Mr Monroe) from a wicked or deceptive mind; but from a weakness, & reposing confidence in my Enemy Lacock &c &c who it is supposed purloined his confidential letter.[2]

The appearence of the Radicals are Gloomy here, their countenance betrays despair, and the news from Pensylvania has destroyed all their hopes; I have every reason to expect all their batteries to be opened against me; and the attack was commenced by the publication that a letter of mine had been read to two senators, advising him to appoint two Federalists & two <senators> republicans in his Cabinet—This was denied by Mr Monroe; and also by myself, and the senator stands in an awkard dilemma—& Mr Monroe not in a pleasant one: But this is a matter between them, that I have, nor intend to have, nothing to do with.[3]

My health is not as good as it has been, but better than when I left you[4]—I have a great deal of writing & you know this is oppressive; however my friend Eaton has acted like a friend; he is worthy of, & shall receve my warmest gratitude so long as I live. I am anxious to hear from you, what markett my cotton has met with—when you receive account of sales advise me. I wish you to close my account with my friend Josiah Nichols to whom present me respectfully. I mean when I say my account, to include yours—I believe there is no other, unless at [James] Stuarts & Co—and I believe not any there, but least there should, I wish you to inquire. Should Mrs. J. have created any account <als> at any other place than at Mr Nichols have it paid, and furnish your aunt with any mony she may want.[5] My Dear Andrew attend to your aunt, & keep her spirits up, & when you receive the account of sales of the cotton advise her of it, as it will be gratefull for her to know it, present me affectionately to her & the young ladies & the two andrews, and when you are at the Hermitage attend to the boys as much as your Leisure will permit.

I have recd a letter from Danl. he is well & doing well, & so is Saml Hays they desire to be presented affectionately to you, your aunt, & all friends.[6]

you will see by the papers that on the 4th of March next Pensylvania will nominate her candidate for President, the present prospects are that she will nominate me; But every nerve will be strained to change her determination, North Carolina will go with her, & Virginia <is to> notwithstanding her Legislative caucus, is wavering[7] The people are beginning to stir, & when they do they will be heard. Newyork will not support Crawford, and I have but little doubt but he will be dropt; when this is done I have no feelings or wishes on the subject—had I a choice—I would prefer a retired life on my farm, for I do assure you there are no happiness for me, in Public life—I find mankind Treacherous, & corrupt, and Virtue to be found amonghst the farmers of the country alone, not about courts, where courtiers dwell. I have just recd a letter from your aunt since I have commenced this letter I shall write her tomorrow,[8] I am your affectionate uncle

Andrew Jackson

P.S. I am anxious to hear the fate of Doctor Butlers Draft I endorsed for him.[9] A. J.

ALS, DLC (10-0483). Published in Bassett, 3:230–32.

1. Donelson's letter has not been found; the enclosures were copies of a portion of Jackson's correspondence with James Monroe from 1816 and 1817.

2. When this charge was repeated in the newspapers, Abner Lacock wrote Monroe on April 24 to deny his involvement in taking the Monroe letter, although he confessed to having discussed Jackson's recommendation before it became a matter of controversy (DLC-Monroe Papers).

3. Jackson was referring to John Binns's report in the Philadelphia *Democratic Press* of January 20 (see above, James Monroe to AJ, February 22).

4. Newspapers reported that Jackson was "severely afflicted with the rheumatism in one of his arms" (*Richmond Enquirer,* February 28).

5. For discussion of Jackson's account with the Nashville merchant Josiah Nichol, see above, AJ to Donelson, January 21. Stewart (d. c1834) was another Nashville merchant. Donelson paid $1,873.25 to Nichol and $100.22½ to Stewart (see his memorandum of accounts, [June]).

6. Letter not found.

7. On February 21, a caucus of 163 of the 236 Virginia legislators convened and supported William H. Crawford for president, giving him 139 votes. John Q. Adams received 7 votes; Jackson and Nathaniel Macon, 6 each; and Henry Clay, 5.

8. See AJ to Rachel Jackson, February 27; her letter has not been found.

9. See AJ to Donelson, February 12, above, and April 4, below.

To John Coffee

City of Washington
March 4th. 1824

Dear Genl

I have Just recd your letter of the 13th ult. I have recd from Bedford & Mackey, accounts of sales of my fifty Bales of Cotton: I am well pleased with the sales, and I will thank you when you write them so to inform them. I will write them as soon as I have leisure—I have ten more Bales Parson wr[i]tes me—which will weigh 5000, this is doing well in Tennessee.[1]

I have not recd any letter from Nicherson It must have been lost by the way.[2]

you will order one of [Eleazer] Carvers Ginns for little Hutchings farm.[3] I do not know that I will have any use for the mony arising from the sales of my little ward Hutchings cotton—you will retain it in your hands untill I return, and if I should have no use for it, if times will authorise a loan of it untill the sales of the land, we will do so. My expences will be pretty heavy next year, I must & will bring Mrs. Jackson on with me, and for this reason untill I return I wish you to hold the mony. It is strange I have not had any letter from my friend James Jackson

My friend A. J. Donelson writes that he has compleated the compromise; but does not tell me the erangement, say to Mr Jackson to write me fully on this subject—and inform me, what amount of costs, if any, I have to provide for. I hope he called upon Mr Darby and had a sight of the articles to which Mr McLamore is a witness before the business was finally closed with Mr Darby I am only anxious on this score, that altho liberality was directed by me to be extended to that Mr Darby might know it was done from feelings of Liberality and not from any right that he Mr Darby had in that suit. Some time since I enclosed Mr McLamores letter to you that you might shew it to Mr Jackson.[4]

I hope it has been finally closed, for when a man begins to forget things of so recent a date as that agreement was, & which was drew by him & Mr McLamore I think it time, to be guarded; and to have to transact business with such a man as Andrew Erwin personally, I would resign any thing before I would do it—Therefore I will be happy if it is done in a way that I will be clear of both, and not sacrafice more than all my claim & Judgts against the heirs of David Allison.

The forfeighted lands will not be sold this year, This will be injurious to your state—But your delegation were all in favour of posponement, and of course I told Mr. Monroe this being the case he had better direct it, which was done[5]

I hope you may receive a good price for your cotton, you have my prayers for your wellfare and that of your amiable family to whom present me affectionately. you will no doubt have seen in the papers the account of the caucus here of less than one fourth of the members. If I am a Judge of human nature this will create *[a re]*action, and prostrate the candidate they have attempted to impose upon the natio*[n]* by a small minority, in open contempt of public opinion. This day the delegates from the whole state of Pensylvania meet to form an Electoral Tickett, This will give tone to the states in the south & west. N Carolina has formed a tickett contrary to the caucus Tickett, which will prevail; Virginia will form one also, and I am sure Virginia will not seperate from both Newyork and Pensylvania—It is thought Newjersy & Maryland will go with Pensylvania—[6]

Present me to Mr James Jackson say to him I have wrote him several letters & have received none from him *[gi]*ve my respects to all my friends in your neighbourhood, Childress, Fulton, [James] Hood &c &c &c, and to Capt J. Donelson & Eliza, to my friend Capt Savage respectfully and believe me your friend.[7]

Andrew Jackson

ALS, THi (10-0512). Published in Bassett, 3:233 (extract).

1. The letters and accounts have not been found. For Jackson's cotton sales, see Account with Bedford & Mackey, January 30.

2. The letter, probably from Malachi Nicholson, has not been found.

3. In 1816 Carver (1785–1866) incorporated the Bridgewater Cotton Gin Company in Massachusetts to manufacture an improved gin that he had developed while residing near Natchez. The gins were reportedly introduced into the Tennessee River Valley of Alabama by Coffee and James Jackson in 1822.

4. See above, AJ to John Coffee, February 15. Donelson's letter has not been found.

5. On the sale of relinquished lands in Alabama, see above, AJ to Andrew J. Donelson, January 21.

6. The convention at Harrisburg on March 4 selected a ticket of Jackson electors for Pennsylvania. In North Carolina, a caucus of about half of the members of the legislature had met on December 24, 1823, and nominated a pro-Crawford slate of electors. Almost immediately, the supporters of John C. Calhoun began a series of district meetings to put forward an opposing "People's ticket." The Calhoun men planned to unite the anti-Crawford forces behind Calhoun by appealing to anti-caucus sentiment and offering minority representation to Jackson and Adams electors, but by February Jackson's supporters had forced an understanding that the ticket would support the strongest anti-Crawford candidate. With Calhoun's withdrawal in the wake of the Pennsylvania results, Jackson men captured the remaining places on the People's ticket. A ticket of Jackson electors for Virginia was formed at a convention in Fredericksburg on June 28.

7. Born in Ireland, Hood (1780–1839) had been a Nashville merchant before moving to the Florence, Alabama, area by 1820. The letters to James Jackson have not been found.

To Samuel Swartwout

Washington
March 4th 1824

Dear Sir

Accept my thanks for your friendly letter of the 1rst Instant which has Just reached me.[1] You are right in supposing me pretty much engaged, not in attending however to Legislative matters, for indeed, there are so many, who by their itch for *discoursing,* seem desirous to enlighten and inform the community and their brethren associates, that I am content rather to be a listener, than an actor: I have however a numerous list of corrispondents to attend to, inasmuch as many of my old soldiers in arms, hearing that I have turned politician, prefer sending their long standing & almost obsolete claims to me, in the hope that I may be able to do something for them. An old soldier you know, should not in time of peace forget his old associates, nor do they permit it, of course I have very many inquiries to reply to, for outstanding and unremunerated services &c—[2]

But notwithstanding this, I have some little leisure time on my hand, when it is a pleasure to me, to hear from, & to answer my friends. It will allways afford me pleasure <to> I assure you, to hear from you; & should I prove in default at any time, you will at once attribute it to the true account—

Regarding the *particular* subject of your letter, you are sufficiently acquainted with me, & with my principles to accord with this remark, that of all men in the country I can know least about matters going on. The world calls me, & the world believes me, a wonderfully ambitious man, bent upon my own purposes, & regardless of all else besides. If I know any thing of myself, I can at least venture to say, that they are greatly mistaken, & that they do not know me.

I have seen & enjoyed much of the honor, the confidence, and regard of my country, and it is gratefull to me, because that it has been extended without any covert solicitation on my part; yet had it never dreamed of me for any higher future post, than that of a private citizen, & suffered me on my own farm, to have been a spectator, rather than an actor, in *events to come,* I should have been contented & happy. Mankind may, or may not, believe it; & surely what I say will not convince them to the contrary; yet with truth can I, & do I say, that in nothing in which I have been engaged; did I ever look to myself. I never yet have been, & hope never to be placed in any situation where fear & trembling shall overtake me, in discharge of my duty; & where that is discovered, with a conviction arising that my country may be benefitted by my acts, I shall proceed regardless of censure. I am getting my dear Sir rather too far advanced in life now, to be goaded by feelings of improper ambition: the alone wish of my heart, is that the country in which I live, & of which I am truly proud, may for all time to come continue free, prosperous, & happy as she is, and has been. A man of fifty seven, should be without any feelings of ambition, except what duty to the interest of his country, & a regard for his own honor & charecter may dictate. I am Sir with great respect & Esteem your most. obdt. servt.

Andrew Jackson

ALS, TNJ (10-0516). Published in Bassett, 3:233–34. Swartwout (1783–1856), whom Jackson had known since the 1807 Burr trial, became a leader of the Jackson campaign in New Jersey and chaired the Jackson convention at Trenton on September 1. Jackson appointed him collector of the port of New York in 1829.

1. Not found.

2. Few of these inquiries have been found. Unsuccessful claims were apparently returned to Jackson, who forwarded the papers to the claimants. The discrepancy between Jackson's reports of the volume of his correspondence and the paucity of letters remaining in the Jackson papers may be partially explained by the absence of pension and claims documents.

Despite Jackson's complaint in the letter below, newspapers supporting the other presidential candidates treated him comparatively gently during the 1824 campaign. In 1822 and 1823 they largely ignored his candidacy or suggested that he was a stalking horse for other contenders. Although editors occasionally commented about Jackson's qualifications, praising his military accomplishments but suggesting that he lacked the civil experience and temperament to be president, more often they simply discounted Jackson as a serious candidate.

*Signs of growing support for Jackson, and especially his nomination by the Pennsylvania convention at Harrisburg on March 4, 1824, forced the editors to criticize him more directly as the campaign progressed. Most criticism continued to focus on the general's martial temperament, but with greater specificity, pointing to the Dickinson duel (*Jackson, *2:77–82, 96–105), the executions of John Wood and the six militiamen (*ibid., *3:47–49, 133–35), the arrests of Louis Louaillier and Dominick A. Hall for violation of martial law at New Orleans (*ibid., *3:298–300), Jackson's comments to James Monroe regarding the Hartford Convention (*ibid., *4:81), the hanging of Alexander Arbuthnot and Robert C. Ambrister (*ibid., *4:196–201), his dispute with Georgia Governor William Rabun over control of the state militia (*ibid., *4:201–203), and his imprisonment of José M. Callava in Florida (see above) as examples of an authoritarian personality that might endanger American liberty if entrusted with the presidency.*

A second thrust attempted to use Jackson's 1816–17 correspondence with Monroe to suggest that Jackson was pro-Federalist, or at least insufficiently Republican (see above, AJ to Monroe, January 16, and to William B. Lewis, February 22; and AJ to George Kremer, [May 6], below). Along *similar lines, opponents pointed to Jackson's support of the limited suffrage provision in the Tennessee Constitution of 1796 to claim he was an "advocate of aristocracy" (*Mobile Commerical Register, *September 28).*

In the southern states, Jackson's tariff position also spawned attacks designed to show that he had betrayed the economic interests of his section, and in Kentucky his complaints about the behavior of the Kentucky militia at the Battle of New Orleans were held against him. Though other issues that would recur in later elections appeared in editorials and pamphlets, the references were scattered and infrequent, and in 1824 Jackson was not subjected to the sustained personal attacks that characterized the 1828 campaign.

To Andrew Jackson Donelson

Washington
March 6th 1824

Dear Andrew

your letters of the 12th & 15th Ult. with mine to Mr Monroe of the 4th march 1817 enclosed, reached me in due course of mail[1]

I should have replied sooner but really I am so pressed with a multiplicity of letters & business; that I am really oppressed, and have scarcely time for necessary rest.

The letters on the subject of Colo Drayton & Mr Adams have been recd, whether they may become necessary or not I cannot say, the battery was unmasked, but has become silent thro fear of exposure as I believe—you know I have allways acted on the defensive & mean to do so now.

I had recd account of sales of my cotton before your letter reached me direct from Bedford & Mackey[2]—I am pleased with the sales; If you should, (which I suppose you will) want any mony, my son use it, I want only oeconomy <now> exercised so that next fall I may have the means of ample support on my Journey hither, & next winter whilst here. you must accompany me <here> next fall, I have been at a loss for some aid in writing. My friend Major Eaton does all he can, but he has his own to attend to, which is very laborious. I have allways wished that my name had not been brought before the nation as President—I should now have been enjoying peacefull retirement; But as it has been brought before the nation, and the Radicals now heap upon me every scurrilous slanderous abuse that falshood can suggest, I am glad my name is before the nation, Truth is allways predominant where reason is left free to combat error, and I have no fear but my charector will stand the test of the most exact scrutiny, both my public & private, and I court it from the nation. They friends of the Caucus candidate think they can by their Vile abuse rous my feelings to some act of Violence; in this they have much mistaken my Charector, These wretches who possess no proper feelings for charector, because they do not know the Vallue of it; having never possessed it themselves, think that the end is worthy of the means, & surely I agree cordially with them, that their cause being a bad one, the means they employ coinside with it. I never read the city Gazzett or the Richmond enquirer, therefore do not know the extent of their abuse—The subjects the embrace, if I am rightly informed, will increase my standing with the nation more than any other course they can pursue; They will elect me, contrary to their wishes, by their *abuse*—I do assure you my young friend, that I would rather be abused by these hireling writers than receive their praise, for the praise of such men would be Viewed by all honest disinterested men, as a cause to suspect my honesty & integrity. When I review my course, my conscience tells me I have acted right—it was a course marked out with the sole View to the good of my country—an honest community View, & approve it as such, & I am at perfect peace with myself.

you will see the result of the Harrisburgh convention of the 4th instant before this reaches you; If unanimous, it creates unanimity in No Carolina, & the sout*[hwes]*t & the people will *elect* the President—you know I have but one feeling, & that is that the caucus candidate may not prevail; I am sure myself that Mr Adams is much stronger than he is.[3]

Present me to your aunt affectionately tell her my health continues good but when I can leave here, I yet cannot say. present me to E. affectionately & all friends write me often & believe me your affectionate uncle

Andrew Jackson

ALS, DLC (10-0526). Published in Bassett, 3:234–36 (extract).

1. Donelson's letters have not been found; for Jackson's letter to James Monroe, see *Jackson*, 4:93–99.

2. Letter not found. For a record of the sales of Jackson's cotton, see Account with Bedford & Mackey, January 30.

3. Official news of the Harrisburg convention reached Washington on March 7. The resolution supporting Jackson for president passed 124 to 1. Many of the general's original supporters, however, were angered by the prominence given to former Calhoun men among the electors and on the committees of correspondence, and some briefly toyed with the idea of reviving the proposed Huntingdon convention to repudiate the Harrisburg nomination of Calhoun for vice-president (he received 87 votes) and to select alternative Jackson electors.

From James Tallmadge, Jr.

Albany March 6th. 1824.

Hond. Sir—

I have hitherto avoided to write on the Presidential question—The peculiar state of things in Newyork induces me to write to you—

The state of N.york is inclined to oppose Mr. Crawford—The 36. votes of this state *can be given* for an opposing candidate to him—and This either—*with*—or *without* the Electoral law now under discussion here.[1] It however becomes indispensible to have a concentration on some one candidate—we can not stand much longer Divided between so many candidates— The People here must have a precise object—In case of a concentration— Genl. Jackson President—Mr. Adams Vice President—or even *vice versa*— the vote of this state may be counted upon—without some concentration— & that shortly—I fear, this state may not continue safe—All is now in our hands—we understand Mr. Calhoun, will not be in the way—

Several friends have urged me to write. we hope *soon* to have a course opened for us to pursue, & to receive information—there is much excitement arising from our electoral Bill & other local causes—The season for acting is at hand—The state administration is acting for Mr. Crawford It must be met—& a definite object, be held up to our People—

I have this Day written, to Mr. Adams—of the same import—[2]

Permit me to tender to you Renewed assurance of the very high Respect entertained by me for your character—I am with great Regard your Obdt. Servt—

James Tallmadge

ALS, DLC (32). Published in Bassett, 3:236. Tallmadge (1778–1853; Brown 1798), a New York legislator and former congressman, would be elected lieutenant governor in November.

1. The New York legislature had under consideration a bill for popular election of presidential electors. On March 10, the senate voted to postpone action on the measure until November.

2. See Tallmadge to John Q. Adams, March 6, MHi.

To James Tallmadge, Jr.

Washington 12 March 1824.

Dr Sir

Your friendly Letter of the 6th. of March was yesterday recvd. and as candor is the language by me always admired, I thank you for the freedom with which you have spoken your sentiments[1]

The subject on which you have written is indeed one of interest, to the american people; the feelings they <manifest> evince, & the excitement manifested thro the nation is confirmatory <evidence> of the fact—I am well pleased to see it, inasmuch as there is evidence in it, that they are awake to the rights that belong to them, nor disposed with passive submission to yield them—

On the subject brought to my consideration by your Letter, I have all along forborne to speak, for the reason of its delicacy; & because any thing to be said by me, might be imputed to selfish consideration; if however I know any thing of myself, no such feeling has, or shall control me. To you however I will speak, as you have done, freely & without reserve.

The principles which have governed me thro life, will I hope not forsake me, in <my> the present situation in which I am placed. I remember not, ever to have solicited an office: my Country it is true has been kind to me, <even> & perhaps beyond any merits of mine; but it has been thro her own voluntary notion, & not from any solicitation of mine; and when my name was presented to the nation, for the important & highly responsible office of Chief magistrate, none certainly less expected it, and none desired it less than I did. I was aware, that, even if elected, the trouble & fatigue <that> which would necessarily devolve, would add nothing to my quiet or happiness; while judging from the past, I foresaw that every little error and indiscretion of <my> life would be treasured, and magnified into crimes of the deepest die <My> A portion of my Country however <unsolicited by me> from no solicitation on my part, have thought proper to consider me worthy of this high post; & acting on the principles which have always governed me, I am content for her to decide without any sort of interference on my part. Should she call me to act I shall, as I always have done, act with that decision and judgment of which I am capable, without any regard to the benefit or injury <it may> to be produced to <me> myself; and <if it> should the choice fall on any other, believe me, my Dear Sir, that not one moments displeasure will be felt by me. I shall then be a private citizen, & in that character, shall <no doubt> understand my duty better than were I to be placed in an high and elevated situation

On the subject of your Letter therefore, I can give no opinion other than what is already offered, that my mind will rest contented at any decision which my Country may freely, & of her own accord pronounce. Could I assure success to myself, by any sort of combination, management or intrigue, I <inform> declare to you most truly, it would not be resorted to—Let my friends therefore every where, adopt that course which, they may believe, will best conduce to the interest of the Country; & whatever it may be, I assure them I shall <be> rest contented

With my best wishes for your health & happiness. I am with great respect Yr Mo Obt

Draft in John H. Eaton's hand endorsed as a copy, DLC (32). Published in Bassett, 3:237–38.

1. See above.

To Rachel Jackson

Washington
March 16th. 1824

My Dear wife

Yesterday being the day that gave me birth; and on which I entered upon my fifty eight year I had a few friends to dine with me amonghst whom, were our friend Govr. Homes of Mississippi, Mr N[athaniel] Macon of the Senate, and Major [William] Bradford of the army, who presented our son with "Coosa" & whom you recollect; they heads of Department with the Honbl Speaker Mr Clay with many others from Boston, Newyork

&c &c &c, our friend Eaton & Call presided & the evening was pleasantly spent, I had like to have forgot to tell you our friend E. Livingston was amonghst the number.[1]

This morning at 11 I was requested to attend Mr Monroe to receive the medle Voted me by Congress on the 27th of Febry 1815.[2] I attended accompanied with Eaton & Call & in the presence of Mrs Monroe, Mrs Hay &c &c &c, and the heads of Departments, & Navy board, with many members of Congress, and my Voluntary aid. E. Livingston, it was delivered in due form—You are aware how disagreable to me these shows of pomp & perade are; & how irksome it is for me to speak of myself—still it was necessary; and I with reluctance performed it—not without a tremor which allways seises me on such occasions—I trust however when you read the sentiments exp[r]essed by me, some of them will be pleasing to you. I therefore have named it, as I know every thing that concerns me is interesting to you.[3]

Tell my son how anxious I am that he may read & learn his Book, that he may become the possessor of those things that a gratefull country has bestowed upon his papa—Tell him that <it is> his <good conduct> happiness thro life, <that> depends upon *his* procuring an education now; & with it, to imbibe proper moral habits that can entitle him to the possession of them. To acquire those proper habits, he must beware religiously on all occasions to adhere to truth, & on no occasion to depart from it—never to make a promise unless on due consideration, and when made, to be sure to comply with it. This rule observed, with a proper attention now to his learning, will make him a great, good, & usefull man, which his papa wishes him, & his little cousin Hutchings, both to become; Having experienced so much inconvenience from the want of a perfect education myself makes me so solictous that his may be perfect; My Dear wife urge this upon him.

My health continues as good as I have aright to expect it—we are now experiencing variable weather not very congenial to my health, but being cautious to preserve it, I hope to pass this month without much injury, and I would to god I could now leave the city; but <of> this is what I cannot do, nor do I yet know when I can. Present me affectionately to the Andrews, <&> to all friends & neighbours & believe me to be your affectionate Husband

Andrew Jackson

P. S. I write in haste & for your own eye—A. J.

ALS, CSmH (10-0559). Published in *Huntington Library Bulletin*, 3(1933):127–28.

1. Macon (1757–1837) was from North Carolina. Bradford (c1771–1826) served with Jackson in the Creek campaign and presented the horse Coosa to Andrew Jackson, Jr., at that time. Other guests among the approximately twenty-five in attendance included John Q. Adams, Samuel L. Southard, and John C. Calhoun.

2. See James Monroe to AJ, March 16.

3. See below.

To James Monroe

[March 16, 1824]

Receiving this emblem of the approbation of my country, from you, who were an eficient & active agent of our Goverment in those scenes of dificulty & danger to which it refers, gives me peculiar pleasure[1]

It brings to my recollection, on the Tocsin of war being sounded, that patriotic ardor which brought Voluntarily to the field thousands of the brave yeomanry of our country to support its Eagles & to protect our frontier from the ruthless savage & the inroads of a British foe. In the name of those patriotic officers & soldiers, who so bravely seconded my Views in the day of Battle, privation, & peril; & who contributed to bring about the happy results to which you refer, I receve this emblem of approbation which the Representatives in congress assembled have conceived me worthy to possess.

That at a period the most critical & alarming, I should have been the humble means, to harmonise the discordant materials of every nation & Tongue; & so to unite them, as to make a successfull defence of the city of NewOrleans, against a superior, well organised Veteran force; & to preserve it from polution & Ravage by an infuriated British soldiery <its "Beauty & Booty"> is remembered as one of the proudest moments of my life. This emblem reminds me of the gratitude we should feel to a kind providence for those happy results.

May you pass thro & retire from the administration of the Goverment with <that> the full approbation of your country, <which> that has hitherto accompanied you—May you be blessed in retirement with all the comforts heaven can bestow, & when life is finished be raised to a happy immortality beyond the grave

AD, DNA-RG 107 (M221-98); ADS draft, THi (10-0561). Published in Washington *National Intelligencer*, March 17.

1. Monroe had presented Jackson with the medal voted by Congress in February 1815 to honor his War of 1812 service.

To Andrew Jackson Donelson

Washington March 19th. 1824

Dear Andrew

yours of the 28th. ult is recd. I sincerely regret the death of Genl Overton, but it was my foreboding & I parted with him, that we should not meet again here below. I have recd a letter from Judge Overton detailing his death & asking about his will[1]

The Genl had made a will & left it in my possession sealed up—it remained with me untill a short time before Major Saml Overton went to Pensacola, it was on the request of the Genl taken to him by me, as he said he wanted to make some alteration in it—Whether the Genl brought it back & left it with me I cannot recollect—but if he did, you will find it in Mrs. Jacksons little Trunk in which my Valuable papers are, ask your aunt to look into it, & if the Genls will is found there make it known to Judge Overton—I should write the Judge now, but I have a bad pain in my left side that makes writing painfull to me. Before this reaches you the result of the Convention in Harrisburgh will be known to you; you will see that the senate of the state of Newyork has posponed the Bill giving to the people the electoral vote for electors—This has kindled a flame in the minds of the people that will not be quenched untill they regain full possession of their rights, and woe to those who have openly dared to usurp the right from them. you may prepare to hear a general expression of indignation throughout the state of Newyork. County & Town meetings will be organised—The caucus candidate cannot get the Vote of that state—and it appears to me that his friends have less common sense than any set of men I ever knew; every step they take is well calculated to destroy their candidate with the people

I have recd a letter from a friend of high standing, who says they *people will come out in newyork in all their strenght*—should the vote be as he calculates it will put an end to the contest, & it cannot get into the house of Representatives.[2]

Great calculations were made by my enemies that I could be irritated, thrown from my equilibrium, and prostrated by some act of rashness & imprudence—The world, or at least that part of it, knew me not—being endowed with common sense & well acquainted with human nature I know when to act to make an impression on mankind, hence I have acted promptly when I discovered the proper time to have arived, & those who could not see the whole ground, have asscribed to the *act, rashness*—I have allways by these acts been successfull, an event not usually attendant on rashness—and when it becomes necessary to philosophise & be meek, no man can command his temper better than I. My friends need not—nor has those who really know me, ever had, any fears on this head; whilst my enemies have become confounded, & dismayed, in not being able to irritate me, & reallise all their slanders ushered forth in the Public Prints.

I am happy you have sold the ballance of my cotton at home, it meets my approbation. Present me to Miss. E. & all friends & believe me your affectionate uncle

Andrew Jacks*[on]*

I write to your aunt by this post[3]

ALS, DLC (10-0567).

1. Letters not found.
2. Letter not found.
3. See AJ to Rachel Jackson, March 19.

To John McLean

Washington March 22nd 1824

Sir

My friend Colo. [George] Chroghan has made known to me his desire of obtaining the office of Postmaster at Neworleans which he is advised will become shortly vacant by the resignation of the present incumbent.[1]

as I am confident he is well qualified; and has high claims upon his country; and having the highest opinion of his charecter, It gives me pleasure to express my wishes that he may succeed in his application.

Should the Colo. not succeed, which I should sincerely regret, I am requested by several Gentlemen from Neworleans to name to you Capt [William Lord] Robeson, Capt [Joseph] Saul, & Capt [Robert D.] Richardson all of whom are well recommended as to good charecter, & fitness for that office[2]

It <having> has been stated to me that Mr Fulwar Skipwith is an applicant for that office; (If <that be> so) I feel it is a duty due to the executive <I owe> to make known his conduct during the <investment of> assault on Neworleans by the British army in the late war. Mr. Skipwith was Speaker of the senate; had been in the confidence of our Goverment, and in consequence thereof, received mine. From his situation I expected much aid from him; You may <Judge> imagine <of> my surprise, when I tell you that instead of being with those who were in defence of the country in the then trying crisis, he was found with those who were engaged in paralysing my defence. <and who> He would neither prorogue the assembly nor adjourn it to Batonrouge—and when the minority abandoned the assembly and tendered their services as Volunteers at my line of defence; Mr Skipwith remained with those who were charged with a <conspiracy> design to deliver the city to, & make terms with the enemy; one part of his conduct it is necessary to detail. When I left the city & marched against the enemy on the night of the 23rd of Decbr. 1814, I was obliged to leave one of my aids in command, having no other confidential officer that could be spared from <his> command; a few days after, Mr Skipwith in person applied to my aid <to obtain my secrets, (that was)> to be informed what would be my conduct if <drove> driven from my lines of defence, & compelled to retreat through Neworleans; whether I would leave the supplies for the enemy, or destroy them. As reported to me by my aid, he wanted this information for the assembly, that in case my intention was, to destroy them, they might make *terms* with the *enemy*, & *save the city*. Obtaining no satisfaction from my aid, a committee of three waited upon me for information on this subject—To them I replied; "If I thought the hair of my head knew my thoughts upon that subject I would cut it off & burn it—<"> To return to their Honourable body and say to them from me, that if I was so unfortunate as to be beaten from the lines I then occupied, & compelled to retreat through Neworleans, they would have *a warm session*." This ended my intercourse with the assembly, untill the evening of the 8th of January, when Mr Skipwith rode down to congratulate me upon the event. <like Judas of old, when he betrayed our saviour with a kiss> From the foregoing you can Judge how much he merits the bounty of his goverment to the exclusion of those, who, have real claims for important service rendered.[3] I am sir with great respect yr. mo. obdt. servt.

Andrew Jackson

ALS draft with revisions in an unknown hand, DLC (32); Copy, DLC (10-0571). Published in Bassett, 3:239–40. McLean (1785–1861) was postmaster general.

1. Croghan (1791–1849; William and Mary 1810), a hero of the War of 1812 who had served under Jackson in the postwar army, obtained the appointment to succeed Thomas B. Johnson.

2. A New Orleans merchant, Robeson (d. 1835) had served as James Winchester's aide at Mobile in 1815 and had married Winchester's daughter Selima (1800–20) in 1817. A banker and president of the Louisiana Insurance Company, Saul (b. c1771) had cooperated in financing Jackson's New Orleans campaign of 1814–15 while cashier of the Bank of Orleans. In 1831 Jackson offered him a position as consul to Tripoli. Richardson (d. 1831) had resigned from the 1st Infantry in 1822 and was at this time editor of the New Orleans *Louisiana Gazette*.

3. Skipwith (1765–1839?), consul-general to France during George Washington's presidency, had authorization to use James Monroe's name in support of his application. Although the *Louisiana Gazette* announced Skipwith's appointment on June 22, Croghan obtained the office and took up the duties in August. When Skipwith again sought the postmaster position in the winter of 1825–26, Jackson's letter on file once more destroyed his chances. Hearing of the letter, Skipwith obtained a copy in late 1826 or early 1827, and he wrote Jackson in May 1827 to protest the general's attack on his character, submitting the protest and an extract of the 1824 letter to the *Richmond Enquirer*, where it was published June 26, 1827. Anti-Jackson papers in 1827 and 1828 used the incident to charge Jackson with unjust character assassination. Jackson's description of Skipwith's conduct, which had previously appeared in Reid and Eaton's *Life of Andrew Jackson*, is supported in part by the affidavit, May 23, 1815, of Thomas Langford Butler (1789–1881), the aide given command in New Orleans by the orders of December 23, 1814. No definite record has been found of the subsequent committee to which Jackson referred, and Jackson may have confused Skipwith's inquiry with the report that led him to close the legislature on December 28 and the committee inquiry into that incident (see *Jackson*, 3:226–27). Regardless of specifics, Jackson obviously had concluded that a portion of the legislature was treasonous (see AJ to Unknown, cMarch 31, 1815, *ibid.*, 3:337–38).

To Samuel Swartwout

Washington March 25th 1824

Dr. Sir

Your kind letter is Just recd.[1] I assure you it would afford me very sincere pleasure, if being an untrammeled man, it was in my power to Vissit the states & cities North of this place. I had for some time before my retirement from the army looked to the period of my release as one, when it would be in my power as a private citizen, to travel into the adjoining states: but we cannot tell what a day or an hour may bring forth: for 'ere after my retirement, I could execute my design & my wishes, did <the Legislature of> my state, take it into <their> her head to exhibit me before the nation for a high, responsible & important office. again there was a barrier interposed to my wishes; for if under such a state of things, I had been found journaying abrod, you are well aware, of the fraternal greetings which the Editors of certain news papers would have extended to me. This you will say a rational man, ought not to regard; & if differently situated, I might argue in the same way; be this as it may, the pleasure & satisfaction to be derived from such a Journey would be entirely lost, if at every Town & Village where I might alight, a suspicion could be indulged, that they considered me there expressly on a pilgrimage after their good opinion

Whether good or bad fortune, I cannot tell, but so it is, my countrymen entertain towards me, if not an unfortunate, at least most singular opinions. Some believe me, as they term it, a most dangerous and terrible man—of savage habits & disposition, and wholly unacquainted with civilised life: Possessing a temper and turn of mind of most incorrigable cast; and that I can break, & trample under foot the constitution of the country, with as much unconcern & careless indifference, as would one of our backwoods hunters, if suddenly placed in Great Britain, break her game laws. The news papers, some of them, circulate these opinions, and many of the people for want of more accurate information do truly believe them.

That it has been my lot often to be placed in situations of a critical kind is true; situations where a man might have been excused, if he had acted first & thought afterwards. My course however was to invert the rule; and altho as has been the case heretofore there was imposed on me the necessity of Violating, or rather departing from, the constitution of the country; yet at no subsequent period has it produced to me a single pang, believing as I do now, & then did, that without it, security neither to myself or the great cause confided to me, could have been obtained. The Violence of this measure, for my enemies prefer to call all my acts by their strongest expressions, added to my Indian Campaigns, have in many parts of the country induced the belief, that I am in fact a sort of raw head & bloody bones, fit only to scar*[e]* children.

To possess the good opinion regard and confidence of ones country should be desired by all: it is this, which prompts onward the statesman & politician, and which encourages the soldier to meet difficulty, & to encounter danger: yet it is not always in <his> our power to obtain it; for after all, strange conceits & wrong impressions will be taken up, which no time or circumstances can eradicate or change. For me to attempt it, would be a fruitless effort, one that would avail nothing; & even could it avail any thing, when lead to the reflection, that the alteration had been brought about by an electioneering exhibit of myself, with such other objects in View as would be imputed, the alteration of opinion would be produced at too great a sacrafic*[e.]*

I never did electioneer, intrigue, or combine for office in my life, I hope never to do it; could I in this way obtain one, even the most distinguished, the pleasure pride, & honor of the post, would be lost in a recollection of the manner after which it was obtained. If the nation shall call me to her first office, it must be her act, not mine. If called, my object & exertions shall be to act on broad national principles, & sedulously to guard her interest & her honor: if any other be called, I shall, as has been ever my endeavour, preserve myself a good citizen.

on reflection then my dear Sir, you & other of my friends will I dare say agree with me, that to travel any where now would be improper, because opening a door to accusation & imputation. True I had designed to travel as far as Philadelphia, because of a desire heretofore had to go to the north; & because, now that her Delegation at Harrisburgh had met, and decided, none of the suggestions I have made could be imputed to me: but it will probably be so late in the season before congress adjourns, that my desire to return home may prompt me to seek to reach it by the nearest & most practicable rout

Pray tender me most respectfully to Mrs. Swartwout to Genl & Mrs. Gains when you shall see them, & to Mr Colden & his lady, & believe me to be with great respect & Esteem yr mo obdt. servt.[2]

Andrew Jackson

ALS, N (10-0586); Draft in John H. Eaton's hand, DLC (32; 10-0590).

1. Not found.

2. Alice Ann Cooper (1789–1874) married Swartwout in 1814. Maria Provoost (d. 1837), daughter of the Right Reverend Samuel Provoost, married Cadwallader D. Colden, Cooper's uncle, in 1793.

To John Coffee

(Private) Washington March 28th. 1824

Dear Genl

It is now the close of March, & congress has not Passed one law of a general nature as yet; The Tarriff bill has engaged the House of Representative for five weeks, and from its progress it will consume five more: Unless it is posponed, I do not expect any thing beneficial will be done this Session—I have thought for some time that if the necessary appropriations were made it would be beneficial to the nation that we should adjourn; there does not appear that spirit of harmony, <for the> that is allways necessary to exist in the deliberations of the Representatives of the nation to produce those beneficial results, that tend to promote the best interests of our common country.[1]

From the papers you will discover, that in that dignified body the senate of the united states, viewed by the constitution to be filled with the sages of our country, for the purpose of reviewing the acts of the Representative branch with calm & dignified deliberation, have so far forgot itself, its dignity of charector, and what is due to the american nation; as to be found debating the Caucus in solemn session; when such debates as this, gets into the senate I loose all hope of any thing beneficial for the nation to be enacted by congress this session, & think it time to adjourn.[2]

I am happy to see the good people of america are puting their faces against these congressional caucuses; & I do hope the one last held will put this unconstitutional proceeding to sleep forever—and leave to the people their constitutional right of free suffrage—should this not be the case, it will introduce into our Goverment, a sistematic system of Intrigue & corruption, first secrete, & last, open & undisguised; that will ultimately destroy the liberty of our country—a central power will arise here; who under the patronage of a corrupt, & Venal administration, will deprive the people of their liberties; and place into the executive chair whom they may will. From what I see in the Public Journals, the feelings of the people are beginning to be aroused to a proper sense of their rights, and I trust they will put down congressional caucuses forever—hereafter. advices from Newyork inform; that they people of that state are about to follow the footsteps of Pensylvania, & to have a general convention: you will have seen that the Carolinas & Georgia are in motion & six weeks will unmasks their course.[3]

I have Just recd a letter from my friend McLamore, enclosing me a coopy of the rough draft of the papers, which clearly shews the acknowledgement of Darby that he nor no other person had any claim or interest in the suit myself against Erwin & others but myself & James Jackson[4]—Darby was bound to have them Registered in Davidson, This he has not done—nor as I am advised, has he ever produced them to Mr James Jackson. I am truly happy that the business is closed & the suit at an end, and I have only introduced the notice of Mr McLamores letter as an evidence to you, how happy I ought to be to get clear of two such men as Erwin & Mr Darby—The latter I had *some* confidence in; you can Judge with what propriety Vested—and I hope it will put Mr Jackson on his guard, which is the design of this letter—for the compromise is made by James fully authorised under my power, and I would fullfil it at all events so far as I have the means—I allways intended Liberality to Mr Darby, I am glad it has been extended, but when extended, it ought to be under its true char*[ec]*ter *Liberality* & *not of right*; & the papers in h*[ere]* will shew it. Colo. Erwin is still here as the agent for the Representatives of Robert Searcy deceased. This business has been brought before the senate & Reported against some time ago—The Colo. still here; whether he will for the whole time here, charge the securities, with his services I cannot say; as my friend James is one of them he had better look out—I expect it will be a Mexican Mission[5]—Present me to Mr James Jackson & family—to your amiable family & my friends in your neighbourhood; for yourself accept my best wishes for your happiness & long life

Andrew Jackson

ALS, THi (10-0604). Published in Bassett, 3:241–42 (extract).

1. The House Committee on Manufactures reported "A bill to amend the several acts for imposing duties on imports" on January 9. Consideration commenced on February 10, and House debates continued until the bill's passage on April 16.

2. On March 18, the Senate began consideration of various joint resolutions proposing constitutional amendments in relation to the election of the president and vice-president. Rufus King took the occasion to warn of the "new, extraordinary, self-created, central power, stronger than the power of the Constitution, which has risen up, at the Seat of Government." His remarks spurred others to defend or attack the caucus, as debate continued until consideration was indefinitely postponed on March 22. Jackson took no part in the debate and did not vote on the postponement resolution (see *Annals of Congress,* 18th Cong., 1st sess., pp. 354–417).

3. *Niles' Register,* March 27, printed extracts of a letter from Albany, New York, reporting that supporters of the electoral law had sent legislators notice of an intention to call a convention to nominate for president, vice-president, governor, lieutenant governor, and presidential electors. Subsequently, legislators favorable to the electoral bill met at Albany on April 7 and called for a convention at Utica on September 21. Jackson was also receiving reports of progress in the formation of the People's ticket in North Carolina.

4. Neither John C. McLemore's letter nor the enclosures have been found.

5. On December 17, 1823, John H. Eaton presented the petition of James Jackson and John C. McLemore, as securities for Robert Searcy, praying for an equitable settlement of his accounts as military paymaster for West Tennessee. The petition was referred to the Committee on Military Affairs, chaired by Jackson, which reported unfavorably on March 8. On March 9, the Senate concurred with the committee's resolution to allow withdrawal of the petition. Jackson was comparing Andrew Erwin's agency on behalf of Searcy's heirs to Erwin's trip to Mexico City in March 1822 as commissioner for a group of Nashville and Kentucky investors to obtain a land grant for what became Robertson's Colony in Texas. Erwin had stayed in Mexico until July 1822, when he left for Nashville expecting rapid progress on the grant, but nothing had as yet resulted from the mission, and the Mexican government did not issue a contract to Erwin's fellow commissioner, Robert Leftwich, until April 1825.

From William Hayden, Jr.

Washington City, March 29th., 1824.

Dr Sir,

I know you will pardon me for troubling you on a subject, which is not, in itself, perhaps, of much importance—but, upon which common justice, <requires> towards those with whom I am connected, during the present session of Congress, requires that I should not permit any erronious impressions to exist.

A copy of the Columbian Observer, a paper printed at Philadelphia, and which contains some animadversions upon my report of your remarks on the bill for the armament of the fortifications, has just been put into my hands. I send, herewith, that paper; together with the Intelligencer containing the Report alluded to. Will you do me the favor, sir, if you have leisure, to look over the Report; and see if, in your opinion, it deserves the censure cast upon it, by the Philadelphia paper.[1]

Our reports of the proceedings of Congress are, upon many subjects, necessarily brief—and, doubtless, often imperfect[2]—It is impossible they should not be so. Those only, who are practically acquainted with the business, can be aware of the difficulty of giving satisfaction to all. The principal consideration, in drafting the Reports, is, *the nature of the subject.* If it is one of great and general <public> interest, it is endeavored to extend the report farther than can be done on questions of a more local or restricted nature. It is always intended, however, that they shall be impartial.

If the remarks in the Observer had applied to the Reporter only, he would not have deemed them of sufficient importance to authorize him to call your attention, from weightier matters, to so humble an object as himself. But as they involve others, to whom the blame, if there be cause for any, ought not to attach, he deems it his duty to request your candid opinion, whether there is any appearance, in the sketch of your remarks, of an intention to mutilate, or misrepresent—and whether they are not given fairly, as taken in connection with the rest of the report on the same subject?

I address you, sir, without the knowledge of Messrs Gales & Seaton—They have never expressed to me a wish, or an intimation, that the character of my reports should be, in any manner, partial. If there be fault, in the present case, it is *mine,* and not *theirs.* I believe neither of those gentlemen were present, during the discussion alluded to. They leave this business to my discretion—And I assert, with the utmost sincerity, that neither the political situation, nor the political opinions, of the member speaking, have ever operated as a reason for the extension or curtailment of his remarks. I have the honor to be, sir, with the greatest respect, Your mo: obt: servant,

W. Hayden Junr, Reporter Nat. Intellr.

Be pleased, if it is not too much trouble, to send <the> me the papers, when you have done with them, at my desk in the Senate Chamber.

W. H.

ALS, DLC (32). Published in Bassett, 3:242–43 (extract). Endorsed by AJ, "to be preserved." Hayden (1795–1880) became Boston city auditor in August and later edited the Boston *Atlas.*

1. On March 9, Jackson had spoken in favor of a bill appropriating $125,000 annually for four years to purchase artillery and bombs for United States fortifications. For Hayden's report of the remarks, see Washington *National Intelligencer,* March 10. A letter dated March 12 from "J.H." to the *Columbian Observer* praised Jackson's address, quoting a portion, and assailed the brevity of Hayden's report, claiming that "the truth is, they desire to inculcate and impress the belief that Jackson is a mere soldier, and to report accurately such a

speech as this might show that he is not an *inferior Statesman to any of them*—therefore must it be kept out of view" (as quoted in the Harrisburg *Pennsylvanian*, March 27).

2. The editors had previously stated that their reporters were in a particularly disadvantageous position to hear the remarks of Jackson and other senators on the right of the chair, with the result that their remarks were "not heard at all, or very indistinctly heard, by the Reporters" (Washington *National Intelligencer*, March 8).

To William Hayden, Jr.

Washington March 30th. 1824

Sir

your note of yesterday, with the two news papers are recd. to which I reply.[1]

I never pretend to recollect, after they are made, remarks offered by me in public debate; and particularly can I not recollect, those inquired of by you; as I had determined to take no part in the discussion; a severe pain in my breast, at the time, I thought forbid me. Contrary to this determination indeed, I was drawn out by a direct appeal made to me by Mr [John] Holmes of Main; my reply therefore, was upon the spur of the occasion, and my remarks such as my mind sugested were proper at the moment.[2] Other Gentlemen can better say whether the report is correctly made than I can, as I pay no attention to such things. There is one thing I can assure you, that I should never ascribe unworthy motives to you, or any one—These are things which should be left, alone to *Him* who can, & has a right to Judge of the causes that control human actions.

Having held no communication with any one on this subject; I should not, could I recollect, interfere in the disputes of public Editors.

I was applied to the other day by Mr Seaton on this subject—The above was substantially my answer.[3] I return the papers as requested, & am Sir with due respect your most obdt. servt.

Andrew Jackson

ALS, OrU (10-0610); ALS copy, DLC (32). Published in Bassett, 3:243 (from the ALS copy).

1. See above.

2. Holmes (1773–1843; Brown 1796) had complained that neither the bill's sponsor nor Jackson, as chairman of the Military Affairs Committee, had supplied the necessary information regarding the state of fortifications to inform a vote on the proposed appropriation for armaments.

3. It is not known whether William W. Seaton's query on the subject was oral or in writing; at any rate, no correspondence with him on this subject has been found.

To William Berkeley Lewis

(Private) Washington March 31rst. 1824

Dear Major

Your letter of the 15th. instant is Just recd. On the subject of the purloined letter spoken of—I have no doubt of the fact—and I am advised that Mr Abner Laycock is suspected—whether this hint is given to shield others, I cannot say; but I have no suspicion that Mr Monroe would connive at such a proceding. It is Mr Monroes letter to me that they have got possession of; mine to him would not suport the information it is alledged, verbally, has been given by Mr Monroe—I stand upon the defensive; and should the attack be made, be assured it will be made to recoil upon its movers.[1] On the subject of the Mexican minister when Mr Crabb was brought forward I was told, the appointment of Mr Brown closed the door against him: and that Mr Edwards would not be appointed—about that time I recd a letter from Genl Stokes, and immediatly pressed his claim upon every ground; & laid before the President, as soon as they reached me, the strong recommendations from his state and had every reason then to conclude that he would have been appointed; when I called again I was then for the first time told that some of the north Carolina delegation had aledged against him what I wrote you—when we meet I think I can give you a clue to this thing.[2]

On the subject of Mr Calhoune, I have no doubt myself, but his friends acted agreable to his understanding & instructions; & that he is Sincere in his wishes—some have doubted this, but I have not—and I can give you when we meet reasons that will convince you I cannot be mistaken—As far as his friends to the South have acted, it is conformable to this; & I have no doubt but both the carolinas will unite in my support—you have seen the result of Pensylvania—Newyork is coming out—and it is said some of the Newengland States; a few weeks will give us the result of the movement of Newyork—if Crawford is not supported in that state I have but little doubt but he will be droped, and from what you will see in the National intelligencer of this morning Mr Clay taken up.[3] I have no doubt <but> if I was to travel to Boston where I have been invited that it would insure my election[4]—But this I can not do—I would feel degraded the ballance of my life—If I ever fill that office it must be the free choice of the people—I can then say I am the President of the nation—and my acts shall comport with that charecter.

I am so constantly engaged with visitors, that I have but little time to write, *[& t]*hat in the night—you must therefore pardon this hasty scrall.

present me to the young Ladies, and accept my best wishes for your health & happiness & believe me your friend.

Andrew Jackson

P.S. Major Eaton is well, sends his respects—I can assure you he has but little time to write to friends—he writes a great deal—Philo Wyomin &c &c &c with many correspondents fills up the measure of his time.[5]

ALS, NN (10-0612). Published in *NYPLB,* 4(1900):195.

1. Lewis's letter has not been found. For earlier discussions of the "purloined letter," see above, James Monroe to AJ, February 22, and AJ to Andrew J. Donelson, February 26.

2. As soon as it became known that Jackson would decline the nomination as minister to Mexico, several prominent Tennesseans headed by Governor William Carroll suggested Henry Crabb for the office. The Brown appointment was probably that of James Brown of Louisiana as minister to France, confirmed on December 9, 1823, but how this affected Crabb's chances is unclear. For Jackson's recommendations of Montfort Stokes, see AJ to Monroe, December 30, 1823, and January 15, 1824. The letter from Stokes has not been found. For the charge against Stokes, see above, AJ to Lewis, February 22.

3. Jackson was referring to the communication, "To 'A Republican,' No. 4," in which "A Democrat" argued that Henry Clay was a stronger candidate than William H. Crawford (Washington *National Intelligencer,* March 31).

4. Invitation not found.

5. The first of the "Philo-Wyoming" letters defending Jackson appeared in Stephen Simpson's Philadelphia *Columbian Observer* and was subsequently reprinted in other papers. See, for example, the Raleigh *Star, and North-Carolina Gazette,* March 19.

To Andrew Jackson Donelson

Washington City april 4th. 1824

Dear Andrew

I have this moment recd your two letters of the 18th. 21rst. ult. with one from your aunt & one from my son.[1] I am much gratified to learn that your aunts health still continues good; mine is improving, could I leave here and have freedom from company; with exercise, I think my health would be good—but as yet, I cannot say when congress will adjourn; or when I can leave here. The Tariff bill has been seven weeks under discussion in the House of Representatives; and when a final vote will be taken on it, in that Branch, is uncertain—The speechmaking mania predominates there. I wrote your aunt on yesterday & will write shortly.[2]

I sincerely thank you for your attention to my business; I assure you it gives me pleasure to find that my private concerns is kept so snug & all my debts paid, & accounts so nearly closed—The news of Doctor Butlers having taken up the Bill is truly pleasing to me. My feelings & reputation is the dearest thing to me; I could meet poverty with firmness, but the loss of reputation I could not bear.[3]

I thank you for the copy of the letter to Mr Monroe of Novbr 1816—I am well prepared for defence; but I suppose, my enemies will shrink from the intended attack—if not I am prepared[4]—you will have seen from the Newyork papers, that on the 8th instant a meeting is to take place in the city on the Presidential question—should it succeed, it is probable it will be followed by similar meetings throughout that state; should this be the case it will put down all candidates but two—Mr Crawford will be droped as I believe; and it is probable all the western states will unite & go with Pensylvania & Newyork: This is my own conjecture—for I hold no correspondence with any one but yourself.[5] I am fearfull my business has interrupted your attention to your profession—This I have regretted much but from my situation I had no person who I could apply to but you. Next fall I will have to bring you on with me; I have been this winter at a great Loss for some confidential friend to aid me; Major Eaton was allways willing but his labours have been great—he has been writing much—I have just learned that he is the author of Wyoming & Philo-Wyoming this for yourself. These pieces I intend having collected in due time & published in pamphlet form—He is now reviewing my life, & a second Edition will soon make its appearence. The moment I can leave here I will do so, & by the most expeditious rout reach home I shall not go through Philadelphia.[6]

Present me to your aunt & the andrews affectionately, to Miss E. & Milbury Donelson & to all my friends & neighbours & believe me to be your affectionate uncle

Andrew Jackson

ALS, DLC (10-0626). Published in Bassett, 3:243–44 (extract).

1. None of the letters have been found.

2. No letter to Rachel of April 3 has been found; Jackson was probably referring to his letter of April 2.

3. Donelson may have reported receipt of William E. Butler's check, which Bedford & Mackey had forwarded to him on March 6 (DLC-32). See above, AJ to Donelson, February 12.

4. See AJ to James Monroe, November 12, 1816 (*Jackson*, 4:73–75).

5. The meeting at Tammany Hall on April 8 passed resolutions nominating Jackson for president and John C. Calhoun for vice-president and endorsing the proposed Utica convention to express the people's choice for president.

6. The series of twelve letters signed "Wyoming," which began appearing in the Philadelphia *Columbian Observer* in mid-March 1823, were republished as *The Letters of Wyoming, to the People of the United States, on the Presidential Election, and in Favour of Andrew Jackson* (Philadelphia, 1824). The "Philo-Wyoming" letters have not been found in pamphlet form. The second edition of John H. Eaton's *Life of Andrew Jackson* was advertised in April for immediate publication. In mid-June, Eaton was in Philadelphia preparing the manuscript for the press.

To James Monroe

Washington April 9th. 1824

Dr Sir

Mr Hay last evening placed a paper in my hand containing the publication of a letter from Mr Lowry of the Senate to you, on the subject of a letter of mine; which he aledges to have been read by you, to him, in the presence of Mr Findly of the Senate, on a certain occasion. I barely cast my eyes over the letter, & returned the paper, & not untill I read the same publication in the Intelligencer of this morning; did I discover that it was not the same shewn me by Mr Hay some time since.[1]

The one published is variant from the one first shewn me by Mr Hay—why the second to you, & not the first, has been published is strange to me—As I may be interested in having the first, I request that you will furnish me with a copy by Major Eaton—The first letter from Mr Lowry to you can alone justify me hereafter, if it should become necessary, to expose the whole to the public without an imputation of violation of confidence.[2]

Mr Lowrys first letter tells you; that he has in possession in your own hand writing, your *confidential* letter to me, recd by way of Richmond, and to which I suppose he alludes when he says; "he has uncontrovertible evidence of the fact,"[3] but does not explain what fact—I cannot understand his having written you two letters so varient, & publishing only the latter; have therefore <for my safety>, to ask you for a copy.

Mr Hay offerred to let me take a Copy of the first letter; but believing all senators honourable men, I refused; but from what I see; I think it necessary now, to have one, which I hope you will please furnish Major Eaton. I am respectfully yr mo obdt servt

Andrew Jackson

ALS, DLC (10-0633); AL draft partly in John H. Eaton's hand, DLC (32). Published in Bassett, 3:245 (from AL draft).

1. The article, first published in the Philadelphia *American Sentinel,* April 6, and subsequently in the Washington *National Intelligencer,* April 9, printed Walter Lowrie to James Monroe, March 15 (DLC-32), giving Lowrie's account of his role in spreading information regarding Jackson's recommendations on Monroe's cabinet.

2. For the first letter, see Lowrie to Monroe, February 21 (DLC-32).

3. Lowrie's cover letter to the editors of the *American Sentinel,* April 1, expressed hope that his current publication would be sufficient, so that he would not have to make public "the incontrovertible evidence within my power."

To James Monroe

Washington
April 10th. 1824

Genl Jackson with best compliments to Mr Monroe acknowledges the recpt of his note of this day, and assures him that it embraces his entire views—It must be a very inexperienced General who unmasks his batteries to his enemy, before he knows the strenght of that enemies Batteries—The Genl will take no step in this case untill Mr Lowry gives to the world his *uncontrovertible proofs.* The Genl will then pursue a course which will be both honourable to himself & to you; & such as our mutual friends, which you have named will approve—The Genl for the present will maintain a dignified silence—[1]

AN, DLC (10-0636).

1. See Monroe to AJ, April 10. Monroe had suggested that George Hay and John H. Eaton should consult regarding the "most expediant" course to follow.

To Andrew Jackson Donelson

Washington City april 11th 1824

Dear Andrew

I have recd your letter of the 27th ult. and the one with the copies of the sec of wars letter to me & mine to him accepting the commission of Major Genl &c &c—My commissions will be found in a red pockett Book, I think in your aunts small Trunk, or my papertrunk in her room—however as I could not receive a copy of them before I leave here; I request you not to forward them—as I shall give no information untill I have all before me as I cannot well see the object of the application—and when I get home I can forward it if I think proper—[1]

I thank you for your strict attention to my business & the manner you have closed it; and your attention to your aunt & they Andrews, to them I ask a continuation of your kind attention.

You will see from the papers that Mr Lowry has come out & him & Mr Monroe is at issue who has told the lye. I see <Mr> the papers have called upon Mr L. to come out with his *incontestible* proof; so soon as this can be dragged from him, I will come out. I cannot before—because he has not published his first letter to Mr Monroe, stating that he had got by the way of Richmond his confidential letter to me—and untill this confidential letter is published by him I cannot move, without placing myself under the imputation of violating *confidence* by publishing private & confidential corespondence. This course I suppose has been recommended to him by his caucus friends—was I to publish my own letters, my enemies would say these are not <any> the ones aluded to; that is witheld—so I have to wait patiently for these Gentry to unmask themselves. Poor Lowry first letter to Mr Monroe must dam him with all honourable men.[2] But as providence has been heretofore kind to me; I trust he will still gard me from the wicked. This is all I ask of him to do, & that truth may prevail. I would not my son conceal a single public act I ever done from the public—If I am elected to fill the Presidential chair it must be by the people; and I will be the President of the nation, & <of> not of a party. I have allways been a republican, and acted with them—but the constitution secures to every man equal rights, & priviledges; and the very moment I proscribe an individual from office, on account of his political opinion; I become myself, a despot, call me by what name you please—because the other has Just as good a right to enjoy his opinion as I have—Therefore as Mr Jefferson said, "*We are all Federalists,* we are all Republicans, and we ought only to inquire is he honest, is he fit, is he capable"[3]—But where a man has shewn his attachment to the constitution & his country by risquing his life, & his all in its defence, is honest, is capable, that he should be unworthy to participate in the offices of his country because him and me differ as to the proper administration—is a species of Democracy, & Republicanism; that I trust in god, I shall never profess, to possess. give my Love to your aunt & all friends & believe me your affectionate uncle

Andrew Jackson

P.S. since commencing this letter Major Eaton has shewn me a letter from Newyork, where on the 8th. instant they have held a meeting, numerous, & unanimous as it respects myself[4]—This to be sure is flattering to me in one sense; but my son I have seen so much treachery & corruption that I am allmost disgusted with mankind—Still I am prepared to say the lords will be done—& if I should be brought into the presidential chair, imploring the benediction of heaven I will endeavour to administer it for the good of the nation regardless of any other consideration—A. J.

ALS, DLC (10-0639). Published in Bassett, 3:246–47 (extract).

1. On March 1, James Monroe informed Jackson of James Madison's request for information regarding Jackson's commissions as brigadier and major general in 1814. Jackson wrote Donelson the same day, requesting copies of the commissions and letters on the subject. Donelson replied on March 25 (not found) that the commissions could not be located, but that the letters indicated, contrary to Jackson's recollection, that he had accepted both commissions. Madison wished the information to prepare a reply to statements attributed to his former secretary of war John Armstrong (1758–1843) in the *Literary and Scientific Repository,* 6(October 1821):502–503 (see *Letters and Other Writings of James Madison* [4 vols.; Philadelphia, 1865], 3:373–85). Regarding Jackson's appointment, see Armstrong to AJ, May 22, and AJ to Armstrong, June 8, 1814 (*Jackson,* 3:75–76, 79). Donelson's letter of March 27 (not found) likely enclosed Bedford & Mackey to Donelson, March 6 (DLC-32), and Jackson's account with Bedford & Mackey, January 30.

2. Jackson was referring to Walter Lowrie's letters reprinted in the Washington *National Intelligencer,* April 9. The reaction in Washington papers to Lowrie's publication was restrained, although the *Washington Republican and Congressional Examiner,* April 9, reprinted a criticism of Lowrie's publication from a New York paper. Jackson here anticipates the publication, signed "P" but by George Hay, in the Washington *National Intelligencer,* April 15, which challenged Lowrie to publish his earlier letter to Monroe and to identify his "incontrovertible evidence." Lowrie's reply in the *National Intelligencer,* April 19, finally published his to Monroe of February 21.

3. The exact source of Jackson's quotation has not been located. He evidently intended to refer to the famous declaration of Thomas Jefferson's first inaugural address: "We are all Republicans, we are all Federalists" (Richardson, *Messages and Papers of the Presidents,* 1:322).

4. Letter not found. The meeting at Tammany Hall passed resolutions nominating Jackson for president and John C. Calhoun for vice-president.

To Rachel Jackson

City of Washington April 12th. 1824

My Dear wife

Your kind letter of the 24th. ult. I have recd;[1] I rejoice to learn that your health is good & your friends are attentive to you, & keep up your spirits. In my last I informed you that I had sent on George to take back our horses left on the road, so that when I left here for home, I would have nothing to detain me; and the horses & servants were a useless expence to us; one with us is sufficient.[2] If the Ohio should keep up for Steam Boat Navigation; I shall go from here in the stage to Wheeling; and from thence to Louisville—& perhaps all the way to Nashville by water. I cannot as yet say when I will be able to leave here; I did hope that last week would have closed the debate upon the Tariff bill; but it is still under discussion, and untill this bill is passed on in the senate & some others, I cannot leave here. we have done nothing yet—I regret to see no national feeling in the majority of congress—every one appears solely to be engrossed with the interest alone of his own section of country—so long as this feeling predominates, it will be unfortunate for our nation—we ought as Legislatures to meet with national feelings, and our Legislation ought to be for the general good; and as far as practicable equity & Justice to all sections of our country—was this <the> course adopted, we would with harmonious feelings, of mutual concessions, soon get through all important questions, which agreable to the present feeling; occasions so much useless debate, to the great injury of our country, <and> the waste of our time; & the public mony. My Love, I hope to leave here in the early part of May—I am truly wearied with lounging here; doing nothing, but feeding on the public funds—we have really done nothing yet beneficial; and for nine weeks has the House of Representatives been engaged debating the Tariff, that could have been as well decided in two. The moment I can say with certainty, the day I can leave here, I will inform you. My health still continues to be as usual; my cough in the morning troublesome; but when we get warm weather; I trust, it will entirely leave me. give my compliments to all friends; to my Dear little Andrews & to Capt A. J. Donelson & believe me to be your affectionate Husband

Andrew Jackson

P S. Mrs. Oneal & daughters request me to present you with their kind compliments & *[goo]*d wishes—A.J.

ALS, DLC (32). Published in Bassett, 3:247–48.
1. Not found.
2. See AJ to Rachel Jackson, April 8.

From Arthur Peronneau Hayne

Confidential. West. Bank 16th. April 1824.

Dear General,

I have received your kind & affectionate letter of the 4th. ult. and for which I beg you will now accept of my most sincere thanks.[1] It would have been sooner answered, but knowing your numerous engagements, I did not wish to trespass too much on your time.

The result of the Harrisburg Convention has afforded me the most sin[c]ere pleasure. However, I never had a doubt, of the part Penna. would take, & therefore was not at all surprised. For two years past, I had perceived this movement. It is the effect of the voice of the people—not of their leaders—& the unanimity is unexampled in that state since the days of Genl. Washington. The part Penna. has taken will affect the adjoining States, Ohio, Maryland, New Jersey & Delaware. My friends from Phila. write thus, "Genl. Jackson's conduct has been truly dignified—this his very enemies admit—*he* has not descended to any unworthy intrigue—nor indulged in any invective against his competitors. In one word, *he has acted like a Washington.*" Of all this, your friends, & those who know you personally, never had a doubt.

I have read with great pleasure that part of your letter on the subject of the Tariff. I think you go far enough. I would not advance a step, beyond the Independence of our Country. Manufacturing establishments, in the *General*, I look upon, as a *Curse* to the *Country*. I am of the opinion, "that Government has never, at any time, interfered to regulate, & direct the employment of private capital, without producing great mischief." I hope the Tariff Bill will not pass this session. Mr. [John] Todd is incompetent to the duties assigned him; the subject is above his comprehension; & be assured by far the greater part of the members of both houses, want information on the subject. The Tariff is a subject of vital importance to the Country, & it shd. be well understood before acted on. I therefore hope, & trust, it will not be acted on, the present session.[2]

I have read my Brothers speech on the Caucus question. I think it conclusive, & just what the Gentlemen deserved. It was of their own seeking. I will admit, that the period has been, when a Caucus was right enough; but from the nature of things, that period never can again occur; at least, it never can be necessary, while there is but one party, in the Nation. If the Federal party shd. again get into favor, in order to unite the Republican party, it may become proper to hold a Caucus. "As a *party* measure, it may in *some* instances, tend to *promote* Union."[3]

In the course of a fortnight, Mrs. [Elizabeth Laura Alston] Hayne & myself will leave Ala. for So. Ca. where we shall pass the Summer.[4] I will thank you to direct your next letter to Charleston. My brother writes me that *So. Ca. will at once take ground in your favor*; & of this I feel perfectly assured. That State, will exhibit the same unanimity, that Penna. has done. I have read McDuffies speech on "*Internal Improvements,*" with peculiar delight, & *Instruction.* I have not had the pleasure of reading your speech on the "*Defences of the Nation.*" My brother informs me it was a *truly eloquent one,* & had *great effect.* I trust the next Mail will bring it on.[5] Mrs. Hayne, unites with me, in her <expressions of> regard, & esteem for you; & believe me to be dear Genl. yours most faithfully & affectionately.

A. P. Hayne

ALS, DLC (32). Hayne (1790–1867) had served with Jackson during the Gulf campaign, as Southern Division inspector general after the war, and as commander of the Tennessee volunteers in the Seminole campaign. He continued to own the West Bank plantation on the Alabama River twelve miles south of Fort Jackson in Autauga County, Alabama, until late 1825.

1. Not found.

2. Tod (1779–1830), of Pennsylvania, was chairman of the House Committee on Manufacturing.

3. Robert Young Hayne (1791–1839) was a senator from South Carolina. For his speech of March 19, see *Annals of Congress,* 18th Cong., 1st sess., pp. 376–86 (quotation, p. 386).

4. Elizabeth L., daughter of William Alston and a niece of Thomas Pinckney, married Hayne in November 1822.

5. Hayne was probably referring to George McDuffie's speech supporting a bill for obtaining road and canal surveys, February 4–5, and Jackson's remarks in favor of an appropriation for fortifications, March 9 (*Annals of Congress,* 18th Cong., 1st sess., pp. 1371–98, 330–31). Jackson's remarks were only briefly reported.

To Andrew Jackson Donelson

Washington april 17th. 1824

Dear Andrew

yours of the 1rst of april is Just to hand[1] The public Journals will shew that the people of Newyork & Virginia are beginning to be alive to the election of the President, & are determined not to yield their constitutional rights to a caucus; or to submit to be sold by their Representatives in Congress for their own agrandisement, under promise to be brought into office by their chief; Mr. Crawford is believed here by all candid men to be prostrate; & must decline—Whether Mr Clay would unite with Mr Crawford I cannot say; but I am sure his Kentucky friends would refuse such a coalition with proper feelings of contempt—It is whispered to me that such a proposal was made to some of them, but properly rejected—

Mr Crawford with all Clays influence could not get one vote for Crawford in the State of Kentucky. all things are progressing well here as far as I know. Mr Lowry you will see; has come out with his letter to the President: you will also see a piece over the signature of *Carlile*; in the Columbian observer, adressed to him. This is severe & pointed; & must bring him out with his *uncontrovertible* proofs—should he be brought out—I will then lay before the nation the whole Budget—Mr Lowry is in a sad dilema—he must fall prostrate before all honourable men.[2]

The Tariff bill passed the House of Representatives yesterday by five of a majority—it will come up to the senate on Monday; so soon as it is acted on by our body; & a few laws pending before congress: I shall leave here for home. since I commenced writing This letter, I have been shewn a letter from a highly respectable charecter in the state of Newyork; The following is an extract—"Mr Clays friends in Newyork has been transferred over by bargain to Mr Crawford; and theres is no doubt but this has been done by Mr Clays consent as it was done by his particular friend Genl [Peter Buell] Porter." from which you will see the corruption of the times.[3] ¿how can a republic last long under such scenes of corruption; nothing but the redeeming spirit of a virtuous people, who will arise in the majesty of their strength, and hurl these Demagogues of corruption from their confidence; can redeem our nation from woe, & our republican Goverment from destruction. I have great hopes in the virtue of they people—and the stir amonghst them at present, is a good omen that they will act for themselves; & if they do, all will be well; and our Country saved from a corrupt rule—I thank you for the information of the health of your aunt & the family present me to her & the andrews & the young Ladies affectionately; tell Mrs. J. that Major [James McMillan] Glassell is with me has come from Philadelphia to see me & has requested me to present him to her in the most kind & affectionate manner[4] should you think it prudent you may make the extract from the newyork letter & put it into the Nashville papers but my name is not to be known I expect Genl Call will have it sent to the west—

I hope to be with you shortly untill then believe me your affectionate uncle

Andrew Jackson

ALS, DLC (10-0649).

1. Letter not found.

2. Jackson was again referring to the publication of Walter Lowrie's letter to James Monroe of March 15. The Carlisle piece has not been found.

3. Jackson's source has not been identified. Apparently he was referring to the April 3 nomination of Samuel Young for governor by a legislative caucus. On April 5, however, Porter (1773–1844; Yale 1791) denied to Henry Clay that any bargain had been made (see *Clay Papers,* 3:731–33).

4. Glassell (1790-1838) had served as one of Jackson's military aides from October 1816 to May 1818.

The A.B. controversy that had engaged the House of Representatives and the partisan press in early 1823 (see above, John H. Eaton to AJ, February 23, 1823) had a sequel just before adjournment in 1824. When, on March 22, William H. Crawford finally complied with a May 8, 1822, House resolution by submitting a lengthy record of treasury department correspondence with banks regarding public deposits, his cover letter cast doubt on Ninian Edwards's testimony before the second of the 1823 committees investigating suppressed documents (ASP, Finance, 4:495). *Edwards, on his way to assume his new position as minister to Mexico, responded with a letter to the House from Wheeling, Virginia, on April 6, in which he defended the veracity of his testimony and went on to avow his authorship of the A.B. letters and to charge "expressly" that Crawford had mismanaged national funds and misled Congress regarding his actions.*

*When Edwards's letter was placed before the House on April 19, it brought squarely to the fore the issue of treasury department mismanagement that had remained in the background of the two A.B. inspired investigations. The letter was referred to a select committee, which voted on April 21 to investigate fully and to require Edwards's attendance. As the session closed, the committee on May 25 offered a preliminary report exonerating Crawford and obtained authority to meet after adjournment to take Edwards's testimony when he arrived. The final report of June 21 concluded that "nothing has been proved to impeach the integrity of the Secretary, or to bring into doubt the general correctness and ability of his administration of the public finances." In the aftermath Edwards resigned his appointment to Mexico (*Annals of Congress, *18th Cong., 1st sess., pp. 2431–50, 2471–79, 2713–56, 2770–2916).*

To Andrew Jackson Donelson

(Private) Washington April 23rd. 1824

Dear Andrew

I have this day recd your letter of the 8th. and one of same date from your aunt[1]—Tomorrow morning I am to meet a joint committee of the H. of Representatives to fix upon a day for Congress to adjourn. from a circumstance that has lately occurred I fear we will not be able to fix as early a day as was a few days ago expected—It is this Mr Edwards who was appointed Minister to Mexico—when he reached Wheeling hearing of a report that was made by Mr Crawford, adressed a memorial to the House of Representatives charging him with various distinct violations of duty; This memorial has been referred to a committee, who has sent for Mr Edwards to prosecute those charges & if the house waits for the Messenger to return with Mr Edwards; Congress cannot rise before the middle of June.[2] I shall not wait for this event—so soon as the Tariff bill now before the senate is acted upon I shall leave here; for if an impeachment should be preferred against Mr Crawford, I would not sit upon his trial and will object to myself. one thing is now certain Mr Edwards must sustain his charges, or he is prostrate forever—If he does Mr Crawford is prostrate forever—It is a subject I intend to take no part in—It is said Mr Edwards is prepared & will positively make good the charges he has made; how this is time will unfold.

I write your aunt tonight[3]—I shall leave here as soon as I can, keep up her spirits as well as you can—give my respects to her, & all the ladies the little Andrews & all friends. yours respectfully

Andrew Jackson

ALS, DLC (10-0679).

1. Letters not found.

2. The House messenger, assistant doorkeeper John Oswald Dunn, reached Edwardsville on May 12 and returned to Washington by May 28, Ninian Edwards arriving on May 31.

3. See AJ to Rachel Jackson, April 23.

As a senator Jackson could hardly avoid the most hotly debated issue of the session: the tariff bill. Although he did not join in the debate, his votes were inevitably the subject of comment by those opposed to his presidential candidacy. Dated on the eve of the bill's consideration by the Senate, the letter to Littleton H. Coleman below, became Jackson's public statement of his tariff position.

To Littleton H. Coleman

Washington City, April 26th, 1824.

Sir:

I have had the honor, this day, to receive your letter of the 21st instant, and with candor shall reply to it.[1] My name has been brought before the nation by the people themselves, without any agency of mine; for I wish it not to be forgotton, that I never have solicited office; nor, when called upon, by the constituted authorities, have ever declined where I conceived my services could be beneficial to my country. But as my name has been brought before the nation for the first office in the gift of the people, it is incumbent on me, when asked, frankly to declare my opinion upon any political national question, pending before, and about which the country feels an interest.

You ask me my opinion on the Tariff. I answer, that I am in favor of a judicious examination and revision of it; and so far as the tariff bill before us embraces the design of fostering, protecting and preserving within ourselves, the means of national defence and independence, particularly in a state of war, I will advocate and support it. The experience of the last war ought to teach us a profitable lesson, and one never to be forgotten. If our liberty and republican form of government, procured for us by our revolutionary fathers, are worth the blood and treasure, at which they were obtained, it surely is our duty to protect and defend them. Can there be an American patriot, who saw the privations, dangers and difficulties experienced for the want of the proper means of defence during the last war, who would be willing again to hazard the safety of our country, if embroiled; or to rest it for defence on the precarious means of national resource to be derived from commerce in a state of war with a maritime power, who might destroy that commerce to prevent us obtaining the means of defence, and thereby subdue us? I hope there is not; and if there is, I am sure he does not deserve to enjoy the blessings of freedom. Heaven smiled upon, and gave us liberty and independence. That same Providence has blessed us with the means of national independence, and national defence. If we omit or refuse to use the gifts which he has extended to us, we deserve not the continuation of his blessings. He has filled our mountains and our plains with minerals—with lead, iron, and copper; and given us climate and soil for the growing of hemp and wool. These being the grand materials of our national defence, they ought to have extended to them adequate and fair protection, that our own manufactories and labourers may be placed on a fair competition with those of Europe, and that we may have, within our country, a supply of those leading and important articles, so essential in war. Beyond this, I look at the Tariff with an eye to the proper distribution of labor, and to revenue; and with a view to discharge our national debt. I am one of those who do not believe that a national debt is a national blessing, but rather a curse to a republic; inasmuch as it is calculated to raise around the administration a monied aristocracy, dangerous to the liberties of the country. This Tariff—I mean a judicious one—possesses more fanciful than real danger. I will ask what is the real situation of the agriculturist? Where has the American Farmer a market for his surplus product? Except for cotton, he has neither a foreign or home market. Does not this clearly prove, when there is no market either at home or abroad, that there is too much labor employed in agriculture; and that the channels for labor should be multiplied? Common sense points out at once the remedy. Draw from agriculture this superabundant labor; employ it in mechanism and manufactures; thereby creating a home market for your bread stuffs, and distributing labor to the most profitable account; and benefits to the country will result. Take from agriculture in the United States six hundred thousand men, women and children, and you will at once give a home market for more bread stuffs than all Europe now furnishes to us. In short, sir, we have been too long subject to the policy of the British merchants. It is time that we should become a little more *americanised*; and, instead of feeding the paupers and labourers of England, feed our own; or else, in a short time, by continuing our present policy, we shall all be rendered paupers ourselves. It is, therefore, my opinion, that a careful and judicious Tariff is much wanted, to pay our national debt, and afford us the means of that defence within ourselves, on which the safety of our country and liberty depends; and last, though not least, give a proper distribution to our labor, which must prove beneficial to the happiness, independence, and wealth of the community.

This is a short outline of my opinion, generally, on the subject of your enquiry, and believing them correct, and calculated to further the prosperity and happiness of my country, I declare to you, I would not barter them for any office or situation, of a temporal character, that could be given me.

I have presented you my opinions freely, because I am without concealment; and should indeed despise myself, if I could believe myself capable of desiring the confidence of any, by means so ignoble. I am, sir, very respectfully, Your most obt. servant.

(Signed) Andrew Jackson.

Printed, Raleigh *Star, and North-Carolina Gazette,* May 28 (mAJs), *Niles' Register,* June 12 (10-0681), and other newspapers. Published in Bassett, 3:249–51. Coleman (d. 1824), a Warrenton, N.C., physician, had chaired a February 21 meeting at Warrenton supporting Jackson for president and was on the committee of correspondence designated at the meeting.

1. Not found. Jackson sent the same answer to a number of inquiries regarding his view of the tariff, and the April 21 letter published by James Parton and subsequent historians as Coleman's inquiry was not Coleman's but a similar communication from a member of the Virginia legislature, most likely Francis Everod Rives of Petersburg (see *Richmond Enquirer,* May 22, 1827).

To Andrew Jackson Donelson

Washington City
April 27th. 1824

Dear Andrew

I had the pleasure this day to receive your letter of the 11th instant:[1] I am still here, the Tariff bill under discussion before us; when we may be able to take a final vote on it; I cannot say—so soon as this is done, & two or three other bills, which have not come up to us yet; I shall leave here.

In my last I named to you an occurrence that would protract the session of congress—I send you herewith the address of Mr Edwards for your perusal, & for the Library. Mr Edwards has been sent for by the committee to whom his memorial has been referred—The Messenger left here on the 14th., as I am informed; and if he has to go to Edwardsville in Illinois; It will be at least the 6th. of May before he can return.[2]

Should Mr Edwards return with him; & Congress determine to investigate the subject this session; It will not rise before July; and as Mr Edwards, as well as Mr Crawfords charector is in Jeopardy; no doubt can be entertained that Mr Edwards will not return, or his charector is prostrate forever—in short, one or the other must fall never to rise again, & both must, or ought to be, anxious for the investigation. Present me affectionately to your aunt and say to her I will be home as soon as I can; but I cannot leave here before I vote upon the Tariff Bill: I have recd many letters on this subject, many as I suppose held forth in *terorum*[3]—I mean to convince those who are not yet acquainted with me; that I cannot be intimidated from doing that, which my Judgment & conscience tells me is right; by any earthly power—I therefore will <vote for> support the Tariff so far as I believe it will tend to *foster*, the means of national defence, and *procure it from own means*; which will insure allways an ample suply within our country in a state of war, beyond this I will view it with an eye to Revenue to meet our national debt; give a proper distribution to labour, by which the agricultural interest will be promoted.

From these hints you will conclude I will vote for the Bill; as I believe it right & proper to feed our own labourers instead of those of Europe, & keep within us that capital that is drawn from us, & creates in part the wealth of England—The British merchants, & British influence has had heretofore too much influence: we must in our politics look more to our national interest. The Bill granting to the Commissioners of Georgia, 5000 acres of land each has this day passed the house of Representatives: and as it has heretofore passed the Senate twice I have no doubt but it will pass our body—give this information to your uncle John with my respects—[4]

My health is tolerable; it has been much better this, than last winter altho it has been much checkered—with my respects to the young Ladies & the andrews believe me your friend

A*[n]*drew Jackson

P. S. The National Intelligencer of this morning gives Senator Lowry a severe dressing over the name of George Hay—this must bring him out—[5]

ALS, DLC (10-0687). Published in Bassett, 3:251 (extract).

1. Not found.

2. See above, AJ to Donelson, April 23. Jackson's reference to the messenger leaving on the 14th must have been in error. The earliest order to Ninian Edwards on the subject was sent by the department of state on April 22 and required only that he await the orders of the House.

3. In legal terminology "in terrorem" means "by way of threat." The surviving portion of Jackson's correspondence does not contain the "many letters" described here.

4. Contrary to Jackson's information, the House bill for relief of the heirs of John Donelson (c1718–86) and others failed on third reading. For subsequent action, see AJ to Rachel Jackson, May 19, below.

5. George Hay's letter of April 26 to the editors of the Washington *National Intelligencer* denied Walter Lowrie's contentions regarding what Jackson had written to James Monroe and upbraided the senator for receiving the stolen letter and attempting to use it to blackmail the president.

To George Kremer

[May 6, 1824]

Dear Sir:

I have received your letter of yesterday; and, with much cheerfulness and candor, shall reply to your inquiry.[1]

It has been repeatedly pressed before the public, that I had written a letter to Mr. Monroe, recommending him to select for his cabinet, "two distinguished republicans and two distinguished federalists;" and that to Mr. Lowrie and Mr. Findlay, Senators from the state of Pennsylvania, the letter had been read. I have not been able to persuade myself, that the fact was so, inasmuch as our correspondence was private and confidential—because Mr. Findlay, who was present, has no recollection of it—because no such letter was ever written by me—and, because the President denies that he read any such letter, or, indeed, any letter at all. I regret that Mr. Lowrie, in presenting this matter, should not recollect one material circumstance. When first it was spoken of, he stated to me, and to others, that a letter purporting, and declared, to be mine, had been read to himself and Mr. Findlay, by the President, which advised that his Cabinet should be formed of "two distinguished republicans, and two distinguished federalists." My reply to him was, that no such letter had ever been written by me; that so far as I could recollect, only one person, Col. Drayton, of South Carolina, had been recommended to him; that I had suggested to the President the propriety of appointing him Secretary of War; for the reason that he was a man of high and honorable feelings, honest, virtuous, and of energetic character Personally, I knew not Col. Drayton: but, from information of his general character, felt satisfied he could do more to correct the feuds which unhappily prevailed in the army, than any other man of whom I had any knowledge. The contents of my letter, as read to him by the President, that two distinguished federalists, and two distinguished republicans, should be selected, was not only stated by Mr. Lowrie to me, but to yourself, and to Mr. Eaton, of the Senate, and to others.

He has changed, however, his ground, and now says, it was a recommendation to the President, to form his Cabinet from the two great leading parties of the country. Both statements are alike unfounded; no such letter was ever written by me; on the contrary, my advice to the President was, that, in the selection of his Cabinet, he should act upon principles like these: consider himself the head of the nation, not of a party; that he should have around him the best talents the country could afford, without regard to sectional divisions; and should, in his selection, seek after men of probity, virtue, capacity, and firmness; and, in this way, he would go far to eradicate those feelings, which, on former occasions, threw so many obstacles in the way of Government; and be enabled, perhaps, to unite a people heretofore politically divided. I gave it as my opinion, that the best evidence of devotion to the government, its constitution, and laws, which any could afford, was, when these were assailed, to venture forth in their defence, and maintain them admidst privations, and at the sacrifice of domestic quiet. That names were mere bubbles; and he who would, as Col Drayton had done, abandon his fire side and the comforts of home, & continue in the defence and protection of his country, through the war, merited the confidence of the government, let him bear what name of party he might: such a man I did recommend to Mr. Monroe; he was one I had never seen; yet one whose conduct, character, and good qualities, entitled him to any and every confidence. As well might the conclusion be adduced, that I had recommended a selection exclusively from one or the other of the parties, as that the cabinet, from a motive of policy, should be kept equally poised, by appointing two of each, for my advice was, to select men of probity, virtue, and talents, without regard to party.

The voice of Washington, in his farewell address to the nation, was, that party animosity was not to be encouraged, because "it was calculated to distract the public councils, and enfeeble the public administration;" and, with his, the voice of every patriot will accord.[2] Virtue being the main pillar of a Republican Government, unless virtuous men shall be drawn into its administration, the fabric must tremble Designing and corrupt men may cover their intrigues under a pretended love for virtue and patriotism; but a truly pure man will be without disguise, verifying, as he passes along, the old adage, that the tree is best known by its fruit.[3]

My letters have, by the President, and with my consent, been placed in the hands of a mutual friend, Mr. Eaton, with permission to publish them whenever he pleases to do so. I care not when it is done, for I am without concealment of any kind. My opinions and sentiments, such as they have been written, or expressed at any time, each and every one are at all times welcome to. In public or in private letters, I but breathe the sentiments I feel, and which my judgment sanctions; and no disposition will ever be entertained by me, either to disguise or to suppress them.[4]

I am, very respectfully, your most obedient servant,

Andrew Jackson.

Printed, Washington *National Intelligencer*, May 7 (10-0705), and other papers.

1. See Kremer to AJ, May 5.
2. See Richardson, *Messages and Papers of the Presidents*, 1:219.
3. A paraphrase of Matthew 12:33.
4. John H. Eaton transmitted copies of Jackson's letters to the Philadelphia *Columbian Observer* on May 9 and sent the originals to the Washington *National Intelligencer* on May 10, resulting in variant texts published in the *Observer* and the *Intelligencer* on May 12.

To William Berkeley Lewis

Washington May 7th. 1824

Dear Major

I have Just recd yours of the 21rst. ult. for which I thank you.[1] Believe me, my Dr Sir, that a man who is Governed by principle, in all his votes, is never in Danger. On the Tariff I am Governed by principle alone—The articles of National Defence, & National Independence, I will with my vote, foster & protect, without counting on cents & dollars; so that our own manufacturers shall stand on a footing of fair competition with the labourers of Europe—In doing this, the articles all being of the product of our own country, tends to promote the agriculturists, whilst it gives security to our nation & promotes Domestic Labour—The ballance of the bill I look to with an eye to Revenue alone, to meet the national debt. These articles of National defence, are Hemp, iron, lead, & coarse woollens and from the experience of last war every patriot will Justify me in this course—& if they do not, my own conscience approves, & I will follow it reguardless of any consequences. All sections of country will approve this course & the south before long, as well as other quarters of the union. To speak upon the subject I once intended; but it is now too late, it is worn out—& I could not expect to have what I said sent forth to the world truly—Joe Gales would not do this—Therefore my votes will speak for themselves, & hereafter I can support my course by all good reasons which will apply to them—

I write in haste—This morning will give you my letter to Mr Kreamer of Pensylvan & it will be followed up with the publication of the letters which has lately passed between me, & Mr Monroe; and then with the whole correspondence—Major Eaton tells me my letter of today is highly approved[2]—fear not; I am cool, & collected, & instead of damagi[n]g me on the Tariff, I am told my enemies, and the enemies of the Tariff, highly approve my course, it being a course of principle—

Major Eaton is not the writer of the Virginian—it is (for yourself) Genl Houston. Major Eaton writes a great deal—and Judge [Jacob C.] Isaacs a little—Wyoming (for yourself) as well as Philo Wyoming, was written by Eaton[3]—My respects to all friends; I shall leave here as soon as I can—May heaven bless you, & yours. adieu

Andrew Jackson

ALS, NN (10-0713). Published in *NYPLB,* 4(1900):196.

1. Letter not found.

2. See above, AJ to George Kremer, [May 6].

3. Isacks (1767–1835), formerly a judge of Tennessee's 3rd circuit, was a Tennessee congressman. The Washington *National Intelligencer,* March 19, published a letter signed "Virginian," defending AJ's qualifications for the presidency from criticisms in the *Richmond Enquirer,* February 26.

From Whitman Mead

NYK May 10 1824

Dear Sir

I deem it unnecessary to make an apology, in addressing you; you no doubt are greatly surprized at the sudden change in the Language of the national Union in the last No.—an Explanation is due. which I trust will be satisfactory, and at the same Time disclose great Baseness on the part of friends of Mr Crawford in this City—

Business compelled me to leave N YK about three weeks since, and the management of the Union was left with the Publisher—repeated attempts had previously been made to purchase the Union by Jacob Barker, and other Crawfordites for the supporting Mr. Crawford; their offers I spurned, but *during my absence* he again applied and Liberally bargained with the Publisher, and yesterday on my arrival in town, to my astonishment I learned that Mr Bark*[er]* had actually agreed to pay 12 dollars a week, & furnish an office, for the Paper—

The reason assigned to me by Mr. [William H.] Clayton the Publisher, that he is poor, and has a large family to support and that the Paper hitherto has been unprofitable[1]—I shall take measures to make public the whole transaction, wh. will exonerate me from every Imputation of a dereliction of Principles, and at the same time subserve the interest of correct measures yrs &c Signed

Whitman Mead

N.B. This letter was shewn to me by Mr. Eaton, he allowed me to copy it—R. K.[2]

Copy in Rufus King's hand, NHi (10-0720). Mead (1792–1833; Yale 1814) was known for his *Travels in North America* (1820).

1. The New York City *National Union,* a Clinton paper in state politics, was published by Clayton, who has not been further identified. Barker (1779–1871), a New York merchant and financier, was one of the founders of Tammany Hall. A statement of the *National Union*'s policy change appeared on May 8: "This paper has hitherto manifested a decided preference for General Jackson over all the other candidates for the Presidency, but without having changed our opinion in relation to that distinguished individual, we feel constrained to admit that the Republican party of this section of the country prefer another for that high office. . . . We shall therefore retire from the present contest." In his *Incidents in the Life of Jacob Barker of New Orleans, Louisiana* (Washington, 1855), Barker related another story, claiming that he established the *Union* to support Clinton and was an early advocate of a shift from William H. Crawford to AJ, following Crawford's illness.

2. King, in return, reported to John Q. Adams that the *National Union* had endorsed Crawford (see entry for May 23 in Charles Francis Adams, ed., *Memoirs of John Quincy Adams, Comprising Portions of His Diary from 1795 to 1848* [12 vols; Philadelphia, 1874–77], 6:351).

From John Freeman Schermerhorn

New York May 14th. 1824

My Dear General

I know you will not be displeased with a line from a country Clergyman, and especially when you see it is from your old friend John F. Schermerhorn who never will forget your kindness & attention to him and his friend [Samuel John] Mills, and who delights to dwell on the scenes, and to call to mind the days of friendly intercourse we have spent together.[1]

I have often, very often, desired & determined to write you & request you at your leisure to drop me a line, but I have not done it; from the consideration, that your time & attention was occupied wholly with the arduous duties of your official station; which you have executed with so much honor to yourself & glory to your country. I need scarce tell you, I have been an anxious & deeply interested spectator of all your movements, for I felt a deep interest in every thing which concerned so worthy a friend, and devoted patriot as Gen Andrew Jackson. And I can truly say that there is nothing in them all, which I have not only uniformly approved, but vindicated, and that not merely in the humble circle of my parish where I move; but in the first circles and greatest men among us, and that at a time when some, who now are friendly, thought it meritorious to vilify Gen. Jackson.

In the county of Schoharie where I now reside, on the second tuesday of June next, during the siting of our circuit court, my fellow citizens have been requested to meet "to nominate a candidate for the presidency." On that occasion, *Deo volente* I shall bear my public testimony to your worth and worthyness to fill the first office in our government.[2] I expect, for this to be assailed & condemned by selfish and interested politicians, but Sir I feel it a duty which I owe you & my country, and under such circumstances I heed no consequences. I have had some doubts whether it will be expedient to allude to the letter of Mr Armstrong the secratary of war in which he orders you to disband your troops at Natchez.[3] your conduct with regard to the transaction I have no difficulty about, but I should no wish to cast an imputation on any other of the administration, for I know not how far they might deserve it, although I very much disapprove & must condemn the conduct of the secratary of war. I have an impression also that on your personal responsibility you raised funds from the Bank of Nashville to pay the necessary advancements for the expedition in the winter of 1812 & 1813. Am I correct?[4]

You have no doubt heard seen much in the papers of the day of the movements & management <in this state.> of the political demagogues & puppets of this state, and no doubt they think all is well for them. But sir if I know any thing, a terrible explosion is at hand, which will confound & defeat all the management of our little U. states senator, whose character I have no doubt you perfectly understand & despise.[5] Governor [Joseph Christopher] Yates is my personal friend not only, but with him I am in habits of confidential intercourse, and rely upon it you can have no true conception of his character & policy from our public papers last winter. He has been represented as an enemy to the people by not recommending the giving the choice of electors to the people. This is not so. He stated in his message expressly that the people ought to have the choice of electors & that he approved of it; but because Congress had this subject before them & it was their duty to pass an act of uniformity on that subject, it was best to wait and see what they would do.[6] Well suppose congress now break up and do nothing on the subject, what inconsistency or impropriety would there be in the Governor should he immediately convene the legislature and say we see congress have done nothing on the subject, and we now recommend the passing of an act giving to the people of this State the choice of electors. And although the Governor has authorised no one to say that he will do so, still I think there is the highest probability it will take place.[7] I had an interview with the Governor yesterday and shall see him again in Albany next week. And I assure you I will do all I can to effect this object, and then I think the State of New York will give you their vote. And I feel it will be of the utmost importance that you return home by the way of N. York & Ohio &c. I want you to appear among us and should the people have the choice of electors I will underwrite for N. York. In such case I should be happy to receive you in my humble dwelling, but as that probably would not be convenient for you I would meet you in Albany. (And nothing but my poverty prevents me from paying you a visit at Washington; for I have a very great desire once more to see you.) And a view of our Canal is certainly an object in itself considered worthy your attention I hope you will consider the importance of returning by N. York as I do, for I believe the feeling in your favour would not only extend but be fixed. I meant to have said something more with regard to Governor Yates. He has been represented as being under the influence of the Bucktail faction of this state, and that through that influence he altered his message with regard to the choice of Electors. Nothing is farther from the truth for he has always kept M. V. Buren, Roger Skinner, Erastus Root, Benj. Knower & Attorney Gen [Samuel Austin] Talcot & Co at a distance & they hate him with all their heart, and for that reason they were glad to get rid of him, *and for no other reason,* did they nominate *[Saml Y]*oung. The Governor is really a good honest *[upri]*ght man, fearful to do any thing that *[is]* wrong & independent enough to dare to do any thing that is right. And I feel persuaded he will act a consistent, correct & dignified manner, and this community will know he is a friend of his country and to the rights of the people.[8]

If our friends manage prudently, (I say *our friends* because your friends in this great matter I consider mine and will act with them) I do not despair, but hope, that Governor Y may be favourable to your election; for

I know he admires you for the independence, integrity and patriotism which you have manifested on so many occasions.

Our worthy citizen DeWitt Clinton is in town, but I have had no interview with him, if I can see Gen. Stephen Van Renselear to day I shall probably call with him on Mr. C. I presume Mr. C. is your friend and is anxious to see you promoted. I wish I was intimately acquainted with him, but I probably never shall be for there is something in his countenance which to me is repulsive & not attractive. Still I a*[dmire]* and wish to see him placed in a sit*[uation]* in which his country may be benef*[itted by]* his talents.[9]

You perceive sir I have written you with all the freedom & frankness of an old confidential friend, and though there is nothing in it which I need to be ashamed that any one may see I wish you to consider <some> those things which I have said with regard to individuals as said in confidence At your leisure I shall be glad to hear from you Direct your letters to me at Middleburgh. Schoharie County N. York. I need not tell you, for I believe you know enough of me to be assured, that whatever may pass between us will be by me considered as in the highest degree confidential & you may if you please write freely and whatever I can do to promote your election in this part of the country shall be done *[c]*heerfully. You will probably hear from me again in a few weeks.

On your return home you will be pleased to mention me affectionately to your worthy <Lady> companion Mrs. Jackson, and our friends Gov. Carroll & Major Haines.[10] May the Lord bless & direct you in all your ways, and at last bring you to his holy hill of Zion with sentiments of the highest respect I am your friend Sir

John F. Schermerhorn

ALS, DLC (32). Schermerhorn (1786–1851) had accompanied Jackson's army to Natchez in early 1813, while touring the West for Connecticut and Massachusetts missionary societies.

1. Mills (1783–1818) accompanied Schermerhorn on the missionary trip.

2. An early June meeting of the grand jury of Schoharie, presumably the one to which Schermerhorn referred, registered ten votes for Adams and nine for Jackson (see *Niles' Register,* June 26).

3. For John Armstrong's order to AJ, February 6, 1813, see *Jackson,* 2:361.

4. When "derangement" in the finances of the paymaster's office delayed the march of Jackson's troops to Natchez in December 1812, he made arrangments with the Nashville Bank to pay his men in bank notes. A subsequent run on the bank led to a further agreement that the bank would pay one-third in specie and two-thirds in notes payable in ninety days (see general orders, December 27 and 29, 1812, DLC-61, and AJ to James Monroe, January 4, 1813, *Jackson,* 2:351–52).

5. Martin Van Buren.

6. Yates (1768–1837), of Schenectady, had been elected with little opposition in 1822, but was not nominated for reelection. For his annual message to the New York legislature, January 6, see Charles Z. Lincoln, ed., *State of New York. Messages from the Governors, Comprising Executive Communications to the Legislature and Other Papers Relating to Legislation from the Organization of the First Colonial Assembly in 1683 to and Including the Year 1906* (11 vols.; Albany, 1909), 3:16–33.

7. Constitutional amendments to provide for the election of presidential electors by congressional districts, or in one case for the abolition of electors, were considered in both houses of Congress in December and January, but none was passed. On June 2, Yates called a special session for August 2 to consider revision of New York's electoral law.

8. The Bucktails were the anti-Clinton faction in New York politics. Skinner (c1772–1825) was United States judge for the northern district of New York. Root (1773–1846; Dartmouth 1793) was lieutenant governor. Knower (d. 1839) was state treasurer. Talcott (1789–1836; Williams 1809) became state attorney general in 1821. Young (1778–1850) was defeated for governor by DeWitt Clinton in 1824.

9. Van Rensselaer (1764–1839; Harvard 1782) was a New York congressman.

10. Probably a reference to Andrew Hynes (1785–1845), a Nashville merchant and manufacturer, who served as Jackson's aide-de-camp during the Natchez expedition.

To James W. Lanier

(Copy) [cMay 15, 1824]

I have recvd your Letter of the 28 of april[1]

Altho I have an adversion particularly at this time to write<ing> letters on political <subjects> matters, yet when my opinions are asked on any subject, I ought not, & do not, forbear freely to give them; & especially on those subjects <about> in which the Country is much interested, and about which there is <much division> great diversity of opinion

In a letter <therefore> it is impracticable to go into detail, and I can therefore only present you with a hasty outline.

On both subjects embraced in your letter, during the present session of Congress we have had occasion to act; & my votes given on them and published will disclose <are> my opinions.[2]

The domestic industry & labor of the Country, coextensive with our national Independence, and national defence in a State of war, should be encouraged & protected. This should be the first design of a Tarriff, and the second a reasonable increase of impost with a view to paying the debt of the Nation, that it may not be entailed on our posterity as has been the case <of> with the English goverment.

As regards internal improvements, Congress can constitutionaly apply their funds to such objects as may be deemed National. They may erect Fortresses & make roads & canals, where they are of a character national, not local. But the general goverment in the prossecution of these objects cannot exercise an exclusive jurisdiction and invade the Soverignty of the States. They have a right to appropriate their funds, and to execute the work where, by the consent of the States thro which a road or canal is to run, <the particular jurisdiction of the State is ended> authority is given. With this limitation I should say that the constitutional power was in Congress Under our Constitution I feel satisfied that the general goverment can not, but with the assent of a state, exercise authority & jurisdiction within the limits of the State <but with its consent>; to concede <power> a different & enlarged power would be to produce in the end a consolidation of the States, to the utter destruction of <liberty as> those checks & balances of power at present existing under our confederation; & which are essential to the maintenance of our <present?> goverment

<This without going into detail, is a hasty & concise outline of my opinions on <the> those <important> subjects *about* which you have requested <my opinion> to be informed>

Jealousy & the fear of encroachment by the general govt. ought not to form a pretext for denying to her the exercise of those powers which may be derived from a liberal construction of the Constitution. She is the Central power around which in their own independent orbits moves the respective states. Strengthen her by encroachment made on the States and despotism may be the consequence, whereas to weaken and render her inefficient by witholding thro any jealous fears constitutional rights which properly belong to her, would be to introduce amongst the States anarchy rivalry & disunion. To keep the soverignty of the States & the general govt properly & harmoniously poised, is the pivot on which must rest the fredom & happiness of this Country This &c—Signed

A. Jackson

Draft in John H. Eaton's hand, DLC (32). Published in Bassett, 3:253. Lanier, president of the town of Franklin, Ohio, also served at times as township trustee, clerk, and justice of the peace. Jackson appointed him postmaster in 1829.

1. See Lanier to AJ, April 28.
2. See Appendix II for Jackson's recorded votes.

To Rachel Jackson

Washington City
Wednesday Evening May 19th. 1824

My Dear wife

The Tariff Bill that has been under discussion so long, and which has retarded all other business; has this day finally passed both houses of Congress—I am now detained only for Genl Call; I hope tomorrow to get his Bills through the Senate and leave here on Sunday morning next—I would leave here tomorrow morn*[ing but]* one of the Bills is to authorise the presiden*[t]* of the u states to order; that the Florida lands shall be survayed—under which I hope to have Colo. Butler appointed survayor-Genl.—and I do not wish, as I have staid so long, to leave here before I see that done, as there are but little relience here to be placed in promises;[1] I have another reason for delay—The act for paying your father & others commissioners under Georgia was lost by intrigue & inattention of its friends in the House of Representatives; Major Eaton Introduced a Bill in the Senate which passed unanimously, & is now before that House; <of Representatives> & I hope it will be acted on tomorrow[2]—and on

Sunday I hope to leave here by the way of Wheeling, Louisvill, & home—But my Love, as it is so uncertain at what day I could reach Louisville—and I might miss you on the way, and being so anxious to see you, & reach home; that I think it will be <well> best for you not to set out, to meet me—If I get a Steam Boat at *[Wheel]*ing when I arive there, I shall, I hope, *[re]*ach you shortly after you receive this letter. give my respects to the andrews, & all friends, & may god take you, & them, in his holy keeping untill I unite with you; is the prayer of your affectionate husband

Andrew Jackson

P.S. we passed a Joint Resolution to day for Congress to rise on the 27th. of this month. I feel happy to believe that I can get away from this place in a few days—My anxiety is great, & I am truly wearied; nothing but imperious necessity has detained me; all the wealth of <Peru> the Indias could not—A.J.

ALS, PPRF (10-0732). Published in Heiskell (2nd Edition), 3:290–91.

1. The House had passed the bill to grant land for the seat of government in Florida and for other purposes on May 18. On May 21, Jackson moved for Senate consideration, and the bill passed on May 22, becoming law on May 24 (4 *U.S. Statutes at Large* 30–31). Butler was confirmed as surveyor on May 24.

2. The House bill for the relief of the heirs of John Donelson (c1718–86) and other Georgia commissioners was rejected on April 27. Eaton's bill, introduced on April 30, passed on May 15. The House approved the bill with amendments on May 21, and the Senate accepted the changes on May 22, the bill also becoming law on May 24 (6 *U.S. Statutes at Large* 313).

To Henry Baldwin

Washington City May 20th 1824

Dr Sir

We have at last after a great deal of unnessary delay & dificulty gotten clear of the Tariff, & concluded to adjourn on the 27th. The two houses had fallen out about two immaterial amendments relative to coarse wollens & cotton bagging; each was obstinate, and untill this morning we had but little expectation of coming to any agreement; we have however by a conferrence settled the disagreement; and all are now thinking <about> of setting out for home, forthwith; with a view to bestow some little attention to our own affairs.[1]

Sunday I shall probably take my departure from this place for Wheeling in hope of meeting a steam Boat there which may carry me to Louisville on my way home. I declare to you I am worn out with the fatigue of legislation—Nature never intended me for any such pursuit I am sure. Day after day talking, & arguing about things that might be decided in a few hours, requires a Job like patience to bear; it does not suit me I assure you. This winter is the most arduous campaign, I have ever been engaged in, and never have I been more solicitous to return to my own Cottage. I should be happy to vissit you at Pittsburgh, but my long absence, and extreme anxiety to return induces a desire to take the nearest rout. You will say it is nothing out of the way, and that the chance of steam boat transportation is as good at one place as the other; This may be very true, but should I enter Pittsburgh I could not do otherwise than remain a day or two there, and this, were you to know my solicitude to get home, you would readily agree could not be done; & besides my good friends, of whom you know I have many, would declare me to be out on an electionering pilgrimage; which altho it would not be true, would yet be a mortifying accusation. I have come to the conclusion therefore, that it is the least exceptionable course, & indeed the most proper, to take the short road home, turning neither to the right, or left, and in this way I may escape those imputations, & censures which otherwise might be made. I should be happy to see you, but shall not. with great respect yr mo obdt. servt.

Andrew Jackson

ALS, PHC (10-0736).

1. The two Senate amendments inserted a provision exempting low-priced woolen goods from any duty above twenty-five percent and struck out the duty on cotton bagging. Jackson served on the conference committee, whose report, keeping the wool exemption except on flannels and baizes and retaining a lowered duty on cotton bagging, was accepted.

From John Coffee

Florence 8th. June 1824—

Dear Genl,

I have this moment seen your arrival at home, announced in the papers, and I take this opportunity by Mr. Simpson, who is going direct to Nashville, to drop you a line[1]—I rejoice to hear of your once more getting safe home to your family, where you may have a little respite from toils and trouble, for I expect the last six months has been a perplexing time to you, as in addition to your duties as Senator, you have seen your name used in various ways, although most generally it has been mentioned in the most flattering and honorable terms, yet by a few Sychophants, attempts has been made to cloud or darken the brilliant prospects, that in every direction illumined your path, but it is very gratifying to your real friends to see how little effect, those attempts have had on public Opinion, it is true that men are not wanting who join the effected alarm to oppose you On account of your vote on the Tariff Bill, but I set it down for granted that most of them, were secretly inimical, but many of them, pretended to be warm friends, I find some shuffeling about this Country, but no One has ventured to say much, nor do I think they will do so, as I am confident the people are steadfast, and not to be moved by sofistry. You have taken your course, you have pursued it steadily, and it is impossible to effect your stand, so long as the people act for themselves, you have therefore nothing to fear.[2]

I did expect untill very lately, that myself and family would be in Ten among our friends at this time, but I have a new Overseer,[3] and one that I fear could not manage my Crop at this season to any good advantage, and I am also at this time pressed with the business of the Surveyors office, which together with some other, but smaller causes, I have determined to put of our visit untill about the last of Sept. by that time the season will be more pleasant, when we anticipate seeing you at your own house—

Doctr. Bedford has sold little Andrews' crop of Cotton, and after paying the freight and charges, and the price of the Baling, he has sent me $2340. in United State bank notes, out of which I have paid his account with Simpson $223—and two or three other small bills, all the residue of the money is now in my hands and subject to your orders—his crop is very promising this year, has an excellent stand of cotton, and corn—The Doctr. has sent up a Carver Gin, *[a]*nd remarked that he had bought on a credit[4]—The worm injured my early planting very much, but the replant does well, upon the whole the prospect of a Crop is good—I have just started my Grist Mill that does very well, which will be a convenience—Our little children has been afflicted with colds and coughs, of late from the changeable weather, Andrew and Alexr. has both suffered by it, but are now nearly well and runing about, Andrew often asks me if I have heard from you. Please say to Mrs. Jackson that our little Rachel Jackson, grows finely, and is more like her Aunt, than any of the connection, I hope to shew her in Sept. in fine plight, as she is very fat and growing—With a tender of respects to Mrs. Jackson—& yourself I remain Dr. Genl. y sevt

Jno. Coffee

ALS, DLC (32).

1. Jackson arrived at the Hermitage on June 4. Coffee's messenger was probably the Florence merchant John Simpson.

2. For an example of the rhetoric by which Jackson's opponents in the South hoped to capitalize on his tariff votes, see "Gen. Jackson and the Tariff," *Mobile Commercial Register,* May 28, which argued that his votes gave "decisive proof that Gen. J. is entirely devoted to this new and oppressive system of taxation, got up for the exclusive benefit of some forty or fifty manufactories." Similarly, the Huntsville *Alabama Republican,* May 21, pointed out that the votes of Jackson and John H. Eaton were essential to passage of the tariff, implying that the senators had betrayed their constituents.

3. Not identified.

4. See accounts with Rapier & Simpson, November 14, 1822, and John Simpson & Co., July 18, 1823. For the gin, see account of Andrew J. Hutchings with John R. Bedford, April 22, 1824.

From Charles Pendleton Tutt

Locust Hill, near Leesburg Via.
June 12th 1824

Dear Sir

I arrived at home three days since from New York, and now after having a little recruited from the fatigues of the Journey, I hasten to acknowledge the receipt of your favor of the 24th ultimo, and at the same time to thank you for the interest you have taken in my matters.[1]

I regretted much that my friend Genl. Houston should have left Loudoun, on the very day on which I arrived at home, as it would have given me great pleasure to have seen him at my house. I however learned that his engagements with Miss [Mariah] Campbell, and his partiality for her society, prevented the Genl. from seeing much of our County, or many of its inhabitants,[2] he has now and will allways have, my best wishes for his prosperity and happiness in this world.

You have, before this will reach you seen, I have no doubt, the proclamation of the Governor of New York, convening the Legislature on the second of August,[3] this measure I do not think will materially affect Mr. Crawfords prospects in that state, for I am well assured that in no possible event could he now, or indeed could he ever, have, obtained the vote of New York. I expressed to you that opinion more than three months ago, and I am now confirmed that I was then correct; to whom the vote of New York will ultimately be given I am unable to say, as much will depend upon the course of Mr. Clinton and his friends, when I last wrote to you I felt confident that you would receive the support of Mr. Clinton and his party,[4] and such may still, and probably will be their course, but I cannot help expressing to you my apprehensions, that Mr. Clinton and his party will wait for the purpose of ascertaining, whether Mr. Adams or yourself be the strongest in New York, and that he will then throw his whole weight and influence with the strongest party, calculating in that way to resuscitate his own popularity, and to obtain once more an asscendancy in that state—I sincerely wish that Mr. Clinton may not have acquired in the New York political school a talent for intrigue, injurious to himself, and disgraceful to the state when tolerated. The above remarks are mere speculations, but knowing as I do, that Mr. Clinton and his party will turn the scale in that great state either in your favor or Mr. Adams's, I cannot help feeling a deep interest, and some share of apprehension in the issue. Mr. Clinton is a great man, and if he would keep an *upright, straight foward* course, he must in time become the first man in our country.

Mr. Van Buren and Governor [Mahlon] Dickerson visited Richmond after the adjournment of Congress for the purpose it is said of ascertain'g, whether in the event of Mr. Crawfords withdrawal from ill health, (which seems quite probable) Virginia could be induced to vote for Mr. Adams. was there ever any thing to equal this in impudence; it seems that Mr. Van Buren not content with the exercise of his talents for intrigue in his own state, must try his powers in the *ancient Dominion,* a place I can assure him where his intrigues will recive no nourishment, but must prove abortions, or if born, will wither and die.[5]

I am apprehensive that I shall fatigue you by the length of this letter, I will therefore close it, by expressing a hope that you have safely arrived at home, and found Mrs. Jackson well, to whom I beg leave to tender my best respects, and with assurances for yourself of the Sincere Esteem and very Great Regard of Yr. Obt. Servt.

Chas. P. Tutt

P. S. I have a Sister, Mrs. [Mildred P.] Jett who keeps the female academy at Shelbyville in your state, her husband has been dissipated, and having spent a large fortune my sister is compelled to support her own family by her exertions, she is a most enterprising woman and did greatly distinguish herself in Winchester Via. and was most unfortunately deluded by great offers to go to Shelbyville, none of which have been complied with. should you ever visit Shelbyville will you do me the favor to call and see her, and extend towards her your advice and protection, I am extremely desirous that she should leave Shelbyville, it is a small place, and not at all suited to the display of her talents—if you should have it in your power in any way to render her any advice or counsel to enable her to obtain in your country a more eligible situation I need not say how greatly I should be your debtor.[6] Tutt

ALS, DLC (32). Published in Bassett, 3:254–55 (extract).

1. Letter not found.

2. William Turnbull wrote Edward G. W. Butler on April 13 that "Genl Houston is trying to make a Miss Campbell from S. Carolina let go her *grip.* I dont think he will succeed" (LNHiC). Campbell was probably in Washington to visit her brother, Robert Blair Campbell (d. 1862; South Carolina College 1809), a representative from the Marlboro District of South Carolina. Though Houston travelled via South Carolina on his return to Washington in the fall, his courtship was unsuccessful.

3. Joseph C. Yates's proclamation was reprinted in the *Richmond Enquirer* on June 11. He called the special session to consider a law to provide for popular election of presidential electors.

4. Letter not found.

5. Martin Van Buren visited Thomas Jefferson at Monticello in May and reportedly stopped at Richmond on his return northward. Many hinted that the trip concerned William H. Crawford's illness, and John Q. Adams surmised that it might indicate a Van Buren shift from Crawford to Henry Clay. The *Richmond Enquirer,* June 11, however, denied that Van Buren and Dickerson (1770–1853; Princeton 1789), a former governor of New Jersey and now a senator, had visited the city.

6. Jett (1788–1826) was engaged to teach at the Shelbyville Female Academy in 1821. She and her husband Birkett D. Jett (1777–1849) continued to reside in Bedford County until her death.

To John Coffee

Hermitage June 18th. 1824

Dear Genl,

Last night I recd your much Esteemed favour of the 8th. instant; informing me of your health & that of your amiable family.[1] I regret much that any circumstances has occurred, & exists, to prevent us the pleasure of seeing you, your lady, & little ones, before next September. I calculated with certainty of meeting you here in all the present month. It is probable that in august I may go out, & come in with you; but of this I will advise you hereafter.

I thank you for your attention to my business relating to my little ward Hutching business; am happy you have recd the amount of the sales of his cotton & has closed the accounts—of that Estate. I have to request that you will retain in your hands the ballance of the proceed*[s]* of Little A. J. Hutchings cotton untill I go o*[ut]* or untill you receive further advice from me. It is true the last six months has been a time of some toil & bustle; I had to see my friends when they called which was often; and altho my health in the early part of the session was much checkered, & not good, still such was the anxiety of the people from Pensylvania Newyork & the Newengland states to see, & converse with me, that I was obliged to indulge them, and have the gratification to believe that they allways left me with good feelings & friendship toward me. Great pains had been taken to represent me as a savage disposition; who allways carried a Scalping Knife in one hand, & a tomahawk in the other; allways ready to knock down, & scalp, any & every person who differred with me in opinion—instead of this they as they expressed found a man of even temper—firm in his opinions advanced, and allways allowing others to enjoy theirs, untill reason convinced them that they were in error—It is true I went there with the determination of a Philosopher, and to take the high ground of open defience of my enemies; allowing them to lye as much as they pleased; but cause it to be well understood that my private charector & feelings were under my own protection & could not be assailed with impunity; that my public charector belonged to the nation & was the fair subject of investigation which I neither feared or wished to prevent, but rather courted than otherwise—and when the Radicals in the Senate brought me out, my reply & remarks gave me peace & quiet for the ballance of the Session; they gon*[t]*lett was never thrown afterwards, and so much was my sentiments approved, tha*[t]* I recd. the public congratulation of Governor [James] Barber of the senate as soon as I sat down—*[My]* health at the time was very bad, and nothing but the conduct of Mr Lowry & Mr Holmes of Main could have induced me to rise at the time.[2]

I have noted your remarks on the subject of some heretofore pretended friends & their attempts to produce an injury to me by commenting on my vote upon the Tariff so called. In this, as on all other occasions, I have pursued the dictates of my matured opinion with the sole view to the Independence, prosperity & happiness of my country; my own conscience approves the course, and when principle is the governing motive & public prosperity & happiness the end; I fear nothing, & no one who pursues this course has any thing to fear. I would like to meet the man who would vallue his liberty & the independence of his country by dollar & cents; leave the defence of his liberty, & Independence, to the precarious means of commerce in a state of war; or for pecuniary gain would become the dupe to the policy of the Holy allience & Great Britain & sacrafice his liberty for ideal pecuniary gain, <*[Labour]* is acknowledged as the wealth of all *[. . .]*> *[b]*y not cherishing & fostering within o*[ursel]*ves the means of national defence by means of our own Labour—Such a man, with such sentiments deserves not to enjoy the blessings of liberty, who would risque it on the precarious means to be procured from commerce in a state of war; when that war, when it h*[appens]* must be with a Superior maratime power.

I am one therefore who think my Liberty is worth protecting—& to protect it; we must procure, & maintain, within ourselves the means of its defence; beyond this I would look to <the> revenue alone to meet our national debt, which out to be extinguished to prevent a monied aristocracy growing up around the administration of our Goverment, dangerous to the perpetuity of our Liberties. These are my Sentiments, & what every american ought to possess. we the cotton growers are protected, & why not the hemp grower, as well as the cotton & sugar grower—why not the wool grower, as well as either, in short sir the agricultural interest must be protected as well as the comercial—protect agriculture & manufactories immediately arise. what does common sense say; If agricultural labour is unproductive because there is no markett for the surplus product either abroad, or at home; why withdraw from it, this surplus labour & apply it t*[o some]*thing else—by which you at once cr*[eate a]* markett at home for the surplus. what is our Situation, Have we a markett for any surplus of agricultural product, but sugar & cotton, & the latter ve*[ry]* precarious; and cannot expect to continue exc*[ep]*t the home markett which has & will be opened for it by the manufacturing of the raw material in america ¿What is the consequence If a home market is not created, there being no foreign markett; I answer the <farmer> agricultural interest must continue to languish, & the farmer must withdraw himself from the consumption of the dutiable article; <The wh> not being able from the product of his labour to pay for it—what becomes then of your revenue from import & Tonnage. The answer is as easy, It must decline as much as the agriculturalists decline the consumption, & be reduced thereby far below the wants of our goverment & must lead to a direct tax for its support & to meet the national debt—and the only way to prevent this, is by a Judicious Tariff protecting & encouraging the agricultural interest, & producing a markett for its surpluss productions, by which they will have the means of procuring & consuming the dutiable articles. It is the course of the anti-Tariff men that must inevitably lead to direct taxation, by *depressing agriculture [fro]m the want of a foreign or home market[t] for their surpluss product,* by which they become unable to procure & consume the dutiable articles. But enough for the present, I am aware of the kind of Demagogues that have taken this course; they cannot hurt me; I fear them not, they never were friends only professors, and I would not abandon my course that I know alone can lead to national Independence & safety for all the offices on earth; and in less than six years the southern states will be unanimous in favour of the measure because the one to be most benefitted by it, being the growers of the raw material. I have never met with one man who has not agreed with me that it is right to protect the great means of national defence—and from the experience of the late war, & the loss of blood & Treasure for the want of them, I do believe there cannot be a true american but unites with me. I shall be glad to hear from you often; I am happy to hear that you have your grist mill in operation—your improvement is now compleat, & you have nothing to attend to but your farm.

My health has improved, has been a little interrupted by a Violent attack of the tooth ache, Jaw ache & head ache—I have <The> fine prospect of cotton, better than I have ever had, & my corn promising. I have not ti*[me]* to write James Jackson, present me to him & say I wish to know when he will be in, as I wish to be at home, that we may finally close the whole business about the Erwin suit, & costs.[3] Present Mrs. J & myself to Polly & the children & kiss sweet little Rachel for us & believe me your friend

Andrew Jackson

P.S. our compliments to Capt Jack & Elisa—I had the law finally passed before I left Congress; allowing the Georgia commissioners their claim viz Donelson Kerr & others—[4]

ALS, THi (10-0791). Published in Bassett, 3:255–57 (extract).

1. See above, Coffee to AJ, June 8.

2. Jackson was probably referring to his March 9 speech regarding arms for fortifications. See above, William Hayden to AJ, March 29, and AJ to Hayden, March 30. Barbour (1775–1842) had served as governor of Virginia, 1812–14.

3. Andrew and James Jackson agreed on settlement of the costs of the Erwin suit in July, but James later tried to reopen the issue, claiming an error in Andrew Jackson's favor (see receipt, July 20; memorandum of costs, [cJuly]; and AJ to James Jackson, June 30, 1825).

4. 6 *U.S. Statutes at Large* 313.

From John Henry Eaton

Philadelphia
22 June 1824

Dr Genl.

Still lingering as you perceive at this gay city, instead like yourself of retiring to the shades of a private residence. I wish indeed I were with you, tho I have no room for complaining or to say that my time is not most agreeably disposed of. The politeness of my acquaintances is great indeed so much so, that it scarcely ever happens that I dine at home, and hence time and things roll pleasurably along

Upon the whole tho I believe it is better that I am away; for judging by our new Radical paper the Whig constant opportunities would be at hand to defend my course at home, on the Tarriff bill. The Whig proclaims <9/10> of the people adverse to the measure, and that a great portion of the residue would unite in opposition only that they do not understand it, which by the bye is quite a pretty compliment to the smartness of the Editors. I should like 1/2 an hours conversation with Messrs Norvell Erwin to see how much they understand of the business: from any remarks I have seen in their paper on the subject it will be quite a difficult matter for any portion of this unformed 1/10 to become more correctly informed than they are.[1] No principle they say can be clearer than to increase the duty will increase the price: now I take it nothing can be more false and the assertion betrays an ignorance of facts. Very good coarse domestic shirting is sold here at 8 Cents; & good enough for any body to wear at 14 Cents even now, this moment, since the Tariff has passed. Cott*[on]* Bagging equal in all respects to the Scotch at 23 Cents These things I see here and know to be facts. The Whig is possitive too that the revenue will be reduced two or three millions. Well it is very possible those gentlemens knowlege in Comercial taste, may be superior to any thing to be met with hereabouts; but so it is <that> the practical men of this section of Country suppose & believe that it will operate to produce a partial increase of the Revenue; but what of that, we dont want money say the anti tarriff men; indeed! it may be so, but if the falling due of large debts in the next four years with nothing to pay with be any proof of their assertion, they will have enough of it. The nation ought to see and know the falacy of these govermental reports which declare 6, 8, or 10 millions to be in the Treasury when in truth not one dollar is there. These paper calculations shewing large balances on hand wont do; the Country is in debt, money is wanting to meet them as they fall due; & these estimated balances on paper wont answer. Some mode therefore of raising cash, & I know of none better than to increase the Tarriff should be resorted to, unless like

England we mean to go on swelling our debt until we shall not have the ability even to discharge the interest

Congress have heretofore proceeded on the principle, that the debt of the Nation should be gradually met & paid, & for this purpose in 1817 remodeled the sinking fund, and made it a sacred pledge for the gradual extinguishment of the nations debt.[2] Seven years has not transpired since and a deficency of nearly twenty millions is found in the disbursement of this fund; over and above which loans during this same period to the amount of twelve or thirteen millions have been made. Still the answer is—we want not money. Very true we can borrow and in that way pay: our credit is very good yet, but if we go on in this way, disregarding too as has been the case the proper application of the sinking fund, we shall leave posterity in an awkard involved and Bankrupt condition. I do not think that fairness & justice to our selves requires a speedy extinguishment of our debt. Many of them have been & yet are applying for the benefit of posterity and they therefore may well be brought in for a share of the burthens The sinking fund set apart is perhaps enough as much as should be appropriated, but this ought to be faithfully applied—not touched for any thing else, or severred in any manner from its purpose; & yet the fact is that it has been severred; that is, there is a deficency in its application towards the extinguishment of the nations debt to an amount little short of twenty millions of Dollars and yet some of our [wise] sage politicians maintain & seriously argue that we have no r*[eal]* need of money

I have recvd. your letter from Louisville and shall attend to your request in procuring you a Copy of Wyoming. One was sent however to Mr Donnelson which will be at your house & may serve until my return home—[3]

My kind remembrance to Mrs. Jackson Dont know when I shall come home. Williams & Rankin are here with me & we are talking of going either to Saratoga or the Bedford Springs[4] with great respect

J. H Eaton

The Democratic meeting here of Jno Binns had about 150 of all ages sorts sizes & colors—it wont do—Presidential matters are proceedi*[ng]* on well—[5]

ALS matched fragments, DLC and ICHi (10-0806).

1. John P. Erwin had joined the editorial department of Joseph Norvell's *Nashville Whig* in October 1823, becoming editor in January 1824. The *Whig* began a series of articles opposing the tariff on May 10. The statement regarding popular opposition to the bill appeared in a brief editorial on May 27.

2. See "An act to provide for the redemption of the public debt," March 3, 1817, 3 *U.S. Statutes at Large* 379–80.

3. Letter not found.

4. Bedford Springs was a summer resort near Bedford, Pennsylvania.

5. A meeting at the courthouse in Philadelphia on June 16 endorsed William H. Crawford for president, denounced the Harrisburg nomination of Jackson, and called for a convention at Harrisburg on August 9 to select a competing electoral slate.

From Caleb Atwater

Circleville O. June 24, 1824

Dear sir,

I now forward the book I promised you sometime since. It is not bound because there is no book binder in this place. It ought to be *well* bound as the mechanical part of it, at least, deserves it.[1]

I regret very much, that I do not know, where to address a letter either to Mr. Eaton or Mr. Call, other wise I should write to them. I would thank you to inform them, that I am doing all I can in the presidential election. Our ticket will be formed before this reaches you, so we have *three* sets of candidates—for Adams, Clay & Jackson. In order to form the latter a state convention will meet a Columbus 2nd July 1824. What the result will be, I pretend not to predict, but will do all I posibly can, for the latter.[2]

We have 7 presses in this state decidedly with us and several *half way* ones & none are hostile to us. So far I have done all I could to effect even this. Ill health and poverty is my excuse for not having done more.[3]

We are gaining *daily* and shall give many thousand votes, next November.

The pamphlets Mr. Eaton sent me, are going through this county & have done much good. I wish I had more of them. My name is on the Jackson ticket as a candidate for elector, though I rather think, Col. [Valentine] Keffer's would do better among the German's and shall endeavor to substitute *his*, in place of *mine*. If Mr. Clay's friends would withdraw him, our work be easily accomplished in Ohio.[4]

I shall visit most of the electors in this county before the election. We are a majority over *all* other*[s]* *now* in this county.

Give my best respects to Messrs. Eaton & Call, and accept for yourself, my best wishes for your health, happiness and success in the approaching presidential election. Your's truly

Caleb Atwater

P. S. I hope Mess. Eaton & Call will write to me.[5]

I have got it bound since writing the above.[6]

Clay is out of the question in this state—The contest is between Jackson & Adams.[7]

Our great state convention will be on the 2nd July at Columbus where delegates from all the counties will nominate Gen. Jackson for President.[8]

ALS, DLC (72). Atwater (1778–1867; Williams 1804) had represented Pickaway County in the Ohio General Assembly and run unsuccessfully for Congress. In February he published the short-lived Chillicothe *Friend of Freedom,* which supported DeWitt Clinton for president, but he had switched to Jackson by April.

1. Atwater's previous communication has not been found. He sent Volume 1 of the *Transactions and Collections of the American Antiquarian Society,* which included his "Description of the Antiquities Discovered in the State of Ohio and Other Western States."

2. A Pickaway County convention met on July 2 and selected Atwater and Valentine Keffer as delegates to the Ohio Jackson convention at Columbus on July 14. At the state convention Atwater was selected to the committee of correspondence, which published *An Address to the People of Ohio on the Important Subject of the Next Presidency* in September.

3. Atwater's exact references can not be established with certainty, but among the most consistently pro-Jackson papers in Ohio were the *Cincinnati Advertiser, Hamilton Intelligencer and Advertiser,* New Lisbon *Ohio Patriot,* Somerset *Perry Record,* West Union *Village Register,* and *Wooster Spectator.* Atwater probably included the Cincinnati *National Republican,* which shifted dramatically from Clinton to Jackson in early April, on his list as well.

4. Keffer (1778–1852), who served several terms in the Ohio General Assembly from Pickaway County, replaced Atwater as Jackson elector on the state ticket.

5. At the bottom of the second page.

6. At the bottom of the first page, marked to correspond with the first paragraph.

7. In the left margin of the first page.

8. In the left margin of the third page.

From George W. Thornton

Boston June 26. 1824—

Sir,

A subject interesting to every citizen of the union, is now before the public; & its result is anticipated with intense solicitude. On this subject it is the province of the humblest individual to express an opinion. Availing myself of this privilege, & having made up my mind I take the liberty to address you. <Before I proceed further, I . . . observe thro' . . .> The subject I allude to is that of the presidency. Personally unacquainted with you, I am not entirely ignorant of your history; from it, I have formed the opinion that yr. claims are superior to any of your competitors. In this quarter very many are of the same sentiment, & but for the publication of yr. correspondence with Mr Monro, you would have been the *most* popular candidate in Massachusetts! An expression which there occurred & which was undoubtedly predicated on unfounded aspersions has caused considerable excitement among many who were previously in yr. favor. I am one of those who believe that the views of the Hartford convention were little short of treasonable. But, Sir, on reflection I cannot conceive of any reasonable construction of the section <Article>, quoted by you, for the <better government of> regulation of the Army, which would have justified the punishment of the leaders of that convention.[1] I have attributed that unfortunate assertion to a premature decision of a proposition involving principles & consequences of magnitude. And, Sir, I sincerely believe a moments reflection would have produced a different opinion. I submit it to you whether it would not be well to explain that obnoxious remark so as to deprive it of its prejudicial character. Such a course would be consistent with your character & would go far to remove the prejudice which that publication has excited. This, Sir, is my object in writing & the only apology I can offer is the solicitude I feel for the welfare of my country. If you condescend to favor me with an explanatory line I flatter myself it will have the effect of removing the prejudice produced by a remark engendered by the false colouring given to the Hartford Convention, at the South, at a time of party excitement.[2] My only anxiety is that your character may be correctly understood & your abilities & judgement be properly appreciated. I am not the apologist of the Hartford Convention. God forbid that I ever should be. But, Sir I believe the anti national principles which dictated that measure have been exagerated & common justice requires that <they> it should be judged of <by> impartially. That the election of President will go to the H. of R. is more than probable—it is morally certain, and it is extremely desirable that the candidates should be divested of every deadweight which does not rightly attach. With these views & the most profound respect for yr. character & sincere anxiety for your welfare, I subscribe myself yr. very humble Servt

Geo' W. Thornton.

ALS, DLC (32). Thornton has not been identified.

1. Jackson's letter to James Monroe of January 6, 1817 (*Jackson,* 4:80–82), had stated that the leaders of the 1814–15 Hartford Convention should have been punished under section 2 of the 1806 act for the government of the army, which concerned spying about fortifications. In a December 25, 1826, letter to Henry Lee, Jackson supported his position by reference instead to articles 56 and 57 of section 1, concerning giving aid to and communicating with the enemy (2 *U.S. Statutes at Large* 366, 371).

2. No reply has been found.

To John Armstrong

Hermitage June 29th 1824.

Sir

Your letter of the 6th Instant is just recd, and I will with my usual frankness answer your enquiries. Permit me here, however to premise, that the words ("*by the weakness or wickedness of our war ministers*") which you have quoted from my letter to Mr Monroe, and underscored in your communication, is not to be found in the copy now in my possession, and printed from the original furnished the Editors of the National Intelligencer.[1]

When I wrote the private & confidential letter to Mr. Monroe, to which you have aluded, I had in my mind, as well as recollection now serves me, the moloncholy list of disasters which had attended our military operations during the late war. Amonghst the rest, I had more particularly in view the surrender of Genl [William] Hull, and the capture of Washington City.[2] When I reflected upon these and other dreadfull calamities which afflicted our common country during the contest with great Britain, proceeding, as was believed, from the imperfect manner in which the campaigns were planned, as well as the fatal <measures> results which followed upon their execution, I was constrained to entertain the opinion which was confidentially expressed to Mr. Monroe in the letter addressed to him on that occasion.

Whether those misfortunes which attended the progress of our arms during a considerable portion of the conflict, were to be ascribed to wickedness, or weakness, or both combined, I have not, in my letter undertaken to determine: Suffice it to say, that my observations was not intended to cast a reproach upon any individual, but were used to enforce the propriety of bringing into office, a man of virtue, talents, and <integrity> energy. I am Sir very respectfully your obdt servt.

Andrew Jackson

ALS draft, DLC (32). Published in 1824 newspapers (extracts) and in Bassett, 3:258.

1. See John Armstrong to AJ, June 6. The quoted phrase from AJ to Monroe, January 6, 1817, was edited out before publication of the letter in the Washington *National Intelligencer,* May 12, 1824. John H. Eaton, however, also supplied a copy of the letter to Stephen Simpson, who published the letter with the offending phrase in the Philadelphia *Columbian Observer,* May 12 (see *Jackson,* 4:80–82).

2. Hull (1753–1825; Yale 1772) surrendered his army at Detroit on August 16, 1812, following a failed invasion of Canada. The British captured Washington on August 24, 1814.

To John Coffee

Hermitage July 1rst 1824

Dr Genl

I have this moment recd from Colo. J Gadsden the letter which I now enclose you & request your attention to the enquiry whether his stock or Lotts can be sold for cash, & at what price & communicate the same to me.[1]

From the urgency of his letter I suppose he is in necessity, & must sell; your early attention to this subject will confer an obligation on me

From a letter recd from Capt Jack Donelson last evening I had the pleasure to hear that you and family are well: we have a good deal of sickness in this quarter—all our relations are well but Milbury D. who is very unwell.[2] I shall be glad to hear something of the adams meeting, who are the prime movers &c &c &c. I am happy to believe that if Tariff principle are right, or wrong Mr Adams is as strong a Tariff man as any—I review my vote on that subject with great complacency; and I well know that no man of sense or my real friend will ever abandon me on that ground, be assured it is a mere pretext for a change, and all I want is really to know them—My friend Capt Savage cannot be amonghst that number—I should regret if he was as I have a sincer respect for the good sense of the man—and even this would only lessen my opinion of his good understanding but fill me with no regret for my votes. I voted from principle & would thus have voted had I have been certain by a change I could have placed myself in the Presidential chair;[3]

A hint from my friend Capt J. Donelsons letter recd last evening has given rise to the foregoing. I have Just recd a letter from Major Eaton from Philadelphia, he says all things are going on *well*—The Legislature of Newyork is called, & if the Electoral Bill passes, it will as it is thought put an end to the contest.[4]

Mrs. J. Joins me in respects to you Polly & the sweet Little ones your friend

Andrew Jackson

ALS, THi (10-0818). Published in Bassett, 3:258 (extract).

1. See James Gadsden to AJ, June 5.

2. Letter not found. Milbery M. Donelson suffered from a bowel complaint that had caused several deaths in the Nashville area (see John Donelson, 1755–1830, to Coffee, June 29, THi).

3. When news of Jackson's tariff vote reached Lauderdale County, John Q. Adams's supporters in the county called for a meeting at Florence on July 10 (see Coffee to John Donelson, 1755–1830, July 8, THi).

4. John H. Eaton's letter has not been found. It apparently discussed the June 2 call for a special session of the New York legislature to consider the popular election of electors. At the session, convened on August 2 and adjourned after five days, Regency legislators coordinated by Martin Van Buren quickly quashed electoral reform by tabling the proposal in the Senate. After the issue contributed heavily to Regency losses in the fall campaign, a law providing for popular election by districts was passed by the new legislature on November 25, too late to influence the 1824 presidential campaign.

To [William Savin] Fulton

Hermitage July 4th. 1824

Dr Sir

I have just recd your friendly letter of the 29th. ult. for which I thank you.[1]

Genl Call writes you by this days mail & will enclose you my letter to Doctor Coleman N. Carolina, which has went the rounds of the papers which will give you fully the outlines of my opinion upon the subject of our national Independence, defence, & Domestic oeconomy, & *the Tariff* with a historical account of the proceedings on the Tariff Bill in both Houses of Congress.[2] There are none so dangerous as hypocritical friends, who profess friendship, but by falshood, & false colouring attempt to assail you under the speces pretext of sorrow & friendship; every one of my intimate acquaintance long since knew my opinion upon the subject of political oeconomy; They knew as long as I had a voice it would be raised in favour of the Independence of our nation, by cherishing & fostering the means of our national defence, that when war came, we would have the means within ourselves of defending our Liberty, of which we boast, our constitution, & our Country—The experience of the late war convinced me that our Liberty was too precious, to be left for the means of its defence upon the precarious supply to be derived from commerce in a state of war, when that war was to be waged with maratime powers who wield the power of the Deep, & who by witholding from us the means of defence, could make us an easy conquest: whoever recollects the distresses of the late war how many of our brave men fell victim to climate for the want of necessary cloathing in the field, & the Hospital, will dispell from his mind all ideas of cupidity, & British influence and prepare our country for defence in time of peace by nourishing & protecting the means of national defence; *at least by a fair protection*, that will place the american labour in a fair competition with that of urope; This is as far as I would go; *Thus far the Bill does not go*—sail Duck, Hemp & iron has not been increased as much as with an eye to revenue they would *well* bear. These are some of the means of national defence, and ought to have been raised as high as Genl Saml Smith in 1817 in his revenue Bill placed them—But Genl Smith altho he acknowledged on the floor that two cents pr lb on hemp and $100 pr ton on iron would be a fair duty on these articles; still he voted against the whole, because *we did not want Revenue*—whilst he was thus declaring, what is the fact; two Bills are presented to us & passed creating stock to the amount of 10,000,000—five to meet the Florida debt & five to meet the 7 pr ct Debt which fall due shortly—Still say the Radicals we do not want Revenue—If a national debt is considered a national blessing then we like great Britain, can get on by borrowing—But as I believe it a national curse, my vow shall be to pay the national debt, to prevent a monied aristocracy from growing up around our administration that must bend it to its views, & ultimately destroy the liberty of our country.[3]

On the subject of my votes were those double faced Hypocritical political friends of mine as a[n]xious in search of truth as they are of falshood; they would find that my votes were bottomed upon national principles, of equality, & perfect reciprocity, to all sections of the union. If they would look at the Journals, they would find in committee of the whole, the bill was laid before us, on all Fabricks of Hemp there were specific duties imposed; on cotton Bagging, & coarse woolings & progressive duty—cotton Bagging 4.1/2. 5.1/2—This being taken up first; my vote reduced cotton bagging to 4.1/2—when sail Duck, Burlaps, & other course fabricks of Hemp—Genl [John] Chandler voted for striking out the whole duty imposed—which left all coarse fabricks of Hemp at 15 prcent advalorum—When the Bill was reported to the house on principles of general Justice I voted to alter the duty on cotton Baggin to an advalorum duty of 25 prct. as the other fabricks were charged to an advalorum duty[4]—I ask Sir, is not here uniformity of principle & of general Justice. The delegation from Alabama will answer in the afirmative, so will those most opposed to the Bill. But the anti Tariff men say this Bill will lead to direct Tax by destroying the Revenue—This is not true, it will promote agricultural labour, create a home markett for it, & add 3 million & a half of revenue. It is the only way to prevent a direct Tax, if we pay the national debt. ¿what is the situation of the american agriculturist—have we at present eithe[r] a home, or foreign markett for the product of agricultural labour, except our cotton, & our sugar—both of which are well protected; and when we take a view of the Spanish main South america, portugal, & Egypt—the foreign markett for our cotton cannot be of long duration—Let me then ask unless a home markett for the surplus labour of agriculture can be made, must not the farmers, live on the product of their own farms, & withdraw themselves from the consumption of dutiable articles: In proportion as the consumption is lessened so is your revenue—which must be made up by internal Revenue, direct or indirect, at a time when the agriculturists are not able, for the want of a markett for their products, to pay a tax—Hence the policy of a Judicious Tariff, to promote the Interest of the agriculturists by opening to them a sure, & safe home markett for the products of their labour—This can only be done by withdrawing the surpluss labour from agriculture & applying it to manufa[c]tories. It is to be regretted that we have two little national feeling, & two much sectional—we are governed too much by British influence, & commercial, to the great injury of our agriculturist, which is the main pillars of our national prosperity, and upon which our Independence & wealth as a nation rests, & out of which manufactures & commerce must grow & prosper, if prosper the do.

I have been amused with the absurdity of the ground taken by the anti Tariff men, they say the Tax upon cotton bagging is onerous & destructive to the cotton growers; now the truth is, the cotton grower does not pay one cent of the duty, it is the buyer—the rope & Bailing is sold as cotton; & last year I made 5 cents & one 8th. upon the rope & 2 cents upon the Bailing—but admit we do—is it not right when we are the only part of the agriculturists that have a foreign, & home markett, for the product of our Labour that we should pay a proportion of the revenue we consume at home better than one sixth of all the cotton that is produced in the union—added to this, 100,000 of foreign cotton last year introduced, the duty paid, & manufactured at our manufactories—Still the southern gentlemen refused to aid Major Eaton who proposed an amendment by the aditional duty on cotton of 3 cents pr lb[5]—the manufacturers in the east are now buying south american cotton in south america, at 6. & 7 cents best quality—in a few years of peace where will be our cotton markett unless we secure it at home—This Tariff & Adams meeting is truly a Farsical thing[6]—Mr Adams, is an open candid man, he has at my Table publickly answered Mr Clay that he was in favour of a *Judicious Tariff*—every person that knows him knows this.[7] now it is the greatest peace of Hypocricy—to say that because I voted as every body who knew me, had read my toasts <votes> for years, knew I would—would make this an objection—I love a candid open enemy, but a hypocritical <professing> friend, who professing friendship <but> acts the hidden enemy, I despise. It is such that can injure most—<& this too who has been aiding in bringing my name before the public without my consent & contrary to my wishes.> I have good feelings toward Mr Adams, & there is no conduct of Hypocritical friends that can alter this feeling—I wish you so soon as the meeting is over to give me the names of those apostate hypocritical friends that I may <note> know them—They can do me no harm—I never have, or will ask any favour of them <all I wished from my friends who brought my name forward—that they would not attempt secretely to slander me but tell the truth & withdraw their support as honourable men—not object to me for doing that that Mr Adams openly avows he is in favour of—> I am & &c &c

A. J.

ALS draft, DLC (32). Published in Bassett, 3:259–61. Endorsed, "To Judge Fulton at Florence."

1. Not found.

2. See above, AJ to Littleton H. Coleman, April 26. Richard K. Call's letter has not been found.

3. Jackson was probably referring to the tariff law of April 27, 1816 (3 *U.S. Statutes at Large* 310–14), for which Smith (1752–1839), then a Maryland representative, had served as floor leader. A senator in 1824, Smith explained his opposition to the new tariff bill in a speech on May 13 (*Annals of Congress,* 18th Cong., 1st sess., pp. 738–43). His acknowledgment that the duties on hemp and iron were fair was not reported. The final 1824 bill incorporated a reduced duty of $35 per ton for hemp and applied $100 per ton to iron nails and wire, not to unmanufactured iron. The two stock bills authorized creation of 4½% stock to pay for claims awarded under the 1819 treaty with Spain and to redeem 6% stock issued in 1812 and coming due in 1825 (4 *U.S. Statutes at Large* 33–34, 73–75).

4. The tariff bill provided for specific duties on some products and assessed ad valorem duties on manufactures not specifically listed. The bill reported to the Senate committee of the whole assessed a 4½ cent duty on cotton bagging to be raised to 5½ cents after June 30, 1825. In the committee Jackson supported William Kelly's motion to delete the proposed increase to 5½ cents, but gave the decisive vote against a subsequent motion to delete the 4½ cent duty. Meanwhile, Chandler (1762–1841) and his Maine colleague John Holmes offered a variety of amendments to reduce the duties on sail duck, a coarse fabric with a value for maritime interests that southerners saw as comparable to their need for cheap bag-

ging. In a series of votes on May 7 the Senate agreed to a specific ad valorem duty on ducks, osnaburgs, ticklenburgs, and burlaps; rejected Jackson's motion to set the duty at 20 percent; and agreed to a duty of 15 percent. On May 11, when the Senate considered the changes made in committee of the whole, Jackson reversed his vote on cotton bagging, and the Senate deleted the specific duty, thus leaving bagging subject to a residual 25 percent ad valorem. The deletion was not accepted by the House, and the cotton bagging duty was finally set at 3¾ cents per square yard. Jackson, who considered the change "immaterial," may have had political reasons for altering his vote on bagging (see above, AJ to Henry Baldwin, May 20; and John C. Fitzpatrick, ed., "The Autobiography of Martin Van Buren," in *Annual Report of the American Historical Association for the Year 1918* [2 vols.; Washington, 1920], 2:240–42).

5. John H. Eaton's amendment, which would have set the duty on cotton, picked or ginned, at six cents per pound, was offered May 10, opposed by four southern senators, and subsequently withdrawn (*Annals of Congress*, 18th Cong., 1st sess., p. 726).

6. Probably referring to the meeting to be held at Florence on July 10.

7. Possibly at Jackson's birthday dinner of March 15. Adams noted in his diary that Henry Clay "became warm, vehement, and absurd upon the tariff" on that occasion (Charles Francis Adams, ed., *Memoirs of John Quincy Adams, Comprising Portions of His Diary from 1795 to 1848* [12 vols; Philadelphia, 1874–77], 6:258).

To Edward Livingston

July 5th 1824 Hermitage

Dr Sir,

your letter of the 11th June is just recd, & I am happy to learn that you are nearly closing the disagreeable duty assigned you, as one of the committee—[1]

Before the receipt of your letter, I had recd. one from Genl Armstrong. my answer to him is enclosed for your information. In my letters to Mr Monroe I have not named Genl A, or any one else; nor have I attempted to ascribe the disasters of the late War, to him alone. The campaign of Genl Hull &c was under another, not him. and when the dates of my letters are adverted to, the public clamor, & the object I had in view, the expressions used must be clearly justified in the necessity which existed of selecting a man of virtue, talents, & energy, to fill the office. As to the talents of Genl A, I have always thought them of the first order, & had he placed himself at the Head of the Army at Bladensburgh, & beat the Enemy (as might have been done) he would have placed himself at the Head of the nation. I have never attempted to determine who was to blame for that catastrophe. In all operations of the military, the War minister has the applause or blame; so with the navy.[2]

Those letters were confidential.[3] How they came before the nation, you know, as well as I. Suffice it to say to you, that I have no heart-burnings as to Genl Armstrong. I had at one time, when I was dismissed from Public service, & ordered to dismiss my volunteers far from home, without the means to provide for my sick &c&c—But so soon as justice was rendered to those men & myself, those feelings were eradicated.[4] I cherished no further unfriendly feelings towards the Genl. I have always believed him a military man of the first order—

with compliments to your Lady & daughter believe me with great respect & Esteem your friend

Andrew Jackson

LS in Andrew J. Donelson's hand, NjP (mAJs); ALS draft and Copy, DLC (33). Published in Bassett, 3:261–62.

1. Letter not found. Livingston sat on the House select committee to investigate the memorial of Ninian Edwards, which continued to meet after adjournment and made its final report on June 21.

2. See John Armstrong to AJ, June 6; and, above, AJ to Armstrong, June 29. William Eustis was secretary of war at the time of William Hull's surrender in 1812. The American defeat at Bladensburg, Maryland, opened the way for the British capture of Washington in 1814.

3. Jackson was referring to his 1816–17 correspondence with James Monroe, made public in 1824.

4. Jackson was referring to dismissal of the Natchez expedition of Tennessee volunteers in 1813 (see *Jackson,* 2:360–61, 383–97).

From William Cocke

Columbus 10th July—1824

Sir,

Our mutual friend Major John Pytchlynn has requested me to inform you that your old friend Pucsenubbe the Oldest chief in the Choctaw nation has been lately much beaten by a party of Indians for haveing agreed to the treaty you last made with the Choctaws & is apprehensave that he is likely to be again maltreated on that account and has requested the major to Solicit you to say what ever you may deem proper on the Occasion the major thinks that any thing like an admonition from you will prevent any attack in future on that good Old man[1] be so good as to make my Compliments acceptable to Mrs Jackson and for your Self accept the best wishes of your H Servant

Wm. Cocke

ALS, DLC (33). Cocke (1748–1828), formerly of Tennessee but now in Mississippi, had served as Chickasaw agent, 1814–18.

1. Pitchlynn (c1756–1835), the father of Choctaw chief Peter Pitchlynn, was a Choctaw interpreter. As a principal or Medal chief, ruling the Northeastern District of the Choctaw nation, Apuckshunnubbe (c1739–1824) signed the 1820 Treaty of Doak's Stand, which Jackson negotiated with the tribe (*Jackson,* 4:391–97). He died in October, after a fall while en route as one of a delegation called to Washington to negotiate adjustments in the western lands given the Choctaws by that treaty. No reply by Jackson has been found.

To Samuel Houston

[cAugust 8, 1824]

[Dr. Sir

Your letter of the 20th. July has been recd. you ask me for "a statement of Capt [Robert] *Campbells of the British army treatment to me whilst a prisoner with]* the British in South Carolina, in the Revolutionary war; his treatment generally to the american prisoners and the character he sustained as an officer & man."[1]

I was captured by Major [John] Coffins corps treated harshly & inhumanly by the officers of that corps. So were all the prisoners who were taken with me. We were marched to Camden, South Carolina & confined in the jail of that village. We were there treated badly & inhumanly, until Genl [Nathanael] Greene advanced upon the British lines, when we were taken from the upper room of the prison, and confined in the cells under ground. The British expecting an attack & canonade. In the day we were permitted to come out of the dungeon & breathe the open air in rear of the Prison. It was in this situation we were visited by the humane Capt. Campbell; who inquiring into our distresses was informed that our rations were witheld from us, and part of them *[applied to feeding the plundered negroes by the provo master, forthwith made it known, as I was advised, to the Commander in chief of the British army Lord Roden, who gave proper orders that the supply rations ordered for the prisoners should be regularly Issued to them & humanely treated]* conduct observed towards them.[2] From this time, until I was exchanged—the Prisoners received the rations in full allowed them. tho scant indeed they were, without any deduction. As far as I was informed Capt Campbell stood well both as an officer & gentleman His appearance was that of a gentlemanly, intelligent officer. He treated the prisoners with great humanity so far as my knowledge extended—I am sir very respectfully, your obt & very Humble servant

Andrew Jackson

LS fragment in Andrew J. Donelson's hand, DLC (75); AL draft, DLC (33); Typed fragment (dated July 30), DLC (72). Date taken from postal notation on the cover of LS fragment, "Fountain of Health. 8th Augst." Missing text, supplied from the AL draft, has been italicized.

1. See Houston to AJ, July 20. From Scotland, Campbell (d. 1820) settled in the Marlboro District of South Carolina after the war and fathered two congressmen, John and Robert B. Campbell. Houston was courting his daughter Mariah (see above, Charles P. Tutt to AJ, June 12).

2. A Massachusetts Loyalist, Coffin (1756–1838) transferred to the southern theater in 1778 and commanded with distinction at the Battle of Eutaw Springs and elsewhere. He continued a career in the British army after the war, rising to the rank of general in 1819.

Greene (1742–86) assumed command of American troops in the Carolinas after the defeat of Horatio Gates at Camden in August 1780. The British commander was Francis Rawdon, later Francis Rawdon-Hastings (1754–1826), first Marquis of Hastings.

Rachel Jackson to Latitia Dalzell Chambers

Hermitage August 12th. 1824.

Dear Mrs. Cambers—

With pleasure I received your Kind and affectionate letter the 2d instant.[1] I was glad indeed to hear from you and that your dear little family wer injoyeing reasonable heath which is more then all wealth of Indias. my health is much better then when you last saw me—I thank you my dear friend for your kind congratulations on the return of my dear Husband. yes I was so rejoised to see him in his own house after an absence of nearly seven monthes. Oh the time was long. but in this wourld we shall have tribulation. Says the [sav] Blessed Saviour, in me ye shall have peace. O glourious hope. Shortly I have to experience an other trial, I must go with him or be as unhappy as I was last winter and how could I bare it. I shall have to go with him. At my time of life it is disagreeable but if the Almighty wills it, with humble submision I can say Amen to the decree. The Genneral sets out next Thirsday to Florence then I trust you will see him to taulk with him about all things you named the Genl loosing some friends on account of the Vote on the Tariff bill. James Jackson, he is gilty of black ingratitude to one of the best friends he ever had. it would take two sheets of paper but I shall not atempt to describe what he has proved him self to be.[2] We have the finest crop of cotten, corn and pittatoes I ever saw and all the country round about & as fare as I have herd. We have had another Camp meeting at the camp you and me went to last sumer Sally Knox never went near she froliks & dances. she lives all with her cousen Rachel.[3] Mr McCulley was here yesterday, Polley has been ill some time but is better. It is very sickly in town I am tould ther died 14 children in one week. Oh the blessed infants. & maney valuable members of socity and in the country it is sickly owing to so much rain the neighbourhood is as when you left us we have no minnister to take charge of this little flock it greives me from day to day but the Lord knows what we are & what is best for us I pray to be fed with that bred that perisheth not but hath life ever lasting. Altho you have journeyed from us I often think of you and youres. how glad I would have been could you have lived neare me. We often conversed on Heavenly things I know I love a Christian O that God may smile on you in temporals, bless you in life and when its his gracious will to call you and give you an inheritence in the Churches of the first Borne assimbles of the just made perfect in the Redeemers righteousness ther I hope to meet you. No more shall we meet and Sigh for parting or absent friends. Ther no more shall I dread the

Wintery blasts those tears that now flows will all be washed away by the hand of my blessed Saviour. I have to bid you adieu for the present. I pray God to bless you with prosperety and health so as to be comfortable in life and beleive me your sincere friend

Rachel Jackson

The Gen sends you his good wishes Rember me to Mr. [Thomas McCutcheon] Chambers.[4]
I would be so glad to see you before I leave the state to go with My dear Husband. Oh shall I returne again that is with Almighty the greate arbiter of faite He will do all thing well, am I his or am I not O decide the doubtfull case—Dr. [Isaac] Watt.[5] R. J.
The Andrews ar well—& poor jon—The Leutenent is not married yet is to be shortly.[6]

Copy, THer (10-0845).

1. Not found.

2. After news of Jackson's tariff votes reached Lauderdale County, James Jackson came out in opposition to the general. For his explanation of his action, see Huntsville *Alabama Republican,* August 20. Some of the Jacksons' friends, however, attributed the switch to James Jackson's dissatisfaction with the Andrew Erwin settlement, rather than to his "avowed" reasons. Others blamed Jackson's support for the marriage of Richard K. Call to Mary L. Kirkman, James Jackson's niece (see John Coffee to John Donelson, 1755–1830, July 8, and John C. McLemore to Coffee, July 28, THi; and John Donelson, 1787–1840, to Edward G. W. Butler, May 9, 1827, LNHiC).

3. Cousin Rachel was probably Sarah Knox's second cousin Rachel Donelson Donelson (1803–24), daughter of Severn and wife of William (1795–1864), who died in September.

4. Chambers (1795–1876), Latitia's husband, remained in Alabama only nine months, and farmed near Princeton, Indiana, Henderson, Kentucky, and Haw Creek, in Missouri, before moving to Oregon (later Washington) Territory, where he became a justice of the peace and county commissioner in Lewis (later Pierce) County.

5. The exact reference has not been established. An 1813 edition of Watts's (1674–1748) *The Improvement of the Mind,* "Presented to Mrs. R. Jackson by her friend Mr. Porter," remains in the Hermitage library.

6. Jon has not been identified; the lieutenant was probably Andrew J. Donelson, who married on September 16.

Despite his many protestations of reluctance and his insistence that friends had brought him forward without his encouragement and contrary to his wishes, Jackson was no passive observer of the presidential campaign. In an apparently wide-ranging correspondence, only a portion of which survives, Jackson monitored political intelligence and passed on to friends and political allies reports favorable to his prospects. Drafts surviving among Jackson's papers suggest that he worked with Samuel R. Overton at the Hermitage in 1824 to devise anonymous replies to editorials opposing his candidacy (see "A Farmer" to Thomas Ritchie, [cJuly]; reply to "Anthony Wayne," [October]; and reply by "Truth," October 12). In addition, Jackson's close relations with George Wilson, editor of the Nashville Gazette, *and William S. Fulton, who wrote for the* Florence Gazette, *enabled him to influence the campaign press. Carefully edited portions of two letters to Jackson appeared in the* Nashville Gazette *as letters to an unnamed Nashvillian (see above, Isaac L. Baker to AJ, February 14 and May 3, 1823). Jackson's letter to Wilson, August 11, records another instance in which Jackson passed on his correspondence for anonymous publication. Unfortunately, only a few scattered dates of the two* Gazettes *are now available, precluding a fuller examination of Jackson's use of newspapers in the campaign.*

In the letter below, Jackson suggested Wilson's response to an unfavorable article in the Richmond Enquirer, *suggestions closely followed by a* Nashville Gazette *editorial (reprinted in the* Cincinnati Advertiser, *September 4).*

To George Wilson

Hermitage, August 13th, 1824.

Dear Colonel:

I received last evening by mail the inclosed letter. I send it for your perusal. I have not seen the paper of [Thomas] Richie, of the 20th ultimo, alluded to; can not, therefore, judge of the necessity or propriety of giving any notice to this publication. Was I to notice the falsehoods and false insinuations of Richie and such unprincipled editors, I could have time for nothing else. Should you, upon reference to the piece alluded to, think it deserves any notice, such a one as the following might be proper: That General Jackson's course requires neither falsehood nor intrigue to support it. He has been brought before the nation by the people, without his knowledge, wishes, or consent. His support is the people. And so long as they choose to support him, as to himself he will not interfere. He will neither resign his pretensions, intrigue, nor combine with any man nor set of men, nor has he ever so combined or intrigued. Mr. Richie may, therefore, be calm. The General or his friends will never adopt the course of intrigue, combination, and corruption pursued by Mr. Richie and his political friends, for any purpose whatever. Their cause requires neither falsehood nor corruption to support it. It is the people's cause. They have brought A. J. before the nation.[1] I am very respectfully your friend,

Andrew Jackson.

Printed, Parton, 3:43 (10-0850).

1. The enclosed letter has not been found. It alluded to "Queries" in the *Richmond Enquirer*, July 20, which suggested the existence of a combination among John Q. Adams, Jackson, and John C. Calhoun to obtain the presidency for Adams, the vice-presidency for Jackson, and some high office for Calhoun. Ritchie (1778–1854) edited the *Enquirer*.

The burgeoning Jackson bandwagon in Pennsylvania picked up fellow travellers from all corners of state and local politics, and behind the unanimity of Jackson's nomination at Harrisburg lay real differences among his supporters. One manifestation of the divisions was the reluctance of some Jackson men to support the nomination of John C. Calhoun for vice-president. The opposition press delighted in pointing out uncomfortable alliances, as editors violently opposed to one another in the 1823 Pennsylvania gubernatorial campaign now found themselves allies in support of Jackson. Northampton County sent two pro-Jackson delegations to the Harrisburg convention, one from each of the opposing gubernatorial factions, and Beaver County also sent two delegations. The letter below reveals local tensions among Jackson supporters in Allegheny County.

From John McFarland

Pittsburgh Aug. 14, 1824.

Dear Sir,

Although I was the first Printer in Pennsylvania, as Editor of the Harrisburg Commonwealth, to advocate your election, I have never had the honor to address you by letter. I have always though sent you a paper and you can see by them, that I have not been wanting in attachment, though I may have been in ability to promote your interest. I would not trouble you at this time, was it not to place you on your guard against to free a correspondence, with concealed enemies or imprudent friends. There are many persons whom you know merely by name, whose forwardness in public meetings and accidental conspicuousness on committees, &c. gives them a kind of fictitious consequence, hurtful alike to the cause they espouse and the man they support. Your answer to H. W. Peterson of Harrisburg last winter, who as *one of the people* was nothing more than a *Bar-keeper,* would have been published as addressed to him, had I not got it in my possession and altered the direction of it to the *Dauphin County Committee*, in which shape it appeared.[1] The same circumstance might attend any communication with Gen. [Edward] Patchel of this place, who to be sure is a warm and zealous supporter of yours, but without either caution or prudence to keep his own secrets. A letter of his which I lately saw addressed to you, is filled with the most strange conceits imaginable. In it, he represents himself as Grand Master of Ceremonies in Pittsburgh and file leader of the Jackson interest. The old man is in his dotage, and in consequence of his warm friendship for you, the caucusites attempted to ridicule the Jackson cause by placing him at the head of affairs. To punish them for this we elected him Brig General, and he is now absolutely of opinion that he is the greatest man in the world excepting yourself. We have a great deal of trouble to keep him in his place, and prevent him from executing martial law on your enemies. From these few hints you will be able to comprehend his character, with the addition that he never spent a cent on your election in his life nor has he the influence of ten votes in the world.[2]

Your efficient friends here, viz: those who are not backward with their purse and who have influence to exercise, are Mr Robert Steele, Commission Merchant, Mr David Lynch, Tobacconist and Robert J[ohn] Walker, Attorney at Law.[3] You have to be sure a vast number of friends ardently attached to your interest and admirers of your character, but confined to the lower and middle classes of society, all they can do is to give you their votes. The leading men in Pensylvania, with very few exceptions, are opposed to you, but your election will create new leaders of as much consequence as they, and you are already secure with the multitude. Your majority in this state will be at least 90.000, depend upon it. I congratulate you on the accession of Louisiana, and as I never had, so I have not yet the least doubt of your ultimate success.[4]

Please excuse the freedom I have taken in this hasty epistle and believe me to be your devoted friend—

John McFarland.
Ed Al. Democrat.

ALS, DLC (72). McFarland (1797–1827), who edited papers in Chambersburg, Carlisle, and Harrisburg before commencing the Pittsburgh *Allegheny Democrat* in June 1824, became notorious for his toast at a Carlisle public dinner: "May the *skins* of the enemies of Jackson be converted into *carpeting,* for his friends to dance upon" (New Orleans *Louisiana Courier,* July 16).

1. See above, AJ to H. W. Peterson, February 23, 1823.

2. See Edward Patchell to AJ, August 7. At the November 14, 1823, Allegheny County meeting, Patchell (c1768?–c1839), a Pittsburgh hatter, was chosen as a delegate to the Huntingdon convention, but at another meeting on January 8, it was announced that he had resigned, and Robert J. Walker was appointed in his place. Although Patchell remained on the Jackson committee of correspondence, he complained publically that he had been excluded from the Jackson electoral ticket by improper means (Pittsburgh *Statesman,* April 17). His election in late May as a brigadier general of Pennsylvania militia appears to have been offered as a consolation. In 1827, when Patchell ran unsuccessfully for the state senate against two other pro-Jackson candidates, he emphasized his laboring status and charged that Jackson had been made "the pack horse for petty politicians and disemblers to hang their budgets upon" (*Pittsburgh Mercury,* July 17, 1827).

3. Walker (1801–69; Pennsylvania 1819), later a senator from Mississippi, represented Allegheny County at the Harrisburg convention. Lynch was probably the Pittsburgh postmaster, 1833–40, also a delegate to the 1843 Pennsylvania Democratic convention. Steele (d. 1825), who served for a time on the Jackson committee of correspondence for Allegheny County, chaired the meeting at which Patchell was nominated for brigadier general.

4. Reports reaching Pittsburgh by August 13 indicated that Jackson supporters had won a majority in the July election of Louisiana legislators.

From William Johnson (1792–1854)

Woodville Augt. 16th. 1824.

Sir,

No doubt you have already discovered from the public prints of this state that a ticket for Electors of President &c has been formed here favorable to your election to that office—I have no doubt myself, but that Genl. Hinds, Genl. [James] Patton & Dr. [Bartlett C.] Barry will be elected, all of whom are pledged to the state, to vote for you, in the event of their success[1]—Govr. Holmes is for you and on him you can rely—Govr. [George] Poindexter is decidedly for Adams, but says that if he thought you could be elected, he would vote for you—However from him you have but little to expect, and less to fear, whatever his professions to the contrary may be[2]—The above information is given you by a soldier, who served under you, in your Artilery-Company, during the greater part of the Creek Campaign, and who wishes you success: still bearing in mind the friendships which were formed in those times of dificulty and danger—Col. Joshua Child is among your warmest supporters here, and deserves much for his exertions &c &c.[3] Very respectfully Your friend

Wm. Johnson

ALS, DLC (33). A lawyer who represented Wilkinson County in the 1820 Mississippi legislature, Johnson chaired a February 23 meeting of Jackson supporters in the county and was appointed to their committee of correspondence. He had served as a private in David S. Deaderick's artillery company, which served as Jackson's guards.

1. Hinds, Patton, and Barry were the Jackson electors. Patton (d. 1831) was lieutenant governor, 1820–22, and a commissioner (along with Hinds) for selecting the site of Jackson, Mississippi, as capital for the state. Barry (d. 1825) was state senator for Wayne, Covington, and Monroe counties.

2. Poindexter (1779–1853) had served as governor, 1819–21.

3. Child, who represented Wilkinson County in the 1819 legislature and served as judge of the first circuit court, 1825–31, had offered resolutions supporting Jackson to the Wilkinson County meeting.

To James Hervey Witherspoon

Nashville
August 17th. [18,] 1824

Dr. Sir

your letter of the 24th. ult. is just recd; and altho an entire stranger to you feel a lively interest in your prosperity & that of your family your lady being the decendant of a distant relation by mariage, <of mine> and one for whom I had a sincere regard, being raised together, I mean your Ladies mother.[1]

I have had a great wish to revisit my native state, & once more mingle with those friends of my juvenile days who may still be living; but I have been hitherto prevented by circumstances over which I had no controle; and I am now prevented from accepting the oppertunity that the friendly invitation of my fellow citizens through you would now afford—for many reasons unnessary now to enumerate; next spring may afford me an opportunity with my family of vissitting the country that gave me birth, when it will afford me much pleasure, and when I shall avail myself of the pleasure of seeing you & your family at your own house; and offering up a prayer for that son of yours, that you have honoured me with his name, that he may long live & be a blessing to his parents in their old age.[2]

As to the question asked, I with pleasure answer, I was born in So Carolina, as I have been told, at the plantation whereon James Crawford lived about one mile from the Carolina road Xg of the Waxhaw Creek, left that state in 1784 was born on the 15th of March in the year 1767—I am truly happy to learn, <where> at what house my mother died, I knew she died near charleston, having vissitted that city with several matrons to afford relief to our prisoners with the British—not her son as you suppose, for at that time my two Elder brothers were no more; but two of her Nephews, William & Joseph Crawford sons of James Crawford then deceased—I well recollect one of the matrons that went with her was Mrs. Boyd—It is possible Mrs [Agnes] Barton can inform me where she was buried that I can find her grave, This to me would be great satisfaction, that I might collect her bones & inter them with that of my father & brothers.[3]

I offer you my thanks for the political information your letter has afforded—

present me affectionately to your Lady kiss my namesake for me; and accept assurances of my high respect & regard yr mo obdt Servt.

Andrew Jackson

ALS draft, DLC (33). Published in Bassett, 3:265 (dated August 11). Witherspoon's reply, April 16, 1825, gives August 18 as the date of the letter received, and extracts of the letter published in 1825 newspapers were also dated August 18. Witherspoon (1784–1842), a Lancaster County planter, served as lieutenant governor of South Carolina, 1826–28.

1. Letter not found. In 1803 Witherspoon married Jane Donnom (1786–1834), daughter of Isaac Donnom (1764–1830) and Sarah Crawford (1764–1805). Sarah was a niece of James Crawford, Sr., and his wife Jenny (Jane, Janet) Hutchinson, Jackson's aunt.

2. Andrew Jackson Witherspoon (1824–91) was born on July 10.

3. Jackson's eldest brother Hugh died at the Battle of Stono Ferry in 1779. His other brother Robert died shortly after release from British imprisonment in 1781. Jackson's mother Elizabeth Hutchinson Jackson died later in 1781, as did Joseph Crawford, the son of James, Sr., and Jenny Hutchinson Crawford. William Crawford (b. c1762) survived the war, and resided in Maury County, Tennessee, by 1828. Mrs. Boyd has not been identified.

Barton (c1757–1846), wife of William, a carpenter who resided about two and a half miles from Charleston, reportedly buried Jackson's mother and delivered her clothes to him. Jackson's father, Andrew, Sr., died shortly before his son's birth in 1767 and was supposedly buried in the Waxhaw Church cemetery.

From Arthur Peronneau Hayne

Private Charleston, South Carolina.
18th. Septr. 1824

My Dear General.

Our mutual friend Coll. Gadsden has just left me. A few days ago he had the pleasure to receive a letter from you.[1] It afford'd me great pleasure to hear of your good health, & that of Mrs. Jackson. My Brother communicated to me on his arrival from Washington your kind message & promise of a letter, which I have not yet received. I have today received a letter from Judge [Thomas] Duncan, written from Pittsburg Penna. under date the 6th. of Septr.[2] The information he communicates is cheering. He writes thus—viz: "Genl. Jackson still holds his ground in Penna.—if the South continues sound, I still consider his election as certain. Appearances are very favorable in New Jersey—in Maryland he will obtain a Majority—Indiana promises well—so does Delaware—Alabama, Mississippi & Louisana we count on. Let what rumours may reach you as to Penna., you may confide in the assurance I now make, *that Penna. will not under any circumstances desert him*"—I need not tell you, that I consider South-Carolina as safe as Tennessee, & of your full & compleat success in North-Carolina, I do not entertain the shadow of a doubt. Indeed Clays withdrawal is all that is wanted to secure your election before it goes into the House. If left to the *People, even in Georgia* you would beat the "*Radical Chief.*"[3] Mr. Clay is no longer looked upon by the *Nation* as a Candidate, & surely under these circumstances his friends will withdraw his Name. Believing as I do, that you are the person pointed out by the *Finger* of *Heaven* to hand down to Posterity the liberties of our Common Country, *Durably Cemented, Improved*, pure & uncontaminated, I confess in common with every other *Patriot*, I feel a deep interest your success. If successful, I confess tho', to you personally, the sacrifice will be a great one, but in the good that will result to the Country, you must look for your reward. The growing Patronage of the Country, as it has been actively employed for the last four years, is no common evil. It threatens destruction to every thing that is great or glorious in the rising Destinies of our Country. This *Hydra must* be *crushed*, else our *Republican principles* & *institutions* will *ere long* be *wrecked* at *its shrine*.

Be pleased to remember me affectionately to Mrs. Jackson, in which Mrs. Hayne unites. Remember me also to Andrew. I shall set out for Alabama in Novr.—I am happy to hear Mrs. J. accompanies you to Washington the ensuing Winter. To my friends in Tennessee be pleased to present me respectfully. I remain, Dear General, yr faithful & affectionate friend

A. P. Hayne

ALS, DLC (33).

1. None of the letters mentioned have been found.

2. Duncan (1760–1827), a justice of the Pennsylvania Supreme Court, was the father of Hayne's first wife, Frances (c1797–1820).

3. William H. Crawford.

To John Coffee

Hermitage. Sept. 20th. 1824

Dear Genl

I have the moloncholy task to inform you that Rachel Donelson, wife of William, is no more; she departed this life on the 16th. instant—the very day on which A & E. Donelson were to be married—They Doctors had held out hopes of her recovery; all things prepared for the marriage—what was to be done in this distressing circumstance, was very perplexing; It was at length concluded to let the parson perform the ceremony, & *it was done*. William, is inconsolable, and all is Gloom & sorrow—we are just informed that Doctor Butler has lost his daughter[1]

I rejoice to learn from Colo Ward that your Mary has recovered & you & family are well—I set out this morning to Murfreesborrugh to the Legislature, and as usual am surrounded with company & have but a moment to write you—¿how does the Irish get on; have they come to their senses; & is peace restored.[2]

I will thank you to say to Mr Nicholson that my Negro fellow Guilbert has ranaway on the 31rst. of august—that I have not heard a word of him since he left me; but from information it is probable he may attempt to go back to Alabama in his neighbourhood & I wish him to keep a look out in that quarter for him.[3]

I will be happy to hear when you will be in, I wish to see, & be with you a few days before I set out.

Mrs. J. Joins me in good wishes to you, Polly, & the family your friend

Andrew Jackson

ALS, THi (10-0894).

1. Mary Jane Butler (c1815–24).

2. To rectify the 1823 Tennessee law regarding presidential electors, which set dates for their election and assembly contrary to those specified by Congress, Governor William Carroll had called a special session of the Tennessee legislature, which convened on September 20. The exact purpose of Jackson's attendance has not been established, but he did meet

with Thomas Washington and Bennett Smith in Murfreesboro to settle the longstanding suit of *Bennett Smith* v. *John Hutchings's Executors.* "Irish" referred to one or more of the Jacksons, Hannas, McCullys, and Chambers of Florence, Alabama, and the Kirkmans of Nashville. In this instance, Jackson probably intended a reference to the hostility of the Jacksons and the Kirkmans to the recent marriage of Richard K. Call and Mary L. Kirkman at the Hermitage. Mary D. Coffee (1812–39) was John's eldest daughter.

3. See advertisement for the runaway slave Gilbert, [September].

From William Johnson (1792–1854)

Woodville Sept. 22<th>nd. 1824—

Sir,

I am *now* in hopes and inclined to think that you will be the next president—Pennsylvania and North Carolina, I think, <are> is now settled

The several numbers of Wyoming have made their appearance here—and I have sent them over the state—and am inclined to think they will have a good effect—Shortly, I will send you in print The reply of my friend Col. Child, to the Honble. Joshua G. Clarke, Chancellor of our state[1]—I am much astonished at Judge Clarke—I had thought him a man of more prudence—However, Sir, he has fallen into the hands of men, who can dispose of him as he should be—Very respectfully

Wm. Johnson

Govr. Poindexter & Govr. [Walter] Leake and their partizans are for Adams[2]—But, sir, the majority of the voters of this state are honest men—And, Sir, consequently the Vote of the state will be for you, a man, who has done more for us than any other since *Washington*—yrs. W. J.

ALS, DLC (72).

1. Clarke (d. 1828), who represented Claiborne County at the 1817 Mississippi constitutional convention, served as judge of the first circuit court, 1818–21, and as chancellor, 1821–28. His letter to the editor of the *Port Gibson Correspondent,* reprinted throughout Mississippi in early September, conveyed a report that Jackson was losing strength to John Q. Adams, who had a majority in the eastern portion of the state. Joshua Child's letter to Johnson, September 18, asserted that Jackson maintained a large majority (see *Woodville Republican,* September 7 and 28).

2. Leake (1762–1825) served as Mississippi governor, 1821–25.

To John Coffee

Hermitage Septbr. 23rd 1824

Dr. Genl

Today I received a letter from Mr H[utchens] Burton Tuscumbia on the subject of the rent of a piece of ground I cultivated near there within the limits of the school land in 1822; when I saw him there and he claimed the rent, I told him if he would produce to me a note from the commissioners that he was entitled to receive it, I would pay a reasonable rent to him, that rent was due to them, it being reserved for the university, and to Justify my paying it to him, I must have their order or permission.

I have wrote him thus, & referred him to you to settle it for me; will you have the goodness to do so—If you should believe that he is entitled, and he cannot produce an order from the commissioners or Trustees, when you collect the mony from those indebted to me pay him a reasonable rent taking his bond to keep me indemnified from the Trustees or commissioners of the school lands.[1]

I have just returned from Murfreesborough, where Mr Washington & myself compleated a final compromise with Major Ben Smith. I have a compleat & final release & he is to have entered satisfaction on the record in Alabama of the Judgt obtained there against J. H Excutors—and on my part as guardian I am to pay four hundred dollars on the first day of June next—This Judge Overton advised me was well for the child; I thought so myself, as it placed his interest on safe grounds, and I was apprehensive of the solvancy of Washington, when you come in I will place this release in your hands for the safety of the Executors and the child.[2]

The Redoubtable *hero*, of *Squating memory, Jessee Benton* has come out with a pamphlet in abuse of Mr Adams & myself, I have not seen it—But am aware that he is only the puppet, moved by the Crawford Junto behind the scene Balch, John P Erwin & Co—it was publis[h]ed by the Editors of the Whig, it has brought upon Norval some contempt & harsh epithets—my hands for the present is tied, I treat it, & intend for the present, with silent contempt they deserve; a time may arise when their mirth may be turned into tears—Balch looks wild, heaving heard that I suspect him as one—when will you be in; I will have to leave hom the first of Novbr. ¿how comes on my particular *friends & Irish relations*[3]

Present us affectionately to Polly & the children & believe me yr friend

Andrew Jackson

The last papers give a flattering prospect of t*[he]* presidencial election—A. J.

ALS, THi (10-0899). Published in Bassett, 3:266 (extract).

1. Letters not found. Burton (1789–1838) resided in the area from at least 1820 until his death. In 1825 Anthony Winston, Jr., paid $50 to Burton for Jackson's rent (see John Coffee to AJ, April 23, 1825).

2. For a discussion of the final settlement of the suit of *Bennett Smith* v. *John Hutchings's Executors* in accordance with the terms discussed here, see AJ to John Coffee, June 6, 1825.

3. Benton (d. 1843), Thomas Hart's brother, had been shot in the buttocks while stooping to avoid fire in a June 1813 duel with William Carroll, and he later shot Jackson in a fracas arising from the duel. His *An Address to the People of the United States, on the Presidential Election* (Nashville, 1824) was published on September 17 (10-0864). It attacked John Q. Adams and Jackson, while supporting William H. Crawford's candidacy. Although Jackson did not respond publicly at this time, he did gather material to answer

Benton, and Jackson's friend William B. Lewis sent a detailed rebuttal for publication in the Philadelphia *Columbian Observer* (see Robert Purdy to AJ, September 29; and Lewis to [Stephen Simpson], September 20, NN). Alfred Balch, reputedly Martin Van Buren's "deputy" in Tennessee, supported Crawford in 1824 (see Lewis to Simpson, September 6, *United States' Telegraph Extra,* September 8, 1832; Balch to William Polk, January 9, Nc, and to John Overton, May 4, THi). The political breach was healed at least by 1826, and Balch served on the Jackson "whitewashing" committee in the 1828 campaign, though he remained a Van Buren partisan.

The letter below is one of several concerning a complicated land dispute between William Martin (1765–1846) and William Brackin (1775–1833) regarding land purchased from Jackson on the middle fork of Drake's Creek in Sumner County, Tennessee. In April 1796 Jackson had sold 160 acres of a 1,000 acre tract (Grant 299) to Jacob Pirkle (Pyrtle, Pirtle, Purtle) of Rockingham County, North Carolina. Since neither Jackson nor Pirkle had seen the land, and, if dates on surviving records are correct, Jackson had not yet completed his purchase of the grant, Jackson gave Pirkle a bond that would allow him to select one of three locations for his purchase. In October of the same year Jackson exchanged the remaining 840 acres with Martin for land closer to Jackson's home, giving Martin a deed that described Pirkle's options. The option was not exercised until 1812, when Brackin, who had purchased Pirkle's bond, obtained from Jackson a deed to 160 acres on the eastern edge of the grant, adjoining property previously owned by Brackin. All seemed well until July 1822, when Martin wrote to inform Jackson that a mistake had been made and some of the land deeded to Brackin lay in a part of the tract not optioned to Pirkle.

Indeed, an error had occurred. Although Jackson believed he had carefully consulted Pirkle's bond in drawing his deeds, Martin's deed described Pirkle's choices in relation to a line running west along the length of the 1,000 acre tract while Brackin's deed referred to a line running south along the tract's width. Thus Martin believed that Brackin was not entitled to the most southern parts of his selection.

When both Brackin and Martin called on Jackson to defend their respective titles, he responded with the same advice he had repeatedly given others since his legal entanglement with Andrew Erwin over the Duck River lands: by all means settle and avoid the courts. He even agreed at least twice to meet with Martin and Brackin in Gallatin to resolve the conflict, though he was ultimately unable to attend either meeting (in October 1825 and February 1826). Efforts at settlement were unavailing, however, and in March 1827 Brackin, himself subject to a suit of ejectment, brought suit against Jackson and Martin in the Sumner County Circuit Court. Jackson was later dropped as a defendent, and his deposition of September 6, 1828, appeared to support Brackin, who obtained the relief he sought in March 1829.

To William Martin (1765–1846)

Hermitage Septbr. 25th. 1824

Dr Sir

yours of the 9th. instant has just come to hand: and I assure you I sincerely regret that you & Mr William Brackin has not accomodated your dispute with regard to the land.[1] I never in my life took more pains to comply with a contract in good faith than in that, and regret that there should exist a dispute therein, when I am sure there ought not to be any; and if a mistake exists, and harmonious & just feelings, the mistake could be easily corrected. I have only to repeat, that having passed the title by convayence to you & to Mr Brackin as the representative of Mr Purtle who held my *special* bond for a convayence there is nothing left in my power. I got only a horse from Mr Purtle, that would now be vallued at from Eighty to one hundred dollars for this land—and if Mr Brakin has received a convayence for land, that from the specialty of my bond Mr Purtle was not to receive, and from the special expressions in the Deed to you recognising the bond to Mr Purtle, a court of chancery will correct this error, if error exists.

This tract of land was as I believe granted to John Rice & convayed to me by Elisha Rice Executor & One of the heirs of John Rice under full power from the other heirs, I believe the grant is recorded in Davidson, perhaps in Sumner, and the convayence to me in Sumner—I think you have the original Grant in your possession as I cannot find it in mine, & I was allways in the habit of delivering the Grant with a convayence made by me. you will find them recorded either in Sumner or Davidson.[2]

How easy it would be for men to steer clear of law, were they disposed so to do; and obtain equal Justice, by submitting ther disputes to arbitration, in this case it appears to me it could be thus well settled.

The land claim so long before congress has been at last granted; The first bill on its third & last reading in the House of Representatives was rejected by the management of Genl Cocke another Bill was originated in the Senate & was finally acted on in both Houses & passed in its present shape by a large majority. The law is very limited in its provisions—the claimants have two years from the passing of this act, under the direction of the secratary of the Treasury to enter five thousand acres each; (original claimant) said claim shall not be located on any lands except those offerred for sale—nor upon any land forfeited or relinquished, nor, for a less quantity than a quarter-section, but may be entered on any *fraction*, confined in the location to the land offices in either of the states of Mississippi or Alabama[3]

I am told it could be well located in the state of Mississippi on the Big Black and its waters, the land there, altho offerred for sale, but little has been sold owing to the charector it has for ill health—The forfeighted lands in upper alabama is to be sold in march next—whether they will all sell or not I cannot say—near to Cahaba, I am told but very little of the forfeighted lands have sold, in that section it might be located advantageously as I have been informed

I cannot close this letter without expressing my regret that the business between you & Mr Brakan cannot be amicably adjusted; I am sure it might be, if harmonious feelings on all sides were to exist, accompanied with Justice—I am sure had I the power, I would step in & effect it.

I regret to hear of your late indisposition am happy to hear of your recovery with due respect & Esteem I am yr mo. obdt. servt.

Andrew Jackson

Photocopy of ALS, TU (mAJs). Martin, a Smith County farmer, had been an officer of Tennessee volunteers on the Natchez expedition and in the early Creek campaign, but his relations with Jackson were strained during the December 1813 "mutiny" of troops. Martin published his side of the dispute during the 1828 presidential campaign and in *The Self Vindication of Colonel William Martin, against Certain Charges and Aspersions Made against Him by Gen. Andrew Jackson and Others . . .* (Nashville, 1829).

1. See Martin to AJ, September 9.

2. Elisha Rice, John's brother, served as a justice of the peace in Davidson County. His September 15, 1796, sale to Jackson of 1,000 acres on the middle fork of Drake's Creek was recorded in Sumner County (1-0445). A copy of thc original grant to John Rice, taken from Davidson County records, was entered into the case file of *Brackin* v. *Martin*, TGSum.

3. Jackson was referring to the law to compensate the heirs of John Donelson (c1718–86) and others for Georgia survey work (see 6 *U.S. Statutes at Large* 313). Martin participated in the claim as an heir of his father, Joseph Martin.

To Samuel Swartwout

Hermitage near Nashville
Septbr. 27th. 1824

My Dear Sir

your letter of the 4th. instant, is this moment received, for which, & the information by it, accept my thanks.[1]

Be assured that the friends of Mr. Adams when they assert that I have "abandoned the field in his favour," not only are guilty of the grossest misrepresentation, but practice an unpardonable outrage upon the principles which I have uniformly carried with me in all my Public Service; viz, never to seek or decline office, but to leave the selection of all incumbents to the free will of the people, untrameled by any exercise of influence inconsistant with the perfect right to Judge the qualifications—as therefore the people have taken up my name in opposition to others, the idea of my being withdrawn has been very properly scouted by yourself. This was hardly to have been looked for by Mr. As friends, nor indeed from any who love the freedom, & sovereignity of the people; or who profess to do so.

Be pleased to present my kind salutations to your lady, & believe me to be very respectfully your friend

Andrew Jackson

ALS, TNJ (10-0902). Published in *Proceedings of the American Antiquarian Society*, 31(1921):77.

1. Letter not found.

To Jacob Call

Hermitage near Nashville T.
Octbr. 9th. 1824

My Dear Sir

yours of the 20th. ult. enclosing the Indiana Jackson Convention reached me yesterday; for the information your letter contains receive my thanks.[1]

It is gratefull to me to be informed that they people are determined to maintain their rights, think & act for themselves, regardless of the intrigues of Demagogues & caucus dictation.

The *Radicals* are in their last agonies of desperation; They have, & will, resort to every means that corruption can devise to promote their chiefs, & their united efforts in malicious & unfounded calumny to detract from others, whom the people have brought forward in opposition to their views: The good sense of the people are not to be led away by the false imputations of secrete, & hired assasins, employed by the combined efforts of the Radical associates for preferment to the Presidential chair.

Being brought forward by the people I rest my pretensions with them, & in their decision I will be content, knowing as far as the people act; it will be with an eye single to the prosperity of the country, & the perpetuity of our happy form of Goverment.

I sincerely wish you success in your election; I will be happy to see you one of the great council of the nation. accept assurances of my respect & Esteem, yr friend,

Andrew Jackson

ALS, InU-Li (10-0912). Call (d. 1826) was elected to fill the Indiana congressional vacancy caused by the death of William Prince, serving from December 23, 1824, to March 3, 1825.

1. Letter not found. On September 16, a convention of eighteen delegates representing fourteen counties met at Salem to form a unified Jackson ticket for the upcoming elections. Call was secretary of the convention. For a report of the proceedings, see the Richmond, Indiana, *Public Leger*, October 9. In the November election, Jackson received about 46.6% of the Indiana vote, a plurality.

From William Gibbes Hunt, George Wilson, and Wilkins Tannehill

Nashville Oct. 9. 1824.

Most Worshipful Sir & Brother,

Previous to the adjournment of the Grand Lodge of Tennessee at its late meeting in this town, the Undersigned were appointed a Committee to carry into effect the following resolution, which was unanimously adopted—

"Resolved that a Committee be appointed to communicate to our late M. W. Grand Master Gen Andrew Jackson the thanks of this Grand Lodge for the zeal he has manifested for the good of the craft, and for the impartiality, judgment and ability with which he has presided over the deliberations of this body—and that said committee be directed to assure him of the respect which is felt by this Grand Lodge for his character as a man and a mason, and of the fraternal regard towards him which is entertained by us, individually and collectively."[1]

In compliance with the above resolution we take this early opportunity to transmit you a copy, and in so doing we beg leave to assure you, that it affords us peculiar pleasure to act as agents for communicating sentiments which are so justly and sincerely entertained towards one who has rendered himself eminent in every situation in which he has been placed, and who in the army, in the state, in the domestic circle, and in the peaceful recess of the masonic temple, is alike useful, distinguished, and esteemed.

Permit us to add assurances of the respect and regard which we individually entertain towards you as a fellow citizen and a member of our order. Yours fraternally,

W. G. Hunt
G. Wilson
W. Tannehill
Committee of the Grand Lodge of Tennessee

ALS in Hunt's hand, also signed by Wilson and Tannehill, DLC (33). Published in Hagerstown, Md., *Torch Light and Public Advertiser,* November 30. Hunt (1791–1833; Harvard 1810), journalist and lawyer, edited the Nashville *National Banner.* Tannehill (1787–1858), merchant, banker, publisher, and mayor of Nashville, 1825–27, was one of Tennessee's most active Masons.

1. Jackson, who earlier belonged to Nashville's Harmony Lodge No. 1 which ceased operation in 1808, was admitted as a member in the Grand Lodge of the State of Tennessee on October 7, 1822, and elected and installed as Grand Master on the same day. In 1823 he presided over a special meeting in April and a portion of the regular October meeting, at which he was reelected. In 1824 he presided over the October 5 session before Tannehill was elected as the new Grand Master on October 6. The resolution of thanks, introduced by Hunt, was voted just previous to adjournment on October 9.

From Caleb Atwater

Glorious News. Circleville Nov. 1st. 1824.

Dear General,

It falls to my happy lot to announce to you, our great and glorious victory over Clay & Adams, in Ohio.

It is done. The victory is our's by thousands.

"The Scioto country" was the seat of Clay's power. It was *here*, that the libellers of your and our country's honor, claimed 15,000 majority. The election is over and Clay has no majority. In this township, a Clay paper said, that myself and three others, were *all* that were for Jackson! 166 voted for you & 56 for Clay! Fairfield county was to give 2000 majority for Clay and you recd 300 majority! Ross county, was to have given 3000 maj. for Clay and you got two to one![1] Clay and Adams are down to rise no more in the West. We have answered your infamous libellers at the polls in a voice louder than thunder. Kentucky will follow and congress are relieved from a burden they wanted to bear.

I thank you a thousand times for all your toils and labors in public and private life, for your patriotic d*[ee]*ds rendered my labors easy & the victory great and effectual.

Your malicious enemies roused every patriotic bosom against them and brought your friends to the polls by thousands. There we met them and treated them as base slanderers and tories.

Such an election never was held in Ohio before. We huzzaed for the vote of every whig and hissed the vote of every ungrateful wretch who dared to oppose you. We want not such another contest, until you have served 8 years. We have got the ground and can keep it in despite of Jesse Benton & Bellamy Storer.[2] I am overjoyed at the event, but must tell you, that my pledge to support you is redeemed. It has occupied all my time, but the pleasure I feel on looking back upon it, is an ample reward.

Stokely Hays Esq. knows how things were when he saw me at Columbus and I know how it now is.

Every officer of both governments, in Ohio 4 postmasters excepted, *opposed* us all they could, but they were prostrated before the majesty of an offended *People*. May God bless you.

Caleb Atwater

Our victory operates on Ky. Inda. Illi. Missouri. Md & Va. I have sent on the glorious news. Expresses carry it into those states. It spreads like wildfire[3]

The cannon are now roaring and the drums beating before my door, and I hear the loud huzzas.

ALS, DLC (33).

1. Atwater's declaration proved premature. Official results gave Clay 48.3% of the votes in Fairfield County, a plurality. In Ross County Clay received almost 75%, and he obtained a bare majority of 50.3% in Pickaway, Atwater's home county. Statewide, Clay won about 38.5% of the vote, a narrow plurality over Jackson.

2. Storer (1796–1875), a Cincinnati lawyer who later became a Whig congressman, was the reputed author of an anti-Jackson handbill circulating in Ohio over the pseudonym "Anthony Wayne." See Cincinnati *National Republican and Ohio Political Register,* September 17, and reply to "Anthony Wayne," [October].

3. Atwater's claims during the campaign were notorious. For example, the Lexington *Kentucky Reporter,* November 15, asserted that Atwater "has doubtless been one of the principal contributors to the Cincinnati Falsehood Manufactory. From that source have originated the reports that Mr Clay had declined—that his cause was hopeless—that Jackson was carrying all before him, &c. &c."

To William Carroll

Hermitage Novr. 2d. 1824

D. Sir,

I have lately been informed that Col. [Nicholas Tate] Perkins has been complaining of my Report, made of his conduct at Enotichopco Creek on the 24th. of Jany 1814; and that he has been industriously circulating Jesse Bentons pamphlet, and making many comments on the injustice done him in that <affair> report.[1]

I am well aware that you have a clear recollection of the occurrences of that day—having been ordered by me to take command of the center column, & charge of the rear Guard, whilst the army was crossing the creek where I expected to be attacked by the Indians, & from the circumstance which occured of Col. Perkins, *contrary* to my *order*, having left his position in the rear with the Guard, before my colums were clear of the fortified encampment, and was attempting to *march through* my columns when I *ordered him back*. It was owing to this <cause> circumstance I <commanded> directed you to place yourself at the head of the center column commanded by Capt [John B.] Quarles, and to remain with the rear until the defile was passed. Your situation gave you an opportunity to see the *entire flight* of the right column commanded by Col.Perkins, as well as the left commanded by Lieut. Col. [John] Stump. I therefore have to request from you a full statement of that affair.[2] I do not know that I shall have occasion to use it; but I wish it for the benefit of the faithful Historian—perhaps it may also, become necessary to use it, in case I shall ever hereafter notice that vile and false production of Jesse's. I am determined, at least, to place it in the power of the future Historian "to render unto Ceasar the *things* that are *Cesars*."[3] I hope therefore you will give a full statement I am sir, with due respect your most Obt svt

Signed, Andrew Jackson

P. S. I have no doubt but you recollect that Col. Perkins was the Senr. officer of the Guard.

Copy, DLC (33).

1. See AJ to Thomas Pinckney, January 29, 1814. Jackson ordered Perkins (1767–1843), who commanded the 1st Regiment of West Tennessee Volunteer mounted gunmen, court-martialed for his conduct during the battle, but he was acquitted. Benton's *Address to the People of the United States* briefly referred to the incident as a case in which volunteer officers were "sacrificed to the vanity and pride of the General" (p. 24).

2. Quarles, a captain in Perkins's regiment, was killed at the battle. Stump (1776–1848), a Nashville merchant who was second in command under Perkins, was court-martialed and cashiered. For Carroll's statement, see Carroll to AJ, November 6.

3. Mark 12:17. Jackson also obtained a copy of the Perkins court-martial in preparation for a possible reply (see James W. Sittler to William B. Lewis, December 12, 1824, DLC-33).

From David Corbin Ker

New Orleans Novr. 23. 1824

Dear Sir

Yesterday the Legislature of this State proceeded to the Election of five Electors of President & Vice President which has resulted in the election of three who will vote for you & two for Mr. Adams[1]—This result is the effect of a compromise between your friends and those of Mr. Adams in the Legislature to prevent as they say Henry Clay from receiveing the vote of the State—As one of the committee appointed by the citizens of this city to promote your election, I protested against this compromise as an abandonment of principle—nor do I think there was any necessity for it; for though several members professed it to be their intention to vote for Clay or Adams, I am convinced they would not have dared to do so & face their constituents afterwards; especially as they had been instructed to vote for you; & I think they only held that language to intimidate your friends & have unfortunately succeeded in depriving you of two votes—At the meeting of the Legislature it is admitted that there was a decided majority in your favor—but every engine of corruption was immediately set in motion & every species of intrigue resorted to by the friends of Clay & Adams aided by your old enemies and by some Apostate friends to seduce members from their duty—Among those who have deserted your Standard and have been most active against you you will be surprised to learn that Judge Joshua Lewis has been most conspicuous, the same man who was a member of Beals Rifle company[2]—The mail is about to close & I have only time to say that I most sincerely wish you health and happiness—respectfully yr. obt. St.

David C. Ker

ALS, DLC (33). As an army surgeon, Ker (1772–1840) had tended Jackson during the New

Orleans campaign. A sometime state legislator, he was on the Jackson committee announced at a June 5 meeting in New Orleans.

1. Two Jackson electors, Pierre R. Lacoste and Jean B. Plauché, and an Adams elector, William Nott, were elected on the first ballot. The third Jackson elector, Sebastian Hiriart, was selected on the fourth ballot, and the second Adams elector, James H. Shepherd, was chosen on the fifth ballot.

2. Following the Jackson meeting of June 5, Lewis (1773–1833), judge of Louisiana's first district court, presided over a meeting of New Orleans citizens opposed to "bound electors" that recommended six candidates for the state legislature. The Jackson forces selected their slate on June 22, and although other tickets were announced, the main contest in New Orleans was between the Jackson and Independent tickets. The pro-Jackson forces elected four legislators, the Independents, two. During the 1815 New Orleans campaign, Lewis had served with the volunteer company of Orleans riflemen commanded by then register of deeds Thomas Beale (d. 1823), but he had become involved in Jackson's post-battle controversy with Judge Dominick A. Hall. Jackson had briefly ordered Lewis arrested after the judge issued a writ of habeas corpus for Hall's release.

From Thomas A. Mera

Caswell North Carolina Decr. 7th 1824.

Dear Sir

Though not being personally acquainted, I think it my duty as a citizen of this commonwealth, and one who holds your services to this Republic, in the highest esteem to let you know or give you a fiew hints, about the conduct of Romulus M Saunders, a member at Congress from this district I have no doubt but he will aim at some place of distinction under the patronage of this government, and I think it not more, than, doing Justice to yourself, and your friends; to stop his career, at least as far as lays in your power—there is no doubt but he is one of those Office hunters zealously attached to the caucus partey as his conduct Towards you fully Testifies it[1]

At all the public Meetings in this district that Mr. Saunders attend his common strain was in the following words, General A Jackson the Warior to be at the head of civil authority if so distruction awaits your republican instutions; he is better suited for the field of Carnage, and bloodshed, than for any civil office within your gift, a man too; who endangered your freedom! by imposeing on the Spanish government, and who has in every act of his like defyed any instructions from the head of department! yes! and the constution of your Country! what can be expected from him but to trample and Barter your freedom like an [Benedict] Arnold? a man too who has shot 7 or 8 of your fellow Citizens! when taken up a fiew miles from the camp upon their way home After serveing their time faithfully as Soldiers and citizens of this country, in short there is nothing to Support this G A. J to this dignifyed place but the Battle at New Orleans, and the Credit of that is not due to him, he had Other brave Officers, who deserves the honours, of that day, and who are entirely forgotten, the peoples ticket they <next> meaning your friends lay hold of. to decry you,

I have seen one nailed to a post a fiew days past, and it and its Suporters should more fitly be carried to the whiping post, or words to this amount all I have stated and various other charges too tedious to mention this mighty civilian! made use of, and can be proven by a respectable Battallion of the Caswell Militia; where he made his last exebition on the 11th. of November last, winding up by saying you had shot deliberately one of the finest young men in the Western Country, and further the rod of vengence is extended towards your Supporters by this great man.[2]

On the first day of December Inst. there was let at Milton in this county the building of a Toll bridge across the dan River Romulus M Saunders president of the bord of directors. this bridge was to be let to the lowest bider according to an advertisement in the milton Gazette; I attended as a bider for the bridge knowing that I could give satisfactory Security! and also knowing that I posessed Sufficient Judgement in the art of building! as I have been engaged in that Occupation the last 14 years and have excuted several Jobs of work both publick & private in this state, and in the state of Virginia, however RMS. had the assurance to tell the Cryer not to Cry my bid, I asked him his reasons and he made no reply, when both my securitys appeared and bid for me, and Offered to be my security for a 100,000$! to secure the bilding of 7000$ worth of a bridge no security would be received nor would my bid. On account of my being a ridgid Jacksonite if this is not trampling on the Rights of free men I know not, what is the day following being the 2nd. Inst he came to apologize but his appology was rejected by me as it should be, (with scorn) demanding Satisfaction for the injury he had done me but the coward refused—this letter, Sir, is not sent to you, in order to agrevate your feelings, nor that you should even notice him? but it is earnestly hoped by, me, and your Other friends, in this neighbourhood, that you'll Check this tyrants career. if he should make any attempts to procure a Sinecure place! under this government! as it is presumed he will. I do assure you that every exertion will be made to keep him at home the ensueing ellection, he calls himself a republican. if so I am much surprized that he would be guilty of such dishonourable conduct, but it is the Oppinion of several of his neighbours that he belongs to the federal Party, but it matters not, what party man he is, this is a fair exposition of his conduct, I should not have troubled you at this important crisis If I had not thought it prudent to let you know one of your Keenest enemies—he is a lordly nabob ever since he maried Judge [William] Johnsons daughter[3]

I trust, Sir, you'll, do me the honour of *[looking]* Silently over this long epistle but mark well the subject it is intended to lay before you I remain Honoured Sir with great Esteem and regard your Obedient very Honble servant

Thomas A Mera

P. S I am glad to see the majority of the freemen of this country coinside with me in sentiment relative to the Presidential Election and earnestly hope you'll sukceed our present chief majestrate—

ALS, DLC (33). Mera has not been identified further.

1. Saunders (1791–1867), who represented North Carolina, 1821–27 and 1841–45, had attended the congressional caucus that nominated William H. Crawford on February 14.

2. Saunders apparently referred to the deaths of the six militiamen, later made infamous by John Binns's *Monumental Inscriptions,* the "coffin handbills" of the 1828 campaign, and either to Jackson's order for the execution of John Wood or to his duel with Charles H. Dickinson. Arnold (1741–1801) was infamous for his treasonable arrangement to surrender West Point to the British in 1780.

3. Saunders had married Anna Heyes Johnson (1800–71), daughter of Supreme Court Judge William Johnson (1771–1834), in May 1823.

To William Berkeley Lewis

Senate chamber Decbr. 8th. 1824

Dr. Major

I reached this city yesterday morning at 11 oclock, all in good health, after a continued travel of 28 days without resting one day—

I enclose you the Presidents message—you will see from the papers the electoral vote. If Louisiana has not voted for Mr Clay he is not in the house—when I have obtained the actual vote & become a little acquainted with the views of the political knowing oncs here, I will give you the speculations on the presidential question.[1]

I am anxious to hear from you—how Jessee has come out &c &c &c—write me.[2]

give me the intelligence how our little sons are, & whether Doctor [Philip] Lindsley has taken charge of the College[3]—with Mrs J. & my compliments to the Ladies of your family, believe me yr friend

Andrew Jackson

ALS, CtHi (10-0965). Published in Parton, 3:52 (extract).

1. For James Monroe's message of December 7, see *Register of Debates in Congress,* 18th Cong., 2nd sess., appendix, pp. 2–8. The Washington *National Intelligencer,* December 8, reported electoral votes from eleven eastern states: 66 for John Q. Adams, 59 for Jackson, 32 for William H. Crawford, and 4 for Henry Clay. Other reports on December 7 and 8 indicated Jackson victories in Illinois and Indiana.

2. Jesse Benton announced as a Crawford elector for Tennessee's western district in July but switched to Clay just before the balloting. Robert H. Dyer, a Jackson elector, won the district by a large margin.

3. Lindsley (1786–1855; Princeton 1804) accepted the presidency of Cumberland College (University of Nashville), taking charge in January 1825.

To Edward George Washington Butler

City Of Washington, December 12th. 1824.

My Dear Edward;

Your letter of the 7th. inst has come to hand announcing the death of my young friend, and your much lamented Brother.[1] Mrs. Jackson & myself tender to you, what we sensibly feel, our sincere condolence on this melancholy occasion. When death comes, he respects no age nor merit; he sweeps from this earthly existence the High and the Low, the rich, and the poor; and should teach us to live, to be prepared for death. Our deceased friend was a youth of great promise, snatched from us at an interesting period of life, and when we least expected it: thereby showing us the great uncertainty of all earthly things: but we have a hope that he is removed from the troubles of this, to a blissful state of immortality, in the next world; and we are taught by the Scriptures "to mourn not for the dead, but for the living."[2] *He is gone*—our tears cannot restore him; and let us be consoled in the hope that he is at rest and happy in the arms of our crucified Saviour. Another consolation may be derived from the letter you have enclosed me stating that whatever could be done during his illness, for his relief and preservation, was cheerfully extended. Be therefore consoled—you have many sincere friends, and some dear relations; and altho' you have experienced the loss of many, still your misfortunes are not greater than those which befal others. you should remember too, that to be reconciled with our Lot is a duty we owe not less to ourselves than to that God, to whose Providence we are all committed. Against his will, it is vain to repine, however trying the affliction, or great the burden; while a calm submission to that will, makes human fortitude triumph over the grave, and conducts us to those happier regions, in which we love to believe our young friend *immortal*, at the same time we are aided in preparation to overtake him *there*

Mrs. J and your friend Mr. Donelson & Lady, are with me, and will be happy to see you at Washington. Will you be here this winter? Mr. D. will write you shortly. Accept, my dear young friend, my best wishes, and those of Mrs. J. and Mrs. & Mr. Donelson, and be pleased to reciprocate to Genl. Gaines, Mrs. Gaines & Mr. [Rawlins] Lowndes[3] our best respects—yrs. affectionately

Andrew Jackson

LS in Andrew J. Donelson's hand, THer (10-0974); Extract, LNT (10-0978). Published in St. Louis *Missouri Republican*, August 7, 1883 (extract). LS endorsed by Edmund P. Gaines, "This letter cannot but be read with great interest; It breathes sentiments worthy of the enlightened head and benevolent heart of its author—sentiments the most appropriate to the melancholy subject to which it has reference; and such as, when carefully treasured up in the mind, will contribute to solace present sorrow, and pave the way for that future *good*, which never fails to follow in the footsteps of affliction and adversity." Also endorsed by Butler.

1. Letter not found. Anthony W. Butler died while on passage from New Orleans to New York.

2. A paraphrase of Luke 23:28.

3. Gaines's aide Lowndes (c1801–77; Military Academy 1820) had been Edward G. W. Butler's classmate at West Point.

To John Overton

City of Washington
Decbr 19th 1824

My Dear friend

I have recd your kind letter of the 28th Ult, & perused it with attention[1]—You will find from the public Journals before this reaches you, that the Electoral vote of Louisiana is not for Mr Clay, & of course he does not go into the House, as the third highest—what may be the result of the vote by the House of Representatives I know not—I hope my friends will <take> continue to take principle for their guide; and let me rise or fall upon the <principle> rule that the people have the right to choose the chief executive of the nation, and a majority of their voices have a right to govern, agreable to the declared principles of the constitution—

Having been supported by the majority of the people, I can have no feelings on the occasion—If party or intrigue should prevail, and exclude me, I shall retire to my comfortable farm with great pleasure—there you know; was the hight of my ambition, there is the only contentment for me, there I could in retirement mingle with my sincere friends. <in rural retirement> should I be selected to preside over the destinies of this great & growing nation—my best Judgt shall be employed for its prosperity & happiness; I am aware of the responsibility of the station—& with my own consent I should never aspired to the responsibility—but, *let the lords will be done*—and if placed in the Executive chair, I shall endeavour, with an honest zeal to discharge the duties of that station & bring to my aid as far as I can command it, the best Talents & Virtue of this nation.

Mrs. Jackson has stood the Journey well, is in good health—and anxious to hear from our little Andrews—will you have the goodness when you are in Nashville to present us to The Revd. Mr Campbell, & Mr J. C McLamore & request of them from me to give us the information of their situation & health—

Mrs. J. Joins me in best wishes for your & Mrs. O. health & happiness, and believe me your friend—

Andrew Jackson

P.S. give our respects to Mrs Genl Overton & family—the Doctor[2] & all our friends A. J.
P. S. I need not say to you I write in great haste the scrall & interlineations & erasure sufficiently evince.

ALS, THi (10-0988). Published in *THQ*, 6(1947):168–69.
1. Not found.
2. Probably a reference to John's nephew James Overton (1785–1865).

Rachel Jackson to Elizabeth Kingsley

[December 23, 1824]

The present moment is the first I can call my own since my arrival in this great city. Our journey, indeed, was fatiguing. We were twenty-seven days on the road, but no accident happened to us. My dear husband is in better health than when we came. We are boarding in the same house with the nation's guest, Lafayette. I am delighted with him. All the attentions, all the parties he goes to, never appear to have any effect on him. In fact, he is an extraordinary man. He has a happy talent of knowing those he has once seen. For instance, when we first came to this house, the General said he would go and pay the Marquis the first visit. Both having the same desire, and at the same time, they met on the entry of the stairs. It was truly interesting. The emotion of revolutionary feeling was aroused in them both. At Charleston, General Jackson saw him on the field of battle; the one a boy of twelve, the Marquis, twenty-three. He wears a wig, and is a little inclined to corpulency. He is very healthy, eats hearty, goes to every party, and that is every night.[1]

To tell you of this city, I would not do justice to the subject. The extravagance is in dressing and running to parties; but I must say they regard the Sabbath, and attend preaching, for there are churches of every denomination and able ministers of the gospel. We have been here two Sabbaths. The General and myself were both days at church. Mr. [Daniel] Baker is the pastor of the church we go to. He is a fine man, a plain, good preacher. We were waited on by two of Mr. [Stephen Bloomer] Balche's elders, inviting us to take a pew in his church in Georgetown, but previous to that I had an invitation to the other. General Cole, Mary, Emily, and Andrew, went to the Episcopal church.[2]

Oh, my dear friend, how shall I get through this bustle. There are not less than fifty to one hundred persons calling in a day. My dear husband was unwell nearly the whole of our journey, but, thanks to our Heavenly Father, his health is improving. Still his appetite is delicate, and company and business are oppressive; but I look unto the Lord, from whence comes all my comforts. I have the precious promise, and I know that my Redeemer liveth.

Don't be afraid of my giving way to those vain things. The apostle says,

I can do all things in Christ, who strengtheneth me. The play-actors sent me a letter, requesting my countenance to them.[3] No. A ticket to balls and parties. No, not one. Two dinings; several times to drink tea. Indeed, Mr. Jackson encourages me in my course. He recommends it to me to be steadfast. I am going to-day to hear Mr. Summerfield. He preaches in the Methodist church; a very highly spoken of minister.[4] Glory to God for the privilege. Not a day or night but there is the church opened for prayer.

[Rachel Jackson]

Printed, Parton, 3:52–53 (10-0996); Copy, DLC (10-0997).

1. Invited by President Monroe, Lafayette arrived at New York on August 15 to begin a triumphal tour that would include a visit to the Hermitage the following May before his return to France in September 1825. While in Washington, he stayed at Gadsby's Hotel, the former Franklin House Hotel, at the northeast corner of I and 21st Streets facing Pennsylvania Avenue. Jackson might previously have seen Lafayette when the Marquis landed at Charleston in June 1777, but not "on the field of battle."

2. Baker (1791–1857; Princeton 1815) was pastor of Second Presbyterian Church in Washington. Balch (1747–1833; Princeton 1774), father of Alfred, was pastor of the Bridge Street Presbyterian Church at 30th and M in Georgetown. "Cole" is almost certainly the copyist's mistranscription of "Call."

3. Philippians, 4:13. The letter has not been found.

4. Probably John Summerfield (1798–1825), a touring Methodist Episcopal preacher resident at this time in Baltimore.

To John Coffee

City of Washington
Decbr 27th. 1824

Dear Genl

Shortly after our arival I wrote you—advising of our safe arival here on the 7th instant all well—after a continual travel of 28 days; My horses stood the Journey well, but as was to be expected, much wearied, & somewhat reduced in flesh.[1]

We have been in a constant bustle since our arival, & will be so for, & during the Holidays, altho Mrs. J & myself goes to no parties

We have had the finest weather thro all this month I ever experienced; this day as pleasant as a may day, & a prospect of a continuation of fine weather. I hope it may have extended to Tennessee, & Alabama—if it has, the cotton planters must have been much benefitted by getting in their crops without injury from rain. I am anxious to hear from you, give me the average of your cotton crops, the prospect of a good price & how Mr Nicholson comes on, & the amount of his present crop of Cotton, with the health of your family, and how my Irish friends comes on; I am fearfull that the information of the electoral vote, & that Georgia has instructed their Representatives in congress, on the event that Mr Crawford is dropped to vote for me, will prove injurious to their health, & spirits;

do console them. I wish you (should you meet with Mrs. James Jackson) to present to her my respects—for her & her children I have a very sincere regard—and the coolness that has taken place between James & me will never be extended to her & the children so long as they treat my name with respect, and altho all intercourse between James & myself is closed, still I will cherish a friendship for Mrs. Jackson & the children.

you will have ere this reaches you, seen the Electoral vote; Mr Clay does not come before the Hous of Representatives, and Mr Crawford it is believed stands no chance;[2] whether his friends may unite with Mr. Adams, and those of Mr. Clay, I cannot say—or whether an attempt will be made to unite Clays friends with Mr. Crawfords and thereby prevent a choice, I cannot say—There are various rumors, on these subjects, but whether any of them is founded in fact I know not, as I do not intermix, or Join in any conversation on the subject of the Presidential election—I do believe that Mr Clay cannot influence the Kentucky Delegation, if he was so disposed—and how the election for President may be decided is very doubtfull, my friends are sanguine, be it as it may, I am contented, I have no feelings on the subject—My happiness & choice would be to return to the Hermitage, enjoy<ing> the sweets of domestic quiett—but *the Lords will be done*—How much your situation are to envied, & how prudent you have been to keep yourself free of political life—surrounded as you are by your lovely children, & amiable wife, you ought not to abandoned it for any thing on earth. Here there is a bustle continually; The man in office greeted with smiles & apparent friendship, <with> his confidence often sought to be betrayed: surrounded thus, where a man must be allways guarded, happiness cannot exist—The best lesson learnt me in my youth, was to pursue principle, & never depart from my own Judgt. when matured—Treat all with complacency, but make confidents of but few, I have profitted much by an adherence to this rule, but still I have been deceived as you know in men—and I have become so well acquainted with human nature, that I am wearied with a public life, & if I could with propriety, would retire—but my Lott is cast, and fall as it may, I must <exercise p> be con*[tent]* should it be that I can retire next M*[arch]* to my home I will be happy—If confined here, I must excercise my best exertions for the public weal, untill the four year runs round—If my life is spared, then I shall claim from my country an exemption from further service or toil.

We are at Mr [John] Gadsbys tavern, well lodged, but *I pay for it*,[3] How my funds may hold out I cannot say—write me, should I want funds whether any of Andrew J. Hutchings present crop can be spared from the purchase of land—I only ask to know, as I allways look ahead in money matters—believing that the clear proceeds of my own crop will be sufficient for my purpose.

all are well & enjoying themselves, the young at parties & Mrs. J. &

myself at home smoking our pipe & all send love to you Polly & the children, your friend

Andrew Jackson

ALS, THi (10-1001). Published in Bassett, 3:269–71.

1. Letter not found.

2. The electoral vote was 99 for Jackson, 84 for John Q. Adams, 41 for William H. Crawford, and 37 for Henry Clay.

3. Previously an innkeeper in Baltimore, Gadsby (1766–1844) took over operation of the former Franklin House Hotel from William O'Neale in 1823.

To William Berkeley Lewis

(Private)

City of Washington
Decbr 27th. 1824

Dear Major

I have not recd a line from any of my friends in Nashville since my arival here, and am very anxious to hear from our little Andrews, & how our College progresses, pray write me; and when you are giving me the above intelligence do I pray you inform how our good friends Jessee Benton & Mr. Balch are.

I am fearfull the result of the electoral vote will derange Jessys head, & Balchs pockett, be this as it may, let me hear from them by you. I have not time or data to give any information certainly on the Presidential question—rumors say that deep intrigue is on foot, that Mr Clay is trying to wield his influence with ohio, Kentucky, Missouri & Elonois in favour of Adams—others say the plan is to prevent an election alltogether this last I do not believe—be it as it may I am content. We are all well, the young at parties—Mrs J & myself at home chatting & smoking our pipe & thinking of our Tennessee friends—all Join in respects to you & the young ladies & wish you the Joys of the Season—your friend

Andrew Jackson

ALS, NNPM (10-1005).

Appendix I

TRANSCRIPTION PREPARED BY JESÚS F. DE LA TEJA

From Catalina Mir Satorios

Charleston 16 de Abril de 1822

Muy Señor mio

Tengo a la vista su mui Apreciable Carta Fecha 28 de Febrero, y Enterada de su Contenidó digo á vmd.— Mucho he sentido su Yndisposision, lo qe. Espero en Dios, qe. Esta le Allare Enteramente Buenó &c.

Sy my Esposo, no se Presento Con su Escritura Reclamando su Esclabo, Como vmd Deceabá fue por motivo de no poderse En Barcar; ny Resistir Ninguna Fatiga por Estar tan á Trasado de Salud, y de Consigiente se tomo la Libertad, de Escrivir á vmd Participando, su Fatal Yndisposision no Cullendo ofender á vmd, sus Cartas Fueron Escritas por Manos del Jues Michel y no tuvo el gusto de una Contesta qe. tanto deceaba el Ynfeliz

Yo no Escrivi á vmd Esperando á vistando el gusto de Presentarme yo Misma en Persona Con es Peranzas de qe. vmd. havia de acender de Governador en la Plaza y Provincia de San Agustin Como vide por los Papeles Publicos pero no he tenido el gusto de ver á vmd Como Pensaba Solo sy qe. tenido el gusto de Recibir sus Cartas las qe. han sido de Mucho Consuelo para my

Devo Creer que el no haverle quitado vmd la vida á hese Negro Yngrato qe. Bien lo Merecia fue porque—Estaba Dispuesto de la Divina Providencia para qe. me sirviese de Aligria en mis Mallores á trasos y no me queda la Menor duda &c

Remito á vmd la Copia de la Escritura de Compra y Escritura de la Benta Como vmd. pide Espero Estara todo á su Gusto tambien Remito un Papel para que vea vmd sy puede mandarme el Dinero en la Forma qe le pido es Favor que de vmd Espero.

Selebrare lo pase vmd sin Novedad y yo siempre quedo a la disposision de vmd—Su Afecta y servidora—Q.S.M.B.

Catalina Satorios

P.D. Estimare á vmd me Remita la Carta al quidado de los Señores MacDoval y Black, para que vengan mas seguras su Afecta Q.S.M.B.

Catalina Satorios

ALS, DLC (31).

Appendix II

Jackson's Recorded Votes in the United States Senate, 1823-25

1823

Dec 22	Against ratification of the 10th article of Treaty of Moultrie Creek, September 18.
Dec 23	For using words "Florida tribes" instead of "Seminole tribe" in resolution ratifying Treaty of Moultrie Creek; for ratifying treaty.
Dec 30	For amendment to limit action of provision for suspending discriminating duties to nations "whose Independence the United States have recognised."

1824

Jan 7	For amendment increasing sum to be granted in bill for relief of Francis Henderson, Jr.
Jan 16	For reversing committee report unfavorable to petition of Alexander A. White.
Jan 23	For bill authorizing a road from Memphis to Little Rock.
Jan 28	For bill setting procedures for adjustment of Spanish and French land claims in Missouri and Arkansas.
Jan 30	For resolution proposing a constitutional amendment to limit president to two elected terms.
Feb 9	For setting appropriation to build sloops of war at $250,000 for present year and $200,000 annually for next three years; for appointment of John Whitehead as collector for Key West, Thompson's Island; against appointment of Alexander [Archibald] W. Hamilton as collector for Pensacola.
Feb 20	For bill to lay out and open public roads in Florida.
Feb 26	Against reversal of committee report unfavorable to petition of directors of New England Mississippi Land Company.
March 3	Against striking appropriation for the purchase of Gridley's farm, on which stood a tavern, near the Military Academy.
March 8	For reversing committee report unfavorable to petition of Sarah

	Easton and Dorothy Storer.
March 9	Against a week's postponement of bill to supply ordnance for fortifications; against reconsideration of language of first section of bill; for third reading of bill.
March 11	For bill for the relief of Dean Weymouth.
March 25	For amendment adding a public agent to appropriation for salaries of commission to settle claims under Article 1 of the Treaty of Ghent.
April 5	For amendment providing that unless a debtor has absconded he can be held to bail only in his state of residence or the state where the debt was contracted.
April 6	Against indefinite postponement of bill to abolish imprisonment for debt.
April 8	For reconsideration of vote to return bill to abolish imprisonment for debt to committee; against indefinite postponement of the bill.
April 9	For bill to abolish imprisonment for debt; against amendment striking appropriation for transportation of military force to Upper Missouri River to protect the fur trade and exclude foreign traders.
April 13	For third reading of bill for relief of Hezekiah Langley and Benjamin M. Belt; against motion to lay on the table a resolution setting adjournment for May 4.
April 19	For a week's postponement of resolution fixing adjournment of Congress; for motion to lay on the table the adjournment resolution; for setting adjournment date of May 15.
April 20	Against referring tariff bill to committee on finance; for bill establishing procedures for settling private pecuniary claims against the United States.
April 21	For bill for the relief of William Duane.
April 22	Against striking out House bill to procure surveys for roads and canals, in preparation for a substitute bill by Thomas H. Benton.
April 23	Against amendment to amendment of road and canal survey bill requiring consent of the state involved prior to any survey; against word change in amendment to survey bill providing that the bill does not affirm congressional power to make roads or canals on own authority; against the amendment re congressional authority; against amendment that money for roads and canals shall be expended in proportion as direct taxes are assessed among states; for third reading of survey bill.
April 24	For bill to provide procedures for settling private pecuniary claims; for bill to procure road and canal surveys.
April 27	Against striking appropriation for fortification at New York City.
April 28	Against amendment striking tariff on iron not manufactured by rolling.
April 29	Against amendment striking two cents per pound tariff on hemp.
May 1	Against amendment adding osnaburgs, ticklenburgs, and burlaps to proposed amendment excepting certain fabrics from duty.
May 3	Against amendment excepting certain fabrics from duty.
May 5	Against amendment striking a proviso setting minimum prices from which duties on even cheaper cotton goods will be figured; against amendment striking additional duty on foreign distilled

spirits; for adjournment.

May 6 Against amendment limiting the prospective increases in duties on unmanufactured wool to 25% ad valorem; for amendment limiting wool increase to 30% ad valorem; for amendment striking out proviso that wools worth no more than ten cents per pound will be charged 15% ad valorem; against amendment specifying 25% ad valorem duty on articles of silk from beyond Cape of Good Hope; for amendment deleting prospective 37½% ad valorem duty on manufactured wool; against amendment excepting duck fabrics from ad valorem and assigning specific duties; against amendment to exempt articles manufactured of flax or hemp from ad valorem duty; against amendment striking duty on cotton bagging.

May 7 Against amendment excepting worsted stuff goods from duty on woolen manufactures; against amendment altering time at which tariff bill will take effect; for amendment lowering duty on worsted stuff goods; against amendment including blankets in amendment lowering stuff goods duty; against amendment excepting ships cleared from ports before passage of tariff bill from its operation; for amendment deleting duty on frying pans; against amendment to alter duty on ducks, osnaburgs, ticklenburgs, and burlaps; for amendment setting altered duty at 20% ad valorem; against amendment setting altered duty at 15% ad valorem; for amendment limiting duty on woolen manufactures worth no more than 33⅓ cents per square yard; for amendment specifying two cents per pound duty on copper; against amendment to alter amendment re iron cables; against amendment to strike out duty on iron cables.

May 8 For amendment changing duties on knives, scythes, sickles, reaping hooks, spades, and shovels from specific to ad valorem; for amendment changing duties on screws from specific to ad valorem; against amendment raising duty on Greek and Latin books; against amendment altering duty on books; for amendment setting altered duty on books at 25% ad valorem; for appointment of Tunstall Quarles as receiver of public moneys for Cape Girardeau district.

May 10 For striking tariff bill section allowing drawbacks on export of some silk or nankeen cloths; against amendment lowering duty on non-Indian silks; against amendments striking out duties on wheat and wheat flour and on potatoes; against striking second section from bill for the relief of Alexander McNair.

May 11 For amendment to delete blankets from lowered duty on worsted stuff goods; against amendment to lower duty on Indian silks; against amendment delaying enforcement against goods shipped from beyond Cape of Good Hope; against amendment striking prospective raises in the duty on manufactured wool; against amendment to alter the duty on hemp; against setting the altered duty on hemp at $45 per ton, for setting it at $37 per ton, and for setting it at $35 per ton; against amendment striking the duty on iron; against amendment striking the duty on foreign distilled spirits; for amendment striking out proviso limiting duty on cheap wool; for amendment striking the duty on cotton bagging.

May 12 Against amendment to alter the duty on Madeira, Lisbon, and

Oporto wines; for third reading of tariff bill.

May 13 For amending language of proposed amendment to reinstate appropriation for military force on Upper Missouri; for passage of tariff bill; for ratification of Cherokee treaty of October 24, 1804.

May 14 Against indefinite postponement of bill for the relief of Mary James.

May 17 For Senate insistence on a proviso re woolen goods, not accepted by House; against Senate recession from its deletion of duty on cotton bagging, not accepted by House; against Senate recession from language re silk drawback, not accepted by House; for bill to provide for punishment of crimes in United States jurisdictions; for revised amendment appropriating for a military force on the upper Missouri River.

May 18 For motion to reduce sum granted in bill for the relief of representatives of John H. Piatt.

May 19 For third reading of bill to improve the navigation of the Ohio and Mississippi rivers; against bill to authorize issuing a register to the brig *William* of New York.

May 21 For third reading of bill for relief of representatives of John H. Piatt; for bill to authorize issuance of $5,000,000 in stock to meet claims under the Spanish treaty of 1819; for amendment to ratification of convention with Great Britain on slave trade to allow either party to renounce the convention on six months notice.

May 22 Against postponing further consideration of the convention on the slave trade until December next; for retaining the words "of America" and "of the West Indies" in lines 4 and 5 of Article 1; for ratification of Article 2; for retaining in Article 7 a section regarding trial of citizens seized on neutral vessels engaged in the slave trade; and for amended resolution ratifying the convention.

Dec 21 For bill granting $200,000 and a township of land to Lafayette for revolutionary services.

1825

Jan 3 Against amendment striking clauses from bill abolishing imprisonment for debt.

Jan 4 Against amendment easing requirements before a debtor can be held on bail.

Jan 5 For ratification of convention with Russia of April 5 (17), 1824, regarding settlement boundaries and trade in the northwest.

Jan 6 For a bill to relieve Thomas L. Ogden and others.

Jan 13 For ratification of convention with the Bey of Tunis of February 24, 1824, amending 1797 treaty; for ratification of treaties with Iowa and with Sauk and Fox Indians, August 4, 1824; for appointments of naval lieutenants.

Jan 17 For bill abolishing imprisonment for debt.

Jan 25 Against bill allowing drawback on export of cordage manufactured from imported hemp.

Jan 26 For third reading of bill authorizing marking of road from Missouri to New Mexico.

Feb 1	Against striking third section of bill for the suppression of piracy.
Feb 3	Against amendment granting aid for merchantmen to arm.
Feb 4	Against amendment striking sections 4–10 from bill for the suppression of piracy; against striking section 2 from bill; against amendment forbidding public armed vessels engaged in piracy suppression from carrying freight.
Feb 8	Against reversing committee report unfavorable to petition of Ebenezer Oliver and others.
Feb 15	Against indefinite postponement of bill to provide three additional U.S. circuit courts.
Feb 16	Against recommitment of bill to provide additional circuit courts.
Feb 17	Against indefinite postponement of bill to provide additional circuit courts; against recommitment of bill to Judiciary Committee; against amendment that the new judges shall not belong to Supreme Court; against amendment reducing new circuits to two.
Feb 18	Against the purchase and distribution of an edition of the journals of the congress of the confederation; for amendment reducing moneys to be appropriated for purchase of a portrait of George Washington.
Feb 21	For amendment appropriating moneys for forts at Beaufort and Cape Fear, North Carolina.
Feb 22	Against amendment to strike first section of bill supplementing the law to enable claimants in Missouri and Arkansas to try the validity of their claims; for third reading of bill; for third reading of bill authorizing purchase of a portrait of Washington; for appointment of Augustus B. Woodward as judge in Florida.
Feb 23	For passage of bill authorizing purchase of a portrait of Washington; against indefinite postponement of bill to extend the Cumberland Road.
Feb 24	Against amendment deleting Illinois and Missouri from action of bill to extend the Cumberland Road; for third reading of bill; for amendment to bill authorizing subscription of stock for the Delaware and Chesapeake Canal to authorize similar subscription for Dismal Swamp Canal Company; for third reading of bill.
March 1	Against laying on the table a bill authorizing occupation of the mouth of the Oregon River; against striking third section of bill to provide for punishment of crimes against the United States; for third reading of bill.
March 7	Against resolution to allow James Lanman to take oath as Connecticut senator; against confirmation of Henry Clay as Secretary of State.
March 8	For removal of injunction of secrecy from proceedings on nomination of Henry Clay; against resolution directing purchase of journals of the congress of the confederacy.
March 9	For ratification of Article 1 of slave trade convention with Colombia of December 10, 1824, giving mutual right of search (2 votes); against ratification of convention with Colombia.

Sources: *Senate Journal,* 18th Cong.; *Senate Executive Proceedings,* vol. 3 (1815–29); *Annals of Congress,* 18th Cong., 1st sess.; *Register of Debates,* 18th Cong., 2nd sess.

Calendar, 1821–1824

1821

Jan 1 To John Caldwell Calhoun. Abstract, DNA-RG 107 (M22-14). Encloses report of Joseph Lovell (not found) re health of troops at Fort Gadsden.

Jan 1 *To James Monroe.* 3

Jan 1 To Thomas Hill Williams. LS, THi (8-0037). Recommends Samuel R. Overton as register of ceded Choctaw land.

Jan 1 Account with Kirkman & Erwin for sundries, freight, and cotton. ADS with AJ endorsement, DLC (31). Runs to May 30, 1822.

Jan 2 To Return Jonathan Meigs, 1740–1823 (enclosure: John C. Calhoun to AJ, Dec 14, 1820). LC, DLC (63). Instructs him re the trial of intruders on Cherokee lands.

Jan 3 To Edward Livingston. ALS, NjP (mAJs). *New York History* 20(1939):457. Introduces Ralph E. W. Earl.

Jan 3 From Edmund Pendleton Gaines. Copy, DNA-RG 107 (M221-89). Reports Spanish reinforcement at Pensacola and smuggling in the area.

Jan 3 From Speaker et al. LS by proxy, DNA-RG 107 (M221-89); Copy, DNA-RG 233 (8-0039). *ASP, Indian Affairs,* 2:503–504. Report disagreements among Cherokees and ask for AJ's intervention; report information that intruders removed by AJ's troops may attempt to return in the spring.

Jan 4 *To John Caldwell Calhoun.* 5

Jan 4 To Richard Keith Call. Photocopy of ALS, TU (mAJs). Discusses plans to interview Thomas Kirkman, apparently regarding rumors against Call's reputation; praises John C. Calhoun's report on army reduction and criticizes House rejection of statehood for Missouri.

Jan 4 To Benjamin Morgan. LS, THer (8-0045). Introduces Ralph E. W. Earl.

Jan 4 Account of Malachi Nicholson with William Griffin for sundries at Andrew Jackson Hutchings's farm. DS by Griffin with AJ endorsement, A-Ar (8-0042). Runs to March 23, 1822.

Jan 5 To John Coffee. ALS, THi (8-0046). Discusses lawsuit, *Bennett Smith* v. *John Hutchings's Executors.*

Jan 8 To Edward George Washington Butler. ALS, NcD (8-0049); Extract, LNT (mAJs). Charles Gayarré, *A Sketch of General*

	Jackson by Himself (New Orleans, 1857), pp. 2–3 (extract). Discusses Butler's trip to Boston, Anthony W. Butler, and the Butlers' landholdings in Robertson County.	
Jan 8	From Speaker et al. ALS by proxy (John Thompson), DNA-RG 107 (M221-89); Copy, DNA-RG 233 (8-0052). *HRDoc* 136, 18th Cong., 1st sess. (Serial 102), pp. 9–10. Introduce Turtle Fields.	
Jan 8	From William Walker. ALS with AJ endorsement, DLC (29). Requests assistance with his claim against the government for wagons used in 1815 by the 39th Infantry.	
Jan 9	From James Craine Bronaugh. ALS, DNA-RG 94 (mAJs). Submits report (not found) on health of Southern Division troops.	
Jan 10	To Ralph Eleazar Whitesides Earl. AL, THi (8-0054). Requests his attendance at the Hermitage for taking AJ's profile.	
Jan 10	From Mary Campbell. ALS with ANS by William Ward, DLC (29). Requests endorsement of her claim to military pension due to the loss of her husband during the revolutionary war and her sons during the War of 1812.	
Jan 10	From [Peter Hagner]. LC, DNA-RG 217 (8-0057). Discusses the claim of Alexander Hamilton, mixed-blood.	
[cJan 10]	Certification of the service of Pierre Denis de LaRonde. DS, DNA-RG 46 (8-0058).	
Jan 11	To Thomas McCorry. Photocopy of ALS, William L. Berry (8-0061). Requests information re land conveyances to David Allison.	
Jan 11	Account with Hoggatt & Overton for farm equipment and sundries. AD with AJ endorsement and ANS by Robert Butler, DLC (31). Runs to April 6, 1822.	
Jan 11	Receipt from John Donelson (1755–1830) for $85 for a bay mare. DS in AJ's hand and with AJ endorsement, THi (8-0059).	
Jan 12	To James Monroe. LS and Extract, NN (8-0063, -0070); ALS copy, DLC (29); Copy, NjP (8-0067). Bassett, 3:35–36. Encloses letters (not found) and recommends George W. Martin and a Dr. [Charles?] Taylor for Florida posts.	
Jan 12	From Willie Blount. AL fragment, DLC (75). Approves Choctaw treaty and discusses changes in Tennessee banking laws.	
Jan 13	From John Caldwell Calhoun. LS, DLC (29); LC (dated Jan 11), DNA-RG 107 (M6-11). *Calhoun Papers,* 5:552–53. Announces ratification of Adams-Onís Treaty and suggests delay in establishing a post on the Sabine; reports receipt of Daniel S. Donelson's application for West Point.	
Jan 13	From William Lee. LC, DNA-RG 217 (8-0071). Discusses account for Choctaw treaty.	
Jan 14	Andrew Jackson Donelson to Daniel Bissell. LC, DLC (63). Expresses pleasure that the court-martial of Thomas J. Ayer will begin shortly.	
Jan 14	Andrew Jackson Donelson to William Lindsay. LC, DLC (63). Regrets the unhealthy conditions at Fort Gadsden, but suggests that troops will likely be moved to Dauphin Island.	
Jan 15	*From Robert Butler.*	6
Jan 16	To Joseph Roffignac. LS, LN (8-0072). Introduces Ralph E. W. Earl.	
Jan 16	From John Caldwell Calhoun (enclosure: Calhoun to Daniel Bissell,	

	July 18, 1820, DLC-29). LS, DLC (29); LC, DNA-RG 107 (M6-11). *TPUS,* 19:256–57. Discusses Robert L. Coomb's conduct.	
Jan 16	From Samuel Spotts. ALS, DLC (29). Requests appointment in the paymaster department.	
Jan 17	Receipt from Malachi Nicholson for $22.20 for pork furnished Andrew Jackson Hutchings's farm. ADS with AJ endorsement, A-Ar (8-0079).	
Jan 18	To John Caldwell Calhoun (enclosures: Speaker et al. to AJ, Jan 3 and 8; Pathkiller to AJ, Dec 11, 1820; Report of meeting with Cherokee Indians, [Jan 18]; AJ to Pathkiller et al., Jan 18). LS, DNA-RG 107 (M221-89); LC, DLC (63); Copy, DNA-RG 233 (8-0081). Bassett, 3:36–38. Discusses meeting with Cherokees and their request for a reservation.	
Jan 18	*To Pathkiller et al.*	7
Jan 18	To Pathkiller et al. Extract, *Cherokee Phoenix,* April 7, 1830 (mAJs). Promises to remove intruders from Cherokee lands if necessary.	
Jan 18	From Daniel Bissell (enclosure: John C. Calhoun to Bissell, Dec 9, 1820). LS, DLC (29). Reports on the location of troops.	
[Jan 18]	Report of meeting with Cherokee Indians. ADS, DNA-RG 107 (M221-89); Copy, DNA-RG 233 (8-0075). *ASP, Indian Affairs,* 2:504–505.	
Jan 19	From David Holmes. ALS, DLC (29). Reports ratification of the Choctaw treaty and discusses army reduction.	
Jan 20	From Daniel Bissell (enclosure: Return of troops under Robert L. Coomb, Oct 1820, DLC-70). LS, DLC (29). Reports detail of Perrin Willis to select a fortification site on the Sabine River.	
Jan 21	To [John Caldwell Calhoun] (enclosure: Edmund P. Gaines to AJ, Jan 3). Copy, DNA-RG 107 (M221-89). Transmits letter.	
Jan 21	To John Caldwell Calhoun (enclosure: James C. Bronaugh to AJ, Jan 9). LS and Copy, DNA-RG 107 (M221-89); LC, DLC (63). Sends letter and discusses abandonment of Fort Gadsden.	
Jan 21	To William Lee. LC, DLC (63). Reports that he has no further information re the arms used by Arthur P. Hayne and the mounted volunteers during the Seminole campaign.	
Jan 21	From John Caldwell Calhoun. LS, DLC (29); LC (dated Jan 5), DNA-RG 107 (M6-11). *Calhoun Papers,* 5:568. Orders court-martial of Talbot Chambers.	
Jan 21	Account with S. Reynder for sundries. DS duplicate, DLC (70). Lexington *Kentucky Reporter,* Aug 13, 1828. Runs to June 15.	
Jan 22	To James Monroe. LS, DLC (8-0091). Recommends Robert P. Currin for collectorship at Pensacola if James Gadsden withdraws.	
Jan 22	From John Caldwell Calhoun (enclosure: Calhoun to Richard I. Easter, Jan 20, DLC-29). LS, DLC (29); LC, DNA-RG 107 (M6-11). Transmits letter denying further delay in settling Easter's accounts.	
Jan 24	*From James Monroe.*	9
Jan 25	From John Caldwell Calhoun. ALS, DLC (29). *Calhoun Papers,* 5:572–73. Discusses army reduction and acquisition of Florida.	
Jan 27	From John Henry Eaton. ALS, DLC (29). Responds to AJ's views	

	(not found) on the admission of Missouri; discusses movement to appoint AJ as Florida governor.
[Jan 27]	From "Helvidius." Printed, *Arkansas Gazette,* Jan 27 (mAJs). Attacks AJ's character and opposes 1820 Choctaw treaty.
Jan 29	From Hugh Lawson White (to AJ and James Jackson). LS, TNJ (8-0095). Reports on his effort to secure a certificate stating the amount paid for Duck River lands.
Jan 29	From Thomas Hill Williams. ALS, DLC (29). Discusses Samuel R. Overton's appointment as register of ceded Choctaw land.
Jan 30	From Samuel Ragland Overton. ALS, DLC (29). Discusses his health and the executions of Alexander Arbuthnot and Robert C. Ambrister.
[Jan– Feb?]	From James Barton Longacre. Copy, DSI (mAJs). Discusses likeness of Jackson he has just completed for the Association of American Artists of Philadelphia.
Feb 3	From Mathew Arbuckle. ALS, DLC (29). Requests recommendation if army is reduced.
Feb 5	From John Nicks (enclosure: Nicks to AJ, [Feb 5]). ALS, DLC (29). Requests retention of rank if army is reduced.
Feb 5	Account with William McKnight for tuition for Andrew Jackson, Jr., Andrew Jackson Hutchings, and Lyncoya. ADS, DLC (29). Runs to November 7.
[Feb 5]	From John Nicks. ALS, DLC (59). Advises that he will accept lesser rank if necessary.
Feb 6	To John Coffee. ALS with ANS by Coffee to John Donelson (1787–1840), THi (8-0099). Discusses legal and financial matters and the ratification of the Adams-Onís Treaty.
Feb 7	From Edward Mitchell. ALS with ANS by AJ that account was returned to Mitchell, DLC (29). Transmits account (not found).
Feb 8	To Henry Atkinson (enclosure: John C. Calhoun to AJ, Jan 21). LC, DLC (63). Orders court-martial of Talbot Chambers.
Feb 8	To Daniel Bissell. LC, DLC (63). Orders completion of survey for fort on the Sabine River and court-martial of Robert L. Coomb.
Feb 8	To John Caldwell Calhoun. LS and Copy, DNA-RG 107 (M221-89); LC, DLC (63). Reports on status of courts-martial of Talbot Chambers and Robert L. Coomb; discusses southern defenses.
Feb 8	From John Thompson (enclosures: Depositions of Benjamin Merrel and John Roark, Jan 27, and of John Snow, [Jan 27]; Return J. Meigs, 1740–1823, to Thompson, Jan 28). ALS, DNA-RG 75 (M208-9). Requests assistance re his claim for reimbursement for the care of John Burke and inquires about fee simple title to his land.
Feb 9	Resolution of the Mississippi legislature thanking AJ and Thomas Hinds for negotiation of the Choctaw treaty. Copy, DLC (29).
Feb 10	From Samuel Ragland Overton. ALS with AJ endorsement, DLC (29). Asks continued support for his appointment as register of ceded Choctaw lands; reports that Winfield Scott regrets his former disagreement with AJ; discusses government deficit and William H. Crawford's political future.
Feb 10	Account with Martha Adams for clothing and sundries. ADS with AJ endorsement, DLC (30). Runs to April 14.

Feb 11 To James Craine Bronaugh. ALS, DLC (29). Bassett, 3:39. States that he has declined appointment as governor of Florida; urges Bronaugh to consider slave speculation in Florida.

Feb 11 *To James Monroe.* 10

Feb 12 To William Lee. LC, DLC (63). Replies further to inquiry re Seminole campaign arms by sending report (not found) re arms stored at Columbia, Tennessee.

Feb 13 To Richard Keith Call. Printed, *The Collector* 19(Nov 1905):1–2 (8-0110). Discusses trip to Alabama and the army reduction bill; announces his acceptance of appointment as governor of Florida.

Feb 14 Account with Benjamin Decker for carpentry work at the Hermitage. DS with AJ endorsement, DLC (29).

Feb 15 To William Flood, to John Randolph Grymes, to William Kenner, to David Corbin Ker, to Benjamin Morgan, to Jacques Philippe Villeré, to Edward Livingston. LSs, DLC (8-0113 to -0129), NjP (mAJs). Introduces Andrew J. Donelson, who travels to New Orleans to study French.

Feb 15 From Mathew Arbuckle. ALS, DLC (29). Relates that John M. Davis will likely file an unfavorable report on the troops at Fort Scott.

Feb 15 From David Emanuel Twiggs. ALS, DLC (29). States that he expects an unfavorable report from the colonel of his regiment and asks to remain in the army.

Feb 16 To Pierre Robin Lacoste, to Jean Baptiste Plauché, to Richard Whartenby. LSs, DLC (8-0131 to -0134); ALS, PBL (8-0138). Introduces Andrew J. Donelson.

Feb 16 From Robert Butler. ALS, DLC (29). Seeks command of a regiment rather than adjutant generalcy in Washington.

Feb 16 From John Haywood. ALS, DNA-RG 59 (M439-8). Wishes to accompany AJ to Florida.

Feb 16 From Joseph Woodruff. ALS, DLC (29). Seeks appointment in East Florida.

Feb 17 From James Craine Bronaugh. ALS, DNA-RG 59 (M439-8). Recommends John Haywood for judge in Florida.

Feb 18 To John Caldwell Calhoun. Typed copy, LU (8-0140). Recommends Robert Butler for command of a regiment.

Feb 18 To Andrew Jackson Donelson. LC, DLC (63). Orders him to obtain a report from Daniel Bissell on the Sabine River fort, to inspect the Rigolets, and to await AJ's arrival in New Orleans.

Feb 18 *From Isaac Lewis Baker.* 11

[Feb 18] Account of James Jackson Hanna with M[ourning] E. Parrish for recapture of the slave, Tom. AD signed by Parrish with AJ endorsement, DLC (58).

[Feb 18] Notice of fees paid by [Mourning E.] Parrish for advertising the capture of Tom in the *Richmond Enquirer* and the Washington *National Intelligencer*. AD, DLC (58).

Feb 19 From William Lee. ALS, DLC (29). Discusses an overpayment to AJ of $691.73.

Feb 19 From Seth Lewis. ALS, DLC (29). Renews correspondence and discusses his conversion to Christianity.

Feb 19	From John Overton. ALS, DNA-RG 59 (M439-8). Recommends John Haywood for judge in Florida.	
Feb 20	To Captain Fennon [Robert Fenner or Alexander C. W. Fanning?]. Printed, TNJ (8-0142). Introduces Andrew J. Donelson.	
Feb 20	From Samuel Kennedy. ALS, DLC (29). Thanks him, on behalf of the Association of American Artists, for sitting for portrait in Philadelphia in 1819 and sends proof impressions from the plate.	
Feb 22	To James Monroe. ALS, DNA-RG 59 (M439-8). Recommends Stockley D. Hays as associate judge in Florida.	
Feb 22	From Daniel Bissell (enclosures: Richard Whartenby to Robert L. Coomb, July 1, 1820; Perrin Willis to Whartenby, Aug 15, 1820; Willis to Commanding Officer at Sulphur Fork, Sept 22, 1820). LS, DLC (29). Reports the arrest of Robert L. Coomb.	
Feb 24	From John M. Davis. ALS, DLC (29). Requests court-martial of Mathew Arbuckle.	
Feb 24	From John Hull (enclosures: Hull to George M. Brooke, [cDec 1820] and n.d.; Brooke to Hull, Dec 5, 1820). ALS, DLC (29). Reports on his relations with Thomas T. Williamson since being reinstated in the army.	
Feb 26	To Hugh Young. ALS, DLC (8-0144). Orders $100 payment to Andrew J. Donelson for a horse purchased from James C. Bronaugh.	
Feb 26	From George Gibson. ALS, DLC (29). Announces his refusal of the Choctaw agency.	
Feb 26	Richard Keith Call to Return Jonathan Meigs, 1740–1823 (enclosures: John Thompson to AJ, Feb 8; Depositions of Benjamin Merrel, John Roark, and John Snow, Jan 27; Meigs to Thompson, Jan 28). ALS, DNA-RG 75 (M208-9). Transmits documents.	
Feb 26	Receipt from Thomas Weston for $5 for labor at the Hermitage. DS in AJ's hand, DLC (29).	
Feb 27	From Daniel Bissell (enclosure: William Lindsay to Bissell, Feb 8, DLC-29). LS, DLC (29); LC, DNA-RG 98 (8-0145). Transmits application for furlough.	
Feb 27	From Stockley Donelson Hutchings. ALS, DLC (29). Reports he has been jailed for an assault on John McKinley.	
Feb 27	From Thomas McCorry. ALS with AJ endorsement, DLC (29). Inquires if AJ still wants papers from the Knox County land registry.	
Feb 28	To Andrew Jackson Donelson. ALS, DLC (8-0146). Reports news from Washington.	
Feb 28	From Richard Ivy Easter. ALS and Copy, DNA-RG 107 (M221-89). States that he is unable to secure his defaulted accounts and resigns from the army.	
[cFeb]	To Richard Keith Call. ALS, DLC (75). Orders him to render postmaster accounts.	
[cFeb]	To Ralph Eleazar Whitesides Earl. Extract, Stan. V. Henkel Catalog 1347 (1924):22 (8-0097). Discusses a slave who may have been stolen by marauding Indians.	
March 1	*To John Caldwell Calhoun.*	13
March 1	*To John Coffee.*	14

March 1	From Frederick Baldwin. ALS, DLC (29). Discusses Cherokee reserves and asks AJ to send military force to remove intruders.	
March 1	From James Jackson Hanna. ALS, DLC (29). Bassett, 3:41–42. Discusses the recapture and proposed sale of Ned, a runaway slave.	
March 1	*From James Jackson.*	16
[cMarch 1]	Account with James Jackson Hanna for business trip to Virginia. AD with AN by AJ, DLC (60). Bassett, 3:41.	
[March 2]	From Edward Jones (enclosure: Account for medical expenses, Nov 24, 1820). ALS with ANS by AJ sending $15, "all I will ever pay," DLC (29). Transmits account.	
March 3	From John Caldwell Calhoun. LS, NjP (8-0153); LC, DNA-RG 107 (M6-11). States that Alexander H. Henderson's youth disqualifies him for appointment to West Point.	
March 3	From Andrew Jackson Donelson. ALS, DLC (29). Reports his arrival in New Orleans; discusses southern defenses and Abner L. Duncan's family.	
March 3	From Thomas Duncan. ALS, DLC (29). Requests that his son, John, be retained in the army.	
March 3	From John Henry Eaton. ALS, DLC (29). Discusses army reduction, national debt, and the Florida governorship.	
March 4	From Caroline S. Butler Bell. ALS, DLC (29). Reports Anthony W. Butler's suspension from Yale and discusses health and family.	
March 4	From Charles Cassedy. ALS, DLC (29). Asks help in acquiring journal of John Donelson (c1718–86) for a history of Tennessee; discusses John Haywood's ability for such a work.	
March 4	From Return Jonathan Meigs (1740–1823). ALS, DLC (29). Acknowledges letter and documents re John Thompson's claim; denounces army reductions.	
March 6	To Thomas McCorry. Photocopy of ALS, William L. Barry (8-0155). Renews request for papers from Knox County register's office.	
March 6	To James Monroe. LS, NN (8-0157). Recommends John W. Overton for associate judge of Florida.	
March 7	From John Caldwell Calhoun. ALS with AJ endorsement, DLC (29). *Calhoun Papers,* 5:662–64. Discusses the political motives for the army reduction.	
March 7	From Andrew Erwin. LS, T (10-0248). Announces that on March 17 he will depose Jenkin Whiteside re *Jackson* v. *Erwin.*	
March 7	From James Hamilton, Jr. LS, THer (8-0174). On behalf of the Charleston City Council, welcomes AJ's proposed visit.	
March 7	From Andrew C. Hays. ALS, DLC (29). Requests Florida appointment.	
March 7	Answer as guardian of William Ferdinand Claiborne in case of *Mary Ann Lewis* v. *William Ferdinand Claiborne, Mary Claiborne, and Micajah Claiborne.* DS and Copy, T (8-0172, -0160).	
March 8	From Thomas Bennett. ALS with AJ endorsement and ALS duplicate, DLC (30). Welcomes AJ's proposed visit to South Carolina.	
March 8	From Charles Coffin. ALS, DLC (30). Acknowledges AJ's inability to donate to Greeneville College; discusses religious matters and	

invites Andrew Jackson, Jr., to attend the school.

March 9 From John Henry Eaton. ALS, DLC (72). Approves AJ's acceptance of the Florida governorship and discusses Robert Butler's army rank.

March 10 To Andrew Jackson Donelson. ALS, DLC (8-0176). Discusses news from Washington, family, and friends.

March 10 Richard Keith Call to Daniel Bissell. LC, DLC (63). Reports AJ's approval for a guard at Sulphur Fork; orders investigation of charges against Robert L. Coomb.

March 10 Commission to take possession of and occupy the Floridas. DS and LC, DLC (30, 63); LC and Copy, DNA-RG 59 (8-0180, -0196); Copy, DNA-RG 46 (8-0179). *ASP, Foreign Relations,* 4:751.

March 10 Commission as governor of Florida, with the powers of captain general and intendant of Cuba. DS and LC, DLC (30, 63); DS, MHi (8-0185); LC and Copy, DNA-RG 59 (8-0181, -0197); Copy, DNA-RG 46 (8-0183). *ASP, Foreign Relations,* 4:751–52.

March 11 From Malachi Nicholson. ALS with ANS by William W. Crawford, DLC (30). Reports on payments made by James Jackson and on activities at the Alabama farm.

March 11 From Samuel Ragland Overton. ALS, DLC (30). Congratulates AJ on appointment as governor of Florida, reports on his health, and discusses news from Europe.

March 11 From Smith Thompson. ALS, DLC (30). Recommends his son, Gilbert L., for Florida appointment.

March 11 From James Winchester. ALS, DLC (30). Recommends Charles Cassedy for Florida appointment.

March 12 From John Quincy Adams (enclosures: Commissions to take possession of the Floridas and as governor, March 10; Adams to James G. Forbes, March 10, DLC-30; Royal order and translation from Ferdinand VII to governor of Cuba, Oct 24, 1820, DLC-29; Form for announcing possession of the Floridas, n.d., DLC-30; Copy of Adams-Onís Treaty, DLC-63; Act of March 3, 1821, putting the treaty into effect, DLC-63). LS and LC, DLC (30, 63); LCs, DNA-RG 59 (8-0188, -0211); Copy with AN by Adams, DNA-RG 107 (M221-88); Copy, DNA-RG 46 (8-0216); Copy fragment, PU (8-0225); Extract in James Monroe's hand, DLC (8-0227). Bassett, 3:42–44. Sends documents and reports that James G. Forbes has been delegated to receive archives at Havana; instructs AJ to appoint Edmund P. Gaines to receive East Florida at St. Augustine; announces that pay will be $5,000 per annum.

March 13 From Washington Jackson (enclosures: William Jones to Jonathan Roberts, Feb 27; Roberts et al. to James Monroe, March 2; Statement of Horace Binney, March 10). ALS, DLC (30). Recommends his brother-in-law, George F. A. Dawson, for Florida appointment.

March 14 To William Lee. LC, DLC (63). Protests stoppage of payment of $691.73 and requests that the secretary of war decide the issue.

March 14 From Daniel Bissell (enclosures: Bissell to Samuel L. Isett, Feb 18; William M. Rivers to Isett, March 3; Deposition of William R. Jouett, March 3; Depositions of George Gray, John Tucker, and

	David S. Barnum, March 5; J[oseph] P. Harrison to Isett, March 7; Isett to Bissell, March 12). ALS, DNA-RG 107 (M221-89). Discusses charges against Robert L. Coomb and requests further orders.	
March 14	From John Clark. ALS, DLC (30). Recommends Joseph Hutchinson for Florida appointment.	
March 14	Account with United States as Choctaw commissioner. AD, DLC (30).	
March 15	From Daniel D. Tompkins. LS, DLC (30). Recommends Gilbert L. Thompson, his son-in-law, for Florida appointment.	
March 16	From William Lee. LC, DNA-RG 217 (8-0230). Requests that AJ pay William Eastin and William E. Butler for forage furnished during the 1820 negotiations out of the Choctaw treaty appropriation.	
March 17	*To John Caldwell Calhoun.*	18
March 18	From James Jackson. ALS, DLC (30). Explains delay in reaching Nashville.	
March 18	*From James Winchester.*	21
March 19	From John Caldwell Calhoun. ALS with AJ endorsement, DLC (30); LC, DNA-RG 107 (M6-11). *Calhoun Papers,* 5:687–88. Accepts Richard I. Easter's resignation.	
March 19	From William Darby. ALS with AJ endorsement noting absence of the enclosure, DLC (30). Sends a copy of *Memoir on the Geography and Natural and Civil History of Florida* (Philadelphia, 1821) and solicits AJ's patronage for a newspaper in Florida.	
March 20	From John Quincy Adams (enclosure: Commission to exercise special powers of removal, March 20). LS and LC, DLC (72, 63); LC, DNA-RG 59 (8-0246); Copy, DNA-RG 46 (8-0250). *ASP, Foreign Relations,* 4:753. Sends document.	
March 20	From Andrew Erwin. ALS, T (10-0252). Announces he will depose Jenkin Whiteside on March 21.	
March 20	Commission to exercise special powers of removal. DS and LC, DLC (30, 63); LC and Copy, DNA-RG 59 (8-0246, -0251); Copy, DNA-RG 46 (8-0252). *ASP, Foreign Relations,* 4:752.	
March 20	Receipt from Alexander Somerville & Co. for $49 for lace and tools. ADS with AJ endorsement, DLC (30).	
March 21	To John Caldwell Calhoun. Abstract, DNA-RG 107 (8-0266). Encloses account of Dr. Hess (not found).	
March 21	Receipt from John Donelson (1755–1830) for $90 for a bay horse. DS in AJ's hand, DLC (30).	
March 22	From John Caldwell Calhoun (enclosures: Thomas S. Jesup to George Bender, March 21; Jesup to Henry Stanton, March 21; George Gibson to John Rogers, March 21, all DLC-30). LS and LC, DLC (30, 63); LC, DNA-RG 107 (M6-11); Copy, DNA-RG 59 (M116-5). *TPUS,* 22:19–21. Orders AJ to proceed to Pensacola via Montpelier, Alabama, and instructs him on taking possession of Florida.	
March 23	*From John Quincy Adams.*	22
March 23	From Edward Ward. ALS, DLC (30). Sends barrel of whiskey.	
March 24	From John Caldwell Calhoun (enclosures: Calhoun to AJ, March	

19 and 22). LC, DNA-RG 107 (M6-11). Sends to Montpelier copies of letters addressed to AJ at Nashville.

March 25 — From Horatio J. Cox. ALS, DLC (30). Inquires about establishing a printing press in Florida.

March 27 — To Daniel Bissell. LC, DLC (63); Copy (dated March 26), DNA-RG 107 (M221-89). Orders Robert L. Coomb released and returned to duty.

March 27 — To John Caldwell Calhoun (enclosures: Daniel Bissell to AJ, March 14; Bissell to Samuel L. Isett, Feb 18; William M. Rivers to Isett, March 3; Deposition of William R. Jouett, March 3; Depositions of George Gray, John Tucker, and David S. Barnum, March 5; J[oseph] P. Harrison to Isett, March 7; Isett to Bissell, March 12, all DNA-RG 107, M221-89). LS, DNA-RG 107 (M221-89); LC, DLC (63). Transmits documents re Robert L. Coomb.

March 27 — From Alexander Outlaw Anderson. ALS, DLC (30). Requests Florida appointment.

March 27 — From Daniel Bissell (enclosures: Bissell to Perrin Willis, Jan 13; Willis to Bissell, Feb 28). LS, DNA-RG 77 (8-0267). Sends correspondence re site for a Sabine River fort.

March 27 — Articles of agreement with Jesse Holt for cedar posts, rails, and logs. DS, DLC (30).

March 29 — Account with James Stewart & Co. for nails, chains, saws, and sundries. ADS, DLC (31). Runs to December 6, 1822.

March 30 — From Henry Atkinson. LS, DNA-RG 94 (M566-138). Orders court-martial of Talbot Chambers.

March 30 — From W[illiam] Brown. ALS, DLC (30). Seeks appointment as sheriff at Pensacola.

March 31 — *To Andrew Jackson Donelson.* 24

March 31 — To Pleasant Moorman Miller. ALS, Thomas F. Stephens (8-0278). *Gulf States Historical Magazine,* 1(1902):46. Discusses Florida governorship and invites Miller to accompany him to Pensacola.

March 31 — From John Caldwell Calhoun (enclosure: Calhoun to Jean A. Pénières, March 31, DLC-30). LS and Copy, DLC (30); LC, DNA-RG 75 (M15-5); Copy, DNA-RG 59 (M116-5). Reports the appointment of Pénières as Indian sub-agent in Florida and urges AJ to seek a formal peace with the Seminoles.

March 31 — From Richard Mentor Johnson. ALS, DLC (30). Introduces Silas M. Noel.

March 31 — From Richard Mentor Johnson. ALS, DLC (30). Introduces Jacob Creath, who accompanies Silas M. Noel.

March 31 — Account of Rachel Jackson with Joseph Litton for shoes, gloves, and combs. DS signed by James Henderson with AJ endorsement, DLC (30).

[cMarch–July] — From Abner Lawson Duncan et al. LS, DLC (31). Recommend Luther Lincoln as pilot, Port of Pensacola.

[cMarch–July] — From Edward Livingston. ALS, DLC (31). Recommends Roger [Selden?] Hearn for Florida appointment.

April 2 — *To John Quincy Adams.* 25

April 2 — To Edmund Pendleton Gaines (enclosure: Commission, April 2). LC, DLC (63). Appoints him to receive East Florida.

April 2 — From Hugh Wallace Wormeley. ALS, DLC (30). Seeks a Florida appointment.

April 2 — Commission appointing Edmund Pendleton Gaines to receive East Florida. LC, DLC (63).

April 3 — From Jacob Creath. ALS with AJ endorsement, DLC (30). Seeks information about settling in Florida.

April 3 — From Silas M. Noel (enclosure: Richard M. Johnson to AJ, March 31). ALS with AJ endorsement, DLC (30). Seeks a Florida appointment.

April 3 — From Jenkin Whiteside. ALS with AJ endorsement and ANS by Stockley D. Hays, DLC (70). Sends form for the transfer of a military land warrant in the name of David Allison to Samuel Wilson.

April 3 — Account with Ingram & Lloyd for record books, paper, and quills. DS, DLC (30). Runs to April 14.

April 4 — From Samuel Brown. ALS, DNA-RG 59 (M439-15). Introduces David Shannon.

April 4 — From William Lee (enclosure: Account for AJ and servants, Oct 1, 1815–April 30, 1816, DLC-19). LS, DLC (30); LC, DNA-RG 217 (8-0286). Explains disallowance of pay.

April 5 — From Malachi Nicholson. ALS, DLC (29). Discusses his account as overseer on Andrew J. Hutchings's plantation.

April 5 — Statement of account with United States for 1820 Choctaw negotiations. ADS, DLC (70).

[April 6] — Power of attorney to Patrick Henry Darby to act in *Jackson* v. *Erwin*. Printed, *Nashville Whig*, April 18 (8-0356).

April 7 — Account of Sally Adams with Harrison Saunders for cloth for Rachel Jackson. ADS, DLC (30).

April 8 — From John Caldwell Calhoun. ALS with AJ endorsement, DLC (30). Bassett, 3:46–47. Expresses pleasure that AJ has accepted the Florida governorship; discusses James Gadsden, Robert Butler, and army reduction.

April 8 — From Richard Ivy Easter. ALS with AJ endorsement, DLC (30). Discusses *Jackson* v. *Erwin* and the disposition of Easter's military accounts.

April 8 — Assignment of land warrant to Samuel Wilson. ADS with ANS by Stockley D. Hays reassigning warrant to AJ, Feb 6, 1823, DLC (32).

April 9 — To John Clark. Extract, Anderson Galleries Catalog 1202 (1916), Item 300 (8-0288). Discusses his trip to Florida and his governorship.

April 9 — From Nathan Reid, Jr. ALS, DLC (30). Inquires about Florida appointment.

April 10 — To John Quincy Adams. LS and LC, DNA-RG 59 (M116-5, 8-0289); LCs, DLC (63); Copy, DNA-RG 46 (8-0291). *ASP, Foreign Relations,* 4:755. Acknowledges instructions re fortifications in Florida.

April 10 — To John Caldwell Calhoun. LS and Copy, DNA-RG 107 (M221-89); LCs, DLC (63); Extract, DNA-RG 94 (M566-139). *TPUS,*

	22:31–32. Announces that he has directed Robert Butler to take possession of East Florida.	
April 10	To John Caldwell Calhoun (enclosure: Daniel Bissell to AJ, March 27). LS, DNA-RG 77 (8-0292); LC, DLC (63). Transmits documents re fortification on the Sabine River.	
April 10	To William Darby. LS, NbO (8-0300). States that he will report on the prospects for a printer in Florida once he has reached Pensacola.	
April 10	To Edmund Pendleton Gaines. LCs, DLC (63). Announces that he has ordered Robert Butler to St. Augustine.	
April 11	*To John Coffee.*	27
April 11	From [Peter Hagner]. LC, DNA-RG 217 (8-0306). Discusses debit of $336 to AJ resulting from the settlement of Milo Mason's account.	
April 11	From Samuel Van Dyke Stout & Co. ALS, DLC (30). Promises to have carriage ready by April 15.	
April 11	Account with United States, with debit from Milo Mason. ADS, DNA-RG 217 (5-1334, 8-0307).	
April 12	To John Quincy Adams. LS and LC, DNA-RG 59 (M116-5, 8-0314); LCs, DLC (63); Copy, DNA-RG 46 (8-0315). *ASP, Foreign Relations,* 4:756. Announces his departure for Montpelier, Alabama, and the dispatch of Richard K. Call to prepare troops assigned to Pensacola.	
April 12	To Robert Butler (enclosures: Provisional commission to receive East Florida, April 12; John Q. Adams to AJ, March 12 and 23; John C. Calhoun to AJ, March 22). LC, DLC (63). *TPUS,* 22:32–34. Appoints him provisionally to receive East Florida and gives instructions.	
April 12	To Richard Keith Call. LCs, DLC (63). Orders him to Montpelier, Alabama, to await AJ's arrival.	
April 12	From William Banks et al. ALS in Banks's hand, DLC (30). Recommend Henry Van Pelt for Florida post.	
April 12	From Thomas Bodley. ALS, DNA-RG 59 (M439-15). Introduces David Shannon and recommends him for Florida appointment.	
April 12	Provisional commission of Robert Butler to receive East Florida. LC, DLC (63). *TPUS,* 22:34–35.	
April 12	Account of Robert Butler as commissioner to receive East Florida. DS duplicate, DLC (70). Runs to August 26.	
April 13	To Edmund Pendleton Gaines. LCs, DLC (63). States that Robert Butler's commission is provisional and that Gaines should receive East Florida if possible.	
April 13	To Sylvanus Thayer. ALS, NHi (mAJs). Introduces Daniel S. Donelson, who enters West Point.	
April 13	From John Caldwell Calhoun. LS, DLC (30); LC, DNA-RG 107 (M6-11). Approves release of Robert L. Coomb.	
April 13	From Robert Wickliffe. ALS (dated 1820), DNA-RG 59 (M439-15). Introduces David Shannon.	
April 13	Agreement among AJ, Jenkin Whiteside, James Jackson, and Patrick Henry Darby for Darby to superintend and arrange their interests in the David Allison estate. ADS in Darby's hand, also signed by AJ, Whiteside, Jackson, and, as witnesses, James B.	

Houston and William B. Lewis, TNJ (8-0316); Copy in James Jackson's hand with ANS by James Jackson, DLC (30).

April 14 To John Caldwell Calhoun. LS and Copy, DNA-RG 107 (M221-89, M222-22); LC, DLC (63). Announces his imminent departure for Montpelier, Alabama; requests transfer of funds to William Eastin and closure of Choctaw treaty account.

April 14 To John Coffee. ALS, THi (8-0320). Discusses Jenkin Whiteside's advice re *Bennett Smith* v. *John Hutchings's Executors.*

April 14 To William Lee (enclosure: Samuel R. Overton draft on John C. Calhoun for $348, Jan 26). LC, DLC (63). Sends $348 for credit to his account and transmits combined receipt of William Eastin and William E. Butler (not found) for forage during Choctaw negotiations.

April 14 From John Jordan Crittenden. ALS, DNA-RG 59 (M439-15). Introduces David Shannon.

April 14 Memorandum of Choctaw treaty and private funds drawn on the branch of the Bank of the State of Tennessee at Nashville. ADS, DLC (30).

April 14 Receipt from George Hewlett for $8 for a bridle. ADS with AJ endorsement, DLC (5).

April 14 Receipt from Craven Jackson for $79.82½ for plastering at the Hermitage. ADS with AJ endorsement, DLC (30).

April 14 Account with Samuel Van Dyke Stout & Co. for carriage repairs. ADS with AJ endorsement, DLC (30). Bassett, 3:48.

April 14 Account current with United States for receiving the Floridas. Copy, DLC (70). Runs to June 13.

April 14 Account with United States as commissioner to receive the Floridas. DS, DNA-RG 217 (8-0323). Runs to August 24.

April 15 From William Taylor Barry. ALS, DNA-RG 59 (M439-15). Introduces David Shannon.

April 15 From Joseph Cabell Breckinridge. ALS, DNA-RG 59 (M439-15). Introduces David Shannon.

April 18 Receipt from Malachi Nicholson for $102, wages as overseer of Andrew J. Hutchings's Alabama farm for 1820. ADS by James Jackson, also signed by Nicholson, with ANS by AJ, A-Ar (8-0357).

April 19 Receipt from William Harvey for $238 for passage of AJ and party from Nashville to Washington, Mississippi. DS, DLC (30).

April 21 From Thomas F. Hunt. ALS, DLC (30). Introduces David Hall, applicant for Pensacola post.

April 22 From John H. Gibson. ALS, DLC (30). Seeks appointment.

April 22 Deed from the estate of William Donelson (1758–1820) for moiety in 640 acres along the Cumberland River in Davidson County. Copy, TNDa (8-0359).

April 22 Account with United States for the transfer of Florida. ADS by James C. Bronaugh, DLC (70). Runs to July 17.

[April 22–27?] Account with Jean Davis for expenses in New Orleans. AD, DLC (70).

April 23 From Martin Gordon et al. DS and Copy, DLC (30, 35). New Orleans *Louisiana Courier,* April 25. Welcome AJ to New Orleans and extol his services to the country.

April 23 — From Daniel Bissell. LS, DLC (30). Regrets that he was unable to greet AJ and requests furlough to attend to personal business in St. Louis.

April 23 — Receipt from Peabody & Chamberlain for $170 for passage on steamboat *Rapide.* ADS, DLC (70).

April 24 — To Albert Gallatin. LS, NHi (8-0367). Introduces Lewis Livingston.

April 24 — From Abner Lawson Duncan. LS, DLC (30). Recommends his nephew, James Nicholson.

April 24 — From James Nicholson. ALS, DLC (30). Seeks appointment.

April 24 — *To John Quincy Adams.* 29

[April 24] — To Martin Gordon et al. Printed, New Orleans *Louisiana Courier,* April 25 (mAJs). Acknowledges welcome.

April 25 — From Henry Stanton. ALS and Copy, DNA-RG 59 (M116-5, 8-0369); Copy, DNA-RG 46 (8-0371). Bassett, 3:50. Reports his failure to secure funds at the New Orleans branch of the Bank of the United States.

April 25 — Toast at public dinner in New Orleans: "The citizen-soldiers of Louisiana—their patriotic devotion to the cause of their country has obtained the applause of their fellow-citizens of that republic into which they have been gloriously incorporated by their valour." Printed, Natchez *Mississippi Republican,* May 8 (mAJs).

April 26 — From Beverly Chew. ALS and Copy, DNA-RG 59 (M116-5, 8-0372); Copy, DNA-RG 46 (8-0374). *ASP, Foreign Relations,* 4:756. States that he cannot advance funds without instructions from the secretary of the treasury.

April 26 — From William Lee (enclosure: Statement of account with United States for 1820 Choctaw negotiations, April 5). ALS, DLC (30); LC, DNA-RG 217 (8-0375). States that AJ's account shows a balance due of $6,011.83.

April 27 — *From Edmund Pendleton Gaines.* 31

April 27 — Rachel Jackson to Elizabeth Kingsley. Printed, Parton, 2:595–96 (8-0377). Discusses trip to and reception in New Orleans.

April [27] — To William Berkeley Lewis. ALS, DLC (30). Reports on arrival and reception in New Orleans.

April 29 — From Joseph Ficklin. ALS, DLC (30). Seeks appointment as Pensacola postmaster.

April 29 — Andrew Jackson Donelson to Chester Root. LC, DLC (63). States that Root's artillery company will occupy Pensacola.

April 29 — Account with John Austin for food and board. AD, DLC (70). Lexington *Kentucky Reporter,* Aug 13, 1828. Runs to May 7.

April 29 — Receipt from Hugh Munro for $270 for passage of AJ and party on sloop *Herald* to Blakely, Alabama. DS, DLC (30).

April 30 — *To José Maria Callava.* 33

April 30 — To José Maria Callava. LC, DLC (63); Copies, DNA-RG 59 (M116-6, 8-0381, -0383), DNA-RG 46 (8-0379), DNA-RG 84 (8-0380); Copies in Spanish by Callava, SpSAG (8-0384, -0385). *ASP, Foreign Relations,* 4:757. Introduces James C. Bronaugh and Henry M. Brackenridge.

April 30 — To Jabez Parkhurst. Copy, DNA-RG 94 (M566-143). Grants furlough.

[April 30] From Cyrus Sibley et al. Printed, Augusta *Chronicle and Georgia Gazette,* June 7 (mAJs). Welcome AJ to Blakely, Alabama.

April 30 To Cyrus Sibley et al. Printed, Augusta *Chronicle and Georgia Gazette,* June 7 (mAJs). Acknowledges welcome.

April 30 From Joseph Ficklin. ALS, DLC (30). States that an army officer wishes to sell Florida land to the United States.

May 1 To John Quincy Adams (enclosures: AJ to José M. Callava, April 30). LS and Copies, DNA-RG 59 (M179-51, 8-0405, M116-6); LC, DLC (63); Copies, DNA-RG 46 (8-0408), DNA-RG 84 (8-0410). Bassett, 3:52–53. Reports his arrival at Blakely, Alabama, and the rumors of slave importation into Florida.

May 1 *To John Coffee.* 34

May 1 From John Caldwell Calhoun (enclosure: William Wirt to Calhoun, April 30, DLC-30). LS, DLC (30); LC, DNA-RG 107 (M6-11); Extract, DNA-RG 59 (M116-5). *TPUS,* 22:40–41. Transmits attorney general's opinion denying AJ's account claim; recommends against immediate removal of the Creek Indians from Florida.

May 1 From William Lee. ALS with AJ endorsement summarizing May 26 reply (not found), DLC (30); LC, DNA-RG 217 (8-0415). Discusses settlement of Choctaw treaty account.

May 1 Andrew Jackson Donelson to Henry Stanton. LC, DLC (63). Orders rations for 500 men.

May 1 Account with John Austin for transportation of James Craine Bronaugh and Henry Marie Brackenridge to Pensacola. DS duplicate by Austin and Bronaugh, DLC (30). Runs to May 7.

May 1 Account with John Austin for use of horse from Blakely to Montpelier, Alabama. DS duplicate, DLC (30). Runs to May 7.

May 1 Account of Henry Marie Brackenridge as translator. DS duplicate, DLC (70). Runs to August 24.

[May 1] Toast at [Blakely, Alabama] public dinner: "The Town of Blakely—May her rising greatness equal the hospitality of her citizens." *Cahawba Press and Alabama State Intelligencer,* June 2 (mAJs).

[cMay 1] To William Brand. Abstract, *The Collector,* No. 390 (April–May 1922), p. 44 (mAJs). Describes a sea trip.

May 3 From Richard Ivy Easter. ALS, DLC (30). Discusses Easter's publications under pseudonym, "Fiat Justitia."

May 3 Richard Keith Call to William Lindsay. LC, DLC (63). Approves furlough.

May 4 From José Maria Callava. Copies (certified by Callava), SpSAG (8-0419, -0424); Translations and Extracts, DLC (63), DNA-RG 59 (M116-6, -5); Extracts, DNA-RG 46 (8-0418), DNA-RG 84 (8-0416). *ASP, Foreign Relations,* 4:760 (extract). States that he must receive instructions from Cuba before discussing Florida transfer.

May 5 To Edgar Hawkins. LC, DLC (63). Grants furlough.

May 7 To John Quincy Adams. LS and Copy, DNA-RG 59 (M116-5, 8-0428); LC, DLC (63). *TPUS,* 22:41–42. Reports that he has directed James Gadsden to sell $3,000 of government bills in New Orleans.

May 7 To John Quincy Adams (enclosures: José M. Callava to AJ, May 4; James C. Bronaugh and Henry M. Brackenridge to AJ, May 7). LS and Copies, DNA-RG 59 (M116-5, -6, 8-0433); LC, DLC (63);

Copies, DNA-RG 46 (8-0429), DNA-RG 84 (8-0431). Bassett, 3:53. Reports on the situation in Florida.

May 7 — To George Mercer Brooke. LC, DLC (63). Orders 4th Infantry to prepare for march to Pensacola.

May 7 — *From James Craine Bronaugh and Henry Marie Brackenridge.* 36

May 7 — From James Grant Forbes. ALS, LS copy, and Copies, DNA-RG 59 (M116-5, -6, 8-0492); LC, DLC (63); Copies, DNA-RG 46 (8-0460, -0461), DNA-RG 84 (8-0463). *ASP, Foreign Relations,* 4:744, 761. Discusses the causes for delay in arriving at Havana.

May 7 — Andrew Jackson Donelson to Henry Stanton. LC, DLC (63). Orders him to New Orleans to procure vessels and supplies for transporting Spanish troops from Pensacola to Havana.

May 8 — From Daniel Parker. LS, DLC (30); LC, DNA-RG 94 (8-0465). Reports the sailing of three artillery companies which await orders for receiving East Florida.

May 8 — Receipt from John Austin for $45 for transportation of baggage. DS duplicate by proxy (John Huff), DLC (70).

May 8 — Receipt from John Austin for $277.75 for food and board. DS duplicate, DLC (70).

May 10 — From Sutton F. Allen. ALS with AJ endorsement, DLC (30). Seeks Florida appointment.

May 10 — *From Richard Ivy Easter.* 39

May 10 — Division order praising the 4th Infantry Regiment. LC, DLC (63). Washington *National Intelligencer,* June 12.

May 11 — To Richard Keith Call (enclosures: AJ to José M. Callava, May 11). Copy, FHi (8-0466). Caroline Mays Brevard, *A History of Florida* (Deland, Fla., 1924), pp. 260–61. Orders him to Pensacola to negotiate the withdrawal of Spanish troops from Florida.

May 11 — To José Maria Callava. LC, DLC (63); Copies, DNA-RG 59 (M116-5, -6, 8-0538); Copy in Spanish (certified by Callava), SpSAG (8-0468). Introduces Richard K. Call.

May 11 — To José Maria Callava. LC, DLC (63); Copies, DNA-RG 59 (M116-5, -6, 8-0539); Copy in Spanish (certified by Callava), SpSAG (8-0469). Bassett, 3:54–55. Discusses arrangements for transportation of Spanish forces following the arrival of instructions from Cuba; inquires about making a deposit of supplies at Pensacola.

May 11 — *To John Coffee.* 41

[cMay 11] — Account of Richard Keith Call for travel expenses. ADS duplicate, DLC (70). Runs to August 24.

May 12 — To Edward Augustus Rutledge. LC, DLC (63). Appoints him translator.

May 12 — From Jacob Knapp. ALS, DLC (30). Seeks appointment.

May 12 — From John McGrigor (enclosure: Joseph D. Smith to AJ, May 14). ALS, DLC (30). Discusses efforts to secure Joseph D. Smith's affidavit re suit *Bennett Smith* v. *John Hutchings's Executors.*

May 12 — Andrew Jackson Donelson to Chester Root. LC, DLC (63). Orders troops deployed to Montpelier.

May 12 — Andrew Jackson Donelson to Chester Root. LC, DLC (63). Orders him to requisition ammunition.

May 12 Account of Edward Augustus Rutledge as translator. DS duplicate with ANS for payment, DLC (70). Runs to November 25, 1822.

May 13 Andrew Jackson Donelson to Chester Root. LC, DLC (63). Countermands order for ammunition.

May 13 Andrew Jackson Donelson to [Joseph] Swiler. LC, DLC (63). Orders him to receive men and baggage for Chester Root.

May 14 From Edward Livingston. ALS with AJ endorsement, DLC (30). Bassett, 3:56–57. Sends volumes for Henry M. Brackenridge on Spanish law and courts.

May 14 From Joseph Dickson Smith. ALS, DLC (30). Recollects a conversation with John Coffee re the debt involved in *Bennett Smith* v. *John Hutchings's Executors* and explains his failure to furnish an affidavit.

May 14 Account with Blue & Shomo for foodstuffs. ADS by Jonas C. Tanner, DLC (70). Lexington *Kentucky Reporter,* Aug 13, 1828. Runs to May 31.

May 15 To Henry Middleton Rutledge. ALS, NjP (8-0476). Expresses pleasure in having Rutledge's son, Edward A., with him and discusses conditions at Montpelier, Alabama.

May 15 From Henry Marie Brackenridge. ALS, DLC (30). Discusses the Adams-Onís Treaty and the United States' rights and claims.

May 15 Elizabeth Kingsley to Rachel Jackson. ALS, DLC (30). Thanks her for letter, praises her religious views, and comments upon the Jacksons' reception en route to Florida.

May 16 From José Maria Callava. LS by proxy in English, FU (mAJs); Copies, DLC (63), DNA-RG 46 (8-0481), DNA-RG 59 (M116-5, -6, 8-0494); Copy (Spanish), SpSAG (8-0479); Extract (English), FHi (mAJs). *ASP, Foreign Relations,* 4:761–62. Expresses his desire for the harmonious transfer of Florida.

May 16 From Nicholas Ware. ALS with AJ endorsement, DLC (30). Asks assistance in petitioning Congress re the claim of the heirs of Thomas Carr and John Donelson (c1718–86) for compensation for survey of lands at the "Bend of the Tennessee."

May 16 Account of William Brand with Abraham H. Inskeep & Co. for wine and foodstuffs. AD, DLC (30).

May 16 Account with Joseph Seignouret for furniture and housewares. AD and Translation with ms insertions by AJ, DLC (30).

May 17 From Robert Butler. ALS, DLC (30). Reports his progress to St. Mary's and discusses his position in the reduced army.

May 17 Andrew Jackson Donelson to Daniel Bissell. LC, DLC (63). On AJ's behalf, grants furlough until June 1 and suggests that Bissell report immediately to the war department.

May 17 Account of William Brand with R[omain] Pamar for glassware and china. AD with ms insertion by AJ, DLC (30).

May 18 To Stockley Donelson Hays. LC, DLC (63). Orders him to Nashville to arrange papers before leaving the army.

May 18 From Daniel D. Tompkins. ALS, DLC (30). Introduces James R. Hanham.

[cMay 18] From [Stockley Donelson Hays]. AL fragment, DLC (75). Reports on the court-martial of James H. Gale.

May 19 *To John Quincy Adams.* 43

May 19 To John Caldwell Calhoun. LC, DLC (63). Encloses recommendation by George M. Brooke for Joseph Shomo as sutler (not found), in which he concurs.

May 19 To David Bannister Morgan. LS, LNHiC (8-0487). Expresses hope that they will meet in Pensacola.

May 19 From John Caldwell Calhoun. ALS (dated 1820), DLC (29). *Calhoun Papers,* 6:130–31. Sends new army register; discusses army reduction, Robert Butler's assignment, and Calhoun's meeting in Washington with Daniel S. Donelson.

May 19 From David Holmes. ALS, DLC (30). Recommends John Garnier for a Florida post.

May 19 From Addin Lewis. ALS, DLC (30); LC, CtY (8-0485). Announces that, absent a collector at Pensacola, he will perform those duties ad interim.

May 20 From Robert Butler. ALS, DLC (30). Reports his arrival at Amelia Island and discusses arrangements for the transfer of East Florida.

May 21 To John Quincy Adams (enclosures: James G. Forbes to AJ, May 7; José M. Callava to AJ, May 16; Richard K. Call to AJ, May 21). LS and Copies, DNA-RG 59 (M116-5, -6, 8-0490); LC, DLC (63); Copy, DNA-RG 46 (8-0489). Bassett, 3:57. Reports arrival from Havana of Gilbert L. Thompson with news that James G. Forbes would leave there shortly; relates that James Gadsden was unable to sell U.S. government bills in New Orleans.

May 21 *To James Gadsden.* 44

May 21 From Richard Keith Call (enclosures: Call to José M. Callava, May 14, and Callava to Call, May 14, DLC-63; Callava to AJ, May 16). ALS and Copies, DNA-RG 59 (M116-5, -6, 8-0497); LC, DLC (63); Copy, DNA-RG 46 (8-0499). *ASP, Foreign Relations,* 4:761. Reports on his mission to Pensacola.

May 21 Commission of James Gadsden to receive Fort St. Marks. Copies, DLC (63), DNA-RG 59 (M116-5, -6, 8-0547).

May 21 Account of Henry Stanton for law books. ADS duplicate with ANS by George Walton, DLC (70). Runs to August 24.

May 22 *To John Caldwell Calhoun.* 46

May 22 To Alexander Campbell Wilder Fanning. LC, DLC (63); Copies, DNA-RG 59 (M116-5, -6, 8-0548). *TPUS,* 22:53. Orders him to Fort St. Marks and instructs him on the disposition of the Spanish cannon.

May 22 From John Quincy Adams (enclosure: List of presidential appointments, n.d., DLC-59). LS, DLC (30); LC and Copy, DNA-RG 59 (8-0502, mAJs); Copy, DNA-RG 46 (8-0505). *ASP, Foreign Relations,* 4:753–54. Announces Florida appointments.

May 23 From John Quincy Adams. LS, DLC (30); Copies, DNA-RG 59 (8-0507, -0510), DNA-RG 46 (8-0509). *ASP, Foreign Relations,* 4:754. Discusses appointments in Florida.

May 23 From James Monroe (enclosures: John Q. Adams to AJ, May 22 and 23). ALS with AJ endorsement, DLC (72); Copy, DLC (8-0513). *TPUS,* 22:53–57. Discusses Florida organization and appointments.

May 23 Account of William Brand with Beaty & Greeves for housewares. AD, DLC (30).
May 23 Account of William Brand with Anthony Rasch for silver. AD with ms insertions by AJ, DLC (30).
May 24 From James Gadsden. ALS, ICHi (8-0518). Reports on purchases in New Orleans and on Spanish troop provisions; details efforts to raise funds and to facilitate the transfer of Florida.
May 25 Account with William Brand for purchases made in New Orleans. DS, DLC (30). Runs to June 1.
May 25 Account of William Brand with William H. Crocker for grain. AD with AJ endorsement, DLC (30).
May 25 Account of William Brand with James N. Hyde for silver. ADS, DLC (30).
May 25 Account of William Brand with Skinner & Grant for hams and lard. AD, DLC (30).
May 26 To John Caldwell Calhoun. Copy, DNA-RG 107 (M221-89). *TPUS,* 22:58–59. Acknowledges Calhoun's view re the Creek Indians in Florida and asks for instructions if the Spanish fail to cede Florida on schedule.
May 26 To Peter Hagner. ALS, Joseph F. Rorke (8-0530). Protests the disallowance of his claim for fuel and quarters while at Washington in February 1819.
May 26 From Edward George Washington Butler (enclosure: Maximilian A. Doyle to Butler, May 2). ALS, DLC (30). Discusses engineering work at Beaufort, North Carolina, harbor; recommends Doyle as translator.
May 26 From James Ramage. ALS, DLC (30). Announces his appointment to convey Spanish officials and troops from St. Augustine to Havana.
May 26 Receipt from Alfred Hennen to Henry Stanton for $152 for law books. ADS, DLC (30).
May 28 To John Caldwell Calhoun. Abstract, DNA-RG 107 (M22-14). Sends memorandum re army wagon not paid for.
May 28 *From James Jackson.* 48
May 29 To John Quincy Adams. DS, DNA-RG 217 (8-0349). Sends $700 bill of exchange in favor of Gilbert L. Thompson.
May 30 To John Quincy Adams. LS and Copies, DNA-RG 59 (M116-5, -6, 8-0534); LC, DLC (63); Copy, DNA-RG 46 (8-0532). Bassett, 3:61–62. Reports no word from James G. Forbes and the rumor of Spanish delay of transfer until August; suggests that if delay continues, he will demand Florida's immediate transfer.
May 31 Division order praising the 4th Infantry. LC, DLC (63).
May 31 Account with Pierre Leroy for six barrels. ADS, DLC (70).
May 31 Endorsement of the firm of McCoy & Scallan. Printed, THi (8-1070).
May Account with Ephraim A. Blaine for food and sundries. DS, DNA-RG 217 (8-0402); DS duplicate, DLC (70). Lexington *Kentucky Reporter,* Aug 13, 1828. Runs to August 7.
[cMay] Account of William Brand with Louis Chesneau for forage. AD, DLC (70).
[cMay] Account of William Brand with John F. Miller for hams. AD, DLC (31).

[May–June] To James Gadsden. Extract, FHi (mAJs). Discusses delays in the transfer of Florida.

June 2 *To Robert Butler.* 51

June 2 From Thomas M. Bradford. ALS, DLC (30). Forwards dispatches from the president.

June 5 Account with Desiderio Lurria for rent of house in Pensacola. DS duplicate, DLC (70). Runs to October 8.

June 5 Cargo manifest for goods shipped by William Brand from New Orleans to Pensacola. Printed form with ms insertions by Brand, DLC (70).

June 7 From Robert Butler. ALS with AJ endorsement, DLC (30). Reports arrival of U.S.S. *Nonsuch* off St. Augustine, purportedly bringing the Spanish commissioner.

June 8 To John Quincy Adams. LS in James Gadsden's hand and Copy, DNA-RG 59 (M116-5, 8-0551); LC, DLC (63). Reports negotiation with Gilbert L. Thompson for a $700 bill of exchange, drawn on the government.

June 8 From Richard Ivy Easter. ALS, DLC (30). Reports on AJ's slaves and crops; regrets the president's Florida appointments; discusses his "Fiat Justitia" publication and Tennessee politics.

June 9 To John Quincy Adams. LS with postscript in AJ's hand and Copy, DNA-RG 59 (M116-5, 8-0553); LC lacking postscript, DLC (63); Copy, DNA-RG 46 (8-0552). *ASP, Foreign Relations,* 4:762 (extract). Reports that he has still received no communication from James G. Forbes.

June 9 *To James Craine Bronaugh.* 52

June 9 To George Poindexter. LS, NN (8-0557). Acknowledges resolution of the Mississippi legislature approving Choctaw treaty.

June 9 From James Grant Forbes (enclosure: Forbes to John Q. Adams, June 9, DNA-RG 59, M116-5). Copies, DNA-RG 59 (M116-5, -6, 8-0555). Announces his arrival at Pensacola.

June 10 To John Quincy Adams. LS and Copy, DNA-RG 59 (M116-5, 8-0561); Copy, DNA-RG 46 (8-0560). Bassett, 3:65. Reports arrival of the *Hornet* and announces his intention to move to Pensacola on the 14th.

June 10 *From José Maria Callava.* 53

June 11 To John Quincy Adams. LS and Copies, DNA-RG 59 (M116-5, -6, 8-0573); LC, DLC (63); Copy, DNA-RG 46 (8-0571). *ASP, Foreign Relations,* 4:763. Questions James G. Forbes's judgment while in Cuba and promises imminent transfer of Florida.

June 11 To Richard Keith Call (enclosure: AJ to James G. Forbes, June 11). ALS, FU (8-0577). *FHQ,* 34(1955):157–58. Discusses plans for Florida transfer.

June 11 To James Grant Forbes. LC, DLC (63); Copies, DNA-RG 59 (M116-5, -6, 8-0581). Inquires why José M. Callava was instructed to turn over West Florida to Forbes.

June 11 From James Grant Forbes. Copies, DNA-RG 59 (M116-5, -6, 8-0585). Explains the appearance of his name in the orders from the governor-general of Cuba and describes archives received in Havana.

June 12 — To Richard Keith Call (enclosure: AJ to José M. Callava, June 12). LC, DLC (63); Copies (one with AJ endorsement), DNA-RG 59 (M116-5, -6, 8-0588). Bassett, 3:69–70. Transmits letter and instructs Call re interpretations of the Adams-Onís Treaty.

June 12 — *To José Maria Callava.* 54

June 13 — To John Quincy Adams. LS and Copy, DNA-RG 59 (M116-5, 8-0600); LC, DLC (63); Copy, DNA-RG 46 (8-0599). *ASP, Foreign Relations,* 4:763. Acknowledges presidential appointments for Florida.

June 13 — *To Robert Butler.* 57

June 13 — To James Monroe. ALS, DLC (8-0601). *TPUS,* 22:70–71. Discusses James G. Forbes's arrival, his own imminent move to Pensacola, and arrangements for the transfer.

June 13 — Account with Lud Harris for forage. ADS duplicate, DLC (30).

[cJune 13] — Memorandum on taking extracts from John Q. Adams's letters of May 22 and 23. ANS, DLC (30).

June 14 — Account of George Brook Tunstall as express rider and printer. ADS duplicate, DLC (70). Runs to August 24.

June 15 — From James Grant Forbes. Copies, DNA-RG 59 (M116-6). Acknowledges AJ's letter of June 11; anticipates no problem with the transfer of East Florida.

June 15 — Account with James Earles for pork and butter. DS duplicate, DLC (70). Lexington *Kentucky Reporter,* Aug 13, 1828.

June 15 — Account with E. Thompson for poultry. DS duplicate, DLC (70). Lexington, *Kentucky Reporter,* Aug 13, 1828.

June 16 — To José Maria Callava. LC, DLC (63); Copies, DNA-RG 59 (M116-6, 8-0605). *TPUS,* 22:73–74. Announces his arrival near Pensacola and requests meeting.

June 16 — From Daniel Bissell. LS, DLC (30). Deplores his discharge from the army and requests endorsement of his military conduct.

June 16 — From José Maria Callava. Translations, DLC (63), DNA-RG 59 (M116-6, 8-0607). *TPUS,* 22:74–77. Denies that cannon in forts are included in the cession and reports his illness.

June 16 — Account with Manuel Gonzalez for forage. DS matched fragments, DLC (70, 75). Lexington *Kentucky Reporter,* Aug 13, 1828. Runs to July 11.

June 17 — To José Maria Callava. LC, DLC (63); Copies, DNA-RG 59 (M116-6, 8-0615). Bassett, 3:70–71. Argues that fortifications include cannon, which are part of the cession.

June 19 — To José Maria Callava. LC, DLC (63); Copies, DNA-RG 59 (M116-6, 8-0619). Reports that he has sent to Pensacola for provisions but that he will remain outside the city until he hears from Callava.

June 19 — From John Caldwell Calhoun (enclosures: Calhoun to AJ, March 31). LS, DLC (30); LC, DNA-RG 107 (M6-11). *TPUS,* 22:81. Transmits copy of letter.

June 19 — *From José Maria Callava.* 59

June 19 — From José Maria Callava. Translations, DLC (63), DNA-RG 59 (M116-6, 8-0624). Bassett, 3:71. Regrets disagreement over cannon and suggests following his recommendation re inventory of same.

June 20 — To Richard Keith Call. AL fragment, FU (8-0626). Requests that

Henry M. Brackenridge and Edward A. Rutledge deliver translations of José M. Callava's letters.

June 20 To José Maria Callava. LC, DLC (63); Copies, DNA-RG 59 (M116-6, 8-0627). Bassett, 3:72–74. Urges expeditious transfer of Florida; discusses provisions for the Spanish troops relocating to Havana; agrees to exchange credentials at transfer ceremony.

June 20 To Henry Stanton (enclosure: AJ to José M. Callava, June 20). Copy and LC, DLC (30, 63); Copies, DNA-RG 59 (M116-6, 8-0641). Orders preparation of boats and provisions for transporting Spanish troops to Havana.

June 20 From José Maria Callava (enclosure: Draft of articles of agreement for evacuation of West Florida, [June 20], DNA-RG 59, M116-6). Translations, DLC (63), DNA-RG 59 (M116-6, 8-0635). Transmits document.

June 20 From Henry Stanton (enclosures: John W. Oddie to Stanton, May 14; Proposal of Hamond & Ogden, May 15; Certificates of James Rinker, May 19, of Daniel T. Patterson, May 23, of Anthony R. Gale, William E. Sheffield, and Carlile Pollock, May 20; J[ohn P.] Cole to Stanton, n.d.; Gale and Sheffield to Stanton, May 21; Stanton to Gale and Sheffield, May 21). ALS and Copy, DNA-RG 59 (M116-6). Discusses arrangements for vessels transporting Spanish troops to Havana.

June 21 From James Grant Forbes. Copies, DNA-RG 59 (M116-6, 8-0643). *TPUS,* 22:83–84. Inquires about transportation to East Florida for Pedro de Alba, who carries instructions for the governor of East Florida.

June 21 From William Peacock. ALS with AJ endorsement, DLC (30). Transmits deposition of Joseph D. Smith (not found) and discusses *Bennett Smith* v. *John Hutchings's Executors.*

June 21 Rachel Jackson to Elizabeth Kingsley. Printed, Parton, 2:597–98 (8-0644). Reports impressions of West Florida.

June 22 From John Quincy Adams. LC, MHi (8-0646). Introduces William S. Smith, his nephew, who has been appointed naval agent at Pensacola.

June 22 *From José Maria Callava.* 60

June 22 From José Maria Callava. Copy (certified by Callava), SpSAG (8-0655); Translations, DLC (63), DNA-RG 59 (M116-6, 8-0652). *TPUS,* 22:84–85. Inquires about orders for the transfer of East Florida, which Pedro de Alba has not conveyed to St. Augustine.

June 23 To José Maria Callava (enclosures: Commission to take possession of and occupy the Floridas, March 10; Revised articles of agreement, [June 23]). LC, DLC (63); Copies, DNA-RG 59 (M116-6, 8-0661). Bassett, 3:76–78. Reiterates his views re inventories of cannon and transportation of Spanish families.

June 23 To Henry Stanton (enclosures: Revised articles, [June 23]). Copy and LC, DLC (30, 63); Copies, DNA-RG 59 (M116-6, 8-0667). Explains conditions for transportation of Spanish families and field artillery.

June 23 From Richard Keith Call. Copies, DNA-RG 59 (M116-6, 8-0658). Bassett, 3:78. Reports that transport ships have gone to St. Marks to bring Spanish troops to Pensacola.

[June 23] Revised articles of agreement between AJ and José Maria Callava for the transfer of the Floridas. Copies, DLC (59), DNA-RG 59 (M116-6). *TPUS,* 22:122–24 (dated July 17).

June 24 To Richard Keith Call (enclosures: AJ to James G. Forbes, June 24; AJ to José M. Callava, June 25). ALS, NNC (8-0671). Transmits letters and instructions re communications with Callava.

June 24 To James Grant Forbes. LC, DLC (63); Copies, DNA-RG 59 (M116-6, 8-0673). *TPUS,* 22:89–90. Orders report on the mission of Pedro de Alba.

June 24 From Arthur Peronneau Hayne. ALS, DLC (30). Announces his imminent departure for Philadelphia and requests AJ's views on establishing in Pensacola a branch of the Bank of the United States.

June 25 To José Maria Callava. LC, DLC (63); Copies, DNA-RG 59 (M116-6, 8-0675); Translation (certified by Callava), SpSAG (8-0678). *TPUS,* 22:90. States that he has requested James G. Forbes to report on mission of Pedro de Alba re transfer of East Florida.

June 25 To William Grafton Dulany Worthington (enclosures: Commission to exercise special powers of removal, March 20; John Q. Adams to AJ, May 22 and 23). LC, DLC (63); Extract, DNA-RG 59 (M116-10). *TPUS,* 22:91–92. Appoints him acting governor of East Florida.

June 25 From José Maria Callava. Translations, DLC (63), DNA-RG 59 (M116-6, 8-0680). Bassett, 3:78–81. Discusses the disposition of cannon.

June 25 From Richard Ivy Easter. ALS, DLC (30). Revises his assessment of Patrick H. Darby's character; discusses Tennessee gubernatorial election and events in Nashville.

June 25 From James Grant Forbes (enclosures: Nicholas Mahy y Romo to Forbes, May 16 and 26). Copies, DNA-RG 59 (M116-6, 8-0689). *TPUS,* 22:95–96. Reports that Pedro de Alba is not the commissioner for the transfer of East Florida.

June 26 *To Robert Butler.* 62

June 26 To José Maria Callava. LC, DLC (63); Copies, DNA-RG 59 (M116-6, 8-0691). Bassett, 3:81 (extract). Agrees on disposition of cannon and discusses Pedro de Alba's role.

June 26 To James Gadsden. LC, DLC (63). Appoints him courier to East Florida.

June 26 From José Maria Callava. Translations, DLC (63), DNA-RG 59 (M116-6, 8-0694). Revises prefatory statement for inventory of disputed artillery and promises response to revised articles of agreement.

June 26 From William D. Gaines. ALS with AJ endorsement, DLC (30). Requests opinion on practicality of a canal connecting the Mobile River and Pensacola Bay.

June 26 From Henry Stanton. Copy, DNA-RG 59 (M116-6). Reports on arrangements for transportation of Spaniards to Havana.

June 27 To John Coffee. ALS, THi (8-0703). Bassett, 3:82 (extract). Discusses delay in Florida transfer; reviews possible sale of his Evans Spring farm and comments upon family matters.

June 27 From John Quincy Adams (enclosure: Commission of James G. Forbes as marshal for Florida, May 18, *TPUS,* 22:45–46). LC and Copy, DNA-RG 59 (M40-17, 8-0701). Transmits commission.

June 27 From John Quincy Adams. LS, DLC (30); LC and Copy, DNA-RG 59 (M40-17, 8-0698); Copy, DNA-RG 46 (8-0696). *ASP, Foreign Relations,* 4:754. Acknowledges receipt of AJ's dispatches through May 30 and discusses delay in transfer of Florida.

June 27 From Alexander Campbell Wilder Fanning. ALS with AJ endorsement, DNA-RG 59 (M116-6). *TPUS,* 22:101–102. Announces transfer of St. Marks.

June 27 From William McClellan. ALS, DLC (30). Reports on trip to the Louisiana-Mexico frontier.

June 27 From Henry Stanton. ALS, DLC (30). States agreement on provisions for Spanish troops and announces impending inspection of field artillery at the Barrancas.

June 28 From José Maria Callava (enclosure: Draft of process verbal, n.d., DNA-RG 59, 8-0718). Translations, DLC (63), DNA-RG 59 (M116-6, 8-0715). Refuses to answer AJ's last letter until AJ accepts change in the inventory of disputed cannon.

June 28 From José Maria Callava. Copy, SpSAG (8-0713); Translations, DLC (63), DNA-RG 59 (M116-6, 8-0711). Suggests that Pedro de Alba accompany James Gadsden to East Florida.

June 28 From José Maria Callava. Translations, DNA-RG 59 (M116-6, 8-0710). Requests information from report of James G. Forbes re Pedro de Alba.

June 28 From José Maria Callava. Translations, DLC (63), DNA-RG 59 (M116-6, 8-0709). Acknowledges receipt of attested copy of AJ's credentials as commissioner.

June 28 James Gadsden to José Maria Callava. ALS, ICHi (8-0725). Announces his imminent departure for St. Augustine.

June 28 From José Maria Callava. Copy (certified by Callava), SpSAG (8-0708); Translations, DLC (63), DNA-RG 59 (M116-6, 8-0707). Requests response to his suggestion that Pedro de Alba accompany James Gadsden to East Florida.

June 29 To John Quincy Adams. LS and Copies, DNA-RG 59 (M116-5, -6, 8-0733); LC, DLC (63); Copy, DNA-RG 46 (8-0730). Bassett, 3:82–84. Reports on the transfer of Florida.

June 29 To John Quincy Adams. LS, DNA-RG 59 (8-0727); LCs, DLC (63), MHi (8-0729). States that he has drawn a bill of exchange for James Gadsden's use and corrects date of bill for Gilbert L. Thompson from June 1 to May 29.

June 29 *To José Maria Callava.* 64

June 29 To José Maria Callava. LC, DLC (63); Copies, DNA-RG 59 (M116-6, 8-0738); Translation, SpSAG (mAJs). Advises that James Gadsden will transmit Pedro de Alba's dispatches for the Spanish governor of East Florida.

June 29 From Richard Ivy Easter. ALS, DLC (30). Relates news from Nashville and congratulates AJ on pending transfer of Florida.

June 29 Rachel Jackson to David Cowan. Abstract, Thomas F. Madigan

	Catalog 55 (1929), Item 70 (8-0742). Agrees to intervene to secure an appointment.	
June 29	Bill of exchange for $4,720 in favor of James Gadsden. DS, DNA-RG 217 (8-0351).	
[June 29]	From José Maria Callava. Translations, DLC (63), DNA-RG 59 (M116-6, 8-0745). Accepts revised articles of agreement and describes proposed transfer ceremony.	
June 30	From José Maria Callava. Translations, DLC (63), DNA-RG 59 (M116-6, 8-0746). Bassett, 3:85. Requests that his name precede AJ's in the left margin in the process verbal.	
June 30	From José Maria Callava (enclosure: Callava to AJ, [June 29]). Translations, DLC (63), DNA-RG 59 (M116-6, 8-0743). Bassett, 3:84. Acknowledges communications and reports agreement on inventory of artillery and transfer procedures.	
June 30	From William Darby. ALS, DNA-RG 59 (M639-3). Introduces Marmaduke Burrough.	
[cJune]	From Daniel Todd Patterson et al. LS, DLC (31). Recommend David Wright as pilot, port of Pensacola.	
July 1	To José Maria Callava. LC, DLC (63); Copies, DNA-RG 59 (M116-6, 8-0748). Bassett, 3:85. Agrees to four copies of the process verbal, two in English, signed first by AJ, and two in Spanish, signed first by Callava.	
July 1	To José Maria Callava. LC, DLC (63); Copies, DNA-RG 59 (M116-6, 8-0750). Bassett, 3:85–86. Discusses transfer ceremony.	
July 1	From Henry Stanton. ALS, DLC (30). Reports imminent arrival of transport from New Orleans and James Gadsden's departure for St. Augustine.	
July 1	Bills of exchange for $520 in favor of James Gadsden. DSs, DNA-RG 217 (8-0340, -0347).	
July 1	Commission of William Grafton Dulany Worthington as acting governor of East Florida. LC, DLC (63). *TPUS,* 22:104–105.	
July 2	From Henry Stanton. ALS, DLC (30). Reports arrival of the transport *Lucy Ann.*	
July 3	*To James Craine Bronaugh.*	66
July 3	To José Maria Callava. LC, DLC (63); Copies, DNA-RG 59 (M116-6, 8-0753). Bassett, 3:86–87. Announces arrival of the *Lucy Ann* and advises Callava to ready Spanish personnel for imminent departure.	
July 3	To Andrew Jackson Donelson. ALS, DLC (8-0758). Bassett, 3:87 (extract). Discusses disciplinary problem with the slave Betty and arrangements for transfer of Florida.	
July 3	To John Donelson (1755–1830). ALS with ANS directing routing by postmaster in Nashville, THi (8-0761). Bassett, 3:87–88. Discusses family business and delays in the Florida transfer.	
July 3	From José Maria Callava. Translations, DLC (63), DNA-RG 59 (M116-6, 8-0756). Bassett, 3:88–89. Agrees to transfer ceremony and to a meeting to approve inventories of artillery and archives.	
July 3	From José Maria Callava. Translations, DLC (63), DNA-RG 59 (M116-6, 8-0755). Agrees to arrangements re process verbal.	

July 4 To John Coffee. ALS, THi (8-0767). Bassett, 3:89 (extract). Encloses statement of Joseph D. Smith (not found) re *Bennett Smith* v. *John Hutchings's Executors* and discusses delays in transfer of Florida.

July 4 From Henry Marie Brackenridge. ALS, DLC (30). Reports on inventory of the archives.

July 4 From John Caldwell Calhoun. ALS, DLC (30). *Calhoun Papers,* 6:239–41 (dated July 3). Discusses the transfer of Florida, James Gadsden's appointment as adjutant general, and the army reduction.

July 4 From José Maria Callava. Translations, DLC (63), DNA-RG 59 (M116-6, 8-0765). Discusses final arrangements for transportation of Spanish personnel to Havana and assures AJ of his desire for a speedy conclusion.

July 4 From Patrick Henry Darby. ALS, DLC (30). Reports on Allison lands and gubernatorial contest in Tennessee.

July 4 Spanish inventory of public documents in Pensacola archives. DS duplicate and Copy, DNA-RG 59 (M116-6, 8-0866).

July 5 *To José Maria Callava.* 67

July 5 From Samuel Meeker (enclosure: Claim against William D. Robinson, July 5). ALS and ALS duplicate, DLC (30). Transmits claim and asks AJ's help in securing payment.

July 5 From Henry Stanton. ALS, DLC (30). Reports that weather has delayed preparations for transportation of Spaniards to Havana.

July 6 To James Craine Bronaugh. ALS, DLC (30). Discusses account of Samuel R. Overton and orders payment of Daniel E. Burch from Choctaw treaty funds.

July 6 To Henry Stanton. Copies and LC, DLC (30, 63); Copies, DNA-RG 59 (M116-6, 8-0774). Bassett, 3:89–90. Instructs him on transportation of Spaniards to Havana; prohibits the transfer to Cuba of an unnamed American prisoner.

July 6 From John Quincy Adams. LS, DLC (30); Copies, DNA-RG 59 (M40-17, 8-0773). Reports that he has remitted $10,000 to the New Orleans branch of the Bank of the United States.

July 7 From Daniel E. Burch. AL, DLC (30). Acknowledges payment and corrects account.

July 7 Account with United States re Florida transfer. DS, DLC (70). Runs to December 1.

July [7] From Henry Marie Brackenridge. ALS, DLC (30). Bassett, 3:90–91. Details inventory of provincial land records and archives at Pensacola; reports on José M. Callava's attitude.

July 8 *To Henry Marie Brackenridge.* 67

July 9 To José Maria Callava. LC, DLC (63); Copies, DNA-RG 59 (M116-6, 8-0780). Announces arrival of Spanish garrison from St. Marks and requests Callava to set the date and hour for the transfer.

July 9 From James Craine Bronaugh. ALS, DLC (30). Transmits Daniel E. Burch's receipt (not found).

July 9 Account with Joseph Shomo for sundries. DS, DLC (70). Runs to October 4.

July 10 To George Mercer Brooke. LC, DLC (63); Copies, DNA-RG 59 (M116-6, 8-0782), T (8-0786). *TPUS,* 22:108–109. Orders preparation to occupy Pensacola.

July 10 To Alexander Campbell Wilder Fanning. LC, DLC (63). *TPUS,* 22:109. Praises him for prompt receipt of St. Marks and orders transfer of American troops from Fort Gadsden to St. Marks.

July 10 To Henry Stanton (enclosure: AJ to Alexander C. W. Fanning, July 10). LC, DLC (63). Orders transport of American garrison from Fort Gadsden to St. Marks.

July 10 From José Maria Callava. Translations, DLC (63), DNA-RG 59 (M116-6, 8-0789). Bassett, 3:91–92. States that he will reply on July 11 with the date for Florida transfer.

July 10 From Daniel Parker. ALS, DLC (30). Asks AJ, as surety for an 1819 note from Robert and [William E.] Butler, to urge them to pay the $5,000, now overdue a year.

July 10 Proclamation of the receipt of East Florida, countersigned by Robert Butler. Printed, *Niles' Register,* Aug 4 (mAJs).

July 11 To James Craine Bronaugh. LS, DLC (30). Discusses account with Daniel E. Burch and comments upon weather.

July 11 From José Maria Callava. Translations, DLC (63), DNA-RG 59 (M116-6, 8-0791). Bassett, 3:92. Suggests July 16 or 17 as the date of transfer and promises a final determination on July 14.

July 12 *To José Maria Callava.* 68

July 12 From James R. Hanham. ALS with AJ endorsement, DLC (30). Applies for appointment to the Pensacola police.

July 12 Invoice of provisions for transport of Spanish personnel to Havana. Copy, DNA-RG 59 (M116-6).

July 12 Receipt of Robert Butler for $520. ADS, DLC (70).

July 13 From José Maria Callava. Translations, DLC (63), DNA-RG 59 (M116-6, 8-0805). Reports delay of artillery inventory.

July 13 From José Maria Callava. Translations, DLC (63), DNA-RG 59 (M116-6, 8-0808). Bassett, 3:94–98. Blames delay in transfer on unprepared transports, misunderstanding between Henry Stanton and the Spanish artillery commander, and his own indisposition; sets transfer ceremony for July 17 at 10:00 a.m.

July 13 To José Maria Callava. LC, DLC (63); Copies, DNA-RG 59 (M116-6, 8-0799). Bassett, 3:98–99. Accepts explanation for delay and agrees to transfer date.

July 13 To José Maria Callava. LC, DLC (63); Copies, DNA-RG 59 (M116-6, 8-0802). Bassett, 3:99–100. Requests description of cannon listed in inventory.

July 13 From David Cowan. ALS with AJ endorsement "to be noted as soon as possession is taken of Pensacola," DLC (30). Seeks appointment, alluding to Rachel Jackson's patronage.

July 14 *To Benjamin Silliman.* 71

July 14 From José Maria Callava. Translations, DLC (63), DNA-RG 59 (M116-6, 8-0817). Discusses completion of artillery inventory.

July 14 From José Maria Callava. Translations, DLC (63), DNA-RG 59 (M116-6, 8-0818). Announces agreement on arrangements and confirms transfer on July 17.

July 15 To José Maria Callava. LC, DLC (63); Copies, DNA-RG 59 (M116-6, 8-0821). Acknowledges letters and expresses satisfaction that disagreements are resolved.

July 15 To José Maria Callava. LC, DLC (63); Copies, DNA-RG 59 (M116-6, 8-0823). States that troops will arrive in Pensacola early on July 17 and that those destined for the Barrancas will not remain for ceremony.

July 15 From José Maria Callava. Translations, DLC (63), DNA-RG 59 (M116-6, 8-0829). Details transfer ceremony.

July 15 *To José Maria Callava.* 72

July 15 *To James Craine Bronaugh.* 73

July 15 To William Lee. LC, DLC (63). Sends receipt of Daniel E. Burch (not found) and expresses hope that this will close AJ's Choctaw treaty account.

July 16 To John Quincy Adams (enclosure: Receipt of Henry Stanton, July 17). LS, DNA-RG 59 (M116-5); LC, DLC (63). *TPUS,* 22:119. Reports that he has drawn $4,620 in favor of Stanton for transportation of Spanish personnel to Cuba.

July 16 From José Maria Callava. Translations, DLC (63), DNA-RG 59 (M116-6, 8-0839). Bassett, 3:101–103. Discusses etiquette and sends Bartholomew Lafon's *Annuaire Louisianais pour L'Anne'e 1809* (New Orleans, 1808), detailing Louisiana transfer ceremony.

July 16 *To José Maria Callava.* 74

July 16 To George Campbell Read. LC, DLC (63); Copies, DNA-RG 59 (M116-6, 8-0846). Orders him to escort Spanish personnel to Havana.

July 16 From Jean Augustin Pénières. Copy with ANS by AJ and Copy, DNA-RG 107 (M221-93); Copy (dated July 19), DNA-RG 107 (M221-92); Extract (dated July 15), DNA-RG 233 (8-0832). *ASP, Indian Affairs,* 2:411–12 (extract). Reports on Indians in Florida.

July 16 Bills of exchange totaling $4,620 in favor of Henry Stanton. DSs, DNA-RG 217 (8-0333).

July 17 To John Quincy Adams. LS and Copies, DNA-RG 59 (M116-5, -6, 8-0849); LC, DLC (63); Copy, DNA-RG 46 (8-0848). Bassett, 3:104–105. Announces transfer of West Florida.

July 17 To Henry Marie Brackenridge. LCs, DLC (63). Appoints him alcalde of and notary for Pensacola.

July 17 To John Caldwell Calhoun. Copy, DNA-RG 107 (M221-93). *Calhoun Papers,* 6:262–63. Announces transfer of West Florida and expresses pleasure at James Gadsden's appointment as adjutant general.

July 17 From Jean Joseph Amable Humbert. LS, DLC (30). Requests endorsement for the publication of Humbert's memoirs.

July 17 Statement by José Maria Callava of the number of Spanish personnel to be transported to Havana. Copy, DLC (70).

July 17 Certification by José Maria Callava of rations for the transport of Spanish personnel to Havana. Copy, DNA-RG 59 (M116-6).

July 17 Process verbal for the transfer of West Florida. DS, Copies, Copies of draft, and Extract, DNA-RG 59 (M116-5, -6, 8-0718, -0860); Extract, DLC (63); Copies, DNA-RG 46 (8-0851), PU (8-0855). *ASP, Foreign Relations,* 4:764–65.

July 17 Proclamation announcing the transfer of West Florida. Printed, Washington *National Intelligencer,* Aug 16 (mAJs).

July 17 Receipt from Ephraim A. Blaine for $146.42 for forage. DS duplicate, DLC (70). Lexington *Kentucky Reporter,* Aug 13, 1828.

July 17 Receipt from Henry Stanton for bills of exchange for $4,620. DS duplicates, DLC (70), DNA-RG 59 (M116-5). *TPUS,* 22:120.

July 18 To John Quincy Adams (enclosure: Process verbal, July 17). AL in James C. Bronaugh's hand and Copy, DNA-RG 59 (M116-5, 8-0860); LC, DLC (63); Copies, DNA-RG 46 (8-0858), PU (8-0859). *ASP, Foreign Relations,* 4:764. Transmits document.

July 18 To John Coffee. ALS, THi (8-0870). Bassett, 3:105. Reports transfer of West Florida and comments on upcoming retirement from public life.

July 18 Ordinance establishing a mayor and council for Pensacola and providing for health and public order. LC, DLC (63); Copy and Broadside (English and Spanish), DNA-RG 59 (M116-6, -7); Copy, DNA-RG 233 (8-0873). *ASP, Miscellaneous Documents,* 2:904–905.

July 18 Ordinance establishing a mayor and council for St. Augustine and providing for health and public order. Printed (Spanish), St. Augustine *Florida Gazette,* Sept 8 (mAJs); Printed (English), *Ordinances, by Major-General Andrew Jackson, Governor of the Provinces of the Floridas . . . ,* St. Augustine, Fla., 1821 (mAJs).

July 18 Account of John V. D. Voorhees for rent of office. DS duplicate, DLC (70). Runs to October 7.

July 19 Commissions of Philo Andrews, John Dubose, Charles Robiou, and Daniel Copp as aldermen for St. Augustine. DSs, DNA-RG 59 (M179-51, M116-5), NPV (8-0876).

July 19 Commissions of Pensacola town officials: William Barnett, alderman and justice of the peace; George Bowie, mayor; James Craine Bronaugh, resident physician; James C. Craig, constable; and Stockley Donelson Hutchings and John Garnier, auctioneers. LCs, DLC (63).

July 19 List of commissions issued for Pensacola. LC with ANS by AJ, DLC (63). *TPUS,* 22:131–32. Runs to July 26.

July 19 Ordinance for the preservation of health in Pensacola. LC, DLC (63); Copy and Broadside (English and Spanish), DNA-RG 59 (M116-6, -7); Copy, DNA-RG 233 (8-0879). *ASP, Miscellaneous Documents,* 2:905.

July 19 Ordinance for the preservation of health in St. Augustine. Printed (English and Spanish), St. Augustine *Florida Gazette,* Sept 1 and 8 (mAJs).

July 19 Account of John Coppinger Connor for transcribing correspondence. ADS duplicate, DLC (70). Runs to September 27.

July 20 From Charles J. Jenkins. ALS, DLC (30). Announces his appointment as Pensacola revenue inspector.

July 20 From John Sommerville. ALS, DLC (30). States that he has transmitted to William Lee the duplicate receipt of William Eastin for $2,000 drawn on the Choctaw treaty account.

July 20 Commission of David Wright as pilot for Pensacola. LC, DLC (63).

July 20 Order establishing pilot rates at Pensacola. DS copy, DLC (63).

July 20 Account of Andrew Jackson Donelson for stationery and writing

	supplies. ADS with ANS by James C. Bronaugh, DLC (70). Runs to October 1.	
July 21	To John Coffee. LS in Richard K. Call's hand, THi (8-0882). Introduces James Scallan.	
July 21	Commission of John V. D. Voorhees as Pensacola health officer. LC, DLC (63).	
July 21	Ordinance for giving effect to the sixth article of the treaty with Spain. LC, DLC (63); Copy and Broadside (English and Spanish), DNA-RG 59 (M116-6, -7); Copy, DNA-RG 233 (8-0889). *ASP, Miscellaneous Documents,* 2:905–906.	
July 21	Ordinance for establishing Florida counties and courts. LC, DLC (63); Copies and Broadside (English and Spanish), DNA-RG 59 (M116-5, -6, -7); Copy, DNA-RG 233 (8-0885). *ASP, Miscellaneous Documents,* 2:906–907.	
[July 21]	*To the Officers and Soldiers Composing the Division of the South.*	75
July 22	To Andrew Jackson Donelson. LC, DLC (63). Orders him to New Orleans on quartermaster business.	
July 23	*Rachel Jackson to Elizabeth Kingsley.*	79
July 23	Commission of Henry D. Peire as sheriff for Escambia County, Florida. LC, DLC (63).	
July 24	From Robert Butler. ALS, DLC (30). Reports transfer of East Florida, receipt of cannon, and his return to Fort Hawkins.	
July 24	From Haden Edwards. ALS, DNA-RG 59 (M116-6). Proposes repair and lease of the Old Barracks, a public building in Pensacola.	
July 24	Commissions of St. John's County, Florida, officials: Philo Andrews, presiding judge, and George Murray, prosecuting attorney. DSs, DNA-RG 59 (M179-51, M116-5).	
July 24	Commissions of Escambia County, Florida, officials: William Barnett, justice of the peace; Washington L. Hannum, prosecuting attorney; Alexander Love, justice of the peace; John Miller, court clerk; David Shannon, presiding judge; and John Garnier, justice of the peace. LCs, DLC (63); DS with AJ endorsement, DNA-RG 217 (mAJs). *TPUS,* 22:662 (8-0896).	
July 25	From John Coffee. ALS with AJ endorsement, DLC (30). Discusses sale of islands in Tennessee River and prospects for sale of AJ's Evans Spring farm in Alabama.	
July 26	*To John Coffee.*	82
July 26	To William Grafton Dulany Worthington (enclosures: Ordinances for establishing the government of East Florida, July 18, 19, 21, and 26; John Q. Adams to AJ, June 27; Commission of James G. Forbes, May 18, *TPUS,* 22:45–46). LC, DLC (63). *TPUS,* 22:133–35. Transmits documents and discusses organization of East Florida government.	
July 26	From Henry Marie Brackenridge (enclosure: Constitutional powers of the alcaldes, n.d., DNA-RG 59, M116-6). ALS and Copy, DNA-RG 59 (M116-6); Copy, DNA-RG 233 (8-0898). *ASP, Miscellaneous Documents,* 2:902–903. Reports on civil administration of West Florida before transfer.	
July 26	Ordinance explaining court procedures. LC, DLC (63); Copies,	

	DNA-RG 59 (M116-6), DNA-RG 233 (8-0910). *ASP, Miscellaneous Documents,* 2:907–908.	
July 27	*To Robert Butler.*	84
July 27	To Haden Edwards (enclosure: Form of a lease, n.d.). LS copy, DNA-RG 59 (M116-6). States that he cannot grant lease for the Old Barracks, but will forward request to Washington.	
July 27	To Henry Stanton. LS, DNA-RG 217 (8-0916). Orders horse and $50 for James R. Hanham, messenger.	
July 27	To William Grafton Dulany Worthington. LC, DLC (63). Discusses East Florida government.	
July 27	Commissions of George Murray and Thomas H. Penn as justices of the peace, St. John's County, Florida. DSs, DNA-RG 59 (M116-5, 8-0915).	
July 28	To James R. Hanham. LS, THi (8-0917). Orders him to St. Augustine.	
July 28	From Zachary Taylor et al. LS, DLC (30). Pensacola *Floridian,* Sept 29. Thank AJ for defense of officers' honor in his farewell to the Southern Division.	
July 29	*To John Caldwell Calhoun.*	86
July 29	To John Caldwell Calhoun. LC, DLC (63). *Calhoun Papers,* 6:294–97. Denounces army position given Henry Atkinson by board of officers overseeing reduction; complains of Jacob J. Brown order re desertions.	
July 30–Aug 14	To John Quincy Adams (enclosures: Henry M. Brackenridge to AJ, July 26; Ordinances of July 18, 21, and 26). LS with AD list of enclosures and Copy, DNA-RG 59 (M116-6, 8-0920); LC, DLC (63); Copy, DNA-RG 233 (8-0959). *ASP, Miscellaneous Documents,* 2:896–901. Transmits documents and discusses the transfer of West Florida and governmental organization.	
July 30	From Henry Stanton. ALS with AJ endorsement and Copy, DNA-RG 59 (M116-6). *TPUS,* 22:155–56. Reports on public buildings in Pensacola.	
[July 30–Aug 15]	Memorandum of documents enclosed in letters to John Quincy Adams of July 30, Aug 9 and 15. AD, DLC (30).	
[cJuly 30]	Memoranda for letter to John Quincy Adams. ADs, DLC (30, 31).	
[cJuly 30]	Ordinance of the Pensacola board of health regarding quarantine. Broadside with AN by AJ, DNA-RG 59 (M116-6). Pensacola *Floridian,* Sept 29.	
July 31	From William Eastin. ALS, DLC (30). States that he has received $2,000 due him; discusses Tennessee gubernatorial contest.	
Aug 1	*From Samuel Ragland Overton.*	89
Aug 1	From Ezekiel Salomon. ALS duplicate with AJ endorsement, DLC (30). Notifies AJ that $10,000 has been credited to AJ's account as governor.	
Aug 2	*To James Jackson.*	91
Aug 2	From Henry Stanton (enclosures: Invoice of provisions, July 12; José I. Cruzat to Stanton, Aug 1, DLC-30). ALS and LC, DLC (30, 63); Copies, DNA-RG 59 (M116-6, 8-0994). Bassett, 3:106–107. Reports José M. Callava's refusal to sign invoice of provisions for Spaniards transported to Havana.	

Aug 3	To James Craine Bronaugh and Henry Stanton. LS, ALS draft, and LC, DLC (30, 63); Copies, DNA-RG 59 (M116-6, 8-0998). Directs them to obtain José M. Callava's agreement to invoice of provisions.
Aug 3	To José Maria Callava. AL drafts, Draft in an unknown hand, and LC, DLC (30, 59, 63); Copies, DNA-RG 59 (M116-6, 8-1006). Bassett, 3:108–111. Denounces Callava's refusal to sign invoice and nullifies the agreement on disputed cannon.
Aug 3	To Bartholomew Schaumburgh. Copy, DNA-RG 94 (8-1016). Assures him that Congress provided for the payment of the "Legion de Francs," volunteers enlisted at New Orleans in 1815.
Aug 3	From James Craine Bronaugh and Henry Stanton (enclosure: Unsigned invoice of provisions, [Aug 3], DLC-30). ALS in Bronaugh's hand and LC, DLC (30, 63); Copies, DNA-RG 59 (M116-6, 8-1001). Report Callava's continued refusal to sign invoice.
Aug 4	To James Monroe. LS, DLC (8-1019); LC, DLC (63). *TPUS,* 22:156–64. Discusses transfer of West Florida, organization of government, conflicts with José M. Callava, qualifications of Eligius Fromentin, and army reduction.
Aug 4	From John R. Bell (enclosures: Bell to José Coppinger, July 30, Aug 2; Coppinger to Bell, Aug 1). LS, DLC (30). Reports on East Florida and transmits documents re provincial archives.
Aug 4	From John Roger Fenwick. ALS, DLC (30). Requests that AJ intercede to prevent the transfer of Edward G. W. Butler to New Orleans.
Aug 4	From Jean Joseph Amable Humbert. LS, DLC (30). Requests help in obtaining Florida land grant.
Aug 7	From William Lee. LS with AJ endorsement, DLC (30); LC, DNA-RG 217 (8-1039). Acknowledges William Eastin's receipt for $2,000 and credits it to AJ's account.
Aug 8	From Robert Butler. ALS with AJ endorsement, DNA-RG 59 (M116-7); LC, DLC (63). *TPUS,* 22:165–67. Announces his arrival in Pensacola and transmits documents re transfer of East Florida.
Aug 8	To Robert Butler. LC, DLC (63). Approves Butler's actions in East Florida and consoles him about his reduced army rank.
Aug 8	From Henry Stanton (enclosures: AJ to Stanton, June 20, 23, and July 6). ALS and LC, DLC (30, 63). Explains his actions re invoice of provisions for Spanish personnel.
Aug 8	To Henry Stanton. ALS draft and LC, DLC (30, 63). Approves Stanton's conduct but recommends caution when dealing with Spaniards.
Aug 8	Receipt from Robert Butler for $1,002.55½ for expenses as commissioner to receive East Florida. ADS duplicate, DLC (70).
Aug 8	Memorandum from Robert Butler re expenses. ADS duplicate, DLC (70).
Aug 9	Account with Desiderio Lurria for foodstuffs. DS, DLC (70). Runs to October 7.
[Aug 9]	To John Quincy Adams. LS and Copy, DNA-RG 59 (M116-7); LC (dated Aug 4), DLC (63); Copy, DNA-RG 233 (8-0986). *ASP, Miscellaneous Documents,* 2:908–909. Reports Robert Butler's arrival in Pensacola and rumors of fraudulent Spanish land grants.

Aug 10 To John Coffee. ALS, THi (8-1040). Describes Pensacola conditions and discusses his intention to resign shortly.

Aug 11 From William Lee. LS with AJ endorsement and Copy, DLC (30); LC, DNA-RG 217 (8-1042). Announces closing of AJ's Choctaw treaty account but reminds him that his military account remains in arrears for $691.73.

Aug 11 Account with Cary Nicholas for postage. DS duplicate, DLC (70). Runs to October 8.

Aug 12 To Robert Butler. LC, DLC (63). Orders him to Nashville to arrange Southern Division adjutant general records, to close quartermaster general accounts, and to report to Edmund P. Gaines for duty.

Aug 13 To William Grafton Dulany Worthington. LC with AN by AJ, DLC (63); LC, PU (8-1048); Copies (one dated Aug 9), DNA-RG 59 (M116-7, -10), DNA-RG 46 (8-1045). *ASP, Foreign Relations,* 4:797. Orders that Spaniards must swear allegiance to the United States if they wish to retain their posts in East Florida.

Aug 13 From David Cowan. ALS, DLC (30). Opposes petition of Pensacola merchants for lower port warden fees.

Aug 13 From James R. Hanham (enclosure: AJ to Robert Butler, July 27). ALS with AJ endorsement, DLC (30). Announces his arrival at St. Augustine and the imminent arrival of William G. D. Worthington; returns dispatch to Robert Butler.

Aug 14 From John R. Bell (enclosures: Jean A. Pénières to AJ, July 16; Horatio S. Dexter to Bell, Aug 12, DNA-RG 233, 8-1055). LS and Copies, DNA-RG 107 (M221-92, -93, M222-22); Copy, DNA-RG 233 (8-1051). *ASP, Miscellaneous Documents,* 2:912. Discusses Indian affairs and general conditions in East Florida.

Aug 15 To John Quincy Adams (enclosure: Petition of Pensacola citizens to the president and board of directors of the Bank of the United States, n.d.). LS in James C. Bronaugh's hand, DNA-RG 59 (M116-7). Bassett, 3:111. Transmits petition.

Aug 15 To Langdon Cheves (enclosure: Petition of Pensacola citizens . . ., n.d., DNA-RG 59, M116-7). Copy, DNA-RG 46 (8-1063). *SDoc* 17, 23rd Cong., 2nd sess. (Serial 267), pp. 249–50. Endorses establishment in Pensacola of a branch of the Bank of the United States.

Aug 15 From James Gadsden. ALS, ICHi (8-1065). Announces his acceptance of adjutant generalcy and the appointment of Robert Butler as lieutenant colonel, 1st Infantry.

Aug 16 Memorandum of Edward Augustus Rutledge, Andrew Jackson Donelson, and Robert Butler re AJ's refusal to accept communication from José Maria Callava until furnished with signed inventory for provisions. LC, DLC (63); Copies, DNA-RG 59 (M116-7). *ASP, Miscellaneous Documents,* 2:813.

Aug 17 From Talbot Chambers et al. LS, DLC (30). Pensacola *Floridian,* Sept 1. Thank AJ for his defense of Southern Division's honor.

Aug 18 Account with Nicholas & Tunstall for printing. DS duplicate, DLC (70). Runs to October 8.

Aug 18	Account with Jonas C. Tanner for paper. ADS duplicate, DLC (70). Runs to October 4.	
Aug 20	To John Quincy Adams. LS, MHi (8-1074). Assures Adams of his efforts on behalf of William S. Smith.	
Aug 20	To John Quincy Adams. LS, DNA-RG 59 (M116-7); LC, DLC (63). Acknowledges deposit of $10,000.	
Aug 20	To Henry Stanton. LC, DLC (63). Orders supply of the Barrancas.	
Aug 20	From John Quincy Adams. LS, DLC (30); LC and Copy, DNA-RG 59 (M40-17, 8-1076); Copy, DNA-RG 46 (8-1080). *ASP, Foreign Relations,* 4:754–55. Requests information to aid organization of Florida Territory.	
Aug 20	From James Ramage. AL, DLC (30). Transmits letter from James Gadsden (not found) and requests permission to remain at the Barrancas until his crew's health improves.	
Aug 20	Ordinance for the better regulation of Pensacola harbor. Printed, *Acts of the Legislative Council of the Territory of Florida . . . 1822* (Pensacola, 1823), pp. xxvii–xxviii (mAJs).	
Aug 20	Receipt from Ephraim A. Blaine for $118.35 as steward. ADS, DLC (70).	
[Aug 20]	Account of AJ and suite for travel expenses from New Orleans to Pensacola. AD in Robert Butler's hand, DLC (70).	
Aug 21	To George Walton, Henry Marie Brackenridge, and John Miller. LC, DLC (63). Bassett, 3:111. Orders them to demand papers in Domingo G. Sousa's possession and to report thereon.	
Aug 21	*From Henry Marie Brackenridge.*	94
Aug 21	Ordinance regulating the fees of justices of the peace. Broadside, DNA-RG 59 (M116-7).	
Aug 22	To George Mercer Brooke. LC, DLC (63); Copy, DNA-RG 59 (M116-7). *ASP, Miscellaneous Documents,* 2:805. Orders preparation of armed detachment.	
Aug 22	*Order to Robert Butler and James Craine Bronaugh.*	94
Aug 22	To Robert Butler and John Miller. LC, DLC (63); Copy, DNA-RG 59 (M116-7). *ASP, Miscellaneous Documents,* 2:804. Orders arrest of Domingo G. Sousa and seizure of papers.	
Aug 22	To George W. Mountz. LC, DLC (63); Copy, DNA-RG 59 (M116-7). *ASP, Miscellaneous Documents,* 2:805. Orders the arrest of José M. Callava and Antoine Fullarat if they refuse to surrender papers.	
Aug 22	From Robert Butler and James Craine Bronaugh (enclosure: Memorandum of documents sought, Aug 22). LC, DLC (63); Copy, DNA-RG 59 (M116-7). *ASP, Miscellaneous Documents,* 2:806. Report seizure of documents and arrest of José M. Callava and Antoine Fullarat.	
Aug 22	From Robert Butler and John Miller. LC, DLC (63); Copy, DNA-RG 59 (M116-7). *ASP, Miscellaneous Documents,* 2:804. Report arrest of Domingo G. Sousa and his transfer of papers to José M. Callava.	
Aug 22	From James Ramage. LS, DLC (30). Reports differences between himself and James E. Dinkins re landing ill naval crew at the Barrancas.	
Aug 22	From George Walton, Henry Marie Brackenridge, and John Miller.	

LC, DLC (63); Copy, DNA-RG 59 (M116-7). *ASP, Miscellaneous Documents,* 2:802–803. Report on interview with Domingo G. Sousa and describe papers in his possession.

Aug 22 Memorandum of documents sought from José Maria Callava and Callava's demand for written request. LC, DLC (63). *ASP, Miscellaneous Documents,* 2:806.

Aug 22 Minutes of the examinations of José Maria Callava, Antoine Fullarat, and Domingo Garcia Sousa. LCs, DLC (63); Copies, DNA-RG 59 (M116-7). *ASP, Miscellaneous Documents,* 2:804–805, 806–807.

Aug 22 Orders for the imprisonment of José Maria Callava, Antoine Fullarat, and Domingo Garcia Sousa. DSs and LCs, DLC (8-1084, 63); Copies, DNA-RG 59 (M116-7). *ASP, Miscellaneous Documents,* 2:807.

Aug 23 *Order to Eligius Fromentin.* 97

Aug 23 *To John Innerarity.* 97

Aug 23 To Ezekiel Salomon. LC, DLC (63). States that he is drawing $5,000 from account in New Orleans.

[Aug 23] To George Walton (enclosure: Order to Eligius Fromentin, Aug 23). LC, DLC (63); Copies, DNA-RG 59 (M116-7, -9). *ASP, Miscellaneous Documents,* 2:823. Transmits order.

Aug 23 From Henry Marie Brackenridge (enclosure: Affidavit of Mercedes Vidal Palao, Aug 23, DLC-63). LC, DLC (63); Copy, DNA-RG 59 (M116-7). *ASP, Miscellaneous Documents,* 2:807–808. Requests order to examine papers at José M. Callava's house.

Aug 23 From James Craine Bronaugh. ALS with AJ endorsement, DLC (30). Bassett, 3:112. Reports interference by George M. Brooke during the confrontation with Callava.

Aug 23 From Eligius Fromentin. ALS copy, DNA-RG 59 (M116-7). *ASP, Miscellaneous Documents,* 2:836. Declines meeting with AJ.

[Aug 23] From [George W. Mountz] (enclosure: Writ of habeas corpus, Aug 23, DNA-RG 59, M116-7). LC dated Aug 24, DLC (63); Copies dated Aug 24, DNA-RG 59 (M116-7, -9). *ASP, Miscellaneous Documents,* 2:822. Reports service of a writ of habeas corpus for the release of José M. Callava.

Aug 23 From George Walton. LC, DLC (63); Copy, DNA-RG 59 (M116-9). *ASP, Miscellaneous Documents,* 2:823. Reports Eligius Fromentin's refusal to meet with AJ.

Aug 23 Order discharging from custody José Maria Callava, Domingo Garcia Sousa, and Antoine Fullarat. LC, DLC (63); Copy, DNA-RG 59 (M116-7). *ASP, Miscellaneous Documents,* 2:809.

Aug 23 Order to Henry Marie Brackenridge to depose José E. and Sebastian Caro. DS with ANS appointing Horatio Biglow and Washington L. Hannum as substitutes in case of illness, DLC (30).

Aug 23 Search warrant for José Maria Callava's house. LC, DLC (63); Copy, DNA-RG 59 (M116-7). *ASP, Miscellaneous Documents,* 2:808.

Aug 23 Return of George Walton, John Miller, David Shannon, and Thomas Brownjohn re search of José Maria Callava's house. LC, DLC (63); Copy, DNA-RG 59 (M116-7). *ASP, Miscellaneous*

	Documents, 2:808.	
Aug 23	Depositions of José E. and Sebastian Caro re Vidal case. DSs, DLC (30).	
Aug 24	To John R. Bell. Copy, DNA-RG 107 (M221-94). Requests report on needed fortifications in East Florida.	
Aug 24	To George Mercer Brooke. LC with AN by AJ, DLC (63). Requests report on fortifications needed in West Florida.	
Aug 24	From Henry Marie Brackenridge. LS with AN and Copy, DNA-RG 59 (M116-7); LC, DLC (63). *ASP, Miscellaneous Documents,* 2:811–12. Summarizes history of the Vidal lawsuit.	
Aug 24	*From Eligius Fromentin.*	98
Aug 24	From Jean Augustin Pénières (enclosure: Pénières to AJ, Aug 27). AL, DNA-RG 107 (M221-92). Explains his delayed arrival at Pensacola and transmits report.	
Aug 24	From Philip Wager. LC, DLC (63); Copy, DNA-RG 59 (M116-7). *ASP, Miscellaneous Documents,* 2:809. Reports the release of José M. Callava, Domingo G. Sousa, and Antoine Fullarat.	
Aug 25	To [Andrew Jackson Donelson]. LS in Andrew J. Donelson's hand, DNA-RG 217 (8-1097). Orders him to New Orleans to withdraw $5,000 from account and return forthwith.	
Aug 25	To Eligius Fromentin (enclosure: Fromentin to AJ, Aug 24). Copy, DNA-RG 59 (M116-7). *ASP, Miscellaneous Documents,* 2:842. Asks that Fromentin correct enclosed statement to show that the request for a writ of habeas corpus was verbal and not written.	
Aug 25	From Thomas John Gantt. ALS, DLC (30). On behalf of the 76 Association of Charleston, transmits a copy of Thomas O. Elliott's *An Oration, Delivered in St. Philip's Church, Charleston, South-Carolina, on the Fourth of July, 1821* (Charleston, 1821).	
Aug 25	*Rachel Jackson to John Donelson (1755–1830).*	99
Aug 26	To John Quincy Adams. LS and Copy, DNA-RG 59 (M116-7); ALS draft and LC, DLC (30, 63). *ASP, Miscellaneous Documents,* 2:801–802. Transmits twenty-three documents relating to the Vidal case and the arrest of José M. Callava.	
Aug 26	To John Coffee. ALS with ANS by Robert Butler, THi (8-1105). Bassett, 3:116. Discusses his financial situation and comments on Tennessee and Alabama gubernatorial elections.	
Aug 26	Receipt from George Walton for $5.50 for blank book. ADS, DLC (70).	
[Aug 27]	From Jean Augustin Pénières. Copy, DNA-RG 107 (M221-92); Extract, DNA-RG 233 (8-1107). *ASP, Indian Affairs,* 2:412 (extract). Reports on Indian land titles in East Florida.	
Aug 28	To John Caldwell Calhoun. Abstract, DNA-RG 107 (M22-15). Sends claim of Sergeant A. Horton.	
Aug 28	To James C. Craig. Printed, *ASP, Miscellaneous Documents,* 2:850 (8-1111). Orders appearance of John Innerarity to answer the Mercedes Vidal Palao petition.	
Aug 28	From William Grafton Dulany Worthington (enclosures: Worthington to Juan de Entralgo, Aug 22; Worthington to the St. Augustine City Council, Aug 27; Worthington to John C. Calhoun, Aug 21). LS draft and Copy, DNA-RG 59 (M116-7). *TPUS,*	

22:193–96. Details organization of city government and conditions in St. Augustine.

Aug 28 Account of Rachel Jackson with F. Pasquier for clothing. DS, DLC (30). Runs to August 31.

[Aug 28] Petition by Mercedes Vidal Palao requesting John Innerarity's compliance with previous court orders. Printed, *ASP, Miscellaneous Documents,* 2:850 (8-1112).

Aug 29 To George Mercer Brooke. ALS copy, DLC (63). Acknowledges report re Edward N. Dulany's mental incapacity and suggests that Dulany be ordered to Washington.

Aug 29 To James C. Craig. Copy, DNA-RG 59 (M116-7). *ASP, Miscellaneous Documents,* 2:852. Grants the Palaos' petition of August 11, 1820.

Aug 29 To John Mellen. ANS, TNJ (8-1114). Grants petition of John Garnier and Charles C. McCarthy and orders James Plunket to testify in matter before the Escambia County Court.

[Aug 29] From Henry Marie Brackenridge and Richard Keith Call. Copy, DNA-RG 59 (M116-7). *ASP, Miscellaneous Documents,* 2:852. On behalf of Severino and Mercedes Vidal Palao, renew petition of August 11, 1820, for execution of judgments against John Innerarity.

Aug 30 From James C. Craig. Copy, DNA-RG 59 (M116-7). *ASP, Miscellaneous Documents,* 2:852. Reports leaving copy of the Palaos' petition with John Innerarity.

Sept 1 To John Quincy Adams (enclosures: AJ to John R. Bell, Sept 1; George J. F. Clarke to Bell, July 25, DNA-RG 59, M116-7). LS, DNA-RG 59 (M116-7); LC, DLC (63). Sends documents.

Sept 1 To John R. Bell. LC, DLC (63); Copies and Extract, DNA-RG 59 (M116-7, -9, -10); Copies, DNA-RG 46 (8-1125), PU (8-1132). *ASP, Foreign Relations,* 4:796–97. Instructs him on continuation of Spaniards in East Florida posts and renews directions on provincial archives.

Sept 1 From George Mercer Brooke. LS, DNA-RG 77 (8-1136). Reports on defenses at the Barrancas.

Sept 2 To John Caldwell Calhoun (enclosures: Jean A. Pénières to AJ, July 16; George M. Brooke to AJ, Sept 1; Horatio S. Dexter to John R. Bell, July 30, DNA-RG 107, M221-93). LS and Copy, DNA-RG 107 (M221-93); LC, DLC (63); Extract, DNA-RG 233 (8-1141). *ASP, Indian Affairs,* 2:414 (extract). Discusses Indian policy in East Florida, Jean A. Pénières, and defenses at the Barrancas.

Sept 2 To John Donelson (1755–1830). ALS, THi (8-1144). Bassett, 3:116–17. Discusses business and family matters, his intention to resign the governorship, and the Tennessee gubernatorial election.

Sept 3 From Eligius Fromentin. ALS and LC, DLC (30, 63); AL copy and Copy, DNA-RG 59 (M116-7, -9). *ASP, Miscellaneous Documents,* 2:820. Denies rumor that he apologized to AJ.

Sept 3 To Eligius Fromentin. LC, DLC (63); Copies, DNA-RG 59 (M116-7, -9). *ASP, Miscellaneous Documents,* 2:820. States that Fromentin acquiesced to AJ's authority.

Sept 3 From Eligius Fromentin. ALS matched fragments and LC, DLC (30, 59, 63); ALS copy and Copy, DNA-RG 59 (M116-7, -9). *ASP,*

Miscellaneous Documents, 2:820–21. Denies acceptance of AJ's authority.

Sept 3 *To Eligius Fromentin.* 100

Sept 3 From James Craine Bronaugh. Copies (one with ANS by Robert Butler), DNA-RG 59 (M116-7, -9); LC with Butler's note, DLC (63). *ASP, Miscellaneous Documents,* 2:821. Supports AJ in controversy with Eligius Fromentin.

Sept 3 From Edward Augustus Rutledge. LC, DLC (63); Copies, DNA-RG 59 (M116-7). *ASP, Miscellaneous Documents,* 2:821–22. Supports AJ re controversy with Fromentin.

Sept 3 From Ezekiel Salomon. ALS, DLC (70). Reports a $5,000 credit to AJ's account.

Sept 3 Receipt from William Brand for $40.75 for food. DS, DLC (70).

Sept 4 Memorandum of John Coppinger Connor attesting to the delivery of AJ's second letter of September 3 to Eligius Fromentin. LC, DLC (63).

Sept 5 From René Edward DeRussy. ALS, DLC (30). Grants leave of absence to Andrew J. Donelson and offers hospitality on the Jacksons' return to Tennessee.

Sept 5 From James Gadsden. ALS, ICHi (8-1149). Discusses AJ's tenure as governor, difficulties with José M. Callava, and Tennessee politics.

Sept 6 Account with David G. Ballard for blacksmithing. DS with AJ endorsement, DLC (70). Runs to September 24.

Sept 6 Order granting further time for the preparation of John Innerarity's defense. Printed, *ASP, Miscellaneous Documents,* 2:854–55 (8-1156).

Sept 6 Ordinance explanatory of the ordinance for the preservation of health in Pensacola. Broadside, DNA-RG 59 (M116-7). Pensacola *Floridian,* Sept 8.

Sept 7 Receipt from Jerremiah Loudan for $5 for wood. AD, DLC (70).

Sept 8 To Ayers P. Merrill. LS, Historic Pensacola (7-1312). Appoints him to Pensacola board of health.

Sept 11 From Daniel Brent. LS, DLC (30); LC and Copies, DNA-RG 59 (M40-18, M116-7, 8-1158). Acknowledges receipt of AJ's letters to John Q. Adams of July 30, August [9] and 15.

Sept 11 Account with Richard Smith for furniture. Printed, *South Atlantic Quarterly,* 21(April 1922):137 (8-1359). Runs to December 3.

Sept 13 From William Harvey. ALS, DLC (30). Recommends William Porter for Florida post.

Sept 14 From James Gadsden. ALS, DLC (30). Discusses AJ's farewell to the Southern Division, army reorganization, and Robert Butler's dissatisfaction with his posting.

Sept 15 Receipt from James Jackson for $976.18 for Andrew J. Hutchings's farm. ADS with AJ endorsement, A-Ar (8-1160).

[cSept 15] Remarks on authority as governor of Florida. Printed, Pensacola *Floridian,* Sept 22 (mAJs).

Sept 16 From James Monroe. ALS, DLC (72). Bassett, 6:475–77. Discusses army reduction, Florida transfer, and appointments; urges AJ to remain as governor.

Sept 17 To John Caldwell Calhoun (enclosure: John R. Bell to AJ, Aug 14).

	LS, DNA-RG 107 (M221-93); LC, DLC (63); Copy and Extract, DNA-RG 233 (8-1164, -1172). *ASP, Miscellaneous Documents,* 2:911–12. Discusses Indian affairs in East Florida and relocation of the Seminoles.
Sept 17	From Duncan Lamont Clinch. ALS, DLC (30). Praises AJ's farewell address to the Southern Division.
Sept 17	Memorandum relinquishing Alabama land for Andrew Jackson Hutchings. ADS copy by Benjamin S. Pope, A-Ar (8-1179).
[Sept 17]	Opinion in *Heirs of Vidal* v. *John Innerarity.* Printed, *ASP, Miscellaneous Documents,* 2:814–18 (8-1174).
[cSept 17]	From George I. Brown. Extract, DNA-RG 59 (M116-8). Discusses Horatio S. Dexter, Edmund M. Wanton, and Indians in East Florida.
Sept 18	To John Garnier. LC, DLC (63). Orders disbursement of provisions to Stephen Richards, interpreter, for the use of Florida Indians.
Sept 18	To William Grafton Dulany Worthington. LC, DLC (63). *TPUS,* 22:209–10. Discusses Indian affairs in East Florida and orders investigation of Horatio S. Dexter and Edmund M. Wanton.
Sept 18	From Daniel Brent. LS, DLC (30); LC and Copies, DNA-RG 59 (M40-18, M116-7, 8-1181). Communicates the president's agreement re disposition of barracks at Pensacola.
Sept 18	Account of Antoine Collins for expenses and board of Florida Indians. ADS by proxy, DLC (70). Runs to September 20.
[Sept 18–20]	Report on talk with Florida Indians. DS (dated Sept 20) and Copy, DNA-RG 107 (M221-93); LC, DLC (63); Extract, DNA-RG 233 (8-1190). Bassett, 3:118–21 (dated Sept 20). Details his exchange with Florida Indian chiefs and his desire for them to live either in Florida or on the Creek reserve.
Sept 19	To William McIntosh. LC, DLC (63); Copies, DNA-RG 107 (M221-93). Orders him to accept Creek Indians now in Florida if they should return.
Sept 19	*From Robert Butler.* 101
Sept 20	To John Caldwell Calhoun (enclosures: AJ to Calhoun, Sept 17; AJ to William McIntosh, Sept 19; Report on talk with Florida Indians, [Sept 18–20]). LS and Copy, DNA-RG 107 (M221-93); LC, DLC (63); Extract, DNA-RG 233 (8-1185). *TPUS,* 22:210–13. Reports on Indian affairs in Florida and on fraudulent Spanish land claims.
Sept 20	From Edward George Washington Butler. ALS, DLC (30). Reports his arrival in New Orleans and reassignment to western military department.
Sept 20	Agreement to sell the Evans Spring farm in Lauderdale County, Alabama, to Richard C. Cross for $7,500. DS (by James Jackson and John Coffee, agents for AJ), Mrs. R. Neal Bass (mAJs).
Sept 20	Account of John Garnier for expenses for Indians. ADS, DLC (70). Runs to October 6.
Sept 21	To William Berkeley Lewis. ALS, NNPM (8-1199). William G. Sumner, *Andrew Jackson* (Boston, 1899), p. 159 (extract). Discusses Tennessee politics, defends his actions in Florida, and announces his expected departure for Tennessee.
Sept 21	To William Grafton Dulany Worthington (enclosures: Report on

talk with Florida Indians, [Sept 18–20]; AJ to William McIntosh, Sept 19). LC, DLC (63). Discusses administration of East Florida and transmits documents.

Sept 21 Memorandum by Horatio Biglow of conversation between AJ and John Innerarity re arrest and interrogation of José Maria Callava. ADS, DNA-RG 59 (M116-7).

[cSept 21–29] Memorandum on controversy re José Maria Callava and Eligius Fromentin. AD, DLC (31).

Sept 22 *To George Bowie and Henry Marie Brackenridge.* 102

Sept 22 To William Berkeley Lewis. ALS, NNPM (8-1204). Introduces John J. Jackson.

Sept 22 To George W. Mountz. LC, DLC (63). Orders report re the arrest of José M. Callava.

Sept 22 From John M. Davis. ALS, DLC (30). Commends AJ's farewell to the Southern Division.

Sept 22 From Fontaine Maury. ALS, DLC (30); LC and Copy, DNA-RG 59 (M40-17, 8-1206). Transmits receipt (not found) crediting AJ's account and requests his signature thereon.

Sept 22 Depositions of John Coppinger Connor and John Jay Jackson re the arrest of José Maria Callava. Copy, DNA-RG 59 (M116-9); LC, DLC (63).

Sept 24 From Daniel Brent. LS, DLC (30); LC and Copy, DNA-RG 59 (M40-18, 8-1208). Acknowledges receipt of AJ's August 26 letter to John Q. Adams.

Sept 24 From George I. Brown. ALS, DLC (30). Thanks AJ for favorable recommendation and commends John C. Connor.

Sept 24 From George W. Mountz. Copy, DNA-RG 59 (M116-9). *ASP, Miscellaneous Documents,* 2:823. Discusses the arrest of José M. Callava.

Sept 25 From Francis Langhorne Dade. Copy, DNA-RG 59 (M116-9). *ASP, Miscellaneous Documents,* 2:824. Discusses the arrest of José M. Callava.

Sept 25 Interrogatories to be put to John Innerarity re the arrest of José Maria Callava. AD draft fragment in AJ's hand, DLC (8-1211); AD in an unknown hand, Ms-Ar (8-1216).

Sept 27 Summons to John Innerarity to appear and answer interrogatories. LC, DLC (63).

Sept 27 From George Bowie and Henry Marie Brackenridge. LC, DLC (63). Report John Innerarity's refusal to answer interrogatories.

[Sept 27] Deposition of John Innerarity re the arrest of José Maria Callava. ADS also signed by George Walton, DNA-RG 59 (M116-7); Copies, Ms-Ar (8-1228).

Sept 27 Receipt from George Walton for $10 for office furniture purchased from Archibald McRae. DS duplicate, DLC (70).

Sept 29 *To the Spanish Officers.* 103

Sept 29 From Langdon Cheves. Copy, DNA-RG 46 (8-1238). *SDoc* 17, 23rd Cong., 2nd sess. (Serial 267), pp. 250–51. States that the Bank of the United States will not open a branch in Pensacola.

Sept 29 *From William McCully.* 106

Sept 29 Answer of John Innerarity to interrogatories re the arrest of José

Maria Callava. DS partially in Innerarity's hand also signed by AJ and Henry M. Brackenridge, DNA-RG 59 (M116-7); AD and Extracts, Ms-Ar (8-1226).

Sept 30 — To John Quincy Adams (enclosures: To the Spanish officers, Sept 29; Opinion in *Heirs of Vidal* v. *John Innerarity,* Sept 17; Pensacola *Floridian,* Sept 29). ALS, DNA-RG 59 (M116-7); LC, DLC (63). Bassett, 3:121–22. Defends the expulsion of Spanish officers and his actions as supreme judicial authority in Florida.

Sept 30 — From Richard Keith Call (enclosures: John Ross to Call, July 30; List by John Johnston of Indian lands needing specifications and warrants, Aug 21). ALS and Copy, DNA-RG 107 (M221-93). Recommends removal of Cherokee subagent James G. Williams and appointment of Thomas C. Hindman.

[Sept] — Receipt from James Jackson for $15.40, final payment on a tract of Andrew Jackson Hutchings's land. DS, A-Ar (8-1123).

[Sept] — Petition of John Innerarity re Vidal case. Translation, *HRDoc* 42, 17th Cong., 1st sess. (Serial 65), pp. 214–15 (8-1117).

[Sept] — Second petition of John Innerarity re Vidal case. Printed, *ASP, Miscellaneous Documents,* 2:854 (8-1156).

[Sept] — Protest of José Maria Callava re his arrest. Printed, New Orleans *Louisiana Courier,* Sept 7 (mAJs).

Oct 1 — To [Abram Eustis]. LS, FU (8-1246). *FHQ,* 33(1954):26–27. Orders compliance with the requisitions of William G. D. Worthington.

Oct 1 — To Spencer Nolen. Facsimile of AL fragment, unidentified newspaper clipping (mAJs). Details duel and death of John Hull, former lieutenant with the 4th Infantry.

Oct 1 — *To William Grafton Dulany Worthington.* 108

Oct 1 — From Abram Eustis. ALS, DLC (30). Announces assumption of command of military forces stationed at St. Augustine.

Oct 1 — Commission of John Miller as mayor of Pensacola. DS, DNA-RG 217 (mAJs). *TPUS,* 22:226–27 (8-1247).

Oct 2 — To John Caldwell Calhoun (enclosures: Richard K. Call to AJ, Sept 30; John Ross to Call, July 30; List by John Johnston of Indian lands needing specifications and warrants, Aug 21). LS and Copy, DNA-RG 107 (M221-93). Transmits documents.

Oct 2 — From DeWitt Clinton. ALS, DLC (30). Sends book: New-York Corresponding Association, for the Promotion of Internal Improvements, *Public Documents, Relating to the New-York Canals, Which Are to Connect the Western and Northern Lakes with the Atlantic Ocean* (New York, 1821).

Oct 3 — Second protest of José Maria Callava re his arrest. Translations, DLC (30), Ms-Ar (8-1249). *ASP, Foreign Relations,* 4:768–76.

Oct 4 — To John Quincy Adams (enclosures: Plans of buildings and maps of East Florida, n.d., DNA-RG 59, M116-8). LS in Richard K. Call's hand, DNA-RG 59 (M116-8); LC, DLC (63). Transmits documents.

Oct 4 — From William Grafton Dulany Worthington. LS, DNA-RG 59 (M116-10); Copies, DNA-RG 107 (M221-94), MdHi (8-1269). *TPUS,* 22:228–29. Inquires about division of authority between himself and military commander Abram Eustis.

Oct 4	Toast at public dinner in Pensacola: "The government of the United States—May its administration always be as wise as its principles are pure." Printed, Pensacola *Floridian,* Oct 8 (mAJs).	
[cOct 4]	From David Shannon et al. (enclosure: Petition of the grand jury of Escambia County, Florida, Oct 4). LS, DNA-RG 59 (M116-8). Request repair of the county jail.	
Oct 5	*To James Monroe.*	110
Oct 5	From James W. Patterson. ALS, DLC (30). Thanks AJ for appointment as district attorney, East Florida.	
Oct [5]	To George Walton. LC, DLC (63). *TPUS,* 22:229–31. Appoints him acting governor of West Florida and gives instructions.	
Oct 6	To John Quincy Adams (enclosure: George I. Brown to AJ, [cSept 17]; Farewell address to the citizens of Florida, Oct 6, DLC-30). LS, DNA-RG 59 (M116-8); Draft (undated) and LC (lacking postscript), DLC (30, 63); Copy, DNA-RG 233 (8-1278). *ASP, Miscellaneous Documents,* 2:909–11. Opposes division of Florida territory; discusses Indian affairs and Spanish land claims.	
Oct 6	To George Mercer Brooke. LC, DLC (63). *TPUS,* 22:238. Orders him to obey George Walton.	
Oct 6	From John Innerarity. Printed, *ASP, Miscellaneous Documents,* 2:865 (mAJs). Petitions for an extension of time in the Vidal estate lawsuit.	
Oct 6	From Chandler Price (enclosure: Cargo manifest of *Orleans,* n.d., DLC-59). ALS and Address page, DLC (30, 31). Sends a pair of shoes for Rachel Jackson; discusses pirate activity in the Gulf of Mexico.	
Oct 6	From William Grafton Dulany Worthington (enclosures: Worthington to Juan de Entralgo, Aug 29, Sept 15; Entralgo to Worthington, Sept 5; Worthington to John R. Bell, James G. Forbes, and Edmund Law, Oct 1; Worthington to Farquhar Bethune, Patrick Lynch, and William Reynolds, Oct 3; Bell, Forbes, and Law to Worthington, Oct 4). LS, DNA-RG 59 (M116-10). *TPUS,* 22:238–41. Transmits documents and discusses the seizure of East Florida archives, health and climate at St. Augustine, and his continuing dispute with the military.	
Oct 6	Farewell address to the citizens of Florida. Printed, Pensacola *Floridian,* Oct 8 (mAJs, 8-1289); AL draft fragment, DLC (59).	
Oct 7	Receipt of Hutchings, a soldier, for $18 for shoeing horse and repairing "sans-susy." DS duplicates by proxy, DLC (70).	
Oct 7	Receipt for $10,000 credit in New Orleans branch bank. DS, DNA-RG 217 (8-0345).	
Oct 8	To Henry Marie Brackenridge. ALS, Robert G. Scott (8-1293). Evert A. and George L. Duyckinck, *Cyclopædia of American Literature* (2 vols; New York, 1866), 1:670. Thanks him for his services and offers aid in securing territorial judicial appointment.	
Oct 8	From John R. Bell. LS and Copy, DNA-RG 107 (M221-93). *TPUS,* 22:245–47. Discusses disagreements with East Florida civil officials.	
Oct 8	From William Christian. ALS, DLC (30). Seeks reinstatement in army or other appointment.	
Oct 8	Judgment against John Innerarity in Vidal case. Printed, *ASP,*	

Miscellaneous Documents, 2:867 (8-1295).

Oct 8 Memorandum by Andrew Jackson Donelson re cost of a seal of office. ADS, DLC (70).

Oct 8 Receipt from Andrew Jackson Donelson for $70 for expenses while in New Orleans. ADS duplicates, DLC (70), DNA-RG 217 (8-0329).

Oct 8 Receipt of George Walton for $24 for chairs purchased from William M. Read. DS duplicate, DLC (70).

Oct 8 Receipt from George Walton for $623 for expenses while acting governor. DS duplicate, DLC (70).

[Oct 8] To John Quincy Adams (enclosure: David Shannon et al. to AJ, [cOct 4]). LS, DNA-RG 59 (M116-8). Transmits document.

Oct 9 From Abram Eustis. ALS and Copy, DNA-RG 107 (M221-93). Reports on St. Augustine fortifications and on housing for troops.

Oct 10 To Richard Keith Call. ALS, DLC (8-1297); Extract, FHi (mAJs). Offers help in securing territorial appointment and instructs him on shipment of furniture to Tennessee.

Oct 14 From Richard Keith Call. ALS, DLC (30). Bassett, 3:129. Thanks AJ for his friendship.

Oct 14 From Richard Keith Call. ALS, DLC (30). Declines recommendation and reports on John Innerarity's actions.

Oct 15 From George Walton (enclosures: James Monroe to AJ, Sept 16; James Gadsden to AJ, Sept 14). ALS, DLC (31). Forwards mail and reports on Callava affair and a meeting at Pensacola.

Oct 15 Deposition of Washington L. Hannum re arrest of José Maria Callava. ADS, DNA-RG 59 (M116-9); LC, DLC (63). *ASP, Miscellaneous Documents,* 2:831.

Oct 16 From Luther A. Hitchcock. ALS, DLC (31). Solicits aid for appointment as teacher in Pensacola.

Oct 19 From John Caldwell Calhoun. LS, DLC (31); LC, DNA-RG 107 (M6-11). *Calhoun Papers,* 6:449–50. Requests that AJ send design for medal commemorating Battle of New Orleans.

Oct 22 From George Walton (enclosures: Jean A. Pénières to AJ, Aug 24 and 27). LS, DLC (31). *TPUS,* 22:259–60. Forwards mail and discusses his authority as acting governor.

Oct 22 Depositions of Henry Marie Brackenridge and John Miller re Vidal suit. ADS and DS with concurring ANS by David Shannon and Furguson H. Nisbet, DNA-RG 59 (M116-9); LCs, DLC (63). *ASP, Miscellaneous Documents,* 2:828–31.

Oct 24 From John C. Mitchell. ALS, DLC (31). Discusses news from Pensacola; appends note to Rachel Jackson and Narcissa Hays detailing social life since their departure.

Oct 26 From John Quincy Adams (enclosures: Adams to Eligius Fromentin, Oct 26, DLC-31; Hilario de Rivas y Salmon to Adams, Oct 6, DLC-30; Protest of José M. Callava, Oct 3; Adams to Joaquin de Anduaga, Nov 2, DLC-31). LS, DLC (31); LC and Copies, DNA-RG 59 (M40-17, M116-8, 8-1301). *ASP, Miscellaneous Documents,* 2:818–19. Upholds AJ's judicial authority but requests explanation for denial of diplomatic immunity to Callava.

Oct 26 From William Grafton Dulany Worthington (enclosures:

	Proclamation by Worthington, Oct 26; Worthington to John C. Calhoun, Oct 9, DLC-30). LS, DLC (31). Discusses Indian affairs and John R. Bell's appointment as Indian agent.
Oct 27	From Mulatto King. LS by proxy (Stephen Richards), William Dearborn (8-1307); Copy, DNA-RG 107 (M221-93). Reports on reception of AJ's talk of September 18–20 and on Indian affairs in West Florida.
Oct 28	From John Caldwell Calhoun. ALS, DLC (31). *Calhoun Papers,* 6:476–79. Explains reorganization of officer corps and discusses Florida's future.
Oct 29	To George Walton. ALS, FU (8-1315). *FHQ,* 33(1954):28–29. Discusses his return to Tennessee and the situation in Florida.
Oct 29	*From "Friend."* 112
Oct 29	From David Shannon. ALS, DLC (31). Reports on affairs in Pensacola and solicits AJ's recommendation as land commissioner.
Oct 29	From George Walton (enclosures: John G. Bird to Walton, Sept 23, DLC-30; Walton to John Q. Adams, Oct 29). LS, DLC (31). Forwards mail; reports two appointments.
Oct 30	From Richard Keith Call (enclosures: Petitions supporting William King for governor of Florida, n.d., DNA-RG 59, M439-10). ALS, DLC (31). Transmits petitions; discusses political import of ball honoring George Walton.
Oct 31	From William Grafton Dulany Worthington (enclosures: James G. Forbes to Worthington, Aug 28 and Oct 3; Report of the committee on St. Augustine public buildings, Sept 9; Resolutions of St. Augustine city council and Board of Health, Sept 27; Worthington to Abram Eustis, Sept 27; Eustis to Worthington, Sept 27; John R. Bell to Worthington, Sept 27; Worthington to Bell, Sept 28; Worthington to Forbes, Sept 29, all DLC-30). LS, DLC (31). Discusses his dispute with Bell over public property.
Nov 2	From William McIntosh. LS by proxy and Copy, DNA-RG 107 (M221-93). Accepts the return of Florida Creeks.
Nov 3	From John Jackson. ALS, DLC (31). Relates his plans to visit New Orleans and Pensacola; introduces Isaac Lewis.
Nov 3	Account with Robert Brownlee Currey for postage as governor of Florida. ADS duplicate, DLC (70). Runs to February 8, 1822.
Nov 4	To Richard Keith Call. Extract, Herbert J. Doherty, *Richard Keith Call, Southern Unionist* (Gainesville, Fla., 1961), p. 22 (8-1328). Discusses Call's courtship of Mary L. Kirkman.
Nov 4	From Henry Marie Brackenridge. ALS, DLC (31). Discusses the Callava and Fromentin controversies.
Nov 5	From John Sommerville et al. LS, DLC (31). *Nashville Whig,* Nov 14. Invite AJ to public dinner and ball.
Nov 5	From George Walton (enclosure: Decree in case of *George Donnely* v. *Henry J. Finch,* Nov 3). LS with AN postscript, DLC (31). Transmits document and reports on the Callava and Fromentin controversies.
Nov 6	To John Sommerville et al. Printed, *Nashville Whig,* Nov 14 (mAJs). Accepts invitation and sets date of dinner for November 9.
Nov 8	From James Gadsden. ALS, DLC (31). Reports Washington

reaction to the Callava and Fromentin controversies and Gadsden's efforts to counter criticism.

Nov 8 Receipt from Rapier & Simpson for $29.40 for leather for Andrew Jackson Hutchings. ADS, A-Ar (8-1331).

Nov 9 From William Grafton Dulany Worthington (enclosures: John R. Bell to Worthington, Aug 27, and Worthington to Bell, Aug 27, DLC-30; Worthington to Abram Eustis, Nov 7, and Eustis to Worthington, Nov 8, DLC-31). ALS and Copy, DNA-RG 59 (M116-10); Copy, DNA-RG 46 (8-1334). *ASP, Foreign Relations,* 4:799. Reports the end of conflict between the civil and military authorities in St. Augustine and the outbreak of yellow fever.

Nov 9 Toast at public dinner in Nashville: "J. C. Calhoun, Secretary of War: An honest man, 'the noblest work of God.'" Printed, *Nashville Whig,* Nov 14 (mAJs).

Nov 11 From Mulatto King et al. LS by proxy (Stephen Richards) and Copy, DNA-RG 107 (M221-93, -96). Announce their wish to deal only with AJ re their relocation and report that general meeting of tribe has not taken place.

Nov 12 From George Walton (enclosures: John R. Bell to AJ, Oct 8; Abram Eustis to AJ, Oct 9). ALS, DLC (31). Reports tranquility of West Florida and the receipt of a pair of shoes for Rachel Jackson.

Nov 12 Deposition of Andrew Jackson Donelson re the Fromentin controversy. ADS, DNA-RG 59 (M116-9); LC, DLC (63). *ASP, Miscellaneous Documents,* 2:822.

Nov 13 To John Quincy Adams (enclosures: Eligius Fromentin to AJ, Aug 24 and Sept 3; AJ to Fromentin, Sept 3; James C. Bronaugh to AJ, Sept 3; Edward A. Rutledge to AJ, Sept 3; Deposition of Andrew J. Donelson, Nov 12; [George W. Mountz] to AJ, [Aug 23]; AJ to George Walton, Aug 23; Walton to AJ, Aug 23). LS, DNA-RG 59 (M116-9); LC, DLC (63). Bassett, 3:126–29. Transmits documents re controversy with Fromentin and defends his actions.

Nov 13 To James Monroe (enclosure: AJ to Monroe, Nov 13). LS, DLC (8-1340); LC, DLC (63). *TPUS,* 22:274–75. Announces his return to Tennessee and discusses controversy with Eligius Fromentin.

Nov 13 To James Monroe. LS with endorsement by Monroe, DNA-RG 59 (M116-9); LC, DLC (63). *TPUS,* 22:275–76. Resigns as governor of Florida.

Nov 13 To George Walton. ALS with ANS by Richard I. Easter, FU (8-1345); LC, DLC (63). *FHQ,* 33(1954):29–31. Approves Walton's conduct in West Florida and discusses Callava-Fromentin affair.

Nov 13 From William Reynolds (enclosure: William G. D. Worthington to John R. Bell, James G. Forbes, and Edmund Law, Nov 7, DNA-RG 59, M116-10). ANS and Copy, DNA-RG 59 (M116-10); Copy, DNA-RG 46 (8-1343). *ASP, Foreign Relations,* 4:799. Explains delay in mailing Worthington's letter of November 9.

Nov 14 To John Quincy Adams. LS, DNA-RG 59 (M116-9). Forwards accounts (not found) of Robert Butler, Richard K. Call, James C. Bronaugh, and John R. Bell for civil duties in Florida.

Nov 14 To Peter Hagner. LS, THi (8-1350); Address page, DNA-RG 217 (5-1327); LC, DLC (63). Protests denial of his claims for fuel and quarters during the Seminole campaign and when in Washington.

Nov 14 To James Monroe. ALS, DLC (8-1354); LC, DLC (63). *TPUS,* 22:276–77. Reiterates his desire to resign and discusses his actions in Florida; acknowledges Monroe's letter of September 16.

Nov 14 From James Gadsden. ALS, ICHi (8-1349). Reports again on Washington reaction to the Callava and Fromentin controversies.

Nov 15 *To Richard Keith Call.* 114

Nov 16 From John Caldwell Calhoun (enclosure: Calhoun to John R. Bell, Sept 25, DLC-30). LS, DLC (31); LC, DNA-RG 75 (M15-5). *TPUS,* 22:278–79. Discusses relocation of Florida Indians.

Nov 16 From John Caldwell Calhoun. ALS, DLC (31). *Calhoun Papers,* 6:511–12. Expresses satisfaction that Jackson's actions in Florida are now correctly understood.

Nov 16 Robert Butler to James Monroe. ALS, DNA-RG 94 (M566-139); Copy, DNA-RG 107 (M221-92). Resigns from army.

Nov 17 To Fontaine Maury (enclosure: Receipt for $10,000 credit in New Orleans branch bank, Oct 7). LS, DNA-RG 59 (M179-52); LC (lacks concluding phrase), DLC (63). Discusses his account with the United States.

Nov 17 To George Walton. LC, DLC (63). Discusses Walton's judicial authority, pirates, and AJ's resignation.

Nov 19 From Richard Keith Call. ALS, DLC (31). Regrets lack of communication from AJ; reports on Florida government and on shipment of AJ's furniture to Nashville via New Orleans.

Nov 19 From James Jackson. ALS, DLC (31). Discusses payment made to Sarah J. Hanna, sale of land in Alabama, and status of crops there.

Nov 19 From George Walton (enclosure: Mulatto King to AJ, Oct 27). ALS, DLC (31). Forwards mail; reports on the arrival of the steamship *Robert Fulton* and on pirates in the Gulf.

Nov 20 From James Gadsden. ALS, DLC (31). Bassett, 3:132–33 (extract). Discusses presidential politics and AJ's rumored support of DeWitt Clinton.

Nov 21 To Jean Augustin Pénières. LC, DLC (63). States that Pénières's reports on Florida Indians will be forwarded to the secretary of war.

Nov 22 To John Quincy Adams (enclosures: Depositions of Washington L. Hannum, John Miller, and Henry M. Brackenridge, Oct 15 and Oct 22). LS, DNA-RG 59 (M116-9); LC, DLC (63). Bassett, 3:133–39. Reviews controversy with José M. Callava.

Nov 22 To Henry Marie Brackenridge. Extract, Henry M. Brackenridge, *Judge Brackenridge's Letters* ([Washington, 1832]), p. 7 (mAJs, 8-1319). Relates James Monroe's satisfaction with Brackenridge.

Nov 22 To John Caldwell Calhoun (enclosure: Jean A. Pénières to AJ, Aug 24). LS, THi (8-1357); LC, DLC (63); Copy (dated Nov 2), DNA-RG 107 (M221-93). Discusses Indian affairs in East Florida.

Nov 23 From William King. ALS, DLC (31). Discusses Pensacola events, including recommendation that King succeed to the governorship of Florida.

Nov 23 From Neamathla and Ninnehamata Tustunnuggee. LS by proxy (Stephen Richards) and Copy, DNA-RG 107 (M221-93, -96). Report on their discussions with William McIntosh.

Nov 23	Toast at public dinner in Nashville for William Carroll: "The venerable Isaac Shelby, late Governor of Kentucky." Printed, *Nashville Whig,* Nov 28 (mAJs).	
Nov 24	From Arkansas correspondent. Printed, *Arkansas Gazette,* Nov 24 (mAJs). Attacks AJ's Florida conduct.	
Nov 24	From David Shannon. ALS, DLC (31). *TPUS,* 22:280–82. Reviews judicial business in Escambia County, Florida, and requests more pay.	
Nov 24	Edmund Pendleton Gaines to James Monroe (enclosure: Robert Butler to Monroe, Nov 16). ALS, DNA-RG 94 (M566-139). Transmits Butler's resignation but appeals for Butler's retention.	
Nov 24	Receipt from Ingram & Lloyd for $13.75 for paper and writing supplies. DS duplicate, DLC (70).	
Nov 26	From Richard Keith Call. ALS, DLC (31). Discusses Mary L. Kirkman and printed attacks on Eligius Fromentin by Cary Nicholas.	
Nov 26	From John Coppinger Connor. ALS, DLC (31). Requests AJ's aid for Florida appointment.	
Nov 26	From John Miller. ALS, DLC (31). Discusses judicial business in Escambia County, Florida, and the Pensacola census.	
Nov 26	From George Walton. LS, DLC (31). Forwards mail; reports on West Florida, Georgia politics, and yellow fever in St. Augustine.	
Nov 30	To James Monroe (enclosures: Petitions supporting William King for governor of Florida, n.d.). LS, DNA-RG 59 (M439-10). Transmits petitions and endorses King.	
Nov 30	From Chester Root. ALS, DLC (31). Reports New York's support for AJ re Callava controversy and AJ's defense of the Southern Division.	
Nov	Receipt from William McKnight for $35 for tutoring Andrew Jackson Hutchings. ADS, A-Ar (8-1326).	
Dec 2	*From James Craine Bronaugh.*	117
Dec 3	To Andrew Erwin. LS by proxy (Patrick H. Darby). T (10-0178). Notifies Erwin of plans to take depositions re *Jackson* v. *Erwin.*	
Dec 3	From James Gadsden. ALS, DLC (31). Renews his approbation of AJ's conduct re the Callava controversy; discusses delay in accepting Andrew J. Donelson's resignation from the army; seeks AJ's oversight of his affairs in Alabama.	
Dec 3	From George Walton (enclosure: Walton to John Q. Adams, Dec 1). LS, DLC (31). Forwards mail and discusses West Florida and Georgia politics.	
[cDec 4]	From James Craine Bronaugh. AL fragment, DLC (75). Reports on election of Philip P. Barbour as speaker of the House of Representatives and on the Florida controversy.	
Dec 5	From Edmund Doyle (enclosures: Mulatto King et al. to AJ, Nov 11; Neamathla and Ninnehamata Tustunnuggee to AJ, Nov 23). ALS and Copy, DNA-RG 107 (M221-93, -96). Discusses Florida Indian affairs and relocation of the Seminoles.	
Dec 6	To John Caldwell Calhoun. LC, DLC (63). Acknowledges Calhoun's agreement on disposition of Florida Indians and suggests military arrangements for same.	
Dec 6	*To James Gadsden.*	120

Dec 6 To George Walton. LC, DLC (63). Approves decision in *George Donnely* v. *Henry J. Finch*; comments on reaction to the Callava controversy.

Dec 8 Robert Butler to James Gadsden. ALS, DNA-RG 94 (M566-139). Reports that the Southern Division adjutant general's records will be sent to Washington.

Dec 8 Receipt from William Perkins for $18.67¼ for work on cotton press. DS in AJ's hand, DLC (31).

Dec 9 *To John Overton.* 123

Dec 10 From George Walton (enclosures: William G. D. Worthington to AJ, Oct 31 and Nov 9). LS, DLC (31). *TPUS,* 22:298–99. Forwards mail, comments upon dissatisfaction in East Florida, and urges AJ to run for president.

Dec 11 From James Craine Bronaugh. ALS, DLC (72). Discusses cabinet reaction to the Florida controversy; reports on civil and military accounts of AJ, Bronaugh, Robert Butler, and Richard K. Call.

Dec 11 From William Grafton Dulany Worthington (enclosures: Resolutions of the St. Augustine city council, Oct 17, 31, and Dec 1; James G. Forbes to Worthington, Dec 1 and 10; Worthington to Forbes, Dec 1; John R. Bell, Forbes, and Edmund Law to St. Augustine city council, Oct 4; Estimate of St. Augustine city council expenses, 1821–22, Dec 10). ALS, DNA-RG 59 (M116-9). Transmits documents re provincial archives and tax matters; discusses Indian relocation.

Dec 12 To John Quincy Adams (enclosure: claim of John R. Bell for pay as acting secretary of East Florida, Oct 7, DNA-RG 59, M179-52). LS, DNA-RG 59 (M179-52); LC, DLC (63). Transmits Bell's account and recommends approval.

Dec 12 To John R. Bell. LC, DLC (63). *TPUS,* 22:303–304. States that Bell's account has been forwarded to Washington and approves Bell's conduct in dispute with William G. D. Worthington.

Dec 12 To John Caldwell Calhoun (enclosures: John R. Bell to AJ, Oct 8; Abram Eustis to AJ, Oct 9). LS and Copy, DNA-RG 107 (M221-93); LC, DLC (63). *TPUS,* 22:302–303. Transmits letters.

Dec 12 To Abram Eustis. LC, DLC (63). Announces transmittal to the secretary of war of Eustis's letter of October 9.

Dec 12 To George Walton. LC, DLC (63). Acknowledges letter of November 12 and decries unreliability of mails.

Dec 12 From Abner Lawson Duncan. ALS, DLC (31). Reports that a relative of AJ's is in transit to Nashville.

Dec 12 From McCoy & Scallan. ALS, DLC (31). Report arrival in New Orleans of James McCully, AJ's supposed Irish relative.

Dec 14 To Richard Keith Call. Extract, Herbert J. Doherty, *Richard Keith Call, Southern Unionist* (Gainesville, Fla., 1961), p. 22 (8-1367). Discusses Call's courtship of Mary L. Kirkman.

Dec 14 Deed to Isaac Lewis Baker for Giles County land and Nashville lot. Copy, TNDa (8-1365).

Dec 15 From James Foster Hull. ALS, DLC (31). Introduces James McCully, AJ's supposed relative, and discusses Hull's early life in Ireland.

Dec 15 Rachel Jackson to Richard Keith Call. Extract, Herbert J. Doherty, *Richard Keith Call, Southern Unionist* (Gainesville, Fla., 1961), pp. 22–23 (8-1367). Describes her meeting with Mary L. Kirkman when returning from Florida.

Dec 17 From Edward George Washington Butler. ALS, DLC (31). Requests advice on joining the Russian army and information about Butler family property in Pennsylvania.

Dec 17 From George Walton (enclosure: Edmund Doyle to AJ, Dec 5). LS, DLC (31). *TPUS,* 22:304–306. Forwards mail and discusses Indian affairs.

Dec 18 From Peter Hagner (enclosure: Account with United States, Dec 18). ALS, DLC (31); LC, DNA-RG 217 (8-1369). Reports a credit of $714.61 to AJ's account.

Dec 18 From William Grafton Dulany Worthington (enclosures: Worthington to John R. Bell, Nov 15; Worthington to Florida Indians, and preliminary articles for a treaty, both Nov 20). ALS, DNA-RG 59 (M116-9). Transmits documents.

Dec 18 Account with United States. AD (endorsed by John C. Calhoun), AD (endorsed by James C. Bronaugh as received, Jan 11, 1822), and LC, DNA-RG 217 (5-1229, -1331, 8-1371); AD, DLC (31).

Dec 19 From James Craine Bronaugh. ALS, DLC (72). Reports on congressional investigation of Callava controversy, on AJ's accounts, and on prospects for appointments of Robert Butler and William King.

Dec 22 From Henry Marie Brackenridge. ALS (dated 1823), DLC (32). Discusses Thomas S. Jesup's visit to Pensacola, George M. Brooke's secret opposition to AJ, and a fight between William W. Lear and Washington L. Hannum.

Dec 22 From James Moore. ALS, DLC (31). Requests information about Florida.

Dec 23 From George Walton (enclosures: Decree in the case of *Timothy Twitchell and N. H. Allen* v. *Pensacola City Council,* n.d., DLC-59; Walton to Florida Indians, Dec 17; Walton to Stephen Richards, Dec 18). LS, DLC (31). Reports reaction to administration support for AJ in Florida controversy.

Dec 24 From Mulatto King and Red Ground Chief. Copy, DNA-RG 59 (M116-10). Complain of depredations by Daniel Perryman and others.

Dec 24 From Stephen Richards. Copy, DNA-RG 59 (M116-10). Requests that AJ address Florida Indians.

Dec 26 From John Quincy Adams. AL in an unknown clerk's hand, DLC (31); LC, DNA-RG 59 (M40-17). Reports $6,156.51 debit in AJ's state department account.

Dec 26 From James Craine Bronaugh. ALS, DLC (31). Reports on AJ's accounts, the appointment of his successor as governor, and William H. Crawford's political intrigues.

Dec 27 From James Craine Bronaugh. ALS matched fragments, DLC (75), ICHi (7-0964). Encloses a letter (not found) for [John] Overton re Crawford's political intrigue, with a view to its publication.

Dec 29 Receipt from Malachi Nicholson for $20, partial wages as overseer

Date	Entry	Page
	on Andrew Jackson Hutchings's farm for 1821. DS with AJ endorsement, A-Ar (8-1373).	
Dec 30	*From James Craine Bronaugh.*	124
Dec 30	From John Henry Eaton. ALS with AJ endorsement, DLC (31). Bassett, 3:141–42 (extract). Discusses presidential politics.	
Dec 31	*From James Monroe.*	126

1822

Date	Entry	Page
Jan 1	From John Quincy Adams (enclosures: Joaquin de Anduaga to Adams, Nov 22, Dec 27, 1821, DLC-31). LS, DLC (31); LC, DNA-RG 59 (M40-17). *ASP, Miscellaneous Documents,* 2:832. Sends translations of letters concerning seizure of Spanish archives in St. Augustine and AJ's actions as governor.	
Jan 1	Receipt of Malachi Nicholson for $250, wages as overseer of Andrew Jackson Hutchings's Alabama farm for 1821. DS, A-Ar (8-1379).	
Jan 2	Account with Rapier & Simpson for general merchandise for Andrew Jackson Hutchings's Alabama farm. ADS with AN by AJ, A-Ar (8-1381). Runs to November 16.	
Jan 4	From Trueman Cross. ALS copy, DNA-RG 107 (M221-93). Discusses erection of barracks at St. Augustine.	
Jan 5	To John Quincy Adams (enclosures: William G. D. Worthington to AJ, Oct 4 and 6, 1821). LS, DNA-RG 59 (M116-10); LC, DLC (63). Forwards reports and recommends salary increases for Florida officials.	
Jan 5	To John Caldwell Calhoun. LC, DLC (63). *Calhoun Papers,* 6:607–608. Discusses the army reduction, the resignation of Andrew J. Donelson, and Winfield Scott's activities.	
Jan 5	To John Caldwell Calhoun (enclosures: William McIntosh to AJ, Nov 2, 1821; Mulatto King to AJ, Oct 27, 1821). LS and Copy, DNA-RG 107 (M221-93); LC, DLC (63). Transmits letters.	
Jan 5	*To Richard Keith Call.*	127
Jan 6	Account with Mary Caffery Knox for hire of slave Lewis to AJ for 1821. DS in AJ's hand, DLC (32). Runs to February 8, 1823.	
Jan 7	*From James Craine Bronaugh.*	128
Jan 7	*From George Walton.*	130
Jan 8	*To Edward George Washington Butler.*	132
Jan 8	Account with Walden Fuller & Co. for ferrying at Florence, Alabama. ADS, THi (8-1393). Runs to December 15.	
Jan 8	Account with Rapier & Simpson for general merchandise. ADS with AJ endorsement, DLC (31). Runs to November 9.	
Jan 8	Memorandum of tools received by Alexander Barksdale, AJ's overseer at Hermitage. AD in AJ's hand signed by Barksdale, DLC (31). Bassett, 3:182 (dated 1823).	
Jan 10	*To James Craine Bronaugh.*	134
Jan 11	To Peter Hagner. LS in Robert Butler's hand, THi (8-1396). Acknowledges letter discussing AJ's military account.	
Jan 12	To John Caldwell Calhoun (enclosures: Mulatto King et al. to AJ, Nov 11, 1821; Neamathla and Ninnehamata Tustunnuggee to AJ,	

Nov 23, 1821; Edmund Doyle to AJ, Dec 5, 1821). LS, DLC (75); Copy, DNA-RG 107 (M221-96). *Calhoun Papers,* 6:618–19. Reveals a scheme of William McIntosh and former Indian agent David B. Mitchell to defraud Creek Indians of their annuity payments.

Jan 12 From William Lee. LS, DLC (31); LC, DNA-RG 217 (8-1398). States that AJ's military account is closed.

[Jan 15] From John Henry Eaton. ALS, DLC (72). Discusses Richard M. Johnson's speech in the Senate on imprisonment for debt.

Jan 16 To William Brand. LS, OClWHi (8-1399). Introduces Richard I. Easter.

Jan 16 To Edward Livingston. LS, NjP (mAJs). Introduces Easter.

Jan 18 To William Grafton Dulany Worthington. LC, DLC (63). Requests copies of correspondence re the Spanish archives at St. Augustine.

Jan 19 From Robert Butler (enclosures: José Coppinger to Butler, June 23 and July [4], 1821; Butler to Coppinger, June 26, July 3, 5, 1821; Butler to John R. Bell, July 11, 1821, DNA-RG 59, M116-10). ALS, DLC (31). Transmits correspondence re the Spanish archives at St. Augustine.

Jan 19 From J[oseph] & R[obert] Woods. ALS with AJ endorsement, DLC (31). Invoice AJ for the shipment of furniture from New Orleans.

Jan 21 From Robert Butler. ALS and Copy, DNA-RG 59 (M116-10); LC, DLC (63); Copy, DNA-RG 46 (8-1402). *ASP, Foreign Relations,* 4:798. Relates his discussion with José Coppinger over the surrender of the archives at St. Augustine.

Jan 22 To John Quincy Adams (enclosures: José Coppinger to Robert Butler, June 23 and July [4], 1821; Butler to Coppinger, June 26, July 3, 5, 1821; Butler to John R. Bell, July 11, 1821, all DNA-RG 59, M116-10; AJ to Bell, Sept 1, 1821; AJ to William G. D. Worthington, Aug 13, 1821; Worthington to AJ, Nov 9, 1821; William Reynolds to AJ, Nov 18, 1821; Butler to AJ, Jan 21). LS and Copies, DNA-RG 59 (M116-10); LC, DLC (63); Copies, DNA-RG 46 (mAJs), PU (8-1404). *ASP, Foreign Relations,* 4:793–96. Discusses removal of the Spanish archives from St. Augustine.

Jan 22 *To Philip Pendleton Barbour.* 137

Jan 22 To James Monroe. ALS with AN by John Q. Adams, DNA-RG 59 (M116-10); LC, DLC (63). Bassett, 3:143. Requests delay in the acceptance of his resignation as Florida governor.

Jan 22 To Smith Thompson. LS, DNA-RG 45 (M124-92). Introduces Mason Wilson.

Jan 22 From Edward George Washington Butler. ALS, LNHiC (9-0001). Thanks AJ for advice and states intention to remain in the U.S. Army.

Jan 24 Account with William Chandler for tuition of Andrew Jackson, Jr., Andrew Jackson Hutchings, and Lyncoya. AD, DLC (31). Runs to January 17, 1823.

Jan 25 From Fontaine Maury. ALS, DLC (31); LC, DNA-RG 59 (M40-17). Informs AJ of a correction to his Florida account.

Jan 26 To John Caldwell Calhoun. Extract, Charles Hamilton Catalog 127 (April 1980), Item 114 (9-0007); Abstract, DNA-RG 94

(M711-3). Complains that William W. Lear has assaulted Washington L. Hannum, a magistrate of West Florida.

Jan 26 Affidavit of Andrew Jackson Donelson re William W. Lear–Washington L. Hannum altercation and Thomas Sidney Jesup's alliance with the Henry Clay–William H. Crawford forces. LC, DLC (63).

Jan 26 Promissory note for $200 to Peter Richardson Booker and Patrick Maguire for one share of stock in the Cypress Land Company on behalf of Andrew Jackson Hutchings. DS signed by AJ and John Coffee, THi (9-0005).

Jan 28 From John Coppinger Connor. ALS, DLC (31). Promises to send copies of documents re the Vidal estate case.

Jan 28 From George Walton (enclosure: Walton to John Crowell, Jan 15). LS, DNA-RG 59 (M116-10). *TPUS,* 22:347–48. Discusses Indian activities, Eligius Fromentin's movements, the John Innerarity case, and the arrival of Edmund P. Gaines.

Jan 29 *To George Gibson.* 139

Jan 29 *To James Monroe.* 140

Jan 30 From James Craine Bronaugh (enclosures: William Lee to AJ, Aug 11, 1821; Lee to Bronaugh, Jan 12). ALS, DLC (31). Reports the settlement of AJ's accounts and relays anti-Crawford rumors.

Jan 31 To John Quincy Adams (enclosures: George Walton to AJ, Jan 7; Walton to Duncan L. Clinch, and to Henry Wilson, Jan 2; Order for arrest of Marcos de Villiers and Arnaldo Guillemard, Jan 2; Memorial of de Villiers and Guillemard, Jan 3; Walton to de Villiers and Guillemard, Jan 5; Certificate of Wilson, Jan 6, DNA-RG 59, M116-10). ALS and Extract, DNA-RG 59 (M116-10); ALS copy, DLC (63); Extracts, DNA-RG 46 (9-0018) and PU (9-0020). Bassett, 3:143–44. Sends documents re Walton's actions in Florida.

Jan 31 From Richard Ivy Easter. ALS with ANS by AJ, DLC (31). Asks to borrow $250 for trip to Mobile.

Jan 31 From J[oseph] & R[obert] Woods. ALS, DLC (31). Report that the shipment of furniture from New Orleans is one package short.

Feb 1 Account with Robert Brownlee Currey for postage. ADS with ANS by AJ, DLC (31). Bassett, 3:168. Runs to August 1.

Feb 2 Richard Keith Call to Rachel Jackson. ALS, DLC (31). Reports on activities and friends in Pensacola.

Feb 2 Receipt of Elizabeth Rucker Donelson for $176.50 paid for seed cotton delivered to AJ's gin. DS in AJ's hand with AJ's ADS receipt for the cotton, DLC (31).

Feb 2 Order from Richard Ivy Easter to pay $150 to Alpha Kingsley, with receipt of Joel Parrish, Jr., for payment, March 25. ADS, DLC (31).

Feb 3 From John Coppinger Connor (enclosures: Opinion in *Heirs of Vidal* v. *John Innerarity,* Dec 10, 1821; Petition asking for review of *Heirs of Vidal* v. *John Innerarity,* n.d.). ALS, DLC (31). Discusses the Vidal estate case.

Feb 4 *From John Sommerville.* 142

Feb 4 From Sylvanus Thayer. Printed form with ms insertions and AJ endorsement, DLC (70). Requests AJ's consent for Daniel S. Donelson to serve five years in army from date of admission to

West Point.

Feb 4 From George Walton. LS, DLC (31). Reports on Vidal estate case, Eligius Fromentin's decision to remain in Pensacola, and Indian affairs.

Feb 6 *To Thomas Jefferson.* 143

Feb 8 *From James Craine Bronaugh.* 145

Feb 9 From Philip Pendleton Barbour. ALS, DLC (31). Bassett, 3:148. States his refusal to put AJ's January 22 letter, as written, before the House of Representatives because of aspersions against some members.

Feb 10 *From John Rhea.* 148

Feb 12 From John Henry Eaton. ALS, DLC (31). Suggests that publication of the documents re the Florida affair has quieted the investigation in the House of Representatives.

Feb 13 To John Quincy Adams. LS, DNA-RG 59 (M116-10). *TPUS,* 22:364. Discusses settlement of AJ's Florida accounts.

Feb 13 To Fontaine Maury (enclosures: Account with Robert B. Currey for postage, Nov 3, 1821; Receipt from Ingram & Lloyd, Nov 24, 1821; AJ to Charles S. West, Feb 14; Receipt from John Sommerville, Feb 15). LS, DNA-RG 59 (M179-53). Discusses Florida accounts.

Feb 14 To Charles S. West (enclosures: Ezekiel Salomon to AJ, Aug 1, Sept 3, 1821; Receipt from John Sommerville, Feb 15). ALS copy, DLC (31); Copy, DNA-RG 59 (M179-53). Directs transfer of funds from AJ's Florida account to the U.S. treasury account.

Feb 14 Receipt from John E. Linn for $10 for tailor's services for Andrew Jackson, Jr., and Andrew Jackson Hutchings. DS in AJ's hand also signed by Robert Butler, A-Ar (9-0027).

Feb 15 Receipt from John Sommerville for $662.37 deposited to the credit of the United States in the branch of the Bank of the State of Tennessee. ADS duplicates, DLC (31), DNA-RG 59 (M179-53); Copy, DLC (63).

Feb 16 *From James Craine Bronaugh.* 149

Feb 18 From William Grafton Dulany Worthington. LS, DNA-RG 59 (M116-10). *TPUS,* 22:364–66. Discusses the problem of the Florida archives; recommends that AJ establish a winter home on the east coast of Florida.

Feb 19 *To Francis Preston.* 151

Feb 20 From William Grafton Dulany Worthington. ALS, DLC (31). Encloses a report (not found) omitted from his letter of February 18.

Feb 22 From John Quincy Adams (enclosure: Adams to George Walton, Feb 22, DLC-31). LS, DLC (31); LC, DNA-RG 59 (M40-17). *TPUS,* 22:367–68. Instructs AJ to forward any official communications from Florida; says that the decision of the department re Joaquin de Anduaga's complaints against AJ will be sent to him as soon as made; transmits documents accompanying presidential message of January 28.

Feb 23 *From James Craine Bronaugh.* 152

Feb 23 From Thomas Washington (1788–1863). ALS, DLC (31); Copy in AJ's hand, THi (9-0033). Explains postponement of action re *Bennett Smith* v. *John Hutchings's Executors.*

Feb 24 From George Walton (enclosures: John R. Bell to AJ, Aug 4; Bell to José Coppinger, July 30, Aug 2, DLC-30; and Coppinger to Bell, Aug 1, DLC-30, all 1821). LS, DLC (31). Discusses the Florida archives and thanks AJ for his advice.

Feb 25 *To John Coffee.* 153

Feb 26 Receipt of Charles S. West for deposit of $5,000 to the account of the United States in the New Orleans branch of the Bank of the United States. ADS, DLC (70).

Feb 27 *To Horace Holley.* 154

Feb 27 From Charles S. West (enclosure: Receipt of West, Feb 26). ALS duplicate, DLC (31). Acknowledges deposit to the credit of the United States.

Feb 28 To John Caldwell Calhoun. LS, NWM (9-0039). Recommends William S. Overton, son of Thomas, for appointment to the Military Academy.

Feb 28 To John Coffee. ALS, THi (9-0040). Instructs him to dismiss Big Spring overseer Stephen Sharrock and to place William W. Crawford in temporary superintendence.

[Feb 28] To Catalina Mir Satorios. Extract, Parton, 2:483–84 (mAJs). Gives history of the acquisition of the slave Polydore (Fernando).

March 2 From James Gadsden. LC, DNA-RG 94 (9-0044). Acknowledges receipt of letter reporting Lear-Hannum fight.

March 2 From Charles S. West (enclosures: Receipt of West, Feb 26; West to AJ, Feb 27). ALS, DLC (31). Transmits duplicates.

March 4 Receipt from George Elliott for $65 for season of mares to Pacolet. ADS with AJ endorsement, DLC (31).

March 5 From Fontaine Maury. ALS with AJ endorsement, DLC (31); LC, DNA-RG 59 (M40-17). Sends receipt (not found) for AJ to sign, acknowledging allowance of $72.95 for postage and stationery.

March 7 From Mason Wilson. ALS with AJ endorsement, DLC (31). Thanks AJ for hospitality and letters of introduction.

March 8 To John Quincy Adams (enclosures: Mulatto King and Red Ground Chief to AJ, and Stephen Richards to AJ, both Dec 24, 1821; George Walton to AJ, Jan 28). ALS, DNA-RG 59 (M116-10); ALS copy, DLC (31). Transmits documents.

March 9 To Sylvanus Thayer. ALS copy, DLC (31). Consents that Daniel S. Donelson commit for five years' service in the army.

March 10 Account with John Decker for foodstuffs. ADS with AJ endorsement, DLC (32). Runs to July 15, 1823.

March 11 From Samuel Houston. ALS and Copy, DNA-RG 107 (M221-93). Asks AJ to intervene with the war department in the settlement of Houston's disputed account for army pay.

March 13 To James Gadsden (enclosure: Samuel Houston to AJ, March 11). ALS, THi (9-0046); Copy, DNA-RG 107 (M221-93). Endorses Houston's claim and requests Gadsden's intervention.

March 13 *From Thomas Gassaway Watkins.* 155

March 14 *To John Coffee.* 157

March 14 Receipt from William White Crawford for $257.56 settling AJ's accounts with him. DS in AJ's hand, DLC (31).

March 15 To Andrew Jackson Donelson. ALS, DLC (9-0052). Expresses satisfaction with Donelson's enrollment to study law at Transylvania University.

March 15 To William Berkeley Lewis. ALS, NNPM (9-0054). Sends draft (not found) of a letter to James Monroe, asking Lewis for suggestions.

March 15 Account with Stephen Upchurch for expenses at Big Spring farm. AD, DLC (37). Runs to July 29.

March 16 To Fontaine Maury (enclosures: Receipt of Charles S. West, Feb 26; West to AJ, Feb 27). ADS abstract, DLC (63); Typed extract, DLC (72). Informs him of deposits made to the account of the United States at the New Orleans branch of the Bank of the United States.

March 19 To John Quincy Adams. ALS, DNA-RG 59 (M116-10); ADS abstract, DLC (63). Discusses the congressional investigation of his conduct as governor.

March 19 *To William Berkeley Lewis.* 159

March 19 *To James Monroe.* 160

March 19 From John Sommerville. ALS, DNA-RG 59 (M179-53). Reports that Joseph Woods has taken charge of the deposit to the United States in the New Orleans branch of the Bank of the United States.

March 20 To John Coffee. ALS, THi (9-0066). Bassett, 3:156. Informs him that Egbert Harris is en route to superintend AJ's farm at Big Spring.

March 20 To Mary Donelson Coffee. AN, THi (9-0068). Asks her to accept a gift of feathers, which William W. Crawford will deliver.

March 20 Announcement of stud season for Young Truxton. Printed, *Nashville Whig,* March 20 (9-0069).

March 21 *To Andrew Jackson Donelson.* 163

March 21 To Fontaine Maury (enclosure: John Sommerville to AJ, March 19). ALS, DNA-RG 59 (M179-53). States that the specie left in his Nashville account has been forwarded to New Orleans in the care of Joseph Woods.

March 21 From Samuel Ragland Overton. ALS with AJ endorsement, DLC (31). Discusses his appointment as land commissioner in Florida and land business.

March 23 Receipt from Stephen Sharrock for $42.18^1/_3$, payment as overseer on AJ's Big Spring farm. DS with AJ endorsement, DLC (31).

March 25 *To Richard Keith Call.* 164

March 25 To Fontaine Maury. ALS, DNA-RG 59 (M179-53); ALS copy, DLC (63). Transmits receipt (not found) for $72.95, paid for postage and stationery expenses.

March 25 Record of mares put to Young Truxton. AD fragment in AJ's hand, DLC (75). Runs to April 18.

March 27 Accounts with Egbert Harris and others for expenses at AJ's Big Spring farm. AD with AJ endorsement, DLC (31). Runs to October 10.

March 27 Receipt from Richard Watkins for $22.22^1/_2$ for cotton delivered to AJ's gin. ADS with AJ endorsement, DLC (31).

March 29 From John Christmas McLemore. ALS, DLC (31). Reports on progress in locating some of AJ's old East Tennessee land warrants; discusses AJ's proposition to sell or trade some of his Memphis land.

March 29 From John Overton. ALS, THi (9-0078). Discusses the plan to divide their Memphis holdings and the compromise and settlement of their dispute re Allison lands.

March 29 — Receipt from Mary Caffery Knox for $50 for a bay filly. DS in AJ's hand, DLC (31).

March 30 — To John Coffee. ALS, THi (9-0086). Commends Coffee's settlement with Stephen Sharrock.

March 31 — Warrant from William Harris Crawford transferring $5,000 from AJ's account as governor of Florida to the United States. Printed form with ms insertions, DNA-RG 217 (9-0089).

[cMarch–April] — Memoranda re William Harris Crawford and the Florida governorship controversies. AD matched fragments, DLC (31, 59). Bassett, 3:148–51 (text from DLC-59 only).

April 1 — To Andrew Jackson Donelson. ALS, DLC (9-0091). Bassett, 3:157 (extract). Discusses Daniel S. Donelson's situation at West Point, slave purchases in Kentucky, and Andrew J. Donelson's educational program.

April 2 — To James Monroe. ALS, DNA-RG 59 (M116-10). Introduces Henry Crabb.

April 2 — Power of attorney to John Overton to conduct business relating to AJ's Memphis landholdings. DS, T (9-0095); Copy, TMSh (mAJs).

April 5 — From John Overton. ALS matched fragments, THi and TNJ (9-0099). Discusses problems regarding the Allison lands and the efforts for compromise of their dispute.

April 6 — From John Caldwell Calhoun. LC, DNA-RG 107 (M6-11). Approves Samuel Houston's claim.

April 7 — From Patrick Henry Darby. Copy, THi (9-0104). Discusses compromise land settlement with AJ, John Overton, John C. McLemore, and others.

April 10 — *From [James Gadsden].* 166

April 11 — *To John Christmas McLemore.* 169

April 11 — Deed from John Overton and AJ to Samuel Ragland Overton for 250 acres in the western district, south of the Tennessee River. Copy, TPHen (9-0108).

April 12 — To Andrew Jackson Donelson. ALS, DLC (9-0110). Bassett, 3:157 (extract). Reaffirms his support of Donelson's educational plans and his view that Daniel S. Donelson should remain at the Military Academy; discusses slave purchase and the Senate's rejection of James Gadsden and Nathan Towson.

April 12 — Bill of sale from Catalina Mir Satorios for the slave Polydore (Fernando), with bill of purchase and affidavits. DS and ADS, DLC (31).

April 13 — *To Egbert Harris.* 170

April 13 — *From James Gadsden.* 171

April 16 — *From James Craine Bronaugh.* 172

April 16 — *From Catalina Mir Satorios.* 173

April 17 — *From John Sommerville.* 175

April 17 — Deed from John Overton and Jesse Wharton for about 1,650 acres in several tracts on or near the Obion River. DS, DLC (31).

April 18 — From Daniel Brent (enclosure: John Q. Adams to Joaquin de Anduaga, April 15). LS, DLC (31). Transmits letter.

April 19 Deed to John Overton for sundry lots in Nashville and several tracts of land on the Obion and Deer rivers. Copies, TPHen (9-0118), TJMad (9-0122).

April 19 Deed of release to John Overton for land claimed by Overton from the David Allison estate. Copy, TPHen (9-0126).

April 19 Deed of release from Patrick Henry Darby, James Jackson, and Jenkin Whiteside to John Overton and Jesse Wharton for land from the David Allison estate. Copy, TPHen, Deed Book A, pp. 74–75 (mAJs).

April 20 Deed of release to James Jackson of all interest in David Allison's lands in Tennessee, excepting those along the Duck River or otherwise conveyed. Copies, TNDa (9-0128), TDWe (9-0129).

April 20 Deed to James Jackson for about 1,650 acres in several tracts on or near the Obion River. Copies, TNDa (9-0131), TUOb (mAJs).

April 22 To Andrew Jackson Donelson. ALS, DLC (9-0133). Reiterates opinion that Daniel S. Donelson should remain at the Military Academy and cancels the order for slaves.

April 23 To John Quincy Adams (enclosures: John Sommerville to Joseph Woods, March 18; Woods to Sommerville, April 3; Sommerville to Thomas T. Tucker, April 15; Sommerville to AJ, April 17). ALS, DNA-RG 59 (M116-10). Complains of the handling of his deposit in the New Orleans branch of the Bank of the United States.

April 24 Advertisement by John Coffee for AJ's runaway slave Gilbert from the Big Spring farm. Printed, *Nashville Whig,* April 24 (9-0136).

April 26 *To Andrew Jackson Donelson.* 176

April 28 From John Christmas McLemore. ALS, DLC (31). Discusses AJ's East Tennessee land claims.

April 30 Account with William Henry Wharton for medical attention to slaves on Big Spring farm. ADS with AJ endorsement, DLC (31). Runs to November 6.

May 1 From John Philippart (enclosure: Prospectus of *The East Indian Military Calendar* and *The Royal Military Calendar,* n.d.). ALS, DLC (31). Requests a narrative of AJ's military engagements and a portrait to publish in a forthcoming edition similar to his *Royal Military Calendar.*

May 2 To John Caldwell Calhoun (enclosure: AJ to James Gadsden, May 2). Copy, DNA-RG 107 (M221-93). *Calhoun Papers,* 7:90. Thanks Calhoun for informing him of the approval of Samuel Houston's claim.

May 2 *To Andrew Jackson Donelson.* 177

May 2 *To James Gadsden.* 179

May 7 From Richard Rush (enclosure: John Philippart to AJ, May 1). ALS, DLC (31). Forwards letter.

May 9 From Henry Middleton Rutledge (enclosure: Catalina M. Satorios to AJ, April 16). ALS, DLC (31). Says that, in the absence of his son Edward Augustus, he translated Satorios's letter.

May 10 To James Glasgow Martin. AN by proxy, DLC (9-0146). Invites him to dinner on May 13.

May 13 Decision in *John, Arthur, and Robert Brooks, administrators of Matthew Brooks* v. *AJ, Thomas Crutcher, and Alfred Balch,*

	executors of William T. Lewis. Copy, T (9-0147).	
May 14	*To Richard Ivy Easter.*	182
May 15	To William Brand. ALS, Joseph F. Rorke (9-0162). Introduces Samuel R. Overton.	
May 15	To Andrew Erwin et al. LS by proxy (Patrick H. Darby), T (10-0296). Announces that in June depositions will be taken of the Allison heirs in Georgia re *Jackson* v. *Erwin.*	
May 15	To Edward Livingston. ALS, NjP (mAJs). Introduces Samuel R. Overton.	
May 16	To Catalina Mir Satorios. Copy with AN by AJ, DLC (31). Sends payment for the slave Polydore (Fernando) and requests a certified bill of sale.	
May 17	To Andrew Jackson Donelson. Extract, Nashville *Republican Banner,* June 22, 1856 (9-0164). Expresses pleasure that Donelson has social contact with Henry Clay and family, towards whom AJ has no enmity.	
May 19	To John Quincy Adams. ALS, DNA-RG 59 (M116-10). Forwards documents (not identified) sent by William G. D. Worthington.	
May 19	To Andrew Jackson Donelson. Extracts, Thomas F. Madigan Catalog (Oct 1935), Item 56 (9-0165), *The Collector* [1988], Item V-662 (mAJs). Reports likely passage of a law re compensation for the heirs of John Donelson (c1718–86) and requests authority to make entry for Donelson and his brother; discusses James Gadsden's rejection by the Senate.	
May 19	To Fontaine Maury. ALS, DNA-RG 59 (M179-54); ADS abstract, DLC (63). Complains again about handling of his account by the New Orleans branch of the Bank of the United States.	
May 20	*To Richard Keith Call.*	183
May 20	*To Andrew Jackson Donelson.*	188
May 22	To Catalina Mir Satorios. Copy, DLC (31). Again requests certified bill of sale for Polydore (Fernando).	
May 22	Account with William Saunders for meals and lodging of AJ and family at the Fountain of Health. DS with AN by AJ, THi (9-0173). Runs to October 25.	
May 29	To James Craine Bronaugh. ALS, DLC (31). Bassett, 3:162–63. Asks Bronaugh's help in securing a Florida post for Hezekiah Niles's son, Samuel; discusses William H. Crawford and the Senate's rejection of James Gadsden and Nathan Towson.	
May 30	*From James Monroe.*	189
[cMay]	From R. & W. Armstrong (enclosure: Bill from Thomas Barron & Co., April 23, DLC-31). AD with AJ endorsement, DLC (58). Bill AJ for wines and other groceries.	
June 1	To James Craine Bronaugh. ALS, DLC (31). Bassett, 3:162 (extract). Withdraws his request for support of Samuel Niles for Florida appointment in favor of Edward A. Rutledge; discusses John Cocke's 1809 duel with Thomas Dardis and James Gadsden's rejection by the Senate.	
June 1	To William Pope Duval. ALS, THer (9-0179). Commends Edward A. Rutledge, Samuel R. Overton, James C. Bronaugh, and Richard K. Call.	

June 2 *To Andrew Jackson Donelson.* 191

June 3 To Samuel Latham Mitchill. LS, Gallery of History, Inc. (9-0188). Introduces John Newnan.

June 3 From Charles McClung. ALS with AJ endorsement leaving further action to McClung's discretion, DLC (31). Discusses surveying of some of AJ's land claims in East Tennessee.

June 5 From Andrew Jackson Donelson. ALS, DLC (31). Empowers AJ to act in his behalf should Congress confirm the Thomas Carr and John Donelson (c1718–86) claim; discusses his trip to Blue Licks spa.

June 5 From Fontaine Maury (enclosure: Certification by Samuel Brook, June 5). ALS, DLC (31); LC, DNA-RG 59 (M40-17). Reports $5,662.37 credit to the United States in settlement of AJ's Florida accounts.

June 5 Certification by Samuel Brook for AJ's deposit of $5,662.37 to the account of the United States. ADS, DLC (31).

June 7 From Catalina Mir Satorios. ALS (Spanish), DLC (31). States that she will secure a proper bill of sale for Polydore (Fernando) as soon as possible.

June 8 From Jean Baptiste Plauché. ALS (French) with AJ endorsement and Translation, DLC (31). Requests that AJ recommend his son, J. J. Alexander, for appointment to West Point.

June 9 From Samuel Ragland Overton. ALS with AJ endorsement, DLC (31). Reports arrival in Pensacola and relates news of New Orleans, Pensacola, and friends in those places.

June 13 Receipt from Malachi Nicholson for $5 for weaving cloth for Andrew Jackson Hutchings's slaves. DS with AJ endorsement, A-Ar (9-0189).

June 25 From John Christmas McLemore (enclosures: William Hill to McLemore, May 17; North Carolina land grants to Stockley Donelson, Nos. 191, 207, 208). ALS, DLC (31). Discusses status of AJ's East Tennessee land claims.

June 25 Certified bill of sale from Catalina Mir Satorios for the slave Polydore (Fernando). DS (Spanish), DLC (31).

June 27 From Felix Grundy. ALS with AJ endorsement, DLC (31). Bassett, 3:163–64. Reports the intention of some Tennessee legislators to nominate AJ for president.

June 28 *To John Caldwell Calhoun.* 192

June 28 *To Andrew Jackson Donelson.* 195

June 29 *To Richard Keith Call.* 197

June 29 *To John M. A. Hamblen.* 200

June 30 From Henry Middleton Rutledge (enclosure: Translation of Jean B. Plauché to AJ, June 8). ALS, DLC (31). Sends translation and expresses his anxiety about Edward A. Rutledge's health during his move to Florida.

June 30 Warrant from William Harris Crawford transferring $662.37 from AJ's account as governor of Florida to the United States. Printed form with ms insertions, DNA-RG 217 (9-0204).

July 1 *To William Berkeley Lewis.* 201

July 2 To James Monroe. ALS, DNA-RG 94 (M688-63). Introduces

	Jean B. Plauché.
July 4	From William Carroll. Printed, *Franklin Independent Gazette,* July 8 (mAJs, 9-0209). Presents the sword voted to AJ by the Tennessee legislature in 1819.
July 4	To William Carroll. Printed, *Franklin Independent Gazette,* July 8 (mAJs, 9-0210). Accepts sword.
July 4	Toast at Fourth of July celebration: "Thomas Jefferson, the Patriot, Sage, and Philanthropist." Printed, *Nashville Whig,* July 10 (mAJs).
July 5	To Andrew Jackson Donelson. ALS, DLC (9-0213). Bassett, 3:167 (extract). Disparages the attacks upon the Kentucky judiciary; urges Donelson to visit at the Hermitage when his studies permit.
July 5	From Samuel Ragland Overton. ALS with AJ endorsement, DLC (31). Discusses Florida appointments and the July 4 celebration in Pensacola.
July 6	From Thomas Gassaway Watkins. ALS, DLC (31). Bassett, 3:167–68 (extract). Discusses national politics, Thomas Jefferson's organization of the University of Virginia, and the possible sale of a slave to AJ.
July 8	From Catalina Mir Satorios. ALS (Spanish), DLC (31). Relates the history of the slave Polydore (Fernando).
July 9	From William Martin (1765–1846). ALS with AJ endorsement "to be carefully preserved," DLC (31). Asks AJ for clear title to land purchased in 1796 and mistakenly deeded in part also to William Brackin.
July 10	To Catherine Donelson Martin. ALS fragment, DLC (72). Discusses arrangements to bring her mother-in-law, Elizabeth G. Anderson, to the Hermitage for a visit.
July 16	To Andrew Jackson Donelson. ALS, DLC (9-0217). Discusses his and Donelson's health and states that he will travel to Murfreesboro to attend the meeting of the Tennessee legislature.
July 16	From James Gadsden. ALS fragment, DLC (75). Writes that he has received AJ's letter of June 28 (not found) but John C. Calhoun has not received the letter mentioned therein.
July 18	*To James Craine Bronaugh.* 202
July 22	Account with James Stewart & Co. for nails and salt. AD, Stanley F. Horn (9-0220).
July 23	From William Saunders. ALS, DNA-RG 94 (M688-26). Seeks recommendation for his son, Pascal Washington, to West Point.
July 24	*From James Jackson.* 204
July 25	To John Caldwell Calhoun. Extracts, Thomas F. Madigan Catalogs (May 1935), Item 202, and (1940), Item 87 (9-0222). Recommends a neighbor's son, probably Pascal Washington Saunders, for West Point.
July 25	*To Andrew Jackson Donelson.* 205
July 26	*To James Monroe.* 207
July 27	*From Egbert Harris.* 208
July 27	Account with James Gray for horseshoeing. DS with AJ endorsement, DLC (32). Runs to April 12, 1823.
Aug 1	*To James Craine Bronaugh.* 210
Aug 1	Account with Thomas Limrick for supplies furnished the Big Spring

	farm. ADS with AJ endorsement, DLC (31). Runs to November 1.	
Aug 3	*From Samuel Houston.*	211
Aug 5	Deposition of John Coffee re *Bennett Smith* v. *John Hutchings's Executors*. ADS copy endorsed as sent to AJ on Oct 12, THi (9-0232).	
Aug 6	*To Andrew Jackson Donelson.*	212
Aug 9	*To James Gadsden.*	215
Aug 9	To Hezekiah Niles. ALS, MeB (9-0245). Compliments Niles's services as an editor; expresses hope that his son received a Florida appointment.	
Aug 10	From James Scallan. ALS, DLC (31). Asks for letters of introduction to AJ's friends in Florence, Alabama.	
Aug 13	From Egbert Harris. ALS with AJ endorsement, DLC (31). Bassett, 3:176–77. Reports on improvements at the Big Spring farm and complains of William W. Crawford's failure to work as promised.	
Aug 14	From Stephen Pleasonton (enclosure: Statement of AJ's account as governor of Florida, Aug 14, DLC-70). LS, DLC (31); LC, DNA-RG 217 (9-0247). Sends document.	
Aug 16	Abstract of AJ's expenditures as governor of Florida, approved by John Quincy Adams. DS, DNA-RG 217 (9-0248).	
Aug 19	To Andrew Jackson Donelson. ALS (dated 1820), DLC (7-1211). Sends money for Donelson's expenses while at Transylvania University and discusses John Haywood's history of Tennessee.	
Aug 19	From Andrew Jackson Donelson. ALS with AJ endorsement, DLC (31). Discusses AJ's nomination for president and offers assistance in the campaign; elaborates on Edward A. Rutledge's claim for payment as translator.	
Aug 19	From James Scallan. ALS, DLC (31). Retracts his request for letters of introduction.	
Aug 19	Approval of AJ's expenses as governor of Florida by the comptroller's office. DS, DNA-RG 217 (9-0251).	
Aug 20	From Joseph Inslee Anderson. LS, DLC (31); LC, DNA-RG 217 (9-0254). Advises that AJ's Florida account has been closed.	
Aug 24	From Egbert Harris. ALS, DLC (31). Bassett, 3:177–78. Reports that he has contracted for installation of a cotton gin at the Big Spring farm.	
Aug 24–26	From Edward Augustus Rutledge. ALS, DLC (31). Reports on activities of AJ's Pensacola friends and on the yellow fever epidemic.	
Aug 27	To James Craine Bronaugh. ALS, FU (9-0255). *FHQ*, 34(1955):21–24. Discusses the prospects of Bronaugh's election as delegate to Congress; laments the weakness of support by Richard K. Call and Richard I. Easter; mentions Edward A. Rutledge's claim.	
Aug 27	From Andrew Jackson Donelson. ALS with AJ endorsement, DLC (31). Acknowledges receipt of $200.	
Aug 28	To Andrew Jackson Donelson. ALS, DLC (9-0259). Bassett, 3:178 (extract). Discusses the completion of Donelson's education and Edward A. Rutledge's claim for translator's fee.	
Aug 28	Account of Egbert Harris with S. & B. Fuqua for lumber at the Big Spring farm. ADS with AJ endorsement, DLC (31). Runs to	

	November 2.	
Sept 2	From Samuel Ragland Overton. ALS, DLC (31). Reports on the yellow fever epidemic in Pensacola, the death of James C. Bronaugh, and the election for territorial delegate.	
Sept 3	From Dolley Gordon. ALS, DLC (31). Requests AJ's attention to the claim of John, her late husband, for a horse and equipment lost on the Seminole campaign.	
Sept 6	*To Andrew Jackson Donelson.*	217
Sept 6	To John Lind Smith. ALS copy, DLC (31). Thanks him for sending checks for Andrew J. Donelson's military pay.	
Sept 9	From John Smith (La.). ALS, DLC (31). Regrets his inability to visit the Hermitage before departing for Louisiana.	
Sept 10	From Samuel Ragland Overton. ALS, DLC (31). Reports on Edward A. Rutledge's instability, Henry M. Brackenridge's appointment as federal judge, the yellow fever epidemic, and the Florida territorial council.	
Sept 20	Nuncupative will of James Craine Bronaugh. Copy in Richard I. Easter's hand, DLC (31). Requests AJ to send Bronaugh's slaves and money to his mother in Virginia.	
Sept 21	From Malachi Nicholson. ALS with AJ endorsement, A-Ar (9-0267). Asks AJ to send sixty pounds of wool to Andrew J. Hutchings's farm.	
Sept 21	Receipt from Malachi Nicholson for $6 for travel expenses to Huntsville to secure injunction against execution in the case *Bennett Smith* v. *John Hutchings's Executors*. DS in AJ's hand, A-Ar (9-0269).	
Sept 22	From Samuel Ragland Overton. ALS with AJ endorsement, DLC (31). Discusses James C. Bronaugh's death, Florida politics, Kentucky's debtor legislation, and presidential campaign.	
Sept 23	Account with Martin & Williams for fabric, clothing, and household goods. ADS with AN by AJ listing various accounts paid, DLC (31). Runs to December 6.	
Sept 24	To Smith Thompson (from AJ and John Henry Eaton). ALS by Eaton also signed by AJ, MdHi (9-0271). Recommend Grey Skipwith as midshipman.	
Sept 27	To Andrew Jackson Donelson. ALS, DLC (9-0273). Reports sickness and death of friends in Pensacola, death of William S. Overton, and marriage of William Donelson (1795–1864); discusses duel between William Cumming and George McDuffie.	
Sept 29	*To John Coffee.*	219
[cSept 29]	To [Richard Keith Call]. Extract, FHi (9-0276). Responds to news of Pensacola epidemic and James C. Bronaugh's death.	
Sept 30	From James Jackson. ALS, DLC (31). Reports death of Jenkin Whiteside; discusses Whiteside's indebtedness, Anthony Winston, Jr.'s offer to buy a portion of AJ's Big Spring land, and overseer problems at the Big Spring farm.	
Sept 30	Account of Egbert Harris with John Secrest for services on AJ's Big Spring farm. DS with AN by AJ, DLC (31). Runs to December 2.	
Sept	Memorandum book of AJ's accounts. ADS, DLC (78). Runs to August 31, 1825.	

Oct 1	From Richard Rapier. ALS, DLC (31). Acknowledges receipt of payment for corn.	
Oct 4	To John Coffee. ALS, THi (9-0280). Introduces Abner E. Calloway and a Mr. Langhorne from Virginia, who are seeking a place to settle.	
Oct 4	To James Monroe (enclosure: William King to Monroe, Aug 1). ALS and Copy, DNA-RG 107 (M221-96, 9-0282). *Calhoun Papers,* 7:293. Supports King's reinstatement in the army.	
Oct 10	From James McMillan Glassell. ALS, DLC (31). Describes the yellow fever epidemic in the army and the fever's effect on the election of a Florida territorial delegate; relates the capture of five pirate ships by a revenue cutter.	
Oct 10	From George Walton (enclosure: Nuncupative will of James C. Bronaugh, Sept 20). ALS, DLC (31). Details Bronaugh's services to the territory in his last days and describes his death.	
Oct 11	*To Andrew Jackson Donelson.*	220
Oct 12	From Robert Butler. ALS, DNA-RG 94 (M688-19). Asks AJ to support Samuel J. Hays's admission to the Military Academy.	
Oct 15	To Richard Keith Call. Printed, *The Collector,* May 1902 (9-0289); Extract, FHi (9-0291). Commends Call's decision not to seek the Florida delegate seat.	
Oct 15	To George Gibson. Extracts, Sotheby Parke Bernet Catalog 4114 (April 1978), Item 134 (9-0293); *Flying Quill* (March–April 1957), Item 74 (9-0294). Discusses military accounts of [Arthur W.] Thornton.	
Oct 15	From Samuel Ragland Overton. ALS, DLC (31). Discusses presidential politics.	
Oct 22	Receipt from William Eastin for $29.50 for transporting rope and baling to Andrew Jackson Hutchings's farm. DS with AJ endorsement, A-Ar (9-0295).	
Oct 23	*To Andrew Jackson Donelson.*	221
Oct 23	To Andrew Erwin. Printed form signed by proxy (Patrick H. Darby), T (10-0318). States that depositions of William B. Lewis and John A. Davis will be taken re *Jackson* v. *Erwin.*	
Oct 28	Account with Anthony Latapie for fabrics. ADS, DLC (32). Runs to March 1823.	
Oct 29	From Thomas Gadsden. ALS, DLC (31). Announces that he has transmitted to AJ the record of the case *Griffith* v. *Frazier.*	
Oct 31	From John Caldwell Calhoun. LS, DLC (31); LC, DNA-RG 94 (M91-1). *Calhoun Papers,* 7:322–23. States that Samuel J. Hays will be considered for the Military Academy at the next appointment date.	
Nov 1	Account with Benjamin P. Person for expenses at the Big Spring farm. DS with AJ endorsement, DLC (32). Runs to March 14, 1823.	
Nov 2	Account with Thomas Limrick for general merchandise for the Big Spring farm. ADS with AJ endorsement, DLC (31). Runs to November 15.	
Nov 2	Receipt from Stephen Upchurch for $11 for labor on the Big Spring farm. DS in AJ's hand, DLC (31).	
Nov 7	From Samuel Kercheval. ALS, DLC (31). Asks AJ to contact John	

	Stump re an unsettled debt of Stump's father, Frederick.	
Nov 9	From Andrew Jackson Donelson. AL draft, DLC (9-0301). Discusses his law classes and denies that eastern law schools are superior to Transylvania.	
Nov 10	From Joseph Philips (1784–1857). ALS, DLC (31). Asks AJ to help secure the appointment as receiver of public monies in Edwardsville, Illinois, for the son of Stephen Winchester.	
Nov 11	From Jean Baptiste Plauché. ALS (French), DLC (31). Thanks AJ for the letter of introduction to James Monroe.	
Nov 11	Receipt of Malachi Nicholson for $15.50 in payment for well digging and hauling lumber at Andrew Jackson Hutchings's farm. DS in AJ's hand endorsed on receipt of James McFarley to Nicholson, September 24, A-Ar (9-0302).	
Nov 14	Account of Andrew Jackson Hutchings with Rapier & Simpson for general merchandise for the farm. ADS by Simpson, A-Ar (9-0304). Runs to June 8, 1824.	
Nov 15	Receipt from A[braham] W. Bell for $51 for work on cotton gin at Andrew Jackson Hutchings's farm. ADS with AJ endorsement, A-Ar (9-0305).	
Nov 15	Receipt from William White Crawford for $100 for work on cotton gin house at the Big Spring farm. DS in AJ's hand, DLC (31).	
Nov 16	From Andrew Erwin. LSs, T (10-0325). Announces that he will take depositions in Tennessee and Georgia re *Jackson* v. *Erwin*.	
Nov 16	Receipt from William Griffin for $120 for millwright's work on the cotton gin house at the Big Spring farm. ADS, DLC (31).	
Nov 16	Account with William Watson for shoes and sundries. DS with AJ endorsement, A-Ar (9-0307). Runs to February 26, 182[3].	
Nov 17	Receipt from Malachi Nicholson for $250, wages as overseer of Andrew Jackson Hutchings's farm for 1822. DS in AJ's hand, A-Ar (9-0309).	
Nov 20	To John Coffee. ALS, THi (9-0311). Reports the death of Rachel D. Eastin in Franklin and his intention to remain for the burial.	
Nov 20	From Daniel Smith Donelson. Copy in AJ's hand, DLC (9-0314). States his desire to resign from the Military Academy because of unjust treatment.	
Nov 20	*From James Gadsden.*	223
Nov 24	From Patrick Henry Darby. ALS with AJ endorsement, DLC (31). Reports his readiness to prosecute *Jackson* v. *Erwin*.	
Nov 25	*To Joseph Norvell and Patrick Henry Darby.*	224
Nov 26	To George Walton. ALS, FU (9-0317). *FHQ,* 34(1955):24–28. Discusses the settlement of James C. Bronaugh's estate; suggests that governmental laxness was partly responsible for the yellow fever epidemic in Pensacola.	
Nov 27	*To Richard Keith Call.*	225
Nov 27	To John Coffee. ALS, THi (9-0326). Reports the reactions of John (1755–1830) and Mary Donelson to death of their daughter Rachel D. Eastin; discusses crops at the Big Spring farm and Richard C. Cross's health.	
Nov 27	To Andrew Jackson Donelson. ALS, DLC (9-0329). Discusses sale of part of Big Spring farm; asks Donelson's opinion about the	

benefit of education at the Transylvania law school.

Nov 28 From William Martin (1765–1846). ALS with AJ endorsement, DLC (31). Asks again for information concerning the land dispute with William Brackin.

Nov 29 From William Davison. ALS, DNA-RG 59 (M439-5). Solicits nomination for marshal of West Florida.

Nov 29 From George Nashee. ALS with AJ endorsement, DLC (72). *Cincinnati Commercial,* Jan 8, 1881. Sends bill for subscription to the Chillicothe (Ohio) *Supporter,* 1813–21, and the *Supporter and Scioto Gazette,* 1821–23.

Nov 30 From Samuel Ragland Overton. ALS with AJ endorsement, DLC (31). In response to AJ's inquiry, discusses situation which led to the yellow fever epidemic.

Dec 2 From Joseph W. McKean (enclosure: Account of Egbert Harris with John Secrest, Sept 30). ALS, DLC (31). Transmits account of Secrest and receipt of Mr. Cummings (not found).

Dec 3 From John Henry Eaton. ALS, DLC (31). Bassett 3:179 (extract). Announces arrival in Washington; comments on presidential ambitions of John Q. Adams, John C. Calhoun, and William H. Crawford.

Dec 5 Deed of partition among AJ, John Overton, James Winchester, and the heirs of William Winchester, for Shelby County holdings of the John Rice grant. DS, T (9-0335).

Dec 6 From Robert Jackson. ALS, DLC (31). Bassett, 3:180. Claims relation to AJ.

Dec 6 Account with John H. Guill for pork. DS partly in AJ's hand, DLC (31). Runs to December 10.

Dec 9 From Anthony Wayne Butler. ALS draft, LNHiC (9-0341). Describes his studies at Yale and his plans to read law.

Dec 10 From James Stewart & Co. ALS, DLC (31). Agree to purchase AJ's cotton crop.

Dec 12 To James Monroe. ALS, Library of the Daughters of the Republic of Texas, San Antonio (9-0351). Recommends Samuel R. Fisher for superintendent of the lead mines of the upper Mississippi River.

Dec 13 To Andrew Jackson Donelson. ALS, DLC (9-0353). Discusses the sale of his Alabama land and again inquires about Donelson's moot court case.

Dec 13 To William Martin (1765–1846). Photocopy of ALS, TU (mAJs). Discusses the land dispute between Martin and William Brackin.

Dec 13 From McCoy & Co. ALS, DLC (31). Bassett, 3:180–81. Discourage AJ from shipping his cotton to New Orleans because of low prices.

Dec 14 From Andrew Jackson Donelson. AL draft, DLC (9-0357). Responds to death of Rachel D. Eastin and AJ's decision to bring slaves from Alabama to the Hermitage; describes the moot court proceedings.

Dec 16 To Andrew Jackson Donelson. ALS, DLC (9-0359). Sends copy of Daniel S. Donelson's letter re leaving West Point.

[Dec 16] From James Gadsden. ALS matched fragments, DLC (75). Reports on his activities in Alabama.

Dec 17 *To George Nashee.* 227

Dec 17 — From James Stewart & Co. ALS, DLC (31). Bassett, 3:181. Offer to buy AJ's cotton at 8 to 8½ cents per pound.

Dec 21 — *To John Coffee.* 228

Dec 22 — From Amos Edwards. ALS, DNA-RG 94 (M688-21). Requests recommendation for his son, Ashmore, to West Point.

Dec 23 — *To Andrew Jackson Donelson.* 229

[cDec 24] — From Samuel Houston. ALS fragment, ICHi (11-0998). Discusses newspaper controversy between Joseph Norvell and Patrick H. Darby.

Dec 25 — From James Stewart & Co. ALS, DLC (31). Agree to take AJ's cotton at the price named in his letter of December 24 (not found).

Dec 27 — *To John Coffee.* 231

Dec 28 — From Shadrach Penn, Jr. Printed form with ms insertions and AJ endorsement of payment on January 21, 1823, DLC (31). Requests payment for the *Louisville Public Advertiser.*

Dec 30 — To James Monroe (enclosure: William Davison to AJ, Nov 29). ALS, DNA-RG 59 (M439-5). Recommends Davison for marshal of West Florida.

Dec 30 — From David Fulton. ALS with AJ endorsement, DLC (31). Discusses the sale of a slave, John Fulton, and encloses receipt for $425 payment.

[cDec 30] — From Andrew Jackson Donelson. AL draft, DLC (9-0379). Expresses doubt that his grandmother, Sarah Michie Smith, or James Sanders will support Daniel S. Donelson's transfer to Yale.

Dec 31 — Account with James Stewart & Co. for the sale of cotton at the Hermitage. ADS, DLC (32). Runs to June 4, 1823.

Dec — To Richard Keith Call. Printed, *The Collector,* November 1905 (9-0333); Extract, FHi (mAJs). Approves Call's decision not to seek the Florida delegate seat; laments the dispute between Richard I. Easter and Henry M. Brackenridge.

1823

Jan 1 — From Edmund Pendleton Gaines. ALS, DLC (31). Reports on inspection tour of territory west of the Mississippi.

Jan 2 — From Henry Baldwin. ALS, DLC (31). Bassett, 3:184 (extract dated Jan 1). Discusses support for AJ's presidential candidacy in Pennsylvania.

Jan 3 — From William Chandler. ANS with Daniel Fowler's receipt, Jan 20, DLC (31). Requests payment of $20 to Fowler.

Jan 3 — From James Stewart & Co. ALS, DLC (31). Transmits bill.

Jan 3 — Account with James Stewart & Co. for baling supplies, wine, sugar, etc. ALS, DLC (32). Runs to April 19.

Jan 4 — From Thomas Glascock. ALS, DNA-RG 59 (M439-18). Introduces Joseph W. E. Wallace.

Jan 7 — From Ephraim Hubbard Foster. Abstract, American Art Association Catalog (April 13, 1927), Item 105A (9-0385). Encloses copy of speech he will deliver at Nashville celebration of the Battle of New Orleans.

Jan 7	Bill of sale from John Smith for a horse, $60. DS in AJ's hand, DLC (31).	
Jan 8	To Andrew Jackson Donelson. ALS, DLC (9-0387). Discusses Daniel S. Donelson's wish to resign from the Military Academy and the Battle of New Orleans celebration in Nashville.	
Jan 8	From Ephraim Hubbard Foster. Printed, *Nashville Whig,* Jan 15 (9-0391). Expresses appreciation for AJ's services to the country.	
Jan 8	To Ephraim Hubbard Foster. Printed, *Nashville Whig,* Jan 15 (9-0393). Thanks Foster and Nashville citizens.	
Jan 8	Toast at public dinner in Nashville: "To General John Coffee, an efficient commander on the day we celebrate." Printed, *Nashville Whig,* Jan 15 (9-0386).	
Jan 8	Account of Malachi Nicholson with William Griffin for machine repair and hardware at Andrew Jackson Hutchings's farm. DS, A-Ar (9-0395). Runs to December 25.	
Jan 9	From Samuel Ragland Overton. ALS, DLC (31). Discusses his disagreements with Nathaniel A. Ware about deliberations of the Florida land claims commission.	
Jan 10	*To John Coffee.*	233
Jan 11	*From John Henry Eaton.*	235
Jan 11	Account with George D. Tracy for suits for AJ, Andrew Jackson, Jr., and Andrew Jackson Hutchings. ADS, A-Ar (9-0401).	
Jan 12	James Stewart & Co. to Mr. Atkinson. ANS, DLC (31). Instructs Atkinson to receive cotton delivered by AJ at Donelson's landing.	
Jan 13	*To Anthony Wayne Butler.*	239
Jan 15	From John Henry Eaton. ALS, DLC (72). Advises against accepting appointment as minister to Mexico; discusses possibility of war in Europe.	
Jan 19	*From Samuel Houston.*	241
Jan 20	From David Adams. ALS, DNA-RG 59 (M439-18). Introduces Joseph W. E. Wallace and recalls childhood friendship with AJ.	
Jan 20	James Monroe to United States Senate. DS, DNA-RG 46 (9-0407). *Senate Executive Proceedings,* 3:325. Nominates AJ as minister to Mexico.	
Jan 21	To Andrew Jackson Donelson. ALS, DLC (9-0409). Discusses Daniel S. Donelson's educational plans.	
Jan 21	*To John Henry Eaton.*	242
[Jan 21]	To James Monroe (enclosure: AJ to John H. Eaton, Jan 21). ALS, NN (9-0419). Sends copy of letter.	
Jan 23	Bill of sale for slave Aaron from Elizabeth Rucker Donelson. DS in AJ's hand, DLC (31).	
Jan 24	To Henry Baldwin. LS, MoIT (9-0425); ALS draft, DLC (32). Bassett, 3:184. Declares his principle neither to solicit nor to decline public office.	
Jan 24	*To John Coffee.*	244
Jan 26	Account with Anthony W. Vanleer & Co. for iron. ADS, DLC (32).	
Jan 27	To John Coffee. ANS endorsed with Malachi Nicholson's receipt, Feb 7, A-Ar (9-0432). Directs him to pay Nicholson $12.	
Jan 27	From James Monroe. DS, DLC (32); Copy, DNA-RG 59 (9-0434). Commissions AJ minister to Mexico.	

Jan 27 Account with Crockett & Adams for bellows and linen. ADS, DLC (32). Runs to June 3.

Jan 27 Receipt from Malachi Nicholson for thirty sheep for Andrew Jackson Hutchings's farm. DS in AJ's hand, THi (9-0435).

Jan 28 From Samuel Ragland Overton. ALS, DLC (32). Discusses Florida politics, the presidential election, and differing opinions on the Florida claims commission.

Jan 28 Receipt from William Chandler (to AJ as agent for Anthony Winston, Jr.) for $6, for tuition of Jesse Thompson in 1822. ADS, DLC (32).

Jan 30 From James Monroe. ALS, DLC (72). Bassett, 6:479–80. Offers appointment as minister to Mexico.

Jan 30 Receipt for $200 from Peter Richardson Booker and Patrick Maguire for one share of Florence stock, purchased by AJ for Andrew Jackson Hutchings. ADS in Booker's hand also signed by Maguire, with AJ endorsement, A-Ar (9-0437).

Jan 31 *To Robert Butler, John Donelson (1755–1830), and Francis Saunders.* 246

Jan 31 From Joel Roberts Poinsett. ALS with AJ endorsement, DLC (32). Discusses political situation in Mexico.

Feb 1 To John Henry Eaton. ALS copy, DLC (32). Discusses claims for cattle seized by the army in the 1814 Pensacola campaign.

Feb 2 Receipt from Jesse Shelton for $25 for hauling a cotton gin from Alabama. DS in AJ's hand, DLC (32).

Feb 3 To Richard Keith Call. Extract, Bassett, 3:185–86 (9-0442). Discusses claims for cattle seized by the army in the 1814 campaign against Pensacola.

Feb 3 From H. W. Peterson. ALS, DLC (32). On behalf of Harrisburg, Pennsylvania, committee, asks AJ's intention concerning presidential candidacy.

Feb 3 Account with William H. Tate for lumber and flooring. ADS, DLC (32). With Tate's receipt, [Feb] 22.

Feb 6 Deed to Patrick Meagher for two lots in Memphis from AJ, John Overton, James Winchester, and the devisees of William Winchester. Copy, TMSh (9-0445). *Goodspeed's History of Hamilton, Knox and Shelby Counties of Tennessee* (Nashville, 1974), pp. 867–68.

Feb 8 To John Caldwell Calhoun (enclosure: Amos Edwards to AJ, Dec 22, 1822). LS, DNA-RG 94 (M688-21). Endorses Ashmore Edwards for appointment to the Military Academy.

Feb 8 To Andrew Jackson Donelson. ALS, DLC (9-0448). Bassett, 3:186–87 (extract). Discusses Kentucky banking legislation in light of the constitutional prohibition against the issuing of paper money by states.

Feb 8 Bill of sale from Rebecca Nowland for slave, John Fulton. DS in William S. Fulton's hand, DLC (72).

Feb 14 To Edward Livingston. LS, NjP (mAJs). Introduces John W. Overton.

Feb 14 *From Isaac Lewis Baker.* 247

Feb 17 *To John Coffee.* 248

Feb 18 Bill of sale from Anthony Winston, Jr., for five slaves for Andrew Jackson Hutchings. ADS, A-Ar (9-0455).

Feb 19	*To James Monroe.*	251
Feb 19	From John Quincy Adams (enclosure: James Monroe to AJ, Jan 27). LS, DLC (32); ALS copy, MHi (9-0457). Bassett, 3:187–88. Transmits commission as minister to Mexico.	
Feb 21	To John Coffee. ALS, THi (9-0462). Discusses accounts with Florence, Alabama, merchants.	
Feb 22	To Andrew Jackson Donelson. ALS, DLC (9-0465). Discusses Daniel S. Donelson and appointment as minister to Mexico.	
Feb 23	*To H. W. Peterson.*	252
Feb 23	*From John Henry Eaton.*	254
Feb 25	From Richard Ivy Easter. ALS with AJ endorsement docketting reply of April 14, DLC (32). Reports on his law practice in Mobile and briefly discusses politics.	
Feb 26	From Isaac Lewis Baker. ALS with AJ endorsement summarizing contents, DLC (32). Reports on activities of Henry Clay's supporters in Louisiana.	
Feb 26	Account with Samuel Green for fencing. DS in AJ's hand, signed by Green, DLC (32).	
March 1	To John Coffee. ALS, THi (9-0467). Discusses settlement of accounts.	
March 1	To James Gadsden. Printed, *Nashville Gazette,* March 21 (9-0471). Discusses the army reduction act and states his understanding that Gadsden could have transferred to a position of the same rank without senatorial consent.	
March 3	To Edward George Washington Butler. Extract, LNT (9-0472). Charles Gayarré, *A Sketch of General Jackson by Himself* (New Orleans, 1857), pp. 4–7 (extract). Gives advice; discusses declination of mission to Mexico.	
March 3	To Sarah F. Chotard. Extract, Rhoda Coleman Ellison, *Bibb County Alabama: The First Hundred Years, 1818–1918* (University, Alabama, [1984]), p. 37 (mAJs). Refuses to use influence with John Coffee and declines gift of lots in Centreville, Alabama.	
March 3	Alexander Donelson's answer in *Winchester* v. *Donelson et al.* DS in AJ's hand with AJ's ADS affadavit about writing the document, TFWi (9-0474); Copy, TNDa (mAJs).	
March 4	Receipt from Samuel Scott for payment for carpentry on barn and slave houses at Hermitage. DS in AJ's hand, DLC (32).	
March 5	To Andrew Jackson Donelson. ALS, DLC (9-0480). Bassett, 3:190–91 (extract). Discusses educational plans of Daniel S. Donelson.	
March 7	From Rebecca Bronaugh. ALS with AJ endorsement docketting reply of March 28, DLC (32). Bassett, 3:191 (extract). Discusses settlement of James C. Bronaugh's estate.	
March 7	From John Rhea. ALS, DLC (32). Bassett, 3:191. Discusses AJ's refusal of the appointment to Mexico.	
March 8	To Andrew Jackson Donelson. ALS, DLC (9-0484). Discusses arrangements for Donelson's return to Nashville from Lexington, Kentucky.	
March 10	*To John Coffee.*	257
March 10	To Andrew Jackson Donelson. ALS, DLC (9-0490). Again discusses	

arrangements for Donelson's return to Nashville.

March 10 Receipt from Thomas Overton for $81, settling all accounts except the hiring of a blacksmith. DS in AJ's hand, DLC (32).

March 11 To Abner Lawson Duncan. Photocopy of ALS, Gary Hendershott Catalog (1992), Item 25 (mAJs); Extract, Kenneth W. Rendell Catalog #100 (1974), Item 60 (9-0491). Introduces James M. Glassell.

March 11 To Alexander Garden. ALS, PHi (9-0492). Thanks him for a copy of his *Anecdotes of the Revolutionary War in America* (Charleston, 1822).

March 11 To James McMillan Glassell (enclosure: AJ to Abner L. Duncan, March 11). ALS, Gerald R. Solomon (9-0494). Discusses Samuel R. Overton's difficulties in settling Florida land claims and movement of troops to Pass Christian, Mississippi.

March 11 Alfred Balch to Thomas Crutcher. ALS with AJ endorsement, DLC (32). Responds to AJ's March 10 letter to Crutcher (not found) by discussing the estate of William T. Lewis.

March 12 *From Alfred Balch.* 259

March 14 To Edward Livingston. LS, NjP (mAJs). Discusses refusal of the Mexican post.

March 15 To John Quincy Adams. LS in James Gadsden's hand, DNA-RG 59 (9-0496); Copy, DLC (32). Bassett, 3:192–93. Declines appointment as minister to Mexico.

March 15 From Anthony Wayne Butler. ALS with AJ endorsement summarizing his reply of April 17, DLC (32). Discusses course of study at Yale and claims his "patrons" pledged to finance law school; requests $100.

March 19 From Samuel Ragland Overton. ALS with AJ endorsement docketting reply of May 3, DLC (32). Discusses Florida politics and endorses George Walton to succeed William P. Duval as governor.

March 20 *From Alfred Balch.* 262

March 20 From Robert Patterson. Printed, *Cincinnati Advertiser,* Aug 16 (mAJs). Sends grass bonnet for Rachel Jackson.

March 20 Robert Patterson to Rachel Jackson. Printed, *Cincinnati Advertiser,* Aug 16 (mAJs). Presents a grass bonnet.

March 21 To Thomas Butler (1785–1847). ALS, LU (9-0499). Introduces Lafayette Saunders.

[March 22] Account with Anthony Latapie for sundries. ADS by Henry Beekman, DLC (32). Runs to July 15.

March 23 *To John Caldwell Calhoun.* 263

March 23 To Natchez gentleman. Printed, *Mississippian and Natchez Advertizer,* April 12 (mAJs). Explains his refusal of the appointment as minister to Mexico.

[cMarch 23] To Mobile friend. Printed, *Niles' Register,* July 5 (9-0502). Heiskell, 1:571–72. Explains his refusal of the post to Mexico.

March 24 *To Edward Livingston.* 264

March 25 Receipt from Thomas W. Creel for $1.12½ for ferriage. ADS, DLC (32).

March 28 From Egbert Harris. ALS with AJ endorsement summarizing his reply, DLC (32). Reports on a brawl in which he was involved at

	Huntsville and requests to borrow AJ's dueling pistols.	
March 30	*From John Caldwell Calhoun.*	266
April 1	Account with James Stewart & Co. and Thomas Barron & Co. for sugar. ADS, DLC (32).	
April 2	From John Rhea. ALS, DLC (32). Reports arrival in Tennessee; discusses the forthcoming meeting of the Tennessee legislature.	
April 4	*To William Savin Fulton.*	267
April 6–11	From John Coffee. ALS with AJ endorsement, THi (9-0515). Discusses AJ's business affairs and presidential prospects in Alabama.	
April 6	From William Gibson. ALS with AJ endorsement, DLC (32). Introduces his son Alfred.	
April 9	From James Gadsden. ALS with AJ endorsement describing reply of April 30, DLC (32). Requests advice on negotiations with Florida Indians.	
April 11	From Alexander Garden. ALS with AJ endorsement to reply after obtaining anecdotes, DLC (32). Requests that AJ ask Thomas Overton for reminiscences to use in a new edition of *Anecdotes.*	
April 12	From John Jay Jackson. ALS with AJ endorsement, DLC (32). Introduces Alfred Gibson.	
April 12	Resolution by Masons of Tennessee's Grand Lodge thanking AJ for presiding over a meeting. Printed, *Proceedings of the Grand Lodge of the State of Tennessee, for the Year 1823* (Nashville, 1823), pp. 23–24 (mAJs).	
April 14	To John McKee. Extract, *Nashville Republican & State Gazette,* June 12, 1827 (9-0520). Congratulates McKee on his candidacy for Congress.	
April 14	To Sylvanus Thayer. LS, NjP (9-0521). Introduces James A. J. Bradford.	
April 15	*To John Coffee.*	270
April 15	From Samuel Ragland Overton. ALS with AJ endorsement docketting reply of May 18, DLC (32). Discusses plans to secure appointment of George Walton to Florida governorship when William P. Duval resigns.	
April 15	From James Robb. ALS, DLC (32). Agrees to suspend lawsuit against Samuel Hogg.	
April 18	From H. M. Johnson. ALS, DLC (32). Asks to buy a tract of land near Memphis if it belongs to AJ.	
April 18	From George Walton. ALS, DLC (32). Reports on political conflict in Florida and asks AJ to support his candidacy for the governorship.	
April 20	From James S. Eldridge. ALS, DLC (32). Asks for money.	
April 20	From Samuel Hogg. ALS, DLC (32). Thanks AJ for help with his legal problems.	
April 21	To Ezra Stiles Ely. Extracts, Ely, *Duty of Christian Freemen to Elect Christian Rulers* (Philadelphia, 1828), pp. 31–32 (9-0531), *Nashville Republican & State Gazette,* April 1, 1828 (9-0529). Asks reinstatement of Thomas B. Craighead from suspension as a Presbyterian minister.	
April 23	From Richard Ivy Easter. ALS with AJ endorsement docketting	

reply of May 18, DLC (32). Discusses presidential politics and his law practice.

April 24 From William Williams. ALS, DNA-RG 94 (M688-32). Reports on educational plans of William D. Chappell.

April 25 From Thomas B. Craighead. LS by proxy, DLC (32). Asks AJ to write the General Assembly of the Presbyterian Church on his behalf.

April 27 From H. M. Johnson. ALS with endorsement regarding July 3 reply asking Johnson to state his terms, DLC (32). Again asks to buy AJ's land near Memphis.

April 28 *To John Coffee.* 272

[April 30] To James McMillan Glassell. ALS fragment, PWbH (9-0538). Discusses refusal of the appointment to Mexico.

May 1 To Edward George Washington Butler. Extract, LNT (9-0541). Charles Gayarré, *A Sketch of General Jackson by Himself* (New Orleans, 1857), pp. 7, 9 (extracts). Advises candor and warns against engaging in litigation.

May 3 *From Isaac Lewis Baker.* 274

May 4 From James Jackson. ALS, DLC (32). Discusses settlement of a lawsuit.

May 4 From George Poindexter. ALS with AJ endorsement docketting reply of May 18, DLC (32). Seeks recommendation for appointment as judge of the U.S. District Court in Mississippi; discusses presidential politics.

May 5 To Catharine Caffery Walker. ALS and Typed copy, THer (9-0547, -0551). Discusses lawsuits, *John Overton* v. *Thomas H. Perkins, William Thomas et al.* (8 *Tennessee Reports* 358) and *Walker* v. *Turner* (9 Wheaton 541).

May 6 From William J. Cart. ALS with Samuel Motheral's receipt for payment, May 23, A-Ar (9-0553). Asks payment of a witness in *Alfred M. Douglass, executor* v. *Jackson & Hutchings.*

May 6 Andrew Jackson Donelson to [George Walker?]. AL draft, DLC (32). Discusses lawsuit, *Walker* v. *Turner* (9 Wheaton 541), before the United States Supreme Court.

May 10 Jane Donelson Hays to Rachel Jackson. ALS, THer (37-0422). Expresses hope for a visit; sends love to family and friends.

May 12 To James Monroe. LS, NN (9-0555). Recommends appointment of a Dr. Lawrence as surgeon of the marine hospital in New Orleans.

May 13 Receipt from Stephen Matthias for $12 partial payment of subscription for Hermitage church. DS in AJ's hand, DLC (78).

May 14 Receipt from William H. Tate for $9.60 for sawing planks. DS in AJ's hand, DLC (32).

May 17 To Robert Patterson. Printed, *Kentucky Gazette,* Aug 21 (9-0558). Thanks him for grass bonnet sent Rachel Jackson and praises domestic manufactures.

May 18 To Anthony Wayne Butler. ALS, LNHiC (9-0559). Reprimands him for ingratitude to Abner L. Duncan and informs him that he cannot count on support for his legal studies.

May 18 To James Monroe. ALS, NN (9-0563). Recommends George

Poindexter for U.S. District Judge of Mississippi.

May 18 From J. C. Cook. ALS, DNA-RG 94 (M688-32). Solicits support for William D. Chappell's appointment to the U.S. Military Academy.

May 18 Rachel Jackson to Robert Patterson. LS by proxy, Anonymous (mAJs); Printed, *Kentucky Gazette,* Aug 21 (9-0562). Thanks him for grass bonnet.

May 19 Certification of the good character of David Campbell (1753–1832). DS, NN (9-0565).

May 23 Statement of money due Samuel Motheral from suit *Alfred M. Douglass, executor* v. *Jackson & Hutchings.* ADS with Jesse Holt's receipt, June 11, THi (9-0566).

May 24 *To John Coffee.* 276

May 24 To Thomas Waters Griffith. ALS, MWiW-C (9-0574). States that he knows of no property owned by James C. Mountflorence in the Nashville area.

May 24 From Samuel Ragland Overton. ALS, DLC (32). Discusses disagreement with Nathaniel A. Ware over Florida land claims.

May 26 To Sylvanus Thayer. Extract, Charles Frederick Heartman, *Rare Americana* (Nov 23, 1929), Item 213 (mAJs); Abstract, *American Book-Prices Current* (1929–30), p. 650 (9-0576). Introduces Samuel J. Hays.

May 27 From N[athaniel] Sanders, William Cage, and Charles Morgan. LS, DNA-RG 94 (M688-32). Testify to the good conduct of William D. Chappell.

May 29 *To Willie Blount.* 278

June 1 From Bolling Gordon. ALS, DLC (32). Reports the imminent death of Richard C. Cross and arrangements to pay Cross's debt to AJ.

June 2 *To Anthony Wayne Butler.* 279

June 2 From William Kenner. ALS, DLC (32). Introduces John Bolton of New York.

June 3 From John Brahan. ALS, DNA-RG 94 (M688-25). Asks recommendation of Edward B. Grayson for appointment to West Point.

June 4 To Andrew Jackson Donelson. ALS, DLC (9-0587). Forwards a copy of new Richmond newspaper, most likely the *Virginia Times.*

June 4 Account with James Stewart & Co. for cotton shipped. ADS, DLC (32).

June 8 From James Gadsden. ALS with AJ endorsement abstracting reply of Aug 15, DLC (32). Reports progress of negotiations with Florida Indians; asks AJ to sell Gadsden's Florence, Alabama, land and stock.

June 8 From Samuel Ragland Overton. ALS, DLC (32). Discusses revolution in Mexico and AJ's presidential prospects.

June 9 *To Pleasant Moorman Miller.* 281

June 9 From John Mead. ALS, DLC (32). Asks help in clarifying his service record.

June 9 Receipt from James Rucker Donelson for $59.50 payment for Elizabeth Donelson's cotton. DS in AJ's hand, DLC (32).

June 10	From Hardy Murfree Cryer. ANS, DLC (32). Sends slave Cyrus for a trial on AJ's farm and possible purchase.	
June 11	Receipt for payment to William T. L. Harwell (in accordance with agreement of January 7, 1823) for repair of barn, gin, mill, and other carpentry at the Hermitage. ADS, DLC (32). Bassett, 3:198.	
June 11	Receipt from Jesse Hall for $70 for cedar logs. DS in AJ's hand, DLC (78).	
June 12	To Bolling Gordon. ALS, THi (9-0594). Acknowledges receipt of partial payment on Richard C. Cross's account.	
June 12	From James Gadsden. ALS, DLC (32). Discusses plans to relocate Florida Indians to the interior, south of Tampa Bay and north of Charlotte Harbor; proposes military force at Tampa Bay; and asks that AJ write the war department in support of those ideas.	
June 13	From John M. A. Hamblen. ALS, DLC (32). Thanks AJ and Rachel for kindness to his daughter, Mary, and to his stepdaughter; praises AJ's presidential candidacy.	
June 13	From John Rhea. ALS, DLC (32). Informs AJ of his decision not to run for Congress.	
June 14	To James Gettys McGready Ramsey. ALS, TU (9-0597). Heiskell, 2:119–20. States that he was not a participant in the Mecklenburg convention.	
June 16	Account with Crockett & Adams for salt and flour. ADS, DLC (32). Runs to July 3.	
June 17	From Samuel Martin. ALS, DLC (32). Urges AJ to visit East Tennessee to put down enemies to AJ's election as president.	
June 17	From Peter Aaron Van Dorn. ALS, DLC (32). Discusses efforts to settle Mary Caffery and Catharine Walker near Port Gibson, Mississippi.	
June 18	Account with the estate of Robert Smiley, tailor. DS, DLC (32). Runs to April 14, 1824.	
June 19	From John Caldwell Calhoun. LC, DNA-RG 94 (M91-1). Acknowledges receipt of AJ's recommendation of William D. Chappell (not found).	
June 19	From Robert Henry Dyer. ALS with AN by [William L. Mitchell], June 19, and ANS by Blackman Coleman, Oct 20, certifying that Dyer's report is correct, DLC (32). Reports on inspection of land John C. McLemore wishes to exchange for AJ's Chickasaw Bluff tract.	
June 22	From William Savin Fulton. ALS, DLC (32). Reports on his efforts to promote AJ's candidacy through the *Florence Gazette.*	
June 24	*From Charles Pendleton Tutt.*	283
June 27	From John Caldwell Calhoun. LC, DNA-RG 94 (M91-1). Informs AJ that Edward B. Grayson will be considered for future appointment to West Point.	
June 27	From Samuel Ragland Overton. ALS, DLC (32). Endorses the restraint of AJ's campaign and reports support in Ohio.	
June 28	From Benjamin W. Johnston. ALS, DLC (32). Solicits introductions to AJ's acquaintances in Mississippi.	
June 28	From Peter Aaron Van Dorn. ALS, DLC (32). Recommends Benjamin W. Johnston to AJ's notice.	

June 29	From Samuel Ragland Overton. ALS, DLC (32). Reports that illness may force his resignation as land commissioner; discusses Florida politics.	
June 30	From James Gadsden. ALS, DLC (32). States that he is sending items by Arthur P. Hayne; reports that Floridians are generally anti-Crawford.	
June 30	From James Jackson. ALS, DLC (32). Discusses efforts to pin down John Williams's anti-Jackson activities.	
[cJune]	From [Anthony Wayne Butler]. AL draft fragment, LNHiC (9-0601). Discusses his financial problems.	
July 1	From Pleasant Moorman Miller. ALS, DLC (32). Encloses statement by Spencer Jarnagin re Miller's quarrel with Patrick H. Darby; discusses drafting of Tennessee's champerty law.	
July 2	From Richard Gilliam Dunlap. ALS, DLC (32). Bassett, 3:199–200. Suggests William G. Blount to oppose John Williams for senator and proposes that AJ advise John Rhea not to be a candidate.	
July 3	To John Coffee. ALS, THi (9-0604). Introduces William McRee, George Talcott, and Roswell Lee, commissioners for locating a western arsenal and foundry.	
July 4	Receipt of Jesse Searcy for $22.32 paid for transportation of John Hutchings's tombstone from Tennessee to Alabama. ADS, A-Ar (mAJs).	
July 5	From Stephen Simpson. ALS with AJ endorsement regarding his answer, DLC (32). Forwards copy of *American Anecdotes, Characters and Incidents* (Philadelphia, 1823), dedicated to AJ.	
July 5	Abner Lawson Duncan to James Gadsden. ALS (addressed care of AJ), DLC (32). Bassett, 3:191. Requests that Gadsden "sound" AJ on the possibility of Duncan's appointment as minister to Mexico.	
July 6	From Abner Lawson Duncan. ALS, DLC (32). Inquires about the presidential campaign.	
July 9	From Frank N. W. Burton, Samuel Hervey Laughlin, and John D. Martin. Printed, *Nashville Whig,* July 21 (9-0608). Invite AJ to a public dinner in Murfreesboro.	
July 9	To Frank N. W. Burton, Samuel Hervey Laughlin, and John D. Martin. Printed, *Nashville Whig,* July 21 (9-0610). Accepts invitation.	
July 10	Toast to literature and science at Murfreesboro public dinner. Printed, *Nashville Whig,* July 21 (9-0612).	
July 12	*To Hardy Murfree Cryer.*	284
July 14	To John Caldwell Calhoun. LS and Copy, DNA-RG 107 (M221-97). *TPUS,* 22:719–20. Complying with James Gadsden's request, suggests site for relocation of Florida Indians and recommends sending an infantry regiment to Tampa Bay to impress the Indians.	
July 14	To George Poindexter. LS, DLC (32). Introduces Benjamin W. Johnston.	
July 15	To George Morton [George Washington Martin?]. Abstract, Parke-Bernet Catalog, Jan 28–29, 1958 (9-0614). Discusses AJ's $1000 note, probably a loan to Morton/Martin.	
July 15	From William Brackin. ALS, DLC (32). Discusses a land dispute with William Martin (1765–1846).	

July 18	From James McMillan Glassell. ALS with AJ endorsement docketting reply of Aug 17, DLC (32). Discusses his medical treatment with Philip S. Physick; reports giving AJ's letter about the Mexican mission to the Philadelphia *Columbian Observer* for publication.	
July 18	Account with John Simpson & Co. for goods furnished Andrew Jackson Hutchings's farm. ADS, A-Ar (9-0616). Runs to June 8, 1824.	
July 20	From R[ichard] R. Royall. ALS, DLC (32). Asks to lease a tract of AJ's land in Alabama.	
July 21	From Richard Ivy Easter. ALS, DLC (32). Reports growing support for AJ's candidacy in southern Alabama.	
July 22	From Samuel Ragland Overton. ALS with AJ endorsement docketting reply of Aug 31, DLC (32). Discusses his efforts to secure appointment as secretary of Florida Territory and the presidential campaign.	
July 23	From Hezekiah Niles. ALS, DLC (32). Acknowledges payment; advises that AJ and John Q. Adams are the strongest presidential candidates in Baltimore.	
July 23	From Lafayette Saunders. ALS, DLC (32). Thanks AJ for letters of introduction; discusses his law practice and Louisiana politics.	
July 23	Andrew Jackson Crawford to Rachel Jackson. ALS fragment, ICHi (9-0619). Extract, *Cincinnati Commercial,* Jan 8, 1880 (9-0622). Discusses his school.	
July 26	From John M. Davis. ALS, DLC (32). Asks for a statement of military services for use in his candidacy for county court clerkship in Georgia.	
July 30	*From James Gadsden.*	285
July 31	From John Caldwell Calhoun. ALS with AJ endorsement, DLC (32). *Calhoun Papers,* 8:200–201. Discusses Florida Indian negotiations, removal of Stephen Cantrell as pension agent, and presidential candidacies of Henry Clay and William H. Crawford.	
[July–Sept]	From Richard Keith Call. AL fragment, DLC (75). Discusses recent session of Florida Legislative Council, James Gadsden's treaty with Florida Indians, and AJ's presidential prospects.	
Aug 2	From DeWitt Clinton. LC, NNC (9-0623). Praises AJ and sends copy of *A Discourse Delivered at Schenectady, July 22d, A.D. 1823, before the New-York Alpha of the Phi Beta Kappa* (Albany, 1823).	
Aug 4	From Edward John Lambert. ALS, DLC (32). Requests a statement of his military service.	
Aug 4	From Sylvanus Thayer. ALS with AJ endorsement docketting reply of Aug 31, DLC (32). Transmits report of Daniel S. Donelson's standing at the Military Academy.	
Aug 6	Deed to Benjamin Foy for a lot in Memphis from AJ, John Overton, James Winchester, and the devisees of William Winchester. Copy, TMSh (mAJs).	
Aug 9	From James O'Hanlon. ANS, THer (mAJs). Presents copy of his *An Oration, Delivered in Lexington Court-House, (S.C.) before an Assemblage of the Inhabitants of That District, on the Fourth of July, 1823 . . .* (n.p., 1823).	

Aug 12	From Benjamin W. Johnston. ALS, DLC (32). Sends thanks for letters of introduction.	
Aug 12	From Samuel Martin. ALS, DLC (32). Asks AJ to endorse the establishment of a farm and a military tactics professorship for Tennessee university students.	
Aug 12	Receipt from James R. Gleaves for $15 partial payment for work on a wagon wheel. DS in AJ's hand with ADS receipt from Charles [Wilkeson], Oct 25, for $2 balance paid, DLC (78).	
[cAug 12]	*To John Caldwell Calhoun.*	287
Aug 13	To Stephen Simpson. Draft in Andrew J. Donelson's hand, DLC (32); Printed, Louisville *Daily Focus,* Oct 21, 1831 (9-0630). Thanks him for the dedication of *American Anecdotes.*	
Aug 13	Mary Donelson Caffery to Rachel Jackson. ALS, DLC (32). Gives news of family members in Mississippi.	
Aug 14	To Anthony Wayne Butler. ALS, LNHiC (9-0633). Informs Butler that he has been unable to raise $100 to help him.	
Aug 14	From George Washington Martin. ALS with AJ endorsement, DLC (32). Asks AJ to pay portion of a debt.	
Aug 15	*To John Coffee.*	289
Aug 15	From Samuel Ragland Overton. ALS with AJ endorsement docketting reply of Sept 10, DLC (32). Discusses Florida affairs and the presidential campaign.	
Aug 15	Receipt for $8 paid for subscription to John Stuart Skinner's *American Farmer,* April 1821–April 1823. Printed form with ms insertions, signed by William F. Redding for Skinner, DLC (32).	
Aug 18	From James G. Lyon. ALS, DLC (32). Discusses recent elections in Alabama.	
Aug 19	To James Monroe. Abstract, *American Book-Prices Current* (1931–32), p. 535 (9-0641). Recommends Mr. Ballow (possibly Thomas Balleau) for midshipman's commission.	
Aug 22	To John Coffee. ALS, THi (9-0642). Bassett, 3:204 (extract). Discusses purchase of cotton bagging and business affairs of Andrew J. Hutchings.	
Aug 22	From [Andrew Erwin]. Copy, T (10-0359). Notifies AJ of his intent to take deposition of Elisha Reynolds.	
Aug 23	Receipt from Stephen Matthias for $30 partial payment of subscription to Hermitage church. DS in AJ's hand, DLC (78).	
Aug 25	*From Edward Ward.*	291
Aug 26	From William Pope Duval. ALS, DLC (32). Attributes abuse against him to AJ's enemies in Florida and states his intention to resign the governorship as soon as he disproves the slanders.	
Aug 26	From Samuel Ragland Overton. ALS with AJ endorsement re letters of Sept 25 to Overton and James Monroe, DLC (32). Asks AJ to expedite recommendations of Overton and George Walton for Florida offices; discusses possible politics behind an act to compensate Florida citizens who suffered depredations by AJ's troops.	
Aug 27	Receipt from Thomas Weston for $20 for labor. DS in AJ's hand, DLC (78).	
Aug 31	To John Caldwell Calhoun (enclosures: Reports of Peter Hagner,	

	April 25, and Richard Cutts, May 20, DNA-RG 107, M221-97). LS, THi (9-0645); ALS draft, DLC (32); AL draft, DLC (19); Copy, DNA-RG 107 (M221-97). Discusses settlement of George Wilson's account with the war department.	
Aug 31	To DeWitt Clinton. LS draft, Draft in Andrew J. Donelson's hand [?], and Copy, DLC (32). Sends thanks for compliments and regrets that he cannot visit New York.	
Aug 31	Receipt from William T. L. Harwell for $45 payment on promissory note. DS in AJ's hand, DLC (32).	
Sept 3	From John McNairy. ALS, DLC (32). Bassett, 3:205–206. Offers to attempt a reconciliation between AJ and John Williams and an accommodation in *Jackson* v. *Erwin.*	
Sept 4	From Moses Foster. ALS, DLC (32). Complains about implementation of ninth article of 1820 Choctaw treaty and asks assistance in obtaining land granted therein.	
Sept 4	From Benjamin Lundy. ALS, DLC (32). Bassett, 3:206–207. Requests for publication AJ's view of gradual emancipation.	
Sept 4	From Sampson Williams. ALS, DLC (32). Urges AJ to attend next session of the legislature to prevent the election of John Williams to the Senate.	
[Sept 6]	*To John McNairy.*	292
Sept 7	From James Titus. ALS, DLC (32). Seeks endorsement of William Edmondson to be Chickasaw agent.	
Sept 8	To Martin, Williams & Co. Photocopy of ALS, MsSM (9-0654). Exchanges wagon boxes for a larger size.	
[cSept 10]	From Thomas Yeatman. ALS with AJ endorsement re payment, DLC (31). Encloses statement of account with AJ.	
Sept 12	To John Coffee. ALS, THi (9-0656). Requests delivery of cotton bagging.	
Sept 15	From Enoch Parsons. ALS, DLC (32). Introduces Edmond B. Corley, a teacher.	
Sept 19	Agreement of AJ and James Jackson with Andrew Erwin, compromising the lawsuit re Duck River lands. Copies, THi (9-0660) and TSBe (9-0667).	
Sept 20	*From William Brady and Thomas Williamson.*	296
Sept 20	From DeWitt Clinton. LC, NNC (9-0671). Sends another copy of *A Discourse Delivered at Schenectady,* which did not reach AJ on previous mailing.	
Sept 20	*From Abram Maury.*	297
Sept 20	From William Polk. ALS with AJ endorsement noting his request that Polk send proceedings of the William Terrell land fraud case to Thomas Claiborne, DLC (32). *North Carolina Historical Review,* 14(1937):363. Regrets inability to meet with AJ in Murfreesboro.	
Sept 20	From Edward Ward. ALS, DLC (32). Asks that his cotton be ginned early so that he can command cash for land purchases.	
Sept 21	*To Abram Maury.*	298
Sept 25	To James Monroe. ALS, NN (9-0674). Recommends George Walton for governor of Florida Territory and Samuel R. Overton for secretary.	
Sept 25	From John Caldwell Calhoun (enclosure: Report of Peter Hagner,	

Sept 22, DNA-RG 217, mAJs). LC, DNA-RG 107 (M6-11). Discusses the George Wilson account.

Sept 26 From Samuel Ragland Overton. ALS, DLC (32). Moderates previous expressions of disappointment with affairs in Florida.

Sept 27 *To William Brady and Thomas Williamson.* 299

Sept 27 From Daniel Smith Donelson. ALS, DLC (32). Writes that he is content to remain at the Military Academy.

Oct 1 From Samuel Ragland Overton. ALS, DLC (32). States that he has published articles supporting AJ for president; reports on Florida affairs.

Oct 2 From Richard Keith Call. ALS, DLC (32). Discusses affairs in Florida: conclusion of Indian treaty, location of the territorial capital, and settlement.

Oct 3 From James Hooper. ALS with AJ endorsement to retain the letter, DLC (32). Discusses dealings with Andrew Erwin regarding contested property deeded to Hooper by AJ.

Oct 4 To Andrew Jackson Donelson. ANS, DLC (32). Directs Donelson to show James Hooper's letter to convince John McNairy of Andrew Erwin's duplicity.

Oct 4 To Thomas Jefferson. LS, Sam Houston Regional Library and Research Center, Liberty, Texas (9-0679). William Carey Crane, *Life and Select Literary Remains of Sam Houston of Texas* (Dallas: William G. Scarff & Co., 1884), p. 35. Introduces Samuel Houston.

Oct 4 *To [John Caldwell Calhoun?].* 300

Oct 4 Certification by William Carroll of AJ's election as United States senator. DS, DNA-RG 46 (9-0677).

Oct 5 *To John Coffee.* 302

Oct 7 From Arthur Peronneau Hayne. ALS, DLC (32). Asks AJ to recommend Abner L. Duncan as minister to Mexico.

Oct 8 To Fielding Lucas, Jr. Facsimile of cover, Robert A. Siegel Auction Galleries, Inc., Sale 750 (May 5, 1993), p. 39 (mAJs); Abstract, Swann Auction Galleries Catalog 29 (Nov 20, 1942), Item 55 (12-0229). Acknowledges receipt of map of Tennessee.

Oct 9 Account with James Stewart for fabric for coat. ADS, DLC (32). Submitted March 18 and paid April 14, 1824.

Oct 10 *To James Monroe.* 303

Oct 10 Receipt from Peter C. Johnson for $17.50 settlement of all accounts. DS in AJ's hand, DLC (78).

Oct 11 To [Willie Blount]. Draft in Andrew J. Donelson's hand?, DLC (72). Thanks him for aid in securing army financing during the War of 1812 and for reporting the deaths of Mary Caffery and Eliza Green.

Oct 12 From Richard Mentor Johnson. ALS, DLC (32). *Register of the Kentucky Historical Society,* 39(1941):186. Congratulates AJ on election to the Senate.

Oct 13 To [Henry Middleton] Rutledge. ALS, PHi (9-0698). Declines invitation to wedding of Rutledge's daughter Mary to Francis B. Fogg, owing to mourning for Mary Caffery and Eliza Green.

Oct 13 Memorandum of agreement with John Christmas McLemore for transfer of AJ's eighth interest in 5,000 acres in Shelby County. DS

	by AJ, McLemore, and witnesses, DLC (32).	
Oct 13	Deed to John Christmas McLemore for undivided eighth interest in 5,000 acres in Shelby County. DS, TMPPM (9-0686); Copy, THi (9-0689).	
Oct 13	Deed from John Christmas McLemore for two tracts of land in Haywood County (enclosures: Grants 18257, Oct 18, 1822, DLC-31, and 18945, April 2, 1823, DLC-32). DS, DLC (32); Copy, TBHay (9-0693).	
Oct 14	To John Caldwell Calhoun (enclosure: Certificate of John B. Nooe, July 28). LS, DNA-RG 94 (M688-28). Recommends William R. Burnley for appointment to the Military Academy.	
Oct 14	From John McKee. ALS, DLC (32). Asks AJ to recommend William P. Gould for register of Tuscaloosa land office.	
Oct 15	*To George Washington Martin.*	305
Oct 16	*From Richard Gilliam Dunlap.*	306
Oct 18	To George Washington Martin. Photocopy of ALS, MsSM (9-0706). Asks Martin to arrange tailoring of clothes for slave George.	
Oct 18	From William Darby. ALS, DLC (32). Inquires about AJ's presidential candidacy; announces he will visit Tennessee on research trip for his geographical dictionary.	
Oct 18	From William McClellan. ALS, DLC (32). Congratulates AJ on election as senator; asks AJ to recommend him for United States marshal of Mississippi.	
Oct 18	Receipt from William Chappell for $35 for a spinning machine. DS in AJ's hand, DLC (78).	
Oct 19	From John Coffee. ALS, DLC (32). Offers to loan horses for AJ's trip to Washington.	
Oct 19	From James Jackson. ALS with AJ endorsement, DLC (32). Discusses Patrick H. Darby's dissatisfaction with the settlement of *Jackson* v. *Erwin.*	
Oct 20	Account with George Crockett for cordage. AD, DLC (32). Runs to February 10, 1824.	
Oct 21	*From James Jackson.*	307
Oct 21	From Pleasant Moorman Miller. ALS, DLC (32). Discusses responses of East Tennesseans to AJ's election as senator.	
[Oct 23]	Memorandum of letter to James Jackson discussing Patrick Henry Darby's interest in the Allison lands. ANS, DLC (32).	
Oct 24	*To John Coffee.*	309
Oct 24	To John Overton. ALS, THi (9-0715). *THQ,* 6(1947):161–62. Asks for a $200 loan.	
Oct 25	From David Campbell. ALS, DLC (32). Asks for help in securing a military appointment.	
Oct 28	*To George Walton.*	311
Oct 28	*From James Jackson.*	312
Oct 30	*To George Washington Martin.*	314
Oct 31	From Thomas Washington (1788–1863). ALS, DLC (32). Discusses possible compromise of *Bennett Smith* v. *John Hutchings's Executors.*	
Oct 31	Acknowledgement of account due O[badiah] Gordon. ANS, DLC (32). With Gordon's receipt for payment, January 22, 1824.	

[Nov 1]	To [Thomas Harding]. AD, NcU (9-0727). Gives direction for trip from Harding's to Keeble's.	
Nov 3	From David McGavock. ALS with AJ endorsement re note given for payment, DLC (32). Requests payment of AJ's $100 subscription to Cumberland College.	
Nov 3	Memorandum of account with Thomas Overton. Photocopy of ADS, TU (mAJs).	
Nov 4	To John Overton. ALS, THi (9-0729). *THQ,* 6(1947):162. Introduces Thomas M. Chambers, a possible overseer.	
Nov 4	*To Unknown.*	315
Nov 5	Account with Miles Blythe McCorkle for medical services for family and slaves. ADS, DLC (33). Runs to July 28, 1824.	
Nov 6	Power of attorney to James Jackson to conclude settlement of *Jackson* v. *Erwin* according to provisions of the agreement. Copy, TSBe (9-0734).	
Nov 6	Account with Love & Lanier for shoes and leather. ADS, DLC (34). Runs to June 13, 1827.	
Nov 6	Account with Woodruff & Smiley for tailoring for George and AJ. AD, DLC (32).	
Nov 6	Account with John Wright for dry goods. AD with AJ endorsement regarding receipt (not found) for payment, July 20, 1824, DLC (33). Runs to June 15, 1824.	
Nov 8	To John Coffee. ALS, AFlT (9-0735). *Journal of Muscle Shoals History,* 1(1973):51–53. Discusses business and legal affairs and announces the marriage of John Donelson (1787–1840) to Eliza E. Butler.	
Nov 8	To Samuel Hodge. ANS, DLC (32). Requests him to make payment to Samuel Scott.	
Nov 8	To John Christmas McLemore. ALS, TMPPM (9-0740). Asks for a written statement of McLemore's recollection of AJ's agreement with Patrick H. Darby regarding the Allison lands.	
N[ov 8]	*To John Overton.*	316
Nov 9	*To John Coffee.*	317
Nov 10	*To Anthony Wayne Butler.*	317
Nov 16	*To Andrew Jackson Donelson.*	319
Nov 16	To Rachel Jackson. ALS, PPRF (9-0756). Describes his reception at Kingston; urges her to be cheerful in his absence.	
Nov 17	From John Crozier et al. Printed, *Knoxville Register,* Nov 21 (9-0760). Invite AJ to public dinner at Knoxville.	
Nov 17	To John Crozier et al. Printed, *Knoxville Register,* Nov 21 (9-0761). Accepts invitation.	
Nov 17	Toast at Knoxville public dinner: "Constitutional Spain—May she successfully resist the combined despotism of the holy alliance, leagued for unholy purposes." Printed, *Knoxville Register,* Nov 21 (9-0762).	
Nov 19	To Rachel Jackson. ALS, DLC (32). Bassett, 3:215. Reports his progress as far as Rogersville, Tennessee.	
[Nov 23]	To Rachel Jackson. ALS fragment, CSmH (9-0764). *Huntington Library Bulletin,* 3(1933):119–20. Urges her to reconcile herself to his absence and to secure necessaries from Josiah Nichol in	

	Nashville.	
Nov 26	From Henry Bowyer. ALS with AJ endorsement to attend to the request when at Washington, DNA-RG 94 (M688-25). Requests cadet appointment for his son Rufus.	
Nov 28	*To Rachel Jackson.*	320
Dec 1	From John Locke (to AJ and John Henry Eaton; enclosures: Peter Hagner to Daniel Rawlings, March 23, 1821; Hagner to John Rhea, Jan 19, 1821). ALS, DNA-RG 46 (9-0774). Discusses claim of the Rawlings estate to compensation for boats furnished during the War of 1812.	
Dec 3	To Rachel Jackson. ALS, CSmH (9-0780). *Huntington Library Bulletin,* 3(1933):120–21. Announces arrival in Washington; describes his reception in Fredericksburg, Virginia.	
Dec 5	To Andrew Jackson Donelson. ALS, DLC (72). Pauline Wilcox Burke, *Emily Donelson of Tennessee* (2 vols.; Richmond, Va., 1941), 1:101. Describes trip to Washington; gives instructions re business in Nashville.	
Dec 5	*To John Overton.*	321
Dec 6	To David Campbell (1779–1859). ALS, NcD (9-0786). Regrets that a resolution to avoid state capitals during legislative sessions prevented a visit at Richmond.	
Dec 7	*To Rachel Jackson.*	322
Dec 7	*To William Berkeley Lewis.*	323
Dec 8	To Thomas Jefferson. ALS, DLC (9-0794). Explains that he could not visit Monticello because he would be accused of political motivation.	
Dec 9	Conversation re Spain with correspondent of Philadelphia *Columbian Observer.* Printed, *Louisville Public Advertiser,* Jan 3, 1824 (mAJs).	
Dec 10	To Rachel Jackson. ALS, DLC (32). Bassett, 3:216. Acknowledges receipt of letter (not found).	
Dec 10	To Fielding Lucas, Jr. LS in John H. Eaton's hand, IGK (9-0796). Returns Lucas's prospectus for a book, signed by Eaton and Richard K. Call.	
Dec 11	*To Rachel Jackson.*	324
Dec 11	*From Winfield Scott.*	325
Dec 11	*To Winfield Scott.*	326
[cDec 11]	*To Andrew Jackson, Jr.*	326
Dec 12	From Waddy Vine Cobbs. ALS, DNA-RG 94 (M567-6). Asks assistance in obtaining furlough extension.	
[Dec 14]	To John Caldwell Calhoun (enclosure: Henry Bowyer to AJ, Nov 26). Abstract, DNA-RG 107 (M22-17). Encloses recommendation of Rufus Bowyer as cadet.	
Dec 15	From Hull & Townsend. ALS with AJ endorsement re answer, DLC (32). Discuss the protest of Anthony W. Butler's note and request payment.	
Dec 15	Motion to refer portion of president's annual message to the Senate Committee on Military Affairs. Abstract, *Annals of Congress,* 18th Cong., 1st sess., p. 37 (mAJs).	
Dec 16	To Samuel Swartwout. ALS, TNJ (9-0806). *Proceedings of the*	

American Antiquarian Society, 31(1921):74–75. Explains his reticence in discussing the presidential election.

Dec 17 From Stephen Pleasonton. LC, DNA-RG 206 (9-0812). Discusses settlement of account of Francis W. Armstrong.

Dec 17 Account with John Nichol for clothing and brandy. ADS by John H. Sommerville for Nichol, DLC (32). Runs to June 7, 1824.

Dec 18 From Thomas Jefferson. ALS draft, DLC (9-0810). Invites AJ to visit Monticello and the University of Virginia on his next passage through Charlottesville.

Dec 18 *John Henry Eaton to Rachel Jackson.* 327

Dec 19 To [Jacob Jennings Brown] (enclosure: Waddy V. Cobbs to AJ, Dec 12). LS, DNA-RG 94 (M567-6). Requests furlough extension for Cobbs.

Dec 19 To Henry Niles. ALS, Norman F. Boas (mAJs). Forwards letter (not found) from John R. Bedford.

Dec 19 Report from the Senate Committee on Military Affairs on army promotions and appointments. Abstract, *Senate Executive Proceedings,* 3:350 (mAJs).

Dec 20 To John Quincy Adams and Louisa Catherine Adams. AN in John H. Eaton's hand, MHi (9-0814). Accepts invitation to a ball on January 8.

Dec 20 To Hull & Townsend. ALS copy, DLC (32). Sends $100 on Anthony W. Butler's protested draft.

Dec 20 From Gerard Alexander. ALS with AJ endorsement, DNA-RG 94 (M688-31). Requests aid in obtaining Military Academy appointments for his son, Thomas L. Alexander, and an orphan, James Dempsey.

Dec 20 From Edward Butler Grayson. ALS, DNA-RG 94 (M688-25). Asks help in securing appointment to the Military Academy.

Dec 20 From Charles J. Nourse. LC, DNA-RG 94 (M565-6). Advises AJ that furlough of Waddy V. Cobbs has been extended.

Dec 21 *To William Savin Fulton.* 328

Dec 21 *To Rachel Jackson.* 330

Dec 21 To John Overton. ALS, THi (9-0821). *THQ,* 6(1947):165. Discusses Richard I. Easter's debt problems and efforts of the caucus faction in Congress.

Dec 22 To William Berkeley Lewis. ALS, NN (9-0825). *NYPLB,* 4(1900):193–94. Discusses settlement of Lewis's accounts with the war department and politics in Washington.

Dec 22 To Thomas Martin Maund. Printed, *Maryland Historical Magazine,* 20(1925):135 (9-0828). Discusses his plans for the holiday recess of Congress.

Dec 22 Receipt from Henry Ewing to Andrew Jackson Donelson for AJ's 1823 state and county taxes. ADS, DLC (32).

[Dec 22] To Stephen Pleasonton (from AJ and John Henry Eaton). ALS in Eaton's hand, DNA-RG 206 (9-0829). Urge settlement of William B. Lewis's account with the war department.

Dec 23 To John Quincy Adams (from AJ and ten Tennessee congressmen). DS, DNA-RG 59 (M439-13). Recommend reappointment of Robert Purdy as marshal of West Tennessee.

Dec 23	From Peter Hagner (enclosures: Rules and regulations governing claims incurred in the Seminole campaign, [1822]; William Wirt to John C. Calhoun, May 22, 1822; statement submitted to the attorney general, [May 1822]). LS, DNA-RG 233 (9-0832). Transmits documents as requested.
Dec 23	From Stephen Pleasonton (to AJ and John Henry Eaton). LC, DNA-RG 206 (9-0843). Discusses terms for settlement of United States claim against William B. Lewis.
Dec 23	Promissory note to Francis Saunders for $1,500. DS, G. Keeling Turner (9-0846).
[cDec 23]	Endorsement on William Wirt to James Monroe, October 20, 1823, regarding revision of accounts previously settled. AD, DNA-RG 107 (M222-23).
Dec 24	To Stephen Pleasonton (from AJ and John Henry Eaton). ALS in Eaton's hand, DNA-RG 206 (9-0848). Accept Pleasonton's proposal re settlement of William B. Lewis's debt to the United States.
Dec 24	From Hull & Townsend. ALS, DLC (32). Acknowledge receipt of $100 on Anthony W. Butler's draft.
Dec 25	From Daniel Munroe Forney (enclosure: Henry Seawell et al. to James Monroe, Dec 24). ALS, DNA-RG 59 (M439-16). Forwards recommendation of Montfort Stokes for minister to Mexico.
Dec 27	*To Thomas Martin Maund.* 332
Dec 27	From Stephen Pleasonton (to AJ and John Henry Eaton; enclosure: Pleasonton to Henry Crabb, Jan 1, 1824). LC, DNA-RG 206 (9-0853). Forwards letter re settlement of William B. Lewis's account.
Dec 28	To Rachel Jackson. Facsimile of ALS (in part), American Art Association Catalog (Dec 7, 1921), Item 712 (9-0854). Bassett, 3:219–20. Describes George Washington's china plate given to AJ by Eleanor Parke Custis Lewis.
Dec 29	From Lyncoya. Copy, THi (9-0857). Robert V. Remini, *Andrew Jackson and the Course of American Freedom, 1822–1832* (New York, 1981), p. 4. Expresses appreciation for AJ's rearing him.
Dec 29	Account of Rachel Jackson with H[arriett] Temple for seamstress work. ADS, DLC (32).
Dec 30	To James Monroe (enclosure: Daniel M. Forney to AJ, Dec 25). ALS, DNA-RG 59 (M439-16). Recommends Montfort Stokes as minister to Mexico.
Dec 30	From Charles Ridgely. Printed, Washington *National Gazette,* Jan 7, 1824 (mAJs, 9-0860). Invites AJ to January 8th ball in Baltimore.
Dec 31	*To John Coffee.* 332
Dec 31	To Charles Ridgely. Printed, Washington *National Gazette,* Jan 7, 1824 (mAJs, 9-0872). Declines invitation to Baltimore celebration.
Dec 31	From William Carroll. Copy, DNA-RG 233 (9-0862). *ASP, Military Affairs,* 4:540. Sends information re possible armory at the Harpeth River Narrows.
Dec 31	Receipt from Jesse Hill to Benjamin P. Person (overseer) for $45.80 payment for pork. ADS, DLC (32).

1824

Jan 1	From George Washington Parke Custis. Abstract, Washington *National Intelligencer,* Jan 6 (mAJs). Presents pocket telescope owned by George Washington.
Jan 1	To George Washington Parke Custis. Abstract, Washington *National Intelligencer,* Jan 6 (mAJs). Thanks him for gift.
Jan 1	To Ezra Stiles Ely. Extracts, Ely, *The Duty of Christian Freemen to Elect Christian Rulers* (Philadelphia, 1828), p. 32 (9-0880); Paul C. Richards Catalog 1 (n.d.), Item 281 (9-0881). *Nashville Republican & State Gazette,* April 1, 1828. Again requests Ely's aid in restoring Thomas B. Craighead to the Presbyterian Church; advises on land redemption.
Jan 1	From [Peter Hagner]. LC, DNA-RG 217 (9-0882). Discusses settlement of George W. Still's account.
[Jan 2]	*To George Washington Martin.* 334
Jan 4	From Henry Forrest. ALS, DNA-RG 46 (9-0889). Discusses petition for relief of Josiah and Jane Watson, parents of William H. Watson, deceased, which Jackson presented to the Senate on January 5.
Jan 5	To John Coffee. ALS, THi (9-0891). Discusses possibility of adding Florida to Coffee's survey district.
Jan 5	To Andrew Jackson, Jr. Printed, Heiskell (1st edition), 1:600 (9-0894). Asks that he write about the farm and the family.
Jan 5	To Rachel Jackson. ALS, DLC (32). Bassett, 3:222. Reports on his health and church attendance.
Jan 6	To Chandler Price. ALS, PHi (9-0898). *Richmond Enquirer,* Feb 7 (extract). States that he will not campaign for president and would be content if another were elected.
Jan 6	From Fontaine Maury. LC, DNA-RG 59 (M40-18). Requests information to aid in the settlement of Alexander C. W. Fanning's account.
[Jan 6]	From [Andrew Jackson Donelson]. AL draft fragment, DLC (9-0895). Reports on his trip to Florence, Alabama.
Jan 7	To [William Lee]. Photocopy of LS, TU (37-0496). Supports claim of Alexander C. W. Fanning.
Jan 7	From [Peter Hagner] (enclosure: Hagner to Bernard M. Patteson, Jan 7). LC, DNA-RG 217 (9-0900). Transmits letter re Patteson's account.
Jan 8	From Charles Fenton Mercer. Printed, Washington *National Intelligencer,* Jan 10 (9-0903). Presents to AJ pistols given to George Washington by Lafayette.
Jan 8	To Charles Fenton Mercer. Printed, Washington *National Intelligencer,* Jan 10 (9-0904). Accepts pistols.
Jan 8	From John Nicholson Moulder et al. Printed, Washington *National Intelligencer,* Jan 13 (9-0905). Praise AJ's services to the country.
Jan 8	To John Nicholson Moulder et al. Printed, Washington *National Intelligencer,* Jan 13 (9-0906). Thanks citizens of first ward, Washington, D.C., for tribute.
Jan 8	From William Robinson. Printed, Washington *National Intelligencer,* Jan 10 (9-0907). Offers gift of George Washington's pistols.

Jan 8 To William Robinson. Photocopy of ALS, TU (mAJs); Printed, Washington *National Intelligencer,* Jan 10 (9-0908). Thanks him for gift of pistols.

Jan 9 From William Lee. LC, DNA-RG 217 (9-0909). Reports adjustment of Alexander C. W. Fanning's claim.

Jan 9 From Greenbury Ridgely Stringer. DS, DLC (32). Notifies AJ that a draft in his favor by William E. and Robert Butler on Wilkins & Linton, October 10, 1823, for $3,000 has been protested.

Jan 10 To Rachel Jackson. ALS, DLC (32). Bassett, 3:222–23. Discusses gifts of Washington's pistols and telescope.

Jan 10 From Major Ridge. Printed, *Cheraw Intelligencer,* June 3, 1825 (mAJs, 10-1066). Extols his friendship with AJ.

Jan 12 Report for Senate Committee on Military Affairs on petition of Thomas Williamson et al. re claims from the 1818 Seminole campaign. Copy, DNA-RG 46 (9-0910). *SDoc* 14, 18th Cong., 1st sess. (Serial 89), pp. 1–2.

Jan 12 Bill from Senate Committee on Military Affairs for relief for soldiers of the Seminole campaign. Copy and Printed, DNA-RG 46 (9-0917).

Jan 13 From John Christmas McLemore. ALS, THi (9-0922). Reviews his understanding of AJ's agreement with Patrick H. Darby for compensation as lawyer in *Jackson* v. *Erwin.*

Jan 14 *To Andrew Jackson Donelson.* 336

Jan 14 To Samuel Lewis Southard. LS, InFwL (mAJs). Encloses letter (not found).

Jan 14 From William Lee. LC, DNA-RG 217 (9-0926). Reports on claim of Hugh Young's father.

Jan 15 To John Caldwell Calhoun. ALS and Copy, DNA-RG 107 (M221-97). Asks whether interest has been allowed to states for advances of funds during the War of 1812.

Jan 15 *To Rachel Jackson.* 337

Jan 15 To James Monroe. ALS, CtY (9-0930). Supports Montfort Stokes for minister to Mexico.

Jan 15 From Joseph Lovell. ALS, DNA-RG 46 (9-0932). Identifies those who recommended Edward Macomb and George P. Todson for army medical appointments.

Jan 16 To Andrew Jackson Donelson. ALS, DLC (32). Asks for copies of some of AJ's 1816–17 letters to James Monroe regarding cabinet posts.

Jan 16 *To James Monroe.* 338

Jan 16 From John Caldwell Calhoun (enclosure: Peter Hagner to Calhoun, Jan 16, DNA-RG 46). LS, DNA-RG 46 (9-0935); LC, DNA-RG 107 (M220-1). Forwards letter reporting that no interest has been allowed to states on money advanced in the War of 1812.

Jan 16 From George W. Hockley. ALS, DNA-RG 59 (M439-17). Introduces Edward Tilghman, who seeks appointment as consul to Tunis.

Jan 16 *From James Monroe.* 339

Jan 16 Speech on war service of Alexander A. White and in support of his petition to the U.S. Senate. Abstract, *Annals of Congress,* 18th

Cong., 1st sess., p. 122 (mAJs).

Jan 17 To William Grafton Dulany Worthington. ALS, James S. Corbitt (9-0941). Regrets that he cannot send information requested, since his papers are in Tennessee.

Jan 17 From John Geddes. Printed, Charleston *City Gazette and Commercial Daily Advertiser,* Feb 12 (mAJs, 9-0940). On behalf of Charleston City Council, asks AJ to sit for portrait by John Vanderlyn.

Jan 17 From Edward Tilghman (enclosure: George W. Hockley to AJ, Jan 16). ALS, DNA-RG 59 (M439-17). Asks help in securing appointment as consul to Tunis.

Jan 18 To John Caldwell Calhoun (from John Henry Eaton and AJ). ALS in Eaton's hand also signed by AJ, DNA-RG 233 (9-0942). Forward papers re establishment of an armory at the Harpeth River Narrows.

Jan 18 *To Andrew Jackson Donelson.* 339

Jan 19 To John Caldwell Calhoun. ALS, NjMoHP (9-0944). Inquires about the revolutionary service of Dr. Samuel J. Axson.

Jan 19 To Peter Hagner. ALS, Gallery of History, Inc. (mAJs). Forwards letter (not found) from James Johnston re claim.

Jan 19 From Peter Hagner. LC, DNA-RG 217 (10-0378). Sends copy of decision re James Johnston's claim.

Jan 19 From Samuel Lewis Southard. LC, DNA-RG 45 (10-0379). Acknowledges receipt of recommendation (not found) of Mr. Sterett for midshipman.

Jan 19 Check from George Brown for $2,500. DS, DLC (32).

Jan 19 Motion to Senate for consideration of bill to pay for horses and equipment lost by Seminole campaign volunteers. Abstract, *Annals of Congress,* 18th Cong., 1st sess., pp. 125–26 (mAJs).

Jan 20 *To Edward George Washington Butler.* 341

Jan 20 *To Chandler Price.* 342

Jan 20 From John Caldwell Calhoun. LC, DNA-RG 15 (mAJs). Reports regarding revolutionary service of Samuel J. Axson.

Jan 20 Report from Senate Committee on Military Affairs on nominations of George P. Todson and Edward Macomb. Abstract, *Senate Executive Proceedings,* 3:358 (mAJs).

Jan 21 *To Andrew Jackson Donelson.* 343

Jan 21 *To Rachel Jackson.* 345

Jan 21 To Samuel Lewis Southard. ALS, Gettysburg National Military Park (10-0391). Forwards letter (not found) of Mary Sterett re her son.

Jan 22 To Hugh Lawson White. ALS, Michael Harris (10-0392). Asks if White wishes to be a candidate for circuit judge of Tennessee and Alabama.

Jan 23 Report for Senate Committee on Military Affairs on bill recommending road from Fort St. Philip to the English Turn. AD, DNA-RG 46 (10-0394). *ASP, Military Affairs,* 3:8.

Jan 25 To John Caldwell Calhoun. ALS and Copy, DNA-RG 107 (M221-97). Forwards Edward Mitchell's claim (not found) and requests information.

Jan 26 From Thomas Carbery. ALS, DNA-RG 59 (M439-12). Recommends

Thomas L. Noyes for state department clerkship.

Jan 26 Account with William Jewell, Georgetown tailor, for clothing. ADS, DLC (32). Runs to April 2.

Jan 27 To Richard Dabbs. ALS, NjP (10-0399). Authorizes payment to Capt. Bradly.

Jan 27 *To John Geddes.* 346

Jan 27 *To Francis Preston.* 347

Jan 27 Amendment to bill for supplying ordnance to fortifications. AD, DNA-RG 46 (10-0404).

Jan 28 Speech on bill for a military road from Fort St. Philip to the English Turn. Abstract, *Annals of Congress,* 18th Cong., 1st sess., pp. 152–53 (mAJs).

Jan 29 To John Quincy Adams (enclosure: Thomas Carbery to AJ, Jan 26). ALS, DNA-RG 59 (M439-12). Recommends Thomas L. Noyes for clerkship in state department.

Jan 29 *To Rachel Jackson.* 348

Jan 30 *To John Christmas McLemore.* 350

Jan 30 Account with Bedford & Mackey for cotton sales. ADS, DLC (32). Runs to March 27.

Jan 31 To Anthony Wayne Butler. ALS, LNHiC (10-0421). Discusses Butler's impecuniousness.

Jan 31 From [Peter Hagner]. LC, DNA-RG 217 (10-0424). Discusses claims of Eli Ballinger and William Balthrepp.

Feb 1 To John Caldwell Calhoun. ALS and Copy, DNA-RG 107 (M222-23); Copy, DNA-RG 156 (mAJs). Requests information on war department funding for use of Military Affairs Committee.

Feb 1 From John Brahan. ALS, DNA-RG 94 (M688-28). Recommends Peyton S. Wyatt for the Military Academy.

Feb 2 From [Peter Hagner]. LC, DNA-RG 217 (10-0428). Discusses Seminole campaign claim of Thomas H. Boyles.

Feb 4 From Henry Marie Brackenridge (enclosure: Brackenridge to William H. Crawford, Jan 30). ALS with AJ endorsement, DLC (32). Discusses claims decisions and officeholders in Florida.

Feb 4 From James L. Edwards. LC, DNA-RG 15 (10-0430). Discusses rejection of James C. Ferguson's pension claim.

Feb 4 From William Grafton Dulany Worthington. ALS, DNA-RG 94 (M688-30). Recommends John Carnan for the Military Academy.

Feb 5 Amendment to bill for a military road from Fort St. Philip to the English Turn. AD, DNA-RG 46 (10-0432).

Feb 6 *To Rachel Jackson.* 351

Feb 6 From John Caldwell Calhoun (enclosure: George Bomford to Calhoun, Feb 6, DNA-RG 156). LCs, DNA-RG 107 (M220-1) and DNA-RG 156 (mAJs). Replies to February 1 inquiry, stating that permanent appropriations for ordnance are preferred to annual.

Feb 7 To Chandler Price. ALS, DLC (75). Denies having written to John Binns regarding the correspondence with James Monroe in 1817 about organizing his cabinet.

Feb 7 From [Peter Hagner]. LC, DNA-RG 217 (10-0439). Discusses rejection of Samuel Cunningham's claim.

Feb 8 From John Jordan Cabell. ALS, DNA-RG 94 (M688-33). Recommends

	John Reid's nephew Samuel Cabell for appointment to the Military Academy.	
Feb 8	From Samuel McCutchon. ALS, DNA-RG 94 (M688-29). Requests appointment of his son Richard B. McCutchon to the Military Academy.	
Feb 8	*From John Henry Eaton to Rachel Jackson.*	353
Feb 9	To John Caldwell Calhoun (enclosure: Petition of George W. Gibbs et al., n.d., DNA-RG 94, M688-30). Abstract, DNA-RG 107 (M22-17). Forwards recommendation of William E. Anderson for the Military Academy.	
Feb 9	*To John Donelson (1755–1830).*	354
Feb 9	To Peter Hagner. Photocopy of ALS, TU (mAJs). Forwards accounts for settlement.	
Feb 9	From Joseph McMinn (enclosure: Black Fox to McMinn, Nov 17, 1823). ALS and Copy, DNA-RG 107 (M221-97). Asks attention to plea for adjustment of Arkansas Cherokee boundary.	
Feb 10	From John Caldwell Calhoun. LC, DNA-RG 75 (M15-6). *Calhoun Papers,* 8:532 (extract). Discusses Edward Mitchell's claim.	
Feb [10]	To John Caldwell Calhoun. Abstract, DNA-RG 107 (M22-17). Transmits recommendations of Edward B. Grayson for the Military Academy.	
Feb 11	Report to Senate of bill to supply ordnance for fortifications. Abstract, *Annals of Congress,* 18th Cong., 1st sess., p. 242 (mAJs).	
Feb 11	Deed to land in Bedford County from AJ, James Jackson, and Patrick H. Darby to Andrew Erwin et al. Copy, TSBe (10-0444).	
[cFeb 11]	From Richard Mentor Johnson et al. ADS signed by twenty-four members of Congress, DLC (72, 9-0878). *Washington Republican and Congressional Examiner,* Feb 12. Oppose nomination of presidential candidate by congressional caucus.	
Feb 12	*To Andrew Jackson Donelson.*	355
Feb 12	To Andrew Jackson, Jr. Typed copy, CCamarSJ (10-0454). Urges him write often and to obey his mother.	
Feb 12	To Rachel Jackson. Photocopy of ALS, THer (mAJs). Discusses health and friends.	
Feb 12	From [Peter Hagner]. LC, DNA-RG 217 (10-0453). Discusses rejection of claims of Henry Hill and Achilles Antorberry.	
Feb 12	From William Lee. LC, DNA-RG 217 (10-0455). Discusses War of 1812 claims of Eli Ballinger and William Balthrepp.	
Feb [12]	To John Caldwell Calhoun. Abstract, DNA-RG 107 (M22-17). Transmits land claim of R. Apperson.	
Feb 13	From James McMillan Glassell (enclosure: Glassell to John Binns, Feb 10). ALS, DLC (32). Discusses a biographical sketch published in James McHenry's *The American Monthly Magazine* and the response to Binns's commentary on AJ's correspondence with James Monroe.	
Feb 15	*To John Coffee.*	357
Feb 16	To John Caldwell Calhoun. Photocopy of LS signed by twenty-five congressmen including AJ, George Webb (mAJs). *Writings of Sam Houston,* 2:3 (dated February 15). Recommend Adam D. Stewart for army paymaster.	

Feb 16	Account with William Watson for shoes. ADS, DLC (33). Runs to November 6.	
Feb [16]	To John Caldwell Calhoun (enclosure: John J. Cabell to AJ, Feb 8). Abstract, DNA-RG 107 (M22-17). Forwards recommendation of Samuel Cabell for the Military Academy.	
Feb 18	From Robert Triplett. ALS, DNA-RG 94 (M688-28). Inquires about the application of William R. Burnley for appointment to the Military Academy.	
Feb 20	To Peter Hagner. ALS, THi (10-0461). Requests copy of Robert Searcy's account as paymaster of West Tennessee militia.	
Feb 20	*To Rachel Jackson.*	359
Feb 20	Speech on bill for the relief of James Johnson. Abstract, *Annals of Congress,* 18th Cong., 1st sess., p. 291 (mAJs).	
Feb 20	Speech supporting bill to open public roads in Florida. Abstract, *Annals of Congress,* 18th Cong., 1st sess., pp. 292–94 (mAJs).	
Feb 20	Account with Anthony Latapie for foodstuff and clothing. ADS, DLC (33). Runs to November 1.	
Feb 21	From [Peter Hagner]. LC, DNA-RG 217 (10-0463). Forwards copy of Robert Searcy's account.	
Feb 22	*To John Coffee.*	361
Feb 22	To John W. Cushman. Printed, Washington *United States' Telegraph,* Aug 4, 1828 (10-0469). Advises on intended removal from New York to Tennessee or Alabama.	
Feb 22	*To William Berkeley Lewis.*	363
Feb 22	To James Monroe. ALS, Uk (10-0474). Washington *National Intelligencer,* May 8. Returns letters and asks their preservation for possible reply to Walter Lowrie.	
Feb 22	*From James Monroe.*	365
Feb 22	From Benjamin Owen Tyler. ALS, DLC (32). Sends portraits of Washington, Franklin, Adams, and Jefferson.	
Feb [22]	To John Caldwell Calhoun (enclosure: John Brahan to AJ, Feb 1). ALS, NcD (10-0425). Forwards recommendations of Peyton S. Wyatt for the Military Academy.	
Feb [22]	To John Caldwell Calhoun. Abstract, DNA-RG 107 (M22-17). Recommends R. H. Lee for the Military Academy.	
Feb [22]	To John Caldwell Calhoun. Abstract, DNA-RG 107 (M22-17). Recommends J. C. Nazro for the Military Academy.	
Feb 23	Account with Samuel Van Dyke Stout for carriage repairs and tack. ADS, DLC (32). Runs to June 30.	
Feb 24	To Ezra Stiles Ely. ALS, MHi (10-0478). Declines invitation to visit at Ely's home in Philadelphia.	
Feb 24	Promissory note to Francis Saunders for $1,500. DS, G. Keeling Turner (10-0480).	
Feb [24]	To John Caldwell Calhoun (enclosure: Joseph McMinn to AJ, Feb 9). Abstract, DNA-RG 107 (M22-17). Transmits letter.	
Feb 25	From Anthony Spengler. ALS, DNA-RG 45 (mAJs). Introduces Dr. Stephen Beattie, who seeks a naval appointment.	
Feb 26	To John Caldwell Calhoun. AL and Copy, DNA-RG 107 (M221-97). Requests copies of AJ to Thomas Pinckney, March 28, 1814, and of war department instructions re 1814 Creek negotiations.	

Feb 26	*To Andrew Jackson Donelson.*	366
Feb 26	Account with John Simpson & Co. for supplies for Andrew Jackson Hutchings's farm. DS, A-Ar (10-0488). Runs to June 18, 1825.	
Feb 26	Account with Bernard Vanleer & Co. for iron. AD, DLC (32).	
Feb 27	To Rachel Jackson. ALS, THer (10-0491). *Historical Outlook,* 14(Jan 1923):11 (extract). Discusses the plight of Elizabeth C. (Love) Watson and family.	
Feb 27	To James Monroe. ALS, DLC (10-0495). Offers to send original of the letter that Walter Lowrie claims to have.	
Feb 27	From John Caldwell Calhoun. LC, DNA-RG 107 (M220-1). Discusses compensation of Robert Searcy during service as paymaster.	
Feb 28	To James Monroe. AL, DLC (10-0497); AL draft, DLC (32). Returns letters; sends original of Monroe to AJ, December 14, 1816.	
[cFeb]	To James Monroe (from AJ, John Henry Eaton, and Richard Keith Call). Extract, Robert F. Batchelder Catalog 45 (1984), Item 55 (10-0427). Recommend Robert Butler for surveyor general of Florida.	
March 1	To Andrew Jackson Donelson (enclosure: James Monroe to AJ, March 1). ALS, DLC (10-0500). Asks Donelson to send documents re AJ's commission as brevet major general in 1814.	
March 1	From Peter Hagner. LC, DNA-RG 217 (10-0504). Discusses settlement of George Selvidge's claim.	
March 1	From Peter Hagner (enclosure: Hagner to Richard M. Johnson, Feb 18, [1823], DNA-RG 107, M222-23). Copy, DNA-RG 107 (M222-23); LC, DNA-RG 217 (10-0505). Discusses the claim of Robert F. Crittenden.	
March 1	From James Monroe. ALS, DLC (10-0506). Forwards request from James Madison for information re AJ's commissions in 1814.	
March 2	To Rachel Jackson. ALS, DLC (32). Bassett, 3:232–33. Gives information re sale of his cotton in New Orleans.	
March 3	To Robert F. Crittenden (enclosure: Peter Hagner to AJ, March 1). ALS, NcD (10-0508). Sends decision of the third auditor re claim.	
March 4	*To John Coffee.*	368
March 4	To Ninian Edwards. AN, ICHi (10-0515). Eli B. Washburne, *The Edwards Papers* (Chicago, 1884), p. 222. Congratulates him on appointment as minister to Mexico.	
March 4	*To Samuel Swartwout.*	370
March 4	From John Caldwell Calhoun. LC, DNA-RG 107 (M220-1). Transmits surgeon general's report (not found) re J. Ponte Coulant McMahon.	
March 6	To John Caldwell Calhoun. ALS, MBU (10-0521); Copy, DNA-RG 107 (M221-97). Requests information re payment to William Duane for military training manuals.	
March 6	*To Andrew Jackson Donelson.*	372
March 6	To Rachel Jackson. ALS, DLC (32). Bassett, 3:236–37. Discusses Ezra S. Ely's invitation to visit Philadelphia.	
March 6	*From James Tallmadge, Jr.*	373
March 7	To Andrew Jackson Donelson. ALS, DLC (10-0531). Urges Donelson to oversee the young Andrews' reading and writing.	

March 7 To Andrew Jackson Donelson. ALS, DLC (10-0534). Reports that Pennsylvania convention has overwhelmingly supported him for president, John C. Calhoun for vice-president.

March 8 From John Caldwell Calhoun (enclosure: [Peter Hagner] to Calhoun, March 8, DNA-RG 217, 10-0537). LC, DNA-RG 107 (10-0536). Transmits report on claim of William Duane.

March 9 To John Quincy Adams. AN in Richard K. Call's hand, MHi (10-0538). Invites him to dinner.

March 9 To Samuel Lewis Southard. AN in Richard K. Call's hand, NjP (10-0540). Invites him to dinner.

March 9 Speech in support of bill to supply ordnance for fortifications. Extract, Harrisburg *Pennsylvanian,* March 27 (mAJs); Abstract, *Annals of Congress,* 18th Cong., 1st sess., pp. 330–31 (mAJs).

March 10 To John Caldwell Calhoun (enclosure: Benjamin Emmons et al. to Congress, Jan 5, DNA-RG 46, mAJs). Photocopy of ALS, THer (mAJs); Copy, DNA-RG 107 (M221-97). Transmits memorial of the trustees of St. Charles, Missouri, requesting that lots reserved for military purposes be applied to support public schools.

March 10 From [James Hamilton, Jr.]. Copy, DNA-RG 233 (10-0545). *HRRep* 105, 18th Cong., 1st sess. (Serial 106), p. 2. On behalf of House Military Affairs Committee, requests information re William Cocke's service in War of 1812.

March 10 To James Hamilton, Jr. LS, DNA-RG 233 (10-0542). *HRRep* 105, 18th Cong., 1st sess. (Serial 106), p. 2 (dated March 16). Discusses William Cocke's military service and endorses his claim.

March 10 Remarks on bill for the relief of Alfred Moore and Sterling Orgain. Abstract, *Annals of Congress,* 18th Cong., 1st sess., p. 334 (mAJs).

March 11 To Joseph Gales. AN, NN (10-0547). Declines dinner invitation.

March 11 To Henry Middleton Rutledge. ALS, PHi (10-0548). Writes that he will be unable to visit South Carolina and Georgia on his way home.

March 12 *To James Tallmadge, Jr.* 374

March 12 John Henry Eaton to John Overton. ALS, THi (mAJs). Bassett, 3:235–36. Requests information about AJ's marriage, to repel rumored attack by the Radicals.

March 13 To Andrew Jackson Donelson. ALS, DLC (10-0551). Bassett, 3:238. Reports on presidential politics in Pennsylvania, New York, and North Carolina.

March 13 From John Caldwell Calhoun. LS, DNA-RG 46 (10-0549); LC, DNA-RG 107 (M220-1). Replies that reserved land in St. Charles, Missouri, is not required for military purposes.

March 14 To John Caldwell Calhoun. AL, InU-Li (10-0553). Requests that medal presentation be postponed to March 16 at 11 a.m.

March 15 To John Caldwell Calhoun (enclosure: Samuel McCutchon to AJ, Feb 8). ALS, DNA-RG 94 (M688-29). Supports appointment of Richard B. McCutchon to the Military Academy.

March 15 Report for Senate Military Affairs Committee on memorial of St. Charles trustees, requesting that the matter be referred to the Committee on Public Lands. AD, DNA-RG 46 (10-0555).

March 16 To Andrew Jackson Donelson. ALS, InU-Li (10-0557). Parton,

3:38 (extract). Describes his birthday celebration and the presentation of his War of 1812 medal.

March 16 *To Rachel Jackson.* 375

March 16 To James Monroe. ALS, DLC (10-0564). Returns "the sketch sent me for our interview of to day."

[March 16] From James Monroe. DS, DNA-RG 107 (M221-98). Washington *National Intelligencer,* March 17. Presents congressional medal awarded for defense of New Orleans.

[March 16] *To James Monroe.* 377

March 16 From Samuel Swartwout. ALS, DNA-RG 94 (M688-35). Asks AJ to recommend Alfred M. Paterson for the Military Academy.

March 18 Receipt from Martin & Williams for $48.30 for clothing. ADS, DLC (32).

March 19 *To Andrew Jackson Donelson.* 377

March 19 To Rachel Jackson. ALS, DLC (32). Bassett, 3:238–39. Discusses his health and his planned route home.

March 22 To John Caldwell Calhoun (enclosure: Samuel Swartwout to AJ, March 16). ALS, DNA-RG 94 (M688-35). Forwards recommendation of Alfred M. Paterson for the Military Academy.

March 22 *To John McLean.* 379

March 23 To John Overton. ALS, THi (10-0580). Fletch Coke, ed., *Dear Judge: Selected Letters of John Overton of Travellers' Rest* (Nashville, 1978), pp. 67–68 (extract). Discusses death of Thomas Overton and congressional debate regarding the caucus.

March [23] From [Anthony Wayne Butler]. AL, LNHiC (10-0575). Discusses the protested note to Hull & Townsend and announces commencement of legal studies.

March 25 To Mobile gentleman. Printed, Raleigh *Star, and North-Carolina Gazette,* June 11 (mAJs). States his views on the tariff.

March 25 To Samuel Lewis Southard. Abstract, *The Collector,* No. 824 [1971–72?], Item F-564 (10-0584). Deals with recommendation of Stephen Beattie.

March 25 *To Samuel Swartwout.* 380

March 26 To John Caldwell Calhoun. ALS, MeSaco (10-0595). Recommends John Peters for paymaster at Harpers Ferry.

March 27 To Andrew Jackson Donelson. ALS, DLC (10-0600). Discusses missing letterbook, presidential politics, and family news.

March 27 To Andrew Jackson Donelson. ALS, DLC (10-0597). Encloses an oration (not found) omitted from previous letter.

March 27 To Rachel Jackson. ALS, DLC (32). Bassett, 3:240–41. Expresses gloom over protracted stay in Washington.

March 27 To William Lee. Extract, Ben Bloomfield List DM-10 (n.d.), Item 36 (mAJs). Supports a claim by Thomas Shields.

March 28 *To John Coffee.* 382

March 29 To [George Bomford]. LS, Gallery of History, Inc. (mAJs). Requests the number of United States rifles and muskets "really fit for service."

March 29 From James L. Edwards. LC, DNA-RG 15 (10-0609). Reports rejection of Hillary Lane's pension application.

March 29 *From William Hayden, Jr.* 384

March 29	From John Preston. ALS, DNA-RG 94 (M688-32). Applies on behalf of his son, eleven years old, for future appointment to the Military Academy.	
March 30	*To William Hayden, Jr.*	386
March 30	From Theodore Newell. ALS endorsed by AJ for preservation, with information about Newell, DLC (32). Praises AJ's character.	
March 30	Account of Rachel Jackson with Hugh Erwin for shoes and gloves. ADS, DLC (33).	
March 31	*To William Berkeley Lewis.*	387
April 1	From George Bomford. LC, DNA-RG 156 (10-0619). Estimates that about 200,000 usable muskets and 16,000 rifles are stored at national arsenals.	
April 2	To Rachel Jackson. ALS, NjMoHP (10-0622). Heiskell, 3:290. States that the tariff bill is delaying the adjournment of Congress.	
April 3	Receipt from George Crockett for $59.80 for rope. ADS, DLC (32).	
April 3	John Overton to [John Henry Eaton]. Broadside with ANS dated May 4, 1827, DLC (mAJs). Gives information about AJ's marriage.	
April 4	*To Andrew Jackson Donelson.*	388
April 5	To Andrew Jackson, Jr. Facsimile of part of ALS, Sotheby's (N.Y.) Sale 5621 (Oct 23, 1987), Item 38 (mAJs); Printed, Heiskell (1st edition), p. 607 (10-0630). Thanks him for letter and urges him to be helpful to Rachel.	
April 5	To Rachel Jackson. ALS, DLC (32). Bassett 3:244. Sends greetings from friends in Washington.	
April 7	To Rachel Jackson. ALS, DLC (32). Bassett, 3:244–45. Informs her that he is starting George home with Mr. Hill of Franklin.	
April 8	To Rachel Jackson. ALS, DLC (32). Bassett, 3:245. Gives instructions for preserving portrait of John H. Eaton.	
April 8	To Rachel Jackson. Printed, Thomas F. Madigan Catalog (1927), Item 139 (10-0631). Discusses property he is sending with George and Senate business delaying his departure.	
April 9	*To James Monroe.*	389
April 9	Account with Josiah Nichol & Co. for merchandise and money advanced. AD matched fragments, DLC (33). Runs to May 26, 1825.	
April 10	From James Monroe. ALS, DLC (32). Bassett, 3:246. Advises publishing nothing in response to Walter Lowrie's attack.	
April 10	*To James Monroe.*	390
April 10	Account with Decker & Dyer for cordials and sweetmeats, with receipt for payment, June 11. ADS, DLC (32).	
April 10	Account with B[ernard] Vanleer & Co. for iron. AD, DLC (32).	
April 11	*To Andrew Jackson Donelson.*	391
April 11	From Pleasant Moorman Miller. ALS endorsed by AJ "to be kept," DLC (32). Suggests policy of excluding members of Congress from government appointments during their terms.	
April 12	To John Caldwell Calhoun (enclosure: John Preston to AJ, March 29). ALS, DNA-RG 94 (M688-32). Forwards Preston's "premature application" for appointment of his son to the Military Academy.	
April 12	*To Rachel Jackson.*	393
April 15	Check to Andrew Jackson Donelson for $12.92. DS by proxy	

	(Donelson), Stanley F. Horn (10-0643).	
April 16	To Andrew Jackson Donelson. ALS, DLC (10-0645). Bassett, 3:248 (extract). Discusses Walter Lowrie's charges, reporting that congressmen who have seen AJ's letters to James Monroe have approved of AJ's advice.	
April 16	*From Arthur Peronneau Hayne.*	394
April 17	*To Andrew Jackson Donelson.*	395
April 17	To George Wilson. Extract, Parton, 3:42–43 (10-0656). Discusses the tariff bill.	
April 17	From Alexander Macomb. ALS, DNA-RG 46 (10-0653); LC, DNA-RG 77 (10-0655). *Calhoun Papers,* 9:37. Discusses possible purchase of Theodore Newell's orrery by the Military Academy.	
April 19	From Peter Hagner. LS, DNA-RG 46 (10-0659); LC, DNA-RG 217 (10-0661). Explains that no claims have been paid to states for clothing militia during the War of 1812 and that a new law would be required to authorize payment.	
[April 19]	Request that the Senate Military Affairs Committee be discharged from further consideration of petition of Julius Willerd and Thomas Childs. AN, DNA-RG 46 (10-0663).	
[April 19]	Report of the Senate Military Affairs Committee re purchase of an orrery. AD, DNA-RG 46 (10-0665).	
April 20	From John R. Mifflin. ALS, DLC (32). Asks help in securing appointment as a collector of customs.	
April 20	Remarks in Senate on bill for the relief of William Duane. Abstract, *Annals of Congress,* 18th Cong., 1st sess., p. 529 (mAJs).	
April 20	Motion in Senate to amend bill for settlement of certain claims by limiting it to claims of twelve years or less standing. Abstract, *Annals of Congress,* 18th Cong., 1st sess., p. 532 (mAJs).	
April 21	To Anthony Wayne Butler. ALS, LNHiC (10-0667). Discusses settlement of note drawn on AJ.	
April 21	From [Francis Everod Rives]. Printed, *Richmond Enquirer,* May 22, 1827 (mAJs, 10-0670). Parton, 3:34. Requests statement of AJ's views on the tariff.	
April 22	To Jacob Jennings Brown. AL in James M. Glassell's hand (signature removed), MHi (10-0675). Asks extension of Major [William] Davenport's furlough.	
April 22	From [Peter Hagner] (enclosure: [Hagner] to Adam Peck, April 22, DNA-RG 217, mAJs). LC, DNA-RG 217 (10-0677). Reports settlement of Peck's account.	
April 22	Account of Andrew Jackson Hutchings with John Robertson Bedford for cotton gin and bagging. AD, A-Ar (10-0673). Runs to February 1, 1825.	
April 23	*To Andrew Jackson Donelson.*	397
April 23	To Rachel Jackson. ALS, DLC (32). Bassett, 3:248–49. Discusses Senate proceedings which delay his departure.	
April 23	From John Caldwell Calhoun. LC, DNA-RG 107 (M6-12). *Calhoun Papers,* 9:48. Forwards information from the commissary general of purchases.	
April 24	Report, on behalf of joint committee of Congress, on business to be	

	completed before adjournment. Abstract, *Annals of Congress,* 18th Cong., 1st sess., p. 570 (mAJs).	
April 26	*To Littleton H. Coleman.*	398
April 27	To Edward George Washington Butler. ALS, Sudeley Castle, Gloucestershire, England (10-0684). Describes visit to Woodlawn plantation in Virginia.	
April 27	*To Andrew Jackson Donelson.*	400
April 27	To Rachel Jackson. ALS, DLC (32). Sends a book per request of Ezra S. Ely.	
April 27	Motion that Senate Committee on Military Affairs be discharged from consideration of bill for relief of Mary James. Abstract, *Annals of Congress,* 18th Cong., 1st sess., p. 577 (mAJs).	
April 27	Promissory note to Francis Saunders for $1,000, payable in sixty days. DS, G. Keeling Turner (10-0692).	
April 28	To Andrew Jackson Donelson. ALS, DLC (10-0695). Reports House rejection of the bill to compensate the heirs of John Donelson (c1718–86) and other Georgia commissioners.	
April 28	From James W. Lanier. ALS with AJ endorsement, DLC (32). Requests for use in the Ohio campaign a statement of AJ's views on internal improvements and the encouragement of manufacturing.	
April 29	From [Peter Hagner]. LC, DNA-RG 217 (10-0698). Reports on settlement of George W. Still's account.	
April 29	Receipted account with Martha Adams for sewing and materials. ADS, DLC (33). Runs to October 15.	
April 30	Report to Senate from the Committee on Military Affairs of bills for relief of Charles Humphrey and Joseph Marechal. Abstract, *Annals of Congress,* 18th Cong., 1st sess., p. 616 (mAJs).	
April	From Allan Ditchfield Campbell. ALS, DLC (32). Sends materials (not found) to be transmitted to Philadelphia on behalf of Thomas B. Craighead; discusses Rachel Jackson's thought of meeting AJ at Louisville.	
May 1	To John Ross et al. Copy, DNA-RG 75 (M234-71). Refers them to the secretary of war for information re pay of Cherokee light horse who helped evict intruders in 1820.	
May 1	Report to Senate from Committee on Military Affairs of bills for relief of Solomon Sibley, David Cooper, and Frederick Perley. Abstract, *Annals of Congress,* 18th Cong., 1st sess., p. 653 (mAJs).	
May 3	From James L. Edwards. LC, DNA-RG 15 (10-0699). Returns John Neely's pension claim for more documentation.	
May 3	Report to Senate of joint committee opinion that Congress can adjourn May 10. Abstract, *Annals of Congress,* 18th Cong., 1st sess., p. 655 (mAJs).	
May 4	Report to Senate from Committee on Military Affairs of bills for exchange of land at Baton Rouge and for relief of Jacob Slough. Abstract, *Annals of Congress,* 18th Cong., 1st sess., p. 674 (mAJs).	
May 5	To Rachel Jackson. ALS, Gallery of History, Inc. (mAJs); Printed, Heiskell (1st edition), p. 599 (10-0700). Expresses distaste for Senate service and support for tariff bill.	
May 5	From George Kremer. Printed, Washington *National Intelligencer,* May 7 (10-0702). Requests information re the AJ-Monroe	

	correspondence discussed by Walter Lowrie.	
May 6	*To George Kremer.*	402
May 7	To John Coffee. ALS, THi (10-0708). Bassett, 3:251–52 (extract). Defends his stand on the tariff bill.	
May 7	*To William Berkeley Lewis.*	404
May 7	Motion to Senate to set ad valorem duty on ducks, osnaburgs, ticklenburgs, and burlaps at twenty percent. Abstract, *Annals of Congress,* 18th Cong., 1st sess., p. 713 (mAJs).	
May 10	To John Caldwell Calhoun. ALS, UPB (10-0717). Introduces Andrew Kinnard and endorses his request for assignment to the topographical corps.	
May 10	*From Whitman Mead.*	405
May 13	To Rachel Jackson. ALS, DLC (32). Bassett, 3:252. Reports on plans for his trip home.	
May 13	From [Peter Hagner]. LC, DNA-RG 217 (10-0721). Explains rejection of James Grimes's claim for compensation.	
May 14	To Andrew Jackson Donelson. ALS, DLC (10-0723). Acknowledges letter, sends encouragement to Andrew Jackson, Jr., and writes of hope to start for home next week.	
May 14	*From John Freeman Schermerhorn.*	406
[May 14]	To Rachel Jackson. Extract, *Flying Quill* (Goodspeed's), May–July 1949, Item 79 (10-0728). Informs her that his departure is delayed by consideration of the tariff bill.	
[May 15]	To Littleton H. Coleman. Copy in John H. Eaton's hand, DLC (36, 10-0726). Grants permission to publish AJ's letter re tariff.	
[cMay 15]	*To James W. Lanier.*	409
May 18	Check to Andrew Jackson Donelson for $200. DS by proxy (Donelson), G. Keeling Turner (10-0729).	
May 19	*To Rachel Jackson.*	410
May 19	From [Peter Hagner]. LC, DNA-RG 217 (10-0730). Discusses payment of claims for transporting officers' baggage.	
May 20	To John Quincy Adams (from AJ and Richard Mentor Johnson). ALS in Johnson's hand, also signed by AJ, DNA-RG 59 (M439-12). Recommend John W. Overton for U. S. district attorney of West Tennessee.	
May 20	*To Henry Baldwin.*	411
May 20	To James Monroe. ALS, DLC (10-0739). Forwards unidentified letter of application for office.	
May 20	To Stephen Simpson. Printed, Louisville *Daily Focus,* Oct 18, 1831 (10-0742). Regrets inability to visit Philadelphia on his way home.	
May 20	To James Telford. Abstract in AJ's hand, DLC (32). Informs Telford of auditor's action on claims to reimbursement for baggage transportation.	
May 21	To Andrew Jackson Donelson. ALS, DLC (10-0744). Discusses preparations for departure from Washington.	
May 21	Motion to take up House bill granting a tract for the seat of government in Florida. Abstract, *Annals of Congress,* 18th Cong., 1st sess., p. 769 (mAJs).	
May 21	Remarks on bill about carrying into effect the ninth article of the 1819 Adams-Onís Treaty. Abstract, *Annals of Congress,* 18th	

Cong., 1st sess., p. 771 (mAJs).

May 22 To James Monroe. ALS, NN (10-0747). Urges immediate nomination of a surveyor of Florida lands.

May 22 To James Telford. Abstract in AJ's hand, DLC (32). Encloses check for baggage transportation reimbursement.

May 22 From Craven P. Luckett. ALS, DLC (20). Requests assistance in procuring Florida appointment.

May 23 From William Pope Duval. Photocopy of ALS, TU (mAJs). Complains of 1823 law confining his movements; compliments AJ's presidential prospects; sends peas.

May 24 To John Quincy Adams (enclosure: William Staughton to Adams, May 24). ALS, DNA-RG 59 (M439-10). Transmits recommendation of Samuel W. Lynd for a clerkship.

May 24 To Samuel Lewis Southard. Facsimile of LS, *Nate's Autographs,* Catalog 2 (Feb 5, 1993), p. 24 (mAJs). Supports Isaac McKeever's request for a Mediterranean command.

May 24 From Edward George Washington Butler. ALS, MoSHi (10-0749). Comments on the publication of AJ's correspondence with James Monroe; gives news of friends in New York.

May 24 From Anderson B. Carr. ALS and Copy, DNA-RG 107 (M221-99). Reports that a commission sent by the president is in the name of Alexander Kerr and requests a replacement.

May 24 Motion to discharge Senate Committee on Military Affairs from considering report on arms furnished to the United States by South Carolina. Abstract, *Annals of Congress,* 18th Cong., 1st sess., p. 775 (mAJs).

May 24 Remarks in the Senate opposing an amendment to a bill amending the Florida territorial government. Abstract, *Annals of Congress,* 18th Cong., 1st sess., p. 778 (mAJs).

May 26 From James Gadsden. ALS, DLC (32). Comments on Florida Indian negotiations and on publication of AJ's correspondence with James Monroe; states intent to retire from public service.

May 27 From James Gadsden. ALS with AJ endorsement docketting receipt and reply, DLC (32). Asks sale of his Cypress Land Company stock.

May 27 Papers in the case of *U.S.* v. *John Overton and AJ, bail of Richard Ivy Easter* (scire facias). Copies, DNA-RG 21 (10-0753). Continued until June 20, 1825, when bail was exonerated.

[May] To James Monroe from forty-four congressmen including AJ. LS, DNA-RG 77 (9-0770). Recommend James Shriver of Pennsylvania for surveyor.

June 5 From James Gadsden. ALS, THi (10-0771). Asks that information be sent to Charleston regarding possible disposition of his Florence, Alabama, stock and lots.

June 6 From John Armstrong. ALS with AJ endorsement to file and preserve, DLC (32). Bassett, 3:254. Asks explanation of AJ's criticism of the "war minister" in the published 1817 correspondence with James Monroe.

June 8 To John Caldwell Calhoun (enclosure: Anderson B. Carr to AJ, May 24). ALS and Copy, DNA-RG 107 (M221-99). Asks correction of Carr's commission to survey a road from Memphis through

Arkansas.

June 8 *From John Coffee.* 412

June 10 From John Caldwell Calhoun. LS, DLC (32); LC, DNA-RG 77 (10-0773). *Calhoun Papers,* 9:154. Reports that the president believes a survey of the Muscle Shoals area cannot be executed this year.

June 10 From Alexander Macomb. LCs, DNA-RG 77 (10-0776, -0777). Relays president's decision re survey of Muscle Shoals area.

June 10 Toast at Nashville public dinner: "Virtue and Intelligence—The sheet anchor of our national Union, and the perpetuity of our national freedom." Printed, *Nashville Whig,* June 14 (10-0780).

June 11 To James Monroe. Copy in Andrew J. Donelson's hand, DLC (32). Again recommends Montfort Stokes for minister to Mexico vice Ninian Edwards, resigned.

June 11 Check to Andrew Jackson Donelson for $30. DS by proxy (Donelson), Stanley F. Horn (10-0785).

[June 11] To Andrew Jackson Donelson. AN, DLC (33, 10-0783). Directs him to prepare a letter to James Monroe re Montfort Stokes.

June 12 *From Charles Pendleton Tutt.* 414

June 13 From Rachel Jackson to John M. A. Hamblen. LS, PHi (10-0788). *Pennsylvania Magazine of History and Biography,* 25(1901):530–31. Mentions that she has seen Hamblen's daughter Mary, then visiting her grandmother, Charity Donelson.

June 14 Check to Andrew Jackson Donelson for $300. DS by proxy (Donelson), Ruth Crownover (37-0497).

June 18 *To John Coffee.* 416

June 19 To Penelope Porter (from AJ and Rachel Jackson). AN in Andrew J. Donelson's hand, THi (10-0799). Invite her to dinner.

June 20 Check to Andrew Jackson Donelson for $10. DS by proxy (Donelson), G. Keeling Turner (10-0800).

June 21 To John Coffee. ALS, THi (10-0802). Discusses collection of debts from Capt. Garner and William Griffin and payment of wages due Malachi Nicholson.

June 22 From Daniel Smith Donelson. ALS, DLC (32). Discusses the spring examinations at the Military Academy.

June 22 *From John Henry Eaton.* 419

June 22 Receipt of William Perkins for $15. ADS, DLC (32).

June 23 Account of Anderson & Knox for glassware, with receipt for payment, June 30. ADS, DLC (32).

June 24 *From Caleb Atwater.* 421

June 24 From Phineas Savery, John Smythe Richardson, and George Flagg Man. LS by proxy, DLC (32). Invite AJ to honorary membership in the Franklin Society, a Brown University forensic group.

June 24 Account of Decker & Dyer for foods, tobacco, cards, and brandy. AD, DLC (32).

June 24 Memorandum of $35 paid to Elizabeth Atwood Hutchings for a horse. ADS, DLC (32).

June 25 From John Caldwell Calhoun. LS, NjP (10-0814); LC, DNA-RG 107 (M6-12). *Calhoun Papers,* 9:178. Informs AJ that he has sent a corrected commission to Anderson B. Carr.

June 26 To Sylvanus Thayer. LS, NWM (10-0815). Introduces Gustave S.

	Rousseau, a new cadet at the Military Academy.	
June 26	From Jacob C. Isacks. ALS, Florida Department of Natural Resources (mAJs). Recommends Leroy May for appointment as a surveyor in Florida.	
June 26	*From George W. Thornton.*	422
June 26	From Thomas Washington (1788–1863). AN, DLC (32). Regrets his inability to attend "this day's festivities" with AJ.	
June 28	From H. Eliott et al. ALS, DLC (32). Announce that the Nashville Guards will escort AJ to the Nashville Independence Day celebration.	
June 29	*To John Armstrong.*	423
June 30	Receipt of J[ohn] Chapman for $50 from Andrew Jackson Donelson for service to AJ. DS, DLC (32).	
June 30	Check to Andrew Jackson Donelson for $200. DS by proxy (Donelson), G. Keeling Turner (10-0816).	
[June]	Memorandum by Andrew Jackson Donelson of accounts paid and monies received for AJ. AD with AJ endorsement, DLC (33, 10-0760).	
[June]	Memorandum by AJ of accounts paid by Andrew Jackson Donelson. AD, DLC (33, 10-0769).	
July 1	*To John Coffee.*	424
July 3	Toast at Nashville Independence Day celebration: "Domestic Economy—The sure road to national prosperity and independence." Printed, *Nashville Whig,* July 5 (mAJs).	
July 4	*To [William Savin] Fulton.*	425
July 5	*To Edward Livingston.*	429
July 5	Receipt of William Chandler for payment of 1823 tuition of Andrew Jackson, Jr., Andrew Jackson Hutchings, and Lyncoya. ADS, DLC (33).	
July 6	Toast at celebration of national independence held at the Fountain of Health: "Our country—May national views and feelings pervade the whole to the exclusion of sectional jealousies." Printed, *Nashville Republican,* July 17 (mAJs).	
July 8	From Paul Allen. ALS, DLC (33). Reports that he is no longer editor of the Baltimore *Morning Chronicle* but is attempting to start another newspaper.	
July 8	From James Gadsden. ALS with AJ endorsement, DLC (33). Discusses Robert Butler's appointment as surveyor general of Florida and AJ's presidential prospects in the Carolinas.	
July 10	*From William Cocke.*	430
July 10	Account of Woodcock & Sledge with Andrew Jackson Hutchings. ADS, A-Ar (10-0821). Runs to September 24, 1825, with receipt for payment by AJ, June 1, 1826.	
July 12	To James Monroe. ALS, NN (10-0825). Forwards letter (not found) of John R. Grymes recommending Joseph Bosque for consul at Tampico.	
July 12	From Charles Caldwell. Printed, *Jackson Gazette,* Aug 28 (10-0823). Claims the superiority of Kentucky bagging for cotton to "Scotch bagging" obtained from New Orleans.	
July 13	From William Edmiston Kennedy. ALS, Florida Department of	

Natural Resources (mAJs). Introduces Romeo Lewis.

July 13 — Account with Francis Saunders for salt, with receipt for payment, July 21. ADS with AJ endorsement, DLC (33).

July 14 — Circuit Court minutes in *Andrew Jackson* v. *Daniel Graham,* ordering a writ of mandamus requiring Graham to adjudicate a Stockley Donelson land grant. Copy, TNDa (10-0827).

July 14 — Receipt from Philip Morris for $30 paid by Andrew Jackson Donelson for service at AJ's ball. DS, DLC (33).

July 15 — Receipt of Malachi Nicholson for his wages as overseer of Andrew Jackson Hutchings's farm in 1823. DS in John Coffee's hand with AJ endorsement, A-Ar (10-0829).

July 17 — To Robert Butler (enclosure: Jacob C. Isacks to AJ, June 26). ALS, Florida Department of Natural Resources (10-0832). Recommends Leroy May as surveyor in Florida.

July 19 — To Robert Butler (enclosure: William E. Kennedy to AJ, July 13). ALS, Florida Department of Natural Resources (10-0834). Forwards letter recommending Romeo Lewis.

July 20 — From Samuel Houston. ALS, DLC (33). *Writings of Sam Houston,* 1:24. Asks AJ to send statement of his treatment as a British prisoner during the Revolution.

July 20 — Receipt of James Jackson for $88.76 as reimbursement of money advanced in settlement of *Jackson* v. *Erwin.* DS in AJ's hand, DLC (33).

July 20 — Receipt of Thomas Weston for $100 for painting and papering house and for furniture. DS in William B. Lewis's hand, DLC (33).

July 22 — From Leonard Pope Cheatham. ALS with AJ's ADS memorandum of July 24 reply, DLC (33). Asks explanation of AJ's refusal of a 1791 bond payable to Thaddeus Holt.

July 24 — To John Donelson (1755–1830). Copy, THer (37-0421). *Nashville Banner,* May 20, 1880. Discusses apportionment of the cost of building a church.

July 26 — From Thomas Claiborne. ANS, DLC (78). Reports purchase of 2,060 acres in western Tennessee from Patrick H. Darby.

[cJuly] — From William Dobein James. Printed, *Jackson Gazette,* Aug 14 (10-0839). Dedicates proposed biography of Thomas Sumter to AJ, an old schoolmate.

[cJuly] — "A Farmer" to Thomas Ritchie. Draft in Samuel R. Overton's hand, matched fragments, DLC (75, 59, 60; mAJs); Printed, *Nashville Gazette,* July 16 (mAJs). Defends AJ's position on the tariff.

[cJuly] — Memorandum of costs in *Jackson* v. *Erwin.* AD in James Jackson's hand with AJ endorsement, DLC (60, 9-0383).

Aug 1 — From James McMillan Glassell. ALS, DLC (33). States that Ellen J. Kirkman sent AJ's correspondence re the marriage of Mary L. Kirkman to Richard K. Call to the Philadelphia *National Gazette & Literary Register,* but the editor Robert Walsh refused publication.

Aug 3 — To Major Walker (enclosure: AJ to Littleton H. Coleman, April 26). AL draft, DLC (33). Defends his view of the tariff.

Aug 3 — Account with Miles Blythe McCorkle for medical treatment of the Hermitage slaves. ADS, THer (10-0841). Runs to October 20, 1825.

Aug 6	From James Gadsden. ALS, DLC (33). Discusses the sale of his Florence, Alabama, assets and his plan to breed horses suited to Florida.	
Aug 7	From Edward Patchell. ALS, DLC (33). Bassett, 3:262–65. Reports on support for AJ in western Pennsylvania.	
[cAug 8]	*To Samuel Houston.*	431
Aug 11	To George Wilson. Typed copy, THi (10-0843). Forwards extract of letter from John H. Eaton for publication in the *Nashville Gazette.*	
Aug 12	*Rachel Jackson to Latitia Dalzell Chambers.*	432
Aug 13	To Robert Butler (enclosure: Samuel Houston to AJ, Aug 13). ALS, Florida Department of Natural Resources (10-0849). Forwards a letter recommending Patton Anderson of Fayetteville, Tennessee.	
Aug 13	*To George Wilson.*	434
Aug 13	From Samuel Houston. ALS, Florida Department of Natural Resources (mAJs). Recommends Patton Anderson, who wishes a position in Florida.	
Aug 14	*From John McFarland.*	435
Aug 16	*From William Johnson (1792–1854).*	437
Aug 17	From Henry Marie Brackenridge. ALS, DLC (33). Reports on difficulties of the Florida claims commission.	
Aug 18	To DeWitt Clinton. Abstract, Dodd, Mead & Co. Catalog 90 (1908), Item 197 (10-0851). Introduces John H. Lewis of Alabama.	
Aug 18	To William Henry Harrison. LS, TxU (10-0853). Introduces John H. Lewis.	
Aug 18	To Stephen Simpson. Printed, Louisville *Daily Focus,* Nov 12, 1831 (10-0856). Introduces John H. Lewis.	
Aug 17 [18]	*To James Hervey Witherspoon.*	437
Aug 18	From Edward George Washington Butler. ALS, DLC (72). Describes the visit of Lafayette to New York.	
Aug 22	Elizabeth C. (Love) Watson to Rachel Jackson. ALS, DLC (11, 10-0858). Discusses news of family and friends; asks AJ to help her son secure a federal clerkship.	
Aug 27	From Western Territory Rucker et al. ALS signed by John H. Woodcock for others, DLC (33). Invite AJ to public dinner in Florence, Alabama.	
Aug 27	To Western Territory Rucker et al. AL draft, DLC (33). Accepts invitation.	
Aug 28	From Anthony Winston, [Jr.], et al. LS by proxy, DLC (33). Inquire about AJ's arrival in Tuscumbia, Alabama.	
Aug 28	Receipt from Henry Garrard for state and county taxes on Andrew Jackson Hutchings's farm in Lauderdale County, Alabama. DS, A-Ar (10-0862).	
[Aug 28]	Toast at Florence, Alabama, dinner: "Gen. La Fayette—the beloved compatriot of our immortal Washington, in the Revolutionary War." Printed, Huntsville *Alabama Republican,* Oct 8 (mAJs).	
Aug 29	To Anthony Winston, [Jr.], et al. ALS copy, DLC (33). Regrets that he will be unable to visit Tuscumbia.	
Aug	From Piomingo (pseudonym). ALS, DLC (33). States support for AJ; suggests a possible financial irregularity in Henry Clay's public service.	

[cAug]	Draft for public letter on tariff, especially on cotton goods. AD draft matched fragments, DLC (59 and 36). Bassett, 3:387 (of DLC-36 fragment).	
Sept 1	From Isaac Shelby. ALS, DLC (72). Frankfort, Ky., *Argus of Western America,* Oct 22, 1828. Inquires about the character of David Smith of Mississippi.	
Sept 4	Check to Andrew Jackson Donelson for $14.75. DS by proxy (Donelson), T (10-0890).	
Sept 6	From Thomas Martin Maund. ALS, DLC (33). Explains circumstances of his sale of the Baltimore *Morning Chronicle.*	
Sept 6	Promissory note for $800 to Francis Saunders, payable November 2. Photocopy of DS, THer (mAJs).	
Sept 9	From William Martin (1765–1846). ALS with AJ endorsement docketting reply, DLC (33). Discusses land transactions.	
Sept 10	To James Monroe. Abstract, Sotheby's (London) Catalog (Dec 15, 1988), Item 194 (mAJs). Introduces bearer.	
Sept 10	To Gilbert du Motier, Marquis de Lafayette. Copy in Andrew J. Donelson's hand, DLC (33). Bassett, 3:266. Welcomes Lafayette to America.	
[cSept 13]	To William Berkeley Lewis. Facsimile of ALS, Paul C. Richards Autographs Catalog 273 (April 1992), Item 285 (mAJs); Extract, Stan. V. Henkels Catalog 951 (1906), Item 584 (10-0891). Invites Lewis and family for dinner preceding the September 16 wedding of Andrew J. Donelson.	
Sept 14	To James Barron. LS, ViW (10-0892). Congratulates him on appointment as commander of the station and navy yard at Philadelphia.	
[Sept 17]	Jesse Benton to the people of the United States. Printed, WHi (10-0864); Extract, DLC (33). In campaign pamphlet form, attacks AJ and John Q. Adams and supports William H. Crawford for president.	
Sept 18	*From Arthur Peronneau Hayne.*	439
Sept 20	*To John Coffee.*	440
Sept 22	*From William Johnson (1792–1854).*	441
Sept 22	Promissory note to Bennett Smith for $400 to be paid June 1, 1825, on behalf of Andrew Jackson Hutchings. DS with Smith's receipt for payment, THi (10-0897).	
Sept 23	*To John Coffee.*	441
Sept 25	*To William Martin (1765–1846).*	444
Sept 27	*To Samuel Swartwout.*	445
Sept 28	Henry Banks to Andrew Jackson Donelson. ALS, DLC (33). Discusses founding of Frankfort, Kentucky, *Western Volunteer,* a pro-Jackson paper.	
Sept 29	From Robert Purdy. ADS with AJ endorsement, DLC (33). Describes events preceding the Jesse Benton–William Carroll duel in 1813.	
[Sept]	Advertisement for the runaway slave Gilbert. AD in Andrew J. Donelson's hand, DLC (10-0881).	
Oct 4	From William Carroll to Andrew Jackson Donelson. ALS with AJ endorsement, DLC (33). Bassett, 1:311–12. States his recollection of AJ's role in Carroll's duel with Jesse Benton in 1813.	

Oct 8	Andrew Jackson Donelson to Joel Parrish, Jr. ALS copy, DLC (33). Requests statement of conversation with Joseph Norvell regarding Jesse Benton's pamphlet.	
Oct 9	*To Jacob Call.*	446
Oct 9	*From William Gibbes Hunt, George Wilson, and Wilkins Tannehill.*	447
Oct 10	To William Gibbes Hunt, George Wilson, and Wilkins Tannehill. ALS copy, DLC (33). Hagerstown, Md., *Torch Light and Public Advertiser,* Nov 30. Thanks them for resolution from the Grand Lodge of Tennessee.	
Oct 10	From Henry Baldwin. ALS with postscript by John J. Audubon, DLC (33). Asks AJ to write letter introducing Audubon to Florida friends.	
Oct 11	Deed of partition for land between AJ and Andrew Jackson Donelson. Copy, TNDa (10-0913).	
Oct 12	Joel Parrish, Jr., to Andrew Jackson Donelson. ALS, DLC (72). States that Joseph Norvell remarked that Jesse Benton's pamphlet "contained *one Hundred and sixty* falsehoods."	
Oct 12	Reply by "Truth" to Jesse Benton's attack on AJ. Draft in Samuel R. Overton's hand and printed broadside, DLC (10-0915, -0938).	
Oct 14	To [Alexander] McCall IV. ALS, ViU (10-0942). Asks him to settle a land transaction between John Stone and McCall's grandfather, Martin Armstrong.	
[Oct 15]	Toast at public dinner in Nashville for John H. Eaton: "The memory of the Baron de Kalb. . . ." Printed, *Nashville Republican,* Oct 23 (mAJs).	
Oct 18	From Gilbert du Motier, Marquis de Lafayette. ALS with AJ endorsement, DLC (33). Bassett, 3:268. States his determination to meet AJ before leaving the United States.	
Oct 19	To Unknown. Typed copy, MoSW (10-0944). States that he has forwarded recommendations for deputy surveyorships in Florida but that no jobs are presently available.	
Oct 19	Receipt from Samuel Van Dyke Stout for $500 in specie paid for a new carriage. DS in AJ's hand, DLC (78).	
Oct 20	Account of Rachel Jackson with H[arriett] Temple for a dress. ADS, DLC (33).	
Oct 21	Check to Andrew Jackson Donelson for $60.00. DS by proxy (Donelson), G. Keeling Turner (10-0945).	
Oct 22	From Richard Ivy Easter. ALS, DLC (33). Introduces Robert C. Lane.	
Oct 22	Deed from AJ and Rachel Jackson to John Donelson (1755–1830) for their one-tenth share of 5,000 acres granted to the heirs of John Donelson (c1718–86). Typed copy, DLC (10-0946); Extract, Parke-Bernet Catalog (Dec 3, 1957), Item 128 (10-0947).	
Oct 27	Account of Rachel Jackson with E. Abbot for dry goods. ADS, DLC (33). Runs to December 31.	
Oct 30	From "Son of Liberty" (pseudonym). Printed with AN, DLC (33). Describes Thomas Jefferson's favorable opinion of DeWitt Clinton.	
Oct 30	Receipt from Jacob D. [Donelson] for a note received for collection. DS in AJ's hand, DLC (78).	

[Oct]	From William Carroll. ALS fragment, ICHi (10-0905). Sends a portion of a letter from AJ to Thomas H. Benton (probably August 4, 1813) re the Benton-Carroll duel.	
[Oct]	Reply to anti-Jackson handbill signed "Anthony Wayne" [Bellamy Storer]. AD draft and draft in Samuel R. Overton's hand, DLC (10-0906, -0908). Bassett, 3:267.	
Nov 1	To William Pope Duval. LS, DLC (10-0948). Introduces John J. Audubon.	
Nov 1	*From Caleb Atwater.*	448
Nov 2	*To William Carroll.*	449
Nov 6	To [Robert Brownlee Currey]. ANS, THi (10-0951). *THQ,* 6(1947):167. Instructs him on the care of AJ's mail during his absence from Nashville.	
Nov 6	To John Overton (enclosure: AJ to [Robert B. Currey], Nov 6). ALS, THi (10-0952). *THQ,* 6(1947):167. Announces departure for Washington and leaves instructions regarding mail.	
Nov 6	From William Carroll. ALS, DLC (72). Reports his recollection of Nicholas T. Perkins's conduct at the Battle of Enitachopko.	
Nov 7	To William Berkeley Lewis. ALS, DLC (72). Informs him that Andrew J. Donelson will forward Carroll's statement on the Battle of Enitachopko.	
[cNov 7]	To Sumner County Citizens. Draft fragment, DLC (59, 10-0963). Acknowledges invitation to stop in Gallatin on his return to Washington.	
Nov 14	From William Field. ALS, DLC (33). Asks AJ to influence the postmaster general in favor of a mail contract for Field's stage line between Nashville and Louisville.	
Nov 15	From Reuben A. Carter. ALS, DLC (33). Asks AJ to support Carter's plan for improvement of the Mississippi River.	
Nov 15	Account with Moses Stevens for Andrew Jackson Hutchings's tuition. ADS, A-Ar (10-0954). Runs to May 17, 1825.	
[Nov 16]	Toast at a Lexington ball: "The venerable Isaac Shelby of Kentucky." Printed, Lexington *Kentucky Gazette,* Nov 25 (10-0956).	
Nov 17	From John H. Coleman et al. Printed, Lexington *Kentucky Gazette,* Nov 25 (10-0957). Invite AJ to a public dinner at Paris, Kentucky.	
Nov 17	To John H. Coleman et al. Printed, Lexington *Kentucky Gazette,* Nov 25 (10-0958). Declines invitation.	
Nov 23	*From David Corbin Ker.*	450
[Nov 24]	Andrew Jackson, Jr., to Rachel Jackson. ALS fragment, ICHi (mAJs). Sends love.	
Nov	From William D. Chappell to Andrew Jackson, Jr. ALS, DLC (33). Asks him to exchange some books at a Nashville bookseller's.	
Dec 1	From Auguste G. V. Davezac. ALS, DLC (33). Recommends Nathaniel Chamberlain for customs appraiser at New Orleans.	
Dec 2	From DeWitt Clinton. LC, NNC (10-0964). Introduces Elbert Anderson, who is pursuing a claim against the war department.	
Dec 2	From Archibald Rhea. ALS, DNA-RG 94 (M688-40). Asks aid in obtaining West Point appointment for his son John S. Rhea.	
Dec 2	Receipt to Hubbard Sanders from Thomas Donoho, agent of Gales and Seaton, for payment for Washington *National Intelligencer,*	

	received through AJ. DS, DLC (33).	
Dec 2	Account of Rachel Jackson with Rachel Williams for a dress, with receipt for payment, December 13. ADS, DLC (33).	
Dec 3	From Willoughby Williams. ALS, DLC (33). Recommends his brother, James G. Williams, as Cherokee agent, vice Joseph McMinn, deceased.	
Dec 7	From William Crockett. ALS, DLC (33). Requests an interview.	
Dec 7	*From Thomas A. Mera.*	451
Dec 7	Account with Tucker & Thompson for a suit. ADS with AJ endorsement, DLC (33).	
Dec 8	*To William Berkeley Lewis.*	453
Dec 9	To Andrew Jackson Hutchings. ALS, THer (10-0970). Instructs him to study, attend church, and write frequently.	
Dec 9	To John Overton (enclosure: James Monroe to U.S. Senators and Congressmen, Dec 7, *House Journal,* 18th Cong., 2nd sess., pp. 9–25). ALS, THi (10-0972). *THQ*, 6(1947):168. Reports arrival in Washington; mentions electoral vote and Lafayette.	
Dec 9	From Trueman Cross (enclosure: Cross et al. to U.S. Senate and House, n.d., 10-1009). ALS, DNA-RG 46 (10-0967). Forwards petition requesting forage allowance for assistant quartermasters.	
Dec 10	From Alexander A. White. ALS, DLC (33). Asks help in securing a federal post.	
Dec 12	*To Edward George Washington Butler.*	454
Dec 12	James W. Sittler to William Berkeley Lewis (enclosure: Proceedings in the court-martial of Nicholas T. Perkins, Jan 27–30, 1814). ALS, DLC (33). Transmits document, as requested by Andrew J. Donelson.	
Dec 14	To Samuel Swartwout. ALS, TNJ (10-0981); ALS copy, DLC (33). Bassett, 3:268–69. Declares that he will not intrigue to secure election.	
Dec 14	From Corbin Lee. ALS, DLC (33). Asks for a job on one of AJ's "western plantations"; inquires whether AJ was wounded in the duel with Charles H. Dickinson.	
Dec 14	Motion to refer a part of the annual message to the Senate Committee on Military Affairs. Abstract, *Senate Journal,* 18th Cong., 2nd sess., p. 34 (mAJs).	
Dec 15	Account with C[hristian] & M[atthew] Hines for two small tubs. Abstract, Forest H. Sweet List [c1927] (10-0985).	
Dec 15	Account of Rachel Jackson with Jared Whitney for shoes, with receipt for payment, March 2, 1825. ADS, DLC (33).	
Dec 18	From Alexander Macomb (enclosure: John C. Calhoun to James Hamilton, Jr., Jan 22, DLC-32). ALS with AJ endorsement, DLC (33); LC, DNA-RG 77 (10-0987). *Calhoun Papers,* 9:452. Forwards letter regarding enlargement and reorganization of corps of engineers.	
Dec 18	From George Wilson. ALS with AJ endorsement, DLC (33). Asks AJ to pursue further a claim against the war department.	
Dec 19	*To John Overton.*	455
Dec 20	To John Pemberton. LS, PHi (10-0991). Declines invitation to celebrate the eighth of January in Philadelphia.	

Dec 20	Jacob Jennings Brown to John Caldwell Calhoun. Copy with AJ endorsement, DLC (33). Proposes improvements in the pay and status of non-commissioned officers.	
Dec 21	Resolution of Nathaniel Macon requesting Military Affairs Committee to inquire into expediency of limiting enrollment at the Military Academy. AD with AJ endorsement, DNA-RG 46 (10-0993).	
Dec 22	Account of Rachel Jackson with Rachel Williams for dressmaking, with receipt for payment January 28, 1825. ADS, DLC (33).	
Dec 23	To John Barney. ALS, T (10-0995). Declines invitation to visit Baltimore.	
Dec 23	*Rachel Jackson to Elizabeth Kingsley.*	456
Dec 23	Report from the Senate Committee on Military Affairs on army promotions and appointments. Abstract, *Senate Executive Proceedings,* 3:398 (mAJs).	
Dec 25	To John Quincy Adams and Louisa Catherine Adams. AN, TNJ (10-1000). Declines invitation to dinner, December 30.	
Dec 27	*To John Coffee.*	457
Dec 27	*To William Berkeley Lewis.*	459
Dec 27	Andrew Jackson Donelson to Stockly Donelson. ALS, Mrs. W. R. Stevens (mAJs). Reports AJ's actions in response to Stockly Donelson to AJ, December 12 (not found); discusses presidential election.	
Dec 29	Motion to refer petition of Thomas R. Broom to Military Affairs Committee, AJ chairman. AD, DNA-RG 46 (10-1007).	
Dec 29	Account of Rachel Jackson with Clagett & Norris for fabric and accessories. ADS, DLC (33). Runs to March 9, 1825.	
Dec 30	To Aaron Dayton (from AJ and Rachel Jackson). Extract, Rosenbach Catalog 17 (1950), Item 379 (10-1017). Invite him to dinner.	
Dec 30	From John Caldwell Calhoun (enclosure: Calhoun to James Hamilton, Jr., Dec 28, DNA-RG 77, mAJs). AL with AJ endorsement, DLC (33); LC, DNA-RG 77 (10-1016). Transmits letter discussing proposed increase in army engineering department.	
Dec 30	Cargo manifest for cotton shipped by AJ as guardian for Andrew Jackson Hutchings. DS, A-Ar (10-1018).	
[Dec]	From William Alexander. ALS, DLC (35, 10-0959). Expresses pleasure at AJ's likely election; discusses claim for revolutionary war services.	

Index

Page-entry numbers between 469 and 575 refer to the Calendar. Numbers set in boldface indicate identification of persons. The symbol * indicates biographical information in the *Dictionary of American Biography;* the symbol †, in the *Biographical Directory of the United States Congress.*